Tolley's
UK Taxation of Tru

While every care has been taken to ensure the accuracy of this work, no responsibility for loss or damage occasioned to any person acting or refraining from action as a result of any statement in it can be accepted by the author, editors or publishers.

Tolley's
UK Taxation of Trusts 2016–17

Twenty-sixth Edition

by
Ian Maston
TEP

Tolley®

Tolley's UK Taxation of Trusts 2016–17

Members of the LexisNexis Group worldwide

United Kingdom	RELX (UK) Limited trading as LexisNexis, 1–3 Strand, London WC2N 5JR and 9–10 St Andrew Square, Edinburgh EH2 2AF
Argentina	LexisNexis Argentina, Buenos Aires
Australia	LexisNexis Butterworths, Chatswood, New South Wales
Austria	LexisNexis Verlag ARD Orac GmbH & Co KG, Vienna
Benelux	LexisNexis Benelux, Amsterdam
Canada	LexisNexis Canada, Markham, Ontario
Chile	LexisNexis Chile Ltda, Santiago
China	LexisNexis China, Beijing and Shanghai
France	LexisNexis SA, Paris
Germany	LexisNexis Deutschland GmbH, Munster
Hong Kong	LexisNexis Hong Kong, Hong Kong
India	LexisNexis India, New Delhi
Italy	Giuffrè Editore, Milan
Japan	LexisNexis Japan, Tokyo
Malaysia	Malayan Law Journal Sdn Bhd, Kuala Lumpur
Mexico	LexisNexis Mexico, Mexico
New Zealand	LexisNexis NZ Ltd, Wellington
Poland	Wydawnictwo Prawnicze LexisNexis Sp, Warsaw
Singapore	LexisNexis Singapore, Singapore
South Africa	LexisNexis Butterworths, Durban
USA	LexisNexis, Dayton, Ohio

© Reed Elsevier (UK) Ltd 2016
Published by LexisNexis

All rights reserved. No part of this publication may be reproduced in any material form (including photocopying or storing it in any medium by electronic means and whether or not transiently or incidentally to some other use of this publication) without the written permission of the copyright owner except in accordance with the provisions of the Copyright, Designs and Patents Act 1988 or under the terms of a licence issued by the Copyright Licensing Agency Ltd, 90 Tottenham Court Road, London, England W1T 4LP. Applications for the copyright owner's written permission to reproduce any part of this publication should be addressed to the publisher.
Warning: The doing of an unauthorised act in relation to a copyright work may result in both a civil claim for damages and criminal prosecution.

Crown copyright material is reproduced with the permission of the Controller of HMSO and the Queen's Printer for Scotland. Parliamentary copyright material is reproduced with the permission of the Controller of Her Majesty's Stationery Office on behalf of Parliament. Any European material in this work which has been reproduced from EUR-lex, the official European Communities legislation website, is European Communities copyright.

Material in Appendix E reproduced by kind permission of STEP and the CIOT.
A CIP Catalogue record for this book is available from the British Library.

ISBN for this volume: 9780754552819

Printed in Great Britain by Hobbs the Printers Ltd, Totton, Hampshire

Visit LexisNexis at www.lexisnexis.co.uk

Preface

Much has changed for trust practitioners since the first edition of this book in 1990. Back then we didn't need to worry about whether an interest in possession trust was 'qualifying' or not. We could create lifetime interest in possession and accumulation and maintenance trusts as potentially exempt transfers. We could hold over gains to settlor-interested trusts. And, of course, non-resident trusts offered plenty of scope for tax planning.

The tax rules for trusts are more complicated now and the opportunities for planning more limited. Likewise, the division between tax evasion and tax avoidance has become blurred and no longer can we expect to rely upon the 'letter' of the law. Much planning needs to be disclosed in advance; 'abusive' planning will fail; tax may need to be paid 'upfront' and the penalties for non-compliance are harsher.

The key changes for trustees in the past year are the abolition of the 10% tax credit, and introduction of new rates of tax, for dividends; the reduction in the rate of capital gains tax to 20% for disposal of most types property; and a new slab system of SDLT for non-residential property transactions. Meanwhile, many of the anti-avoidance measures announced last year are now on the statute book (although not all are yet in effect), including the introduction of a 60% GAAR penalty effective from Royal Assent of Finance Act 2016. Accelerated payments notices have now collected £3 billion of disputed tax (it was only £1 billion this time last year!). On an international level, the extensive multilateral agreement in relation to the OECD's common reporting standard remains a game-changer in the field of information exchange.

The inheritance tax nil-rate band is still at £325,000; however, the rules for an addition nil-rate band for family homes (to be phased in from 2017) have been finalised. So too, at long last, has the long-running 'simplification' project in relation to the taxation of 'relevant property' trusts.

This is only my third year of authorship and much of the commentary was originally contributed by the previous author Matthew Hutton. Matthew had been responsible for the UK Resident Trusts chapters from the 9th edition (taking over from Tony Sherring) and the non-UK Resident Trust chapters from the 16th edition (following Ian Ferrier). My influence over the style and content will accumulate year on year: This year I have re-ordered Chapter 7 in relation to Capital Gains Tax. Readers will hopefully not miss the commentary that I have discarded as no longer relevant. I have retained the convention of quoting the most relevant tax year for the purposes of rates, reliefs and exemptions. Where, for example, the context is one of compliance, attention is focused on tax year 2015/16 – as advisers will now be completing the self-assessment return for that year. On the other hand, where planning is in issue reference is made to the current year 2016/17.

Part 2 on Non-UK Resident Trusts has historically comprised only a small part of the book and that continues to be the case, at around 15% of the text. These five chapters are certainly not intended to provide more than a basic overview of the subject, which is handled substantively in a number of excellent books. Although the proposed changes are still in consultation, I have included as much details as is available about the proposed new deemed domicile rules from 2017/18 and the likely effects of these for the settlors of Non-UK Resident Trusts.

I have reproduced the text of certain HMRC and former Inland Revenue Statements of Practice, Extra-statutory Concessions and press releases in the Appendices. I have also included a reproduction of Form SA 900 – Trust and Estate Tax Return for the year ended 5 April 2016. This is by kind permission of The Stationery Office.

It goes without saying that the masculine gender includes the feminine (and vice versa) wherever used in the text.

Finally, I should like to record my sincere gratitude to Project Manager Fergus Burdon, and Content Developer Charlene Edwards, each of whom has played their part in what has been a relatively easy process of production. Needless to say, any technical errors that remain are entirely my responsibility.

I believe that I have taken account of all changes in the law down to the end of July 2016.

Ian Maston
Litton Cheney, September 2016

About the Author

Ian Maston BA, TEP, Solicitor (Non-Practising)

Ian Maston is the owner of Mastoni Tax Ltd, an independent consultancy specialising in private client taxation. Previously head of BDO's London trust team and a founder partner of Gabelle LLP, over the last 20 years Ian has written, lectured and advised on all aspects of inheritance tax, estate planning and trusts. He is a member of the *Legal Network TV* Legal Expert Panel and *Tax Journal's* long-running *Ask an Expert* Panel. He lives in West Dorset with his wife and two sons and can be contacted at ian@mastonitax.com or on 01308 482205.

Contents

Preface	v
About the Author	vii
Abbreviations and References	xxv
Table of Statutes	xxix
Table of Statutory Instruments	xli
Table of Cases	xliii

PART I: UK RESIDENT TRUSTS

Chapter 1   Setting the Scene

Inheritance tax: the 2006 bombshell	1.4
Capital gains tax	1.7
Income tax	1.10
Stamp taxes	1.12
High-value UK residential property	1.13
Non-domiciliaries	1.16
Anti-avoidance	1.17

Chapter 2   Types of Trust

General	2.1
Will trusts	2.4
Lifetime settlements	2.14
Dispositive powers within trusts	2.24
Implied trusts	2.29
Trusts in practice	2.30
Discretionary trusts	2.31
Interest in possession trusts	2.38
Bare trusts	2.44
Accumulation and maintenance trusts	2.49
Charitable trusts	2.51
Disabled trusts	2.52
Employee trusts	2.53

Contents

Chapter 3   Interests of Beneficiaries

A mere spes	3.2
Vested interests, whether in possession or in reversion	3.3
Contingent interests	3.4
The accumulation of income	3.6
Intermediate income	3.13

Chapter 4   Anti-Avoidance Rules Affecting the Settlor

Income Tax	4.2
Overview	4.2
An 'interest' under a settlement	4.3
'Settlor' and 'settlement'	4.5
Exceptions	4.10
Heritage maintenance funds	4.13
Settlements on children	4.14
Bare trusts	4.20
Chargeability of the trustees to tax	4.23
Waiver of dividends	4.24
Capital sums	4.26
The Pre-owned Assets Regime: income tax charge from 2005/06	4.32
Capital gains tax	4.33
The flip-flop scheme	4.34
Sub-funds	4.36
Deeds of variation	4.37
Inheritance tax	4.38
The Pre-owned Assets Regime	4.39

Chapter 5   The Position of Trustees

Personal liability	5.1
Tax liabilities in the ordinary course	5.4
'Relevant trustees'	5.4
Income tax	5.5
Settlor-interested trusts	5.11
Capital gains tax	5.18
Inheritance tax	5.19
Tax liabilities: unusual events to be wary of	5.21
Capital gains tax: recapture of held-over gains	5.21

Emigration	**5.25**
Inheritance tax	**5.26**
Failed potentially exempt transfers	**5.28**
Residence of trustees	**5.29**
The Non-UK Resident Landlord Scheme	**5.30**
The 'rule in *Hastings-Bass*'	**5.31**
Rectification	**5.48**
Mistake: the equitable jurisdiction of the court	**5.51**
Chapter 6 Income Tax	
Interest received	**6.1**
Bank and building society interest	**6.4**
The accrued income scheme	**6.7**
Stock dividends	**6.20**
Enhanced stock dividends	**6.21**
Transfers of income streams	**6.22**
Deductibility of expenses	**6.23**
Fixed interest trusts	**6.24**
Accumulation and discretionary trusts	**6.26**
The case law and the statutory framework	**6.28**
Trust management expenses	**6.31**
Payment of interest by trustees	**6.41**
Non-UK resident beneficiary	**6.44**
Interest in possession trusts	**6.45**
Discretionary and accumulation trusts	**6.50**
The standard rate band	**6.52**
The special rates	**6.55**
Deceased estates	**6.59**
Income which is charged at the special rates	**6.60**
Exceptions	**6.63**
Discretionary payments to beneficiaries: the grossing up regime	**6.65**
Tax pools	**6.68**
Income or capital?	**6.80**
Making payments to beneficiaries of discretionary and accumulation trusts	**6.86**
Payments to beneficiaries of fixed interest trusts: the tax voucher	**6.91**

Taxation of land transactions	**6.96**
Flat management companies	**6.99**
Assessment	**6.101**
Non-UK resident beneficiaries	**6.104**

Chapter 7 Capital Gains Tax

Occasions of charge	**7.1**
Connected persons	**7.3**
Absolute entitlement	**7.6**
Gains	**7.6**
Losses	**7.15**
Appointments and distributions	**7.19**
Demergers	**7.21**
Termination of a qualifying life interest	**7.25**
Rate of tax	**7.33**
The annual exemption	**7.36**
Allowable expenditure	**7.40**
Base values at death	**7.40**
Expenses	**7.43**
Interaction with inheritance tax	**7.46**
Taper relief (for disposals before 2008/09)	**7.48**
Main residence relief	**7.51**
Hold-over relief	**7.60**
Business assets	**7.62**
Non-business assets	**7.71**
Chargeable transfers etc	**7.72**
'Flip-flop' schemes	**7.75**
Relevant property settlements	**7.76**
'Melville' arrangements: Mark I and Mark II (before 10 December 2003)	**7.78**
Gifts to heritage maintenance trusts	**7.83**
Accumulation and maintenance settlements	**7.84**
The claim	**7.91**
Anti-avoidance rules for non-UK residents	**7.92**
Instalment relief	**7.94**
The potential for double taxation	**7.95**

Disposal following earlier hold-over (the half-gain rule): before 2008/09	**7.96**
Enterprise Investment Scheme (EIS)	**7.97**
Seed Enterprise Investment Scheme	**7.101**
Entrepreneurs' relief	**7.102**
Conditions	**7.103**
Extension to trustees	**7.104**
Investors' Relief	**7.107**
Deeds of variation and post-death appointments	**7.112**
Sub-funds	**7.118**
The accrued income scheme and capital gains tax	**7.123**
High value disposals of residential property	**7.126**
Miscellaneous	**7.129**
Administrative rules	**7.129**
Valuation of shares in unquoted/unlisted companies	**7.132**
Pooling land	**7.133**
Interests under a settlement	**7.134**
Variation of trusts	**7.135**
Chapter 8 Inheritance Tax: Definitions	
'Settlement'	**8.2**
'Interest in possession'	**8.6**
'Qualifying interest in possession'	**8.7**
'Immediate post-death interest'	**8.8**
'Trust for bereaved minors'	**8.9**
'Age 18-to-25 trust'	**8.13**
'Disabled person's interest'	**8.16**
'Transitional serial interests'	**8.17**
'Excluded property'	**8.23**
Excluded property settlements	**8.24**
FOTRA securities	**8.26**
Reversionary interests	**8.28**
'Relevant property'	**8.29**
'Payment' and 'Quarter'	**8.31**
'Potentially exempt transfer'	**8.32**
'Gift with reservation'	**8.36**

Protective trusts	8.41

Chapter 9 Inheritance Tax: Relevant Property Settlements — The Ten-Year Charge

Overview	9.1
The ten-year anniversary	9.8
The amount which is chargeable	9.12
Relevant property	9.12
Accumulations of income	9.13
Expenses	9.14
Latent capital gains tax	9.15
Business and agricultural property reliefs	9.17
Valuation principles: liabilities	9.18
Heritage property	9.21
The calculation of the tax	9.23
The ten-year charge (simple case)	9.24
The deemed chargeable transfer	9.24
The deemed cumulative total	9.25
The effective rate	9.28
The rate of ten-year charge	9.29
Accumulations of income	9.30
Undistributed income	9.33
Related settlements	9.37
Same-day additions	9.44
Relevant and non-relevant property combined	9.49
Finance (No 2) Act 2015 simplification	9.55
Property is added to the settlement	9.57
Property changing character within the settlement	9.65
Settled legacies	9.66
Trusts of pension death benefits	9.68
Anti-avoidance measures	9.69
Property moving between settlements	9.69
Excluded property	9.71
Some practical difficulties	9.77
Identification	9.77
Failed potentially exempt transfers	9.78

Gifts with reservation of benefit	**9.81**
The impact of Finance Act 2006	**9.83**

Chapter 10   Inheritance Tax: Relevant Property Settlements — The Exit Charge

Introduction	**10.1**
The occasions of charge	**10.3**
Exemptions from the exit charge	**10.8**
Excluded property	**10.8**
Gratuitous transfers	**10.10**
Transfers within the first quarter	**10.11**
Other exemptions	**10.14**
The amount chargeable	**10.17**
The rate of charge	**10.20**
Exit charge before first ten-year anniversary	**10.21**
The deemed chargeable transfer	**10.21**
The deemed cumulative total	**10.24**
Rate of charge	**10.25**
Exit charge between ten-year anniversaries	**10.28**
The 'age 18-to-25 trust' charge	**10.32**

Chapter 11   Inheritance Tax: Accumulation and Maintenance Settlements

Historical Background	**11.1**
What is an accumulation and maintenance trust?	**11.4**
The historical position	**11.4**
Two sets of statutory conditions	**11.6**
The inheritance tax consequences	**11.16**
The 2006 changes	**11.19**
The main changes	**1.19**
The options in the transitional period	**11.21**
The 'continuing' accumulation and maintenance trust	**11.22**
The 'age 18 to 25 trust' accumulation and maintenance trust	**11.23**
The 'relevant property' accumulation and maintenance trust	**11.25**
Deciding between these options	**11.26**
The charge to tax on failure	**11.29**

Chapter 12　Inheritance Tax: Qualifying Interest in Possession Trusts

The charge on death	12.3
The charge on lifetime termination	12.8
Reverter to settlor	12.13
Reversionary interests	12.17
Reservation of benefit	12.19
Disguised interests in possession	12.23
Miscellaneous anti-avoidance	12.28

Chapter 13　Stamp Taxes: Liability and Compliance

Summary	13.1
Stamp Duty Land Tax	13.5
Bare trusts	13.5
Settlement	13.10
Trustees' responsibilities	13.12
General	13.12
Who are the 'responsible trustees?'	13.13
Recovery of tax from trustees	13.14
Filling in the land transaction return or self-certificate: the 'relevant trustees'	13.16
Enquiry	13.17
Appeals	13.19
Scottish trusts and offshore trusts	13.20
Exercise of power of appointment or discretion	13.22
Chargeable consideration	13.23
Non-residential or mixed use land	13.25
Residential land	13.27
Additional Residential Properties	13.29
The 'ATED' SDLT charge	13.34
Other points	13.35
Land and Buildings Transaction Tax	13.37
The Annual Tax on Enveloped Dwellings (ATED)	13.40
Stamp duty	13.46
Application of the disclosure regime to SDLT	13.48

Chapter 14   Charitable Trusts

Introduction	14.1
Definition of a charity	14.4
Exemptions on setting up or giving to charities	14.10
Stamp duty and stamp duty land tax	14.10
Inheritance tax	14.12
Capital gains tax	14.14
Income tax	14.15
Transfer of family shareholdings to charities	14.28
Tax exemptions for charities	14.31
Charities: the 'fit and proper persons' test in FA 2010	14.43
Anti-avoidance	14.47
Charities: the 'purpose of establishment condition'	14.51
Non-qualifying expenditure	14.53
Substantial donors (before 1 April 2011)	14.57
Tainted donations (after 31 March 2011)	14.58
Abnormal dividends	14.60
Spotlights	14.62
Gifts of qualifying investments: avoidance arrangement blocked by statute	14.65
Latest developments	14.66
Time charities	14.67
HMRC administration	14.68
Disaster funds	14.74
Miscellaneous	14.76
Some background to the 2006 and 2011 reforms	14.76
Cessation of charitable use	14.78
Schools	14.79
The Trust (Capital and Income) Act 2013	14.80

Chapter 15   Trusts for Disabled or Vulnerable Persons

Overview	15.1
Disabled person	15.3
Inheritance tax	15.7
A capital gains tax uplift?	15.12
No transfer of value?	15.13

Contents

Income and capital gains tax	**15.14**
Electing for special treatment	**15.17**
Administration	**15.18**
Trusts compensating asbestos victims	**15.19**
Chapter 16 Trusts for Employees	
Overview	**16.1**
Employee benefit trusts (EBTs)	**16.3**
A corporation tax deduction?	**16.4**
Inheritance tax	**16.6**
Income tax	**16.11**
Capital gains tax	**16.23**
The deductibility of a loan from an EBT	**16.32**
Settlement opportunity	**16.35**
Employee Ownership Trusts (EOTs)	**16.36**
Qualification conditions	**16.37**
Capital gains tax	**16.38**
Income tax	**16.41**
Inheritance tax	**16.42**
Chapter 17 Starting a Trust: Tax and Tax Planning	
Overview	**17.1**
Compliance on setting up a trust	**17.6**
Form 41G (Trust)	**17.8**
Capital gains tax	**17.9**
Hold-over relief	**17.13**
Payment of tax	**17.18**
Inheritance tax	**17.20**
The small exemptions	**17.21**
Compliance issues	**17.22**
DOTAS	**17.24**
Stamp taxes	**17.25**
Charities	**17.27**
Tax planning	**17.28**
The nil-rate band trust: inheritance tax planning	**17.33**
Agricultural and business property	**17.36**

Bare trusts	17.40
Defeasible absolute interests: 'non-settlements'?	17.41
Sales at an undervalue	17.42
Exceeding the nil-rate band	17.45
Life assurance trusts and IHT mitigation	17.47
The discounted gift trust	17.51
The gift and loan arrangement	17.55
The flexible reversionary trust	17.57
Avoidance	17.59
Chapter 18 Running a Trust: Tax Planning	
General principles and overview of the chapter	18.1
Avoiding aggregation	18.2
The age of the donee	18.4
Married couples and registered civil partners	18.5
Residence nil rate band	18.11
'Having your cake': pre-March 1986 settlements	18.17
Family companies	18.18
Business property relief	18.28
Relevant business property	18.29
AIM shares	18.32
Disqualified and qualifying businesses	18.34
Excepted assets	18.48
Groups	18.51
Minimum period of ownership	18.54
Sales and liquidations	18.55
Agricultural property relief	18.56
Agricultural property	18.57
Farmhouses	18.58
The alternative occupation and ownership tests	18.64
Claw-back of business and agricultural property reliefs	18.66
Treatment of liabilities for financing relievable property: anti-avoidance rules	18.71
Hold-over relief for capital gains tax	18.72
Planning considerations	18.73
Future considerations	18.75

Contents

Income tax planning	**18.77**
Own share purchases	**18.84**
The second home: washing the gain?	**18.85**
The family home: 'double trust' arrangement rendered ineffective	**18.90**
Avoidance of double charges	**18.92**

Chapter 19   Ending a Trust: Tax Planning

Overview	**19.1**
Inheritance tax	**19.3**
Capital gains tax	**19.10**
Other taxes	**19.14**
Income tax	**19.14**
Stamp taxes	**19.20**
Planning points	**19.21**

Chapter 20   Compliance: Income Tax and Capital Gains Tax

Returns for income tax	**20.1**
Notification of liability	**20.9**
Trusts with no income	**20.12**
Payment of tax	**20.17**
Estimates	**20.20**
Finality for deceased estates	**20.21**
Clearance	**20.22**
Policy for trustees	**20.23**
Discovery	**20.25**
The beneficiaries	**20.31**
Deceased estates	**20.32**
Completing the Trust and Estate Tax Return — SA900	**20.37**
Toolkit	**20.70**
The foreign supplementary pages: dividends from non-UK companies	**20.71**
The non-residence etc supplementary pages: statutory residence test	**20.73**
Trust and Estate capital gains	**20.74**

Chapter 21   Compliance: Inheritance Tax

Determination of tax chargeable	**21.3**
The Inheritance Tax Account (other than on death)	**21.3**

Payment of tax	**21.6**
De minimis provisions: excepted transfers and excepted settlements	**21.8**
The settlor's chargeable gifts history	**21.12**
Late payment of tax	**21.14**
Reporting requirements	**21.15**
Determination	**21.17**
Quick succession relief	**21.18**
Payment of tax by instalments	**21.19**
Liability for tax	**21.26**
National heritage property	**21.30**
Self assessment and electronic delivery	**21.31**
Chapter 22 Compliance: the Interest and Penalty Regimes	
Interest	**22.3**
Inheritance tax	**22.6**
Penalties	**22.7**
For late filed returns: income tax and capital gains tax	**22.7**
Inaccuracies in a return: the FA 2007 regime	**22.9**
Fixed penalties under inheritance tax	**22.19**
Unpaid tax	**22.21**
Fixed penalties under income tax and capital gains tax prior to 1 April 2011	**22.21**
The FA 2009 Sch 56 penalty	**22.22**
Inheritance tax	**22.23**
Offshore penalties	**22.24**
Criminal Sanctions	**22.28**
Policy developments	**22.31**
Chapter 23 Anti-avoidance	
Overview	**23.1**
Inheritance tax anti-avoidance	**23.4**
The General Anti-Abuse Rule	**23.11**
DOTAS	**23.15**
Inheritance tax	**23.17**
SDLT	**23.24**
High risk promoters, follower and accelerated payment notices	**23.27**

PART II: NON-UK RESIDENT TRUSTS

Chapter 24 Residence and Domicile

Introduction	24.1
Basic concepts	24.3
Residence of individuals (before 2013/14)	24.4
The comprehensive statutory test for residence (from 2013/14)	24.9
The rules	24.10
Temporary non-residence	24.21
Residence of trustees	24.22
Domicile	24.26
Non-UK domiciliaries: policy developments	24.39
The FA 2008 revisions	24.41
The quantum of the RBC charge	24.44
The Summer Budget 2015 proposals	24.46
Companies	24.51

Chapter 25 Income Tax

Liability to UK tax	25.1
Identifying the income of the beneficiary	25.4
Anti-avoidance	25.13
The 2008/09 reforms	25.16
Transfer of assets abroad	25.18
Transactions in land	25.46
Deduction of tax	25.51
Temporary non-residents	25.53

Chapter 26 Capital Gains Tax

Introduction	26.1
Three heads of charge	26.4
The exit charge	26.5
The settlor charge	26.17
The capital payments charge	26.33
The 2008/09 changes	26.47
Proposed changes from 2017/18	26.53
Temporary non-residents	26.57
The 'flip-flop' schemes	26.59
Situs of assets	26.62

Information powers and requirements	26.63
Capital gains tax for non-residents holding UK residential property	26.66

Chapter 27 Inheritance Tax

Domicile the determining factor	27.1
Excluded property	27.2
Settled property situated outside the UK	27.4
The settlor	27.7
Liabilities and excluded property	27.9
Deemed domicile	27.13
Situs of property	27.21
Avoidance blocked	27.24
Reversionary interests	27.27
Exempt gilts	27.28
A proposed 'look through' for UK residential properties	27.39
Double tax treaties	27.53
Reporting obligations	27.55
Executors and trustees	27.59
Enforcement: the *Clore* case	27.62
The Pre-owned Assets Regime	27.63

Chapter 28 Tax Planning Issues for Offshore Trusts: An Overview

Protection and establishment of domicile	28.5
The trust document and its contents	28.7
The family context	28.12
Non-UK resident children's trusts	28.15
The location of the trust	28.17
Planning opportunities for non-UK domiciled individuals	28.20
Information exchange	28.27
Disclosure facilities	28.29
Multinational initiatives	28.32

APPENDICES

A	Press Releases and Statements of Practice
B	Extra-statutory Concessions
C	Checking Liabilities and the Tax Pool etc in 2015/16
D	Trustee Act 1925, ss 31–33
E	Questions by STEP/CIOT and answers from HMRC to FA 2006, Sch 20 (revised October 2008)
F	Form SA900—Trust and Estate Tax Return 2015/16
G	Residence and Ordinary Residence of Individuals Before 2013/14
H	Appendix H: Trust Management Expenses Table
Index	

Abbreviations and References

Abbreviations

ACT	Advance Corporation Tax
AIM	Alternative Investment Market
App	Appendix
APR	Agricultural Property Relief
ATED	Annual Tax on Enveloped Dwellings
BES	Business Expansion Scheme
BPR	Business Property Relief
CA	Court of Appeal
CA(NI)	Court of Appeal (Northern Ireland)
CG	Inland Revenue Capital Gains Manual
CGT	Capital Gains Tax
CGTA 1979	Capital Gains Tax Act 1979
Ch D	Chancery Division
CIOT	Chartered Institute of Taxation
CIR	Commissioners of Inland Revenue ('the Board')
col	column
CJEC	Court of Justice of the European Community
CRT	Composite Rate Tax
CS	Court of Session
CTA 2010	Corporation Tax Act 2010
CTO	Capital Taxes Office
CTT	Capital Transfer Tax
DTR	Double Taxation Relief
EBT	Employee Benefit Trust
ECHR	European Convention on Human Rights
EIS	Enterprise Investment Scheme

Abbreviations and References

EOT	Employee Ownership Trust
ESC	Extra-statutory Concession
FA	Finance Act
FICO	Financial Intermediaries and Claims Offices
FOTRA	Free of tax to residents abroad
FURB	Funded Unapproved Retirement Benefit Scheme
GAAR	General Anti-Abuse Rule
HL	House of Lords
HMRC	Her Majesty's Revenue and Customs
ICAEW	Institute of Chartered Accountants in England & Wales
IRC	Inland Revenue Commissioners
ICTA 1988	Income and Corporation Taxes Act 1988
IHT	Inheritance Tax
IHTA 1984	Inheritance Tax Act 1984
IRPR	Inland Revenue Press Release
ITEPA 2003	Income Tax (Earnings and Pensions) Act 2003
ITTOIA 2005	Income Tax (Trading and Other Income) Act 2005
KB	King's Bench Division
LBTT	Land Buildings Transaction Tax
OECD	Organization for Economic Co-operation and Development
para	paragraph
PC	Privy Council
PET	Potentially Exempt Transfer
Pt	Part
QB	Queen's Bench Division
s	section
Sch	Sch [Sch 4 para 2 = 4th Schedule, paragraph 2]
SDLR	Stamp Duty Land Tax
SI	Statutory Instrument
SNRB	Settlement Nil-Rate Band
SO	Stamp Office
SP	Inland Revenue Statement of Practice

SpC	Special Commissioners' decisions
SSCBA 1992	Social Security Contributions and Benefits Act 1992
STEP	Society of Trust and Estate Practitioners
TCGA 1992	Taxation of Chargeable Gains Act 1992
TIOPA 2010	Taxation (International and Other Provisions) Act 2010
TMA 1970	Taxes Management Act 1970
TSEM	Inland Revenue Trusts, Settlements and Estates Manual
UK	United Kingdom
USM	Unlisted Securities Market

References

AC	Law Reports, Appeal Cases
All ER	All England Law Reports
EG	Estates Gazette
JLR	Jersey Law Reports
LR Sc & D	Law Reports, Scotch and Divorce (HL)
SpC	Special Commissioners
STC	Simon's Tax Cases
STC (SCD)	Simon's Tax Cases, Special Commissioners Decisions
STI	Simon's Tax Intelligence
TC	Official Reports of Tax Cases

Table of Statutes

1881 Customs and Inland Revenue Act
   s 38(2)A 23.5
1925 Law of Property Act
   s 175 .... 3.14
1925 Settled Land Act
   .... 18.42
   s 64 .... 7.135
1925 Trustee Act 1.3; 2.14
   s 31 ... 2.25; 3.13, 3.15, 3.8; 4.22; 5.3;
        6.64; 8.18, 8.21; APP C; APP D
    (2) .... 6.85, APP E
   32 .... 2.24, 2.25; 8.9; APP D, APP E
    (1) 2.26
   33 .... 8.41; APP D
   57 .... 2.24; 2.26; 2.27; 7.135
    (1) 2.28
   68(17) 2.6
1958 Trustee Act (Northern Ireland)
   s 33 .... 8.9
1958 Variation of Trusts Act
   .... 2.18, 2.24, 2.26; 7.135
1964 Perpetuities and Accumulations Act
   .... 2.16, 2.17
1965 Finance Act
   s 42 .... 26.1
1969 Family Law Reform Act
   .... 2.15
1970 Taxes Management Act
   s 7 .... 20.9
    (9) 5.4
   8 .... 20.14
   8A 20.14, 20.15A
   9A 20.24, 20.27
   9ZA, 9ZB 20.11
   12AA 20.14
   12B 20.23
   13 .... 5.8
   19A 20.24
   20(8A) 28.30
   28A 20.24
   29 .... 20.24, 20.25, 20.27; APP G
   33 .... 16.26
   34 .... 20.26
   36 .... 20.22, 20.26
   42 .... 20.15A
   43(1) 7.91
   76 .... 5.8
   93 .... 22.7
   98 .... 26.64
   99 .... 22.8
   106B-106D 22.28
   106E(1), (2) 22.29
   106F(2) 22.29
   106F(4) 22.28
   106H(4) 22.28
   107A 7.129; 20.15A
   Sch 1A

1970 Taxes Management Act – *cont.*
   Sch 1A – *cont.*
    para 3 .... 7.91
1973 Domicile and Matrimonial Proceedings Act 24.27
1973 Education Act
   s 2 .... 14.78
1973 Finance Act 6.82
1975 Finance Act
   Sch 5
    para 6(2) 27.33
1975 Inheritance (Provision for Family and other Dependants) Tax Act
   .... 28.16
1982 Administration of Justice Act
   s 20, 21 .... 5.49
1982 Finance Act
   s 129 .... 14.10
1984 Inheritance Tax Act
   s 1A .... APP E
   2(3) 21.1, 21.18
   3 .... 17.20
    (1) 10.5; 27.2
    (2) 27.2, 27.6
    (3) 10.7
   3A 5.28; 17.20; 8.32; 9.71
    (1A)(c)(iii) 8.33
    (3) 8.35
    (4), (5) 21.12
   4(1) 9.60
   5(1)(a)(i) .... APP E
    (b) 27.2
    (1A) 13.14C
    (1B) 12.28
   6 .... 24.25; 27.28
    (1) 27.27
    (2) 8.26; 10.8
   7(2) 9.28
    (4) 8.34
   8A 12.26; 18.6
   8D-8M 18.11
   10 .... 13.14C; 16.8; APP E
   11 .... 28.16
   12 .... 16.4, 16.8, 16.9
   13 .... 16.8, 16.24
   13A 16.42, 16.43
   15 .... 4.25
   16 .... APP E
   18(1) 8.8
    (2) 7.29; 27.7
   19 .... 17.21
    (3A) 9.71
   21 .... 17.21
   23 .... 14.12; APP A
   24 .... 10.14; APP A
   25 .... APP A

1984 Inheritance Tax Act – *cont.*

s 28	16.10, 16.24
28A	16.42
40	APP A
Pt III (ss 43–93)	9.70
s 43	9.39
(2)	2.20, 2.21, 2.22; 8.2, 8.5; 9.61, 9.67; 17.41
(b)	APP E
(3)	8.3; APP A
44(1)	27.7
(2)	8.4; 9.77; 27.7
45	5.20
46A	8.33
(4), (5)	APP E
46B	8.33
(1)–(3)	APP E
(5)	APP E
48	27.3
(1)	8.28; 12.17, 12.18; 27.27
(2)	8.28; 12.18
(3)	8.4; 9.64, 9.72; 27.6, 27.25
(a)	27.4, 27.27, 27.32, 26.63
(b)	27.27
(3A)	9.64, 9.72
(3B), (3C)	8.24; 9.75; 27.25
(3D)–(3F)	8.25, 27.26
(4)	8.26; 9.75, 9.77; 27.28, 27.30, 27.37
(b)	27.33, 27.35
(5)	9.77; 27.35, 27.37
(6)	9.77
49(1)	4.46; 5.19; 8.21; 9.41, 9.66; 12.10, 12.11; 18.95 21.20; APP E
(1A)	APP E
(c)	8.21; 9.72
49A	8.8; APP E
49B	8.8, 8.17
49C	8.8, 8.17, 8.19
(1)–(3)	APP E
49D	8.8, 8.17; 9.72
49E	8.8, 8.17
50	5.19
(1)	12.6
(2)	APP E
(3)	12.6; APP E
(4), (5)	APP E
(6)	APP A
51	5.19
(1)	APP E
52	5.19
(1)	12.6, 12.9, 12.10; APP A, APP E
53	5.19
(1)	27.2
(2)	8.6; 12.9; APP E
(2A)	8.6; APP E
(3)	12.13
(4)	12.13
(a)	12.7
(5)–(8)	12.13, 12.16

1984 Inheritance Tax Act – *cont.*

s 54	5.19; 12.13; 26.35
(1)(b)	APP E
(3)	12.16
54A	9.53; 12.29
(1A)	APP E
54B	9.53; 12.29
55, 56	5.19
57	5.19; 12.12
57A	5.19
Pt III Ch III (ss 58–85)	APP E
s 58	5.19; 8.30
(1)(b)	8.15
(d)	9.68
(ea)	8.29
(f)	8.29; 27.2
s 58(2A)	9.68
59	5.19
60	5.19; 9.8
61	5.19
(1)	9.8
(2)	9.9
(3), (4)	9.8
62	5.19; 9.37, 9.40
62A	9.44
62A(1)(d), (e)	9.45
62B	9.44
62B(1)	9.46
(3), (4)	9.45; 9.48
62C	9.44, 9.45, 9.47
(4)	9.48
62D	9.44
63	5.19; 8.31
64	5.19; 9.29, 9.30, 9.77
(1A)	9.33, 9.34
(1B), (1C)	9.33, 9.35
(2)	9.12
(2A)	9.33, 9.36
65	5.19
(1)	7.72
(a)	10.3; 27.32
(b)	10.3; APP A
(2)	9.77; 10.17
(3)	7.72
(4)	7.85; 10.11; 18.72; 19.3; APP E
(5)	10.10
(6)	10.5
(7)	10.8; 27.32
(7A)	27.32
(8)	10.8; 27.14
(9)	10.7
66	5.19; 9.55
(1)	9.28, 9.29
(2)	9.30, 9.51, 9.84; APP E
(4)(b)	8.30; 9.49; 10.19
(c)	9.38; 10.19
(5)	9.25
(a), (b)	9.65
(6)	9.25; 9.27

1984 Inheritance Tax Act – *cont.*

s 67	2.21; 5.19; 9.59
(1)	9.57
(2)	9.58
(3)	9.57
(6), (7)	9.65
68	5.19; 9.55, 9.84; APP E
(1)	10.17, 10.25
(2)	10.25
(3)	10.27
(b)	7.72
(4)(b)	10.24
(5)	10.21
(a)	8.30; 10.17, 17.39
69	5.19; 9.55
(1)	9.84; 10.28, 10.29
(2), (3)	9.83, 9.84; 10.31
(4)	7.72; 9.84; 10.28
70	5.19; 14.7, 14.67
(3)–(5)	APP E
(6)	11.31; APP E
(7)	APP E
(8)	11.31; APP E
(10)	APP E
71	5.19; 8.14; 11.19; APP E
(1)	7.89
(a)	APP B
(b)	6.66
(1A)	APP E
(3)	11.31
(4)	7.87 11.29; APP E
(5)	11.31
71A	8.9, 8.11, 8.12
(4)	APP E
71B	8.8
(2)(b)	8.12; APP E
(3)	APP E
71C	8.8; APP E
71D	8.11, 8.12; 10.34
(1)(a)	APP E
(2)	APP E
(3)(b)(i)	APP E
(4)	APP E
(5)(b)	APP E
(6)	8.15
(a)	APP E
(7)	APP E
71E	7.88; 8.13, 8.14; 10.34
(1)	10.32
(2)	10.32
(b)	8.15; APP E
(3)	10.32; APP E
(4)	APP E
(5)	10.32
71F	8.14, 8.15; 9.55
(2)	10.32
(3), (4)	10.34
(5)	10.34
(a)	APP E
(7)–(9)	10.34
71G	8.14; APP E

1984 Inheritance Tax Act – *cont.*

s 71H	APP E
72	5.19; 16.7, 16.42
(3A)	16.42
73	5.19
74	5.19
74A, 74B	8.25, 27.26
75	5.19; 10.14
75A	16.42
76	5.19; 14.12
(1)	10.16
(a)–(c)	10.14
(1A), (1B)	12.18
(3)–(8)	10.16
77, 78	5.19
79	5.19; 9.22
(8), (9)	9.21
80	5.19; 9.7, 9.54, 9.64; 9.71, 9.72, 9.74, 9.76
(1), (2)	9.67
81	5.19; 9.70, 9.71, 9.73; 10.26; 19.4
81A	23.10
82	5.19; 9.64, 9.71, 9.74
83	5.19; 9.63, 9.64; 9.66; 27.59
84	5.19
85	5.19; 12.18
86	5.19; 8.29, 16.6, 16.7; 16.8, 16.9; 23.17
(3)(d)	16.42
87	5.19; 8.29
88	5.19; 8.29, 8.42
89	5.19, 5.39, 5.52; 8.16
(2)	7.35
89A	8.16
(1)(c)	APP E
(2), (3)	APP E
89B(1)(c)	8.16
90	5.19; 18.25
91	5.19; 27.59, APP E
92	5.19; APP E
93	5.19
Pt IV (ss 94–102)	9.18
s 94	16.8, 16.9
102(1)	16.8
103(1)	9.17
(3)	18.62
104	18.40; 21.13
(1)(a)	18.42
105(1)	16.9
(a)	18.42
(1ZA)	18.32
(3)	18.34, 18.35, 18.36, 18.37, 18.39, 18.40, 18.47
(4)(b)	18.34, 18.51, 18.53
(5)	18.55
106	18.42, 18.54
107	18.31, 18.42, 18.54
108	18.31, 18.54
109	18.54
110(b)	9.19

1984 Inheritance Tax Act – *cont.*

s 111	18.51
112	18.17, 18.48
113	18.54, 18.55
113A	7.47
113A(1), (2)	18.67
(3)(b)	17.37; 18.66
(3A)	18.66
(b)	17.35
113B	18.66
115(1)	9.17; APP E
(2)	18.57, 18.58
(3)	18.59
117	18.64
(a)	17.38
124A	18.66
(1), (2)	18.67
124B	18.64
124C	18.57
141	21.18
142	4.37; 8.88; 18.3, 18.9; 27.1; APP E
(1)	7.115
(2)	9.10
144	7.72, 7.117; 10.11; APP E
(3)	7.56
(c)	10.12
(4)(a)	12.26
160	9.14; 18.63
161	7.40; 14.29; 21.20
162	9.14
(4)	9.18; 18.56
162A	23.10; 27.9
162B	18.56, 18.71; 23.10
162C	18.56, 18.71
165	7.47, 7.94; 18.72
175A	16.33; 23.10
178–186	7.41
186A, 186B	7.41
187–189	7.41
190–198	7.42
199	21.26; APP A
(1)(a)	21.12
(c)	5.28
(2)	21.12, 21.13
200	21.26
(1)(c)	APP E
201(1)(a), (b)	21.13
(c)	21.26
202, 203	21.26
204	5.26; 21.26
(1)	26.61
(2)	5.28; 26.61
(5)–(8)	21.12
205	21.26
Pt VIII (ss 215–261)	
	21.1
s 216	5.19; 27.57
(1)(b)	21.3
(c)	21.3
(6)	21.4

1984 Inheritance Tax Act – *cont.*

s 216(7)	21.4
218	5.20; 27.55, 27.56
(3)	21.16
219	21.15
219A	21.15
221–223	21.17
226	22.3
(1)	21.6
227	21.19, 21.20
(1)	21.25
(b)	10.22
(3)	21.25
(4)	21.24
228, 229	21.20
233	21.14
(3)	6.42
234	21.21, 21.23
235	21.14, 21.29
237	21.26
239(4)	21.27
245	22.13, 22.19
(2)(a)	27.57
(3)	27.57
(5)	22.19
245A	22.13; 22.19, 27.57
247, 248	22.13, 22.19
260	10.26
267	8.24, 8.27; 9.72; 10.9; 21.16; 24.25, 24.37, 24.41; 27.13; 28.3
(2)	27.14
(3)	27.14, 27.25
(5)	27.14
267ZA, 267ZB	7.29; 27.7
268	9.39; 12.11; 23.4
272	7.78, 7.79; 14.5; 18.32; 26.60
Sch 2	
para 1A	9.80
3	10.30
Sch 3	4.13; 10.14; APP A
Sch 4	4.13
para 16	10.14
Sch 6	
para 2	12.7
Sch 20	
para 3(3)	APP E

1986 Finance Act

s 102	4.1; 7.115; 8.36, 8.37; 18.17
(1)(b)	23.5
(4)	7.78; 8.39; 9.81; 27.6
(5)	12.20
102ZA	8.21, 8.37; 12.19
102A–102C	8.37; 23.7
103	16.32; 18.92
104	18.93
Sch 19	
para 46	8.35
Sch 20	4.1; 7.115; 8.37
para 6(1)(c)	23.4
para 8	17.38

Table of Statutes

1986 Insolvency Act
- s 30-32 .... 7.135
- s 283 .... 17.40
- 423 .... 28.19

1987 Family Law Reform Act
- s 1 .... APP D
- 19(1) .... APP D

1987 Landlord and Tenants Act
- 6.100
- s 42 .... 6.99

1987 Reverter of Sites Act
- 14.78

1988 Income and Corporation Taxes Act
- s 18
  - Schedule D
    - Case III 25.8
    - Case IV. 25.4, 25.8
    - Case V. 25.4, 25.8
- s 213–218 .... 7.21
- 219 .... 5.6; 18.84
- 220–229 .... 5.6; 18.84
- 235 .... 14.60
- 278 .... APP B
- 336 .... APP G
- Pt XV (ss 660–694)
  - .... APP A
- s 686 .... APP A
  - (2)(b) 5.11
    - (ii) 6.61, 6.72
- 687 .... 6.81
  - (1) .... APP B
  - (2) .... APP B
- 790 .... 25.15
- Sch 20 .... 14.33

1988 Finance Act
- s 66 .... 24.51

1989 Finance Act
- s 43 .... 16.5
- 151 .... 6.101

1990 Finance Act
- s 126 .... 8.29

1991 Finance Act 27.1
- s 121 .... 8.29

1992 Charities Act
- 14.76

1992 Finance (No 2) Act
- 14.29
- s 27 .... 14.23

1992 Taxation of Chargeable Gains Act
- 26.66
- s 2(1) 1.9; 7.1; 26.2
- (2) 7.18; 26.17; 28.23
- (4) 5.40
- 2B–2F 7.127
- 3(3) 7.36
- (7) 7.38
- 10 .... 7.98; 25.45; 26.2, 26.4
- 10A .... 24.17; 26.19, 26.57, 26.59; 28.23; APP G
- 12 .... 24.26; 26.62

1992 Taxation of Chargeable Gains Act – cont.
- s 12(1), (2) 28.20
- 13 .... 24.43; 26.3, 26.44
  - (10) 26.42
- 14A 24.43; 26.43, 26.43, 26.44
- 16(2) 7.131
- 16(2A) 7.5, 7.41
- 16A 7.17, 7.18
- 17 .... 7.3
  - (1) 16.25
  - (2) 7.23
- 18(1), (2) 7.3
  - (3) 17.12
- 19 .... 14.30
- 28 .... 7.106
- 37 .... 7.124
- 38(1)(b) .... 7.44; APP A
  - (2)(b) 7.45
- 60 .... 2.44;7.9; 13.6
  - (2) 7.10, 7.12, 7.89
- 62 .... 17.5
  - (1) 7.40
  - (4) 2.7; 7.117
  - (6) 4.37; 7.112; 26.25
    - (b) 7.116
  - (7) 7.112
  - (9) 7.116
- 65(1) 7.129
  - (b) 18.75
  - (4) 5.4; 7.129; 18.72
- 68 .... 2.11; 5.18
- 68A 7.36
- 68C 4.37, 7.112
- 69 .... 2.11; 5.34; 16.23; 24.16, 24.23; 26.10
  - (1) 5.18; 7.62
- 70 .... 2.11
- 71 .... 2.11; 7.14, 7.117, 7.117
  - (1) .... 7.5, 7.6, 7.14, 7.122; 18.82; 19.13; APP A
  - (2) 7.4, 7.5, 7.6, 7.12, 7.15, 7.16, 7.40
  - (3) 7.12
- 72 .... 2.11; 7.27, 7.31; APP A
  - (1) .... 7.26; APP E
    - (a) 7.28
    - (b) 7.99
- 73 .... 2.11; 7.26, 7.29
  - (1)(a) 7.6, 7.99; 19.13
    - (b) 19.13
  -) 7.6
- 74 .... 2.11; 7.29; 19.13
- 75 .... 2.11
- 76 .... 2.11; 26.11, 26.13
  - (1) 7.134
  - (1A) 7.134
  - (2) 7.25
- 76A 7.134
- 76B 2.11, 7.75

xxxiii

Table of Statutes

1992 Taxation of Chargeable Gains Act – cont.
s 77 .. 2.11, 4.1, 4.33, 4.34, 4.37; 7.75, 7.98, 7.112, 7.115; 12.22; APP B
   (1) 18.82, 18.85
   (2) 26.17
   (8) 4.35
78 .... 2.11, APP B
   (3) 26.18
79 .... 2.11; APP B
79A 2.11, 6.43; 7.12, 7.16
80 ..... 2.11, 7.93; 23.4; 26.5, 26.12, 26.14
81 .... 2.11, 26.4, 26.7
82 .... 2.11, 26.4, 26.8
83 ..... 2.11, 7.93; 23.4; 26.10, 26.12
83A 2.11, 24.25
84 .... 2.11, 26.14
85 .... 26.11, 26.15
   (1)–(9) 26.12
86 .... 2.11, 5.32; 7.98, 7.114, 7.115, 8.127; 12.22; 16.23; 24.43, 26.3, 26.54, 26.64; 28.15; APP B
   (1)(c) 26.21
   (4) 26.17
     (b) 26.18
86A 2.11, 26.19; 24.18
87 ..... 1.9; 2.11, 5.40; 7.115, 8.127; 16.23; 20.58; 24.17, 24.43; 26.1; 26.24, 26.33, 26.39, 26.42, 26.43, 26.44, 26.45, 26.54
   (2), (3) 26.18
   (7) 26.34
   (9) 26.34
88 .... 2.11, 26.36, 26.42
89 .... 2.11, 26.37, 26.42
90 .... 2.11, 26.38, 26.42
   (5) 26.57
91 .... 2.11; 19.19; 26.3, 26.45
92–95 .... 2.11, 26.4
96 .... 2.11, 26.39
   (5) 26.40
97 .... 2.11
   (1)(b) 26.41
   (5) 26.57
   (6) 26.41
98 .... 2.11, 26.42
98A 2.11
106A 26.16
115 .... 7.123
119 .... 7.123
144(3) 16.25
144ZA–144ZD 16.25
149A 16.25
150E–150G 7.107
Pt 5 (ss 152-169A)
.... 7.107
152 .... 7.62, 23.4; 26.5, 26.14

1992 Taxation of Chargeable Gains Act – cont.
s 165 ..... 4.34; 5.22, 5.24; 7.29, 7.47, 7.81, 7.82, 7.91, 7.122; 10.13; 17.14, 17.17; 18.33, 18.87, 18.89; 19.13; 26.6
   (3) 7.64
   (d) 7.51, 7.73, 7.73, 10.26; 18.72, 18.88
   (4) 7.62
   (5) 7.62
   (6) 7.62
   (9) 7.66
   (10) 7.46
165A 7.66
   (14) 7.66
166, 167 .... 7.92
168 .... 5.223; 7.50, 7.93
   (4) 5.21
   (5) 5.21
   (7) 5.21
   (9) 5.21
169 .... 26.10
169B 10.26; 17.15
169C 7.81; 17.15
   (6) 5.24
169D(1) 7.83
169F(4B) 5.24
169H, 169I 7.102
169J 7.102, 7.104
169K 7.102
169K(1) 7.103
169L 7.102
169M 7.102, 7.105
169N 7.102
169O 7.102, 7.105
169P–169S 7.102
222 .... 7.51, 7.54; 25.47; 17.11
   (5)(a) 7.17
222B, 222C 17.11; 26.68
223 .... 7.51; 17.11
   (1) 7.50, 18.85, 18.89
   (2)–(4) 7.58
224 .... 7.51; 17.11; 25.47
   (3) 25.47
225 ..... 7.51, 7.52, 7.54, 7.55, 7.56, 7.57; 17.11; 18.85, 18.87
   (5)(a) 7.53; 18.85
225A–225D 17.11
225E 7.59
226 .... 17.11; 25.47
226A 17.11; 7.82
226B 17.11
236H 16.37, 16.38
236I–236N 16.37
236O, 236P 16.37, 16.39
236Q–236U 16.37
239 .... 16.24
241 .... 18.42

1992 Taxation of Chargeable Gains Act – cont.

s 248A–248E	7.133
251(1)	17.11
252	17.19, 17.10
256	14.31, 14.53
(2)	14.78
257	14.14
257A	14.58
258	7.71
260	5.22, 5.24; 7.51, 7.60, 7.73, 7.74, 7.76, 7.79, 7.81, 7.82, 7.91, 7.83, 7.91; 9.82, 9.84; 10.13; 17.14, 17.16;18.72, 18.85, 18.87, 18.88; 19.13, 19.21; APP E
(2)	7.72
(a)	7.97, 7.122
(d)	7.72, 7.87
(db)	7.72
(db)	7.97
(3)	26.6
(5)	17.43
(7)	7.46
261ZA	5.22; 7.50
261	7.92
269	17.9
272	7.40
274	7.40, 7.41
275A	26.62
281	7.94
286	7.3
(a)	17.12
288(1)	7.93
Sch A1	
para 21	7.50
Sch 1	
para 1	7.36
2(5)	7.36
(7)	7.36, 7.37
Sch 4	7.95
Sch 4A	7.95
Sch 4B	7.75, 26.59
Sch 4C	26.51, 26.59
Sch 4ZA	7.118; 19.13
para 19	7.122
para 20(1), (2)	7.122
Sch 5	26.17; APP B
para 1(3)	26.44
2	26.20
(3)–(6)	26.21
3–5	26.22
6	26.24
8	26.20, 26.23
9	26.26, 26.27
(3)	APP E
10	26.64
Sch 5B	
para 3(5)	7.99
para 17	7.97, 7.98; 18.33
Sch 5BB	7.101

1992 Taxation of Chargeable Gains Act – cont.

Sch 7	7.62
Pt I	
para 1	7.122
para 1(1)(a)	7.67
2	7.69, 7.122
para 3, 4	7.122
Pt II	18.87
para 7	7.70

1993 Charities Act

	14.4, 14.76

1995 Finance Act ... 1.3; 4.35

s 138(1)	14.36
154, 155	18.57

1995 Law Reform (Miscellaneous Provisions) Act ... 2.19

1996 Finance Act

s 154	27.31; APP B
199	18.32
200	24.35
Sch 28	
para 7, 8	27.31
Sch 38	18.32

1996 Trusts of Land and Appointment of Trustees Act

s 12	7.55, 7.56

1997 Finance Act

s 94	18.54

1998 Finance Act ... 4.33; 7.64; 27.1

s 132	26.27
143	21.30
Sch 22	26.28
Sch 23	26.29
Sch 25	21.30

1999 Finance Act

s 64	2.45
Sch 13	
para 1(3A)	13.46

2000 Finance Act ... 1.12; 14.40; 26.57

s 38	14.15
46	14.35
90	7.75
146, 147	28.28
Sch 25	26.15
Sch 26	26.15, 26.59

2000 Trustee Act ... 1.3; 5.3; 6.43

2002 Finance Act ... 1.12

s 52	7.112
97	14.23
119	7.78, 7.79; 9.81
Sch 18	14.4

2003 Finance Act

s 42–44	1.12
(4)	13.8
45	1.12
46	1.12
47	1.12; 7.133
48–54	1.12

Table of Statutes

2003 Finance Act – *cont.*
  s 55 .... 1.12
    (2) 13.23
  56–67 .... 1.12
  68 .... 1.12; 14.10
  69–75 .... 1.12
  75A–75C 13.1
  76 .... 1.12; 13.8
  77–104 .... 1.12
  105 .... 1.12; 13.1
  106–118 .... 1.12
  119 .... 1.12; 9.82
  120–124 .... 1.12
  163 .... 7.75
  185 .... 12.21
  186 .... 27.32
    (3) 9.75
  Sch 3 .... 1.12
    para 1 .... 13.36
  Sch 4ZA 13.30
  para 10-13 .... 13.31
  Sch 4 .... 1.12
    para 8(1) 13.11, 13.35
    8(1A), (1B)
    .... 13.11
    16A,16B 13.36
  Sch 5–Sch 7 .... 1.12
  Sch 8 .... 1.12; 14.10, 14.11
  Sch 9–Sch 15 .... 1.12
  Sch 16 .... 1.12; 13.1
    para 1(1) 13.8, 13.10
    (2) 13.5
    2(a) 13.20
    (b) 13.21
    3 .... 13.10
    4 .... 13.11
    5(1), (2) 13.14
    (3) 13.13
    (4) 13.15
    6(1), (2) 13.16
    (3) 13.17
    (4) 13.18
    (5) 13.19
    7 .... 13.22
  Sch 17 .... 13.10
  Sch 18 .... 1.12
  Sch 29 .... 7.75
2003 Income Tax (Earnings and Pensions) Act
  Pt 3, Ch 3 (ss 173–191)
  .... 16.11
  s 26A 24.20
  181 .... 4.43
  312A–312I 16.41
  Pt 7, Ch 5 (ss 471–484)
  .... 16.25
  Pt 7A (ss 554A–554Z21)
  .... 16.15, 16.16
  s 713–715 .... 14.15
2004 Finance Act 1.7
  s 168(1) 9.68

2004 Finance Act – *cont.*
  Pt VII (ss 290–302)
  .... 27.58
  s 302 .... 14.10
  306(1)(c) 23.17
  308 .... 23.25
  Sch 15 .... 4.39
    para 3–5 .... 4.42
    6 .... 4.43
    7(2) 4.43
    8 .... 4.44; 17.49
    9 .... 4.44
    10 .... 4.45
    11 .... 4.46
    12 .... 26.63
    13 .... 4.47
    16 .... 4.48
    21 .... 4.49; 18.93
    22, 23 .... 4.49
  Sch 21 .... 7.81
  Sch 22 .... 7.82, 18.86, 18.87
2005 Finance Act 1.9
  s 30–32 .... 7.128
  Sch 1A 7.59
2005 Finance (No 2) Act
  Sch 5 .... 16.25
2005 Income Tax (Trading and Other Income) Act
  .... 20.4
  s 8 .... 25.3
  38–44 .... 16.4
  54 .... 6.42
  277 .... 6.59, 6.96
  Pt 3, Ch 6 (ss 322–328B)
  .... 18.43
  s 325 .... 18.87
  397A 6.48; 20.71
  398 .... 6.48
  399 .... 25.11
  484, 485 .... 17.49, 17.50
  487, 488 .... 17.49, 17.50
  515–526 .... 17.49, 17.50
  535–537 .... 17.54, 17.50
  Pt 4 Ch 8 .... 5.6
  Pt 5 Ch 2 (ss 578–608)
  .... 14.35
  Pt 5 Ch 5 (ss 619–645)
  .... 4.2; 5.11, 5.17; 16.22
  s 619 .... 4.1, 4.11
  620 .... 4.1, 4.11
    (1) 4.4, 4.24
    (2), (3) 4.5
  621 .... 4.1, 4.11
  622 .... 4.1, 4.11; 20.54, 20.57
  623 .... 4.1, 4.11
  624 .... 4.1, 4.3, 4.11, 4.13
    (1) 4.23; 5.11; 6.88
  625 .... 4.1, 4.11, 4.23
    (2) 4.10
    (5) 4.3

2005 Income Tax (Trading and
    Other Income) Act – cont.
  s 626 .... 4.1, 4.11, 4.23
  627, 628 .... 4.1, 4.11, 4.23
  629 .... 2.45; 4.1, 4.11; 28.15
    (1) . 4.16, 4.21, 4.23, 4.24; 12.22;
                                20.54, 20.57
      (a) 4.14
      (2) 20.54, 20.57
      (3) 4.15
  630 .... 4.1, 4.11, 4.23
  631 .... 4.1, 4.11, 4.23
  632 .... 4.1, 4.9, 4.11, 4.23
  633 .... 4.1, 4.11, 4.26; 17.43
  634 ...... 4.1, 4.11, 4.26, 4.27; 17.43
  635, 636 ...... 4.1, 4.11, 4.26; 17.43
  637 .... 4.1, 4.11, 4.26; 17.43
    (8) 4.29
  638 ...... 4.1, 4.11, 4.26, 4.37; 17.43
  639 .... 4.1, 4.11, 4.26; 17.43
  640 .... 4.1, 4.11, 4.26; 17.43
  641 .... 4.1, 4.11, 4.26; 17.43
    (1) 4.29
  642 .... 4.1, 4.11, 4.26; 17.43
  643 .... 4.1, 4.11, 4.26
  644, 645 .... 4.1, 4.11
  Pt 5 Ch 7 (ss 646–648)
    .... 6.5
  s 646 .... 4.1, 4.11
    (5) 6.60, 6.61
    (8) 4.23; 5.11
  647 .... 4.1, 4.11
  648 .... 4.1, 4.11
    (1) 4.9
    (3) 5.17
  Pt 5, Ch 6 (ss 649–682A)
    .... 5.10
  s 649 .... 2.7, 2.11
  650 .... 2.7, 2.11
    (3), (4) .... APP A
    (6) .... APP A
  651 .... 2.7, 2.11
    (1)–(3) .... APP A
  652–654 .... 2.7, 2.11
  655 .... 2.7, 2.11
    (1) .... APP A
  656 .... 2.7, 2.11; 20.33
  657–661 .... 2.7, 2.8
  662 .... 2.7, 2.8; APP A
  663 .... 2.7, 2.8; APP A
    (1) 20.33
  664–678 .... 2.7, 2.8
  679 .... 2.7, 2.8
    (2), (3) .... APP A
  680 .... 2.7, 2.8, APP A
  681 .... 2.7, 2.11; 20.35
  682 .... 2.7, 2.11
    A 2.7, 2.11, 20.36
  685A 6.88, 6.89
  Pt 5 Ch 8 (ss 687–689)
    .... 6.97

2005 Income Tax (Trading and
    Other Income) Act – cont.
  s 713–715 .... APP G
  832 .... 24.26; 28.20
  869 .... 6.42
  878(1) 14.5
2006 Charities Act
    ... 14.4, 14.8, 14.47, 14.61, 14.76,
                                      14.77
2006 Companies Act
    .... 18.30, 18.51
2006 Finance Act ... 1.4, 1.9; 2.11, 2.46;
                          4.36; 5.19; 7.84; 8.8,
                          8.10, 8.16, 8.17, 8.22,
                          8.29; 17.23; 21.8; APP E
  s 74 .... 26.16
  157(2) 27.25
    (4)–(6) 27.25
  165 .... 13.8
  173 .... 28.28
  Sch 12
    Pt II 7.103
  Sch 20 .... 7.51, 7.72; APP E
    para 3 .... APP E
2007 Finance Act
  s 66 .... 4.50
  109 .... 18.32
  809C 24.26
  809D 24.26
  809VA 24.42
  Sch 24 .... 22.9
    para 1A(2) 22.12
         3(1) 22.13
  Sch 26 .... 18.32
2007 Income Tax Act
  s 10 .... 5.6
  13(1)(c) 20.71
  14(1)(c) 20.71
  19(2)(b) 20.71
  24 .... 5.6
  Pt 4 Ch 4 (ss 117–127)
    .... 5.6
  s 131–151 .... 18.33
  Pt 5A Ch 5A (ss 257A-257HJ)
    .... 7.101
  Pt 8 Ch 1 (ss 383–412)
    .... 5.7
  s 383 .... 6.41
  390 .... 6.41
  392 .... 6.41
  396 .... 6.41
  401 .... 6.41
  403–405 .... 6.42
  Pt 8 Ch 2 (ss 413–430)
    .... 14.15
  s 416(7) 14.17
  417–421 .... 14.17
  429 .... 14.25
  431–434 .... 14.26

Table of Statutes

2007 Income Tax Act – *cont.*
  Pt 8 Ch 4 (ss 447–452)
    .... 6.65
  s 466–468 .... 4.6
  469 .... 4.6
  469B 6.83
  470, 471 .... 4.6
  472 .... 4.6, 4.17
  473 .... 4.6
  474 .... 4.6; 24.21
  475 .... 4.6; 16.20; 24.16, 24.21
  475(6) 24.22
  476 .... 4.6; 16.20; 24.21
  477 .... 7.121; 24.21
  Pt 9 Ch 3 (ss 479–483)
    ...... 4.14; 5.6; 5.17; 6.42, 6.56, 6.92;
                    20.16; 25.11
  s 479 ..... 2.11; 6.28, 6.42, 6.59, 6.67,
                6.70, 6.72; APP C
    (1) 6.60
  480 .... 2.11, 6.60
    (1) 6.66
    (3)(a) 6.62
    (c) 6.100
  481 .... 2.11; 6.59, 6.67
  482 .... 2.11, 6.12, 6.59; 18.84
  483 .... 2.11
  484 .... 6.62
  485(5)(a) 6.36
  486 .... 6.29
  487 .... 25.11
  491, 492 .... 6.52
  Pt 9 Ch 7 (ss 493–498)
    .... 6.12, 6.91; 20.56; 25.12
  s 493 .... 6.73, 6.75, 6.85
    494(1) 6.105
    (3) 6.105
  496 .... 6.67, 6.72, 6.75, 6.83
  496A 16.20
  496B .... ; 16.20, 16.21
  497 .... 6.74
  498 .... 6.58A, 6.67, 6.71
  499–503 .... 25.52
  508 .... 4.13
  521 .... 14.53
  522 .... 14.27, 14.31, 14.53
  523 .... 14.31, 14.53, 28.14
  524, 525 .... 14.31, 14.53
  526 .... 14.31, 14.35, 14.53
  527 .... 14.53
  528 .... 14.35, 14.53
  529 .... 14.53
  530 .... 14.35, 14.53
  531, 532 .... 14.31, 14.53
  533–539 .... 14.53
  540(3) 14.53
  541–542 .... 14.53
  543 .... 14.48, 14.53, 14.55
  544–548 .... 14.48, 14.55
  549–557 .... 14.48

2007 Income Tax Act – *cont.*
  Pt 12 (ss 615–681DP)
    .... 6.7
  s 615 .... 7.123
  s 615(3) 9.68
  s 616-618 .... 7.123
  s 619 .... 6.7, 7.123
  632(1) 6.15
  636 .... 6.15
    (2) 6.19
  639–650 .... 6.7
  651 .... 6.7, 6.15
  652–664 .... 6.7
  666 .... 6.15
  667 .... 6.15, 6.60
  674 .... 6.10
  Pt 13 Ch 1 (ss 682–713)
    .... 14.60
  s 683 .... 14.60
  705 .... 14.60
  Pt 13 Ch 2 (ss 714–751)
    .... 25.18; 28.15, 28.24
  s 720 .... 5.6
  721(5) 25.23
  723(3) 25.23
  726 .... 25.18
  730 .... 25.18
  731 .... 25.22
  732 .... 25.22
    (1)(c) 25.32
  733–735 .... 25.22, 25.37
  735A 25.37
  736 .... 9.73; 25.24, 25.28
  737 .... 9.73; 25.24, 25.28
  738 .... 9.73; 25.24, 25.28
    (1), (2) 25.29
  738(3) 25.30
    (4) 25.29
  739 .... 9.73; 25.24, 25.28
  740–742 ... 9.66; 25.24, 25.28, 25.31
  748–750 .... 26.42
  Pt 13 Ch 3 (ss 752–772)
    .... 6.97; 25.46
  s 756(5) 25.48
  764 .... 5.6
  767 .... 25.47
  768 .... 25.50
  770 .... 25.50
  809A 28.3, 28.20
  809C, 809D 24.25, 28.3, 28.20
  809E–809L 28.3, 28.20
  809M 25.17, 28.3, 28.20
  809N–809Z 28.3, 28.20
  809Z1–809Z6 .... 28.20
  809ZH–809ZR 14.58
  811, 812 .... 6.104
  813 .... 6.104; 25.52
  814 .... 6.104
  829, 830 .... APP G
  831 .... 24.4, 24.7
    (1)(b) .... APP G

2007 Income Tax Act – *cont.*
  s 832 .... 24.4, 24.7; 28.20
    (1)(b) .... APP G
  833, 834 .... APP G
  837 .... 4.18
  Pt 15 (ss 847–987)
  .... 6.105
  s 853–857 .... 25.51
  899(5)(d) 6.105
  964 .... 20.48
  971 .... 5.30
  989 .... 14.53
2008 Finance Act 1.7; 24.3; 24.25,
           24.41; 25.54; 26.1; 26.47
  s 2(2) 26.51
  58 .... 26.42
  67 .... 4.38
  98 .... 13.46
  141 .... 8.17
  135 .... 8.13; 21.14
  188 .... 17.17
  Sch 2
    para 5 .... 26.17
         74 .... 7.96
  Sch 7 .... 28.1, 28.3, 28.23
    para 108 .... 26.34
         111 .... 26.57
  Sch 19
    para 3 .... 14.24
  Sch 29
    para 12 .... 17.17
  Sch 32 .... 13.46
  Sch 36
    Pt 1 .... 26.64
    para 1–3 .... 21.15
  Sch 39
    para 12 .... 7.91
  Sch 40 .... 22.9
2009 Corporation Tax Act
  s 14 .... 24.51
    1290–1297 .... 24.51
2009 Finance Act 24.32
  s 94 .... 22.27
  s 96 .... 21.15
  122 .... 1.24
  Sch 19 .... 6.67
  Sch 25 .... 6.22
  Sch 55 ·
    para 3–6A 22.20
  Sch 56 .... 22.23
    para 1 .... 22.22
         3 .... 22.22
         9(1) 22.22
         10 .... 22.22
         16 .... 22.22
2009 Perpetuities and Accumulations Act
  .... 2.13, 3.9; 18.75, 18.80
  s 14 .... 2.16
2010 Corporation Tax Act
  s 191(7) 14.17

2010 Corporation Tax Act – *cont.*
  s 196–198 .... 14.17
  199 .... 14.31
  448–450 .... 26.25
  449 .... 4.30
  454 .... 26.25
  471, 472 .... 14.53
  Pt 6 .... 14.27
  473 .... 14.31, 14.53
  474 .... 14.31, 14.53
  475–477 .... 14.53
  478, 479 .... 14.31, 14.53
  480 .... 14.35, 14.53
  481 .... 14.53
  482 .... 14.35, 14.53
  483, 484 .... 14.53
  485, 486 .... 14.31, 14.53
  487–491 .... 14.53
  Pt 11 Ch 4 (ss 492–517)
  .... 14.33
  s 492 .... 14.48, 14.55
  493 .... 14.48, 14.55
    (3) 14.53
  494, 495 .... 14.48, 14.55
  496 .... 14.48, 14.53, 14.55
  497–501 .... 14.48, 14.55
  502–510 .... 14.57
  574 .... 28.14
  584 .... 14.36
  658(1) 17.57; 14.4
  Pt 16 Ch 1 .... 6.22
  939A–939I 14.58
  1033 .... 5.6, 6.59, 18.84
  1034–1048 .... 5.6, 18.84
  1073–1099 .... 7.21
  1119 .... 14.53
2010 Finance Act 1.24, 14.2; 23.10
  s 4 .... 7.97
  31 .... 14.2, 14.65
  53(3) 13.14C
    (b) 12.28
  Sch 6 .... 14.6; 28.20
    Pt 1 .... 14.5
    para 1 .... 14.43
         2, 3 .... 14.43
         4 .... 14.43, 14.44
    Pt 3 .... 14.2
    para 30 .... 14.4
         32 .... 14.4
  Sch 7 .... 14.65
  Sch 8
    para 8 .... 14.2
2010 Finance (No 2) Act
  Sch 1 .... 26.52
2010 Finance (No 3) Act
  Sch 14
    para 2 .... 15.19
2010 Taxation (International and Other
         Provisions) Act
  s 6(3) 26.8

Table of Statutes

2010 Taxation (International and Other Provisions) Act – *cont.*
  s 8–18 .... 25.15
  Pt 8 .... 5.6
2011 Charities Act
    ..... 1.3; 14.4, 14.28, 14.47, 14.61
  s 3 .... 14.9
    4(2) 14.77
  Pt 11 (ss 204–250)
    .... 14.8
  s 228–234 .... 14.8
2011 Finance Act 7.102
  s 9 .... 7.97
    52 .... 1.24
  Sch 14 .... 1.24, 7.63
    para 2 .... 18.89
2012 Finance Act 23.10; 24.42
  s 38 .... 7.101
  s 51 .... 14.16
    209 .... 14.13
    210 .... 8.25
    214 .... 13.34
    223 .... 22.8
  Sch 6 .... 7.101
  Sch 15 .... 14.16
  Sch 33 .... 14.13
  Sch 35 .... 13.34
2013 Finance Act .. 23.10; 24.21; 25.36, 25.37
  s 26 .... 25.34
    43C 23.14
    62 .... 26.44
    63 .... 4.13
    71D 8.15
    71E 8.15
    86 .... 8.29; 10.14
    94–174 .... 13.40; 18.71
    178 .... 27.7
    194–197 .... 17.25, 13.2
    206–211 .... 23.11
    212A 23.11, 23.14
    213–215 .... 23.11
    218 .... 24.8
    219 .... 24.20
    233 .... 20.14
  Sch 10 .... 25.34
  Sch 33 .... 13.40; 18.71; 20.14
  Sch 34 .... 13.40; 18.71
  Sch 35 .... 13.40; 18.71

2013 Finance Act – *cont.*
  Sch 36 .... 27.10
    para 5(3)(a), (b)
    .... 18.71
  Sch 39 .... 17.25, 13.2
  Sch 40 .... 17.25, 13.2
  Sch 41 .... 17.25, 13.2
  Sch 43C 23.14
  Sch 44 .... 8.10, 8.15
  Sch 45 .... 24.8
    Pt 1 .... 24.8
    Pt 2 .... 24.8; 24.12; 24.14
    Pt 3 .... 24.8
    Pt 4 .... 24.8
    Pt 5 .... 24.8
  Sch 46 .... 24.8; 25.18, 25.33
    para 114 .... 27.28
  Sch 51 .... 20.14
2013 Trust (Capital and Income) Act
  .... 14.80
2014 Inheritance and Trustees' Powers Act
  .... 2.23, 2.25
2014 Finance Act . 9.4; 13.2, 13.32; 19.4
                19.6; 23.10, 23.27; 25.37
  Sch 24 .... 13.47
  Sch 25
    para 5 .... 21.2
  Sch 37 .... 16.36, 16.42
2015 Finance Act 24.44; 27.39
  s 66 .... 14.41
    117 .... 23.16, 23.18
    120 .... 22.25
    121 .... 22.26
  Sch 17 .... 23.16, 23.18
  Sch 21 .... 22.26
2015 Finance (No 2) Act
  .... 9.6
  s 13 .... 9.76
2016 Charities (Protection and Social Investment) Act................ 14.66
2016 Land and Buildings Transaction Tax (Amendment) (Scotland) Act
  .... 13.38
2016 Finance Act
  s 162 .... 22.25
  s 163 .... 22.27
  s 165 .... 22.27
  Sch 20 .... 22.25

Table of Statutory Instruments

1987/1130 Inheritance Tax (Double Charges Relief) Regulations 1987 .... 4.52; 8.39, 9.74; 18.92
1987/516 Stamp Duty (Exempt Instruments) Regulations 1987 .... 13.36
1990/2231 Income Tax (Building Societies) (Dividends and Interest) Regulations 1990 .... 25.47
2002/1731 Inheritance Tax (Delivery of Accounts) (Excepted Transfers and Excepted Terminations) Regulations 2002 .... 21.8
2002/1732 Inheritance Tax (Delivery of Accounts) (Excepted Settlements) Regulations 2002 .... 21.11
2005/724 Charge to Income Tax by Reference to Enjoyment of Property Previously Owned Regulation 2005
  reg 3 .... 4.43
  6 .... 4.52; 18.93
2005/3441 Inheritance Tax (Double Charges Relief) Regulations 2005 .... 18.93
2006/875 Stamp Duty Land Tax (Amendment to the Finance Act 2003) Regulations 2006 .... 13.28
2007/3000 Income Tax (Benefits Received by Former Owner of Property) (Election for Inheritance Tax Treatment). Regulations 2007 .... 4.49
2008/605 Inheritance Tax (Delivery of Accounts) (Excepted Transfers and Excepted Terminations) Regulations 2008 .... 21.9, 21.11
2008/606 Inheritance Tax (Delivery of Accounts) (Excepted Settlements) Regulations 2008 .... 21.11
2008/2682 Income Tax (Deposit-Takers and Building Societies) (Interest Payments) Regulations 2008 .... 25.47
2009/403 Finance Act 2008, Schedule 39 (Appointed Day, Transitional Provision and Savings) Order 2009 .... 7.129, 7.12; 17.17
  art 10 .... 7.91
2009/511 Finance Act 2008, Schedule 41 (Appointed Day and Transitional Provisions) Order 2009 .... 22.9
2009/1029 Substantial Donor Transactions (Variation of Threshold Limits) Regulations 2009 .... 14.56
2009/3001 Offshore Funds (Tax) Regulations 2009 .... 7.123
2010/1879 Taxes and Duties (Interest Rate) Regulations 2010 .... 17.19
2010/1904 Taxes (Definition of Charity) (Relevant Territories) Regulations 2010 .... 14.2
2011/170 Inheritance Tax Avoidance Schemes (Prescribed Descriptions of Arrangements) Regulations 2011 .... 23.17
2011/702 Finance Act 2009, Schedules 55 and 56 (Income Tax Self Assessment and Pension Schemes) (Appointed Days and Consequential and Savings Provisions) Order 2011 .... 20.6
2011/2446 Taxes and Duties, etc (Interest Rate) Regulations 2011 .... 17.19
2012/735 Finance Act 2010, Schedule 6, Part 1 (Further Consequential and Incidental Provision etc) Order 2012 .... 14.2, 14.5
2012/736 Finance Act 2010, Schedule 6, Part 2 (Commencement) Order 2012 .... 14.2, 14.5
2012/2395 Stamp Duty Land Tax Avoidance Schemes (Prescribed Descriptions of Arrangements) (Amendment) Regulations 2012 .... 23.25
2012/2396 Stamp Duty Land Tax (Avoidance Schemes) (Specified Proposals or Arrangements) Regulations 2012 .... 23.25
2013/938 Small Charitable Donations Regulations 2013 .... 14.18
2015/1378 Inheritance Tax (Electronic Communications) Regulations 2015 .... 21.31

Table of Cases

A

Abacus Trust Co (Isle of Man) Ltd v National Society for the Prevention of Cruelty to Children [2001] STC 1344, 3 ITELR 846, [2001] 35 LS Gaz R 37, (2001) Times, 25 September, [2001] All ER (D) 207 (Jul) .... 5.26, 5.29, APP A
Aberdeen Asset Management plc v Revenue and Customs Comrs [2013] CSIH 84, [2014] STC 438, 2014 SC 271 .... 15B.12
Aikin (Surveyor of Taxes) v Macdonald's Trustees (1894) 3 TC 306, 32 SLR 85, Exch Ct 6.26, 7.22
Allfrey v Allfrey [2015] EWHC 1717 (Ch), [2015] WTLR 1117, [2015] 2 P & CR D43, [2015] All ER (D) 245 (Jun) 2.17A, 7.3P, 7.11, 2.18
Allnutt v Wilding [2007] EWCA Civ 412, 9 ITELR 806, [2007] All ER (D) 41 (Apr) 5.42
American Leaf Blending Co Sdn Bhd v Director General of Inland Revenue (Malaysia) [1979] AC 676, [1978] 3 All ER 1185, [1978] 3 WLR 985, [1978] STC 561, [1978] TR 243, 122 Sol Jo 641, PC 16.41,18.50
Anderson (R) v Revenue and Customs Comrs [2013] UKFTT 126 (TC), [2013] SWTI 1812 .... 6.43, 17.50
Archer Shee v Baker [1927] 1 KB 109, 11 TC 749, CA; revsd sub nom Baker v Archer-Shee [1927] AC 844, 96 LJKB 803, 71 Sol Jo 727, 137 LT 762, 43 TLR 758, [1927] All ER Rep Ext 755, sub nom Archer-Shee v Baker 11 TC 749, HL 22.4, 22.5, 22.6, 22.10, 22.13, 22.55
Archer-Shee v Garland (Inspector of Taxes) [1931] AC 212, 100 LJKB 170, 144 LT 508, 47 TLR 171, sub nom Garland (Inspector of Taxes) v Archer-Shee 15 TC 693, HL 22.4, 22.5, 22.7, 22.10, 22.13, 22.55
Arnander (executors of McKenna, dec'd) v Revenue and Customs Comrs (SpC 565) [2006] STC (SCD) 800, [2007] RVR 208 .... 16.54, 18.61
Association belge des Consommateurs Test-Achats ASBL v Conseil des ministres: C-236/09 [2012] 1 WLR 1933, [2012] All ER (EC) 441, [2011] 2 CMLR 994, [2011] Lloyd's Rep IR 296, [2011] NLJR 363, [2011] All ER (D) 07 (Mar), ECJ 6.46
Atkinson and Smith (executors of the Will of William Atkinson dec'd) v Revenue and Customs Comrs [2010] UKFTT 108 (TC), [2010] SWTI 2123; revsd sub nom Revenue and Customs Comrs v Atkinson and Smith (executors of the Will of William Atkinson dec'd) (FTC/61/2010) [2011] UKUT 506 (TCC), [2012] STC 289 ... 16.58, 18.65

B

Bainbridge v Bainbridge [2016] EWHC 898 .... 5.49B
Baird's Executors v IRC [1991] 1 EGLR 201, [1991] 09 EG 129, 10 EG 153, 1991 SLT (Lands Tr) 9 .... 16.56, 18.63
Baker v Archer-Shee. See Archer Shee v Baker
Bambridge v IRC [1955] 3 All ER 812, [1955] 1 WLR 1329, 36 TC 313, 34 ATC 281, [1955] TR 295, 99 Sol Jo 910, L(TC) 1754, HL 22.20
Barclay's Bank Trust Co Ltd v IRC (SpC 158) [1998] STC (SCD) 125 .... 16.41, 18.48
Barclays Private Bank and Trust (Cayman) Ltd v Chamberlain (2005) 9 ITELR 302 .... 5.32
Barclays Wealth Trustees (Jersey) Ltd v Revenue and Customs Commissioners [2015] EWHC 2878 (Ch), 165 NLJ 7677, [2015] WTLR 1675, [2015] All ER (D) 89 (Nov) 2.20, 2.21, 27.5
Barlow Clowes International Ltd v Henwood [2008] EWCA Civ 577, (2008) Times, 18 June, [2008] BPIR 778, [2008] All ER (D) 330 (May) 21.28, 24.29
Barr's Settlement Trusts, Re, Abacus Trust Co (Isle of Man) v Barr [2003] EWHC 114 (Ch), [2003] Ch 409, [2003] 1 All ER 763, [2003] 2 WLR 1362, 5 ITELR 602, (2003) Times, 28 February, [2003] 13 LS Gaz R 27, [2003] All ER (D) 79 (Feb) ..... 5.29, APP A

Table of Cases

Beckman v IRC [2000] STC (SCD) 59 .... 16.22, 18.29
Beneficiary v IRC (SpC 190) [1999] STC (SCD) 134 .... 22.28
Best (executor of Buller, dec'd) v Revenue and Customs Comrs [2014] UKFTT 77 (TC), [2014] WTLR 409 .... 16.38, 18.45
Billingham (Inspector of Taxes) v Cooper [2000] STC 122, [2000] 06 LS Gaz R 36, 144 Sol Jo LB 85; affd [2001] EWCA Civ 1041, [2001] STC 1177, 74 TC 139, [2001] All ER (D) 60 (Jul) 23.41
Bird v Revenue and Customs Comrs (SpC 720) [2009] STC (SCD) 81 .... 4.28
Bond (Inspector of Taxes) v Pickford [1983] STC 517, 57 TC 301, CA . 7.3H, 7.11, 7.122, 8.41, 8.104, 16.87, 18.82, APP A
Bosanquet v Allen (Inspector of Taxes) [1985] AC 1082, [1985] 2 All ER 645, [1985] 2 WLR 1010, [1985] STC 356, 59 TC 125, 129 Sol Jo 381, HL 6.28, 7.24
Brander (representative of James (dec'd), Fourth Earl of Balfour) v Revenue and Customs Comrs [2009] UKFTT 101 (TC), [2009] SFTD 374; affd sub nom Revenue and Customs Comrs v Brander (Executor of the Will of the late Fourth Earl of Balfour) [2010] UKUT 300 (TCC), [2010] All ER (D) 94 (Aug) 16.35, 18.42
Breadner v Granville-Grossman [2001] Ch 523, [2000] 4 All ER 705, [2001] 2 WLR 593, 2 ITELR 812 .... 5.27, APP A
Brodie's Will Trustees v IRC (1933) 17 TC 432, 12 ATC 140 .... 6.79, 7.73, 7.75, 7.78
Brooke v Purton [2014] EWHC 547 (Ch), [2014] WTLR 745, [2014] All ER (D) 262 (Mar) 5.42A
Broome v Revenue and Customs Comrs [2011] UKFTT 760 (TC), [2012] SWTI 39 .... APP G
Brown's Executors v IRC (SpC 83) [1996] STC (SCD) 277 .... 16.40, 18.47
Brumby (Inspector of Taxes) v Milner [1976] 3 All ER 636, [1976] 1 WLR 1096, [1976] STC 534, 51 TC 583, [1976] TR 249, 120 Sol Jo 754, L(TC) 2609, HL 6.82, 7.76
Bulmer v IRC [1967] Ch 145, [1966] 3 All ER 801, [1966] 3 WLR 672, 44 TC 1, 45 ATC 293, [1966] TR 257, 110 Sol Jo 654, L(TC) 2211 .... 4.11
Burgess v Revenue and Customs Commissioners [2015] UKUT 578 (TCC), [2016] STC 579, [2015] All ER (D) 209 (Nov) 20.28A, 20.30
Burns v Revenue and Customs Comrs [2009] STC (SCD) 165 .... 22.26
Burrell v Burrell [2005] EWHC 245 (Ch), [2005] STC 569, 7 ITELR 622, [2005] All ER (D) 351 (Feb) .... 5.31, APP A
Burton (Ernest) v Revenue and Customs Comrs (TC00156) [2009] UKFTT 203 (TC), [2009] SFTD 682, [2009] SWTI 2632 .... 23.58
Buzzoni (M) (Kamhi's Executor) v Revenue and Customs Comrs [2013] EWCA Civ 1684, [2014] 1 WLR 3040, [2014] 1 EGLR 181, [2014] WTLR 421 .... 20A.8, 23.7

C

Carver v Duncan (Inspector of Taxes) [1985] AC 1082, [1985] 2 All ER 645, [1985] 2 WLR 1010, [1985] STC 356, 59 TC 125, 129 Sol Jo 381, HL . 6.34, 7.24, 7.26, 7.29, 7.30
Caton's Administrators v Couch [1997] STC 970, sub nom Couch (Inspector of Taxes) v Caton's Administrators 70 TC 10, [1997] 30 LS Gaz R 29, CA 7.45, 8.9
Civil Engineer v IRC (SpC 299) [2002] STC (SCD) 72, [2002] WTLR 491 ... 21.28, 21.37, 24.29
Clark (executors of Clark dec'd) v Revenue and Customs Comrs [2005] STC (SCD) 823 .... 16.31, 18.38
Clinch v IRC [1974] QB 76, [1973] 1 All ER 977, [1973] 2 WLR 862, [1973] STC 155, 49 TC 52, 52 ATC 201, [1973] TR 157, 117 Sol Jo 342 .... 23.42
Clore (No 3), Re, IRC v Stype Trustees (Jersey) Ltd [1985] 2 All ER 819, [1985] STC 394, sub nom IRC v Stype Trustees (Jersey) Ltd [1985] 1 WLR 1290, 129 Sol Jo 832 .... 23.63, 26.65
Clore (No 2), Re, Official Solicitor v Clore [1984] STC 609 ..... 21.38, 24.38, 24.42, 25.7, 27.62
Clore's Settlement Trusts, Re, Sainer v Clore [1966] 2 All ER 272, [1966] 1 WLR 955, 110 Sol Jo 252 .... 12.1H
Congreve and Congreve v IRC [1948] 1 All ER 948, 30 TC 163, 27 ATC 102, 41 R & IT 319, [1948] LJR 1229, 92 Sol Jo 407, L(TC) 1457, HL 22.20, 22.21

Coombes v Revenue and Customs Comrs [2007] EWHC 3160 (Ch), [2008] STC 2984, [2007] All ER (D) 324 (Nov) 23.20
Couch (Inspector of Taxes) v Caton's Administrators. See Caton's Administrators v Couch
Crossland (Inspector of Taxes) v Hawkins (1960) 39 TC 493, 39 ATC 461, 53 R & IT 758, [1960] TR 297; on appeal [1961] Ch 537, [1961] 2 All ER 812, [1961] 3 WLR 202, 39 TC 493, 40 ATC 126, [1961] TR 113, 105 Sol Jo 424, CA 4.6
Crowe v Appleby (Inspector of Taxes) [1975] 3 All ER 529, [1975] 1 WLR 1539, [1975] STC 502, 51 TC 457, 54 ATC 177, [1975] TR 151, 119 Sol Jo 776, L(TC) 2561; affd [1976] 2 All ER 914, [1976] 1 WLR 885, [1976] STC 301, 51 TC 457, [1976] TR 105, L(TC) 2584, CA .... 7.3I, 7.11, 8.41, 17.22, APP E
Cunard's Trustees v IRC [1946] 1 All ER 159, 27 TC 122, 174 LT 133, CA 6.79, 7.73, 7.75, 7.78
Customs and Excise Comrs v Fisher (Lord) [1981] 2 All ER 147, [1981] STC 238, [1981] TR 59 .... 16.36, 18.43

D

D S Sanderson v HMRC [2016] EWCA Civ 19 .... 20.28, 20.29
Davies (Inspector of Taxes) v Hicks [2005] EWHC 847 (Ch), [2005] STC 850, (2005) Times, 27 May, [2005] All ER (D) 167 (May) 23.16
De Vigier v IRC [1964] 2 All ER 907, [1964] 1 WLR 1073, 42 TC 24, 43 ATC 223, [1964] TR 239, 108 Sol Jo 617, HL 4.46, 4.48A
Dextra Accessories Ltd v MacDonald (Inspector of Taxes) [2002] STC (SCD) 413, SCD; affd sub nom MacDonald (Inspector of Taxes) v Dextra Accessories Ltd [2003] EWHC 872 (Ch), [2003] STC 749, [2003] 25 LS Gaz R 47, (2003) Times, 25 April, [2003] All ER (D) 299 (Apr); revsd [2004] EWCA Civ 22, [2004] STC 339, 77 TC 146, (2004) Times, 3 February, 148 Sol Jo LB 150, [2004] All ER (D) 256 (Jan); affd [2005] UKHL 47, [2005] 4 All ER 107, [2005] STC 1111, (2005) Times, 11 July, [2005] All ER (D) 85 (Jul) 15B.5
Diana (Lady) Hood v HMRC [2016] UKFTT 59 .... 23.8B, 23.8
Dreyfus (Camille and Henry) Foundation Inc v IRC [1956] AC 39, [1955] 3 All ER 97, [1955] 3 WLR 451, 36 TC 126, 34 ATC 208, 48 R & IT 551, [1955] TR 229, 99 Sol Jo 560, 1955 SLT 335, HL 15.3C, 25.15, 28.14

E

Edge v Pensions Ombudsman [2000] Ch 602, [1999] 4 All ER 546, [2000] 3 WLR 79, [2000] ICR 748, 1999] PLR 215, [1999] 35 LS Gaz R 39, [1999] NLJR 1442, CA .... APP A
Edwards (Inspector of Taxes) v Roberts (1935) 19 TC 618, CA 15B.11
European Commission v Kingdom of Spain C-127/12 (3 September 2014), ECJ 1.25
European Commission v United Kingdom: C-112/14 (2014) ECLI:EU:C:2014:2369, [2015] 1 CMLR 1515, [2015] STC 591, (2014) Times, 17 December, [2014] All ER (D) 146 (Nov), ECJ 23.44

F

Farmer (Farmer's Executors) v IRC [1999] STC (SCD) 321 .... 16.27, 16.41, 18.35
Faulkner (Trustees of Adams) v IRC [2001] STC (SCD) 112 .... 13.12
Faye v IRC (1961) 40 TC 103, 40 ATC 304, [1961] TR 297 .... 21.28, 24.29
Ferguson v Revenue and Customs Comrs [2014] UKFTT 433 (TC), [2014] SFTD 934, [2014] SWTI 2474 .... 14.50, 15.42
Figg v Clarke (Inspector of Taxes) [1997] 1 WLR 603, [1997] STC 247, 68 TC 645, [1996] 10 LS Gaz R 21, 140 Sol Jo LB 66 .... 7.3E, 7.8, 8.38

xlv

Fox v Stirk; Ricketts v Registration Officer for the City of Cambridge [1970] 2 QB 463, [1970] 3 All ER 7, [1970] 3 WLR 147, 68 LGR 644, [1970] RA 330, 134 JP 576, 114 Sol Jo 397, CA 7.57, 8.21
Frankland v IRC [1997] STC 1450, CA 10.72J, 11.12, 11.12A, 14.60
Freedman v Freedman [2015] EWHC 1457 (Ch), 18 ITELR 586, (2015) Times, 23 June, [2015] WTLR 1187, [2015] SWTI 1735, [2015] All ER (D) 197 (May) 5.49B
Furness v IRC [1999] STC (SCD) 232 .... 16.27, 18.35
Furse, Re, Furse v IRC [1980] 3 All ER 838, [1980] STC 596, [1980] TR 275 ...... 21.37, 24.37
Futter v Futter, Futter (No 3 and No 5) Life Interest Settlements, Re [2010] EWHC 449 (Ch), [2010] STC 982, 12 ITELR 912, [2010] All ER (D) 52 (Apr); revsd sub nom Futter v Futter [2011] EWCA Civ 197, [2012] Ch 132, [2011] 2 All ER 450, [2011] STC 809, 13 ITELR 749, [2011] 2 P & CR D20, [2011] All ER (D) 101 (Mar); revsd in part sub nom Futter v Revenue and Customs Comrs [2013] UKSC 26, [2013] 3 All ER 429, [2013] 2 WLR 1200, [2013] STC 1148, (2013) Times, 10 June, [2013] All ER (D) 106 (May) 5.25, 5.34, 5.36, 5.37, 5.38, 5.41, 5.45

G

Gaines-Cooper v Revenue and Customs Comrs [2007] STC (SCD) 23, 81 TC 61, 9 ITLR 274, SCD; affd [2007] EWHC 2617 (Ch), [2008] STC 1665, 81 TC 61, 10 ITLR 255, [2007] All ER (D) 212 (Nov) .... 25.7, 28.6; APP G
Garland (Inspector of Taxes) v Archer-Shee. See Archer-Shee v Garland (Inspector of Taxes)
Gee, Re, Wood v Staples [1948] Ch 284, [1948] 1 All ER 498, [1948] LJR 1400, 92 Sol Jo 232 .... 16.18, 18.25
Genovese v Revenue and Customs Comrs [2009] STC (SCD) 373, SCD .... APP G
Gilchrist (as trustee of the J P Gilchrist 1993 Settlement) v Revenue and Customs Comrs [2014] UKUT 169 (TCC), [2014] STC 1713, 164 NLJ 7605, [2014] WTLR 1209, [2014] All ER (D) 25 (May) 6.20, 7.16
Glyn v Revenue and Customs Comrs [2013] UKFTT 645 (TC) .... 21.6; APP G
Glyn v Revenue and Customs Commissioners [2015] UKUT 551 .... 24.8
Golding v Revenue and Customs Comrs [2011] UKFTT 351 (TC) 16.55, 18.62
Grace v Revenue and Customs Comrs [2008] STC (SCD) 531, SCD .... APP G
Grace v Revenue and Customs Comrs [2011] UKFTT 36 (TC), [2011] SFTD 669, [2011] SWTI 1581 .... APP G
Green v Cobham [2002] STC 820, 4 ITELR 784 .... 5.28
Green (Anne Christine Curtis) v Revenue and Customs Comrs [2015] UKFTT 236 (TC), [2015] SWTI 2486 .... 16.38, 16.39,18.45
Gulbenkian's Settlement Trusts (No 2), Re, Stevens v Maun [1970] Ch 408, [1969] 2 All ER 1173, [1969] 3 WLR 450, 113 Sol Jo 758 .... 3.6B, 10.29

H

Hampden Settlement Trusts, Re [1977] TR 177, [2001] WTLR 195 .... 12.1H
Harding (executors of Loveday) v IRC [1997] STC (SCD) 321 .... 11.12
Harris (trustee of Harris Family Charitable Trust) v Revenue and Customs Comrs [2010] UKFTT 385 (TC), [2010] SFTD 1159 .... 14.16, 15.11
Hart (Inspector of Taxes) v Briscoe [1979] Ch 1, [1978] 1 All ER 791, [1978] 2 WLR 832, [1978] STC 89, 52 TC 53, [1977] TR 285, 293, 121 Sol Jo 852, L(TC) 2663 .... 9.69, 10.58, 16.87, 18.82
Hastings-Bass, Re, Hastings-Bass v IRC [1975] Ch 25, [1974] 2 All ER 193, [1974] 2 WLR 904, [1974] STC 211, 53 ATC 87, [1974] TR 87, 118 Sol Jo 422, CA ... 5.25, 5.26, 5.27, 5.28, 5.29, 5.30, 5.31, 5.32, 5.33, 5.34, 5.35, 5.36, 5.38, 5.39, 5.40, 5.41, 5.42, 5.44, APP A
Hawksley v May [1956] 1 QB 30 .... 2.37H, 2.48
Herman v Revenue and Customs Comrs (SpC 609) [2007] STC (SCD) 571 ... 23.56, 26.60
Higginson's Executors v IRC [2002] STC (SCD) 483 .... 16.52, 18.58

Table of Cases

Hoare Trustees v Gardner (Inspector of Taxes) [1979] Ch 10, [1978] 1 All ER 791, [1978] 2 WLR 839, [1978] STC 89, 52 TC 53, [1977] TR 293, 121 Sol Jo 852, L(TC) 2663 .... 7.3H, 7.11, 8.41
Howard de Walden (Lord) v IRC [1942] 1 KB 389, [1942] 1 All ER 287, 25 TC 121, 111 LJKB 273, CA 22.19
Howarth's Executors v IRC [1997] STC (SCD) 162 .... 5.21
Howell v Trippier (Inspector of Taxes) [2004] EWCA Civ 885, [2004] STC 1245, 76 TC 415, (2004) Times, 17 August, 148 Sol Jo LB 881, [2004] All ER (D) 220 (Jul) . 6.20, 7.16
Hutchings (Timothy Clayton) v Revenue and Customs Comrs [2015] UKFTT 9 (TC) 19.13, 20.16A

I

Inchyra (Baron) v Jennings (Inspector of Taxes) [1966] Ch 37, [1965] 2 All ER 714, [1965] 3 WLR 166, 42 TC 388, 44 ATC 129, [1965] TR 141, 109 Sol Jo 356 . 22.8, 22.10
Income Tax Special Purposes Comrs v Pemsel [1891] AC 531, 3 TC 53, 55 JP 805, 61 LJQB 265, [1891–4] All ER Rep 28, 65 LT 621, 7 TLR 657, HL 15.3A
Inglewood (Lord) v IRC [1983] 1 WLR 366, [1983] STC 133, 127 Sol Jo 89, CA 12.1I
Ingram (executors of Lady Ingram) v IRC [2000] 1 AC 293, [1999] 1 All ER 297, [1999] 2 WLR 90, [1999] STC 37, [1999] 03 LS Gaz R 32, [1998] EGCS 181, 143 Sol Jo LB 52, HL 20A.7, 23.6
IRC v Botnar [1998] STC 38; affd [1999] STC 711, 3 TC 205, [1999] All ER (D) 658, CA 4.5, 22.24
IRC v Brandenburg [1982] STC 555, 126 Sol Jo 229 .... 24.27, 24.30, 27.34
IRC v Buchanan [1958] Ch 289, [1957] 2 All ER 400, [1957] 3 WLR 68, 37 TC 365, 36 ATC 36, 50 R & IT 223, [1957] TR 43, 100 Sol Jo 502, L(TC) 1823, CA 4.8
IRC v Bullock [1976] 3 All ER 353, [1976] 1 WLR 1178, [1976] STC 409, 51 TC 522, [1976] TR 179, 120 Sol Jo 591, L(TC) 2598, CA 21.29, 21.36, 21.37, 24.30
IRC v Challenge Corpn Ltd [1987] AC 155, [1987] 2 WLR 24, [1986] STC 548, 131 Sol Jo 46, PC 22.24
IRC v Duchess of Portland [1982] Ch 314, [1982] 1 All ER 784, [1982] 2 WLR 367, [1982] STC 149, 54 TC 648, [1981] TR 475, 3 FLR 293, 126 Sol Jo 49 ..... 21.26, 24.27
IRC v Eversden [2002] EWHC 1360 (Ch), [2002] STC 1109, 75 TC 340, [2002] 36 LS Gaz R 40, (2002) Times, 18 July, [2002] All ER (D) 154 (Jul); affd sub nom IRC v Eversden (exors of Greenstock, dec'd) [2003] EWCA Civ 668, [2003] STC 822, 75 TC 340, [2003] 27 LS Gaz R 38, 147 Sol Jo LB 594, (2003) Times, 30 May, [2003] All ER (D) 198 (May) 4.62, 13.2R, 13.2S
IRC v Executors of Dr Richards [1971] 1 All ER 785, [1971] 1 WLR 571, 46 TC 626, 50 ATC 249, [1971] TR 221, 115 Sol Jo 225, 1971 SC (HL) 60, 1971 SLT 107, HL 7.43, 8.7, 8.8
IRC v George. See Stedman's Executors v IRC
IRC v Gray (Executor of Lady Fox) [1994] STC 360, [1994] RVR 129, CA .. 16.55, 18.63
IRC v Hawley [1928] 1 KB 578, 13 TC 327, 6 ATC 1021, 97 LJKB 191, 138 LT 710 .... APP E
IRC v Helen Slater Charitable Trust Ltd [1982] Ch 49, [1981] 3 All ER 98, [1981] 3 WLR 377, [1981] STC 471, 55 TC 230, [1981] TR 225, 125 Sol Jo 414, CA 14.48, 15.40, 25.15, 28.14
IRC v Levy [1982] STC 442, 56 TC 68, 126 Sol Jo 413 .... 4.11
IRC v Lloyds Private Banking Ltd [1998] STC 559, [1998] 2 FCR 41, [1999] 1 FLR 147, [1999] Fam Law 309, [1998] 19 LS Gaz R 23, 142 Sol Jo LB 164, [1998] All ER (D) 124 .... 13.11A
IRC v Macpherson [1989] AC 159, [1988] 2 WLR 1261, 132 Sol Jo 821, sub nom Macpherson v IRC [1988] 2 All ER 753, [1988] STC 362, HL 11.6
IRC v Matthew's Executors [1984] STC 386, 58 TC 120, 1984 SLT 414, Ct of Sess 7.3J, 7.11, 8.42
IRC v Mills [1975] AC 38, [1974] 1 All ER 722, [1974] 2 WLR 325, [1974] STC 130, 53 ATC 34, [1974] TR 39, 118 Sol Jo 205, L(TC) 2506, HL 4.6
IRC v Plummer [1980] AC 896, [1979] 3 All ER 775, [1979] 3 WLR 689, [1979] STC 793, 54 TC 1, [1979] TR 339, 123 Sol Jo 769, HL 4.11

Table of Cases

IRC v Regent Trust Co Ltd [1980] 1 WLR 688, [1980] STC 140, 53 TC 54, [1979] TR 401, 124 Sol Jo 49 .... 22.11
IRC v Stannard [1984] 2 All ER 105, [1984] 1 WLR 1039, [1984] STC 245, 128 Sol Jo 400 .... 24.41, 27.61
IRC v Stype Trustees (Jersey) Ltd. See Clore (No 3), Re, IRC v Stype Trustees (Jersey) Ltd
IRC v Universities Superannuation Scheme Ltd [1997] STC 1, 70 TC 193 .... 15.52
IRC v Willoughby [1995] STC 143, 70 TC 57, CA; on appeal [1997] 4 All ER 65, [1997] 1 WLR 1071, [1997] STC 995, 70 TC 57, 1 OFLR(ITLR) 103, [1997] 29 LS Gaz R 28, [1997] NLJR 1062, HL 20A.2, 22.23, 22.24, 23.2

J

Jager (Theodor) v Finanzamt Kusel-Landstuhl: C-256/06 [2008] ECR I-123, [2008] SWTI 137, [2008] All ER (D) 65 (Jan), ECJ 1.24
Jefferies (I S and A L) v Revenue and Customs Comrs [2009] UKFTT 291 (TC), [2010] SFTD 189, [2010] SWTI 234 .... 7.50, 8.14
Jenkins (Inspector of Taxes) v Brown [1989] 1 WLR 1163, [1989] STC 577, 62 TC 226 .... 7.133, 8.124
Jenkins v IRC [1944] 2 All ER 491, 26 TC 265, 171 LT 355, CA 6.38, 17.44
Jiggens v Low [2010] EWHC 1566 (Ch), [2010] STC 1899, [2010] All ER (D) 243 (Jun) 5.35
Joseph Nicholas Hanson as Trustee of the William Hanson 1957 Settlement v Revenue and Customs Comrs [2012] UKFTT 95 (TC), [2012] SFTD 705, [2012] SWTI 1388; affd sub nom Revenue and Customs Comrs v Joseph Nicholas Hanson (Trustee of the William Hanson 1957 Settlement) [2013] UKUT 224 (TCC) 16.51, 18.57
Judge (personal representatives of Walden, dec'd) v Revenue and Customs Comrs [2005] STC (SCD) 863 .... 13.14, APP E

K

Karim v Revenue and Customs Comrs [2009] UKFTT 368 (TC), [2010] SWTI 1289 .... APP G
Keeler's Settlement Trusts, Re, Keeler v Gledhill [1981] Ch 156, [1981] 1 All ER 888, [1981] 2 WLR 499, 125 Sol Jo 170 .... 16.19, 18.26
Kimber v Revenue and Customs Comrs [2012] UKFTT 107 (TC), [2012] SWTI 1462 .... APP G
Kwok Chi Leung Karl v Comr of Estate Duty [1988] 1 WLR 1035, [1988] STC 728, 132 Sol Jo 1118, PC 24.15, 27.22

L

Laerstate BV v Revenue and Customs Comrs (TC00162) [2009] UKFTT 209 (TC), [2009] SFTD 551, [2009] SWTI 2669 .... 21.49, 24.52
Langham (Inspector of Taxes) v Veltema. See Veltema v Langham (Inspector of Taxes)
Lawson v Rolfe [1970] Ch 612, [1970] 1 All ER 761, [1970] 2 WLR 602, 46 TC 199, 48 ATC 557, [1969] TR 537, 114 Sol Jo 206 .... 22.10
Lee, Re, Sinclair v Lee. See Sinclair v Lee
Leedale (Inspector of Taxes) v Lewis [1982] 3 All ER 808, [1982] 1 WLR 1319, [1982] STC 835, 56 TC 501, 126 Sol Jo 710, HL 23.1
Levene v IRC [1928] AC 217, 13 TC 486, 97 LJKB 377, [1928] All ER Rep 746, 72 Sol Jo 270, 139 LT 1, 44 TLR 374, HL .... APP G
Lloyd's TSB (personal representative of Antrobus, dec'd) v IRC [2002] STC (SCD) 468 .... 16.51, 16.52, 18.58
Lloyd's TSB Private Banking plc v Revenue and Customs Comrs DET/47/2005 (10 October 2005, unreported) 16.52, 18.59
Lobler v HMRC [2015] UKUT 0152 .... 5.47A, 5.49C

Lobler (Joost) v Revenue and Customs Comrs [2013] UKFTT 141 (TC), [2013] SWTI 1777 .... 6.43, 17.50
Lorber (P A) v Revenue and Customs Comrs [2011] UKFTT 101 (TC) 4.30

M

McCall (personal representative of McClean, dec'd) v Revenue and Customs Comrs [2008] STC (SCD) 752 .... 16.32, 18.39
McCall (personal representative of McClean, dec'd) v Revenue and Customs Comrs [2009] NICA 12, [2009] STC 990, NI CA 16.32, 18.39
MacDonald (Inspector of Taxes) v Dextra Accessories Ltd. See Dextra Accessories Ltd v MacDonald (Inspector of Taxes)
McKelvey (personal representative of McKelvey, dec'd) v Revenue and Customs Comrs (SpC 694) [2008] STC (SCD) 944 .... 25.17, 28.16
Macpherson v IRC. See IRC v Macpherson
Mansworth (Inspector of Taxes) v Jelley [2002] EWCA Civ 1829, [2003] STC 53, 75 TC 1, [2003] 10 LS Gaz R 29, (2002) Times, 20 December, [2002] All ER (D) 156 (Dec) 15B.23, 15B.24, 15B.25, 15B.26, 16.25, 16.26, 16.27, 16.28
Marley v Rawlings [2014] UKSC 2, [2014] 1 All ER 807, [2014] 2 WLR 213, 16 ITELR 642, [2014] 2 FLR 555, [2014] Fam Law 466, 164 NLJ 7592, (2014) Times, 28 January, [2014] All ER (D) 132 (Jan) 5.43
Marquess of Linlithgow v Revenue and Customs Comrs [2010] CSIH 19, [2010] STC 1563, 2010 SC 391, 2011 SLT 58 .... 6.17, 12.1B, 17.23
Marshall (Inspector of Taxes) v Kerr [1995] 1 AC 148, [1994] 3 All ER 106, [1994] 3 WLR 299, [1994] STC 638, 67 TC 56, 138 Sol Jo LB 155, HL .. 4.55, 7.112, 7.113, 8.87, 8.89, 8.92, 23.25
Melville v IRC [2000] STC 628, 74 TC 372, [2000] NPC 70, [2000] LS Gaz R 38, [2000] All ER (D) 832; affd [2001] EWCA Civ 1247, [2002] 1 WLR 407, [2001] STC 1271, 74 TC 372, 4 ITELR 231, [2001] NPC 132, [2001] 37 LS Gaz R 39, [2001] All ER (D) 453 (Jul) 7.78, 8.65, 8.66, 8.67, 8.68, 10.70
Mettoy Pension Trustees Ltd v Evans [1991] 2 All ER 513, [1990] 1 WLR 1587 ..... 5.25, 5.36, 5.38, APP A
Minden Trust (Cayman) Ltd v IRC [1985] STC 758, CA 24.28, 24.30, 27.35
Monro v Revenue and Customs Comrs [2008] EWCA Civ 306, [2009] Ch 69, [2008] 3 WLR 734, [2008] STC 1815, 79 TC 579, [2008] All ER (D) 126 (Apr) 15B.24, 16.26
Montagu Trust Co (Jersey) Ltd v IRC [1989] STC 477 .... 9.27, 24.29, 24.30, 27.36
Moxon's Will Trusts, Re, Downey v Moxon [1958] 1 All ER 386, [1958] 1 WLR 165, 102 Sol Jo 124 .... 12.1H
Murray Group Holdings v Revenue and Customs Comrs [2012] UKFTT 692 (TC), [2013] SFTD 149, [2013] SWTI 492, [2012] All ER (D) 295 (Nov); affd in part sub nom Murray Group Holdings Ltd v Revenue and Customs Comrs [2014] UKUT 0292 (TCC), [2015] STC 1, [2014] All ER (D) 109 (Jul) 15B.13, 16.13

N

Nelson Dance Family Settlement, Re, Trustees of the Nelson Dance Family Settlement v Revenue and Customs Comrs [2008] STC (SCD) 792; affd sub nom Revenue and Customs Comrs v Trustees of the Nelson Dance Family [2009] EWHC 71 (Ch), [2009] STC 802, 79 TC 605, [2009] All ER (D) 185 (Jan) 15B.9, 16.33, 18.40
Nightingale Ltd v Price (Inspector of Taxes) (SpC 66) [1996] STC (SCD) 116 . 14.33, 15.26

O

Ogden v Trustees of the RHS Griffiths 2003 Settlement [2008] EWHC 118 (Ch), [2009] Ch 162, [2008] 2 All ER 654, [2009] 2 WLR 394, [2008] STC 776, [2008] All ER (D) 267 (Jan) 5.39, 5.44, 5.44
Ogilvie v Allen (1899) 15 TLR 294, HL 5.37, 5.45

P

Padmore v IRC [1989] STC 493, 62 TC 352, [1989] 28 LS Gaz R 42, CA 23.9
Page (Inspector of Taxes) v Lowther [1983] STC 799, 57 TC 199, 127 Sol Jo 786, CA
.... 6.97, 7.91, 22.44, 25.49
Paul and Annette Galbraith (t/a Galbraith Ceramics) v Revenue and Customs Comrs
(TC02639) [2013] UKFTT 225 (TC), [2013] SFTD 857, [2013] SWTI 2221 ..... 18.6, 20.6
Pawson v Revenue and Customs Comrs (TC01748) [2012] UKFTT 51 (TC); affd sub
nom Revenue and Customs Comrs v Lockyer and Robertson (personal representatives
of Pawson, dec'd) [2013] UKUT 50 (TCC), [2013] STC 976, [2013] NLJR 291,
[2013] All ER (D) 36 (Mar) 16.36, 16.37, 16.38, 18.43,18.44
Pearson v IRC [1981] AC 753, [1980] 2 All ER 479, [1980] 2 WLR 872, [1980] STC
318, [1980] TR 177, 124 Sol Jo 377, HL .... 2.37, 2.40, 9.6, 9.18, APP E
Pepper (Inspector of Taxes) v Hart [1993] AC 593, [1993] 1 All ER 42, [1992] 3 WLR
1032, [1992] STC 898, 65 TC 421, [1993] ICR 291, [1993] IRLR 33, [1993] NLJR
17, [1993] RVR 127, HL 22.20
Persche (Hein) v Finanzamt Ludenscheid: C-318/07 [2009] ECR I-359, [2009] All ER
(EC) 673, [2009] 2 CMLR 819, [2009] STC 586, [2009] PTSR 915, (2009) Times,
3 February, [2009] All ER (D) 213 (Jan), ECJ 1.24, 15.1, 15.2, 15.3C
Peter Clay Discretionary Trust (Trustees of) v Revenue and Customs Comrs [2007] STC
(SCD) 362, 9 ITELR 738 .... 6.32, 6.34, 7.26, 7.29, 7.32, 7.34, 7.35
Phillips (executors of Phillips, dec'd) v Revenue and Customs Comrs [2006] STC (SCD)
639 .... 16.31, 18.38
Piercy (executors of, dec'd) v Revenue and Customs Comrs [2008] STC (SCD) 858
.... 16.34, 18.41
Pilkington v IRC [1964] AC 612, [1962] 3 All ER 622, [1962] 3 WLR 1051, 40 TC 416,
41 ATC 285, [1962] TR 265, 106 Sol Jo 834, HL 2.27, 12.1H
Pitt v Holt [2010] EWHC 45 (Ch), [2010] 2 All ER 774, [2010] 1 WLR 1199, [2010]
STC 901, 12 ITELR 807, (2010) Times, 24 February, [2010] All ER (D) 149 (Jun);
revsd [2011] EWCA Civ 197, [2012] Ch 132, [2011] 2 All ER 450, [2011] STC 809,
13 ITELR 749, [2011] 2 P & CR D20, [2011] All ER (D) 101 (Mar); revsd in part sub
nom Pitt v Revenue and Customs Comrs [2013] UKSC 26, [2013] 3 All ER 429,
[2013] 2 WLR 1200, [2013] STC 1148, (2013) Times, 10 June, [2013] All ER (D) 106
(May) 5.25, 5.33, 5.36, 5.37, 5.38, 5.41, 5.45
Pollen Estate Trustee Co Ltd v Revenue and Customs Comrs [2013] EWCA Civ 753,
[2013] 3 All ER 742, [2013] 1 WLR 3785, [2013] STC 1479, [2013] 2 P & CR D48,
[2013] All ER (D) 256 (Jun) 15.5

R

R v Inspector of Taxes, Reading, ex p Fulford-Dobson [1987] QB 978, [1987] 3 WLR
277, 60 TC 168, 131 Sol Jo 975, [1987] LS Gaz R 2197, sub nom IRC, ex p Fulford-
Dobson [1987] STC 344 .... APP G
R (on the application of Davies) v Revenue and Customs Comrs [2010] EWCA Civ 83,
[2010] STC 860, [2010] 09 LS Gaz R 17, (2010) Times, 23 February, [2010] All ER
(D) 197 (Feb); affd sub nom R (on the application of Davies) v Revenue and
Customs Comrs [2011] UKSC 47, [2012] 1 All ER 1048, [2011] 1 WLR 2625, [2011]
STC 2249, 81 TC 134, [2011] NLJR 1483, (2011) Times, 24 October, [2011] All ER
(D) 157 (Oct) .... APP G
R (on the application of Gaines-Cooper) v Revenue and Customs Comrs [2010] EWCA
Civ 83, [2010] STC 860, [2010] 09 LS Gaz R 17, (2010) Times, 23 February,
[2010] All ER (D) 197 (Feb) .... APP G
R (on the application of Huitson) v Revenue and Customs Comrs [2010] EWCA Civ
558 .... 22.49
R (on the application of Huitson) v Revenue and Customs Comrs [2011] EWCA Civ
893, [2012] QB 489, [2012] 2 WLR 490, [2011] STC 1860, 14 ITLR 90,
[2011] All ER (D) 225 (Jul) 22.50
R (on the application of Shiner) v Revenue and Customs Comrs [2010] EWCA Civ
558 .... 22.49

l

Table of Cases

R (on the application of Shiner) v Revenue and Customs Comrs [2011] EWCA Civ 892, [2012] 1 CMLR 237, [2011] STC 1878, 14 ITLR 113, [2011] All ER (D) 226 (Jul) 22.50
Rahman (Abdel) v Chase Bank (CI) Trust Co Ltd 1983 JLR 1, 1984 JLR 127, 1985–86 JLR N-5, 1987–88 JLR 81, [1990] JLR 59, 36 .... 25.10, 25.12, 25.30
Rahman (Abdel) v Chase Bank (CI) Trust Co Ltd 1991 JLR 103 . 25.10, 25.12, 25.30, 28.9
Ramsay v Liverpool Royal Infirmary [1930] AC 588, 99 LJPC 134, [1930] All ER Rep 127, 143 LT 388, 46 TLR 465, HL 21.28, 24.29
Ralph Hely-Hutchinson v HMRC [2015] EWHC 3261 .... 16.31
Reed (Inspector of Taxes) v Clark [1986] Ch 1, [1985] 3 WLR 142, [1985] STC 323, 58 TC 528, 129 Sol Jo 469, [1985] LS Gaz R 2016 .... APP G
Revenue and Customs Comrs v Anson [2012] UKUT 59 (TCC), [2012] STC 1014, 14 ITLR 601 .... 22.27
Revenue and Customs Comrs v Atkinson and Smith (executors of the Will of William Atkinson dec'd). See Atkinson and Smith (executors of the Will of William Atkinson dec'd) v Revenue and Customs Comrs
Revenue and Customs Comrs v Bower (executors of Bower (dec'd) [2008] EWHC 3105 (Ch), [2009] STC 510, 79 TC 544, [2009] All ER (D) 68 (Jan) 6.46, 17.53
Revenue and Customs Comrs v Brander (Executor of the Will of the late Fourth Earl of Balfour). See Brander (representative of James (dec'd), Fourth Earl of Balfour) v Revenue and Customs Comrs
Revenue and Customs Comrs v Charlton [2012] UKUT 770 (TCC) 20.28
Revenue and Customs Comrs v Grace [2008] EWHC 2708 (Ch), [2009] STC 213, [2008] All ER (D) 90 (Nov); affd [2009] EWCA Civ 1082, [2009] STC 2707, [2009] All ER (D) 280 (Oct) .... APP G
Revenue and Customs Comrs v Joseph Nicholas Hanson (Trustee of the William Hanson 1957 Settlement). See Joseph Nicholas Hanson as Trustee of the William Hanson 1957 Settlement v Revenue and Customs Comrs
Revenue and Customs Comrs v Lansdowne Partners Ltd Partnership [2011] EWCA Civ 1578, [2012] STC 544, 81 TC 318, [2011] All ER (D) 175 (Dec) 18.27, 20.27
Revenue and Customs Comrs v Lockyer and Robertson (personal representatives of Pawson, dec'd). See Pawson v Revenue and Customs Comrs
Revenue and Customs Comrs v Trustees of the Nelson Dance Family. See Nelson Dance Family Settlement, Re, Trustees of the Nelson Dance Family Settlement v Revenue and Customs Comrs
Revenue and Customs Comrs v Trustees of the Peter Clay Discretionary Trust [2008] EWCA Civ 1441, [2009] Ch 296, [2009] 2 All ER 683, [2009] 2 WLR 1353, [2009] STC 469, 79 TC 473, 11 ITELR 672, (2009) Times, 2 January, [2008] All ER (D) 255 (Dec) 6.35
Robert Ames v HMRC [2015] UKFTT 337 .... 7.85D, 7.100
Robson v Dixon (Inspector of Taxes) [1972] 3 All ER 671, [1972] 1 WLR 1493, 48 TC 527, 51 ATC 179, [1972] TR 163, 116 Sol Jo 863 .... APP G
Roome and Denne v Edwards (Inspector of Taxes) [1982] AC 279, [1981] 1 All ER 736, [1981] 2 WLR 268, [1981] STC 96, 54 TC 359, [1981] TR 1, 125 Sol Jo 150, HL .... 7.3H, 8.41, 21.23, 24.24, APP A
Rose, Re, Midland Bank Executor and Trustee Co Ltd v Rose [1949] Ch 78, [1948] 2 All ER 971, [1949] LJR 208, 92 Sol Jo 661 .... 6.17, 17.23
Rosser v IRC (SpC 368) [2003] STC (SCD) 311 .... 16.51, 16.54, 18.60
Royal Bank of Canada v IRC [1972] Ch 665, [1972] 1 All ER 225, [1972] 2 WLR 106, 47 TC 565, 51 ATC 233, [1972] TR 197, 115 Sol Jo 968, L(TC) 2429 .... 23.42
Rumbelow v Revenue and Customs Comrs [2013] UKFTT 637 (TC) .... APP G
Rysaffe Trustee Co (CI) Ltd v IRC [2002] EWHC 1114 (Ch), [2002] STC 872, 5 ITELR 53, [2002] All ER (D) 520 (May); affd [2003] EWCA Civ 356, [2003] STC 536, 5 ITELR 706, [2003] 22 LS Gaz R 31, (2003) Times, 29 April, 147 Sol Jo LB 388, [2003] All ER (D) 295 (Mar) 10.36, 10.39, 20A.5, 23.4

S

St Dunstan's v Major (SpC 217) [1997] STC (SCD) 212 .... 14.16, 15.11

Table of Cases

Sanderson v Revenue and Customs Comrs [2013] UKUT 623 (TCC), [2014] STC 915, [2014] All ER (D) 91 (Jan) 18.28
Sansom v Peay (Inspector of Taxes) [1976] 3 All ER 375, [1976] 1 WLR 1073, [1976] STC 494, 52 TC 1, 120 Sol Jo 571, sub nom Sansom and Bridge v Peay (Inspector of Taxes) [1976] TR 205 .... 7.54, 8.18, 9.6
Seaborn (George) v Revenue and Customs Comrs [2014] UKFTT 086 (TC) 20.10
Seddon (Trustees of Mrs M Seddon Second Discretionary Settlement) v Revenue and Customs Comrs [2015] UKFTT 140 (TC), [2015] SFTD 539 .... 6.20, 7.16
Shah v Barnet London Borough Council [1983] 2 AC 309, [1983] 1 All ER 226, [1983] 2 WLR 16, 81 LGR 305, 127 Sol Jo 36, HL .... APP G
Shepherd v Revenue and Customs Comrs [2006] EWHC 1512 (Ch), [2006] STC 1821, 78 TC 389, [2006] All ER (D) 191 (May) .... APP G
Sheppard (Trustees of the Woodland Trust) v IRC (No 2) [1993] STC 240, 65 TC 724, [1993] 14 LS Gaz R 44 .... 14.60, 15.52
Sieff v Fox [2005] EWHC 1312 (Ch), [2005] 3 All ER 693, [2005] 1 WLR 3811, 8 ITELR 93, [2005] All ER (D) 273 (Jun) .... 5.34; APP A
Sinclair v Lee [1993] Ch 497, [1993] 3 WLR 498, [1994] 1 BCLC 286, sub nom Lee, Re, Sinclair v Lee [1993] 3 All ER 926 .... 7.3S, 7.22, 8.111
Smallwood v Revenue and Customs Comrs [2009] EWHC 777 (Ch), [2009] STC 1222, 11 ITLR 943, [2009] 17 LS Gaz R 15, [2009] All ER (D) 122 (Apr); revsd sub nom Trevor Smallwood Trust, Re, Smallwood v Revenue and Customs Comrs [2010] EWCA Civ 778, [2010] STC 2045, 80 TC 536, 12 ITLR 1002, [2010] All ER (D) 99 (Jul) 21.24, 24.25
Southgate v Sutton. See Sutton v England
Stanley v IRC [1944] KB 255, [1944] 1 All ER 230, 26 TC 12, 113 LJKB 292, 170 LT 140, 60 TLR 209, CA 6.89, 7.83
Starke v IRC [1996] 1 All ER 622, [1995] 1 WLR 1439, [1995] STC 689, [1996] 1 EGLR 157, [1995] 23 LS Gaz R 32, [1996] 16 EG 115, 139 Sol Jo LB 128, CA 16.51, 18.57
Stedman's Executors v IRC [2002] STC (SCD) 358; revsd sub nom IRC v George [2003] EWHC 318 (Ch), [2003] STC 468, (2003) Times, 18 March, [2003] All ER (D) 376 (Feb); revsd [2003] EWCA Civ 1763, [2004] STC 147, 75 TC 735, [2004] 03 LS Gaz R 34, (2003) Times, 9 December, [2003] All ER (D) 102 (Dec) . 16.29, 16.30, 16.37, 18.36, 18.37
Stephen Norman Rumbelow [2013] UKFTT 637 (TC) 21.7
Stevenson (Inspector of Taxes) v Wishart [1987] 2 All ER 428, [1987] 1 WLR 1204, [1987] STC 266, 59 TC 740, 131 Sol Jo 744, [1987] LS Gaz R 1574, CA . 6.80, 7.74, 7.75
Stonor & Mills (Dickinson's Executors) v IRC (SpC 288) [2001] STC (SCD) 199 . 7.42, 8.6
Strathalmond (Lord) v IRC [1972] 3 All ER 715, [1972] 1 WLR 1511, 48 TC 537, 51 ATC 188, [1972] TR 171 .... 23.9
Sutton v England [2009] EWHC 3270 (Ch), [2010] WTLR 335; revsd sub nom Southgate v Sutton [2011] EWCA Civ 637, [2012] 1 WLR 326, [2011] 2 P & CR D37, [2011] WLR (D) 182, [2011] All ER (D) 291 (May) 2.25, 2.26, 2.28, 7.90, 8.75
Swales v IRC [1984] 3 All ER 16, [1984] STC 413, [1984] LS Gaz R 2300 .... 9.6
Swires (Inspector of Taxes) v Renton [1991] STC 490, 64 TC 315 . 7.3H, 7.11, 8.41, 8.108

T

Thomas v Lord Advocate (1953) 32 ATC 18, [1953] TR 19, 1953 SC 151, 1953 SLT 119, Ct of Sess 6.17, 17.23
Trennery v West (Inspector of Taxes). See West (Inspector of Taxes) v Trennery and other appeals
Trevor Smallwood Trust, Re, Smallwood v Revenue and Customs Comrs. See Smallwood v Revenue and Customs Comrs
Trustee of the Georgia Vickery, Franki and Mia Settlement v Revenue and Customs Comrs (TC02688) [2013] UKFTT 282 (TC) 18.6, 20.6
Trustees of David Zetland Settlement v Revenue and Customs Comrs [2013] UKFTT 284 (TC), [2013] SWTI 2424 .... 16.38, 18.45
Trustees of the PL Travers Will Trust v Revenue and Customs Comrs [2013] UKFTT 436 (TC), [2014] SFTD 265 .... 6.59, 7.48

Trustee One Ltd v Amos-Yeo [2015] EWHC 2480 .... 5.47A
Tucker (a bankrupt), Re, ex p Tucker [1990] Ch 148, [1988] 1 All ER 603, [1988] 2
  WLR 748, 132 Sol Jo 497, [1988] 15 LS Gaz R 33, CA 23.63
Tuczka v Revenue and Customs Comrs [2010] UKFTT 53 (TC), [2010] SWTI 1594
  .... APP G
Turberville v Revenue and Customs Comrs [2010] UKFTT 69 (TC), [2010] SWTI
  1619 .... APP G
Two Settlors v IRC (SpC 385) [2003] STC (SCD) 45 .... 7.80, 8.67

U

Udny v Udny (1869) LR 1 Sc & Div 441, 7 Macq 89, HL 21.27, 24.28

V

Van Der Merwe v Goldman and HMRC [2016] EWHC 926 (Ch) 5.49B
Veltema v Langham (Inspector of Taxes) [2004] EWCA Civ 193, [2004] STC 544,
  (2004) Times, 11 March, 148 Sol Jo LB 269, [2004] All ER (D) 436 (Feb), sub nom
  Langham (Inspector of Taxes) v Veltema 76 TC 259 .... 18.26
Vestey v IRC (No 2) [1980] AC 1148, [1979] 3 All ER 976, [1979] 3 WLR 915, [1980]
  STC 10, 54 TC 503, [1979] TR 381, 123 Sol Jo 826, HL 22.19, 22.21, 22.23, 25.32
Von Ernst and Cie SA v IRC [1980] 1 All ER 677, [1980] 1 WLR 468, [1980] STC 111,
  [1979] TR 461, 124 Sol Jo 17, CA 24.26, 24.30, 27.33

W

W T Ramsay Ltd v IRC [1982] AC 300, [1981] 1 All ER 865, [1981] 2 WLR 449,
  [1981] STC 174, 54 TC 101, [1982] TR 123, 125 Sol Jo 220, HL 20A.3, 23.3, 24.15
Wagstaff v Revenue and Customs Comrs [2014] UKFTT 43 (TC), [2014] WTLR 547,
  [2014] SWTI 883 .... 7.52, 8.16
Walker's Executors v IRC [2001] STC (SCD) 86 .... 16.22
Walton v IRC [1996] STC 68, [1996] 1 EGLR 159, [1996] RVR 55, [1996] 21 EG 144,
  CA 16.56, 18.63
Watkins (D M) & Harvey (CJ) (Mrs K M Watkins' Executors) v Revenue and
  Customs Comrs (TC01582) [2011] UKFTT 745 (TC), [2012] SWTI 38 .... 6.46, 17.53
Weight v Salmon (1935) 19 TC 174, 14 ATC 47, [1935] All ER Rep 904, 153 LT 55, 51
  TLR 333, HL 15B.11
West (Inspector of Taxes) v Trennery and other appeals [2003] EWCA Civ 1792, [2004]
  STC 170, 76 TC 713, 148 Sol Jo LB 56, (2004) Times, 23 January, [2003] All ER (D)
  329 (Dec); revsd sub nom Trennery v West (Inspector of Taxes) [2005] UKHL 5,
  [2005] STC 214, 149 Sol Jo LB 147, (2005) Times, 1 February, [2005] All ER (D) 257
  (Jan), sub nom West (Inspector of Taxes) v Trennery [2005] 1 All ER 827, 76 TC
  713 .... 4.52
Weston (Weston's Executors) v IRC [2000] STC (SCD) 30 .... 16.27, 18.35
Weston (Weston's Executors) v IRC [2000] STC 1064, [2000] All ER (D) 1870 ..... 16.27,
  18.35
Whitney v IRC [1926] AC 37, 10 TC 88, 95 LJKB 165, 134 LT 98, 42 TLR 58, HL
  .... 22.1
Williams (Surveyor of Taxes) v Singer [1921] 1 AC 65, 7 TC 387, 89 LJKB 1151, 64 Sol
  Jo 569, 123 LT 632, 36 TLR 661, [1920] All ER Rep Ext 819, HL 5.8, 22.3, 22.13
Wilson v Turner (1883) 22 Ch D 521, 53 LJ Ch 270, 31 WR 438, 48 LT 370, CA
  .... 12.1G
Winans v A-G [1904] AC 287, 73 LJKB 613, [1904–7] All ER Rep 410, 90 LT 721, 20
  TLR 510, HL 21.36, 24.36
Wolff v Wolff [2004] EWHC 2110 (Ch), [2004] STC 1633, [2004] All ER (D) 28
  (Sep) 5.30, 5.39, 5.44

Wood v Holden (Inspector of Taxes) [2006] EWCA Civ 26, [2006] 1 WLR 1393, [2006] STC 443, 78 TC 1, 8 ITLR 468, [2006] 2 BCLC 210, (2006) Times, 20 February, 150 Sol Jo LB 127, [2006] All ER (D) 190 (Jan) 21.48, 21.49, 24.51
Woodhall (personal representatives of Woodhall) v IRC [2000] STC (SCD) 558 ...... 13.12

X

X v A [2005] EWHC 2706 (Ch), [2006] 1 All ER 952, [2006] 1 WLR 741, [2006] 2 P & CR D7, 8 ITELR 543, [2006] 3 FCR 148, (2006) Times, 10 January, [2005] All ER (D) 379 (Nov) 12.1H

Y

Yuill v Fletcher (Inspector of Taxes) [1984] STC 401, 58 TC 145, [1984] LS Gaz R 1604, CA 22.43, 25.48
Yuill v Wilson (Inspector of Taxes) [1980] 3 All ER 7, [1980] 1 WLR 910, [1980] STC 460, 52 TC 674, 124 Sol Jo 528, HL 22.43, 25.48

Part I:

UK Resident Trusts

Chapter 1

Setting the Scene

[1.1] Trusts have a long and venerable history in the countries which now comprise the United Kingdom. They are a well-established part of the financial planning armoury of the well-advised family. The reasons for making a trust are and have been varied, though asset protection has always been at the vanguard. While tax mitigation should not be the driving force, the tax implications of adopting or indeed continuing a particular type of trust should always be appreciated. This book explains the UK taxes to which trusts, whether resident in or (the subject of Part II) outside the United Kingdom, can be liable.

[1.2] This is a book about the taxation of trusts rather than tax planning through trusts. However, the reader will find from time to time (and especially in CHAPTERS 17, 18 and 19) suggestions as to tax efficiency.

[1.3] The book does not deal with the few situations where Scottish Law or Northern Irish Law in particular require attention; for example, references to the *Trustee Act 1925* and to the *Trustee Act 2000* (which has no application in Scotland or in Northern Ireland) should be disregarded by its Scottish and Northern Irish readers. Similarly, the *Charities Act 2011* (and its predecessors) applies only in England and Wales. Likewise, readers in Northern Ireland and, particularly, Scotland should proceed with caution generally given the accelerating pace of the devolution of tax legislation. The author has tried to make reference to relevant differences wherever possible – see, for example 13.37 and 13.38 on Land and Buildings Transaction Tax.

Inheritance tax: the 2006 bombshell

[1.4] The apparently benign attitude taken by the then Labour Government to inheritance tax completely changed on 22 March 2006, with the Budget proposals for 'aligning the inheritance tax treatment of trusts', that is as between interest in possession and discretionary or accumulation trusts. Although in the course of Committee Stage and Report Stage amendments, the regime for Will trusts which would have substantially curtailed the availability of the spouse exemption on the first death was very significantly watered down, no one should be in any doubt as to the impact of those changes. This now makes it inheritance tax inefficient (as opposed to merely neutral) to use trusts in their traditional guise for asset protection as opposed to tax mitigation. A position exacerbated by further changes announced recently (see 1.5).

[1.5] We continue to rely on the continuation of the *Finance Act 1975* rates for taxing relevant property (including discretionary) trusts, that is, based on the lifetime rather than the death rates for inheritance tax, as indeed on the 100% rates of relief for qualifying business and agricultural property remaining unchanged. However, following proposals at Budget 2012, a series of consultations were launched on simplifying the basis of calculating the 10-year and exit charges to inheritance tax in relevant property trusts, with a view to introducing amending legislation in *Finance Bill 2014*. The specific proposals touched on three areas: the calculation of the 10-yearly and exit charges, a statutory rule on how long income can remain undistributed without being accumulated and the alignment of filing and payment dates for inheritance tax with those in place for income tax and capital gains tax. Amending legislation for the latter two changes was included in *Finance Bill 2014* (see **9.34–9.36** and **21.4–21.7**) and (it has to be said, minor) changes to the calculation of 10-yearly and exit charges were included in *Finance (No 2) Act 2015* (see **9.22** and **9.44**).

[1.6] The fundamental difficulty with all this is of course that estate planning in general and the use of trusts in particular is a long-term exercise and the interests of the client are hardly well served by a succession of changes over a relatively short period.

Capital gains tax

[1.7] Significant changes in 2008/09, have simplified things for practitioners. Gone are taper relief with all its complications and also indexation allowance. With the removal of halving relief and the kink test for such taxpayers, the base cost simply becomes March 1982 value or the acquisition cost or market value at date of acquisition if later – this 1982 base date, at more than 30 years ago, is surely ripe for reform. Happily, the collection of general reliefs remains, hold-over relief, roll-over relief and main residence relief chief among them.

[1.8] The introduction of entrepreneurs' relief at a relatively late stage in the 2008 reform announcement process was intended as something of a sop to those who had complained with some justification that the removal of business assets taper would leave them dramatically worse off under the new regime. Of course, with a current lifetime limit of £10 million of chargeable gains (increased from £5 million on 6 April 2011, having started at £1 million in 2008), those realising significantly in excess of this amount are not really assisted but there will certainly be very few of them. From a technical point of view it is perhaps a pity that the 2008 legislation looked to the repealed retirement relief for general concepts and definitions. And, following as it does retirement relief, the application of entrepreneurs' relief to trustee disposals is, however, profoundly unsatisfactory (see **7.104–7.106**).

[1.9] Capital gains tax changes following the Emergency Budget on 22 June 2010 took effect from 23 June 2010. This introduced a top rate of 28% for (broadly) higher rate taxpayers, trustees and personal representatives, and a rate of 18% applying to the chargeable gains of individuals to the extent that when added to the taxable income for the year do not exceed the income tax basic rate threshold. For 2016/17, the 28% rate has reduced to 20% for most disposals (and with a corresponding 10% rate for individuals); however, the 28% rate remains for disposals of residential property that do not qualify for private residence relief, and for disposals of the share of gains made by private equity fund managers (so-called 'carried interests').

Income tax

[1.10] For the purposes of both substantive tax liability and compliance, there is a significant difference in the income tax treatment of trusts which are interest in possession on the one hand and discretionary/accumulation on the other (see **6.60–6.79**). In particular, the example at **6.73** illustrates the potential additional impact for an additional rate taxpaying beneficiary of receiving dividend income through a discretionary trust to the extent that there is no available tax pool. Even where the beneficiary pays tax at no more than the basic rate (or is in a tax repayment situation), the additional burdens in terms of cash flow and professional time in the trustees first having to pay the tax and then the beneficiary's reclaiming it makes discretionary/accumulation structures unattractive, except perhaps in cases where they are the right form to adopt in the overall context of things.

[1.11] It should be noted that the taxation of dividend income has changed significantly from 2016/17, with the abolition of the 10% dividend tax credit, the introduction of new rates and of a new dividend allowance for individuals but not trustees. The impact of these changes is very different for interest in possession and discretionary/accumulation trusts (see **6.46** and **6.51**).

Stamp taxes

[1.12] Meanwhile, of course, the importance of stamp taxes has been increasing, with recent increases in both the rates of stamp duty land tax and residential property values. *FA 2000* and *FA 2002* introduced a number of statutory reversals of anti-avoidance arrangements. *FA 2003, ss 42–124* and *Schs 3–18* (subject to subsequent amendments) introduced a comprehensive revision to the structure of stamp taxes, whereby from 1 December 2003 they have been restricted to charge (a) value passing under transfers of UK land and buildings (whether or not effected electronically) or under agreements to transfer UK land and buildings (through stamp duty land tax); and (b) transfers of, or (through stamp duty reserve tax) agreements to transfer, chargeable securities. More recently, the SDLT 'slab system' of thresholds and charges has been replaced by a more graduated charge regime for residential properties from 4 December 2014 and other properties from 17 March 2017. From 1 April 2015, SDLT has been replaced by a new Land and Buildings Transactions Tax in Scotland. (See generally Chapter **13**.)

High-value UK residential property

[1.13] While not specifically relevant to trustees, the three measures (including SDLT) introduced in 2012/13 and 2013/14 should be mentioned, as underlining the Government's determination both to stamp out perceived avoidance of this tax and to discourage the holding of residential property within corporate structures, especially outside the UK. First, the rate of stamp duty land tax on residential property, having become 5% for acquisitions for more than £1 million on or after 6 April 2011, was increased to 7% where the

[1.13] Setting the Scene

consideration exceeds £2 million for acquisitions on or after 22 March 2012 (see **13.34** – and note that since 4 December 2014 entirely new rules apply). Second, where certain types of 'non-natural persons' (though not including trustees) acquire an interest in a single UK dwelling for a chargeable consideration of more than £2 million on or after 21 March 2012, a rate of 15% SDLT applies (see **13.40–13.44** – and this rule continues despite the changes to the general SDLT rates from 4 December 2014). Third, from 2013/14, the Government introduced an annual tax on enveloped dwellings (or ATED) where such a property is 'enveloped' subject to specified exceptions, together with a charge to capital gains tax where a non-natural person wherever resident disposes of a UK dwelling for more than £2 million, to the extent that a gain has arisen since 6 April 2013 and the dwelling has been within the charge to ATED (see **7.126–7.128**). It was announced in Budget 2014 that the ATED and related capital gains tax charge would be extended to properties worth more than £1 million from 2015/16, and to properties worth more than £500,000 from 2016/17, and at the Autumn Statement 2014, a 50% hike in all but the new £1 million rate charges was announced, as from 2015/16. While the expression 'non-natural person' does not include trustees, trustees may well be indirectly affected by these new charges, insofar as they hold shares in such a non-natural person (typically where the trustees are non-UK resident).

[1.14] Tax planning in relation to UK residential property remains high on the anti-avoidance agenda, as witnessed by two further changes. First, Autumn Statement 2013 announced a new CGT charge for non-residents holding UK residential property and, following a formal consultation between 28 March and 21 June 2014, legislation was included in *Finance Act 2015, Sch 7* making consequential amendments to *TCGA 1992* and other relevant statutes (see **26.66**). Peter Vaines summed up the complexity that this brings in the following commentary from the Squire Sanders March 2014 Tax Bulletin:

> 'For a UK resident who has an offshore company and makes a gain on a property which it has owned for some time, it is going to be a bit complicated. The gain up to April 2008 will probably not be taxable if he is a non dom; the gain up to April 2013 will be taxable on him personally under *section 13*; the gain up to April 2015 will be taxed on the company under the ATED rules and the gain after April 2015 will be subject to the new CGT charge in the company. Or maybe not. One or more of these charges might not apply - in which case one of the others will probably apply instead. I hope this is clear.'

[1.15] Secondly, Summer Budget 2015 announced a specific change to the inheritance taxation of residential property held through an offshore holding structure – effectively treating the structure as transparent. Thus, as from 2017/18 (the proposed introduction date), inheritance tax will be due on UK residential property, however it is held (see **27.39–27.48**). The imperative to de-envelope properties held through holding structures has thus increased considerably, as from 6 April 2017 such structures are likely to incur a significant annual ATED charge but with no associated tax advantage of any sort. One of the difficulties for taxpayers, however, is that there is often a tax cost involved in the de-enveloping process itself (particularly CGT or SDLT) and therefore there has been a reluctance to de-envelope (see further **27.49–27.50**).

Non-domiciliaries

[1.16] Perhaps as a result of it being an election year, with all UK parties wanting to 'look tough' on tax avoidance, non-UK domiciliaries have take a few big hits in the last year. First, in the Autumn Statement of 2014, significant increases to the Remittance Basis Charge (RBC) were announced from 2015/16, including a new RBC charge rate of £90,000 for any non-UK domiciliary resident in the UK for 17 out of 20 tax years (see **24.45**). Shortly after its introduction, however, the death of this change was foretold because in the Summer Budget 2015 (following the election of a Conservative majority Government), a new deemed domicile rule for all taxes was announced for anyone resident in the UK for more than 15 out of the past 20 tax years from 2017/18. A new deemed domicile rule for 'the returning UK dom' was announced at the same time. Extensive commentary on these changes is included in CHAPTERS 24, 25, 26 and 27.

Anti-avoidance

[1.17] The final word should go to anti-avoidance. Initiatives to make life harder for those seeking to avoid and evade tax continue to be announced – be they in relation to penalties, the disclosure of tax schemes, the GAAR, or the targeting of those facilitating or promoting such planning, or those using such planning as a 'cash flow' deferral device. These topics will hopefully be irrelevant to most readers of this book but in terms of 'setting the scene', they cannot be ignored. The 'scene' is very much against all but the most vanilla planning and there is no sign of a change under the new Conservative Government. These topics are covered in more details in CHAPTERS 22 and 23.

Chapter 2

Types of Trust

General

[2.1] It is essential that, for the tax year in question (that is, for the purposes of this book, largely 2015/16 or 2016/17) or on occasion even for the day in question, the practitioner is aware of the character of the particular trust for tax purposes. For income tax purposes, the trust may be 'fixed income' or 'interest in possession', that is the income belongs to the beneficiary (or beneficiaries) as it arises (see **6.45–6.49**); alternatively, the income may be subject to accumulation or to distribution at the trustees' discretion, in which case a special income tax regime applies (see **6.50–6.64** and **15.17**). For capital gains tax all types of trust are treated in the same way. For inheritance tax, the principal distinction is between a 'qualifying interest in possession' under which the capital underlying the interest is treated more or less as if it were owned by the beneficiary (see CHAPTER **12**) and the 'relevant property' regime which has a separate system of ten-year and exit charges (see CHAPTERS **9** and **10**).

[2.2] While the terms 'trust' and 'settlement' are, in practice, used interchangeably, a 'settlement' can be wider than a trust for tax purposes. For example the funding of a bank account by different individuals where the account is owned outright will be a settlement for income tax purposes, though not a trust. Also, the manner of creation may distinguish between the two. A settlement presupposes a settlor to create it. A trust can arise in many ways and, often enough, without a trust instrument (as in an intestacy, where trusts may arise in terms laid down by statute). Trusts can also come into being where assets are misappropriated: the holder is trustee for the rightful owner. A firm's clients' account is held in trust for the clients whose balances are held in that account. The purchaser of goods under a *Romalpa* (or retention of title) clause can be a trustee. Therefore, while there is no precise legal definition, the following well-respected definition is a very good description:

> 'A trust is an equitable obligation, binding a person (called a trustee) to deal with property (called trust property) owned by him as a separate fund, distinct from his own private property, for the benefit of persons (called beneficiaries or, in old cases, *cestuis que trust*), of whom he may himself be one, and any one of whom may enforce the obligation . . . Any act or neglect on the part of a trustee which is not authorised or excused by the terms of the trust instrument, or by law, is called a breach of trust.'
>
> (Underhill and Hayton, *Law of Trusts and Trustees*, 18th edn, p 2)

This is not the only definition. A very narrow definition is to be found in the Hague Convention on the Recognition of Trusts:

> 'The term "Trust" refers to the legal relationships created – inter vivos or on death – by a person, the settlor, when assets have been placed under the control of a trustee for the benefit of a beneficiary or for a specified purpose.'

[2.2] Types of Trust

Bearing in mind that the purpose of the Convention is to ensure that this method of holding property is accepted in jurisdictions where trusts are not acknowledged, this definition will do. The purpose is to prevent such occurrences as the German authorities claiming death duties because the trustees of a UK settlement have bought a flat in Berlin for the use of a beneficiary and one trustee has died.

[2.3] A trust can arise under a Will. Both Will trusts and lifetime settlement deeds are referred to as trust instruments.

Will trusts

[2.4] A Will 'speaks from' death. That is to say that it is construed as if it had been written on the date of the testator's death. The appointment of an executor is also immediate, so that the grant of probate (which is the authority of the court) simply validates any previous acts of the executor.

[2.5] The beneficiaries have no legal entitlement to their legacies etc before the executor gives his assent or transfers the cash or other subject-matter of the legacy or bequest; until that point, they have merely a 'chose in action', that is a right to have the estate properly administered and, in course of time, their entitlement made over to them.

[2.6] An executor is not a trustee. It is customary for a Will which appoints settled legacies and/or trusts of residue to appoint the same individuals as executors and as trustees. It may not always be easy to see which they are at any given moment. This can be important in terms of general law as executors and trustees have different powers. Having said this, *Trustee Act 1925*, s 68(17) extends the meaning of 'trustee' to include a personal representative. However, the functions are quite different. A personal representative also includes an administrator of an intestate estate.

[2.7] The distinction between executor and trustee is also important for tax. In the context of capital taxation, it is more logical to date an inheritance back to the date of death rather than to the date of assent and so, for instance, *TCGA 1992, s 62(4)* ensures that a specific legacy will generally date back to the death, so that the assent is not a disposal for capital gains tax purposes. However, following the death the executor has to assume control of the assets, pay debts, taxes and so on. Whilst this is going on, the estate is said to be 'in the course of administration'. During this period the provisions of *ITTOIA 2005, Pt 5, Ch 6 (ss 649–682A)* apply for the purposes of income tax. Those sections attempt to bridge the gap between the general rules of executorship (which sometimes take a different view of what is income and what is the amount due to the income beneficiary) and the income tax rules. The beneficiaries' income is calculated more or less on a receipts basis.

[2.8] When does the administration period come to an end? Once the residue of the estate has been ascertained and all due debts and taxes paid or reserved for in a quantified amount, the administration is complete. The date on which the estate accounts are signed by the residuary beneficiaries (if this occurs) can be taken as a convenient 'cut-off' point for the estate administration, though there may be arguments in a particular case that it came to an end at some other date. The issue was discussed in HMRC Capital Taxes IHT Newsletter of December 2001, though no guidance additional to the above comments was given. At one time, a good rule of thumb was the time when the final corrective account was filed. However, where the spouse exemption prevents there being a charge to inheritance tax, the original account is little more than a statistic for government and it is clear that corrective accounts are not always filed. 'Administration period' is discussed in the glossary to TSEM, but with no greater clarity.

[2.9] Once the administration period has come to an end, then, to the extent that the Will provides for settled legacies or settled shares in residue, the income will become trust (rather than estate) income. Where there is a discretionary settlement in a Will, equal, for example, to the nil-rate band for inheritance tax, it is those assets which have been appropriated, valued for the purposes of the administration at the date of appropriation (albeit for inheritance tax at their value at date of death), which form part of the settlement at any particular time.

[2.10] Therefore it becomes important to know when an estate is in administration and when a Will trust commences. Taking the second question first, the Will trust comes into existence when, and to the extent that, capital has been appropriated – whether in whole or part. If an estate is in course of administration and there is a settled legacy for infants, the executors may well feel safe in putting a few thousand pounds into investments designated as part of the infants' legacy. That brings into existence the trust for the children. Later, the balance of the legacy may be added and that, too, will become subject to the trusts of the settled legacy. So, once there is trust property separately identified and managed, there is a Will trust. It can exist alongside the estate in course of administration and the executors can be trustees of the settled legacy.

[2.11] There can be planning points in choosing the moment when an executor becomes a trustee and there is some room for manoeuvre as to when that takes place. It will usually be up to the executors to decide: the self assessment literature contains no useful guidance on the issue. HMRC will generally be content to follow the decision taken by the executors (see HMRC's Trusts, Settlements and Estates Manual at TSEM7360). In applying *ITTOIA 2005, ss 649–682A*, there can be no assessment under the 'special rates' for discretionary and accumulation settlements (per *ITA 2007, Pt 9, Ch 3, ss 479–483*), until the executors become trustees. *Finance Act 2006* has generally conformed the definitions for purposes of subjecting trust income and gains to income tax and capital gains tax respectively, although there do remain compliance as well as substantive differences between the two taxes. *TCGA 1992, ss 68–98A* apply only to trustees. A discussion of the planning possibilities, depending upon the family, type of asset etc, is beyond the scope of this book, which is about trusts and not about deceased estates.

[2.12] What happens when, with an estate not now in course of administration, some new asset comes to light, perhaps shares in a company which had been overlooked because dividends had not been paid for many years, or perhaps some benefit from another estate? Once the original administration period has come to an end, the estate ceases to be in course of administration. The settled estate will have become a trust and it cannot revert back into an estate in course of administration just because some new asset turns up or some event causes tax to be paid, etc.

[2.13] An estate can spawn a trust. This is of considerable importance for income tax purposes, with two different sets of rules for beneficiaries' income according to whether the income is that of an estate in course of administration or is trust income. The beneficiaries of an estate are taxed more or less on a receipts basis, the income falling into the year of receipt (see 20.32–20.36). However, apart from discretionary and accumulation settlements, income beneficiaries of trusts are taxed on a 'see through' basis. This means that the income of the trustees is apportioned through to the beneficiaries. The tax year of the income of a settlement is the year in which the trustees receive it or are assessed upon it, not the year of payment to the beneficiary. This can be quite significant where there has been a deed of variation. These deeds have no effect for income tax until they are executed and under the pre-1995 rules this left an untidy area between the date of death and the date of the deed, where the income for tax purposes and the income awarded by the deed might differ. This element of untidiness has largely gone under the receipts basis. Now, if a deed seems likely, it is usually sensible to hold back any payments of income until the deed has been executed.

Lifetime settlements

[2.14] A settlement will normally be constituted by a deed. One reason is that a deed validates a transaction which would otherwise fail for lack of consideration. An oral declaration by the settlor can create a settlement. In the offshore tax jurisdictions, trusts are often constituted by a declaration of trust by the trustees who have already received the capital to be settled. This means that a settlement can be made without the settlor being physically present. With the introduction of anti-money laundering legislation, the need for ancillary support services in those offshore jurisdictions, eg opening bank accounts, may often require at least an initial visit by the settlor. However, in most cases where UK practitioners are concerned, there will be a trust instrument, either a settlement deed or a Will. Occasionally, by reason of intestacy, there will be a settlement with no trust instrument. Sometimes there will be a Will amended by a deed of variation. There are still in being UK trusts executed before the coming into force of *Trustee Act 1925* and, here and there, there may be imported trusts where the governing law of the trust is not that of the UK. In general, the UK practitioner is more likely to be looking at a post-war English law settlement, made by deed or by Will. An accountant who prepares a working epitome of the trust instrument should ask the solicitor who drafted the document to confirm that the epitome is correct. The annual trust accounts may usefully summarise that epitome.

[2.15] A trust instrument executed at any time over the last forty years or so will often have been based on a standard precedent and so should be relatively familiar in its terms. That said, each individual trust deed should be carefully read to ensure that its terms are clearly understood. Occasionally, some legislative change throws up an issue of interpretation. For instance, when the *Family Law Reform Act 1969* reduced the age of majority to 18, it enacted that the age of majority should be taken to be 21 when construing documents dated before 1 January 1970.

[2.16] A current issue arises since 1 April 2010 when the *Perpetuities and Accumulations Act 2009* came into force, which, in particular, specifies a single perpetuity period of 125 years and a general rule (subject to some limitations) abolishing the rule against excessive accumulations of income. A trust (other than a charitable trust) cannot last 'in perpetuity': hence the rule against perpetuities.

[2.17] There are now three different periods within which all interests under the trust must vest, depending upon when the particular trust was created.

- First, for a settlement made before 16 July 1964 whether *inter vivos* or by Will, the common law rule applies. That is, any possibility of all or part of a trust vesting more than 21 years after the death of all those living at the date of the settlement will make the limitation void.
- Second, a settlement made or coming into effect on death which takes effect after 15 July 1964 and before 1 April 2010 will be governed by the *Perpetuities and Accumulations Act 1964*. Any limitation which is valid under the common law is valid. In addition, the 'wait and see' provisions of the 1964 Act may help to save an otherwise void limitation. That is, in broad terms, you 'wait and see' whether in the circumstances the trust does vest within the, typically lives in being (royal lives, usually) or 21 years thereafter at the date of the settlement.
- Third, settlements made or coming into effect on or after 1 April 2010 will have a single perpetuity period of 125 years.

In addition, for trusts effective before 1 April 2010, the trustees may substitute a period of 100 years, subject to three conditions:

(a) the trust instrument specifies a perpetuity period defined by reference to the lives of persons in being when it takes effect;
(b) the trustees believe that it is difficult or not reasonably practicable for them to ascertain whether the lives in being have ended and therefore whether the perpetuity period has ended; and
(c) they execute a deed stating such belief and that the 2009 Act shall apply.

[2.18] Under the terms of the *Variation of Trusts Act 1958* it is possible, inter alia, to ask the court to extend a trust's perpetuity period (see, for example, *Allfrey v Allfrey* [2015] EWHC 1717 (Ch), [2015] WTLR 1117, [2015] 2 P & CR D43).

[2.19] Another example of a problem solved by legislation is the effect of divorce on the entitlements of children under the Will of the first of the ex-spouses to die. Before 1 January 1996, any such gifts to the children could fail if the Will made them contingent on the prior death of the former spouse and he/she was still alive. In these circumstances, the entitlements of the children would, in effect, pass to the Crown. That problem was solved by the *Law Reform (Miscellaneous Provisions) Act 1995* under which the ex-spouse is treated as having pre-deceased the testator for all purposes. The same position applies following the dissolution of a civil partnership, where the surviving partner is treated as having pre-deceased the first to die.

[2.20] Once a settlement has been made, it is open to anyone (whether or not the original settlor) to add property to it. That said, it is generally preferable, especially for inheritance tax but also for purposes of the income tax and capital gains tax anti-avoidance legislation, if the principle 'one settlement, one settlor' is followed. Generally speaking, the addition of property to a settlement will not create a new settlement for either income tax or capital gains tax purposes. However, there is an issue in the context of inheritance tax. The expression 'settlement' is defined in *IHTA 1984, s 43(2)* to mean 'any disposition or dispositions of property . . . '. So, as HMRC Trusts and Estates have argued, the addition of property to an existing settlement can itself create a new settlement for inheritance tax purposes. While this becomes something of an absurdity where, say, capital within the annual exemption of £3,000 is merely added to an existing discretionary trust, the point may become rather more material in other contexts.

[2.21] Consider an excluded property settlement which is made by someone domiciled outside the UK for all inheritance tax purposes when the settlement was made and the trust fund consists in property situated outside the UK (see 27.4). If, having become actually or deemed domiciled in the UK, the original settlor adds property to that settlement, HMRC Trusts and Estates will argue for one of two analyses. First, that the settlor may have created a new settlement for inheritance tax purposes, even if the property concerned is situated outside the UK. Second, and perhaps more typically, HMRC will say that there remains a single settlement, part of which continues to benefit as excluded property and the other part of which falls within the chargeable transfer regime. Generally, see 9.57–9.64. The 'added property' provisions of *IHTA 1984, s 67* envisage that it is possible to add property to a discretionary settlement without (presumably) that addition constituting a new settlement for purposes at least of the special regime for relevant property trusts. However, HMRC will not hesitate to apply the section 43(2) analysis in a case where a now UK domiciled individual adds property to a settlement created when he or she was non-domiciled, and in the case of *Barclays Wealth Trustees (Jersey) Ltd v HMRC* [2015] EWHC 2878 (Ch) the High Court has now endorsed this view (see 27.5).

[2.22] A second area where it is important to determine whether a new settlement has been created is where 'additions' are made to interest in possession trusts established prior to 22 March 2006. On 29 October 2013 HMRC published updates to its inheritance tax manual (at IHTM 16074–16078) providing extensive examples of how they will approach this issue in practice. The key areas covered are as follows:

(a) *Mixed funds* Where funds have been mixed, HMRC will accept an apportionment that is fair and reasonable (see IHTM16075).
(b) *Maintenance or improvement* The guidance distinguishes between expenditure by a life tenant on the *maintenance* of his home (which would not normally be an addition of property) and expenditure by a life tenant or settlor on *improvements* to the property (which would

normally give rise to an addition of relevant property and would require an apportionment of the value of the improved property). Additions of property for maintenance expenditure is covered extensively in IHTM16078 and a number of different scenarios are addressed. IHTM16077 deals with an 'improvement'.

(c) *Loans* HMRC do not give any definitive guidance on whether a loan made after 22 March 2006 gives rise to an addition of relevant property, as noted in the following example given in IHTM16077.
What would be the case if instead of transferring the £50,000 to the trustees Sheila had loaned the money to the trustees at arm's length? The question of whether loans made after 22 March 2006 to a settlement in which an interest in possession subsists before that date may give rise to relevant property is complex. Any case where this applies should be referred to Technical.

[2.23] HMRC Trusts and Estates have said that the payment of premiums on a life policy settled before 22 March 2006 is not an addition of property to a settlement, but rather the enhancement of property already in the settlement (even if the terms of the settlement are altered on or after 22 March 2006, provided that that is authorised by the trust deed) and an amendment to *Finance (No 2) Bill 2006* at Report Stage expressly so provided.

Dispositive powers within trusts

[2.24] Trust instruments commonly include dispositive powers (ie powers which are not merely administrative). Two common powers of this sort are as follows:

(a) *Appointment* This is a power to declare fresh trusts within the framework of the main trust instrument. So, a discretionary trust may well contain powers to appoint funds in favour of a beneficiary or a class of beneficiaries selected by the trustees. The result is usually a sub-trust. It is not a separate trust (unless the deed of appointment makes it one). It is a fund within the trust designated for its own beneficiary/beneficiaries.

(b) *Advancement* This is a power to hand over capital to a beneficiary. If the trust instrument is silent, then *Trustee Act 1925, s 32* (see APPENDIX D) will apply to permit an advancement of capital. Until 1 October 2014, the statutory power enabled the trustees to advance up to one half of the presumptive share of the favoured beneficiary. When the *Inheritance and Trustees' Powers Act 2014* came into force on 1 October 2014, *section 32* was amended to allow an advancement of the whole (see **2.25**). A modern trust instrument normally permits advancement of the whole share. Conditions may be imposed. Advancement is not a casual payment. It is some substantial preferment, something to give a start in life or to consolidate a beneficiary's position once a start has been made. To pay for education is advancement. So is the handing over of a substantial block of shares. To pay living expenses is not. Note generally that capital cannot be advanced under the statutory power (whether or not extended) unless the beneficiary in question has a right to capital, whether or not contingent. That is, if the beneficiary is only an income beneficiary, an express power to pay capital to him is required in the deed (as otherwise there is no such power).

[2.25] Following recommendations published by the Law Commission in December 2001, the Government issued a draft *Inheritance and Trustees' Powers Bill* in March 2013. This received Royal Assent in May 2014 as the *Inheritance and Trustees' Powers Act 2014* and came into force on 1 October 2014. The main interest of the Act lies in changes to the distribution of a deceased's estate on intestacy (outside the scope of this book). However, other provisions amend *Trustee Act 1925, ss 31 and 32* to extend the statutory powers of trustees to apply income and capital.

[2.26] Somewhat complex facts were considered in a High Court decision (*Sutton v England* [2009] EWHC 3270 (Ch), [2010] WTLR 335 which has been reversed in part by the Court of Appeal (see **2.28**)). Under the terms of a 1940 settlement trustees currently held the capital in five unequal shares or stirpes. The problem was that the beneficiaries under each stirps did not have a share in the income of a specified part of the fund. Rather, they had a specified share in the income of the whole of the fund. Because in particular the beneficiaries under one stirps (the Southgate stirps), some of whom are now US resident, faced severe US tax liabilities without relief for UK tax liability, the trustees were seeking to create a distinct sub-trust under the settlement in favour of the original assignor of that stirps (the daughter of one of the settlors) and her issue, with US resident trustees. So the judge Mann J was being asked to order that the trustees should have a power of appropriation (which did not exist in the settlement), so as to appoint the creation of a sub-fund for the beneficiaries of the Southgate stirps, being a proportionate share of the overall fund as corresponded to their final share. While Mann J was satisfied that such an appropriation would be expedient, the problem was that all the parties had accepted that such an appropriation would vary the beneficial interest in the fund and this could not fall within the scope of *Trustee Act 1925, s 57*. The judge did observe that the result could be achieved by a variation of the trust following an application under the *Variation of Trusts Act 1958*, though this seems not to have been possible because of inter-family relations. There was a further point, namely whether the trustees could exercise the power of advancement under *Trustee Act 1925, s 32(1)*, which power the trustees had. However, they wanted some kind of confirmation from the Court that the proposed exercise would be appropriate. Again, this was not forthcoming from the judge because the proposed acts did not fall within the statutory power. The trustees were seeking not an advancement of capital, but a variation of the trust to exclude a contingent interest, for which there was no authority. The proposed advancement related not to the application of capital money, but to the variation of an interest under the trust.

[2.27] The facts of *Sutton v England* are very complex and bear careful study. Two particular concerns with the High Court decision were raised in professional circles (and do not seem to have been addressed by the Court of Appeal's decision in **2.28**):

(a)   the ruling that a power of appropriation cannot extend beyond purely administrative matters so as to embrace dispositive issues; and

(b) as to the decision on advancements, that the power cannot be used to advance interests as opposed to actual assets. This goes against what practitioners have being doing in practice for very many years (in reliance on the House of Lords decision in 1964 in *Pilkington v IRC* [1964] AC 612, [1962] 3 All ER 622, HL: see **11.8**).

Does (b) provide support for the view that the House of Lords got it wrong in *Pilkington* in allowing settled advances? Mann J noted that *Trustee Act 1925, s 57* does not require consents, which might have been the issue here, in that not all the beneficiaries agreed with what was proposed. This seems to have been the case in that apparently an application under the *Variation of Trusts Act 1958* was not possible because of inter-family relations.

[2.28] The Court of Appeal subsequently reversed the point on *Trustee Act 1925, s 57* (*Southgate v Sutton* [2011] EWCA Civ 637, [2012] 1 WLR 326, [2011] 2 P & CR D37). The Court held that the partition of a trust fund did not necessarily have more than an incidental impact on, or necessarily involve a variation or rearrangement of, the beneficial interests in it. The Court therefore had power, in appropriate circumstances, to grant an application by trustees under *section 57(1)* for the appropriation and partition of trust property. Mummery LJ said that the court should be satisfied on two main points before exercising its discretion on an application under *Trustee Act 1925, s 57*. First, the powers sought should be for the purposes of a transaction 'in the management or administration of any property vested in trustees'; second, the transaction should, in the opinion of the court, be 'expedient', meaning that it should be in the interests of the trust as a whole. While a variation of the beneficial interests under a trust was not as such a matter of 'the management or administration' of the trust property', an application under *section 57(1)* fell within the court's jurisdiction if the exercise of the powers conferred might only incidentally affect the beneficial interests in the trust property. In this case, that test was held to be satisfied and the application was granted.

Implied trusts

[2.29] Reference is sometimes made to trusts which are resulting, implied or constructive. This really means reading into a trust something which is not already written there or finding that a particular transaction results in a trust. Resulting, etc trusts do occur in family settlements where there is a defect in the draftsmanship. For instance, a fixed interest (ie not discretionary) trust might have successive interests for life, but, because the draftsman omitted to provide for it, no beneficiary is named to receive the capital on the death of the last life tenant. There is then a resulting trust for the settlor. He gave away everything except for the right to receive the capital, so he must have retained that right. Needless to say, whatever tax planning was intended will have been defeated if there is a resulting, etc trust for the settlor. Accordingly, for income tax purposes he will be taxed on the income (as explained at **4.3** and **4.5**) and for capital gains tax purposes he will not be able to hold over a gain arising on transfer of an asset to a trust (see **7.81**). For inheritance tax purposes the reservation of benefit rules explained at **8.36–8.37** may also apply. These adverse effects can be prevented for the future, though not for the past, by execution of a deed under which the settlor irrevocably releases or assigns any such interest and so that the trust shall be construed as if the settlor had died.

Trusts in practice

[2.30] The types of trust normally encountered in practice are:

(i) Discretionary trusts;
(ii) Interest in possession trusts;
(iii) Bare trusts;
(iv) Accumulation and maintenance trusts;
(v) Charitable trusts;
(vi) Disabled trusts; and
(vii) Employee trusts.

A summary of each of these is provided below. The first three are found in many practical situations and further commentary about them is included throughout this book. The remaining four each have (or, in the case of accumulation and maintenance trusts, had) a particular function in practice and are the subject of their own short chapter. Other trusts, with even more specific roles, are discussed at different places throughout the book – particularly within CHAPTER 8.

Discretionary trusts

[2.31] The essence of discretionary trust is that the trustees have a discretion as to what they do with the *income* of the trust, as it arises. Typically they will have a power or duty to distribute the income amongst a defined class of beneficiaries, none of whom has any *right* to income. Alongside this there is usually a power or duty to accumulate any income that is not so distributed (although for many older trusts there will be a finite period during which such accumulations can be made – see 3.9).

[2.32] This discretion over income is in direct contrast to the position for an interest in possession trust, where the trustees are obliged to distribute income to one or more identified beneficiaries.

[2.33] The trustees of most discretionary trusts would also have a discretion over the distribution of the capital of the trust, enabling them (by the exercise of the one of the dispositive powers described at 2.24) to make payments of capital to beneficiaries or, as importantly, to declare new trusts of income. Such powers are not, however, exclusive to discretionary trusts, as the trustees of many interest in possession trusts have such powers too (see 2.39).

[2.34] In tax terms, a *standard* discretion trust would fall into the 'relevant property' regime for inheritance tax purposes (see CHAPTERS 9 and 10) and, correspondingly and most importantly in tax planning terms, the assets of the trust would not be treated as comprised in the estates of any of the beneficiaries.

[2.35] Likewise the income of a discretionary trust is not treated as the income of any beneficiary as it arises and is instead charged at the special rates applicable to trusts (see CHAPTER 6).

[2.36] The capital gains tax treatment of discretionary and interest in possession trusts is the same, in so far as in both cases it is the trustees who are assessed to tax on any gains rather than the beneficiaries. The application of certain capital gains tax reliefs does, however, vary between the two types of trust (see CHAPTER 7).

[2.37] Finally, it needs to be remembered that certain of the other trusts described in this book take the form of a discretionary trust – for example most employee trusts and many disabled trusts – but certain factors about those trusts (most typically the identity of their beneficiaries) trigger different tax consequences. A list of these 'favoured' trusts can be found at 8.29.

Interest in possession trusts

[2.38] An interest in possession trust is a trust with fixed interests in income. There will be one or more beneficiaries currently entitled to income, subject only to the due payment of tax and expenses. The commonest may be a Will trust giving the income to the widow for life and the capital to the children upon her death. But lifetime trusts creating fixed interests for adult beneficiaries were also extremely common before 22 March 2006, used as an alternative to an outright gift of property.

[2.39] The right to income of the life tenant may be defeasible. That is to say that the right can be brought to an end. Common cases of defeasible interests are as follows:

(i) Income is left to a widow(er) during widow(er)hood. Not only death, but also re-marriage, could bring her or his interest to an end.
(ii) A class gift has been made, one member of the class has become entitled to an interest in possession in his putative share and the class is enlarged. An obvious illustration is where capital is left to 'such of my grandchildren as shall attain the age of 25, if more than one in equal shares'. There are three grandchildren, one over 18 with an interest in possession in one-third and two others under age. A fourth grandchild is born. The interest in possession is now in one-quarter and not in one-third, ie the interest in possession to the extent of one-twelfth (owned by the grandchild over 18) has come to an end.
(iii) An overriding power of appointment or advancement has not been invoked. That is to say, the trustees cannot withhold income from the life tenant once they have received it, but at some future time they could exercise one of their overriding powers in favour of beneficiaries other than the life tenant.

[2.40] In all these cases the fact that the right to income is defeasible does not prevent the trust being an interest in possession trust for as long as the defeasance has not taken place. The phrase 'interest in possession' is not defined in any statute but has been explored in *Pearson v IRC*, [1981] AC 753, [1980] 2 All ER 479, HL: it may be taken as meaning 'present right to present enjoyment' (see **8.6**) and it is the 'present' right which is the key. When identifying whether any interest in possession exists the question that should be asked is: 'Is anyone entitled to the income as it arises?' If they are then it is an interest in possession trust and, if not, it will be either be a standard discretionary trust or some form of favoured trust.

[2.41] In tax terms, the inheritance tax position for an interest in possession trust will be determined by whether or not it is a so called 'qualifying' interest in possession trust. If it is, the assets of the trust will be deemed to form part of the life tenant's estate. If it is not then, just as for discretionary trusts, the relevant property regime will apply (see CHAPTERS 9 and 10).

[2.42] The inheritance taxation of qualifying interest in possession trusts (and how to identify them) is covered in CHAPTER 12.

[2.43] Typically, the income of an interest in possession trust, whether or not a 'qualifying' interest in possession, will be taxed on the trustees at the basic rate and on the life tenant at his or her marginal rate (and subject to a tax credit for the basic rate paid by the trustees) (see CHAPTER 6).

Bare trusts

[2.44] A bare trust is a form of nominee arrangement were a trustee simply holds assets on behalf of someone else, the actions of a bare trustee being the actions of his principal. The trustee may self-assess for income tax, but not for capital gains tax which is dealt with in the name of the principal and at his/her tax district. This approach is confirmed by *TCGA 1992, s 60* (see **7.11**).

[2.45] The most common form of bare trust may be the portfolio of shares held by a stockbroker's nominee company for his client. The next commonest may well be assets in settlements where the beneficiaries are entitled to them but, for some reason or other, the actual transfer has been delayed. Parents have sometimes set up bare trusts for their infant children. Generally, the intention would be to recover tax on the infant's personal allowance and use his exemptions and lower rates. However, this device was countered by *FA 1999, s 64* in relation to trusts established, or capital transferred to existing trusts, on or after 9 March 1999 [*ITTOIA 2005, s 629*]. From that date, income from such capital has been treated as the parent's, whether or not paid out, subject to the existing £100 de minimis limit per child per tax year: see **4.15**. Any gains of the trust do, however, benefit from the infant's annual capital gains tax exemption, whenever the trust was set up. Problems are more likely to arise in the field of administration rather than tax. If there is income and a tax recovery there must be cash and somebody must manage it. If the gift of capital was made by a parent before 9 March 1999 then, in order to avoid assessment on the parent, the income must be retained and invested by the trustees, for the beneficiary to receive on attaining the age of 18.

[2.46] For inheritance tax purposes a bare trust is treated as if the property concerned was owned beneficially by the infant (or other beneficiary). There was in the course of 2006 a debate with HMRC as to whether or not a bare trust for an infant should be regarded as a substantive settlement under the *FA 2006* regime for trusts. Happily, in early March 2007, HMRC agreed that there was no substantive settlement. This analysis means, of course, that in the event of the death of the infant under the age of 18, the property in the bare trust forms part of his chargeable estate for inheritance tax purposes. And, on attaining the age of 18, the transfer of the property to the infant will have no inheritance tax (or capital gains tax) implications.

[2.47] It is to be hoped that the trustees' investment policy is approved by the infant when he attains majority. Because an infant lacks contractual capacity, shares etc should not be put into his name. Perhaps the company registrar would not notice but, for example, an infant cannot transfer shares, nor take up a 'rights' issue. Banks will open savings accounts for minors but the facility of a cheque book is generally denied. In a book of this sort it is not sensible to attempt a list of the administrative problems of bare trusts for infants, but the reader should be aware that there are issues.

[2.48] Those in whom legal ownership of investments and other property is registered should also appreciate that they have an obligation when the infant attains 18 to inform him of his entitlement (see *Hawksley v May* [1956] 1 QB 30) and, if demanded, to transfer the capital to him. In that case the plaintiff beneficiary became entitled to income on attaining age 21. The court held that the trustees had a duty to inform the beneficiary on reaching the then age of majority that he had an interest in the capital and income of the trust fund. It was also their duty to disclose to the beneficiary on demand any deed or document relating to the trust (including an opinion by counsel as to its effect), though with no obligation on the trustees to give to the beneficiary legal advice or to inform him of his right to sever. And the trustees had to pay to the beneficiary the income from his share of the trust fund on his attaining majority without any demand from him.

Accumulation and maintenance trusts

[2.49] An accumulation and maintenance trust was a favoured type of discretionary trust – ie outside the relevant property regime – used extensively before 22 March 2006 as a vehicle for a gift to children or grandchildren under the age of 25. A detailed commentary on their inheritance tax treatment can be found at CHAPTER 11.

[2.50] A typical accumulation and maintenance trust would provide for income to be held at the trustees' discretion below a defined vesting age of no older than 25, and during this time the income tax treatment was the same as for a standard discretionary trust. If a beneficiary did not take an absolute interest at the vesting age, an interest in possession trust needed to apply from that point and, likewise, the income tax treatment of that trust would be that for a standard interest in possession trust.

Charitable trusts

[2.51] Charitable trusts are covered in detail in CHAPTER 14.

Disabled trusts

[2.52] Special income tax and inheritance tax rules apply to certain trusts – which can now be both discretionary or interest in possession – for disabled beneficiaries. Disabled trusts are covered in detail in CHAPTER 15.

Employee trusts

[2.53] Trusts for the benefit of employees generally have no special treatment for either income tax or capital gains tax purposes but, for inheritance tax purposes, special provisions exclude such trusts from the relevant property regime. Employee trusts are covered in detail in CHAPTER 16.

Chapter 3

Interests of Beneficiaries

[3.1] An interest of a beneficiary may be:

(i)   a mere *spes*;
(ii) vested;
(iii) contingent;
(iv) in possession; or
(v)   in reversion.

The differences can be important for tax purposes.

A mere spes

[3.2] A mere *spes* is a hope, the right to be considered as a beneficiary under a discretionary settlement. Its value does not form part of the beneficiary's estate for inheritance tax purposes. However, the existence of such a right for either the settlor or spouse/civil partner may trigger anti-avoidance legislation: see CHAPTER 4.

Vested interests, whether in possession or in reversion

[3.3] A vested interest is one to which a person is entitled for the time being. It may be defeasible, that is subject to removal by the trustees. Sometimes a vested interest which is defeasible looks very like a contingent interest (see **3.4**). A vested interest in income can be either in possession or in reversion. Vested in possession means that the beneficiary is entitled to the current enjoyment of the income from the capital: either he is the life tenant or he is an annuitant. Vested in reversion means that, although the beneficiary has a right which forms part of his estate, there is some prior right, for instance, as under a simple trust such as 'to my widow for life and, upon her death, to our children in equal shares'. Here the widow has a *vested* interest in possession and each child has a vested interest in reversion. An adult son or daughter can transfer such an interest whilst it is still in reversion: there will be good inheritance tax reasons for so doing (see **12.17** and **12.18**).

Contingent interests

[3.4] A contingent interest requires the satisfaction of a pre-condition. Therefore, the gift in the illustration in **3.3** would have different consequences if it were instead 'to my widow for life and, upon her death, to such of our children as are then living, in equal shares.' This formula gives each child a *contingent* reversionary interest – ie the right of each is conditional upon he or she being alive at the date of the mother's death. Should their mother wish to release her life interest she could effectively pass only the right to income to her children. They would then receive the income during her lifetime (called an interest 'pur autre vie') and the capital would be divided among the survivors at her death.

[3.5] A further illustration is: 'To my son for life, with remainder to his children at 25 and subject thereto to my daughter'. The son has a vested interest in possession. His children have contingent reversionary interests because any of them who does not reach the age of 25 gets nothing. The daughter has only a contingent reversionary interest because she gets nothing if any of her nephews and nieces attains the age of 25.

The accumulation of income

[3.6] 'Accumulations' are not the same as 'undistributed income'. Where trustees have a discretion to distribute income, there will always be a time lag between the receipt of the income and its distribution. Income does not 'accumulate' pending distribution. Income is 'accumulated' when it becomes capital. This would typically be because the trustees have resolved to use it as capital ('resolved to accumulate it'); however, HMRC can also argue that income which has remained undistributed for a long period of time accumulates automatically – albeit that they acknowledge that the law on *when* this happens is not clear.

[3.7] The point in time when money changes from being undistributed income into an accumulation is not easy to determine. Sometimes it becomes obvious from a transaction, because, say, income has been used to purchase an investment. At other times it will depend upon the behaviour of the trustees. For instance, if accounts are made up to 5 April 2015 and no positive steps were taken during the year to accumulate, then it is unlikely that the trustees will consider the matter until the autumn. Thus it might be possible to say by 31 December 2015 that the trustees had resolved not to distribute the income of 2014/15 and that that was when accumulation took place. That is not conclusive, of course – and, indeed, depending on the terms of the trust, it might be possible for trustees to retain income as undistributed for a year or two before deciding whether either to distribute or to accumulate it. Dilatory trustees could easily defer the decision for months. In the end they must make their minds up because they have a fiduciary duty. Very occasionally, in the past at least, income could be undistributed for years and still not have been accumulated. This arose in the *Gulbenkian* case (see 9.32). However, under the self assessment regime, such a situation is now going to be improbable in the extreme.

[3.8] Modern precedents generally include a power to accumulate income. The *Trustee Act 1925, s 31* also provides a statutory power of accumulation where property is held on trust for a child under the age of 18. There is, however, no general implied power to accumulate and therefore if the trust instrument is silent and *section 31* does not apply, income cannot be accumulated.

[3.9] For trusts made before 1 April 2010, the periods of accumulation are limited. Twenty-one years is a standard period. For trusts made on or after

1 April 2010 (which is the effective date of the Perpetuities and Accumulations Act 2009), the old rules against 'excessive accumulations' do not apply and so a direction in a trust deed made on or after 1 April 2010 to accumulate income for longer than the minority of any particular beneficiary, or, say, for longer than a period of 21 years from the date of the settlement is valid. (See **2.16** for the perpetuities provisions of the Act.)

[3.10] Sometimes, albeit rarely, trustees have no option and the terms of a trust compel them to accumulate income ie they have no power to distribute it to beneficiaries. More typically trustees might be compelled to accumulate if they decide not to distribute. Likewise, many modern precedents would allow the trustees to distribute accumulations as if they were income: see **6.80–6.85**).

[3.11] There are tax consequences of the accumulation of income because:

(a) in a children's trust, the accumulations can typically be applied by the trustees as income if the income of the trust fund is inadequate and they then become income of the current year;
(b) once the children become entitled to the accumulations otherwise than by way of augmentation of income, they receive them as capital;
(c) the ten-year charge for inheritance tax is levied on accumulations in a special way (see **9.30–9.33**). Historically, it has not been charged at all on undistributed income; however, new deeming rules apply to income undistributed for five years or over from 6 April 2014 (see **9.34–9.36** and see also *Inland Revenue Statement of Practice SP 8/86* reproduced in APPENDIX A).

[3.12] The above said, the self assessment regime, which requires (in the normal case) submission of returns and payment of tax, on or before the 31 January following the end of the tax year, encourages the timely turning of the trustees' minds to the issue of accumulation among others. While there will always be exceptions, it is likely that the decision whether or not to accumulate income will have been taken within nine months less five days after the end of the tax year, at the latest.

Intermediate income

[3.13] The interests of the beneficiaries must be clearly understood. The most common case where this causes confusion is where there is a trust for children at age 25 and some are over 18 and therefore by reason of *Trustee Act 1925, s 31* are in receipt of income (subject to an overriding accumulation period). The trust instrument can overrule *section 31* but, if it does not, a child who has only a contingent interest is entitled to the income of his putative share at age 18. This is so even if the share is revocable.

[3.14] A popular type of accumulation and maintenance settlement (made before 22 March 2006) was for 'such of the beneficiaries as attain the age of 25, if more than one in equal shares' and with a power to accumulate income up to that age. In such a case the child who is over 18 can receive the income, but only if the trustees choose not to accumulate it (given that there is still a permitted accumulation period). Occasionally one sees an old Will which provides for capital to be divided equally among a class of children, but so that no child shall receive his share until age 25. This is not a contingent gift; all that happens is that vesting is deferred. From the age of 18 the child is entitled to his income.

[3.15] Where a gift is not immediate but is to take effect at a future time or is contingent, then there is always a question as to who gets the income in the meantime. This income is known as the intermediate income. The rules are complicated. To some extent they depend on case law, but there are also statutory provisions in *Trustee Act 1925, s 31* (see APPENDIX D) and *Law of Property Act 1925, s 175*. The upshot is that all future and contingent gifts carry the intermediate income unless:

(a) the settlor or testator has expressed a wish to the contrary (eg to accumulate); or
(b) the gift is a deferred or contingent pecuniary legacy; or
(c) the gift is a deferred residuary gift of personalty (ie not 'realty' but real property).

Chapter 4

Anti-Avoidance Rules Affecting the Settlor

[4.1] Even though property has been successfully settled, it is still possible for tax referable to either the property or income from it to fall upon the settlor. Given a modern precedent correctly used by the family solicitor who is not driven to daring draftsmanship by the provocative wishes of the settlor, this should not happen. The principal dangers are for the trust to be caught: (a) for income tax by *ITTOIA 2005, Pt 5, Ch 5 (ss 619–648)*; (b) for capital gains tax by *TCGA 1992, s 77* (up to and including 2007/08, but not from 2008/09); and/or (c) for inheritance tax as a gift with reservation of benefit under *FA 1986, s 102, Sch 20*. Furthermore, there is, from 6 April 2005, an annual income tax charge on the benefit of enjoying 'pre-owned assets' of which a gift had been made since 18 March 1986, whether or not involving a settlement structure: see 4.39–4.51. See also CHAPTER 26 for the capital gains tax charge on certain settlors of non-UK resident trusts.

Income tax

Overview

[4.2] The regime has been consolidated in *ITTOIA 2005 Ch 5, Pt 5* and applies whenever the settlement was made. The target is the settlor who retains 'an interest' under the settlement (as defined).

An 'interest' under a settlement

[4.3] Income of the trustees is treated as that of the settlor unless it derives from property in which he has no interest [*ITTOIA 2005, s 624*]. He is deemed to have an interest in property if it or any related property could be applied for his benefit or the benefit of his spouse/civil partner. 'Related property' is defined quite straightforwardly, as 'in relation to any property, . . . income from that property or any other property directly or indirectly representing proceeds of, or of income from, that property or income from it' [*ITTOIA 2005, s 625(5)*]. Subsections ensure that those who are not currently a spouse (which, from 5 December 2005, includes the other member of a registered civil partnership) can be ignored, as can interests in property derived from insolvency, premature death of beneficiaries and so on.

[4.4] The scope of 'related property' is illustrated by *IRC v Botnar*, CA [1999] STC 711. Mr Botnar had made a settlement in Liechtenstein. He was excluded from benefit, but there was a clause in the settlement deed which permitted capital to be transferred to any other trust fund. Therefore, it became possible for Mr Botnar to benefit as a beneficiary of that other trust fund. The income of the settlement was, accordingly, properly assessed upon him.

'Settlor' and 'settlement'

[4.5] For income tax purposes the definitions of 'settlor' and 'settlement' are extremely wide. The word 'settlor' means any person by whom the settlement was made and 'settlement' is defined as including 'any disposition, trust, covenant, agreement, arrangement or transfer of assets' [*ITTOIA 2005, s 620(1)*]. Accordingly the shadow settlor (ie an individual who provides funds indirectly) is caught. Further, the person who provides funds indirectly and those who make reciprocal arrangements for the making of settlements are specifically caught [*ITTOIA 2005, s 620(2), (3)*]. TSEM4125 more or less repeats this, with an example. The point is illustrated in both *Crossland v Hawkins*, CA 1961, 39 TC 493, and *IRC v Mills*, [1974] STC 130, HL. HMRC consider that a loan to trustees on non-commercial terms would be a settlement.

[4.6] Somewhat curiously, there remains no general definition of 'settlement' for income tax purposes, other than in relation to the anti-avoidance provisions (see **4.5**). The expression 'settled property' means broadly any property held in trust other than nominee or bare trustee situations (*ITA 2007, s 466*), which was derived from capital gains tax. General definitions of 'settlor' and the identification of the settlor in the cases where there are transfers between settlements or where there is a variation of a Will or an intestacy are now found in *sections 467–473 of ITA 2007*. In particular, *sections 472–473* identifying the settlor where there has been a post-death variation of a Will or intestacy do more than restate the rule before 2006/07. In broad terms (as before), where it is the original beneficiary who varies the Will or intestacy, he is the settlor for income tax purposes. However, this does not apply when the property was itself settled under the Will and as a result of the variation becomes comprised in another settlement; in such case the deceased is treated as the settlor. *Section 474* imports, again from capital gains tax, the notion that trustees are a single person (distinct from the persons who are trustees from time to time) and, though with no substantive change for residence purposes, the residence rule for trustees mentioned in CHAPTER 24 is in effect applied by *sections 475–476* to that deemed person who constitutes the body of trustees.

[4.7] A Will is not a settlement (*IRC v Buchanan*, CA (1957), 37 TC 365), though a deed of variation may give effect to a settlement.

[4.8] There was a period when the question of paying the debts of the settlor seemed to be a trap, in circumstances where the trustees paid the capital taxes on making the settlement. It has always been possible for the trustees to pay the inheritance tax or capital gains tax occasioned by the making of the settlement. These taxes are the liability of the settlor. However, he can make a settlement of assets subject to payment by the trustees of either or both taxes. The risk of the trustees being attacked for having paid the capital taxes of the settlor receded when Inland Revenue Statement of Practice SP 1/82 (now obsolete) was published.

[4.9] Income has its usual meaning for tax purposes, although it is extended to include offshore income not otherwise assessable [*ITTOIA 2005, ss 632, 648(1)*]. *Section 632* charges 'offshore income gains'.

Exceptions

[4.10] The primary limitation, as found in case law, is that these anti-avoidance provisions catch only those settlements where bounty is given. (*IRC v Levy*, Ch D [1982] STC 442; *IRC v Plummer*, [1979] STC 793, HL; *Bulmer v IRC*, Ch D (1966), 44 TC 1). Therefore, fully commercial transactions are not vulnerable. There are also statutory exceptions to the scope of the rule, ie where the settlor or spouse/civil partner can benefit only on: the bankruptcy of an actual or potential beneficiary; an assignment of/or charge on the property made or given by such a person; in the case of a marriage settlement or civil partnership settlement, the death of both parties to the marriage or civil partnership and all of the children of the family of the parties to the marriage; or the death of a child of the settlor who had become entitled under the settlement at an age not exceeding 25 [*ITTOIA 2005, s 625(2)*]. A further exception to the rule was introduced by *FA 2012, s 12* for income arising on or after 21 March 2012: to counter arrangements which had been established to make the settlor-interested rule work in favour of the taxpayer by having income treated as arising to a corporate settlor, it will not now apply in cases where the settlor was not an individual.

[4.11] Allocations of pension rights are not affected by *ITTOIA 2005, ss 619–648*, nor are settlements related to divorce or separation, nor trading payments, nor charitable covenants which pre-dated Gift Aid (though some may well continue). If a settlement is caught and the settlor then takes remedial action so that he no longer has an interest, his liability ceases from the end of that tax year (ie not retrospectively). It will be clear that it is quite safe to use a discretionary settlement where the surviving spouse/civil partner can benefit after the death of the settlor. This can be important where the settlor is the breadwinner whose death will reduce the family's income.

[4.12] A settlor must be living at the time income is assessable if it is to be deemed to be his.

Heritage maintenance funds

[4.13] There is a special rule where a maintenance fund has been established within *IHTA 1984, Sch 4* to ensure proper preservation of heritage property. In particular, for the first six years of the settlement, none of the trust fund can be applied otherwise than (a) for the maintenance, repair or preservation of, or making provision for public access to, properly which is qualifying property etc; or (b) by meeting trustee expenses, though income not so applied or accumulated can be paid for the benefit of a national body or qualifying charity within *IHTA 1984, Sch 3*. That apart, the settlement may well be settlor-interested, and so the income would normally be assessed on the settlor under *ITTOIA 2005, s 624*. However, the trustees have power to elect for any year that the income should be treated not as that of the settlor but rather of the trustees [*ITA 2007, s 508*]. The election must be made on or before the first

[4.13] Anti-Avoidance Rules Affecting the Settlor

anniversary of the usual filing date for the tax year. With common marginal rates of tax this would not usually make much difference, though if the settlor has losses or is not otherwise a higher or additional rate taxpayer, less tax might be payable if the income is assessed on the settlor, who would have the usual right of recovery for the tax paid against the trustees. A legislative correction to prevent the anomaly of an effective double income tax liability on payments by the trustees where an election is in place was made by *FA 2013, s 63*, with effect from 2012/13: see **7.83**.

Settlements on children

[4.14] A second set of rules catches settlements where income is used to benefit an infant child of the settlor who is unmarried or (from 5 December 2005) not in a civil partnership (subject to the de minimis mentioned at **4.15**). The scope of the legislation was widened from 9 March 1999. For capital settled before that date, it remains the income paid to or for the benefit of the child which is treated as income of the settlor. Income accumulated from capital settled before 9 March 1999 is safe, although if it is drawn down later and used as income while the child is under 18, it will be taxed on the settlor. However, income arising from capital settled on or after 9 March 1999 (whenever the settlement was made) is assessable on the parent settlor, in the year in which paid to the child [*ITTOIA 2005, s 629(1)(a)*]. The *accumulation* of income in a parental settlement (like any other settlement) brings a liability to what are called the 'special rates' of tax in *ITA 2007, Pt 9 Ch 3, ss 479–483* (see **6.55** and **6.60–6.64**).

[4.15] There is a de minimis relief where the income of an infant child does not exceed £100 per annum (*ITTOIA 2005, s 629(3)*) and this is available to each parent's settlement (including any income from any other statutory settlement made by that parent for that child), separately: once the threshold is exceeded, the whole of the income is taxable on the parent.

[4.16] There may be a danger of a parent joining in an 'arrangement' and so becoming a settlor without knowing. Then, if income is spent on his infant children, *ITTOIA 2005, s 629(1)* is triggered. In a Special Commissioner's case, Sir Stephen Oliver QC held that the parental settlement provisions applied to company dividends paid on shares owned by three minor children for which their parents had subscribed (*Bird v Revenue and Customs Comrs (SpC 720) [2009] STC (SCD) 81*). However, perhaps rather surprisingly, he went on to find that HMRC were not entitled to raise an out-of-time assessment on the grounds of the taxpayers' fraudulent or negligent conduct, because reference neither to the notes to the tax return, nor to the legislation, would have indicated to the assumed reasonable compliant taxpayer that in such a case the parents had indirectly provided funds for the purpose of the arrangements which included the payment of the dividend.

[4.17] Those advising on deeds of variation should bear this problem of settlements on infant children in mind, because it is not unknown for parents to re-direct legacies under a Will from themselves to their children without appreciating that in so doing they have become 'settlors' for income tax purposes. Believing that the income is from, say, grandfather's estate, they allow it to be spent on their own infant children and are caught. Not unnaturally HMRC are interested in cases where money moves to an infant child of the settlor who is unmarried or (from 5 December 2005) not in a civil partnership. This includes capital payments as well as income. The point received express statutory confirmation from 2006/07 with what may be found in *ITA 2007, s 472*.

[4.18] In a situation where HMRC contend that income-producing funds for a minor derive from a parent, evidence that the funds were given by (say) a grandparent should dispel the contention. So it was in *Lorber (PA) v Revenue and Customs Comrs* [2011] UKFTT 101 (TC), where the First-tier Tribunal accepted Mr Lorber's contention that the money in several building society accounts had come from his children's grandfather (for whom he held a power of attorney and who had died before the hearing of the appeal).

[4.19] It is not always clear where the parental settlement borderline is to be found. The case of *Butler (Inspector of Taxes) v Wildin* [1989] STC 22, 61 TC 666, Ch D illustrates this. Two brothers wished to benefit their infant children who had money which had come from their grandparents. The money was invested in a £100 company which had a development site and this became valuable. The purchase of the site was financed by a bank loan guaranteed by the brothers. The brothers gave their services to the company free of charge. This scheme was held to be an 'arrangement' (ie a settlement for the purposes of what is now *ITTOIA 2005, s 620(1)*). However, that was a High Court decision. The case went to the Court of Appeal, but was settled by agreement. Therefore there is no report of the case except in the High Court. It is thought that the High Court might have been overruled had the case proceeded.

Bare trusts

[4.20] A single 'bare trust' for a child might be a trust of income only or also a trust of capital. In the latter case the capital belongs absolutely to the child and he can call for it on attaining the age of 18 (see **2.44–2.48**). In either case, the income belongs absolutely to the child and, though it may be paid to him or applied for his benefit while under the age of majority, more usually the income will be retained by the trustees until the child is old enough to give a valid receipt at 18.

[4.21] Until 9 March (Budget Day) 1999, what is now *ITTOIA 2005, s 629(1)* did not apply to such income which was not paid out and, instead, the income was treated as that of the child. Income from trusts established on or after 9 March 1999 is now assessed upon the parent settlor, subject to the £100 de minimis limit. This applies whether or not the income is paid out, though the settlor has a statutory right of indemnity for the tax from the trustees.

[4.22] The rule is not retrospective and income from pre-9 March 1999 settlements continues to benefit from the old rule (although income from capital added to such settlements on or after 9 March 1999 will be caught). The new rule also applies in a case where the child's right is to income only – ie an interest in possession settlement. Interest in possession trusts for minor children are rare but not unknown and it is, of course, important that *Trustee Act 1925, s 31* is excluded for such trusts.

[4.23] Anti-Avoidance Rules Affecting the Settlor

Chargeability of the trustees to tax

[4.23] If in any case *ITTOIA 2005, s 624(1) or s 629(1)* applies to treat income under a parental or settlor-interested settlement as that of the parent settlor, the trustees still continue to have income tax liability. *ITTOIA 2005, s 646(8)* provides that nothing in *ss 624–632* is to be construed as excluding a charge on the trustees as persons by whom any income is received. The rules, which are somewhat complex, are covered at **5.11**.

Waiver of dividends

[4.24] If all the shareholders who are *sui juris* (ie of full age and capacity) waive their dividends from a family company and the result is an increase in the dividend to trustees, the waivers will be 'arrangements' and the individuals making them are settlors [*ITTOIA 2005, s 620(1)*]. Similarly, if the trustees make payments to or for infant children (who are not married or, from 5 December 2005, in a civil partnership) of one of these settlors and these can be connected to the waiver, *ITTOIA 2005, s 629(1)* can cause the 'parent settlor' to be assessed.

[4.25] There is usually no inheritance tax issue. The waiver of a dividend is not a transfer of value if made within twelve months before the right to the dividend has accrued [*IHTA 1984, s 15*]. A waiver before then would almost certainly be a disposition because there would be a fall in value of the donor's estate.

Capital sums

[4.26] Specific provisions are aimed at settlements from which capital sums reach the settlor or the settlor's spouse/civil partner, having been funded from trust income [*ITTOIA 2005, ss 633–643*]. Originally, the abuse consisted simply of borrowing money from the accumulated income of the family settlement. As strategies were caught by legislation, the schemes became more sophisticated, culminating in the settlement owning shares in a company which accumulated its income and made loans to the ruling family. These days, such loans are highly unlikely. Both company law and tax law militate against them.

[4.27] It is easiest to look first at the simple case where there is no connected company. It is the payment of a 'capital sum' to the settlor or spouse/civil partner which activates the rule. A 'capital sum' means a loan, a repayment of a loan or any other payment not being income and not paid for full consideration [*ITTOIA 2005, s 634*]. In such a case, the first comparison is of the capital sum and the undistributed income of the trust. If the capital sum is less than the income which has not been distributed, the capital sum will be assessed on the settlor. If the capital sum is greater, the undistributed income is assessed. Running totals need to be kept, so that every year when there is income which is within the total of capital sums, that too is assessed. It is the income which is the real target, not the capital sum.

[4.28] A case which shows how easy it is to fall within the rule is that of *De Vigier v IRC* [1964] 2 All ER 907, [1964] 1 WLR 1073, HL where, in order to take up a rights issue, the trustees borrowed from Mrs De Vigier, the settlor's wife. Within the year, the trustees had repaid the loan. The trust had undistributed income and Mr De Vigier was assessed. This is an easy trap to fall into, even now, nearly 50 years after the House of Lords decision. The amount of the repayment will be assessed on the settlor to the extent that it falls within the income available up to the end of that tax year or the following ten years. The charge to tax will be on the relevant amount grossed up, in 2014/15 and 2015/16 at 45% (though with a 45% tax credit).

[4.29] The extension of this anti-avoidance legislation to the case where there is a company involved requires that:

(a) the trustees hold shares in a company (or are participators in any other way);
(b) the company is a close company (or would be if UK resident) or is controlled by such a company [*ITTOIA 2005, s 637(8)*];
(c) a capital sum is paid to the settlor by the company; and
(d) a capital sum etc is or has been paid to the company by the trustees.

[*ITTOIA 2005, s 641(1)*]

[4.30] The various payments must fall within the same period of five years. Payments by or to an associated company (within *CTA 2010, s 449*) are caught as if they were made by or to the company concerned.

[4.31] The likeliest trigger for the capital sums regime nowadays is some simple transaction like that in the *De Vigier* case above. That said, however, the teeth of the regime are drawn by *section 640* in the simple case where the settlor makes a loan to the trustees and is repaid. In broad terms the income tax paid by the trustees in respect of undistributed income which is taxed on the settlor is credited to the settlor. The only exposure therefore would seem to be in respect of dividend income where (in 2014/15 and 2015/16) the trustees will have paid tax at 37.5% but the settlor will be assessed at 45% or where the capital sum is matched with income of a year with a lower trust rate (such as 2009/10 when the rate was 40%).

The Pre-owned Assets Regime: the income tax charge from 2005/06

[4.32] Although an income tax matter, this subject is dealt with below at 4.39–4.51 under inheritance tax insofar as it has been presented as an anti-avoidance measure in relation to the reservation of benefit regime.

Capital gains tax

[4.33] Following the alignment of the rates of income tax and capital gains tax in the *FA 1988*, it became necessary to protect HMRC from settlements where the settlor or his spouse/civil partner could benefit from the resultant capital gains tax anomalies. In 2006/07 and 2007/08 (but not since 2008/09) the settlor was also taxed on the trustees' gains in the case where the beneficiaries included his minor children who were not married or in a civil

[4.33] Anti-Avoidance Rules Affecting the Settlor

partnership, as well as the settlor and spouse/civil partner. Plainly the risk to HMRC was whether the settlements were new or old. Therefore the anti-avoidance legislation aimed at UK resident trusts [*TCGA 1992, s 77*] applied regardless of when a settlement was made. (See CHAPTER 26 for anti-avoidance provisions affecting non-UK resident trusts.) There was far less interest in this type of operation from 2004/05 to 2007/08, since trustees paid the 40% rate of capital gains tax whatever the type of trust. Nevertheless, up to 2003/04, the section still operated to impose an additional 6% in settlor-interested cases where the settlor was a higher rate taxpayer. Bear in mind that if the settlor was no more than a basic rate taxpayer the application of *section 77* brought an advantage, as it did in the case where he had allowable losses or had his annual exemption available. Given the alignment of capital gains tax rates from 2008/09, *section 77* has been repealed from 2008/09: see 4.40–4.43 of the nineteenth edition of this book for the impact of the rule. The fact that a settlement is settlor-interested does still have one capital gains tax consequence: gains cannot be held over on transfer to the trustees (see 7.81).

The flip-flop scheme

[4.34] A so-called 'flip-flop scheme' was decided against the taxpayer in 2004. This was an arrangement popular during the 1990s, at least while the rate of capital gains tax on life-interest trusts was only 25% or less, to ensure enjoyment by the settlor of the proceeds of sale of private company shares, when the sale had been made by trustees of a settlement in which the settlor had no interest throughout the tax year of sale. The arrangement proceeded as follows. Shortly before the end of the tax year the settlor would give the shares to the trustees of a life interest trust for himself (Trust 1), holding over the gain under *TCGA 1992, s 165*. Suppose that the shares were worth £10 million. Trust 1 would borrow £7.5 million from the bank against the security of the shares, with no personal guarantees by the settlor. The trustees of Trust 1 would advance the £7.5 million to Trust 2, another life interest trust for the settlor (with power to advance capital). Just before the end of the tax year the trustees of Trust 1 would irrevocably exclude the settlor and his spouse from benefit, converting the Trust into a life interest trust for the settlor's children. No binding agreement to sell the shares would have been made. At the beginning of the following tax year Trust 1 would sell the shares, paying off the bank loan and paying capital gains tax at 25%, as a trust not caught (it is argued) by *section 77*. The sale proceeds net of tax at 25% would be available for enjoyment by the settlor through Trust 2. The taxpayers were successful before the Special Commissioners, HMRC's appeal was upheld in the High Court, the Court of Appeal found for the taxpayers (*West (Inspector of Taxes) v Trennery and other appeals* [2003] EWCA Civ 1792, [2004] STC 170, 76 TC 713) but the House of Lords allowed HMRC's appeal ([2005] UKHL 5).

[4.35] The five members of the appellate committee of the House of Lords were unanimous in finding for HMRC. The substantive judgments were delivered by Lord Millett and by Lord Walker of Gestingthorpe. Having traced the legislative history of *section 77* and examined the changes made by *FA 1995*, Lord Walker found that the taxpayers' argument on the meaning of 'derived property' faced an insuperable objection. That is, if (as the Court of Appeal had decided) property in Trust 2 could not include derived property in relation to the trust fund of Trust 1, 'the whole elaborate definition of "derived property" in *section 77(8)* could have been replaced by a simple reference to any capital or income of the property comprised in the chargeable settlement'. Accordingly, to give meaning to *section 77(8)*, HMRC's case had to be correct. (See also *Bowring v Revenue and Customs Comrs* [2015] UKUT 550 (TCC)).

Sub-funds

[4.36] One feature which historically has seemed unfair relates to settlements which contain separate funds or sub-settlements. If there is only one fund where the settlor or spouse/civil partner may benefit, that is enough to bring the whole settlement within the legislation and so the settlor can be assessed on gains from which he is totally excluded. To address this problem, *FA 2006* introduced a new sub-fund regime whereby an election can be made to treat a sub-fund as a separate settlement for capital gains tax (and indeed income tax) purposes, subject to certain conditions: see **7.118–7.122** for details.

Deeds of variation

[4.37] As stated at **4.7**, a deed of variation may give effect to a settlement. Where the donor of a deed of variation continues to enjoy the redirected property, it is not treated as a gift with reservation for inheritance tax, but is rather deemed to be a gift by the deceased not by the true donor [*IHTA 1984, s 142*]. For capital gains tax, *TCGA 1992, s 62(6)* applies, but this deems the gift to have been made by the deceased only for the purposes of that section (ie in relation to a deemed disposal on death). If the original beneficiary has an interest in a settlement which results from a deed of variation, *section 77* applies (before 2008/09) and the trustees' gains are assessed on him. (*Marshall (Inspector of Taxes) v Kerr* [1995] 1 AC 148, [1994] 3 All ER 106, HL and see **7.112–7.117**.) Specifically, from 2006/07, *section 68C* of *TCGA 1992* provides that, in effect, it is the original beneficiary who is the settlor of a settlement which arises under the variation of a Will or intestacy, unless the property being varied was itself settled under the Will or intestacy (in which case it is the deceased who is the settlor).

Inheritance tax

[4.38] The inheritance tax charge on gifts with reservation operates on a death. Where property is settled, the charge falls upon the trustees. Therefore, although gifts inter vivos which are gifts with reservation can affect the estate of the settlor, the charge on trusts is discussed in later chapters (see CHAPTERS 9, 10 and 18).

The Pre-owned Assets Regime

Summary

[4.39] The regime legislated by *FA 2004, Sch 15*, creates a charge to income tax from 2005/06. The charge is applied to the value of the benefit of enjoying 'pre-owned assets' at any time from 2005/06 onwards. These, generally, are assets which were previously owned by the taxpayer and which have been disposed of in whole or in part since 18 March 1986. According to the Finance Bill 2004 Standing Committee Report, the declared target of this new charge is: ' . . . the range of schemes that allow wealthy taxpayers to give their assets away, or achieve the appearance of doing so, and so benefit from the inheritance tax exemption for lifetime gifts, while in reality retaining continuing enjoyment of and access to those assets, much as before.' HMRC provide guidance on the regime in their Inheritance Tax Manual at IHTM44000-44116.

[4.40] Separate rules apply to:
- land;
- chattels; and
- intangible property comprised in a settlement where the settlor retains an interest.

Land

[4.41] There will be an income tax charge where a taxpayer occupies any land, whether alone or with others, and the disposal condition or the contribution condition is met. The meaning of occupation of land or (see **4.43**) use or possession of a chattel is explained in technical guidance issued by HMRC in March 2005 as amended. Reference should be made to HMRC's Inheritance Tax Manual at IHTM44003 for HMRC's current view on the meaning of 'occupation' for these purposes. The disposal condition is that the taxpayer has after 17 March 1986 disposed of all or part of his interest in the land, other than by an excluded transaction. The contribution condition is that at any time after 17 March 1986, he has directly or indirectly provided (other than by an excluded transaction) any of the consideration given by someone else for the acquisition of an interest in the land.

[4.42] Where the regime applies, it is the 'appropriate rental value' which is charged to income tax, less any payments made in pursuance of a legal obligation. That rental value equates broadly to the rent payable on a landlord's repairing lease [*FA 2004, Sch 15, paras 3, 4 and 5*].

Chattels

[4.43] Principles similar to the above (under *FA 2004, Sch 15, paras 6 and 7*) apply for chattels except that:
- instead of occupation the test is possession or use of a chattel; and
- instead of the appropriate rental value the charge is on the appropriate amount, which is the official rate of interest at the beginning of the relevant tax year, ie 4.00% for 2012/13 and 2013/14 [*ITEPA 2003,*

s 181; FA 2004, Sch 15, para 7(2); Charge to Income Tax by Reference to Enjoyment of Property Previously Owned Regulations 2005, SI 2005/724, reg 3].

Intangible property comprised in a settlement where the settlor retains an interest

[4.44] Here the charge under *paras 8* and *9* of *Sch 15* is based not on the enjoyment of benefits but rather on the satisfaction of a set of circumstances (with no let-out for any payments made by the chargeable person). The set of circumstances is:

- under the settlement any of the income arising would be taxed on the settlor;
- any such income would be treated as so taxable, disregarding benefits received by his spouse/civil partner; and
- that property includes any 'relevant property' ie intangible property which is or represents a property settled by or added to the settlement by the chargeable person after 17 March 1986.

Intangible property would include cash and investments (though not land or chattels). The purpose of this charge is to catch inheritance tax avoidance schemes based on, in particular, the *Eversden* decision, though not (as explained by HMRC's technical guidance) under established arrangements such as gift and loan trusts or discounted gift trusts or under certain 'business trusts'. Where *para 8* applies, the charge is on the official rate of interest at the beginning of the relevant tax year applied to the capital in the settlement.

Exclusions

[4.45] These are defined by *Sch 15, para 10* separately for the disposal and contribution conditions respectively (and in any case apply only to land or chattels). Broadly speaking, these embrace the following:

- there was a disposal of the individual's whole interest in the property except for any right expressly reserved by him, whether by an arm's length transaction with an unconnected person or by a transaction as might be expected to be made at arm's length between unconnected persons;
- the transfer of a property to his spouse/civil partner (or former spouse/civil partner under a Court Order);
- a disposal to an interest in possession trust in which his spouse/civil partner or (under a Court Order) former spouse/civil partner continues to have an interest in possession (except on the death of the beneficiary);
- the disposal was one within the exemption from inheritance tax for dispositions for the maintenance of the family; or
- the disposal is an outright gift to an individual which is wholly exempt from inheritance tax under either the annual exemption or the small gifts exemption.

An important additional exclusion in the case of the contribution condition is:

- the contribution consisted of an outright gift of money made at least seven years before the occupation of the 'relevant property' begins.

An exemption adding to the first of the above exclusions was made by regulations issued in March 2005. A disposal of part of the individual's interest in the property (except for any right expressly reserved) will be exempt provided that either it occurs under an arm's length transaction with an unconnected person or, if the transaction is between connected persons, it is one such as might be expected to be made at arm's length between unconnected persons and, when made after 6 March 2005, it was not for a consideration in money or readily convertible assets.

Exemptions

[4.46] Again, the drafting is complex, but the exemptions under *Sch 15, para 11* (which apply to all three categories within the regime) are, broadly:

- the taxpayer's estate for inheritance tax purposes includes the relevant property (or property which derives its value from the relevant property). Note that, from 5 December 2005, this exclusion will not apply where the relevant property is treated as within the taxpayer's estate because the donee has made a reverter to settlor trust on the original donor. Of course, following the introduction of the new inheritance tax regime for trusts from 22 March 2006, this would no longer be possible with a trust made on or after that date in any event, as the trust would fall within the 'relevant property' regime, even if on a life interest, and the trust fund would not be treated as part of the taxpayer's estate within *IHTA 1984, s 49(1)*;
- the property would be treated as part of the taxpayer's estate as property subject to a reservation of benefit;
- the property would be subject to a reservation of benefit apart from certain prescribed exemptions, eg gifts to charities;
- the relevant property would be treated as a gift with reservation but for the exception for co-ownership arrangements under inheritance tax, ie insofar as the chargeable person has given part of their interest to someone with whom they share occupation (and, broadly, pays no less than their share of the running expenses, on a *pro-rata* basis);
- the relevant property would fall to be a gift with reservation of benefit but for an exemption which allows occupation as a result of a change in circumstances which was unforeseen when the gift was made, the donor cannot maintain himself through old age, infirmity or otherwise and the occupation represents a reasonable provision by the relative donee for the donor's care and maintenance; or
- the relevant property would fall be to be a gift with reservation of benefit but for, in the case of land or chattels, the payment of full consideration for the taxpayer's occupation or enjoyment.

De minimis exemption

[4.47] There is a very small *de minimis* exemption under *Sch 15, para 13* where the aggregate of the amounts otherwise chargeable under the regime does not exceed £5,000. If it does exceed that sum the whole amount is taxable.

Post-death variations

[4.48] A person who disposes of property received under a Will or intestacy by an inheritance tax protected variation is not caught by the new regime (*Sch 15, para 16*).

Transitional provisions

[4.49] A person who is caught by the new regime can make an irrevocable election under *Sch 15, paras 21–23* to opt into the reservation of benefit regime. This means that the property concerned is treated as part of his estate on death with a liability for inheritance tax for the donee (primarily) or for the donor's personal representatives. The election must be made before the 31 January following the end of the tax year in which the new regime first applies. The form for making the election is IHT 500, although prior to its issue no regulations were released to promulgate the form, as was envisaged by the legislation, under which an election is to be made 'in the prescribed manner'. HMRC have confirmed that elections made for 2005/06 by 31 January 2007 are valid notwithstanding that it was not until 19 October 2007 that the requisite enabling regulations (*The Income Tax (Benefits Received by Former Owner of Property) (Election for Inheritance Tax Treatment) Regulations 2007, SI 2007/3000*) were issued. Against HMRC's settled view that the late appearance of the regulations does not affect the validity of elections previously made, one should note that the election itself refers expressly to the provisions of *FA 2004, Sch 15, paras 21–23*, which require that the election is made 'in the prescribed manner'.

[4.50] It was in large part the professional furore at the lack of regulations which led to the enactment of *FA 2007, s 66* which authorises HMRC to accept at their discretion a late election, whether for 2005/06 or for later years, and HMRC have published guidance as to the circumstances in which they will accept a late election (see HMRC's Inheritance Tax Manual at IHTM44077).

Scope

[4.51] Although the regime is specifically targeted at schemes made with a view to avoiding the reservation of benefit regime, whether in relation to houses, land, chattels or insurance policies, the breadth of the rules will mean that many 'innocent' arrangements will also be caught. A careful review was required before 6 April 2005 of all action taken since 18 March 1986 which might produce an income tax charge under the new regime, to decide what should be done in vulnerable cases: ie whether:

(a) to pay the income tax charge;
(b) to pay to the donee such an amount each year as will escape the charge;
(c) to bring the benefit to an end (most probably as a deemed potentially exempt transfer for IHT purposes); or
(d) to opt into the reservation of benefit regime, with an IHT liability for the donee (primarily) or for the donor's personal representatives following the donor's death.

[4.52] However (as an issue beyond the scope of this book), the way in which the regime applies to particular past arrangements is not always certain and taxpayers must take their own advice as to the extent to which a particular arrangement is caught and, if so, what action now to take. If either option (c) or option (d) above is chosen, the issue of possible double charges to inheritance tax must be borne in mind, ie if the transferor under the original arrangement dies within seven years of setting it up. Consider first whether the *Inheritance Tax (Double Charges Relief) Regulations, SI 1987/1130* mentioned at **9.81** will assist. Otherwise, the *Charge to Income Tax by Reference to Enjoyment of Property Previously Owned Regulations 2005, SI 2005/724, reg 6* may help, but only where the arrangement adopted was a 'double trust' Scheme and the taxpayer has gone for option (d) above. Further regulations were made on 14 December 2005, to apply from 4 January 2006, by the *Inheritance Tax (Double Charges Relief) Regulations 2005, SI 2005/3441* to cover cases where a double trust arrangement is unscrambled within the terms of the trust rather than by electing into reservation of benefit.

Chapter 5

The Position of Trustees

Personal liability

[5.1] While trustees manage a trust in much the same way as directors manage a company (and both trustees and directors may be held to account for any failures or defaults in so doing), there any similarity ends. Under the doctrine of the 'veil of incorporation' a company is a distinct legal entity, with its own legal personality. It is distinct from both its directors and its shareholders. By contrast, there is no such separation between a trust and its trustees. In a very real sense, a trust *is* its trustees for the time being. Jointly and severally, the trustees have unlimited personal liability for the debts and defaults of the trust, whether relating to tax or to anything else. An invitation to act as a trustee therefore requires very careful consideration before it is accepted.

[5.2] The principle of personal liability is tempered to some extent by the general rule is that a trustee may be indemnified out of the trust assets for any liabilities which fall upon him/her as a trustee. Insofar as any such liabilities were due to the trustee's own negligence or active default (and subject to any indemnity provisions in the trust deed), it would be open to any or all of the beneficiaries to claim against the trustee for the loss to the trust fund. That aside, plainly if the trust fund were not enough to meet substantial tax (or other) liabilities, that would leave the trustee with a liability to be discharged out of personal capital.

[5.3] It goes without saying that a trustee may act in relation to a settlement only insofar as he or she has power to act in a particular way. Such powers may be conferred by statute (eg *Trustee Act 1925* or *Trustee Act 2000*) but, more specifically, the trust deed, especially if relatively recent (that is, drawn over the last 30 years or so) should provide for the trustees to have extensive powers. It has been quite common for settlements and indeed Will trusts to incorporate by reference the so called STEP standard provisions which comprise a wide range of administrative powers for trustees. First published in 1992, the second edition is the current version. The Senior District Judge of the Family Division of the High Court issued a practice direction on 30 January 2013, enabling the incorporation of the STEP standard provisions second edition into Wills by reference.

[5.4] The Position of Trustees

Tax liabilities in the ordinary course

'Relevant trustees'

[5.4] The term 'relevant trustees' is used to signify those trustees who hold office, when income arises or in the year of assessment when a capital gain arises. Trustees who are subsequently appointed are also 'relevant trustees'. It is the relevant trustees who are responsible to HMRC and are liable for tax, interest and penalties [*TMA 1970, s 7(9)* and *TCGA 1992, s 65(4)*].

Income tax

[5.5] Income tax is assessed upon the person who receives the income (with exceptions where caught by anti-avoidance legislation):

ITTOIA 2005	
sections 8, 230, 245, 271, 332, 338, 348, 352, 371, 404(1), 425, 549, 554, 581, 611, 616, 685 and *689*	the provisions for income charged under the Act: tax to be charged on 'the person receiving or entitled to the profits'.
TMA 1970	
section 71	which states that 'every body of persons shall be chargeable to income tax in like manner as any person is chargeable under the Income Tax Acts'.
section 72 [before 2012/13]	which makes the trustee of an incapacitated person assessable and chargeable to income tax.
section 73 [before 2012/13]	which makes parents and guardians liable for the income tax liabilities of infants.

Other sections can be found which repeat this general rule, namely, that whoever is the recipient of income is assessable. It is this general rule which makes trustees assessable and there is no separate code for them.

[5.6] Trustees are not 'individuals'. Therefore, except in the case of a bare trustee or the receiver etc for an incapacitated person, there can be no personal allowances. Personal reliefs are amounts to which an individual is entitled (see *ITA 2007, s 24*). And it is made clear by *ITA 2007, s 10* that only individuals are charged at the higher or the additional rate. Therefore the general rule is that trustees are assessable at the basic rate of 20% (for 2015/16 and 2016/17) on the full amount of their statutory income, except that dividend income is charged at 10%, satisfied by the tax credit in 2015/16 (see **6.1** – and note too the fundamental changes to the taxation of dividends from 2016/17). There are special provisions charging (in 2015/16 and 2016/17) an extra 25%, or for dividends 27.5% (in 2015/16), and a fixed rate of 38.1% in relation to dividends (in 2016/17) on the income of discretionary and accumulation settlements (see **6.55**), on items assessed upon trustees under the accrued income scheme (see **6.15–6.18**) and also under the rules relating to offshore roll-up funds and relevant discounted securities [*ITA 2007, Pt 9, Ch 3, ss 479–483; TIOPA 2010, Pt 8, ss 354–363A* and *ITTOIA 2005, Pt 4, Ch 8, ss 427–460*]. Where trustees have shares in a company which buys them back, then, unless capital treatment applies under *CTA 2010, ss 1033–1048*, formerly *ICTA 1988, ss 219–229*), there will be an effective tax rate of 30.555% for 2014/15 and 2015/16 – see **6.60**.

[**5.7**] Trustees may claim non-personal reliefs and losses (eg trading losses, capital allowances etc). Business losses from property income (see *ITA 2007, Pt 4, Ch 4, ss 117–127A*) can be carried forward. Income tax relief for interest paid by trustees is often misunderstood. Limited allowance is given (see **6.28** and **6.41–6.42**). The general point (developed at **6.41**) is that most of the provisions in *ITA 2007, Pt 8, Ch 1 (ss 383–412)*, for example interest on loans to buy an interest in a close company or to invest in a partnership are restricted to individuals and are not extended to trustees. This different treatment as between individuals and trustees was confirmed by the CIOT with HMRC in 2010.

[**5.8**] Income can be *mandated* to the income beneficiary, in which case the trustees should report to their HMRC Officer, giving the name and address of the beneficiary and so on. The result will be that the income will not be assessed on the trustees. Where the income is not taxed at source the beneficiary should self assess (TSEM3040). Naturally there will be no relief for trust expenses. The legislation in *TMA 1970, ss 13, 76* has been repealed from 2012/13 onwards, apparently because of the introduction of HMRC's general data-gathering powers. Occasionally, this principle may alter the amount of tax (as in *Williams (Surveyor of Taxes) v Singer* [1921] 1 AC 65, (1920), 7 TC 387, HL, where UK trustees mandated US income to a non-UK resident beneficiary). This fits with the general rule that it is the recipient of income who is assessable.

[**5.9**] It is possible for trustees to suffer a deficiency of income in a given year, perhaps because of exceptional expenses. If these are properly chargeable against income, the consequence may be that the income beneficiary has no trust income that year and may also have a reduced income in the following year. Any such deficiency can be carried forward to reduce the statutory income of the next year.

[**5.10**] Statutory and equitable apportionments will not normally affect trustees. They do appear in estates in the course of administration; usually where there is an intestacy. The consequences are blended into the income tax system by *ITTOIA 2005, Pt 5, Ch 6, ss 649–682A* which cause the income for tax purposes to be related to that for executorship.

Settlor-interested trusts

[**5.11**] Any income treated as that of the settlor under *ITTOIA 2005, Pt 5, Ch 5* is not to be treated as the income of any other person [*ITTOIA 2005, s 624(1)*]. However, *ITTOIA 2005, s 646(8)* provides that 'nothing in the relevant provisions is to be read as excluding a charge to tax on the trustees as

[5.11] The Position of Trustees

persons by whom any income is received'. Therefore the trustees have a liability to pay, if necessary by self assessment, tax at the basic rate on income caught by the anti-avoidance regime, except in relation to income which has been mandated to the beneficiary (see **5.8** and **5.15**). Even if the settlor were to pay the whole of the liability himself, whether or not he exercises his statutory right of reimbursement under *ITTOIA 2005, s 646*, the trustees must both file a self assessment return and pay their tax due.

[5.12] It seems that the purpose of the original provision was to preserve the old *Schedule D* charge under *ICTA 1988, s 59* on persons 'receiving' the income; now that *Schedule D* has been repealed, the rule appears in *ITTOIA 2005, s 8*. However, if trustees are in receipt of income, there is a question as to the rate at which they are liable, that is whether in addition to the dividend or basic rate they are also liable at 'the special rates for trustees' income' to be found in *ITA 2007, Pt 9, Ch 3* and discussed at **6.55–6.64**. Excluded from these rates is income which, before being distributed, is 'the income of any person other than the trustees' (*ITA 2007, s 480(3)(a)*). With bare trusts of income from capital settled before 9 March 1999 in cases where *Trustee Act 1925, s 31* has been excluded (see **4.14** and **4.21**), it is the child's income and therefore there is no charge on the trustees under *ITA 2007, s 479* (given *s 480(3)(a)*). Prior to 2006/07, for such income, it was the act of distribution which might create chargeability on the settlor: therefore, the precursor to the special rates (the 'additional rate') would not apply, as the income was that of the child. Income from capital settled on or after 9 March 1999 would, if within *section 629(1)*, be taxed on the settlor (subject to the £100 de minimis relief) whether or not it was distributed and again therefore the additional rate would not apply. However, from 2006/07 *ICTA 1988, s 686(2)(b)(ii)* was repealed.

[5.13] *FA 2006, Sch 13, para 2* removed from the list of income which did not attract the additional rate, income which is treated as that of a settlor. It is therefore only the income of a person other than the trustees which does not attract that rate. And income which is received by the trustees but is deemed to be the income of a settlor does not fall within that description. We therefore have the curious result that, where a discretionary or an accumulation trust is concerned, there is a special rate tax liability on the trustees at 45% (with different rates for dividends) in 2015/16 and 2016/17, and that same income is also assessed on the settlor at up to those rates, whether under *section 624(1)* or under *section 629(1)* of *ITTOIA 2005*. No credit mechanism is provided by statute. HMRC have said that, to alleviate the charge to double taxation, the settlor will be given a credit for the tax paid by the trustees in his own self assessment, though there is no statutory authority for this proposition. The mechanism, according to HMRC, was an informal one, prior to 2010/11. That is, the trustees will inform the settlor of the income tax which they have paid, to be reported by him as such on his own self assessment return. All this seems an unnecessary complication, with significant administrative burdens for both HMRC and taxpayer and adverse cash-flow implications if the settlor is no more than a basic rate taxpayer.

[5.14] As from 2010/11 a settlor who is not liable at rates above the basic rate must return to the trustees the benefit of the excess tax paid by the trustees [*ITTOIA 2005, s 646(5)*, as amended by *F(No 3)A 2010, s 7*]: any such payments will accordingly be disregarded for inheritance tax purposes. From 2006/07 to 2009/10 inclusive this obligation arose only in respect of a repayment in respect of 'an allowance or relief'. Accordingly, if the settlor did in those years transfer to the trustees any tax repayment received by him, this would have been a chargeable transfer for inheritance tax purposes (except insofar as covered by eg his annual exemption or the normal expenditure out of income exemption). HMRC say that this obligation, from 2010/11, is in respect not merely of a cash sum repaid by HMRC to the settlor, but also to the extent that his tax liability is less than it would have been but for the settlor-interested income. HMRC's Trusts, Settlements and Estates Manual has an example which illustrates the operation of the rule in *section 646*, at *TSEM4550*.

[5.15] HMRC have developed Form R185 (Settlor) to address this need, for returns for 2009/10 and for later years. Note that the only exception to what is described at **5.13–5.14**, whether from or before 2010/11, is the case where the trustees have mandated the income to a particular beneficiary, so that the trustees cannot be said to have received it. In that event trustees have no liability either to complete a self-assessment form (assuming that they have not been sent one) or to pay any tax.

[5.16] A curious rule was introduced by *FA 2006* which is found at *section 685A* of *ITTOIA 2005*. In broad terms this provides that in a settlor-interested settlement (where the income is treated as that of the settlor and of no other person (see *ITTOIA 2005, s 624(1)*) and a distribution of income is made to someone other than the settlor as an annual payment, the recipient is treated as having paid additional rate income tax (higher rate before 2010/11), albeit this is tax which he cannot either recover or set off against a tax liability on other income. It is clear from the notes to Form R185 (Trust Income) for 2006/07 (which had to be corrected) that, according to HMRC, this means that the recipient must enter on his self assessment or repayment claim form the net (and not the gross) amount of the payment, although this does not seem clearly to follow from *section 685A*. This left open the analysis that the recipient was for general income tax purposes treated as being in receipt of income of the grossed-up amount of the annual payment, which might otherwise have the effect of increasing the rate of tax on other income or indeed on chargeable gains of the year. This problem has been addressed and rectified by *FA 2008, s 67* which, with retroactive effect to 2006/07 and subsequent tax years, treats such deemed income as, generally, the highest slice of his total income, with the exception of purposes of the top slicing rules for life assurance gains [*ITTOIA 2005, 685A(5A), (5B)*]. The thinking behind the *FA 2006* innovation is somewhat puzzling, although the author has been told that it was prompted by the tax credits regime, to prevent a person receiving tax credits which would otherwise be covered by the annual payment on which he is not subject to income tax.

[5.17] Income may be received by UK resident trustees of a discretionary or an accumulation trust where the income is caught by the regime, but the settlor either is domiciled outside the UK or is not resident or (before 6 April 2013) not ordinarily resident in the UK. In the case of income arising from trustees outside the UK which is not remitted to the UK, *ITTOIA 2005, s 648(3)* provides that such income will not be 'income arising under a settlement' for purposes of *ITTOIA 2005, Pt 5, Ch 5*. This will of course leave a liability on the trustees at 45% (for 2015/16 and 2016/17) or on dividend income at 37.5% (2015/16) or 38.1% (2016/17) under *ITA 2007, Pt 9, Ch 3*. Suppose, following payment by the trustees of their liability, the income is then remitted to the UK, there is no statutory provision for the settlor to credit the tax paid by the trustees against his personal liability. In such circumstances, however, tax paid by the trustees should be credited by HMRC against the liability of the settlor (see 5.13).

Capital gains tax

[5.18] The expression 'settled property' is defined as any property held in trust where the trustee is not a nominee or a bare trustee [*TCGA 1992, s 68*]. *Section 69(1)* provides that trustees are to be treated as a single and continuing body of persons. Therefore, retirements and appointments of new trustees do not of themselves give rise to disposals.

Inheritance tax

[5.19] The inheritance tax legislation does not carry a definition of 'trustees'. There is a definition of non-UK resident trustees in *section 218*, but that relates to the report to HMRC which is required to be made by any professional person, other than a barrister, who has been concerned with the making of a settlement whose settlor is domiciled within the UK, but where the trustees are not or will not be resident in the UK. There is also one other definition, in *section 45*, which covers what must be an exceptionally unusual situation, in providing that if there is settled property without trustees then the person managing the property is deemed to be a trustee.

[5.20] There is a separate group of sections [*IHTA 1984, ss 49–93*] which deals with the inheritance on settled property. As discussed extensively in other parts of this book, the key distinction is between trusts subject to the 'relevant property' regime and those where a life tenant is deemed to own the assets for inheritance tax purposes. In both cases the requirement to report on and pay inheritance tax can fall upon the trustees.

Tax liabilities: unusual events to be wary of

Capital gains tax: recapture of held-over gains

[5.21] In most cases, an election for hold-over relief can be made only where the transferee is UK resident. So trustees might advance an asset to a beneficiary and together elect to hold over the gain. However, the legislation envisages the possibility that the transferee might become non-UK resident within a certain time and sell the asset tax-free, so converting a deferral into an exemption. If this happens in the remainder of the year of assessment during which the transfer took place or within the following six tax years, the held-over gain is immediately crystallised [*TCGA 1992, s 168(4)*]. If the transferee's work takes him temporarily away from the UK and he returns within three years, there will be no charge [*section 168(5)*]. The assessment is made upon the transferee and is therefore at his tax rates. Should he fail to pay within twelve months of the due date, the transferor is liable, in the context of this paragraph this would be the trustees [*section 168(7)*]. The transferor has a right of recovery from the transferee [*TCGA 1992, s 168(9)*]. If the transferee, whilst resident in the UK, has disposed of all or some of the assets on which hold-over relief was claimed, then the gains thereon are not caught again by *section 168* to that extent.

[5.22] The one exception to the above rule is in relation to gifts of UK residential property interest on or after 6 April 2015 [*TCGA 1992, s 261ZA*]. As such interests are, since 6 April 2015, subject to UK capital gains tax in the hands of non-residents, any held-over gains could come into charge at some future point. Of course, the conditions for hold-over relief to be available must still be met. It would be unusual for a UK residential property to qualify as a 'business asset' such that relief under *TCGA 1992, s 165* would be available – perhaps if the property qualified as a 'furnished holiday let' – and it would be more likely for relief to be claimed under *TCGA 1992, s 260* on a chargeable transfer to or from a trust.

[5.23] The potential liability under *TCGA 1992, s 168* can be guessed with sufficient accuracy for most people. The gain held over is capable of exact calculation. The guesswork is as to the transferee's rate of tax in a future year. The maximum rate of tax was 18% in 2008/09, 2009/10 and for disposals prior to 23 June 2010 (though before 2008/09 it could have been up to 40%); it was increased to 28% for disposals after 22 June 2010 and has been reduced to 20% from 6 April 2017 (except in relation to residential property, which remains at 28%) (see further CHAPTER 7). It may be possible to cover this risk by insurance. An indemnity from a member of the family may turn out to be worthless. The safest course may be for the trustees to retain legal (but not beneficial) ownership of sufficient of the assets to cover the liability.

[5.24] A claw-back charge can also arise following the entry of an asset *into* a settlement under hold-over election. Hold-over relief, whether under *section 165* or under *section 260*, is precluded if the settlement is settlor-interested (see **7.81**) and a claw-back charge applies under *TCGA 1992, s 169C* if, although not settlor-interested at the time of the transfer, the settlement *becomes* settlor-interested within the prescribed period (broadly six years after the end of the tax year in which the transfer took place). The effect of the claw-back would be to disapply the hold-over, thereby increasing the base cost in the hands of the trustees (to market value at the date of transfer) and retrospectively to impose a chargeable gain on the settlor, unless he has died before the date of the charge [*TCGA 1992, s 169C(6)*].

EXAMPLE

On 10 January 2011 Gerald made a wide-discretionary settlement for the benefit of his children and children-in-law, all of whom are over 18, excluding his wife Gina and himself from benefit. Gerald elected to hold over the gain arising on the transfer of the assets to the trustees. Gina is tragically killed in a car crash in the course of 2012. On 1 September 2013 Gerald remarries Gertrude who has two teenage children, who as Gerald's step-children are not excluded from benefit under the settlement. The settlement is therefore now settlor-interested, which means that were Gerald to transfer any asset into the trust at a time while one of his step-children (or indeed children) under the age of 18 can benefit, he would not be able to hold over the gain. However, could the gain in 2011 which was held over now be clawed back under *section 169C*? Happily, the answer is negative, given the protection of *section 169F(4B)*.

Emigration

[5.25] Where migration of a trust is possible, so that the trustees cease to be UK resident, there is a deemed disposal and reacquisition at market value of all the trust assets (see **26.5**). In such case the whole question of indemnities takes on a different aspect and appropriate legal advice is required.

Inheritance tax

[5.26] For inheritance tax the issue of personal exposure is resolved by *IHTA 1984, s 204*. That *section* applies equally to personal representatives and trustees and restricts their liability to the value of the capital of the estate or trust. The *section* first limits the liability to 'so much of the property as he has actually received etc' and then qualifies that by a reference to the value of any property which might have been available but for his neglect or default. The other taxes have no similar provision.

[5.27] A decided Special Commissioner's case on liability for inheritance tax in a deceased estate presents a salutary warning; although it concerns personal representatives rather than trustees, a similar point could well catch out unwary trustees (*Howarth's Executors v IRC*, [1997] STC (SCD) 162). The executors were Mr Stephen Howarth, Mrs Susan Howarth and an employee of the family's solicitors. The testatrix died in 1985 and the executors were due to pay capital transfer tax, as inheritance tax then was, over 10 years. Assets were transferred to beneficiaries following an election to pay tax by instalments on qualifying property and Mr Howarth duly paid the instalments of tax down to October 1994. He was made bankrupt in May 1995. Notices of determination were issued by the then Inland Revenue so as to enable them to collect tax from the solicitor's employee. As a defence it was said that the Revenue should have registered a land charge on the deceased's property. That would have protected the employee from the problems which arose as a result of the sale of the property without payment of the outstanding tax. The Special Commissioner found that no charge need have been registered and that, as the tax is a personal liability of the executors (on a joint and several basis), the determination was valid.

Failed potentially exempt transfers

[5.28] Death within seven years of the maker of a potentially exempt transfer will cause the transfer to become chargeable [*IHTA 1984, s 3A*]. For instance, if the settlor of a relevant property trust had first made a potentially exempt transfer, then set up the trust and subsequently died within seven years of the potentially exempt transfer, there could well be an inheritance tax charge on the trustees (see **9.78–9.80**). Another example is that of the beneficiary of a qualifying (or 'estate') interest in possession trust who surrenders his interest, with the effect of advancing the interest next in line under the settlement, say his daughter aged 30 as remainderman. The beneficiary makes a potentially exempt transfer, but if he dies within seven years the transfer becomes chargeable. While the daughter is primarily liable for the tax, the trustees are also liable in the event that HMRC fail to collect the tax from her, to the extent of the trust assets in their hands [*IHTA 1984, s 199(1)(c) and s 204(2)*].

Residence of trustees

[5.29] The question of the residence of the trustees is very important, because liability to UK tax will depend upon residence to a large extent. This is dealt with in CHAPTER 24.

The Non-UK Resident Landlord Scheme

[5.30] Under this scheme, the rent paid to such a landlord bears tax by deduction at source, unless a certificate has been obtained from HMRC authorising the payment of rent gross [*ITA 2007, s 971*]. The problem stems from the scheme's definition of residence (in terms of 'usual place of abode') which is different from other definitions. HMRC advised on their website on 14 May 2013: 'If you are a letting agent acting for landlords based outside the UK, you must complete NRLY Annual Return even if you have not deducted any tax under the Non-Resident Landlord Scheme. You must also do so if you are a tenant who has deducted tax under the scheme.' HMRC then proceed to give help and guidance on completing the relevant form.

The 'rule in *Hastings-Bass*'

[5.31] What happens when trustees of a settlement exercise a power only to discover later that unforeseen results have ensued, especially adverse tax implications? The principle established in *Hastings-Bass, Re, Hastings-Bass v IRC* [1975] Ch 25, [1974] 2 All ER 193, CA might have helped in the past, the essential principle being stated in the later case of *Mettoy Pension Trustees Ltd v Evans* [1991] 2 All ER 513, [1990] 1 WLR 1587 as follows: 'Where a trustee acts under a discretion given to him by the terms of the trust, the Court will interfere with his action if it is clear that he would not have acted as he did had he not failed to take into account considerations which he ought to have taken into account.' However, in a decision issued on 9 March 2011 in the conjoined cases of *Pitt v Holt and Futter v Futter* [2011] EWCA Civ 197, [2012] Ch 132, [2011] 2 All ER 450, the Court of Appeal found in favour of HMRC in dramatically restricting the scope of the *Hastings-Bass* doctrine (see **5.42**). Meanwhile paras 5.32–5.46 give a summary of the cases decided between 2000 and 2010, now largely of historical interest.

[5.32] The original *Hastings-Bass* decision was concerned primarily with the validity of powers which trustees had purported to exercise. The cases mentioned below illustrate the then willingness of the courts to consider seriously assisting trustees faced with unexpected tax consequences. In *Abacus Trust Co (Isle of Man) Ltd v National Society for the Prevention of Cruelty to Children* [2001] STC 1344, 3 ITELR 846, Ch D, the trustees made an appointment of capital with catastrophic effects for the settlor in rendering him liable to the charge on the trustees' gains under *TCGA 1992, s 86*. Leading counsel had advised that the appointment should not be made until after 5 April 1998, the trustees having acted on 3 April. The Court ruled that, since their failure to take leading counsel's opinion into account was highly material to the trustees' decision and because the appointment would not have been made had they taken that advice into account, the exercise of the power of appointment was invalid and of no effect.

[5.33] However, limits to the principle were set. In *Breadner v Granville-Grossman* [2001] Ch 523, [2000] 4 All ER 705, Park J refused to set aside a power of appointment exercised by trustees one day after the time limit for its exercise had expired. The learned judge said that to set aside the exercise of the power in this case would be an unwarranted extension of the *Hastings-Bass* principle. It would not be declaring a decision of the trustees to be void, but rather declaring that they should be treated as having exercised it at some other time: 'It cannot be right that whenever trustees do something which they later regret and think that they ought not to have done, they can say that they never did it in the first place.'

[5.34] In *Green v Cobham* [2002] STC 820, 4 ITELR 784 the *Hastings-Bass* principle was successfully applied. In that case the trustees as a body became resident in the UK by reason of the retirement of an individual from professional practice, though he continued to act as a trustee. Under the rule in *TCGA 1992, s 69* the whole of the trust immediately became UK resident in a tax year during which there was the exercise of an appointment. There the Court said that there was no room to doubt that, had the then trustees of the Will trust had regard to the possible capital gains tax consequences of the proposed appointment, they would not have gone ahead with it. This was a clear case of the application of the *Hastings-Bass* principle. The Court accordingly declared the deed to be an invalid exercise of the power and therefore void in its entirety.

[5.35] An application for the rule in *Hastings-Bass* to be applied was partially successful when made by *Abacus Trust Co (Isle of Man) Ltd* in a 2003 case. An appointment of 60% of the trust fund on discretionary trusts was made in 1992 in pursuance of what the trustees thought to be the settlor's wishes. In fact, the settlor had wanted only 40% of the fund to be appointed on discretionary trusts. The High Court found that insofar as the error lay in the transmission of the settlor's wishes to the trustees the trustees themselves had made no error. However, because the person who conveyed the settlor's wishes to the trustees fell within the wider business structure of the trust company, it could be said that the trustees were responsible for the fault. The settlor was arguing that the appointment was void, whereas counsel for the sons to whom discretionary payments had been made since 1996 argued that the appointment was merely voidable, so as to be declared void as from the current date. It was left to the parties to reach agreement on whether or not the appointment should now be voided and if so on what terms. Inheritance tax implications will also have followed from the decision. (*Abacus Trust Co (Isle of Man) Ltd and Colyb Ltd v Barr*).

[5.36] The *Hastings-Bass* principle has been employed to unscramble a tax avoidance scheme where the participants did not fully understand what was involved. But this will apply only if the applicant had made a sufficiently serious mistake as to the legal effects of the transaction. Mr and Mrs Wolff sought in 1997 to mitigate the potential inheritance tax liability on their house by effecting a reversionary lease scheme. However, they did not appreciate at the time that, once the reversionary lease fell in after 20 years, they had no right to stay in the property and were at the effective mercy of the lessees, their daughters. Their application to have the arrangement set aside was allowed by Mann J in the High Court. He held that evidence of a gift more than the donors had intended was sufficient ammunition for the claim to succeed. (*Wolff v Wolff* [2004] EWHC 2110 (Ch), [2004] STC 1633).

[5.37] In *Burrell v Burrell* [2005] EWHC 245 (Ch), [2005] STC 569, 7 ITELR 622 the trustees of a discretionary settlement successfully applied to set aside part of a deed of appointment which had been made in November 2000. This was on the footing that they had failed to appreciate, consider and take into account the fact that that appointment generated very considerable liabilities to inheritance tax. They argued that they would not have executed the deed had they appreciated those liabilities. No argument to the contrary was advanced for the defendants and the High Court, again Mann J, applying the *Hastings-Bass* rule, found that it was clear that the trustees would not have acted as they did had they appreciated the true fiscal position.

[5.38] A case was reported from the Cayman Islands in 2005, *Barclays Private Bank and Trust (Cayman) Ltd v Chamberlain* (2005) 9 ITELR 302. A settlement had been created in 1994 by an individual who was a UK resident for UK capital gains tax purposes. The settlor was the principal beneficiary, and the trust was governed by the laws of the British Virgin Islands. In 2000 two investments were made from the settlement into a Guernsey protected cell company. Before the second investment was made the UK tax legislation changed, but the trustee was unaware of the change. The second investment therefore went ahead, under which the trustee made a loan of £712,000 to a company. The result of the change in tax legislation was to impose a substantial tax liability upon the settlor. When this became apparent the trustee applied to the Court for a declaration that the trustee's decision to accept the loan was void or voidable under the *Hastings-Bass* principle. The Judge in the case accepted that there was an inadvertent tax problem, ruled that the loan was void from the beginning and agreed the mitigation sought. The case fell within the *Hastings-Bass* principle for the following reasons:

(a) the whole purpose of the investment had been to defer capital gains tax; and
(b) the change in the UK legislation was plainly a relevant consideration which the trustees did not consider.

[5.39] More recently, Mr Pitt suffered serious head injuries in a road accident so that he was unable to manage his own affairs. The sum of £1.2 million was paid to Mrs Pitt as his receiver under a structured settlement. On advice (as it turned out, as to the income tax and capital gains tax but not, somewhat oddly, the inheritance tax implications), Mrs Pitt created a discretionary settlement to hold the £1.2 million with herself and her children as beneficiaries. This of course resulted in a substantial chargeable transfer with inheritance tax payable at 20% on top of the nil-rate band, whereas it would have been possible to avoid this through the creation of a disabled trust under *IHTA 1984, s 89*. In reliance on the *Hastings-Bass* principle the High Court held that Mrs Pitt could unravel the settlement and the assignment of the funds made by her as receiver, in that had the inheritance tax position been taken into account she would not have acted as she did (*Pitt v Holt* [2010] EWHC 45 (Ch), [2010] 2 All ER 774, [2010] 1 WLR 1199. HMRC were joined as a party to the proceedings in accordance with the Tax Bulletin statement (see **5.42**), arguing that the *Hastings-Bass* principle which had been only a first instance decision was either mistaken or had been taken too far by the decided cases. However, the High Court was bound by authority and any decision restricting the scope of the *Hastings-Bass* principle had to be for the Court of Appeal in that or in any future case.

[5.40] A second case decided in 2010 concerned a misapprehension relating to the capital payments rule for offshore trusts under *TCGA 1992, s 87*. At issue were two settlements made in 1985 by Mark Futter which were wound up in April 2008 through exercise of powers of enlargement and advancement in favour of Mark Futter and his children. At that stage each settlement had substantial 'stockpiled gains' for capital gains tax purposes. Advice had been received that personal losses of the relevant beneficiaries could be set off against the attributed gains. Unfortunately, however, this is expressly prohibited by *TCGA 1992, s 2(4)*. Notwithstanding various arguments presented by HMRC Norris J held that he had simply to apply the rule in *Hastings-Bass*. HMRC opposed the application on the grounds that the rule had been carried to almost absurd lengths and that, as Lloyd LJ had said in *Sieff v Fox* [2005] EWHC 1312 (Ch), [2005] 3 All ER 693, [2005] 1 WLR 3811, the rule should be kept within reasonable bounds. The two deeds were set aside on the footing that they were void and not voidable. The recipients of the funds were ordered to return them to the trustees with an account of all income received, Norris J stating in conclusion:

> 'The trustees must be treated as if the property with which they parted has at all material times formed part of the trust fund: and they must pay whatever tax, interest and penalties are due on that footing. The property so returned may be the subject of a fresh and valid exercise of the respective powers of enlargement and advancement.'

(*Futter v Futter, Futter (No 3 and No 5) Life Interest Settlements, Re* [2010] EWHC 449 (Ch), [2010] STC 982, 12 ITELR 912).

[5.41] Later in 2010 the High Court in England and Wales granted yet another request by a family to void a trust deed of appointment under the *Hastings-Bass* principle, upon the (apparently mistaken) supposition that the deed had inadvertently triggered substantial capital gains tax liabilities for the trustees and the two young beneficiaries (*Jiggens v Low* [2010] EWHC 1566 (Ch), [2010] STC 1899).

[5.42] On 9 March 2011 the Court of Appeal unanimously allowed the appeal of HMRC in the cases of *Pitt v Holt* and *Futter v Futter*. The Court held that the so-called rule in *Hastings-Bass* was not a correct statement of the law, deriving as it did not from the ratio of that case but from the subsequent decision in *Mettoy* (see **5.31**). The Court distinguished between acts of trustees which were void and acts which were voidable. A purported exercise of the discretionary power on the part of trustees would be void if what was done was not within the scope of the power. By contrast, if an exercise by trustees of a discretionary power was within the terms of the power, but the trustees had in some way breached their duties in respect of that exercise, then (unless it was a case of a fraud on the power) the trustees' act was not void, but it might be voidable at the instance of a beneficiary who was adversely affected. The two cases under appeal concerned acts which were within the powers of the trustees, but which were said to be vitiated by the trustees' failure to take into account a relevant factor to which they should have had regard, usually tax consequences, or by their taking into account some irrelevant matter. The Court stated that the principled and correct approach to these cases was, first, that the trustees' acts were not void, but, second, that they might be voidable. They would be voidable if, and only if, they could be shown to have been performed in breach of fiduciary duty on the part of the trustees. While fiscal considerations would often be among the relevant matters which trustees ought to take into account, if the trustees had sought advice (in general or in specific terms) from apparently competent advisers as to the implications of the proposed course of action and followed the advice obtained, then in the absence of any other basis for a challenge, the trustees were not in breach of the fiduciary duty if it turned out that the advice given to them was materially wrong.

[5.43] In *Futter* the exercise of the trustees' powers of enlargement and advancement was not only not void (because they were within the relevant powers of the trustees), but they were also not voidable (because the trustees committed no breach of fiduciary duty). In *Pitt* Mrs Pitt had fulfilled any duty of skill and care she was under by looking for advice to her solicitors, either to advise her or to see that she got whatever advice she needed from another source. In entering into the settlement, she had not been acting in breach of her fiduciary duties owed to her husband and so the settlement and the assignment to the trustees of the £1.12 million were not voidable. The Court went on to consider the doctrine of mistake (see **5.51**). Here, the test as to the gravity of the mistake was set very high. For a voluntary disposition to be set aside, there had to be a mistake on the part of the donor, either as to the legal effect to the disposition or as to an existing fact which was basic to the transaction. Moreover, the mistake had to be of sufficient gravity as to satisfy the test in *Ogilvie v Allen* (1899) 15 TLR 294, HL: under this decision, in the absence of all circumstances of suspicion, a donor could obtain back property which he had given away only by showing that he was under some mistake of so serious a character as to render it unjust on the part of the donee to retain the property given to him. While Mrs Pitt had been under a mistaken belief when she made the settlement as to the tax consequences, and it was a mistake of sufficient gravity to satisfy the *Ogilvie vAllen* test, nonetheless it was not a mistake as to

[5.43] The Position of Trustees

the legal effect of the disposition and so could not attract the equitable jurisdiction for mistake (*Futter v Futter*) and (*Pitt v Holt* [2011] EWCA Civ 197).

[5.44] The Court of Appeal refused leave to appeal to the Supreme Court, although the taxpayers applied direct and were granted leave by the Supreme Court on 1 August 2011. The Supreme Court heard the appeal in March 2013 and took two months to determine their decision in favour of HMRC, as had been widely anticipated. The fact that the appeal was heard by a panel of seven Law Lords rather than the usual five, is testament to the significance of the issue. The principal judgment was delivered by Lord Walker of Gestingthorpe which was unanimously accepted by his colleagues. Specifically disapproving *obiter dicta* of Buckley LJ in *Hastings-Bass* itself and *obiter dicta* of Warner J in the subsequent case of *re Mettoy*, Lord Walker ruled that a Court should intervene in setting aside trustees' decisions only where trustees had acted in such a way as to amount to a breach of their fiduciary duty. That is, it was not sufficient to show that the deliberations of the trustees had fallen short of the highest possible standards or, had the trustees surrendered to the Court the exercise of their discretions, the Court would or might have acted in a different way. Further, it would be contrary to both principle and authority to impose a form of strict liability on trustees who had conscientiously obtained and followed apparently competent professional advice which turned out to be wrong, in making a decision which they had power to make. On the facts of *Futter*, the trustees' exercise of their power of advancement had been valid and there were no grounds for the Court to intervene. The Court delivered the same judgment on the *Hastings-Bass* principle in the conjoined case of *Pitt v Holt*, although in the latter case judgment was in fact given for the appellants on the grounds of mistake (see 5.52). Lord Walker said that in neither of the two cases had the trustees personally failed in the exercise of their fiduciary duties by following incorrect advice (*Futter v Revenue and Customs Comrs and Pitt v Revenue and Customs Comrs* [2013] UKSC 26, [2013] 3 All ER 429, [2013] 2 WLR 1200).

[5.45] HMRC will be content that some brake has been applied to the tendency of the Courts to allow application of the *Hastings-Bass* doctrine; however, the doctrine is not dead. In *Kennedy v Kennedy* (2014) EWHC 4129 Ch, the High Court agreed to set aside a clause in a trust deed that inadvertently created a £650,000 capital gains tax liability and specifically applied the tests articulated by Lord Walker in the Supreme Court. The Court decided that on balance it was 'unconscionable in principle' not to correct the appointment and, perhaps most interestingly, they set aside only the *clause* which triggered the capital gains tax liability, rather than the entire appointment.

[5.46] It is worth noting that an amendment to Jersey's trust law came into force in October 2013, effectively incorporating the *Hastings-Bass* rule into statute. The *Trusts (Amendment No 6) (Jersey) Law 2013* confirms the Jersey Royal Court's ability to provide discretionary relief where beneficiaries find themselves materially prejudiced by a trustee's decision.

[5.47] In *HCS Trustees Ltd v Camperio Legal and Fiduciary Service plc* the Guernsey Royal Court has held that the *Hastings-Bass* rule forms part of

Guernsey law, but without confirming the precise nature of the rules in Guernsey (as reported by Andrew Goldstone in *Tax Journal* on 18 September 2015).

Rectification

[5.48] An alternative to an application to the Court under the *Hastings-Bass* principle would be an application for rectification. However, the circumstances in which an order would be made are strictly circumscribed and it must be shown that the document executed by the settlor was that which he intended to execute. The remedy was not available in a recent case (*Allnutt v Wilding* [2007] EWCA Civ 412, 9 ITELR 806). There the mistake claimed (which came to light only after the death of the settlor, Mr Strain, more than 7 years after he had made the settlement) was that in executing a settlement for his children he had intended to make a potentially exempt transfer, whereas instead the effect of the settlement was to create a chargeable transfer, so triggering a liability to lifetime inheritance tax on a transfer of £550,000 to the trustees. The Court of Appeal, upholding the High Court, refused to grant rectification, because there was no evidence that the settlor's true intention had been to execute a settlement in a different form, even though the settlement actually made had not achieved the object of mitigating the inheritance tax which he had hoped to avoid. In this case Rimer J considered that the transaction (namely the creation of the settlement) which the applicants sought to effect by virtue of the Court Order was fundamentally different from the one effected by the original settlement and he stated:

> 'The case is therefore one in which I find that Mr Strain intended to execute a Settlement in exactly the form that Mr Wilding drafted. Insofar as he was labouring under any sort of mistake when he did so, his mistake was not as to the language, terms, meaning or effect of the Settlement. His only mistake was that a payment of the £550,000 to it would be a potentially exempt transfer. In my judgment a mistake of that nature is not one which the Court has any jurisdiction to rectify.'

[5.49] Two interesting cases touching on the issue of rectification were reported in early 2014. In *Marley v Rawlings* [2014] UKSC 2, [2014] 1 All ER 807, a couple had intended to sign simple 'mirror' Wills but, following a mix-up at the point of execution, Mr Rawlings signed Mrs Rawlings' Will and she signed his. The Supreme Court, overturning the decisions of both the High Court and the Court of Appeal, allowed Mr Rawlings' Will to be rectified (he had died second and the issue had not come to light on the first death) on the grounds, inter alia, that a 'clerical error' had occurred, and that this concept was not limited to textual errors in the document. In *Brooke v Purton* [2014] EWHC 547 (Ch), [2014] WTLR 745) the testator had intended for all his assets to be held upon discretionary trusts; however, the Will prepared for him included only a nil-rate band discretionary trust. There then arose a question as to whether his business assets (qualifying for 100% relief from inheritance tax) should be subject to that trust? The High Court held that the drafting was sufficiently ambiguous for extrinsic evidence about the testator's intentions to be relevant, this evidence clearly showed that the testator wanted the business assets to be subject to the trust, and therefore rectification (under *Administration of Justice Act 1982, s 20*) would have been possible. However, in this case, there was a simpler option as the court simply exercised its jurisdiction under *Administration of Justice Act 1982, s 21* to interpret the Will so as resolve the ambiguity – ie reading it so that the business assets should be subject to the trust.

[5.50] More recently, in both *Lobler v HMRC* [2015] UKUT 0152 and *Prowting 1968 Trustee One Ltd v Amos-Yeo* [2015] EWHC 2480 the Upper Tribunal and the High Court have both allowed the relief in cases involving (*Lobler*) the partial surrender of life policies and (*Prowting*) shares acquisition agreements. It has been suggested that *Lobler* was wrongly decided (see **5.55**).

Mistake: the equitable jurisdiction of the court

[5.51] A somewhat curious High Court decision in 2008, not involving trusts, allowed a gift made by a taxpayer at a time when he was terminally ill, though unaware of the fact, to be set aside as voidable (*Ogden v Trustees of the RHS Griffiths 2003 Settlement* [2008] EWHC 118 Ch, [2009] Ch 162, [2008] 2 All ER 654). Following tax planning advice, Mr Griffiths made three substantial potentially exempt transfers which he hoped to survive for seven years (or at least for three years). At the time of the last of the three, in February 2004, he was suffering from lung cancer which was diagnosed in Autumn 2004 and which led to his death in April 2005. It was established that Mr Griffiths would not have made the gift (of £2.6 million) in 2004 had he known of his medical condition, as the inheritance tax of over £1 million would not have been payable had the funds been left in his estate to pass to his wife as spouse exempt. The judge, Lewison J, said that a mistake of fact is capable of bringing the equitable jurisdiction of the Court into play provided it is sufficiently serious. That was established in this case. It was then necessary to show that had Mr Griffiths been aware of the true facts he would not have acted as he did, which the Judge also found. This finding is not an application of the *Hastings-Bass* principle discussed at **5.31–5.44**, though it was applied in the *Wolff* case mentioned at **5.36**. It remains to be seen whether the principle could be applied in other contexts as well and it is likely that in future such cases HMRC will ask to be joined as a party. The moral perhaps of the case is that an individual should not have a medical examination before a gift if an adverse outcome might dissuade him from making the gift; if the donor survives the seven year period, all well and good, but if not, there remains the argument that he was then suffering from a terminal disease which had he known about it would have dissuaded him from making the gift.

[5.52] Overturning the Court of Appeal on the issue of mistake, the Supreme Court unanimously allowed the appeal of Mrs Pitt in *Pitt v Revenue and Customs Comrs* [2013] UKSC 26, [2013] 3 All ER 429, [2013] 2 WLR 1200. They held that it was possible to set aside a voluntary disposition on the grounds of equity where a mistake had been made which was sufficiently serious to satisfy the conditions laid down by the House of Lords in the 1897 case of *Ogilvie v Allen*. The Court had to make a valuation judgment as to whether it would be unconscionable or unjust to leave the mistake uncorrected and had to form a judgment about the justice of the case. On the facts, Mr Pitt acting through his wife as his receiver had had an incorrect conscious belief, or had made an incorrect tacit assumption, that the proposed settlement would have no adverse tax effects (which unfortunately followed from the fact that the settlement was an immediately chargeable transfer by Mr Pitt). The settlement could have been drawn so as to comply with the requirements for relief under *IHTA 1984, s 89* (disabled trusts), so removing the trust from the relevant property regime, with no element of artificiality of abuse of the statutory relief. Indeed, this was precisely the sort of settlement for which *section 89* had been enacted. The only true requirement, said Lord Walker, was that there was a causative mistake of sufficient gravity, which was satisfied in the present case. The Court ordered that the settlement should be set aside.

[5.53] The last 12 months have seen a number of cases where the courts continue to demonstrate their willingness to set aside transactions on the basis of mistake, even where the essential mistake was as to the tax consequences.

[5.54] *Freedman v Freedman* [2015] EWHC 1457 (Ch) and *Van Der Merwe v Goldman and HMRC* [2016] EWHC 926 (Ch) both involved transfers of residential property into trust, where the transferors were not aware of the immediate inheritance tax charges arising. In each case, the court found that the mistake was sufficiently grave or serious for it to be unconscionable for the donees to benefit from the mistake by retaining the property. In *Bainbridge v Bainbridge* [2016] EWHC 898, the donees received advice that the transfer of three parcels of farmland into trust would not trigger a capital gains tax liability. In fact, it triggered a liability in excess of £200,000 and the court again found that it would be unconscionable to allow the transfers to stand, notwithstanding that the trustees had subsequently sold some of the parcels. For an analysis of the case and the way in which the court dealt with the practical matter of restoring the donors to their original positions, see Arabella Murphy's *Bainbridge: tracing the proceeds of a mistake* in Tax Journal, 17 June 2016.

[5.55] In *Lobler v HMRC* [2015] UKUT 0152 the taxpayer withdrew funds from various Zurich Life policies in a way which triggered significant income tax charges in relation to partial surrenders, when it would have been possible to complete the withdrawal documentation in a way which avoided this (by effecting the full surrender of specific policies). In this case, the court refused to set aside the transactions on the basis of a mistake 'because the party receiving the benefit of the mistake is not Zurich but a third party to the policy contract, HMRC'. It did, however, allow rectification as an alternative remedy (see 5.50). In his article *Lessons from Lobler on rectification and mistake (Tax Journal, 15 May 2015)*, Timothy Jarvis argues persuasively that the court got this wrong on both fronts – that HMRC's benefit should not have prevented rescission for mistake as a remedy, and that rectification should not have been available because there was no real dispute between the words of the withdrawal documentation and the taxpayer's intention to effect partial surrenders. Nevertheless, the case demonstrates again the courts' willingness to help out taxpayers who find themselves with unexpected tax burdens.

[5.56] Of course, it is still too early to draw definitive conclusions from these cases albeit that they are a very helpful indication that taxpayers who find themselves in a mess might have an escape route. We will need to see whether any of them are appealed and, if so, what the appellate courts make of them, and we will need to see a few more cases where rescission for mistake is denied, before determining quite where the limits of the Supreme Court's decision lie.

Chapter 6

Income Tax

[6.1] In taxing income received by trustees, the fundamental distinction is between income which is payable to one or more beneficiaries as of right (an interest in possession) and income which is payable at the trustees' discretion or which may be accumulated (discretionary or accumulation income). A single trust may receive both types of income. Whereas the former cannot be taxed in 2015/16 and 2016/17 at more than the basic rate of 20%, the latter may be taxed at up to 45%.

[6.2] It should be noted particularly that the taxation of dividend income has changed significantly from 2016/17, with the abolition of the 10% dividend tax credit, the introduction of new rates and of a new dividend allowance for individuals but not trustees. The impact of these changes is very different for interest in possession and discretionary/accumulation trusts.

[6.3] The alternative regimes are described at **6.45–6.49** and **6.50–6.64** respectively. First, however, this chapter considers certain types of income and deductible expenses for tax purposes.

Interest received

Bank and building society interest

[6.4] Up to and including 2015/16, most bank and building society interest had income tax deducted at source at the basic rate of 20%. In relation to interest in possession trusts, there was no additional tax to pay and (subject to the £1,000 standard rate band) trustees of discretionary and accumulation trusts had to pay an additional rate of 25% (to ensure that the full 45% rate applicable to trusts was payable).

[6.5] Up to and including 2015/16, where there were no UK resident *beneficiaries* interest could also be paid gross (see **25.51–25.52**). In such a case the term 'beneficiary' extended only to people who, at the time the definition is applied, were identified as beneficiaries. People who might become beneficiaries could therefore be ignored. Interest from the National Savings Bank was also received gross.

[6.6] From 2016/17, all bank and building society interest is paid gross and trustees will therefore need to pay tax at the rate applicable to their trust (20% or 45%). The new personal savings allowance (PSA) also introduced from 2016/17 is not available to trustees but could be available to the beneficiaries of interest in possession trusts, where the income they receive from the trustees retains its character as interest. The beneficiaries of discretionary/accumulation trusts receive income as 'trust income' (not interest) and their PSA would not therefore be available in relation to it.

The accrued income scheme

[6.7] Trust law requires the cost of securities bought *cum* interest to be paid out of capital and the proceeds of sale to be a capital receipt. However, for tax purposes, the accrued income scheme (see *ITA 2007, Pt 12, ss 615–681DP*) does not work like that. Securities are defined [*ITA 2007, s 619*] and include loan stocks of governments, public and local authorities and companies, which are interest-bearing as well as, from 25 July 1991, certain qualifying building society shares. Shares, national savings certificates, zero coupon bonds, and certificates of deposit are excluded. There is a de minimis exemption for individuals, disabled trusts and personal representatives (securities of £5,000 nominal value) [*ITA 2007, ss 639–640*], but there is no such exemption for other trustees. The aim of the accrued income scheme is to ensure that each person pays income tax on the interest on securities which accrues during his period of legal ownership. Therefore, tax is charged on an accruals basis and by reference to legal, rather than beneficial, ownership. (See also **6.15**.) Although the income tax aspects of offshore resident trusts are dealt with in CHAPTER 25, it is worth noting that non-UK resident trustees will generally escape the accrued income scheme [*ITA 2007, s 643*].

The 'rebate amount'

[6.8] When trustees purchase interest-bearing securities *cum* interest, they are deemed to have purchased the interest which had accrued by the settlement day for the transfer. The accrued interest is called the 'rebate amount'. A gift to trustees produces the same result. Relief is given in respect of the rebate amount, either against the next interest received from that security or against the accrued interest on sale, whichever comes first. The relief can be given in a different year of assessment from that in which the purchase is made.

The 'accrued amount'

[6.9] Similarly, when the trustees sell *cum* interest they are deemed to have received the accrued interest as income. This is known as the 'accrued amount'. There should be no problem in discovering the accrued interest, as it is shown on the stockbrokers' contract note for transactions in fixed interest securities. The accrued amount is assessable upon the trustees.

EXAMPLE 1

24 May 2013
    Purchase £40,000 5% Treasury Stock 2018.
    Accrued interest therein is £427.40 (7 March to 24 May).

7 September 2013	£
Interest (gross)	1000.00
Relief for accrued interest in the purchase	(427.40)
Income for tax purposes	£572.60

EXAMPLE 2

24 May 2013
    Purchase as in Example 1.
24 June 2013
    Investment is sold.

	£
Accrued interest	
On sale 106 days	580.82
On purchase 78 days	(427.40)
Assessable (as miscellaneous income under *ITTOIA 2005, Pt 5, Ch 7*)	£153.42

'Settlement day'

[6.10] The expression 'settlement day' is defined [*ITA 2007, s 674*]. For Stock Exchange transactions, there should be no problem as dealings in government stocks are normally for settlement on the day following the transaction. For dealings in eurosterling, settlement falls three days after the transaction; for domestic loan stocks and debentures, it is five days after the transaction. If the transaction is not through The Stock Exchange, 'settlement day' means:

(a)   the due date for payment if the transaction is for cash; or
(b)   the date of transfer in any other case.

Fixed interest trusts

[6.11] If there is a beneficiary entitled to income, trust law accords him the whole of the interest received. Therefore most trustees would give the income plus the tax recovery to the income beneficiary in *Example 1*. Others believe that if they are to pay tax on accrued income out of capital (see **6.12**), they should retain the recovery on the rebate amount. The two treatments may be compared:

(i)   The trustees receive:

	£
Gross interest	1,000
less tax	(200)
Net	£800
Recovery of tax on rebate amount	
£427.40 at 20% =	£85.48

(ii)   If the beneficiary receives the tax recovery as well as the interest, he has £885.48.
(iii)   If the trustees withhold the recovery, he has £800.

HMRC are not concerned whether one or the other method is used. The statutory income is £572.60 (see *Example 1*) either way. Where interest is mandated to the life tenant and relief is due against an interest payment, that relief is given to the life tenant by HMRC.

Rate of tax

[6.12] Where trustees are assessable upon the accrued interest on sale, they suffer tax at 45% in 2015/16 and 2016/17 (ie the special trust rates), regardless of the type of settlement (ie there need be no power to accumulate or exercise discretion and there may be a life tenant) [*ITA 2007, s 482*]. Because trust law requires the proceeds to be received as capital, this tax will be paid out of capital. It is only when *ITA 2007, Pt 9, Ch 7* applies and causes it to form part of the tax pool (see **6.68–6.79**) that the tax can reappear as tax on the income of an individual. The rate is 20% (for 2015/16 and 2016/17) for an estate in course of administration.

[6.13] The charge on the accrued amount is not really a charge on income. It is only a charge on income accrued and that is capital so far as trustees are concerned. Therefore, the accrued income does not become part of the income of the income beneficiary and he receives no credit for the tax paid thereon. Occasionally, someone may benefit from a discretionary trust and the tax voucher he is given will include the tax assessed on the accrued amount, but this will be very rare.

[6.14] Were it possible for trustees to deal in loan stocks only at a time when no interest had accrued, they could avoid the conflict between trust law and tax law. This suggestion is impractical, however.

Occasions of charge

[6.15] A further problem for trustees is that, although the prime purpose of the scheme is to deal with sales *cum* interest, it is enacted in relation to transfers [*ITA 2007, s 632(1)*]. A gift into settlement, an appropriation, a conversion of securities, the change from being a personal representative to being a trustee and the retirement and appointment of trustees are all technically within the charge (subject to the £5,000 *de minimis* limit in certain cases: see **6.7**). Following representations, it is clear that a change of trustee will usually be ignored by HMRC. If the change of trustees takes the trust offshore, however, that will be caught. There is no transfer when a beneficiary becomes absolutely entitled as against the trustees, perhaps on fulfilling a contingency or on the termination of a life interest. This is because the legal ownership does not change. Thereafter, the trustees are bare trustees and the transfer to the beneficiary is then exempt. However, the transfer to a beneficiary in any other case is within the legislation. The coming to an end of the administration period will convert the personal representatives into trustees. That, too, is an occasion of charge. Prior to 6 April 1996, a death caused a deemed transfer: no longer, however [*ITA 2007, s 636*]. There will be a transfer of securities if a person declares himself a trustee of the securities [*ITA 2007, s 651*]. Transfers by or to nominees or bare trustees are treated as transfers by or to the beneficial owner [*ITA 2007, s 666*]. Where trustees make 'qualifying accrued income profits' those profits are treated as income arising under a settlement for purposes of the settlor-interested income tax regime [*ITA 2007, s 667*].

[6.16] Somewhat curiously, a settlor will be charged on the accrued income when he/she gives away securities and there is no provision for reimbursement of the resultant tax by the donee trustees. Perhaps even odder is the rule that, even though the income might escape tax, the accrued amount is still assessable. Therefore a gift of securities to a charity would produce an assessment on the donor. The sale by trustees of exempt gilt-edged securities where the life tenant is non-UK resident (FOTRA securities) also produces an income tax liability.

[6.17] When making a transfer without going through The Stock Exchange, a trustee must bear in mind that the fact that the security has gone *ex-div* is irrelevant except to The Stock Exchange. The transferee will be entitled to the next interest payment on a private transfer, so that the transferor is handing over a stock carrying the accrued interest.

[6.18] Occasionally, the allowance on a rebate amount is found to be stranded. If trustees purchase a security *cum div* and, before the next interest is due, that security becomes one to which a beneficiary is absolutely entitled, nobody is entitled to the allowance.

Personal representatives

[6.19] Personal representatives have a limited opportunity to avoid an assessment on accrued income if they transfer securities in specie to a legatee shortly after the death of their deceased: 'shortly after' means in the same interest period as that in which the death occurred [*ITA 2007, s 636(2)*]. Again, there is no equivalent relief for trustees.

Stock dividends

[6.20] Stock (or 'scrip') dividends have generally lost their tax attractions since 5 April 1999 with the abolition of ACT, although they may still be found from time to time. The shareholder accepts shares in lieu of his cash dividend. The stock and the cash amount are of much the same value. Trustees would not accept a stock dividend unless they had power to accumulate and wished to add to an existing holding without dealing costs. An election by trustees of a discretionary or an accumulation trust to receive a stock dividend as an alternative to cash, carries, unsurprisingly, a tax liability at the dividend trust rate, ie 37.5% in 2014/15 and 2015/16: this was confirmed by the Court of Appeal in *Howell v Trippier (Inspector of Taxes)* [2004] EWCA Civ 885, [2004] STC 1245. For inheritance tax, it was held in the case of *Gilchrist (as trustee of the J P Gilchrist 1993 Settlement) v Revenue and Customs Comrs* 2014 UKUT 0169 (TCC), [2014] STC 1713, 164 NLJ 7605 (and more recently followed in*Seddon (Trustees of Mrs M Seddon Second Discretionary Settlement) v Revenue and Customs Comrs* [2015] UKFTT 140 (TC), [2015] SFTD 539) that a stock dividend share is capital for the purpose of the inheritance tax ten-year charge (see CHAPTER 9). Generally, see CHAPTER 55, 'Stock Dividends' in *Tolley's Tax Planning 2014/15*.

Enhanced stock dividends

[6.21] Enhanced stock dividends were popular in 1993/94, but since then have, in practice, come to an end. They are unlikely to be seen after 5 April

1999 because they were a device which helped dividend-paying companies to escape advance corporation tax (ACT).

Transfers of income streams

[6.22] *CTA 2010, Pt 16, Ch 1, ss 752–757* (formerly *FA 2009, Sch 25*) charges a disposal of a right to income as an income tax receipt equal to the market value of the right disposed of if that is less than the actual consideration received. In response to the Tax Faculty's representations on Finance Bill 2009, HMRC confirmed that Sch 25 does not apply to:

- the creation of an interest in possession (IIP) by the trustees of a discretionary trust;
- the transfer by the trustees of an existing IIP from one life tenant to another; or
- the sale of an interest in a discretionary trust or of an IIP trust by the beneficiary.

Thus, not all trust transactions are caught. The text of the correspondence was published in TAXGUIDE 5/09 (*TAXline August 2009 – Issue 8 p 8*).

Deductibility of expenses

[6.23] Within a property business or a trade carried on by trustees, expenses will be deductible from property and trading income in the ordinary way. It should be noted that the limit on income tax reliefs which are otherwise uncapped introduced by *FA 2013, s 16, Sch 3* with effect from 2013/14 applies only to individuals and not to trustees.

Fixed interest trusts

[6.24] In a trust which is not discretionary etc, the trust management expenses which are properly chargeable to income are deducted from the net trust income to arrive at the net income of the beneficiary. This can then be grossed up to find the beneficiary's statutory income (see APPENDIX C). If income were to fall, the trust management expenses could create a deficit on income account. That can be carried forward to the next fiscal year.

[6.25] If income is mandated to the life tenant, the trustees cannot deduct expenses from it; they will have to pay them from capital.

Accumulation and discretionary trusts

[6.26] Trust management expenses reduce the amount of tax when calculating the special rates on accumulation and discretionary trusts (see **6.31–6.40**). They have to be allowed for when calculating the income of a beneficiary of any other trust. Sometimes the result can look wrong as in *Aikin v Macdonald Trustees Ex (S)* (1894) 3 TC 306 where trustees taxed on income from foreign possessions on a remittance basis could not obtain relief for their UK expenses which did, in part, relate to that income. However, in general, the results seem correct. The expenses of an accumulation or discretionary trust are not available to the beneficiaries, whether by way of income distribution or as capital when accumulations are paid out, and so income used to pay those expenses does not suffer any additional tax.

[6.27] APPENDIX C contains an example of the manner in which the incomes of beneficiaries with discretionary and vested interests in income are calculated, and provides a practical illustration of the manner in which expenses affect the statutory income of beneficiaries. This example is drawn on the traditional basis (ie does not follow the HMRC form) and illustrates a practical method of checking the HMRC calculation. This can be beneficial for a higher or additional rate taxpayer and unsatisfactory for one with a very small income.

The case law and the statutory framework

[6.28] In deciding what is chargeable to income (given the exception from the special rates at 6.63 (b)), general law is applied rather than income tax law and any special provisions of the trust instrument are ignored. This was particularly relevant in two leading House of Lords cases, heard together, *Bosanquet v Allan; Carver v Duncan*, HL [1985] STC 356. In those cases life assurance premiums were, by reason of special clauses in the trust deed, chargeable to income and the trustees sought to have the income needed to pay the premiums excused from tax under what has become *ITA 2007, s 479*. They were unsuccessful. By contrast, interest paid by trustees which is not deductible for tax is an expense properly chargeable to income. The income used for such a payment is, therefore, not assessable under *section 479*.

[6.29] In 2015/16 trustees would have received up to three categories of income. The expenses are set against net income in a particular order (as prescribed by *ITA 2007, s 486*):

(1) UK dividends and deemed income where a scrip dividend has been received or where a company has written off a debt;
(2) foreign dividends; and
(3) other income, charged at the 20% rate.

This order is that which is most beneficial to the beneficiary.

[6.30] The author understands that this same order will continue for 2016/17 notwithstanding the change to the way dividends are taxed.

Trust management expenses

[6.31] Professional costs can be treated as expenses only if properly chargeable to income: this is a problem area. In the past, as a general rule, accountants have traditionally charged fees, etc, against income in the accounts. Supported by the instructions in their standard charging clauses, the banks have tended to do the opposite. Solicitors generally fall somewhere in the middle. The HMRC view has traditionally been quite restrictive, insofar as they have expressed a view, and there has always been a risk of challenge to claims for substantial expenses: see **6.36–6.40** for the present position. In *Carver v Duncan* Lord Templeman said: 'The general rule is that income must bear all ordinary outgoings of a recurrent nature, such as rates and taxes, and interest on charges and encumbrances. Capital must bear all costs, charges and expenses for the benefit of the whole estate.' HMRC consider that what Lord Templeman meant by 'for the benefit of the whole estate' is that the expenses must be regarded as capital if they affect the future capital and future income of the trust (even if they are of a recurrent nature). However, the Court of Appeal in the *Peter Clay* case found against HMRC's stance (see **6.35**).

[6.32] In their Trusts, Settlements and Estates Manual as revised, at TSEM 8120, HMRC state:

> 'There are three categories of trust expenses: those incurred for the benefit of the estate as a whole, because they are incurred for the joint benefit of income and capital beneficiaries,
> 1. those incurred for the benefit exclusively of income beneficiaries;
> 2. those incurred for the benefit exclusively of capital beneficiaries.
>
> The Court of Appeal decision in *HMRC v Peter Clay* sets out explicitly how 1 and 2 are to be treated:
> 1. Expenses for the benefit of the whole estate, where the purpose or object for which they are incurred is to confer benefit both on the income beneficiaries and on the capital beneficiaries. Such expenses are wholly chargeable to capital in general trust law. They cannot be charged to income, and they cannot be apportioned to income.
> 2. Expenses that are exclusively for the benefit of the income beneficiaries, where the purpose or object of the expenses incurred is to confer benefit solely on the income beneficiaries. Such expenses are chargeable to income in general trust law.
> 3. Implicitly, expenses incurred for the benefit exclusively of capital beneficiaries must be charged wholly to capital.
>
> *Clay* also established that where an expense that is exclusively for income beneficiaries is not separately recorded, but the time related to these activities has been specifically recorded, the overall expense can be apportioned to income on a time basis. If there are no time records, the trustees can make a realistic estimate.'

[6.33] The actions of the trustees may affect both current and future beneficiaries. The illustration below clearly affects both. The author has heard mentioned a figure for expenses as low as 10% of the income as typically accepted by HMRC, in the past at least. The amount of the expenses can have a significant effect on the special rates of tax, thus (in 2015/16 and disregarding the standard rate band – see **6.52–6.54**):

	20% Income
Gross income (non-dividend)	100.00
Tax at basic rate	(20.00)
Net income	80.00
Special rate tax	(25.00)
Net for beneficiary, etc	£55.00

If 50% of the net income had been used to pay tax-deductible expenses, there would be a corresponding reduction in the special rate tax as follows (though with a very substantial effect on the beneficiary's income):

Net income	80.00
Expenses	(40.00)
Special rate tax	(12.50)
Net for beneficiary, etc	£27.50

The *Peter Clay* case

[6.34] The test case on trust management expenses was decided by Special Commissioners Adrian Shipwright and Dr John Avery-Jones in favour of the taxpayers (*Trustees of the Peter Clay Discretionary Trust v HMRC* [2007] STC (SCD) 362 Sp C 595). HMRC appealed to the High Court on the substantive issues decided against them by the Special Commissioners, whereas the trustees cross-appealed on the two minor points decided against them. The High Court decided in large part for HMRC, on the basis of the principle in *Carver v Duncan* [1985] AC 1082 (see **6.31**). Appeals were made to the Court of Appeal. There were originally five categories of fees at issue: the trustee fees (substantially of the executive trustee, but also to a lesser extent those of the fixed non-executive trustees), the investment managers' fees, the custodian fees, the bank charges and the accountancy fees.

[6.35] By the time of the hearing, of the five categories of fees noted at 6.34, it was only the executive trustee's fees and the investment managers' fees which were in issue. As to the latter, the Court said that the Special Commissioners had correctly decided that once the trustees had resolved to accumulate the income, those monies should properly be regarded as capital. Accordingly, expenses incurred in connection with the investment of the money could not be said to be chargeable to income. As to the substantive issue on the trustees' fees, the Court of Appeal held that the High Court had been correct to hold that the Special Commissioners had erred in law in disregarding the principle established by the House of Lords in *Carver v Duncan* 'in the light of the general principle of fairness'. However, the Court went on to find that a proper apportionment between income and capital for the fees charged by the executive trustee was appropriate: if professional fees incurred by the trustees for accountancy services could properly be apportioned on a time basis between fees dealing with income and fees dealing with capital, the fees charged by the executive trustee should be approached in the same way. Furthermore, although the fees paid to the non-executive trustees were fixed and did not vary, they should too be in principle capable of apportionment. And so it was correct that the Special Commissioners needed to make a finding whether and to what extent in the present case the non-executive trustees did devote part of their time addressing matters which were exclusively for the benefit of the income beneficiaries. (*Revenue and Customs Comrs v Trustees of the Peter Clay Discretionary Trust* [2008] EWCA Civ 1441, [2009] Ch 296, [2009] 2 All ER 683). The decision is final.

HMRC's guidance

[6.36] In the course of 2004 and 2005 HMRC were reviewing the law and practice on Trust Management Expenses (TMEs) in discretionary and interest in possession (IIP) trusts. Recognising that the guidance provided on TMEs in the Trusts, Settlements and Estates Manual was not as comprehensive as it could be, HMRC obtained full legal advice on the issue. That legal advice confirmed that TMEs had been claimed inappropriately in many cases. For example, trustees of discretionary trusts had made substantial claims for items such as providing beneficiaries with a benefit in kind, which are not expenses but distributions of income; trustees' fees, which are not 'expenses of the trustees' as provided by *ITA 2007, s 484(5)(a)*; and expenses which are capital in nature.

[6.37] In February 2006 HMRC finalised their 'explanatory note' on TMEs, the essential parts of which are now to be found in their Trusts, Settlements and Estates Manual at TSEM8000 and following entitled 'Trust Management Expenses'. The 2006 note put trustees and their advisers on notice of HMRC views which may not always have been reflected in claims for expenses in the past. Divergence from HMRC views should (as always) be noted in the white space in the SA return. That said, however, following what is the final decision in the *Peter Clay Discretionary Trust* test case announced on 19 December 2008, HMRC have had to refine their guidance as set out below.

[6.38] The first, general, point is that allowable TMEs are those to be taken into account for tax purposes to tax accumulation/discretionary trustees at lower than the special trust rates and to arrive at the net amount of an interest in possession beneficiary's income. It is emphasised that some payments out of a trust are distributions which are not allowable, calculated to benefit the beneficiary, as against an expense which is a payment out of the trust which is, broadly, calculated to maintain or improve the level of the income or capital in it. Distributions are never allowable TMEs.

[6.39] In the SA 950 Trust and Estate Tax Return Guide for 2014/15, HMRC's notes on trust management expenses following *Peter Clay* now read as follows at page 22, under the heading 'What expenses are deductible for trustees?':

> 'Trustees cannot deduct management expenses against income taxable only at the dividend rate (10%) or basic rate (20%).
>
> You can deduct the expenses of managing the trust from trust income chargeable at the special trust rates, provided the expenses are under general trust law properly chargeable to income. To be properly chargeable to income, the expenses must be incurred exclusively for the benefit of the income beneficiaries.
>
> You cannot deduct expenses that are incurred for the benefit of the whole estate, for example, legal expenses, the cost of investment advice or of changing trust investments. Under trust law such expenses are properly chargeable to capital.
>
> You can find more guidance on what are allowable trust management expenses for trustees at www.gov.uk/guidance/trusts-and-income-tax.'

The final link ultimately refers readers on to *Helpsheet 392 Trust Management Expenses* which now also includes a useful table setting out HMRC's view of what can and what can't be deducted. The table is reproduced at Appendix H.

[6.40] At one level the above may appear fairly unobjectionable, but at another, the sentence 'you cannot deduct expenses that are incurred for the benefit of the whole estate . . . ' seems excessively restrictive in terms of what the Court of Appeal said about apportionment. Trustees will need to have their wits about them, making appropriate use of the white space in case of any doubt.

Payment of interest by trustees

[6.41] The payment of interest by trustees is often misunderstood. The general rules are now found in *ITA 2007, Pt 8, Ch 1, ss 383–412*. While the introductory provision in *section 383* refers to 'a person', most of the specific reliefs are restricted to 'an individual'. Although *section 383* (loan to buy plant or machinery for partnership use) has no restriction to an individual, *section 390* (loan to buy plant or machinery for employment use) obviously does. *Section 392* (loan to buy interest in close company) somewhat restrictively refers to 'an individual', as does *section 396* (loan to buy interest in employee/controlled company). Again, *section 398* (loan to invest in partnership) refers to an individual. And *section 401* (loans to invest in co-operative) is also restricted to an individual. As the author understands it, a few claims to relief by trustees on interest paid on borrowings for example to acquire an interest in a close company or to invest in a partnership, were accepted by HMRC in the past, though he has heard other reports of disallowance. Certainly there is no published concession. This somewhat surprising discrepancy of treatment as between individuals and trustees was raised by the CIOT with HMRC, who have confirmed that the legislation is clear and will not be amended.

[6.42] While not strictly germane to the subject-matter of this book (as relating to deceased estates rather than to trusts), a brief discursus is made into *ITA 2007, ss 403–405* (loans for paying inheritance tax). Unfortunately, the allowance relates only to a loan which is used to obtain a grant in respect of personal (ie not real) property, and then just for twelve months, and not to subsequent borrowings. The fact that no tax relief is available does not change the nature of the interest paid: it is still an expense. Interest on tax paid late is disallowed by *ITTOIA 2005, ss 54* and *869* and *IHTA 1984, s 233(3)*. The sections are similar and prevent any deduction for such interest in a tax computation. Although not strictly a matter for trustees, it is interesting to see the consequences in estates generally. The first case is an estate in course of administration where there is a limited interest (ie a life tenant). In that case the income of the beneficiary is based on the amounts paid to him. As the interest will have reduced, the money available for him it will make his income less. The second case is an estate in course of administration where there is an absolute interest. In such a case the personal representatives keep two running totals, one being the payments made, the other the residuary income (ie the income for tax purposes). The payments made are income to the extent that they are within the residuary income. The interest on tax cannot be deducted from the residuary income and so does not reduce the income. The third case is an interest in possession trust where the interest paid is an expense. The fourth case is a discretionary or accumulation trust where that which is needed for *ITA 2007, Pt 9, Ch 3* is the amount of income not used for expenses. Insofar as the income is a deductible expense (see **6.31–6.40**), it will affect the taxable amount for purposes of the special rates. The words in the Trust and Estate Tax Return Guide (page 23 re box 13.19 for 2014/15) are clear, although there is no specific reference to interest on tax.

[6.43] The *Trustee Act 2000* does not appear to have particular relevance to the subject-matter of this book, other than to extend the range of expenses which are permitted under trust law and therefore which might be thought to be allowable under tax law (eg trustees' remuneration and certain other expenses).

Non-UK resident beneficiary

[6.44] Where the beneficiary is non-UK resident there are special rules (see **25.4–25.12**).

Interest in possession trusts

[6.45] What follows is subject to the special regime for trusts with vulnerable beneficiaries – which is now covered in CHAPTER 15.

[6.46] The key points of income taxation for the trustees of an interest in possession trust are as follows:

- The income of the trust is *due* to a beneficiary (or beneficiaries) and therefore the *ultimate* income tax liability (eg after the beneficiary has been given credit for any tax paid by the trustees (which may be reclaimed in appropriate circumstances)) will be determined by the recipient beneficiary's tax position.
- The trustees are themselves liable to income tax on anything that they *receive* but only at *basic rate*.
- If trustees receive income which they then pass on to the beneficiary, they must provide the beneficiary with a tax voucher detailing the income tax that they have deducted (see **6.91–6.95**) and the income then retains its character in the hands of the beneficiary (eg as bank interest, dividend etc).
- It is open to the trustees to *mandate* income directly to a beneficiary. In such a case, the trustees have no liability to income tax and the beneficiary is simply taxed directly in relation to the income received.

[6.47] For 2015/16, the trustees of interest in possession trusts receiving bank or building society interest would be most likely to receive that interest net of basic rate tax deducted at source. Likewise, any dividends would be received with a non-deductible 10% tax credit, but which would nevertheless satisfy the trustees' basic rate income tax liability. Any other income received gross would be subject to tax at 20%.

[6.48] For 2016/17 onwards, there are two significant changes:

- Bank and building society interest is now received gross, so the trustees would need to pay 20% income tax at basic rate.

- The dividend tax credit has been abolished so the trustees will also need to pay basic rate tax in relation to any dividends received. The new tax regime for dividends comprises three rates – for basic rate taxpayers: 7.5%; for higher rate taxpayers: 32.5%; and for additional rate taxpayers: 38.1%. As the trustees of an interest in possession trust can only be taxed at basic rate, they will pay 7.5% on any dividend income received (regardless of quantum).
- It should be noted that although the trustees are not entitled to the new (from 2016/17) *personal savings* or *dividend* allowances, these may be available to the beneficiary entitled to the trust income.

Again, the trustees would be liable to tax at 20% on any other income (eg rental income).

[6.49] In 2008/09 the 10% tax credit was extended to foreign dividends from a company in which the shareholder owns less than 10% (*ITTOIA 2005, s 397A*). The 10% limitation was then removed from 2009/10, provided that the dividend-paying company was resident in a jurisdiction with which the UK has a double tax treaty with a non-discrimination article. Up to and including 2015/16, a double grossing up exercise was then required by section 398, so that the cash dividend was grossed up first by the foreign tax suffered (whether withholding or underlying) and is then grossed up again by the 10% UK tax credit. From 2016/17 onwards the 10% tax credit is also abolished for foreign dividends.

Discretionary and accumulation trusts

[6.50] What follows is subject to the special regime for trusts with vulnerable beneficiaries – which is now covered in CHAPTER 15.

[6.51] The key points of income taxation for the trustees of a discretionary/accumulation trust are as follows:

- The income of the trust is not *due* to a beneficiary and therefore the income tax regime operates to ensure that trustees themselves are fully taxed (thereby defeating any simple attempt to mitigate income tax by directing income to trustees). As such, trustees are liable to tax on all the income *due* to the trust whether or not it is received by them and, subject to a relatively modest *standard rate band*, at *special rates*, which ensure that trustees pay income tax at the highest possible marginal rate – being, for 2016/17 onwards 38.1% for dividend income (and see further below for the position in earlier years) and 45% for all other income.
- Because no beneficiary has any entitlement to income, they receive income from the trust only at the trustees' discretion. When receiving such income they are again entitled to a tax voucher from the trustees (see 6.86–6.90) but the income does not then retain its character in the hands of the beneficiary (eg as bank interest, dividend etc). Instead, the beneficiary received 'trust income' and the tax voucher must account

for 45% tax paid. The fact that the income does not retain its character means that a beneficiary cannot take advantage of the new (from 2016/17) *personal savings* or *dividend* allowances.
- Trustees must ensure that they have a sufficient 'tax pool' to cover the 45% tax voucher given to a beneficiary, and where trustees have paid tax at less than 45% great care is required.

The standard rate band

[6.52] The standard rate threshold for discretionary/accumulation trusts is £1,000 [*ITA 2007, s 491*]. This threshold of £1,000 is divided equally among all the settlements made by the same settlor up to a maximum of five [*ITA 2007, s 492*]. Note that this rule is, somewhat curiously, subtly different and more extensive than the anti-fragmentation rule for purposes of the annual exemption from capital gains tax (see **7.36**). Income which is otherwise taxable at a special trust tax rate is to be disregarded if an amount of that description is already chargeable at the basic rate or the dividend ordinary rate [*ITA 2007, s 491*].

[6.53] Allowable trust management expenses (see **6.31–6.40**) are obviously deducted before arriving at the amount falling within the standard rate band.

[6.54] For most income sources, the standard rate is 20%, subject to any income tax deducted at source (eg on bank and building society interest in 2015/16). For dividend income received in 2015/16 the standard rate is covered by the 10% notional tax credit. For dividend income received in 2016/17, the standard rate is 7.5% (see **6.48**).

The special rates

[6.55] Trustees of settlements where there is a discretion over income or a power to accumulate are subject to the 'special rates' of tax (*ITA 2007, Pt 9, Ch 3*). (The first £1,000 of income is exempted on the special rates as within the standard rate band (see **6.52–6.54**).)

[6.56] The rate for non-dividend income is 45% for 2015/16 and 2016/17 but the income tax payable will depend on whether tax has been deducted at source, so for building society interest which has suffered a 20% deduction (ie in 2015/16), a further 25% will be payable, whereas for gilt interest or rental income which has been received gross, the full rate of 45% would be payable.

[6.57] For 2015/16, the special rate for dividend income, is 37.5% but given the non-repayable 10% tax credit the effective rate paid on dividend income is 27.5% for 2015/16. This, of course, is in relation to the gross dividend – ie including the 10% nominal credit – which works out to an effective 30.56% in relation to the net dividend received. For 2016/17, the 10% tax credit is abolished and instead a special rate of 38.1% will apply to the net dividend received. This represents an increase in the effective tax rate of 7.54%.

[6.58] In the 2003 consultation on the modernisation of trusts there was a proposal that income retained by the trustees would be taxed much as it is at present, whereas income distributed by the trustees on or before the 31 December following the end of the tax year of receipt (called 'streamed income') would be assessed on the recipient beneficiary. This proposal did not become law and appears now to have been long abandoned.

EXAMPLE

A discretionary trust receives gross interest income of £2,000 in tax year 2013/14. The trustees incur qualifying management expenses of £300 (gross equivalent), leaving them with £1,700. Tax at the basic rate of 20% is deducted from the interest. The computation is as follows:

	£
Interest income (gross)	2,000
Less allowable management expenses	(300)
Less standard rate band	(1,000)
Charged at the special rate	700
Tax liability at 45%	315
Tax liability on standard rate band	200
Less tax paid at source	(400)
Further tax payable by the trustees	£115

Deceased estates

[6.59] Where a discretionary settlement is set up by a Will, there will be a period during which the administration of the estate takes place. During this period the settlement has not been created and therefore the special rates do not apply. However, when the administration period ends, income from that point becomes that of trustees rather than executors and so there will be a liability at the special rates on the income, under *ITA 2007, s 479*. In most cases the same people will be both executors and trustees, though the two capacities are different.

Income which is charged at the special rates

[6.60] The income which is to be charged at the special rates (ie on top of the standard rate band) is as follows:

(a) Income which is to be accumulated or which is payable at the trustees' discretion [*ITA 2007, s 479(1) and s 480*]. Specified elements of deemed income are brought within the scope of the special rates [*ITA 2007 ss 481–482*]. One example is a premium on a lease lasting for no more than 50 years, part of which would be income for tax by virtue of *ITTOIA 2005, s 277* but is not income for trust purposes. Another is the proceeds of sale of shares bought by a company from trustees which are not subject to capital gains tax under *CTA 2010, s 1033*. In a situation where the proceeds of sale are treated as income for tax purposes, the qualifying distribution represented by the excess over the nominal value is treated as attracting the special rates. The gross amount of such a distribution is subject to the special rate for dividends in the relevant year. There are exceptions for charities and pension funds. In the case of a settlor-interested trust where in the settlor's self assessment the amount received is all taxed at the higher or additional rate, the special rate will apply in the trustees' assessment, for which the settlor will be given credit in his own self assessment (see **5.13**). However, to the extent that the payment falls within the settlor's basic rate band, he will secure a repayment from HMRC for which from 2010/11 he must account to the trustees [*ITTOIA 2005, s 646(5)*]. The legislation applies to interest in possession trusts as well.

(b) Amounts assessed under the accrued income scheme (whether or not a discretionary or accumulation and maintenance settlement) [*ITA 2007, s 667*].

(c) Royalties received under an exclusive copyright licence granted by the original licensor (whether or not a discretionary or accumulation and maintenance settlement) but not those from a subsequent assignment (see *Trustees of the PL Travers Will Trust v Revenue and Customs Comrs* [2013] UKFTT 436 (TC), [2014] SFTD 265).

[6.61] Interestingly, had a settlor in 2008/09 or 2009/10 paid over to the trustees the repayment of tax occasioned by his being only a basic rate taxpayer in such circumstances, then presumably he would have made a chargeable transfer (subject to any applicable annual exemptions). The inheritance tax point is expressly closed off for the future see **5.14**. That he might have done on the basis of mistaken professional advice. As to the scope of *s 646(5)*, at all events the amounts will have been relatively small – and the point could not have applied before 2008/09, at a time when *TA 1988, s 686(2)(b)(ii)* applied to ensure that the trustees could not be liable on trust income at more than the basic rate.

[6.62] On a separate issue, but in the context of chargeable transfers for inheritance tax, one should remember the possibility that where the settlor is a beneficiary but does not receive the income, he has a statutory right of recovery from the trust for any tax paid by him. If he fails to exercise the right, he makes a chargeable transfer. This has been less likely since 2008/09, insofar as the tax is primarily collected by HMRC from the trustees.

Exceptions

[6.63] There are exceptions to the charge which brings the total up to the special rates, so that no assessment is made upon the following:

(a) income which is the income of some person other than the trustees before it is distributed [*ITA 2007, s 480(3)(a)*]. (See **6.64**); and
(b) income used to defray the expenses which are properly chargeable to income [*ITA 2007, s 484*]. (See **6.31–6.40**.)

[6.64] In relation to the first exception from the special rates (see **6.63**(a)), the income of an infant's legacy is outside the charge provided the gift to the infant is outright. In such a case the trustees act as managers of the capital and income, but the infant is the owner of the income and were he to die it would form part of his estate. If the gift is contingent in any way, it is not within this protection. See also **4.14–4.19** for the liability and compliance position for parental settlements for minor children and the change for income from funds provided on or after 9 March 1999. If income from funds provided before 9 March 1999 belongs to the beneficiary absolutely (and is retained by the trustees pending attainment of the age of 18), that is a bare trust of income, the income is assessed on the child and so the special rates do not apply. This might happen either under a life interest trust which disapplies the accumulation provisions for minors under *Trustee Act 1925, s 31* or under a bare trust of capital.

Discretionary payments to beneficiaries: the grossing up regime

[6.65] When a payment is made under a discretionary power and it is income of the recipient for tax purposes, *ITA 2007, Pt 9, Ch 4, ss 484–487* does not apply. Instead the payment comes within CHAPTER 7 of *ITA 2007, Pt 9, ss 493–498*. The net payment is grossed up in 2015/16 and 2016/17 at 45% (ie at the special rate) and a tax voucher R185 (Trust Income) can be given for that tax.

[6.66] Payments to or for the beneficiaries of accumulation and maintenance settlements where their shares of income have not vested will be made pursuant to a discretionary power, because, by the terms of such a settlement, the income must be ' . . . accumulated so far as not applied for maintenance, education or benefit of a beneficiary' [*IHTA 1984, s 71(1)(b)*]. The application of the income is therefore at the discretion of the trustees until the beneficiary becomes entitled to the income of his share. Once a beneficiary is entitled to his income as it arises the special rates do not apply, as there is no discretion. Similarly, the special rates (see **6.55–6.64**) upon the income of the settlement which the trustees must hand over to such a beneficiary will also no longer apply. This is because the income has ceased to be income which must be accumulated' or which 'is payable at the discretion of the trustees' [*ITA 2007, s 480(1)*]. The manner in which this distribution charge is eliminated from the income of a settlement where there are still beneficiaries not yet entitled to their income is illustrated in the example in APPENDIX C where the incomes of Alice and Belinda are excluded from the extra charge.

[6.67] Where a payment is made to or for a beneficiary of an accumulation and maintenance settlement (ie one whose share of income has not vested) it must be for his 'maintenance, education or benefit'. Where significant sums are involved this must put some limit upon the amount which can be expended, although the author has never heard of a case being challenged by HMRC.

Tax pools

[6.68] Where a discretionary payment is made to a beneficiary, an assessment is made upon the trustees to collect the 45% (in 2015/16 and 2016/17) under *ITA 2007, s 496* to the extent that it is not covered by the tax pool. Trustees must take this into account when making net payments to beneficiaries, and should ensure that they have paid enough tax (and therefore have a large enough 'tax pool') to cover the tax credit at the special rates. The tax pool for 2015/16 comprises:

(i) the balance from 2014/15;
(ii) tax on income (except as mentioned at (iii) or at (iv) below) charged at 37.5% or at 45%;
(iii) tax at 27.5% on any UK dividends, UK stock dividends or tax charged on the release of a loan to participators in a close company, on any of which tax is charged at the dividend trust rate under *ITA 2007, s 479*;
(iv) tax at 27.5% on other amounts charged at the dividend trust rate under *ITA 2007, s 481*;
(v) any tax on income which falls within the £1,000 standard rate; and
(vi) tax on any income charged under the vulnerable persons regime (see CHAPTER 15).

[6.69] There is provision for double tax relief to flow through, so that the beneficiary can claim a credit for the foreign tax paid on taxed overseas income, to the extent that it is included in a payment to him.

[6.70] For 2015/16, the tax credit on a dividend is 10%. Dividends received by trustees who are within ITA 2007, s 479 are taxed at the dividend ordinary rate (ie 10%) and at the dividend trust rate of 37.5%. The 10% tax credit on dividends does not enter the tax pool, although the extra 27.5% which makes it up to the dividend trust rate does go into the pool.

[6.71] As discussed above, from 2016/17, trustees will pay the special rate on dividend income at 38.1% with no tax credit. An amendment to *ITA 2007, s 498* introduced at the Committee Stage of the passage of *Finance Act 2016* through Parliament ensured that this will be included within the types of tax to be included in a trustees' tax pool.

[6.72] Tax on non-dividend income flows through and the 45% thereon for 2015/16 and 2016/17 will go into the tax pool. This may affect the trustees' view of their investment portfolio. If only the 27.5% (in 2015/16, or 38.1% in 2016/17) goes into the tax pool where dividends are received, should the trustees buy debentures or gilts, income on which attracts the 45%? Any capital growth may cover the difference. There is of course a further point, ie the relative balance of income tax at 45% and capital gains tax (at 28% in 2015/16 and 20% in 2016/17). There is a fiscal incentive at least to invest for capital growth rather than income, in terms of what might be called the overall return to the portfolio. This is quite apart from the tax disincentive illustrated at 6.73 of the receipt by discretionary or accumulation trustees of dividend income in circumstances where they make distributions and there is no or an insufficient brought forward tax pool.

[6.73] There is a problem over payments to beneficiaries which are within the regime for grossing up and tax payments. The 45% due from the trustees under *ITA 2007, s 493* has to be deducted from them and then compared with the tax pool to see if any further tax is due [*ITA 2007, s 496*]. Any existing discretionary or accumulation trusts will have a tax pool from the past and they may be unaffected for a while. However, a new discretionary trust or one with a small brought forward tax pool would be caught if it relied on dividend income (on which, historically, only 27.5% entered the pool (and likewise only 38.1% from 2016/17)) to fund payments from which 45% is deducted. By way of illustration (for 2015/16):

	£	£
Dividend received by trustees		90.00
Add tax credit		10.00
Gross income		100.00
Special rate tax thereon at 37.5% dividend trust rate:		
Met by tax credit	10.00	
Paid by trustees	27.50	37.50
		62.50

The problem is that £62.50 cannot simply be distributed to the beneficiary. The tax credit has met part of the trustees' own liability under *section 479 of ITA 2007* but cannot be used to frank the tax under *section 493* which they are liable to deduct on making the distribution.

	£	£
Net income of trust		62.50
Liability at 45% under *section 493* on gross payment of £90 to beneficiary	40.50	
Met by trustees' payment above	(27.50)	
Remaining liability of trustees	13.00	(13.00)
Available for distribution to beneficiary		49.50
Grossed up under *section 494* at 45%		40.50
Gross income of beneficiary		90.00
Tax thereon at 45% (met by trustees)		40.50
Net income of beneficiary		49.50

It should be noted that this does not affect an accumulation settlement. That will pay the additional 27.5%, but no more. It is only the discretionary settlement, invested in equities and making income payments to beneficiaries, which is caught.

[6.74] The way in which the tax pool works is well set out in *ITA 2007, s 497*. The system ensures that, to the extent that tax paid by the trustees in any year (excluding the non-payable 10% tax credit on dividends, for 2015/16) exceeds the tax due from the trustees on the grossed up amount of any payments of income, such excess is not wasted and remains available to frank the trustees' liability for tax on making income distributions should there otherwise be a shortfall. The existence of any mismatch between the tax pool and the distributable cash is a point which trustees should consider before making a distribution. In the past, tax pools have tended to cover a larger distribution than is permitted by the accounts, although that has now changed (see 6.77).

[6.75] If there is an assessment on the trustees under *section 496*, there can be no set-off against a future year. That is to say, if tax on the distributions of income in 2015/16 exceeds the total of the tax credits of that year, etc, together with the tax pool brought forward from 2014/15, then there will be a *section 493* charge and the fact that there may be accumulated income in 2016/17 does not give rise to a recovery of the tax so charged in 2015/16.

[6.76] The income tax return for trustees of accumulation and maintenance and of discretionary settlements is the standard Self assessment Trust and Estate Return with its Guide and Tax Calculation Guide. This is explained in CHAPTER 20.

[6.77] Tax pools have been used as reservoirs against the advent of a suitable beneficiary. For instance, if all possible beneficiaries were adult higher or additional rate taxpayers in years 1 and 2 and in year 3 a child were added to the class, the trustees might accumulate in years 1 and 2 and distribute something in year 3, so giving to the new beneficiary income of years before he was born. The fact that tax rates change from year to year does not affect the balance brought forward in the tax pool.

[6.78] Stripping the tax pool is important in the years before a discretionary settlement ceases to be such. The tax pool exists only so long as the grossing up and tax payment regime applies to payments made by trustees and, as the changeover from an accumulation and maintenance settlement to a life interest settlement or a series of absolute interests takes the trustees out of that regime, the tax pool will then disappear.

[6.79] The disappearance of the tax pool is not gradual. If the trust is within the special regimes, the tax pool is there to be used. Once the trust ceases to be within those regimes, there is no tax pool. One curiosity is that if there are several beneficiaries of an accumulation or discretionary settlement, the fact that one of them attains a right to income does not reduce the tax pool. Had there been separate settlements, one for each beneficiary, the total of the tax pools would have been less.

Income or capital?

[6.80] For the grossing up and tax payment regime to apply, two tests must be satisfied.

(a)   Is the payment made by trustees in the exercise of a discretion?
(b)   Is the sum income of the recipient for tax purposes?

Trustees generally have a power to advance capital and any such advancement would satisfy the first test. HMRC may then consider the possibility of the money being the income of the beneficiary. The cases which are of general application are *Brodie's Trustees v IRC* (1933), 17 TC 432 and *Cunard's Trustees v IRC* (1945), 27 TC 122. In both cases there was a 'topping up' provision which could be used for the maintenance of the usual standard of living of the beneficiary. Therefore, trust capital was converted into income.

[6.81] The case of *Stevenson v Wishart (Levy's Trustees)* [1987] STC 266, CA concerned a discretionary settlement. The trustees had the usual dispositive powers. They gave away the entire income of the trust to charity for a short period of years. They then appointed capital to a woman aged over 90. In this way they expended £109,000 of capital on her medical expenses and nursing home fees. Anybody with capital might reasonably meet such expenses from it so that, although used for the maintenance of the beneficiary, the money was not income in her hands. Therefore, there was no *section 687* assessment upon the trustees. Fox LJ: ' . . . there is nothing in the present case which indicates that the payments were of an income nature except their recurrence. I do not think that is sufficient. The trustees were disposing of capital in exercise of a power over capital. They did not create a recurring interest in property. If, in exercise of a power over capital, they chose to make in their discretion regular payments of capital to deal with the specific problems of Mrs Henwood's last years rather than release a single sum to her of a large amount, that does not seem to me to create an income interest. Their power was to appoint capital. What they appointed remained capital.'

[6.82] The provisions of the trust instrument in *Brodie* and *Cunard* did not permit the use of capital save as a support for income. Therefore the regime is much less a danger to trustees than was thought to be the case before *Stevenson*. Indeed, the *Stevenson v Wishart* principle might be useful in a case where trustees want to avoid the adverse impact of the current (the taxation of dividend income is set to change from 2016/17 – see 6.45) tax regime for dividends on distributions to a higher rate beneficiary, where there is no available tax pool. They could accumulate the dividend income for several years and then, using powers in the trust deed, appoint the accumulated income as capital to the beneficiary. Provided the circumstances are not such that HMRC could legitimately treat the distribution as income in the hands of the beneficiary, such a strategy should be effective and is supported by the Trust and Estate Tax Return Guide: see 6.85. There could incidentally be, albeit minor, inheritance tax implications of such a course, insofar as such advances of capital would constitute the exit of relevant property from the discretionary regime; accumulations form part of the capital of the trust as confirmed by Inland Revenue Statement of Practice SP 8/86 (reproduced in APPENDIX A).

[6.83] There have been cases where employees benefited from capital settled for them. If the trustees distribute surplus capital to beneficiaries who can receive it only because of their employment, it becomes income in their hands, ie it forms part of the emoluments of their employment (*Brumby v Milner*, HL [1976] STC 534). Any reader referring to this case should bear in mind that the grossing up and tax payment regime originated in the *FA 1973* and that the events in *Brumby v Milner* took place earlier. The winding up of settlements for employees can easily produce double taxation, ie the realisation of investments gives rise to a capital gains tax charge and the distribution of the net proceeds is received as income and is thus taxable under *ITA 2007, s 496*.

[6.84] Where income is used to fund payments which will be employment income taxed as such, *ITA 2007, s 496B* (enacting HMRC extra-statutory concession A68) provides for the tax deducted to be set against the tax pool. This prevents double taxation for income tax.

[6.85] The Trust and Estate Tax Return Guide for 2015/16 deals on page 25 in discussing boxes 14.1 to 14.14 with payments made on the exercise of the trustees' discretion which were income of a beneficiary. It says 'Payments out of trust capital including out of accumulated income or deemed income are not usually regarded as the income of a beneficiary irrespective of the purposes for which they are made and should not normally be included'. The official view is that where a payment is made out of capital or accumulations it can only be income in the hands of the beneficiary if it is a 'topping up' payment as in *Brodie* and *Cunard* or if it is paid as an annuity. Traditionally a relaxed view is taken as to when accumulation takes place (although, strictly speaking, undistributed income will retain its character until the trustees decide on accumulation). Normally this would be left for the trustees to decide. Therefore, if the trustees carried forward undistributed income for a year or two without accumulating it, there should be no argument: in practice, however, especially under self assessment, they are likely to make a decision in the autumn following the end of the year of assessment (see also 3.7). This official view is at odds with the *Trustee Act 1925, s 31(2)* (see APPENDIX D) which contemplates accumulations being drawn down as income. It is based on the characterisation of the money in the hands of the trustees, although *section 493* of *ITA 2007* refers to its character in the hands of the recipient ('income of the beneficiary').

Making payments to beneficiaries of discretionary and accumulation trusts

[6.86] Payments of income to beneficiaries of discretionary and accumulation settlements (rather than payments on behalf of them) will be made in practice only to adult beneficiaries, because only they can give a 'good receipt' to the trustees. In general they will be beneficiaries entitled to the income of their share or putative share by reason of attainment of the age of 18 or some higher age specified in the trust instrument. The beneficiary's statutory income will depend upon his entitlement to capital. This is a 'see through' situation and the tax voucher given to the beneficiary should show special types of income separately eg income with foreign tax deducted or interest on a National Savings account. Indeed, the form R185 (Trust Income) shows different categories of trust income separately (see **6.87**).

[6.87] A single form R185 (Trust Income) is used by trustees of both discretionary and fixed income trusts. Similarly, form R185 (Estate Income) has been revised to make it clearer. Tax deducted from rent to pay to a non-UK resident landlord should be notified on form NRL6. Form R185 (Trust Income) distinguishes between discretionary payments (from, separately, non settlor-interested and settlor-interested trusts) and non-discretionary entitlements (separating out non-savings income taxed at basic rate, savings income taxed at basic rate, income taxed at dividend rate, untaxed income, foreign income and stock/scrip dividends). Form R185 (Estate Income) is drawn similarly, albeit not in exactly the same terms.

[6.88] In a case where the settlement is settlor-interested, the income is that of the settlor and of no other person [*ITTOIA 2005, s 624(1)*]. So a payment of income made to a beneficiary other than the settlor will have no income tax implications. The introduction into *ITTOIA 2005* of *s 685A* with effect from 2006/07 makes the point express. However, somewhat curiously, the section treats the beneficiary of an annual payment as having paid additional rate income tax, which is of course not repayable and cannot be credited against any other tax liability of his. See **5.16** for this provision.

[6.89] Another oddity about *section 685A* is that it applies expressly only to a discretionary settlor-interested trust. Although the beneficiary will not have further tax to pay, HMRC confirm in para TSEM3757 of their Trusts, Settlements and Estates Manual that the income 'remains part of the beneficiary's total income and may therefore affect tax reliefs and benefits which are mean [*sic*] tested (eg Age allowance, Student loan repayments)'. However, if the trust is interest in possession in structure, the provision seems not to apply, making the beneficiary of a settlor-interested interest in possession in a better tax position than one of a settlor-interested discretionary trust. Nothing is said in the Manual and the trust page on an individual's tax return has no box in which to report the income. The point was noted on the Trusts Discussion Forum in a posting on 9 September 2009 by Felicity Whitley of Hall Barn Consultants Ltd.

[6.90] Advancements of capital to adult beneficiaries with a vested interest in income may be made without income tax consequences. Payment of accumulations upon majority is a capital payment (*Stanley v IRC* (1944) 26 TC 12).

Payments to beneficiaries of fixed interest trusts: the tax voucher

[6.91] Where there is a vested interest in income the beneficiary will be either a life tenant or an annuitant. In both cases the payment of income is nearly always quite straightforward. The trustee pays over the appropriate income and gives a tax voucher for the year of payment showing the gross income, tax at basic rate and the net sum to which the beneficiary is entitled. The payment of income to a life tenant may be in the year following the year of receipt. The details on the voucher will be those of the year of receipt. This is a transparent situation. The income of the trustee is not his; it is the income of the beneficiary, subject only to necessary outgoings. This transparency does not mean that capital sums which are deemed to be income of the trustees become income of the income beneficiary. Therefore, lease premiums assessed as property income (see **6.96**), charges under the accrued income scheme, etc, although income of the trustees in the fiscal sense, do not become income of the life tenant, etc. The transparency extends to foreign beneficiaries where there is income which is exempt to them. So the trustees will arrange for interest on exempt gilts (FOTRA) to be received gross, which they will pay over to the non-UK resident without paying or deducting tax.

[6.92] An annuitant receives his annuity under deduction of tax. So far as the trustees are concerned, the annuity is a charge on income, or, if income is insufficient, on capital. Tax is deducted under *ITA 2007, Pt 9, Ch 4* as an annual payment. This rule applies to the extent that it is not out of income.

However, there is, on the face of it, a problem with dividend income. HMRC Centre for Non-UK Residents (previously FICO) has confirmed that the trustees are given credit for the 10% non-repayable tax credit, though there will, of course, be an additional 10% liability for the trustees to pay, which again they will deduct from the payment to the annuitant, net of 20% basic rate tax (in 2015/16).

[6.93] In trusts created by Wills, it is not uncommon to see a 'top up' clause. This is a clause requiring the trustees to make payments out of capital if income is inadequate. Often the words in the trust instrument are imprecise, perhaps saying no more than that capital may be paid to a beneficiary if income is not sufficient for her to maintain her normal standard of living. This brings into question the character of the payment. This has already received attention (see 6.80–6.85).

[6.94] A trust deed may provide a right for the beneficiary to occupy a property. The occupation itself has no income tax consequences, at least with UK trusts, ie there is no assessment of a notional income. Payments of rates and outgoings by the trustees are liabilities of the beneficiary and the sums paid out are net sums. The gross equivalent will form part of the beneficiary's income.

[6.95] Payments to beneficiaries with less than a vested interest have already been touched upon and the treatment of management expenses has been considered in 6.31–6.40.

Taxation of land transactions

[6.96] Premiums on leases for no more than 50 years can be assessed to income tax. The rate of tax is the trust rate of 45% for 2014/15 and 2015/16, whatever the type of trust, increased from the basic rate in 2006/07 [*ITTOIA 2005, s 277*].

[6.97] In a case where a capital sum is received on selling or developing land, there can be an assessment to income tax (which arises under *ITTOIA 2005, Pt 5, Ch 8*). The charging provision is *ITA 2007, Pt 13, Ch 3, ss 752–772*. The regime extends to arrangements or schemes which enable gains to be realised by an indirect method. The provision is aimed at traders in property who regularly managed to avoid the appearance of trading in the years before the introduction of capital gains tax. There then being no tax on capital gains, if they could avoid income tax, they escaped tax altogether.

[6.98] The leading case for trustees is *Page v Lowther*, CA [1983] STC 799. In that case, trustees owned 2.6 acres in Kensington. They granted a building lease to a developer who was to clear the site and erect 28 houses, 33 flats, garages etc. As these were sold, a proportion of the proceeds was payable to the trustees. In this way the trustees received over £1 million. This transaction was not trading, nor were the trustees in the habit of trading. They were simply realising a valuable property in the most rewarding manner. They were caught by the section.

Flat management companies

[6.99] *Landlord and Tenant Act 1987 (LTA 1987), s 42* provides that a Flat Management Company (FMC) can be treated as a discretionary and accumulation trust. This means that interest paid on a deposit made by a FMC should have tax deducted despite the 'company' status. There will be no trust deed in these cases. Banks and building societies will need to hold evidence before they begin making net payments to a company. As there is no trust deed HMRC suggest that banks etc obtain a signed declaration from the company certifying that the funds to be held in the bank account are, under *LTA 1987, s 42*, held by the company in its capacity as a trustee of a trust to hold service charges.

[6.100] On the whole the point made at **6.99** should not be a particular concern in that FMCs do not tend to have large cash deposits. The only exception might be a sinking fund. Worse than the requirement for the bank to deduct basic rate tax might be the liability of the FMC (as a deemed discretionary trust) to the special rates of income tax. Happily, however, TSEM5710 gives comfort both that there will be no further tax liability on top of the basic rate deducted at source and indeed that in many cases the *LTA 1987* regime will not apply. Specifically, *ITA 2007, s 480(3)(c)* provides that income from service charges paid in respect of dwellings in the UK and which are held on trust are exempted from the charge at the trust rate and the dividend trust rate. For 2007/08 and later years such income is charged at the standard rate, so that if the only income is bank interest with tax deducted at source there will be no further tax to pay.

Assessment

[6.101] As a matter of practice, HMRC select one trustee and direct assessments to that trustee. Usually HMRC choose the first-named in the trust instrument. This was given statutory backing [*FA 1989, s 151*], now repealed as unnecessary. The trustee selected will be one of the 'relevant trustees' (see **5.4**).

[6.102] Trustees of a bare settlement can self assess (see **2.44**). Then their figures are incorporated in their principal's return. They can self assess income only, however; capital gains must be reported by the beneficial owner.

[6.103] The manner in which expenses affect the calculation of the income of beneficiaries has already been explained (at **6.58**). Income paid to the beneficiaries will be marshalled in the way which gives them the greatest benefit, ie the first sums which reach them are from basic rate tax which could be repaid, then lower rate repayable tax and finally non-repayable basic rate. Beneficiaries will want their tax vouchers early in the tax year because many of them will not want to self assess. They will wish to file their returns on or before 31 October and let HMRC compute their tax liability.

Non-UK resident beneficiaries

[6.104] The general rule for a person not resident in the UK in a particular year of assessment is that (apart from trading or professional income carried on through a branch or agency or property income) the UK income tax liability cannot exceed the tax deducted at source [*ITA 2007, ss 811–814*]. This provision works by removing from charge any 'excluded income' (and also ignoring personal allowances given either under a double taxation treaty or to Commonwealth citizens or citizens of the Republic of Ireland and certain others). The expression 'disregarded income' which is defined in *ITA 2007, s 813* includes savings or investment income.

[6.105] Consider income arising to trustees from a property business. If the trust is interest in possession, the beneficiary being absolutely entitled to the underlying income could be liable to higher or additional rate tax on the net income. By contrast, if the trust is discretionary, any payments to the beneficiary would be taxed as savings or investment income. Distributions made to a beneficiary of a discretionary trust are governed by *ITA 2007, s 494(1)*, which provides that 'the discretionary payment is treated as if it were made after the deduction of a sum representing income tax at the trust rate on the grossed up amount of the discretionary payment'. Distributions of income from UK discretionary trusts to non-UK resident beneficiaries will in the normal case not be liable to any tax above the basic rate. The definition of 'qualifying annual payment' in *ITA 2007, s 899(5)(d)* excludes 'a payment in relation to which income tax is treated as having been paid under *section 494(3)* (income tax treated as paid by beneficiary or settlor in relation to discretionary trust)' from the deduction of income tax at source requirements of *ITA 2007, Pt 15*. Generally, see 24.9–24.20 for the new statutory residence test from 2013/14.

Chapter 7

Capital Gains Tax

Occasions of charge

[7.1] The charge to capital gains tax is based on disposals and deemed disposals by persons resident in the UK in any part of the tax year in which the disposal or deemed disposal takes place [*TCGA 1992, s 2(1)*]. CHAPTER 24 explains the concept of 'residence', including a summary of the comprehensive statutory residence test which applies from 2013/14. From 2015/16 non-residents have also been liable for capital gains tax on the disposal of UK residential property (see **26.66–26.67**).

[7.2] The transfer of assets by the settlor to the trustees, whether on creation of the settlement or subsequently, will constitute a disposal by him for capital gains tax purposes (even if he has a beneficial interest under the settlement). Except where those assets are sterling cash, the disposal may trigger a chargeable gain or an allowable loss [*TCGA 1992, s 71*]. The normal dealings of trustees will produce disposals with gains taxable or losses allowable in the normal way. Additionally, on the transfer of an asset out of the settlement, there is a deemed disposal and re-acquisition by the trustees at market value (see **19.6**). Before the application of any reliefs (as discussed later in this chapter), the gain or loss must be computed. This will involve deducting from the gross sale proceeds the acquisition cost or, where acquired before 1 April 1982, the value at 31 March 1982, with deductions for allowable expenditure and incidental costs of acquisition or disposal.

Connected persons

[7.3] Trustees of a settlement and the settlor are 'connected persons'. This extends to persons connected with the settlor. Sometimes a family company can be connected with the trustees [*TCGA 1992, s 286*]. There are two practical consequences as follows:

(a) Transactions (including the settlement of capital) between the settlor and the trustees are deemed to be at market value [*TCGA 1992, ss 17, 18(1)(2)*].
(b) Any loss incurred by the settlor on transferring assets to the trustees can be used only against a chargeable gain arising from some other transaction with the same trustees [*TCGA 1992, s 18(3)*].

[7.4] The most common area of difficulty is with losses. A loss on a disposal to a connected person can be set off only against a gain made on a disposal to the same person. In the February 1993 Issue 6, page 56, of the *Inland Revenue Tax Bulletin* it was made clear that:

(a) the settlor and the trustees are connected at the moment when the settlement comes into existence;
(b) once the settlor is dead the connection is broken;
(c) the transfer of losses to beneficiaries under *section 71(2)* is not inhibited by *section 18(3)*.

[**7.5**] The possibility of transfer of losses from the trust under *section 71(2)* arises in circumstances where the value of an asset to which a beneficiary has become absolutely entitled has fallen during the period from the date of acquisition by the trustees to the deemed date of disposal legislated by *section 71(1)*. The resultant loss is transferred to the beneficiary. Loss claims now have to be calculated by the taxpayer and a claim made [*TCGA 1992, s 16(2A)*]. See **7.15** and **7.16** and, for the targeted anti-avoidance rule from 5 December 2006, see **7.17–7.18**.

Absolute entitlement

Gains

[**7.6**] When a person becomes absolutely entitled to settled property as against the trustees (other than on the death of a life tenant before 22 March 2006 – see **7.31** for the position on a death after 21 March 2006: *TCGA 1992, s 73(1)(a)*), there is a charge to capital gains tax on the deemed disposal. This will normally be the case where a life interest comes to an end without there being another life tenant. It will also take place where a contingent interest vests. For instance, an accumulation and maintenance settlement may provide for a child to take his share of capital on reaching the age of 18 (typically reduced from 25 before 6 April 2008), although in such a case it is to be hoped that hold-over would still be available (see **7.72(c)**, **7.87**). The charge is calculated as if the disposal had been at market value at the date when the beneficiary became absolutely entitled [*TCGA 1992, s 71(1)* and see also **7.25**].

[**7.7**] Where two or more beneficiaries become absolutely entitled to settled property at the same moment, this can affect the valuation. For instance, there might be unquoted shares comprising 60% of a company's capital and they might be split between two beneficiaries. The valuation required is of 60%, as confirmed by HMRC's Capital Gains Manual at CG37370.

[**7.8**] A High Court case in 1996 considered the date when beneficiaries became absolutely entitled as against the trustee. There had been a class gift, so that settled property was held for such of the settlor's children as might attain the age of 21. Therefore, the answer to the question when the class closed (ie when no further children could be added) would determine when the children became absolutely entitled. The settlor was paralysed from the chest down as a result of an accident in 1964. He died in 1990. HMRC took the view that the settlor's incapacity was not relevant in determining the beneficial interests in the settlement. Therefore the children did not become absolutely entitled until 1990. The court found in favour of HMRC (*Figg v Clarke (Inspector of Taxes)* [1997] 1 WLR 603, [1997] STC 247, Ch D).

[7.9] The trustees often continue to hold an asset of this sort pending transfer and then they do so as bare trustees. The subsequent transfer to the beneficiary is a non-event for capital gains tax. Similarly, a transfer directed by the beneficiary is treated as a transfer by him [*TCGA 1992, s 60*]. The rule that the moment when a person becomes absolutely entitled is the occasion of a deemed disposal is intended, amongst other things, to ensure that all beneficiaries are treated equally. The actual date of transfer by the trustees is then irrelevant.

[7.10] Sometimes, the trustees will be able to hold over a gain when a beneficiary becomes beneficially entitled (see 7.60–7.74) – and it matters not if the trust is settlor-interested. Where hold-over is available to the trustees, they should protect themselves against the recapture of the relief should the beneficiary become non-UK resident within the six years following the year of his acquisition (see 5.21–5.24). It is possible for the legal ownership of the assets to be left with the trustees as security. The trustees then hold those assets as bare trustees [*TCGA 1992, s 60(2)*].

[7.11] There are decided cases on the subject of what is meant by becoming absolutely entitled as against the trustees and the reader may find help in: *Hoare Trustees v Gardner (Inspector of Taxes)* [1979] Ch 10, [1978] 1 All ER 791, Ch D; *Roome and Denne v Edwards (Inspector of Taxes)* [1982] AC 279, [1981] 1 All ER 736, HL; *Bond (Inspector of Taxes) v Pickford* [1983] STC 517, 57 TC 301, CA and *Swires (Inspector of Taxes) v Renton* [1991] STC 490, 64 TC 315, Ch D.

[7.12] The case of *Crowe v Appleby (Inspector of Taxes)* [1976] 2 All ER 914, [1976] 1 WLR 885, CA is important. Freehold property was held by trustees of a Will in equal undivided shares for the children of the deceased, upon life interest trusts. When one of the children died, the Court of Appeal held that her children had not become absolutely entitled against the trustees, despite them having attained absolute interests under the Will. This was on the basis that there were still shares in the property held in trust for the deceased's surviving children and as the property was a single indivisible asset, the children of the deceased child could not compel the trustees to transfer their share to them. Note that absolute entitlement includes a case where a person would be so entitled but for being under the age of 18 or otherwise under a disability [*TCGA 1992, s 71(3)*]. The definition of 'absolutely entitled' in *TCGA 1992, s 60(2)* shows that the right to the assets should only be subject to expenses, taxes and other outgoings. A power of appointment is not, of itself, a right to the assets. It may become one when exercised.

[7.13] In *IRC v Matthew's Executors* [1984] STC 386, 58 TC 120 trustees allocated an area of land with development potential equally among the twelve charities which were the beneficiaries. The trustees then entered into a contract for the sale of the land as agents for the beneficiaries. They told the charities later. It was held that the allocation of the land was of no effect and that the land was not held on trust for the beneficiaries absolutely as against the trustees.

[7.14] See also HMRC Statement of Practice SP 7/84, reproduced in Appendix A, for the HMRC view as to when the exercise of a power of appointment or advancement falls within the deemed disposal rules of *TCGA 1992, s 71*.

Losses

[7.15] Upon a beneficiary becoming entitled absolutely to an asset standing at a loss, which cannot be offset by the trustees against past trust gains, the loss is available to the beneficiary only for offset against a subsequent gain arising to him on disposing of that asset or, if the asset is land, on disposing of that asset or any asset derived from it [*TCGA 1992, s 71(2)*]. Before 1999, the beneficiary was able to offset trust losses which were imputed to him generally on an advance of capital against other capital gains which might arise to him in that or a future tax year.

[7.16] The *FA 1999* restriction of the loss rule under *TCGA 1992, s 71(2)* encouraged the development of an arrangement to use the trustees' losses. A person would transfer to a trust under hold-over relief business assets with a large inherent gain, having acquired the right to become a beneficiary. The trustees would then realise the assets, triggering the gain which they would offset against their own losses. There would subsequently be an advance of capital out of the trust to the transferor as a beneficiary. Now, under *TCGA 1992, s 79A* (inserted by *FA 2000, s 93*) there is a restriction of the set-off of trustees' losses against capital gains arising on the disposal by trustees of assets transferred to them, in circumstances where gains arising on that transfer have been deferred under a hold-over claim. The restriction applies where the transferor of the asset or any connected person has purchased an interest in the trust or entered into any arrangement to purchase such an interest. The rule applies for trust gains arising on or after 21 March 2000.

[7.17] Trustees, as also individuals and personal representatives, are potentially affected by an anti-avoidance rule which takes effect from 6 December 2006 [*TCGA 1992, s 16A* inserted by *FA 2007, s 27(3)*]. A loss is not an allowable loss if it accrues 'directly or indirectly in consequence of, or otherwise in connection with, any arrangements [which includes any agreement, understanding, scheme, transaction or series of transactions (whether or not legally enforceable), and the main purpose, or one of the main purposes, of the arrangements is to secure a tax advantage.' The expression 'tax advantage' is defined to mean: relief or increased relief from tax, repayment or increased repayment of tax, the avoidance or reduction of a charge to tax or an assessment to tax, or the avoidance of a possible assessment tax, and 'tax' means capital gains tax, corporation tax or income tax.

[7.18] HMRC guidance on the 2006 rules can now be found within HMRC's Manuals at CG/App9. For example, a body of trustees sell a capital asset and realise a capital gain. In the same tax year, they also sell an asset which is standing at a loss in order to crystallise that loss. The loss can be set against the gain and so no capital gains tax is payable in the year. That is Example 11 in the guidance, in which HMRC state that the losses are allowable and that there is no tax avoidance purposes: 'the tax consequences of the transactions match the real change in the economic ownership of both assets'. Again, in Example 14, trustees having realised a chargeable gain transfer a loss-making asset to a beneficiary in the same tax year. The loss which the trustees incur on the transfer of the second asset is set against the gain arising on the transfer of the first. HMRC comment that the two disposals have been made not to secure a tax advantage, but with a view to taking advantage of the statutory relief in *TCGA 1992, s 2(2)* 'in a straightforward way'. *Section 16A* will not apply and the losses will be available to set against the chargeable gain. Despite the helpfulness of the guidance, there will be many permutations of various possible structures and extreme caution is required in both effecting and reporting any transaction which may be affected by the new rule.

Appointments and distributions

[7.19] Care is needed where discretionary trustees make an appointment. If the result is a sub-trust, there is no occasion of charge (unless a sub-fund election is made: see **7.119–7.122**). However, if the appointed capital leaves the settlement, there is an occasion of charge (even though it may be possible to hold over the gain). The distinction between the two types of appointment has received judicial scrutiny and the present position is explained in Inland Revenue Statement of Practice SP 7/84 (see APPENDIX A). This distinction can still create uncertainty: see *Allfrey v Allfrey* [2015] EWHC 1717, 64 TC 315, Ch D. Generally, see CHAPTER 19 for the capital gains tax and other tax implications of capital leaving a trust.

[7.20] In a protective trust, the principal beneficiary's interest can be forfeited by his seeking to anticipate income, to borrow against his interest and so on. The termination of the life interest in such a case is ignored for capital gains tax.

Demergers

[7.21] Demergers make use of the provisions in *CTA 2010, ss 1073–1099*, formerly *ICTA 1988, ss 213–218*. The first were, probably, BAT Industries PLC and the demergers of Argos PLC and Arjo Wiggins Appleton PLC and, secondly the Racal/Vodafone demerger. Then came ICI and Zeneca. There is a line of trust cases in which the courts held that, for anything of value to come from a company as capital, it must be capital under company law (eg a liquidation, a reduction of capital). Anything else must be income. Very probably there is an income connection in that companies do put profits to reserve and it is accumulations of past profits which provide the capital for growth or for a distribution which looks like capital to the recipient. The purchaser of shares looks upon the company's reserves as being capital and they will be reflected, in a way, in the price paid for the shares. From his viewpoint any distribution which is not a dividend must be capital.

[7.22] When demergers were devised, it was commonly thought that the demerged shares were income and belonged to the life tenant. This was unreal when over 40% of the value might be in the demerged shares. However, the ICI/Zeneca demerger was unique in that ICI PLC transferred the Zeneca business to Zeneca PLC in exchange for that company issuing its shares to the holders of shares in ICI PLC. This has become known as an indirect demerger, in contrast to a direct demerger where the principal company distributes shares in a subsidiary to its shareholders. The indirect demerger of Zeneca PLC was considered in *Lee, Re, Sinclair v Lee* [1993] 3 All ER 926, Ch D. The court was able to distinguish indirect demergers and to hold that the shares in Zeneca PLC would be capital. In the judgment it was said that if the earlier decisions 'would produce a result manifestly inconsistent with the presumed intention of the testator or settlor, the court should not be required to apply them slavishly. In origin they were guidelines . . . '.

[7.23] Trustees have to decide how to account for the demerged shares. In a direct demerger will they hand the demerged shares over to the life tenant? If they do, there is no question of a charge under *TCGA 1992, s 71* because they are owned by the life tenant *ab initio* and they never form part of the trust capital. There has been no disposal by the trustees. There is no suggestion that the life tenant should be assessed to income tax on the value of the shares. If on a direct demerger the life tenant is entitled to the shares, his base value is the market value at the date of the demerger [*TCGA 1992, s 17*]. If, on an indirect demerger, the life tenant receives the demerged shares then, again, there is no disposal by the trustees and the life tenant has a nil acquisition value [*Section 17(2)*]. This must be exceptional perhaps because the law of the trust is not that of England or because there is a clause permitting the trustees to ignore case law in allocating special distributions, etc. The base value of the shares in the old company is undisturbed.

[7.24] If the trustees retain the shares, then it will be with the acquiescence, at the least, of the life tenant and that must amount to a settlement by him. That will not affect the income tax position. If the settlement resulted in a gain exceeding the life tenant's £11,100 annual exemption (for 2015/16 and 2016/17), etc then that would trigger a charge on the life tenant. That probably means that in small cases the trustees will retain the demerged shares without there being any immediate tax consequences. They would have to be sure that there was general agreement among the family of course. The HMRC view is fully explained in the October 1994 edition of their *Tax Bulletin*, Issue 13, p 162.

Termination of a qualifying life interest

[7.25] The termination of a qualifying life interest is a deemed disposal if it results from a death or if the consequence is that a beneficiary becomes absolutely entitled against the trustees. The rules set out in this paragraph and in 7.26–7.31 apply only to 'qualifying' interests in possession which are treated for inheritance tax as though the beneficiary were entitled to the underlying assets. They do not apply to cases where there is an interest in possession, as a right to receive income, which is not a 'qualifying' interest: see 7.31. Termination can also occur when an original life tenant buys out the remainderman and so becomes absolutely entitled to the settled property. In such a case there is a charge on the trustees under *TCGA 1992, s 71(1)* and market value will be substituted for the consideration which would, in any case, have gone to the remainderman. The remainderman is not chargeable. There is no charge under *section 76(2)*. A similar situation emerges if the remainderman buys out the life tenant. The identification of assets subject to an interest in possession is explained in SP D10 as amended (see APPENDIX A).

[7.26] Termination on death is in principle a no gain/no loss situation. Normally the base values of those assets which supported the life interest are changed to the market value at the date of death. If the life interest is in part of a fund, then this provision applies to an appropriate part. Where the property reverts to the settlor, there is no chargeable gain, but the deemed disposal is at a value such as to ensure that neither a gain nor a loss arises to the trustees (ie not at market value) [*TCGA 1992, ss 71–73*].

Example

Two sisters, Anne and Kate, are life tenants of a single block of shares with a base value of £50,000. Anne dies when the market value is £100,000. The trustees' base value alters as follows:

	£
Old base value of one half (Kate's share)	25,000
Base value of one half on Anne's death	50,000
Revised base value of holding	75,000

The base value of each individual holding alters because the proportion attributable to the life interest of the deceased life tenant is updated [*TCGA 1992, s 72(1)*].

[7.27] There are interests in possession which are not life interests within the definition in *TCGA 1992, s 72*. For instance, a beneficiary might have an interest in the income which terminates on his reaching a particular age. Since 1996 (and 1993 by concession) the death of such a beneficiary has been treated in the same way as the death of a beneficiary having a life interest [*TCGA 1992, ss 72 and 73*]. Accrued but unrealised gains and losses are effectively cancelled by the capital gains tax-free rebasing to market value at death.

[7.28] Sometimes the trust instrument requires assets to be appropriated to a capital beneficiary on the death of one of two life tenants. Therefore, until the appropriation is made it is not known what is the 'corresponding part' mentioned in *TCGA 1992, s 72(1)(a)*. In such a case the base value of each individual holding is not altered as in the Anne and Kate illustration above. Instead it is the base value of the appropriated assets which alters. So, for instance, if trustees had holdings of equal value in two companies and the life tenant of one half of the settlement died, given a power of appropriation, they could appropriate one holding. Only that holding's base value would change. See CG37530–37532.

[7.29] Where trust assets were received subject to hold-over relief, the held-over gain is brought into charge on the death of the life tenant [*TCGA 1992, s 74*]. If possible, the trustees will hold over this amount a second time under either *section 260* or *section 165*: it is only where a UK domiciled surviving spouse/civil partner inherits non-business assets that a further hold-over claim will not be possible. If the deceased was UK domiciled for inheritance tax purposes but the survivor was not (nor deemed to be under the terms of a post-death election under *IHTA 1984, ss 267ZA and 267ZB*), there will be a chargeable transfer enabling a *section 260* election [*IHTA 1984,* *s 18(2)*]. The base value will then be the value at death reduced by the amount held over. If hold-over is not possible, the trustees were on a disposal before (but not since) 6 April 2008 able to benefit from:

(i) re-basing. Effectively this meant that there was no charge under *section 74* if the gain was held over prior to 1 April 1982; or
(ii) the half-gain rule (see **7.96** and **6.82** of the 19th edition of this book).

[7.30] The clawback on death is a reasonable precaution so far as HMRC is concerned. Their worry would be the use of elderly people of little means as life tenants purely so as to wash out a capital gain. See CG36510–CG36513 for the hold-over of a clawed-back gain, including two examples.

[7.31] The introduction from 22 March 2006 of the current inheritance tax regime for trusts (generally see CHAPTERS **9** and **10**) has some consequential effects for capital gains tax. These are found in *FA 2006, Sch 20, Pt 4*, which amends the relevant *TCGA 1992* provisions. The treatment of the termination of a life interest on the death of the beneficiary given by *TCGA 1992, s 72* is modified from 22 March 2006. Only certain life interests will, on termination, attract the treatment described at **7.25** and **7.26**. These are cases where there is a 'qualifying' interest in possession, ie:

(a) the termination of an interest in possession in being at 22 March 2006;
(b) the termination of a 'transitional serial interest' (see **8.17–8.22**);
(c) the termination of a disabled person's interest (see **15.7–15.11**);
(d) the termination of an 'immediate post-death interest' arising under a Will (see **8.8**) and
(e) the termination of a life interest arising under a trust for bereaved minors (again, see **8.9–8.12**).

Otherwise, the termination of a life interest will fall within the 'relevant property' regime for inheritance tax – and this will comprise the majority of such trusts created since 22 March 2006. The principles set out at **7.6–7.14** will apply in the event that someone becomes absolutely entitled to the settled property as against the trustees; otherwise, there will be no capital gains tax implications (and, in particular, no opportunity for capital gains tax-free uplift of the base cost to market value).

[7.32] For the position in relation to a disabled trust see CHAPTER **15**.

Rate of tax

[7.33] For disposals on or after 23 June 2010, and up to and including 2015/16, a fixed rate of 28% has applied to trustees and personal representatives.

[7.34] For 2016/17 the fixed rate has reduced to 20% for most disposals; however, the 28% rate remains for disposals of residential property that do not qualify for private residence relief, and for disposals of the share of gains made by private equity fund managers (so called "carried interests").

[7.35] The capital gains tax rate for trustees is disapplied, subject to an election, in the case of trusts for the most vulnerable: see **15.16**.

The annual exemption

[7.36] Trustees are entitled to an exemption equal to half that of an individual, £5,550 (= ½ of £11,100) for 2015/16 and 2016/17. Where there is a group of settlements made by the same settlor, the annual exemption for each is the amount obtained by dividing half the individual's exemption by the number of settlements, but with a minimum of one-tenth of the individual's exemption for each of them (ie £1,110). For this purpose 'settlor' is defined in *TCGA 1992, s 68A*. When counting the number of settlements the taxpayer can exclude non-UK resident settlements, charitable settlements and trusts of registered pension schemes and the like [*TCGA 1992, Sch 1, para 2(7)*]. He should however include any settlor-interested trust and a trust of a term life policy taken out for inheritance tax protection. This sharing of exemptions does not apply to settlements made before 7 June 1978. Those settlements each have a £5,550 exemption for 2015/16 and 2016/17 [*TCGA 1992, Sch 1, para 2(5)*]. A disabled person's trust has the full individual exemption [*TCGA 1992, Sch 1, para 1*]. The annual exemptions are index-linked [*TCGA 1992, s 3(3)*]. This index-linking can be prevented by Parliament and has been so prevented. When not prevented the index-linking takes place by reference to the September of the preceding fiscal year.

[7.37] Is a settlement of a funded unapproved retirement benefit scheme (FURBS) a 'qualifying settlement' for anti-fragmentation purposes? Typically, a company establishing such a FURBS will ensure that each employee has a settlement of which the discretionary beneficiaries will be himself and various members of his family. According to HMRC, if the employer has made any contribution to the scheme which is not taxable on the employee (for example expenses of administering or setting up the unapproved scheme), it will be a qualifying pension scheme and therefore an 'excluded settlement' within *TCGA 1992, Sch 1, para 2(7)*. This will almost certainly have been the case and the existence of such a settlement for any particular employee will not therefore affect the exemption available to other settlements which he may have established and the trustees of the FURBS settlement will be entitled to the full annual exemption of £5,550 for 2015/16 and 2016/17.

[7.38] Where an estate is in course of administration and will, in due time, become a trust, the personal representatives have an annual exempt amount equal to that of an individual. This is restricted to the year of death and the next two years of assessment [*TCGA 1992, s 3(7)*]. If the administration continues beyond that period then, until a trust is set up, there is no annual exemption at all.

[7.39] If there are separate funds within one trust, this does not mean that there are two taxpayers. There may well be two files with HMRC because there are, say, two funds, one for a discretionary, the other for a life tenant's fund. He will often start by making two assessments but this is wrong. One trust is one taxpayer for capital gains tax (subject to making a sub-funds election from 2006/07: see **7.118–7.122**). There can be fiduciary problems where there are separate funds. Should the trustees take a loss in one fund and set it against a gain in another without compensation, for instance?

Allowable expenditure

Base values at death

[7.40] Where the disposal is of assets acquired by inheritance on death, the acquisition value of the assets is market value at death [*TCGA 1992, s 62(1)*]. If the value of an asset in the deceased's estate has been ascertained for capital transfer tax or inheritance tax, that is the market value at the date of death [*TCGA 1992, s 274*]. The word 'ascertained' is important. If no inheritance tax is due, HMRC Trusts & Estates will close their file without agreeing anything. In such a case the value has not been ascertained. Since 1992 there has been an increase in the number of cases where there has been no negotiation with either the District Valuer or the Shares Valuation Division because the maximum rate of business and agricultural property relief have been increased to 100%. Where there is no such negotiation, that will inevitably alter the basis on which the acquisition value of shares (or other relevant business property) and of agricultural property held by the trustees of the Will is calculated. The application of *section 274* can bring benefits to the taxpayer, in circumstances where for example the effect of the related property provisions of *IHTA 1984, s 161* can be to increase the value over and above market value. Where no value has been ascertained for inheritance tax purposes, it is market value which must be established [*TCGA 1992, s 272*].

[7.41] When the asset is listed shares or units in an authorised unit trust and the market has fallen in the year following death, the executors may well have taken advantage of the relief for the sale of shares from the deceased's estate contained in *IHTA 1984, ss 178–189*. An election for that relief results in the substitution of gross proceeds of sale for the original market value at death. Cancellation or suspension of a quotation can be treated as a sale where the death occurs on or after 16 March 1992 [*IHTA 1984, ss 186A, 186B*]. The resulting revised probate value also becomes the ascertained value for *TCGA 1992, s 274*. A small capital gains tax loss must always result. This is because the revised base value is the gross proceeds of sale. The disposal for capital gains tax is the net proceeds of sale. The loss is therefore the difference, ie the dealing costs.

[7.42] A similar relief operates on the sale of land during the four years following the death, albeit subject to more complex conditions [*IHTA 1984, ss 190–198*]. Note that (in the view of the author) the revaluation rule for inheritance tax can apply where, within three (not four) years after death, there is a sale of the land for a consideration lower than *or* greater than market value at death, provided that an inheritance tax value has to be 'ascertained', that is some inheritance tax is or may be payable. This principle was affirmed in *Stonor & Mills (Dickinson's Executors) v IRC* (SpC 288) [2001] STC (SCD) 199, although the taxpayer was unsuccessful in securing relief in that case, as the residuary beneficiaries were charities and so there was no inheritance tax issue. However, HMRC have announced that in their view the revaluation rule will, as with the corresponding rule for sales of listed shares and units in authorised unit trusts, within 12 months after death, apply only where the sale is made at a loss. Specifically, HMRC consider that in *Stonor* the Special Commissioner implied that a revaluation could occur only where the sale was made at a loss. Of course, it could be equally possible to argue that any increase in value post-death is just that. In such a case, any increase would be subject to capital gains tax. In any case where the increase in the value of the land as at the date of death is subject to a 40% inheritance tax charge, it is likely to be cheaper to adopt this view (and pay the capital gains tax); however, personal representatives also need to be aware that they are under a duty to correct any errors in an inheritance tax return and they will therefore need to take a view as to whether any increase in value is a real post-death increase, or simply reflective of an initial 'date of death' valuation which was too low.

Expenses

[7.43] Personal representatives can add the costs of obtaining probate to the probate value in calculating their base value for capital gains tax (*IRC v Executors of Dr Richards* [1971] 1 All ER 785, [1971] 1 WLR 571, HL). A scale has been published in Inland Revenue Statement of Practice SP 2/04 following meetings between the Board of HMRC and professional bodies, so that a reasonable figure can be added to the probate value without the necessity of agreeing the actual costs incurred. SP 2/04 is reproduced in APPENDIX A.

[7.44] Allowable expenditure includes expenditure on enhancement of value and on establishing title etc [*TCGA 1992, s 38(1)(b)*]. That subsection refers to expenditure by the owner and is strictly interpreted by HMRC. Therefore, for instance, although the executors may claim the probate costs (as in the *Richards' Executors* case), they would not be available to a legatee.

[7.45] The costs of valuation are incidental to a disposal and so are an allowable expense [*TCGA 1992, s 38(2)(b)*]. HMRC regard only the costs of making a valuation (and any necessary appointment for tax purposes) as being within the *section*. The costs of negotiating a value with the District Valuer or Shares Valuation Division will therefore be disallowed. This principle was confirmed by a 1997 valuation case (*Caton's Administrators v Couch* [1997] STC 970, CA). Incidental costs of trustees could include the cost of varying a settlement so as to produce a termination and fees in respect of discharges (but not insurance premiums and not bank trust company's withdrawal fees except as covered by an agreement with the clearing banks). See the *HMRC Capital Gains Manual* at CG15260 and CG16615.

Interaction with inheritance tax

[7.46] Generally speaking, inheritance tax and capital gains tax are 'chalk' and 'cheese', taxing as they do different events, and do not overlap. However, there is one circumstance where a credit for inheritance tax paid is available to reduce a chargeable gain, namely where a disposal on which hold-over relief is claimed is also a chargeable transfer for inheritance tax and inheritance tax is paid. There can be a charge to inheritance tax on the making of a settlement. This may be because of the premature death of the settlor who has made a potentially exempt transfer (typically, before 22 March 2006). It can be because the gift to the trustees is an immediately chargeable transfer. Whatever the reason and whether the inheritance tax is paid by the settlor or by the trustees, it is effectively treated as part of the trustees' base value [*TCGA 1992, s 165(10), s 260(7)*].

[7.47] Note that:

(a) capital transfer tax was treated in the same manner;
(b) the inheritance tax is discounted if it would otherwise result in a capital gains tax loss on disposal. The result will be a no gain/no loss situation;
(c) the gift by the settlor must have been made after 5 April 1980; and
(d) if the inheritance tax was paid on the making of the settlement and the settlor dies within seven years, an additional assessment will be made on the trustees. This also attracts the relief.

Where a donor settles shares but there is no capital gain at the time of the gift, could he simply go through the motions of making a claim under *TCGA 1992, s 165*, so that if the trustees have to pay any inheritance tax it can be added to the base value of the shares? It is thought that this question must be answered negatively, simply because both hold-over relief sections seem to be drawn on the basis that a chargeable gain is produced by the disposal.

EXAMPLE

On 1 March 2008 Harry settled a business asset worth £500,000 on a qualifying interest in possession trust. He elected for hold-over relief, with the result that the trustees inherit his acquisition cost of £250,000. The transfer to the settlement is potentially exempt, but Harry died on 1 March 2011 (making the transfer chargeable). The clawback under *IHTA 1984, s 113A* retrospectively denies business property relief (as the trustees were no longer using the asset for business purposes when Harry died). The trustees pay the inheritance tax due (on the footing that no part of Harry's nil-rate band for inheritance tax at death was available in respect of the gift to the trustees). The trustees sold the asset in 2013/14 for £600,000, producing a chargeable gain as follows:

	£	£	£
Sale proceeds			600,000
Original market value	500,000		
Gain held over	(250,000)	250,000	
Inheritance tax at 40% on £500,000		200,000	
			(450,000)
Chargeable gain			£150,000

Taper relief (for disposals before 2008/09)

[7.48] The taper relief, for disposals after 5 April 1998, applied to trustees and personal representatives just as it did to individuals. The relief was repealed from 2008/09, so that any taper accrued but not realised as at 6 April 2008 is effectively been forfeited. Where the relief applied, a chargeable gain was tapered according to the length of time the asset had been (or was deemed to have been) held. The steepness of the taper depended upon whether the asset was a business asset or a non-business asset, the maximum rate of taper being achieved after ten years for non-business assets and (since 6 April 2002) two years for business assets, reduced from four years for disposals on or after 6 April 2000. Non-business assets acquired (or deemed to have been acquired) before 17 March 1998 qualified for an addition of one year to the period of whole years for which they are held after 5 April 1998. For trustees and personal representatives, the maximum rate of taper resulted in a tax rate, for 2007/08, of 10% in relation to business assets and 26% for non-business assets held at 17 March 1998 (ie attracting the 'bonus year'). There was apportionment in any case where the use of an asset changed over the period of ownership.

[7.49] For an overview of taper relief as it applied to trustees readers are referred to **6.16–6.21** of the 19th edition of this book. In the course of 2009/10 there was a significant First-tier Tribunal decision relating to a controversial mixed use issue which, albeit not involving trustees, deserves mention.

[7.50] The issue is the application of taper relief on a gain arising on the disposal of a single asset which was used both for main residence purposes (subject to relief from capital gains tax) and, in this case, as an hotel or indeed any other business use. Mr and Mrs Jefferies agreed with HMRC that the hotel had been used as to 65% for private occupation and as to 35% for business purposes. 65% of the gain was therefore wholly relieved under *TCGA 1992, s 223(1)*. The taxpayers argued that the gain attributable to business purposes attracted full business assets taper and therefore was subject to an effective rate of tax of 10%. HMRC on the other hand contended that the business gain should be further split 35/65, with the appropriate rates of business and non-business taper applied accordingly to the resulting figures. The Tribunal Judge took a pragmatic approach, noting that HMRC's argument created an anomalous result whereby the portion of the business gain was treated as arising from the non-business proportion of the asset, which had already been excluded from charge under *section 223*. She applied the specific requirement in *paragraph 21 of TCGA 1992, Sch A1* that apportionment for taper relief purposes should be made on 'a just and reasonable basis', deciding that the whole of the business gain should be treated as eligible for business asset taper relief (*Jefferies (I S and A L) v Revenue and Customs Comrs* [2009] UKFTT 291 (TC), [2010] SFTD 189, [2010] SWTI 234).

Main residence relief

[7.51] The familiar main residence relief for individuals is extended to trustees by *TCGA 1992, s 225*. Provided that during all or part of the trustees' period of ownership, the dwelling-house is occupied as his only or main residence by a person entitled to do so under the terms of the settlement, the provisions of *ss 222–224* are applied to the trustees' gain. On a disposal after 9 December 2003, no relief is given under *section 225* where the gain on entry of the asset to the settlement was held over under *section 260* (though not under *section 165*, eg where the property concerned qualified as furnished holiday accommodation). While, prior to 22 March 2006, there were planning opportunities presented by the combination of the *section 165* hold-over and *section 225* main residence relief, these have now disappeared following enactment of the present inheritance tax regime for trusts [*FA 2006, Sch 20*]. This is because practically every lifetime transfer into trust will be a chargeable transfer for inheritance tax purposes and so will attract *section 260* hold-over, which takes priority over *section 165* hold-over [*TCGA 1992, s 165(3)(d)*].

[7.52] *Section 225* relief depends upon occupation of the house by a beneficiary by virtue of entitlement under the settlement, which would include the exercise of powers given to the trustees. However, relief would not extend to the case where the trustees grant a tenancy of the property to an individual under their powers of management in the settlement deed, so that the individual, albeit a beneficiary, occupies as a tenant rather than as a beneficiary. This point was at the heart of the dispute in *Wagstaff v Revenue and Customs Comrs*, [2014] UKFTT 43 (TC), [2014] WTLR 547. HMRC argued that the arrangements between the parties amounted to the creation of a tenancy, but the First-tier Tribunal preferred the taxpayer's arguments that they created a trust. HMRC accept that a beneficiary occupying as such, and not as a tenant, can pay rent to the trustees for the occupation of the house without prejudicing the future application of main residence relief to the trust. Such a payment could, for example, be useful either to meet expenses of maintaining the property or indeed to compensate other beneficiaries under the settlement.

[7.53] If there is any question of a main residence election being made under *section 222(5)(a)*, it must be the subject of a joint notice by the trustees and the beneficiary. The interesting thing about *section 225* is that there is no pro rata test. That means that where, whether in an interest in possession or a discretionary trust, there is is more than one beneficiary, occupation by just one of them can secure the relief for the whole gain accruing on disposal of the dwelling house.

[7.54] The case of *Sansom v Peay (Inspector of Taxes)* [1976] 3 All ER 375, [1976] 1 WLR 1073, Ch D established that *section 225* relief is available in a case where trustees permit a beneficiary to live in a house belonging to a discretionary settlement. In this case the power to permit beneficiaries to live in a dwelling held within the settlement was 'for such period and generally upon such terms as the trustees in their discretion think fit'. The trustees bought a house and permitted beneficiaries to occupy it as their principal place of residence. The question was raised as to whether they occupied the house as of right or only at the trustees' discretion. The judgment showed that there had been a valid exercise of a power and that the beneficiaries were entitled to occupy the house as of right until permission was withdrawn. Accordingly, the main residence exemption was available to the trustees on selling the house at a gain [*TCGA 1992, ss 222, 225*]. If it was intended that a beneficiary shall have a permanent home, then this could before 22 March 2006 have caused inheritance tax problems by creating an interest in possession. This subject is further discussed in Inland Revenue Statement of Practice SP 10/79 (see APPENDIX A).

[7.55] There has over recent years been some professional discussion, especially on the Trusts Discussion Forum, about the availability of *section 225* relief in the case where the trustees own only a part interest in the house or flat. This might arise in a situation where husband and wife together own the matrimonial home and the husband dies leaving his share on trusts which has the inheritance tax effect that the substantive value is not aggregated with the wife's estate on the second death. The wife continues to occupy the house alone, being a co-owner with the trustees. Traditionally most professional advisers would have said that on a sale of the house at a gain the trustees should obtain main residence relief under *section 225* given that a beneficiary, ie the wife, has occupied it throughout her period of ownership under the terms of the settlement. However, a potential problem is presented by the *Trusts of Land and Appointment of Trustees Act 1996, s 12*. There has been a concern that under the statutory trust of land the trustees themselves do not have a right to occupy the land and therefore have no such right which they can confer on a beneficiary. Assume that the prospective occupying beneficiary were other than the widow, it would follow on this basis that he or she could enter into occupation only on the basis of a personal licence from the widow, which then would hardly satisfy the conditions for *section 225* relief. Until publication of the article referred to at 7.56, the better view seemed to be that main residence relief should be available to the trustees in such a situation where the terms of the settlement give the widow a right to occupy under an interest in possession, (albeit not a 'qualifying interest in possession' for inheritance tax purposes), but not where the trusts are discretionary.

[7.56] In the case where the trustees of a discretionary Will trust co-owned the house with a widow/widower, granting a licence to occupy to her/him, clear confirmation of HMRC's view is found from an article in *Trusts and Estates Law & Tax Journal* May 2009 by Gill Steel and Richard Dew. HMRC stated that, whether the trust is discretionary or interest in possession in form, their position is that the trustees still have rights of occupation as co-owners. It appears therefore that in neither case is *TLATA 1996, s 12* an impediment to giving relief under *TCGA 1992, s 225* if the trustees have the power to allow occupation under the terms of the settlement. Remember that if the Will does provide for a discretionary structure and the circumstances are such that an immediate post-death interest (IPDI: see 8.8) arises in the two years following death, the reading back provisions of *IHTA 1984, s 144(3)* inserted by *FA 2006* will result in a spouse-exempt IPDI arising on death. As a non-tax point, such a discretionary structure, typically where the widow is not the only occupant of the house, that is someone else (whether or not a member of the family) lives there to look after her, is helpful in the context of the care home fees issue. The value of the house owned by the Will trustees which the widow occupies is effectively nil. These observations apply equally to a civil partnership and a surviving civil partner.

[7.57] There has, over the last four or five years, been a significant number of cases before the First-tier Tribunal on eligibility for main residence relief, albeit involving individuals and none involving trustees. The principles affirmed by those cases are of interest in establishing the requirements of entitlement to the relief, where the disposal is made by trustees just as where it is made by an individual. The key theme that has emerged from these cases, is that intention of the occupier is central when determining whether a property is occupied as a 'residence'. In *Fox v Stirk; Ricketts v Registration Officer for the City of Cambridge*[1970] 2 QB 463, [1970] 3 All ER 7, CA, Lord Widgery described a residence as '...a place where a man is based or where he continues to live, the place where he sleeps and shelters and has his home . . . ' and where there is ' . . . some assumption of permanence, some degree of continuity, some expectation of continuity...'. It is the need for this 'assumption' and this 'expectation' that enables the intentions of the parties to be considered.

[7.58] The significance of being able to evidence a qualifying period of occupation is that, as relevant also to trustee ownership and disposals, there may be relieved from capital gains tax not only the gain attributable to the actual period of occupation but also the gain attributable to the final few months (see 7.59) of ownership [*TCGA 1992, s 223(2)*], to a qualifying period of letting [*section 223(4)*] and to a qualifying period of absence [*section 223(3), 3A* and *3B*] or indeed a delay of up to 12 months after acquisition in taking up occupation (Extra-statutory Concession D49).

[7.59] Until 2014/15, the gain attributable to the final 36 months of ownership of any property which qualified for main residence relief would be relieved. This was reduced to 18 months from 2014/15 but subject to two caveats:

- Where contracts are exchanged before 6 April 2014, the 36 month exemption will apply as long as the conveyance is made before 6 April 2015.
- Where a disposal is made by a disabled person (as defined in *FA 2005, Sch 1A*), or a long-term resident in a care home (or their spouse or civil partner), the final period of exemption will remain at 36 months [*TCGA 1992, s 225E*]. A 'long-term resident in a care home' is someone who is resident in, or can reasonably be expected to be resident in, an establishment that provides accommodation together with nursing or personal care for at least three months. This extended period does not apply where the relevant individual has an interest in another dwelling house (or an entitlement to occupy a dwelling house under a trust) where main residence relief would be available.

Hold-over relief

[7.60] There are two principal heads of hold-over: *section 165* for business assets (see 7.62–7.70) and *section 260* for chargeable transfers etc for inheritance tax purposes (see 7.72–7.82). Where both heads could apply, *section 260* takes priority (*TCGA 1992, s 165(3)(d)*). However, with effect from 10 December 2003, a gain arising on a transfer to a settlor-interested trust (or to a trust which becomes settlor-interested within broadly six years) can no longer be held over (see 7.81).

[7.61] Neither head of hold-over relief is generally available unless the transferee is UK resident. The one exception to this rule is in relation to gifts of UK residential property interest on or after 6 April 2015 [*TCGA 1992, s 261ZA*]. This topic is covered in more detail at 5.21–5.24.

Business assets

[7.62] The settlor can settle defined business property and hold over the gain [*TCGA 1992, s 165(4),(5), Sch 7*]. For years up to and including 2002/03, business property was defined in similar terms to property which qualified for retirement relief. As from 2003/04, with the demise of retirement relief, the taper relief definitions were imported into hold-over relief. As from 2008/09, with the repeal of taper relief, the relevant definitions (as drawn from taper relief) find their way into a new *section 165A* positioned, it may be observed, just where they belong in the context of hold-over relief. Broadly, 'business assets' are trading assets and shares in trading companies.

[7.63] The status of property let as qualifying furnished holiday accommodation was to have changed for capital gains tax (and income tax) purposes from 2010/11, as announced at Budget 2009. No longer would it have been deemed as a trade and therefore would no longer qualify for business assets hold-over. Meanwhile, since 2009/10, the deemed trading treatment applies not just to property in the UK but to property situated throughout the European Economic Area. However, *clause 65* of *Finance Bill 2010* which would have affected the repeal was withdrawn before Royal Assent was given on 7 April 2010 and the Chancellor's Budget statement on 22 June 2010 confirmed that deemed trading treatment would continue. That said, however, the availability of the reliefs has been tightened up, following a consultation document issued on 27 July 2010. In particular, from 2011/12 no longer is sideways loss relief available, to offset furnished holiday lettings losses against general income; they can be carried forward only to set against profits from the same business, a UK business being a separate business from one carried on elsewhere in the EEA. As from 2012/13 the property has had to be available for letting to the public for 30 weeks (rather than, as previously, 20 weeks) and actually let for 15 weeks (rather than 10 weeks) in the relevant 12 month period [*FA 2011, Sch 14*].

[7.64] A gain on shares or securities which are transferred to a company cannot be held over [*TCGA 1992, s 165(3)*]. This rule does not apply in the case of disposals to a trust with a corporate trustee. The trustees of a settlement are treated for capital gains tax purposes as being a single and continuing body of persons (distinct from those who may from time to time be the trustees) [*TCGA 1992, s 69(1)*]. Therefore such a transfer is treated for all capital gains tax purposes as a transfer to trustees and not as transfer to a company (*Inland Revenue Tax Bulletin*, Issue 50, December 2000, p 815).

[7.65] Business assets intended to be used by a life tenant would not normally be settled. This is because roll-over relief [*TCGA 1992, s 152*] would not be available upon their replacement. That relief requires the assets and the trade to be in the same proprietorship.

[7.66] The word 'etc' is added to the word 'trade' to signify that professions, vocations, woodlands and agriculture are included (see *sections 165(9)* and *165A(14)*), and to 'personal company' and 'unlisted trading company' to indicate that group structures are acceptable (see *section 165A*). It is added to 'shares' to signify that securities also qualify. 'Listed' includes the AIM. (Note this is not the same treatment for inheritance tax, see **18.32**). A personal company is one where not less than 5% of the votes are exercisable by the individual. A 'trading company' is one that does not have substantial non-trading activities. Substantial is not defined but is taken to be more than 20%, as confirmed by HMRC's Capital Gains Manual at CG64090.

[7.67] Agriculture is defined by reference to the meaning for inheritance tax (see *TCGA 1992, Sch 7, para 1(1)(a)*). It is only the definition which is borrowed in this way and provisions such as those which prescribe a minimum period of ownership in order to qualify for the inheritance tax relief are not imported for the hold-over relief. Nor indeed, in a case where the 'agricultural value' of the agricultural property is less than its market value with agricultural property relief being given on the agricultural value only, is there any limitation on the amount of the gain which can be held over [*TCGA 1992, s 165(5), Sch 7*].

[7.68] As family trusts are not commonly concerned with listed companies whether on the AIM or not, the question as to whether the company is a personal company or not will rarely have to be answered except in the unusual case where assets used in a 'personal company' are transferred. The upshot is that the settlement of shares in a family company will usually be possible with the benefit of hold-over relief.

[7.69] So far as transfers by trustees are concerned, a similar result is achieved by *TCGA 1992, Sch 7, para 2*. The shareholding test is that the trustees have 25% of the votes if the company is listed (including the AIM). There is no minimum holding requirement if the company is not listed.

[7.70] Only partial hold-over is possible on a transfer of trading company shares where:

(i) the company holds assets which are not business assets (defined as not used in its trade); and
(ii) the transferor at some point in the previous 12 months held at least 25% of the votes or is an individual and the company is his personal company.

One looks at the chargeable assets of the company at the time of the disposal of the shares (see *TCGA 1992, Sch 7, para 7*). The fraction which qualifies for hold-over is:

$$\frac{\text{Company's chargeable business assets}}{\text{Company's chargeable assets}}$$

Non-business assets

[7.71] Where other (ie non-business) assets are transferred in specie, there can still be hold-over where the gift is of a work of art or other heritage asset which is:

(a) the subject of a private treaty sale to an approved museum or other body; or
(b) accepted by HMRC in lieu of tax; or

(c) the subject of a conditionally exempt transfer for inheritance tax purposes (including a gift to a maintenance fund for an historic building).

[TCGA 1992, s 258]

Chargeable transfers etc

[7.72] More important in the context of family trusts is the fact that assets may also be transferred in and out of trusts subject to hold-over in certain cases [TCGA 1992, s 260(2)], provided always that, with transfers into trust since 10 December 2003, the trust is not settlor-interested. The scope of 'settlor-interested' trusts is summarised at **4.33**. Note in particular the extension within this category from 2006/07 of settlements under which the settlor's minor unmarried children not in a civil partnership can benefit. Section 260 hold-over applies to the following cases:

(a) the disposal constitutes a chargeable transfer for inheritance tax purposes or would be if not covered by the annual £3,000 exemption. Potentially exempt transfers which fail by reason of the donor's premature death do not qualify for this hold-over relief. The inheritance tax regime for trusts introduced by FA 2006, Sch 20 from 22 March 2006 has dramatically increased the numbers of disposals for capital gains tax purposes which may attract hold-over relief under this head, as being chargeable transfers for inheritance tax purposes. This will cover not only traditional discretionary settlements, but also new interest in possession settlements (excluding, in all cases, settlor-interested trusts (see **7.81**));

(b) the disposal is a deemed chargeable transfer by reason of the property leaving a discretionary or other 'relevant property' settlement. When a discretionary legacy in a Will is closed out within the two-year period (ie so as to use *IHTA 1984, s 144*), this is not a deemed chargeable transfer and this form of hold-over relief is not available in such a case. There can be technical arguments where the personal representatives are also trustees of the Will. The personal representatives cannot exercise the discretions which will come to them as trustees until they are trustees. A well drafted Will will allow the trustees to make an appointment before residue has been ascertained (or even before application has been made for probate). The likelihood is that the appointment will be exercised shortly after the death, before there has been time for a chargeable gain arising on assets vesting absolutely, so that in a case where there is a surviving spouse/civil partner the appointment and the Inheritance Tax Account can be submitted at the same time, obviating the need to pay over inheritance tax and then reclaim it subsequently. The Chartered Institute of Taxation and HMRC have corresponded on this subject (see *Taxation Practitioner* (now *Tax Adviser*) of September 1995). The official view is that discretionary trustees can exercise their power of appointment at any time, but that there is no capital gains tax effect if this occurs before there is an assent to the trustees (see **7.117**);

There is one exception to the general principle that hold-over relief is available on a transfer out of a relevant property trust. This is where the absolute entitlement occurs either on or within one quarter following the date of a ten-year anniversary (or indeed the commencement of the trust). This is the consequence of *IHTA 1984, s 69(4)*, effectively disapplying *IHTA 1984, s 65(1)* (and *(3)* which brings in *IHTA 1984, ss 68–69*. *Section 68(3)(b)*, requiring a quarter to be counted whether complete or not, is dealing with the precise situation where the exit date follows within three months after a quarter day which is **not** a ten-year anniversary date; and

(c) the disposal is by the trustees of an accumulation and maintenance trust when a beneficiary attains the age of 18 (or, before 6 April 2008, 25) or other lower specified age, without a prior right to income (and see 7.84) [*TCGA 1992, s 260(d)*];

(d) the disposal is by the trustees of a 'bereaved minors' or 'age 18-to-25' trust [*TCGA 1992, s 260(da), (db)*].

[7.73] Transfers of relevant business property and agricultural property (as defined for inheritance tax) can attract 100% business or agricultural property relief. Where the transfer would be a chargeable transfer in the ordinary way, it is still regarded as a chargeable transfer (but no tax is payable). This means that hold-over under *section 260* is available. There will be cases where this gives a better position than that under *TCGA 1992, s 165*. This is because there can be non-business chargeable assets which restrict *section 165* but not *section 260*. Where both sections could apply, *section 260* takes precedence [*TCGA 1992, s 165(3)(d)*].

[7.74] Prior to 22 March 2006 (in particular) trustees of discretionary settlements had to have regard to the fact that, once the discretion had gone, so too had the power to hold over gains under *TCGA 1992, s 260*. Now that most post-21 March 2006 non-charitable settlements (with are not disabled trusts) will fall into the relevant property regime, together with an increasing number of pre-22 March 2006 settlements which were originally set up as either interest in possession or accumulation and maintenance trusts, the scope of *section 260* hold-over has been widened.

'Flip-flop' schemes

[7.75] *FA 2000, s 90* counteracted the so-called 'flip-flop' scheme, with effect from 21 March 2000. This scheme was intended to circumvent the settlor-interested trust rules under *TCGA 1992, s 77* by means of two trusts, the first of which would borrow cash commercially against the security of an asset (typically shares in a private company) which was to be sold at a substantial gain. Some 75% of the funds would be transferred by the trustees to the second trust which would be settlor-interested. The settlor and spouse would then be excluded from benefit under the first trust, so that when the sale was made the gain would not be assessed on the settlor and any tax on the trustees (which used to be at 23%) would be paid out of the proceeds of sale, which would also enable repayment of the bank loan (see **4.34–4.35** for a case decided in 2005 by the House of Lords in favour of HMRC). Now, if there is a transfer by trustees of funds to another person at a time when the trustees are in debt and

Hold-over relief **[7.78]**

any borrowed money is not used wholly for normal trust purposes, there will be a disposal and reacquisition of the settled property at that time [*TCGA 1992, s 76B* and *Sch 4B*]. The increase in the rate of capital gains tax to 34% effected by *FA 1998* made these schemes less attractive for UK trusts; however, they continued to be used with offshore trusts, which are also made ineffective by *FA 2000*, until *FA 2003, s 163* and *Sch 29* further closed off the planning possibilities: see **26.59–26.61**.

Relevant property settlements

[7.76] Because of the availability of *section 260* hold-over relief discretionary and other 'relevant property' settlements are very interesting to estate planners, though, since 10 December 2003, the facility for hold-over is denied where the transfer is to a settlor-interested trust (see **7.81**). The nil-rate band settlement has been with us for some time and, if annual exemptions for inheritance tax are available, this can (for 2016/17) be a settlement of £328,000, where only the current year's exemption is available, or £331,000 if the exemption for 2015/16 was unused and can be brought forward. However, the settlement of business or agricultural property with 100% business property relief or agricultural property relief is even more worthwhile.

[7.77] Because trustees can themselves make disposals with hold-over, a conduit effect can occur, assets being put into a discretionary settlement and, later, being passed to beneficiaries. This point is, of course, subject to general anti-avoidance principles and, since 10 December 2003, to the restriction that (at least, on the transfer in) the trust must not be settlor-interested (see **7.81**).

'Melville' arrangements: Mark I and Mark II (before 10 December 2003)

[7.78] While the anti-avoidance rule in *FA 2002, s 119* goes back more than six years, it is so fundamental that it is worth recording the case decided in favour of the taxpayer which led to its introduction. Before 10 December 2003 (the date of that year's pre-Budget Report) it was possible under *section 260* to hold over gains on such assets entering a discretionary settlement, even where the settlement was settlor-interested and even where the value fell within the nil-rate band for inheritance tax, because there was a chargeable transfer. Interestingly, the 1991 Inland Revenue Consultative Document on the Income Tax and Capital Gains Tax Treatment of UK Resident Trusts (withdrawn in 1993) proposed that this facility be limited to cases where an actual liability to inheritance tax arose, though this has not (yet, at least) been enacted. Of course, to the extent that the transfer into the discretionary settlement causes the settlor to exceed the nil-rate band, an actual liability to inheritance tax will arise at 20%. To avoid this unwelcome consequence, in cases where substantial value (and gains) are involved, advisers had for some years been limiting the amount of the transfer of value to within the nil-rate band by having the settlor retain valuable rights under the settlement: typically, this would be through a general power exercisable at any time after the expiry of 90 days from the date of the settlement (and before the vesting day) to require the trustees inter alia to transfer to the settlor the whole of the trust fund absolutely. In *Melville v IRC* [2000] STC 628, 74 TC 372, the High Court affirmed that this right was property within the meaning of *IHTA 1984, s 272* and that therefore on the 'estate before less estate after' principle the amount of the transfer of value was very significantly reduced from the gross value of the property transferred. The settlor would of course reserve a benefit within the meaning of *FA 1986, s 102*. However, after the expiry of the 90-day period, he would have been relieved of his right either by act of the trustees or by release by the settlor. This would be treated as a potentially exempt transfer under *section 102(4)*, with no inheritance tax consequences if the settlor survives for seven years. HMRC's appeal against this decision was rejected by the Court of Appeal on 31 July 2001 ([2001] STC 1297).

[7.79] The effect of the *Melville* decision was counteracted by *FA 2002, s 119*. The result is achieved by removing from the definition of 'property' in *IHTA 1984, s 272* the newly defined 'settlement power' such as was found in the *Melville* case. The effect is, therefore, that under the *Melville Mark I* structure, there will be a substantial initial charge to inheritance tax at 20% of the excess of the amount of the trust fund over the nil-rate band available to the settlor. Interestingly, however, it remained in principle possible (until 10 December 2003) to achieve the same object by a different discretionary structure (so-called *Melville Mark II*), eg a discretion over income for a fixed period of, say, twelve months, following which there would be an outright reversion to the settlor, albeit perhaps subject to the contingency that he was still alive at expiry of the fixed period (see **7.80**). The gift into settlement would in principle attract hold-over relief without an immediate charge to inheritance tax in the same way and during the discretionary period the settlor would give away his reversionary interest to another settlement from which he was excluded from benefit. At the end of the twelve-month period the trust fund would automatically revert to the trustees of the second settlement with the ability to hold over the gain under *section 260*. *Finance Act 2002, s 119* did also address a further aspect of the *Melville* decision by ensuring that, on the death of the settlor of a revocable settlement, the right to revoke has never been counted as property for inheritance tax purposes. That said, however, *section 119* does *not* provide that the release of such a power to revoke in the seven years before death is prevented from being a potentially exempt transfer which becomes chargeable for inheritance tax.

[7.80] There remains a particular technical issue on the effectiveness of *Melville Mark II* schemes. It may well be critical whether or not the interest of the settlor in remainder on expiry of the fixed period is contingent. There is an argument that if the settlor does not have to survive any period there is no transfer of value at all. The issue arose in a curious Special Commissioner's case, *Two Settlors v IRC* (SpC 385) [2003] STC (SCD) 45, the initial proceedings of which were struck out because the case was heard as one concerning inheritance tax and not, as the Special Commissioner ruled it should have been, capital gains tax. It is possible that another such case will come before the Courts again in a capital gains tax guise. In that case two discretionary settlements were created to receive a transfer of shares, with a view to limiting the transfer of value within the nil-rate band but claiming hold-over relief. HMRC's argument is that, if there is no transfer of value, as they contended, then there can be no hold-over claim under *section 260*.

Hold-over relief [7.82]

The 10 December 2003 restrictions

[7.81] As an effective block on *Melville Mark II*, hold-over relief is precluded, whether under *section 260* or under *section 165*, on a gain arising on a gift to a settlor-interested trust on or after 10 December 2003 [*FA 2004, Sch 21*]. The rule applies not only to gifts into trust which are settlor-interested at the time of the gift. It also catches cases where within six years after the end of the tax year in which the gift was made the settlement becomes settlor-interested, in which case there is a claw-back of the hold-over relief already given. Note that this anti-avoidance rule (found in *TCGA 1992, s 169C*) has no *pro rata* or *de minimis* limitations.

[7.82] A further restriction on the use of hold-over relief, with effect from 10 December 2003, is contained in *TCGA 1992, s 226A* (inserted by *FA 2004, Sch 22*). It is no longer possible to combine the advantages of holding over a gain on a second home into a discretionary trust with main residence relief for the gain realised by the trustees (including the held-over gain) on subsequent sale. Transitional rules preserve relief accrued before 10 December 2003 for a qualifying period of beneficiary occupation. The following example illustrating the operation of the transitional rules, is taken from paras 82–89 of the *Finance Bill Explanatory Notes* on *Sch 22*. However, *Schedule 22* does not catch the combination of *section 165* hold-over and *section 225* relief: see 18.19–18.20 for a tax planning suggestion here, although one which can no longer be used, at least in its original form, from 22 March 2006, though which, in its revised form, remains effective now that deemed trade treatment continues for furnished holiday lettings (see 18.21).

EXAMPLE – TRANSITIONAL RULE

The new provisions apply where there is a disposal of a private residence on or after 10 December 2003. However, where all the claims for gifts relief under *section 260* that affect the computation of the gain on that disposal relate to transfers made before 10 December 2003, the bar on private residence relief applies only to that part of the gain referable (on a time basis) to the period from 10 December 2003 to the date of the disposal. An example of the operation of this transitional rule is given below.

Geoffrey owned a house that he had never occupied as a residence. On 10 December 2001 it was worth £300,000, and on a disposal for that sum he would have realised a gain (before any taper relief) of £200,000 for the purposes of capital gains tax.

On 10 December 2001 Geoffrey transferred the house to the trustees of a settlement that is not a settlor-interested settlement. He claimed gifts relief and the gain of £200,000 was held over.

The trustees allowed Helen, Geoffrey's daughter, to occupy the house, under the terms of the settlement, as her only residence from 10 December 2001 to 10 December 2004. On 10 December 2011 they sold the house for £750,000 (net of incidental costs).

The trustees had a gain on the sale of £650,000 (sale proceeds £750,000 less allowable acquisition costs, net of held-over gain, of £100,000). Because their allowable expenditure was reduced as a result of Geoffrey's claim to gifts relief, they cannot cover the whole of the gain by private residence relief in respect of Helen's occupation of the house throughout their period of ownership.

But because the gifts relief related to a transfer before 10 December 2003, the transitional rule applies. Gifts relief is available to the trustees on the gain relating to the period from 10 December 2001 to 9 December 2003 (2 years).

Their total period of ownership was 10 years. So they are entitled to private residence relief of £130,000 (£650,000 × $^2/_{10}$). They remain chargeable on a gain of £520,000.

It should be noted that private residence relief is not available in respect of the period from 10 December 2008 to 10 December 2011, even though that is the final three years of their ownership of the house. The transitional rule specifically prevents any period on or after 10 December 2003 from qualifying for relief as part of the final three years of ownership.

Gifts to heritage maintenance trusts

[7.83] Before 2012/13 the making of a hold-over election by the transferor of property to a heritage maintenance fund, which was settlor-interested, depended upon the trustees having elected for the income of the fund to be taxed on them rather than to be taxed on the settlor (see **4.13**). The disadvantage of that was that when trustees made payments to the settlor for use in the house opening business, the payment was treated as a taxable receipt. From 2012/13 the settlor can claim hold-over relief on the transfer not just where the trustees have made the income tax election but also where they could make such an election [*TCGA 1992, s 169D(1)*, amended by *FA 2013, s 63(1)*]. This means that the settlor can defer the capital gains tax charge on the gift in circumstances where the trustees can reimburse the settlor for expenditure made on repairing and maintaining the heritage property without those payments constituting taxable receipts for the settlor.

Accumulation and maintenance settlements

[7.84] The reader will be aware of the dramatic changes made by *FA 2006* to the inheritance tax regime for trusts in general and to accumulation and maintenance settlements in particular, which are described in CHAPTER **11**. Now that 6 April 2008 has passed, any accumulation and maintenance settlement made before 22 March 2006 and still in being at 6 April 2008 will (with two caveats noted below) have entered the 'relevant property' regime *on that date*.

[7.85] The first caveat is that if an interest in possession arose in any part of the capital between 22 March 2006 and 6 April 2008, that share in capital will then have become subject to the relevant property regime, ie with the possibility of holding over a gain arising upon a transfer out of settlement from that point.

[7.86] The second caveat is that no hold-over is possible on an exit from the relevant property regime which occurs in a quarter beginning with the day on which the settlement commenced or with a ten-year anniversary, because there is then no chargeable transfer for inheritance tax purposes [*IHTA 1984, s 65(4)*]. This means that the cost of securing capital gains tax hold-over shortly after a ten-year anniversary is the payment of say one quarter's worth of exit charge (at a maximum rate of 0.15%). This carries the advantage for purposes of capital gains tax hold-over that, even where the trust fund comprises non-business assets, it will generally be possible to hold over any gain arising on absolute advance of the trust assets to one or more beneficiaries under *section 260* (see the last paragraph of 7.72(b)).

[7.87] There have traditionally been problems in connection with hold-over and transfers out of accumulation and maintenance settlements. Hold-over of

Hold-over relief **[7.89]**

the gain on a non-business asset is not available if the beneficiary already has a 'qualifying interest in possession' (see **8.7**). This is because the disposal has to be one which 'by virtue of *subsection (4)* of *section 71* of *IHTA 1984* does not constitute an occasion on which inheritance tax is chargeable under that section' [*TCGA 1992, s 260(2)(d)*]. When a beneficiary becomes a life tenant by reason of attaining 18 years there is neither disposal nor chargeable transfer. If he then becomes entitled to the capital at age 25, that is a disposal but not one which is within *IHTA 1984, s 71(4)*. Generally, this is a problem which will have ceased with the coming to end of the transitional period on 6 April 2008. However, conceivably, it could still be a problem for the future in the case where the absolute vesting age has been changed to 18, so as to secure continuing accumulation and maintenance status and (albeit improbably) an interest in possession arises before that age.

[7.88] As to what happened on 6 April 2008, two exceptions were mentioned above to the general principle that the relevant property regime will apply. The first is the case just mentioned where the age of vesting has been changed if necessary to age 18, in which case the protection of the accumulation and maintenance regime from the relevant property regime continues in relation to any share in the trust fund attributed to a beneficiary under the age of 18 for the time being. The second exception is when the capital entered an 'age 18-to-25 trust' (see **8.13–8.15**) on or before 5 April 2008; the trust property does not become relevant property, but is subject to an exit charge to inheritance tax on absolute entitlement under *IHTA 1984, s 71E*. Any gain arising on exit may be held over under *TCGA 1992, s 260(2)(a)*. Hold-over is available also if the beneficiary dies under the age of 18 [*TCGA 1992, s 260(2)(db)*], even though no inheritance tax charge arises.

[7.89] So far so good. The problem, however, is a technical trust point which touches on the time at which it can be said that a particular beneficiary becomes absolutely entitled as against the trustees. It will be usual for the trust deed to empower the trustees to appropriate any part of the trust fund in its actual condition towards the satisfaction of the share or interest of any person in the trust fund as the trustees shall seem just and reasonable, according to the respective rights of the persons interested in the trust fund. Until the trustees make that appropriation, the argument is that the beneficiary concerned does not have ' . . . the exclusive right . . . to direct how that asset shall be dealt with' as provided in *TCGA 1992, s 60(2)*. Therefore, in the absence of a deliberate exercise by the trustees of the power of appropriation, *IHTA 1984, s 71(1)* does not apply. This is the analysis in CG37530–1:

> 'If the trustees have an express power to decide which assets should go to a beneficiary in satisfaction of his or her beneficial interest, no beneficiary should be regarded as having becoming absolutely entitled to the appropriate share of any such assets until the last contingency is fulfilled. . . .
>
> If, however, the trustees, before the last contingency, appropriate specific assets to a beneficiary whose share has vested, there is a *Section 71(1)* occasion of charge in relation to those assets at the date of appropriation. The reason for this is that if the trustees have an express power of appropriation they can decide which assets a particular beneficiary is to receive as his entitlement. Until this power is exercised, the beneficiary cannot claim any specific asset and therefore it cannot be said that he or she is absolutely entitled to a fractional share of everything'.

[7.90] This point may come as some surprise to practitioners, as possibly representing a change of practice within HMRC. The argument against this view would seem to be that a power of appropriation is an administrative power only and not a dispositive power, which was supported by the High Court decision in *Sutton v England* [2009] EWHC 3270 (Ch), [2010] WTLR 335, although reversed by the Court of Appeal, but without touching on that specific point (see **2.26–2.28**). Of course, if the HMRC view is applied to its logical conclusion, any assets to which the beneficiary is presumptively entitled having attained the age of absolute entitlement will remain settled property for capital gains tax purposes until such time (if ever!) as the trustees exercise their power of appropriation. The moral is, for trustees wanting to ensure a valid hold-over claim, that on or before the date of absolute entitlement the relevant appropriation is made. If, during the discretionary period, the trust fund has been appropriated to different shares within the settlement, each called, for example, the 'appointed fund' of one of the children prospectively entitled, the worrying point raised in **7.89** does not arise.

The claim

[7.91] The usual rules for making a hold-over election apply, now on Helpsheet HS 295. Note the need to specify whether the claim is made under *TCGA 1992, s 165* or under *s 260*. For claims before 1 April 2010, the time limit is five years and ten months from the end of the year of assessment in which the disposal was made [*TMA 1970, s 43(1)*]. With effect from 1 April 2010, the time limit has been reduced to four years from the end of the year of assessment. (*FA 2008, Sch 39, para 12* and *The Finance Act 2008 Schedule 39 (Appointed Day, Transitional Provisions and Savings) Order 2009, SI 2009/403, art 10*). A claim once made cannot be amended after 12 months have expired from the date of the claim, though no amendment may be made while there is an outstanding enquiry [*TMA 1970, Sch 1A, para 3*]. The moral of this strict rule is that care should be taken on the timing of a hold-over claim if there is any doubt as to whether it should be made, recognising that if made after the due date for payment of the capital gains tax, the tax will first have to be paid and then recovered on the making of a subsequent hold-over claim. (There is also power in *paragraph 3* for HMRC to give notice to the claimant to amend the claim so as to correct any obvious errors or mistakes.)

Anti-avoidance rules for non-UK residents

[7.92] Hold-over relief is not available to transfers to non-UK residents [*TCGA 1992, ss 166, 261*] or to foreign-controlled companies [*TCGA 1992, s 167*].

[7.93] In addition, any previously held-over gains will crystallise if the donee(s) become(s) non-UK resident or cease(s) to be liable to UK tax as a result of becoming dual resident for the purposes of a double tax treaty, in either case within six years after the end of the year of assessment in which the transfer under hold-over took place. See **5.21–5.24** and **26.12** [*TCGA 1992, ss 80, 83, 168, 288(1)*].

Instalment relief

[7.94] In certain cases where a disposal made by way of gift does bear capital gains tax and no hold-over claim is available, the tax may be paid by equal instalments over ten years. There is no interest exemption, ie interest accrues on the unpaid tax and the interest to date must be added to each instalment. The instalment cases are where the asset is:

(a)   land (or an interest in land);
(b)   a controlling shareholding;
(c)   any other shares or securities not listed on a recognised stock exchange (for example, OFEX).

[TCGA 1992, s 281]

The potential for double taxation

[7.95] The avowed intention of the restrictions on hold-over explained above was to ensure that gifts were not, in effect, exempted from both capital taxes by being potentially exempt transfers and disposals sheltered by hold-over at the same time. Unfortunately, a form of double taxation now arises. It is possible to make a gift which is not subject to hold-over and so capital gains tax is paid; the donor does not pay inheritance tax at the time (perhaps it is a potentially exempt transfer), but because of the donor's premature death (within seven years) the donee does have to pay that tax. The capital gains tax will reduce the donor's estate and to that extent there will be no double counting. However, the total tax which is related to the one gift can be substantial. Perhaps this will encourage the making of gifts where the donee pays the capital gains tax. This has the effect of reducing the amount of the chargeable transfer for inheritance tax (see *IHTA 1984, s 165*).

Disposal following earlier hold-over (the half-gain rule): before 2008/09

[7.96] Before 2008/09, where trustees received an asset subject to a hold-over by the settlor a special relief may have been available. To qualify:

(a)   the trustees must have acquired the asset after 31 March 1982,
(b)   the settlor must have acquired the asset before 31 March 1982,
(c)   the settlor must have given the asset to the trustees before 6 April 1988, subject to a hold-over election, and
(d)   the trustees' disposal must have been after 5 April 1988 and before 6 April 2008.

The relief operated as a restriction of the deduction from the base value by reason of the hold-over. The deduction was reduced to one half. The relief had to be claimed within two years of the end of the fiscal year of disposal although extensions could be requested. With the reform of capital gains tax from 6 April 2008, the half gain rule was repealed, except for corporation tax purposes [*TCGA 1992, Sch 4*, amended by *FA 2008, Sch 2, para 74*].

Enterprise Investment Scheme (EIS)

[7.97] The old reinvestment relief provisions which gave relief to some trustees before repeal of that regime from 1998/99 have been carried over into the present EIS deferral regime [*TCGA 1992, Sch 5B, para 17*]. In broad terms, the gain on the disposal of any chargeable asset can be deferred by reinvestment. This requires a subscription for 'eligible shares' in a qualifying 'trading company' within twelve months before or three years after the disposal. In the case of a discretionary trust, all the beneficiaries must be individuals. With an interest in possession trust, relief is given if any of the beneficiaries are individuals. If there are non-individual beneficiaries, then (as under reinvestment relief) pro rata relief is obtained according to the proportion of the individual interests in possession borne to all the interests in possession. While the term 'individuals' includes charities, interests in possession do not include interests for a fixed term.

[7.98] Since it is the trustees who realise the gain, it is they who must make the qualifying EIS investment. There might be thought to be (or, rather, have been) a problem with a settlor-interested trust, since, while it will be the trustees who have made the disposal, the tax is assessed on the settlor, either under *section 77* in a UK resident trust (before 2008/09, when *section 77* was repealed) or *section 86* in a non-UK resident trust. However, in the UK resident case, HMRC accept that the scheme of *TCGA 1992, Sch 5B, para 17* is that a qualifying reinvestment by the trustees effectively franks their gain, so that (if in full) there was no residual trust gain to be assessed on the settlor under *section 77*. The same, however, does not apply in the non-UK resident trust case, where the pre-relieved gains are assessed on the settlor under *section 86*, assuming of course that for the year of assessment in question, he is UK resident and domiciled and has an interest in the settlement. There could conceivably be cases where the non-UK resident trust is not subject to *section 86* but the trustees are still liable to capital gains tax on the gain, for example because it arises from the disposal of chargeable assets used in a trade carried on in the UK under *TCGA 1992, s 10*. In such a case, an EIS investment would be open to the non-UK resident trustees.

[7.99] An interesting question arises if the trustees of a qualifying interest in possession trust have claimed EIS reinvestment relief and the life tenant dies before sale of the EIS shares or before the occurrence of some other event which triggers the deferred gain. Under general principles there will be a deemed disposal and reacquisition at market value under *TCGA 1992, s 73(1)* or *s 72(1)*, according to whether the settlement comes to an end or it continues. The disposal is deemed and not actual and the EIS shares themselves either will pass to the remaindermen or will continue in the trust for the succeeding life tenant. The question is whether or not the deferred EIS gain is charged on the deemed disposal. Clearly, had the life tenant owned the EIS shares beneficially, any such charge would have been excluded by *TCGA 1992, Sch 5B, para 3(5)*, ie on the death of the 'investor', whereas, in this case, it is, of course, the trustees who are the investors. On the other hand, both *section 72(1)(b)* and *section 73(1)(a)* provide that no chargeable gain shall accrue on the disposal. The EIS legislation treats a chargeable gain as accruing at the time of the chargeable event. The question, therefore, is whether the provisions in the main body of the Act have the effect of excluding this gain, which would at the least appear equitable. If, on the other hand, such a gain might arise, well-advised trustees may wish to consider insuring against the possibility of such crystallised deferred gains.

[7.100] The recent case of *Robert Ames v HMRC* [2015] UKFTT 337 highlights the need for an EIS claim to be made before the fifth anniversary of the self-assessment filing date for the tax year.

Seed Enterprise Investment Scheme

[7.101] Trustees are not eligible for the Seed Enterprise Investment Scheme established for shares issued on or after 6 April 2012. By *FA 2012, s 38, Sch 6* (and extended by *FA 2014, ss 54 and 55*), inserting *ITA 2007, Part 5A* and *TCGA 1992, s 150E–150G, Sch 5BB*, the relief is limited to individuals.

Entrepreneurs' relief

[7.102] To compensate taxpayers adversely affected by the repeal of business assets taper relief from 2008/09, *FA 2008, Sch 3* introduced entrepreneurs' relief (*TCGA 1992, ss 169H–169S*). In broad terms this relief re-introduces the provisions of retirement relief. Prior to 23 June 2010, gains qualifying for entrepreneurs' relief were reduced by $^4/_9$ to produce an effective rate of tax of 18%, up to a maximum of £1 million of qualifying gains over a lifetime, starting with 6 April 2008. For disposals on or after 6 April 2010, the lifetime limit was increased to £2 million (*FA 2010, s 4*). For disposals on or after 23 June 2010 the lifetime limit was further increased to £5 million and the applicable rate of tax specified as 10% [*F(No 2)A 2010, Sch 1*, amending *TCGA 1992, s 169N*]. For disposals on or after 6 April 2011 the lifetime limit has become £10 million [*FA 2011, s 9*].

Conditions

[7.103] The relief is available on the following:
- the disposal of all or part of a trading business carried on by an individual whether alone or in partnership;
- a disposal of assets that were in use for the business at the point the business ceased and where disposal is made within three years;
- a disposal of shares in or securities of a company where the individual was an officer or employee and had a minimum of 5% of the nominal value of ordinary shares plus voting rights of the company (for disposals on or after 6 April 2013 of shares acquired via an Enterprise Management Incentive ('EMI') the 5% requirement has been removed); and
- a disposal of an asset owned by an individual used for the purposes of a business carried on by a partnership in which the individual is a partner or by the individual's company in which shares are held

('associated disposal'). There must be a disposal of business assets of a partnership or of shares in a company which qualifies as a material disposal and is made as part of a withdrawal by the individual from participation in the business of the partnership or the company. HMRC have confirmed that a withdrawal from participation in the business is a reference to equity participation and not a reference to time spent: that is the individual could continue to work full-time in the business without prejudicing the entrepreneurs' relief (see CG63995). Budget 2015 introduced a 5% minimum equity disposal effective from 18 March 2015 [*TCGA 1992, s 169K(1)* amended by *FA 2015, s 41*] (and Finance Bill 2016 has introduced some minor technical changes – see the article by Martin Mann *Tax Journal* 22 April 2016).

Generally speaking, the conditions must be satisfied for a period of 12 months either ending with the disposal or in certain cases ending at a time which falls within three years after the disposal. (For EMI shareholders the 12-month period commences from the date the option is granted.) There is no minimum age (or indeed working time requirement for an officer or employee of a company).

Extension to trustees

[7.104] Gains realised by trustees can attract entrepreneurs' relief, the extension given by *section 169J*. The availability of relief relies, however, upon the entrepreneurs' relief qualifying status of a qualifying beneficiary (ie an individual who has an interest in possession (not including a fixed term) in the whole of the settled property or a part which contains the settlement business assets of which the trustees dispose). That being the case, relief for the disposal of a trust's business assets, which may be either shares or securities of a company or assets used for purposes of a business, will be available subject to the following additional conditions:

- Where the disposal is of shares of a company, for a period of one year ending not earlier than three years before the disposal, the company must be the 'personal company' of the qualifying beneficiary who must also be an officer or employee. That is, the 5% minimum requirement for shares and votes must be met by the beneficiary, not by the trustees.
- Where it is a disposal of business assets, the assets were in use by the beneficiary for the purposes of the business whether alone or in partnership for the period of one year not earlier than three years before the disposal and the beneficiary ceases to carry on the business at that time or ending three years before.

It is interesting, and somewhat curious, that, as a corollary of the point that it is in relation to the beneficiary that the standard qualifying conditions have to be satisfied, there is no particular statutory requirement for any qualifying period for the interest in possession. It is provided simply that at the date of disposal there must be 'an individual who is a qualifying beneficiary'. While this seems to be a lacuna, it can give rise to interesting planning possibilities by securing successive interests in possession for different beneficiaries in the same settlement (albeit not for a fixed term), subject always perhaps to the General Anti-Abuse Rule from 2013/14.

[7.105] *Section 169O* contains further provisions in the case where more than one beneficiary has an interest in the relevant settled property. An apportionment is made by reference to the proportional entitlement of the qualifying beneficiary to the income of the relevant settled property. Where the relief is to be claimed by the trustees, *section 169M* provides that there is a joint claim by the trustees and the qualifying beneficiary, which ensures that his relevant maximum of qualifying gains per individual (currently £10 million) is not exceeded.

[7.106] The Tax Faculty of the ICAEW published in February 2012 a useful 23-page document, 'ICAEW Tax Guide 1/12 Entrepreneurs' Relief – Practical Points', comprising a series of questions and answers with HMRC. Generally, the responses of HMRC appear cast in a favourable light to the taxpayer and, indeed, go beyond the strict letter of the legislation, which HMRC say they are interpreting on a purposive basis. For example, a traditional difficulty can arise where the taxpayer (whether an individual or trustees) contracts to sell a business but continues to carry on the business between contract (which determines the date of disposal for capital gains tax purposes) and completion. That will deny entrepreneurs' relief from gains realised on disposing of assets used in the business, even within the three-year period following the date of cessation. However, HMRC say (at para 59) that 'if the facts indicate there was a genuine business disposal linked to a genuine business cessation, ER should not become unavailable where the strict application of section 28 determines the date of disposal to be before the date of cessation'.

Investors' Relief

[7.107] Budget 2016 included an announcement that 'Entrepreneurs' relief [would] be extended to external investors in unlisted trading companies'. In fact, this *extension* takes the form of an entirely new *Investors' Relief* created by *Finance (No 2) Bill, clause 76* by the introduction of new clauses within TCGA 1992, Part V.

[7.108] As for Entrepreneurs' Relief, where available, the new Investors' Relief will apply a 10% rate of Capital Gains Tax subject to a lifetime cap of £10 million (which is in addition to the Entrepreneur's Relief cap in the same amount). It applies only to *newly issued* ordinary shares in an unlisted trading company for new consideration on or after 17 March 2016 and where the shares are subsequently held for *three years*.

[7.109] Originally the relief was to be available only to individuals who were not employees and officers of the company; however, the restrictions in relation to employees and officers were subsequently watered down by government amendments during the passing of the Finance Bill, and the relief was also extended to trustees (see **7.110**). For more information generally about this new relief, readers are referred to the articles in *Taxation* magazine by Kevin Slevin, *Gains from investment*, 7 April 2016, and John Endacott, *Encouraging Growth*, 14 July 2016.

[7.110] As for Entrepreneurs' Relief, trustees do not qualify for relief in their own right but must, in effect, piggyback off an 'eligible beneficiary', whose £10 million limit is then used by the trustees. To be an 'eligible beneficiary' the following conditions must be met:

- Immediately before the disposal, the beneficiary must have had an interest in possession (but not for a fixed term) in the trust holding the shares, and they must have had this for a period of three years;
- The beneficiary must have avoided any of the restrictions in relation to employees or officers throughout that three-year period; and
- The beneficiary must have elected to be treated as an eligible beneficiary. In other words, the individual could deny the trustees use of his or her £10 million exemption if the circumstances so dictated.

[7.111] The obvious attractions of Investors' Relief over Entrepreneurs' Relief are the absence of any minimal shareholding percentage and of the need to be an officer or employee in the target company. Less attractive is that it applies only to newly issued shares rather than to transferred shares (and in the context of trusts, of course, shares are often gifted), and that the qualifying period is three years rather than one. It is unfortunate that the relief applies only to interest in possession trusts, the logic for which would appear to be the need to link the £10 million cap to individuals only.

Deeds of variation and post-death appointments

[7.112] Deeds of variation are effective for capital gains tax where, within two years of an individual's death, dispositions of his property effected by Will or intestacy are varied or a benefit is disclaimed. There has to be a written deed of variation and, for instruments made before 1 August 2002, an election had to be made to the Board (generally within six months of the date of the deed). For deeds made on or after 1 August 2002, the position has become simpler and no notice is required to be given to HMRC: rather, the deed must contain a statement that the parties thereto intend that the capital gains tax relieving provisions apply [*FA 2002, s 52*]. The variation is then treated as if it had been made by the deceased in his Will [*TCGA 1992, s 62(6),(7)*]. The effect is limited, however, and in particular, as established by the House of Lords case of *Marshall v Kerr* (see **7.113–7.116**), a variation of a Will or intestacy which creates a settlement produces the result for both capital gains tax and income tax (though not for inheritance tax: see **7.115**) purposes that the original beneficiary is the settlor. That makes the settlement 'settlor-interested', for UK resident trusts under *TCGA 1992, s 77* and, as in *Marshall v Kerr*, for non-UK resident trusts under *section 86*. This is provided, from 2006/07, expressly by new *section 68C* inserted by *FA 2006, Sch 12, para 1* into *TCGA 1992*. Note, however, that where there is a variation of a settled gift into another settlement, it will generally be the deceased (rather than the beneficiary who effects the variation) who is regarded as the settlor. While *section 77* has been repealed from 2008/09, there remains the restriction that hold-over relief cannot be claimed on a transfer by the settlor into a trust in which he is interested (see **7.81**).

[7.113] It would seem obvious that deeds of variation should be used to roll gains away to taxpayers with the benefit of either allowable losses or an annual exemption. However, an attempt to re-route a gift to take advantage for capital gains tax purposes of the deceased's non-UK residence status failed in *Marshall (Inspector of Taxes) v Kerr* [1995] 1 AC 148, [1994] 3 All ER 106, HL.

[7.114] The testator had died in 1977 resident and domiciled in Jersey. His daughter, Mrs Kerr, was resident and domiciled in England. In 1978 she settled the half of the estate to which she was entitled by a deed of variation. As the law was understood at the time, this caused the testator to be deemed to be the settlor so that the result was a Jersey settlement made by a Jersey settlor. This view was challenged. In June 1994 the House of Lords found Mrs Kerr to be the settlor for the purposes of what is now *TCGA 1992, s 86* so that the settlement turned out to be one made by a UK resident, etc. The House of Lords found that two tacit but unjustified assumptions had been made by the lower courts: first, that Mrs Kerr could settle the assets concerned (whereas during the administration she had only the right to have the estate duly administered); second, that the assets were those which the testator was deemed to dispose of on his death (while the executors might themselves acquire and dispose of assets during the administration).

[7.115] Interestingly, it was in the High Court that the most straightforward reason was given as to why the taxpayers had to fail. *TCGA 1992, s 62(6)(b)* states expressly that where a valid election is made and notice is duly given: 'this section shall apply as if the variation had been effected by the deceased'. In other words, *section 62* leaves untouched the rest of the capital gains tax regime which in the case of settlements depend on who was the settlor (*section 77* (since repealed) in the case of a UK resident settlement and *sections 86* and *87* for a non-UK resident settlement). By contrast, the deeming provisions for inheritance tax purposes in *IHTA 1984, s 142(1)* state that: 'this Act shall apply as if the variation had been effected by the deceased'. That means, of course, that in considering the application of the reservation of benefit provisions in *FA 1986, s 102* and *Sch 20*, the disposition is treated as having been made by the testator and not by the beneficiary.

[7.116] It is worth observing that the legislation in force when the House of Lords delivered their decision in *Marshall v Kerr* has since been changed, in particular by the insertion of *TCGA 1992, s 62(9)*, which provides that *section 62(6)* 'applies whether or not the administration of the estate is complete or the property has been distributed in accordance with the original dispositions'.

[7.117] Where property is held by the personal representatives on discretionary trusts, they may appoint assets to a beneficiary within two years of the death. *IHTA 1984, s 144* prevents that being an occasion of charge for inheritance tax. There is no equivalent provision for capital gains tax so that, the beneficiary having become absolutely entitled as against the estate [*TCGA 1992, s 71*], there is an occasion of charge. However, there is a distinction between the case where, on the one hand, the personal representatives assent the asset or assets concerned to the trustees who then make the appointment and, on the other, there is an appointment by the trustees *before* the assets have been assented to them. Only in the former case is there a capital gains tax disposal. In the latter, the trustees being entitled at that point only to the chose in action which every beneficiary under a Will acquires at date of death, the effect of the appointment is simply to declare the trustees as bare trustees for the beneficiary. When the assent takes place there is no disposal and the acquisition date and acquisition cost of the beneficiary are read back to the date of death in the normal way under *TCGA 1992, s 62(4)*.

Sub-funds

[7.118] A new regime was introduced by *FA 2006, Sch 12, Pt 2* (to be found in *TCGA 1992, Sch 4ZA*). Where a single settlement has more than one 'sub-settlement' or 'sub-fund', even with separate trustees, the gains or losses on those sub-settlements or funds form part of the overall computation of chargeable gains which is assessed on the trustees of the main settlement. In broad terms, the new regime allows trustees of the 'principal settlement' to elect that a fund or other specified portion of the settlement shall be treated for capital gains tax purposes as a separate settlement. The creation of a sub-fund will involve a disposal by the trustees of the principal settlement. The election cannot take effect from a date earlier than that on which it is made. The four conditions are as follows:

(1)   the principal settlement is not itself a sub-fund settlement;
(2)   the sub-fund does not comprise the whole of the property in the principal settlement;
(3)   there is no asset an interest in which is comprised both in the sub-fund settlement and in the principal settlement; and
(4)   no person is a beneficiary under both the sub-fund settlement and the principal settlement.

Conditions (1)–(4) must be satisfied when the election is made. Conditions (2)–(4) must be satisfied throughout the period from when the election is treated as taking effect and ending immediately before the election is made.

[7.119] HMRC have provided a form (SFE1) for making a sub-fund election. No election may be made after the second 31 January after the year of assessment in which the effective date falls. The sub-fund election must contain certain declarations, statements and information and it may not be revoked.

[7.120] Following on the disposal which the trustees of the principal settlement are treated as having made, the trustees of the sub-fund settlement are treated as having acquired the relevant property at the date of the election taking effect and for a consideration equal to the then market value of the relevant assets.

[7.121] For income tax purposes there are corresponding provisions in *ITA 2007, s 477*.

[7.122] HMRC's Capital Gains Manual comments at CG33331 are as follows:

> 'Except for the purposes of the annual exempt amount (see CG18115) the sub-fund becomes a new separate settlement on "the specified date" (see the end of TSEM3510).

Otherwise the basic principle is that the tax consequences should be the same as those which would apply if the trustees had exercised their powers to transfer assets to the trustees of a separate settlement. The legislation provides the same possibilities in the case where such powers are not available to them. For example there may only be a power in 'narrower form'. See the discussion in Bond v Pickford 57 TC 301, and CG37841.

There is a deemed disposal under TCGA 1992, s 71(1) by the trustees of the principal settlement at the beginning of the specified date and reacquisition by the trustees of the sub-fund settlement on the specified date. See TCGA 1992, Sch 4ZA para 19 and para 20(1) and (2)).

If however a particular asset meets the business asset test or agricultural property test "gifts hold-over relief" may be available under TCGA 1992, s 165 or Sch 7, paras 1 to 4. See CG66940+.

It is also accepted that if the transaction creating the sub-fund settlement is a chargeable transfer for inheritance tax, and the specified date is the same day, the conditions of TCGA 1992, s 260(2)(a) can be met. For example one might have a Will trust where currently there is an immediate post-death interest for A, the son of the testator, see CG36542. The trustees exercise a power to declare discretionary trusts for A's children, B,C and D, in respect of part of the settled property. This is a chargeable transfer for IHT. Assuming the property held on discretionary trusts meets the conditions for there to be a sub-fund, an election might be made under which the specified date is the date of the exercise of the power. In this situation section 260(2)(a) could apply unless any of B, C and D are under 18.'

EXAMPLE
The Bergh Trust, made five years ago, comprises a wide portfolio of rented property, quoted investments and a variety of shareholdings in private trading companies. The beneficiaries are in broad terms the grandchildren and remoter issue of the settlor. For various administrative reasons, the trustees want for 2015/16 to hive off into a separate settlement run by separate trustees (though this is not necessary under the legislation) the shares in the private trading companies. So this they do, ensuring that the beneficiaries are restricted to the children of the settlor's elder daughter and that those beneficiaries cannot in future benefit under the principal settlement. Separate trustees are appointed. The trustees of the principal settlement are treated as making a disposal. However, because the event constitutes a chargeable transfer for inheritance tax purposes, the gain can be held over by election by the trustees of the principal settlement under TCGA 1992, s 260.

The accrued income scheme and capital gains tax

[7.123] Gilt-edged securities and qualifying corporate bonds (see *TCGA 1992, s 115*) are exempt from capital gains tax but fall within the accrued income scheme. Other securities (but not shares) (see *ITA 2007, s 619*) are within both capital gains tax and the accrued income scheme under *ITA 2007, Pt 12, ss 615–681DP*. The position for these is covered by *TCGA 1992, s 119*. This is aimed at producing a clean price for capital gains tax by deducting accrued interest from, or adding the rebate amount to, the consideration for the disposal. See **6.7–6.19** for the income tax effects of the accrued income scheme.

[7.124] There are numerous special cases covered by the legislation, but these are rare. For instance, a convertible security may be converted into equity so that the accrued income scheme creates an assessment to income tax, but there is no disposal for capital gains tax. For items of this sort, the reader is referred to the legislation.

[7.125] Where the disposal of an investment in an offshore roll-up fund (subject to the new regime introduced by *FA 2009*, with effect from 1 December 2009) is made and income tax is assessed under the*Offshore Funds (Tax) Regulations 2009 (SI 2009/3001)*, there are no capital gains tax consequences so far as the gain is deemed to be income [*TCGA 1992, s 37*].

High value disposals of residential property

[7.126] As from 2013/14 a new capital gains tax charge at a rate of 28% for disposals by non-natural persons of UK residential property for a consideration of more than £2 million (and which threshold has since reduced – see 7.128) has applied. This was the third limb of the special avoidance code for structures under which non-natural persons hold UK residential property, the other two limbs being the increased entry charge to stamp duty land tax (see **13.34**) and the Annual Tax on Enveloped Dwellings (ATED) described at **13.40–13.45**. The charge to capital gains tax will apply only where, and to the extent that, the property is within the charge to the ATED, and applies whether or not the non-natural person is UK resident. While this new charge is not directly relevant to trusts as, expressly trusts and trustees are not non-natural persons as defined, the charge may of course indirectly affect trusts insofar as they hold shares in or own interests in relation to such a non-natural person.

[7.127] For these purposes the acquisition value of the property is rebased to 6 April 2013. The legislation contains a specific tapering principle to avoid the 'cliff edge' effect which would otherwise have the effect that selling a property for just over the threshold would produce rather less net than selling the property for just under it. Additionally, it may be that the availability of one or more of the reliefs through the ATED listed at **13.44** will disapply the charge to capital gains tax. Likewise, there will be time apportionment. For example, if a £2 million property held at 6 April 2013 by a non-natural person is sold on 6 April 2018 for a consideration of £3 million but was within the charge to ATED for only three of those five years, the chargeable gain will be £600,000 (ie 3/5ths of the £1 million gain) [*TCGA 1992, ss 2B–2F, inserted by FA 2013, Sch 254*].

[7.128] As announced in Budget 2014, the ATED charge and this related capital gains tax charge was extended to properties worth more than £1 million from 2015/16, and to properties worth more than £500,000 from 2016/17.

Miscellaneous

Administrative rules

[7.129] The 'relevant trustees' defined for capital gains tax purposes are the same relevant trustees as appear in the income tax legislation (*TMA 1970, s 107A*), namely those who are trustees in the year of assessment when the chargeable event takes place and those who subsequently become trustees [*TCGA 1992, s 65(4)*]. Anything done by one relevant trustee is treated as being done by them all and any or all of them can be assessed. There is a modest protection for liabilities accruing prior to appointment. HMRC may assess any trustee on behalf of all the trustees [*TCGA 1992, s 65(1)*, as amended].

[7.130] A capital loss must be calculated and claimed. The claim is typically (though need not be) claimed in the self assessment return. For claims made on or after 1 April 2010, the time limit is four years after the end of the year of assessment in which the loss arose, replacing the traditional time limit of five years and 10 months (*Finance Act 2008 (Schedule 39 Appointed Day, Transitional Provisions and Savings) Order 2009, SI 2009/403*). The losses of 1996/97 and subsequent years are relieved in priority to pre-1996/97 losses brought forward.

[7.131] Generally, a loss will be allowable if the disposal of that asset at a gain would have been taxable [*TCGA 1992, s 16(2)*]. Allowable losses realised in the same year as a taxable gain *must* be deducted from those gains in computing the taxable amount for the year (even if the effect is to 'waste' the annual exemption). By contrast, losses in a given year, which are not used, for example, because there are no gains against which to offset them, may be carried forward. Such brought forward losses need not 'waste' the annual exemption and the taxpayer trustees can choose to utilise only so much of the losses as are necessary to bring the gains down to the annual exemption threshold. Any losses remaining can then be carried forward further.

Valuation of shares in unquoted/unlisted companies

[7.132] A company is unlisted where none of its shares are listed on any recognised stock exchange. Trustees often have holdings in unlisted companies which are really the only reason for the settlement and so date back some time. Rebasing to 31 March 1982 is still part of capital gains tax and can cause doubts if the trustees dispose of part of an old holding and want to rebase the value of the shares disposed of. The worry is whether the whole holding should be rebased or just the number of shares disposed of. The HMRC Capital Gains Manual makes it clear that the whole holding is to be revalued (CG50901, CG50904 and CG50905).

Pooling land

[7.133] Occasionally, a family pools its assets in order that they can be managed as one unit. This will arise with holdings in a company or landed estates. The trusts which are used as the vehicle for the pooling tend to be bare trusts for tax purposes. The most recent case was *Jenkins (Inspector of Taxes) v Brown* [1989] 1 WLR 1163, [1989] STC 577, Ch D. A published concession (ESC D26), has been enacted from 2010/11 in *TCGA 1992, ss 248A–248E*, inserted by *SI 2010/157, art 8*: this relates to exchanges of interests in land where individuals have property in joint ownership and wish to separate their financial affairs. Stamp duty land tax is charged on each side of the transaction [*FA 2003, s 47*].

Interests under a settlement

[7.134] The disposal by a beneficiary of his interest under a settlement does not trigger a chargeable gain [*TCGA 1992, s 76(1)*]. This provision would, for example, protect the gift of a reversionary interest for inheritance tax mitigation purposes. The protection is given to an original beneficiary or anyone else who did not acquire his interest for a consideration in money or money's worth (other than consideration consisting of another interest under the settlement). Since 6 March 1998, this rule applies only if the settlement has never been resident outside the UK [*TCGA 1992, s 76(1A), (1B)*]. FA 2000, s 91 provided a further limitation to this principle from 21 March 2000 by inserting a new *TCGA 1992, s 76A* and *Sch 4A*. These new provisions create a charge to capital gains tax in certain circumstances where a beneficiary sells his interest in the trust on or after 21 March 2000. The type of trusts caught are those which are settlor-interested or where any of the trust property is derived from a trust which was a settlor-interested trust at any time in the previous two tax years. If the rules apply, the assets underlying the interest are treated as though they are disposed of and immediately re-acquired by the trustees at market value.

Variation of trusts

[7.135] There are times when it would suit everybody concerned to vary a trust. Some variations are made to correct drafting or typing mistakes, others to vary the entitlement of beneficiaries. Also, there are the variations when some new administrative power is needed, perhaps to delegate investment matters to an investment manager or to put investments in the names of nominees (perhaps a stockbroker's nominee company). In general, anything directed at beneficiaries' rights will require an application under the *Variation of Trusts Act 1958* and may prove to be expensive. Administrative matters can be dealt with, probably at far less expense, by the use of *Trustee Act 1925, s 57*. Very occasionally the variation may be under *Settled Land Act 1925, s 64*. The ability to vary a trust can be important, in that the taxpayer is still the same even though there may have been some redirection of wealth. The variation is not a disposal and is not the occasion of a capital gains tax charge, whereas resettlement must involve the trustees in capital gains tax and inheritance tax implications. Variations which have greater tax consequences are disclaimers, assignments and surrenders. Any of these will attract the attention of HMRC (see TSEM1840, 1845 and 1850). Following the introduction of the vulnerable beneficiaries regime (*FA 2005, ss 30–32*) – see CHAPTER 15 – there may be a case for an application under the *Variation of*

Trusts Act 1958 in order to secure beneficial tax treatment for a beneficiary of a trust who currently is the only disabled one of a number of beneficiaries within the terms of the trust set up specifically for him/her but including siblings, etc. This would ensure that the disabled beneficiary benefited from the new rules. Such action would imply exclusion from the trust of the other beneficiaries. The balance of advantage here would have to be weighed up: it may be possible to create separate trusts for the non-disabled beneficiaries.

Chapter 8

Inheritance Tax: Definitions

[8.1] The legislation provides a number of definitions which are fundamental to an understanding of the inheritance tax legislation. These are examined below, in an order which (albeit not alphabetical) is logical in the context of the structure of inheritance tax.

'Settlement'

[8.2] 'Settlement' means any disposition of property, however effected, where the property is held:

(a) in trust for persons in succession; or
(b) for any person subject to a contingency; or
(c) on trust to accumulate income; or
(d) on trust with power to make payments at the discretion of the trustees with or without power to accumulate surplus income; or
(e) to fund an annuity or other periodical payment.

[*IHTA 1984, s 43(2)*]

[8.3] A lease of property for life or for lives is also treated as a settlement where made for less than full consideration [*IHTA 1984, s 43(3)*].

[8.4] It is possible for trustees to receive gifts from someone other than the original settlor. The most common scenario is probably where each of two spouses or civil partners makes transfers to the same trust. The possibility of more than one settlor is covered by *IHTA 1984, s 44(2)*. This provision treats each transferor as a separate settlor and his or her gifts as separate settlements. There will then be issues of identification. This is a topical point in relation to two situations in particular. First, with excluded property settlements (see 8.24), an addition of property to an excluded property settlement by the settlor who at the time of the addition has become actually or deemed domiciled in the UK may constitute a new settlement for inheritance tax purposes and therefore not one excluded from the scope of inheritance tax by *IHTA 1984, s 48(3)*. Second, in relation to the current regime for trusts introduced on 22 March 2006, the addition of property to an interest in possession settlement in being at 22 March 2006 will not, as a new settlement within the 'relevant property' regime, get the benefit of the transitional rules (but see 2.22 for the circumstances in which HMRC consider that an addition has been made). The 'relevant property' regime recognises the concept of adding to a settlement (see 9.57–9.64), but with the requirement to adjust the rate of tax applicable at the following ten-year anniversary, following *IHTA 1984, s 67*.

[8.5] There may arise the issue of the status of a non-UK law trust for purposes of English Law, and specifically inheritance tax. Among these is a 'usufruct' which confers a right to occupy a property for a period of time, whether defined in years or by reference to a life. In their Trusts and Estates Newsletter of April 2013 HMRC set out their long-held view that a usufruct will more than likely fall to be treated as a settlement under *IHTA 1984, s 43(2)*. HMRC recognised that arrangements differed from jurisdiction to jurisdiction and that the circumstances of each case needed to be considered but that effect will be to treat a usufruct as giving rise to an interest in possession in the property concerned, with the inheritance tax implications varying according to whether the interest arose before or since 22 March 2006. Responses to this article on the Trusts Discussion Forum (in particular) questioned HMRC's view; however, it has been reiterated again in the Trusts and Estate Newsletter of September 2015, which states:

> 'IHT treatment of usufructs
>
> HMRC can confirm that its approach to the treatment of a usufruct remains as stated in the April 2013 Newsletter.
>
> Since April 2013, HMRC has dealt with a small number of cases where the estate included a usufruct and in each case, the facts were less than straightforward. HMRC applied its approach to the facts of each case as it understood them to be, and in each case, the difference between the value reported by the taxpayer and the value that emerged following HMRC's approach was not sufficient to warrant pursuit. So in accordance with its Litigation and Settlement Strategy, HMRC adopted the value reported by the taxpayer.
>
> But HMRC remains of the view that, generally, a usufruct should be treated as giving rise to a settlement for IHT purposes and will pursue the collection of tax on that basis.'

'Interest in possession'

[8.6] 'Interest in possession' means the interest of a person who has the *immediate* entitlement (subject to expenses or other similar outgoings) to any income produced by the settled property as it arises. The fact that this interest could be revoked or defeated in any way does not matter. Practitioners will generally treat this as meaning a life interest or an annuity. Interest in possession is not defined in the legislation but the meaning has been tested in *Pearson v IRC* [1981] AC 753, [1980] 2 All ER 479, HL. The official view as to the meaning of 'interest in possession' may be found in HMRC's Inheritance Tax Manual at IHTM16062 which states: 'The main authority for the definition of an interest in possession is the House of Lords case *Pearson v IRC*: a person has an interest in possession when they have 'a present right of present enjoyment' or an immediate right to the income or enjoyment of property (irrespective of whether the property produces income). In contrast, the beneficiary (or object) under a non-interest in possession settlement has only the right to be considered by the trustees if and when they distribute any income or benefits.' Reference has already been made to the case of *Sansom v Peay (Inspector of Taxes)* [1976] 3 All ER 375, [1976] 1 WLR 1073, Ch D (see 7.54) and HMRC Statement of Practice SP 10/79 (see Appendix A). These show that an interest in possession in the family home can be created by the trustees of a discretionary settlement who allow exclusive occupation of the property by a beneficiary. It would not follow that the lending of any asset or the existence of a standing order for the payment of income to a beneficiary would have the same effect. The latter point was considered in *Swales v IRC* [1984] 3 All ER 16, [1984] STC 413, Ch D. The identification of an interest in possession has become especially important in the context of the 'transitional serial interest' regime (see **8.17–8.22**). In particular, the legislation recognises the possibility that there may be successive interests enjoyed by the same person which are not the same interests in possession: see *IHTA 1984, s 53(2)*. Budget 2008 cleared up an uncertainty first raised in August 2007 in relation to the interpretation of *IHTA 1984, s 53(2A)*. The upshot is that where within the transitional period (which ended on 5 October 2008) an interest in possession existing at 22 March 2006 is replaced with another interest for the same beneficiary, that will be a transitional serial interest, triggering no chargeable event for inheritance tax purposes.

'Qualifying interest in possession'

[8.7] 'Qualifying interest in possession' is the technical term used, since 22 March 2006, to describe an interest in possession trust which is outside the relevant property regime. In other words, its assets are treated as belonging to the life tenant(s). Prior to that date, all interest in possession trusts were taxed in this way. See CHAPTER **12**.

'Immediate post-death interest'

[8.8] An 'immediate post-death interest' or IPDI is a creature of *FA 2006*, inserting new *section 49A* into *IHTA 1984*. Such a settlement can arise only by Will or under the intestacy rules; the person beneficially entitled to an interest in possession must have become so entitled on the death of the testator or intestate; the trust property has been neither a bereaved minors trust nor a disabled person's interest (see below) at all times since the interest in possession arose. The much more restrictive conditions for an IPDI originally introduced into *Finance (No 2) Bill 2006* were removed by Government amendment at Report Stage. This has the effect that practically every interest in possession trust under a Will, whether or not for a surviving spouse/civil partner, will qualify as an IPDI and, if for a surviving spouse/civil partner, will attract the spouse/civil partner exemption under *IHTA 1984, s 18(1)* [*IHTA 1984, s 49A and ss 49A–49E*].

EXAMPLE

A husband's Will leaves, after various legacies and bequests, residue on a life interest trust, split as to two thirds to his wife and one third to his daughter. Each of the two interests in residue is an IPDI, that for the widow qualifying for the spouse exemption and that for the daughter attracting any remaining balance of the nil-rate band (along with non-charitable legacies and bequests). This analysis would not be affected if the trustees had a power to terminate either or both of the IPDIs during the beneficiary's lifetime. If they were so to act, in favour of an individual absolutely, this would cause the beneficiary to make a PET. If the terms of the appointment were that a successive trust interest arose, whether on discretionary or on life interest terms, that would trigger a chargeable transfer by the beneficiary and the ensuing trust would enter the relevant property regime.

'Trust for bereaved minors'

[8.9] A trust for a bereaved minor (TBM) is defined in *IHTA 1984, s 71A* introduced by *FA 2006*. A TBM is a trust established under the Will or by reason of intestacy of a deceased parent or step-parent or of a person having 'parental responsibility' of a bereaved minor for him or established under the Criminal Injuries Compensation Scheme (or, from 8 April 2010, the Victims of Overseas Terrorism Compensation Scheme), which satisfies three conditions. First, the bereaved minor will, on or before attaining the age of 18, become absolutely entitled to the settled property, any income arising from it and any accumulated income. It has been confirmed by HMRC that for these purposes, although the legislation refers to bereaved minor in the singular, the singular includes the plural (response to question 1 from STEP/CIOT of the 'trusts for children' series questions posed to HMRC, with the answers released on 29 June 2007, reproduced in APPENDIX E). Second, while the bereaved minor is alive and under the age of 18, any of the settled property which is applied for the benefit of a beneficiary is applied for the benefit of that bereaved minor alone. Third, as long as the bereaved minor is alive and under the age of 18, either he is entitled to all the income arising or no such income may be applied for the benefit of any other person (though see **8.10** for the minor concession for settlements made on or after 8 April 2013). However, somewhat qualifying conditions 2 and 3, HMRC's response referred to above states that 'it is not necessary to fix the shares in which each child takes income and capital while they are all under 18. Hence it is possible to pay out income and capital to the minor children in unequal shares. The same point applies, mutatis mutandis, to age 18-to-25 trusts with the substitution of the age 25.' It has to be said that not all commentators agree with this interpretation, though it is hard to see how it would be challenged as incorrect. A trust is not prevented from being a TBM by reason only of the statutory powers of advancement conferred on the trustees by either *Trustee Act 1925, s 32* or *Trustee Act (Northern Ireland) 1958, s 33* [*IHTA 1984, ss 71A–71C*].

[8.10] Draft legislation for FB 2013 published in January 2013 would have removed TBM (and age 18-to-25 trust) status from settlements made on or after 8 April 2013 which included statutory or express powers of advancement. Happily, responding to concerns raised by the professional bodies, *FA 2013, Sch 44* confirms the continuation of the FA 2006 position. Further, for property settled on or after 8 April 2013 such powers may also be used for the payment of small amounts of income or capital to beneficiaries other than the bereaved minor (or the age 18-to-25 beneficiary), without prejudicing its favoured status. That small amount (or 'annual limit') is the lower of £3,000 and 3% of the maximum value of the settled property during the period in question: see **15.10**.

[8.11] Some important points (going both to drafting and to substance) are made by HMRC's answer to Question 1 of the 'trusts for children' series of questions. While there is considerable flexibility to vary the presumptive share of a bereaved minor beneficiary while under the age of 18, there is one point of substance which should be noted. HMRC consider that, whether under a *section 71A* or (see **8.13–8.15**) a *section 71D* trust, where a power is exercised to exclude a particular beneficiary revocably, that individual is no longer a beneficiary within the meaning of the relevant section. Unless therefore such a decision is to be made irrevocably, it is as well to reduce such a beneficiary's presumptive share to, say, 5%, leaving room for manoeuvre subsequently before he attains age 18 (or, under a *section 71D* trust, 25). Once he becomes 18 (or 25) there is no possibility of divesting him of his share through a power of appointment. However, up to that age, the trustees could always exercise a power of advancement.

[8.12] HMRC's answer to Question 2 of the 'trusts for children' series of questions makes clear that, to be valid, the class of potential beneficiaries under either regime must close when the trust arises, whether in the case of *section 71A* on the death of the testator (other than where it is a deceased father with a child *'en ventre sa mere'*) and in the case of a *section 71D* trust either on death where created by Will or on the date of conversion from a Budget Day 2006 accumulation and maintenance trust (see **11.21**).

EXAMPLE

Amending the example at 8.8, the one-third share in residue is left to such of the husband's children as shall attain the age of 18 years and if more than one in equal shares absolutely. When the husband dies, his son is aged 16 and his daughter 13. This should be a qualifying TBM, given that the Will provides that while a child is alive and under the age of 18 any income from their prospective share is paid to that child alone (though see HMRC's generous interpretation at 8.9–8.10). If the daughter dies at say 17, the capital, then being paid to the son at age 20, would not have been the subject of an absolute gift at age 18. However, the gift should still have satisfied *section 71A*, by analogy with traditional HMRC practice on *section 71* accumulation and maintenance trusts: the assumption is made that a beneficiary will reach the specified age. IHTA 1984, s 71B(2)(b) ensures that no inheritance tax will be payable on the daughter's death.

'Age 18-to-25 trust'

[8.13] This may be regarded as an 'add-on' to the bereaved minors regime (see **8.9–8.12**) introduced by the Government at Committee Stage of the *Finance (No 2) Bill 2006*. It applies where the bereaved minor becomes entitled to the capital on or before attaining the age of 25 (*IHTA 1984, s 71E*). Note that there is no requirement that income be paid out at age 18: there could, for example, be a subsisting accumulation period. Otherwise, the conditions applying to TBMs apply (see **8.9–8.10**), mutatis mutandis; note in particular the flexibility mentioned at 8.9 in relation to payment of income and capital in unequal shares while all the beneficiaries are under the age of 25, in the case of an age 18-to-25 trust. Once the child reaches 25, his share must be fixed, though leaving it open in relation to the shares of his siblings under the age of 25 to continue to pay out income and capital among those siblings in unequal shares.

[8.14] The *section 71E* regime is extended to the case where a Budget Day 2006 accumulation and maintenance trust was converted so as to secure the protection of the regime before the earlier of 6 April 2008 and the date on which the *section 71* status ends. At that time the individual prospectively entitled to a share in the capital must have been below the age of 25. In that event the special charging regime provided by *sections 71E, 71F and 71G* will apply, from the later of the date on which the beneficiary attains the age of 18 and the date on which the special regime starts to apply until the age at which capital vests (not later than age 25).

[8.15] Specifically, note that property within an age 18-to-25 trust is not 'relevant property' and so there can be no ten-year anniversary charge during this period [*IHTA 1984, s 58(1)(b)*]. HMRC's guidance mentioned at **8.9–8.12** applies equally to this type of trust, with a substitution of 25 for 18 as the age below which the presumptive share of a beneficiary may be varied. Similarly, see **8.10** for the minor concession which applies equally to age 18-to-25 settlements made on or after 8 April 2013.

EXAMPLE

Developing the example at **8.12**, suppose that the husband's Will were written so that a one third share in residue was to be held for such of his children as were living at the date of his death and if they had attained age 25 or older absolutely, but if under the age of 25 on the following trusts: income from the share may be accumulated until the later of the expiry of 21 years from the date of the father's death and the beneficiary's attaining age 18 or it may be paid out; income arising thereafter before the child attains the age of 25 is to be paid out and, on attaining the age of 25, capital together with any accumulations of income is paid to him absolutely. That would amount to a qualifying 'age 18-to-25 trust', so that the capital underlying a presumptive share would not enter the special charging regime until such time as the child attained the age of 18. If the beneficiary dies before attaining the age of 18, *IHTA 1984, s 71E(2)(b)* precludes a charge to IHT. Should he die between ages 18 and 25, the terms of the Will and the circumstances then prevailing will dictate the inheritance tax analysis. If the capital continues to be held on age 18-to-25 trusts for the benefit of surviving siblings, that regime will continue and there will as yet be no exit charge (see *IHTA 1984, s 71D(6)*). If, however, on the beneficiary's death, the age 18-to-25 trust comes to an end, there will be an exit charge calculated under *section 71F*. For an illustration of the way in which the exit charge operates under the special charging regime, see the example at **11.21** (c).

'Disabled person's interest'

[8.16] See CHAPTER 15.

'Transitional serial interests'

[8.17] There are three categories of transitional serial interest (TSI). The first category is an interest in possession which arises *before* 6 October 2008 and which replaces an interest in possession in being at 22 March 2006. Second, if an interest in possession in being at 22 March 2006 is replaced, *after* 5 October 2008, by an interest in possession in favour of the first life tenant's widow or widower (or civil partner) on death of the life tenant, that replacement interest in possession will also be a TSI. Third, replacement life interests of life assurance policies in being at 22 March 2006 will be TSIs, in the circumstances corresponding to the above two categories. Under *FA 2006* the transitional period ended at 6 April 2008, but this was extended by *FA 2008* to 6 October 2008. None of a bereaved minor trust, or an age 18-to-25 trust nor a disabled person's interest can be a TSI [*IHTA 1984, ss 49B–49E; FA 2008, s 141*]. Under the new regime it becomes important to identify what is an interest in possession (see **8.6**) and to be able to distinguish one interest in possession from another, where held for the same beneficiary. HMRC have been asked for their views on various aspects of this issue and the exchange of correspondence (in May 2007) is reproduced at APPENDIX E.

[8.18] The underlying theme of HMRC's responses to the seven scenarios is that the expression 'interest in possession' is regarded as meaning *'present right to present enjoyment'* (following the House of Lords decision in *Pearson v IRC* [1981] AC 753, [1980] 2 All ER 479, HL). So, under Example 1, where as at 22 March 2006 a beneficiary has an interest in possession not expressly under the settlement but by virtue of *Trustee Act 1925, s 31* (his having reached age 18 and there being no subsisting accumulation period), there will not be a new interest in possession when, say, an express right arises at age 25, but rather a continuation of the Budget Day interest. The analysis is the same where on attaining the specified age the beneficiary acquires a right to capital, albeit not absolutely but only so as to pay him the income, with power for the trustees to advance capital, and subject thereto capital going after his death to his children, whether that 'engrafted trust' is contained in the same or in a different clause of the deed. Equally, the same interest continues where on attaining an age a contingent interest in capital is replaced by a vested but defeasible interest in capital. And that point applies also where it attaches not to a Budget Day 2006 interest in possession but to a TSI.

[8.19] The rationale behind HMRC's answers to those first five situations is that the relevant interest arises under the terms of the settlement and not from the exercise of the trustees' powers. Here they make a distinction (see their answer to Question 6 of the 43 Questions reproduced in APPENDIX E) in the case where the trustees exercise a power of advancement extending a Budget Day 2006 interest in possession, which does, according to them, give rise to a different interest. However, it is far from clear that this is the case; if before 6 October 2008, it could well be a *section 49C* TSI and if after 5 October 2008 in favour of the surviving spouse or civil partner of the Budget Day beneficiary a *section 49D* TSI (see **8.17**).

[8.20] Question 6 deals with the case of an interest *'pur autre vie'*. Assume that A has the right to receive income during X's lifetime, A dies while X is still alive and A's son B becomes entitled (before 6 October 2008) to income for the rest of X's life: HMRC confirm that this is a TSI, ie that A's interest has 'come to an end' as required by the section. Question 7 deals with a Budget Day 2006 A&M settlement of one or more life policies which are converted into age 18 to 25 trusts before 6 April 2008. Value added by payment of premiums after conversion simply serves to increase the value of the age 18-to-25 trust and does not create a separate relevant property settlement.

[8.21] The significance of these issues (and HMRC's confirmation) is really twofold. First, because one can have only one bite at the TSI cherry, the fact that a beneficiary who was entitled under *Trustee Act 1925, s 31* at 22 March 2006 became entitled before 6 October 2008 to an express interest in possession left it open to appoint a TSI before 6 October 2008. Second, if that express interest in possession arises on or after 6 October 2008, the *section 49(1)* 'fiction' will continue without the underlying trust property entering the relevant property regime. The only qualification here is the point made at the penultimate sentence of **8.19**, where HMRC's view is certainly open to challenge.

EXAMPLE

Jane, aged 75, was the life tenant under a Will trust made by her late husband who died ten years ago. Feeling fairly healthy and thinking of inheritance tax mitigation of her own estate, she reckoned that she could do without the income from the Will trust. So before 6 October 2008 and at Jane's request the trustees exercised their powers to terminate Jane's interest in favour of a continuing interest in possession for Jane's son Gerald aged 49. That created a TSI for Gerald and so an interest to which Gerald is treated as beneficially entitled under *IHTA 1984, s 49(1A)(c)*. The only qualification is that if Jane continues to enjoy a benefit from any of the trust property (whether bricks and mortar or not), she will be treated under *FA 1986, s 102ZA* as having made a gift with reservation of benefit.

[8.22] There was a fourth exchange of correspondence between STEP/CIOT and HMRC, in the context of *FA 2006* and transitional serial interests. This is to do with HMRC's statement of practice SP 10/79 (reproduced in Appendix A) which sets out, in broad terms, the circumstances in which HMRC will regard the occupation of a dwelling-house owned by trustees of a discretionary trust as creating an interest in possession. There were five questions and answers in the exchange of correspondence. Readers are referred to the exchange reproduced at the end of Appendix E. The first issue is whether it can be established in a particular settlement that there was an interest in possession as at 22 March 2006. The second is whether the interest in possession in any particular case relates to the whole trust fund or only to a particular dwelling-house, such that when the dwelling-house is sold or the beneficiary vacates the property, the trust re-enters the relevant property regime.

'Excluded property'

[8.23] 'Excluded property' has a special meaning so far as the trustees of settlements are concerned. Excluded property is property excluded from the charge to inheritance tax. See also **27.2–27.9** and **27.27–27.38** for further discussion of excluded property. See **7.112–7.117** for a note on the variation of a Will to introduce a non-UK domiciliary as settlor of an offshore trust, effective for inheritance tax but not for capital gains tax purposes.

Excluded property settlements

[8.24] Where the settlor was domiciled outside the UK when the settlement was made, non-UK situs property in the settlement is excluded property. When the settlement was made on or after 10 December 1974, the extended meaning of domicile set out in *IHTA 1984, s 267* is used (see **27.2–27.13** and

27.21–27.22). The broad definition of excluded property settlements is qualified by *FA 2006*, from 5 December 2005. The trust property will not be excluded property if a UK domiciliary is or has been beneficially entitled to an interest in possession at any time and that entitlement arose directly or indirectly as a result of a disposition made on or after 5 December 2005 for a consideration in money or money's worth, regardless of who gave the consideration. It is expressly provided that disqualification includes a case where the entitlement arose under a Will or intestacy [*IHTA 1984, s 48(3B–C)*].

[8.25] The *Finance Act 2012, s 210*, with effect from 22 March 2012, added to the inheritance tax downside of tax avoidance schemes under which an individual treated as UK domiciled for inheritance tax purposes has acquired an interest in an excluded property settlement with a view to converting chargeable property into excluded property. Where there is an arrangement under which a UK domiciliary acquires or is enabled to acquire an interest in what would otherwise be excluded property with the result that there is a reduction in the value of the chargeable estate, the settled property acquired is prevented from being excluded property [*IHTA 1984, s 48 (3D)–(3F)*]. Furthermore, that event will trigger a chargeable transfer for inheritance tax purposes and the relevant assets in the offshore settlement will become liable to ten year and exit charges [*IHTA 1984, s 74A and s 74B*]. The charge largely replicates the tax treatment that a UK-domiciled individual would suffer if the assets within the offshore trust, which are 'excluded property' and which would otherwise be ignored for IHT purposes, had instead been transferred to a UK trust. There is an element of retrospective taxation in that, where such an arrangement was put in place before 22 March 2012, the assets concerned will attract ten year and exit charges in relation to events arising after 21 March 2012. In circumstances where *section 74A* triggers a charge to inheritance tax the individual who acquires the interest is among the persons who are liable for the tax [*IHTA 1984, s 201(4A)*].

FOTRA securities

[8.26] A large number of government securities has been issued free of tax while in foreign ownership [*IHTA 1984, s 6(2)*]. These are now known as FOTRA securities (ie free of tax to residents abroad). Before 6 April 1996 the tax exemption depended upon domicile and ordinary residence. Now it depends upon compliance with conditions under which the securities are issued [*IHTA 1984, s 6(2) and s 48(4)* (ie the conditions set out in the prospectus)]. From 6 April 1996 all gilt-edged securities issued previously are FOTRA securities. This may mean that, where held by or for non-domiciliaries, they are excluded property.

[8.27] Further, all gilts (with one exception relating to War Loan) are now excluded property where held by or for individuals not ordinarily resident in the UK, wherever they may be domiciled. This applies before 2013/14, from which year the concept of ordinary residence has been repealed. The change from being ordinary assets to excluded property is not an occasion of charge. So far as the trustees of a discretionary settlement are concerned, such gilts are excluded property provided that the objects of the discretion are within the conditions. If held by the trustees of an interest in possession or an accumulation and maintenance settlement, they are excluded property to the extent that there is a qualifying interest in possession (see **2.34** and **8.7**) in them and the beneficiary is within the conditions. They can also be excluded property if all possible beneficiaries are within the conditions. The test of domicile is that of the general law and not the special one in *IHTA 1984, s 267*. Schemes are sometimes based on FOTRA securities. It is known that the Treasury is unwilling to see anything happen which could be regarded as going back on the promises made when the securities were issued. However, if there is the slightest weakness in any scheme based on FOTRA securities, it will fail in its purpose (see, for instance, *Montagu Trust Co (Jersey) Ltd v IRC* [1989] STC 477, Ch D).

Reversionary interests

[8.28] Reversionary interests under settlements are also usually excluded property. See **12.17–12.18** for further discussion on this point [*IHTA 1984, s 48(1),(2)*].

'Relevant property'

[8.29] 'Relevant property' is settled property in which there is no 'qualifying interest in possession' (see **8.7**), subject to certain other exclusions. *Section 58* lists certain settlements without an interest in possession which are also excluded from the relevant property regime. They are the standard favoured trusts:

(a) charities;
(b) accumulation and maintenance trusts;
(c) bereaved minor trusts and age 18-to-25 trusts (see **8.9–8.12** and **8.13–8.15**);
(d) protective trusts where the failure or determination occurred before 12 April 1978. See **8.41–8.42** for the treatment of a discretionary trust arising under a protective trust, with the principal beneficiary being treated as entitled to a deemed interest in possession. Amendments made by FA 2006 ensure that this treatment applies in a case where the trust was made before 22 March 2006 and the actual trust becomes discretionary after 21 March 2006; in that event the principal beneficiary is treated as entitled to an interest in possession in being at 22 March 2006 [*IHTA 1984, s 88*];
(e) certain trusts for disabled persons set up before 10 March 1981, together with the four categories of disabled person's interest listed at **15.9**;
(f) employee trusts within *IHTA 1984, s 86*, unless there is a non-favoured interest in possession in the trust fund to which either an individual or a certain type of company is beneficially entitled;
(g) maintenance funds for historic buildings, within *IHTA 1984, Sch 4*;
(h) pension funds and superannuation schemes;

(i) trade or professional compensation funds (such as that established by the Law Society);
(j) newspaper trusts (such as that which owns The Guardian), within *IHTA 1984, s 87*;
(k) football club trusts, to the extent that their capital represents pools payments for ground improvements [*FA 1990, s 126*, now repealed by *FA 2012, Sch 39, para 19* with effect from 6 April 2013];
(l) sports and games trusts, to the extent that their capital represents the reduction in pools betting duty from 40% to 37.5% [*FA 1991, s 121*, now repealed by *FA 2012, Sch 39, para 20* with effect from 6 April 2013];
(m) property comprised in an asbestos compensation settlement [*IHTA 1984, s 58(1)(ea)*];
(n) property comprised in a decommissioning security settlement (added by *FA 2013, s 86*); and
(o) excluded property (see **8.23–8.24** and **27.2–27.3**).

[*IHTA 1984, s 58(1)(f)*]

[8.30] Therefore when *section 58* refers to 'relevant property', it is referring to property, not being a qualifying interest in possession or falling within any of the above exceptions, which is contained in a settlement. There is a trap where a relevant property trust, established by a non-UK domiciliary, contains both UK situs and non-UK situs property. The latter would be excluded property. However, its existence in the settlement, and specifically its value immediately after the settlement commenced, has, to date, been taken into account in computing the rate of tax either on exit or at each ten-year anniversary (see *IHTA 1984, s 66(4)(b)* and *s 68(5)(a)*). It is proposed that this trap will disappear from the date of Royal Assent of the Second Finance Act of 2015, as the final elements of the project to simplify relevant property trust charges become law (see CHAPTER 9).

'Payment' and 'Quarter'

[8.31] 'Payment' includes a transfer of assets other than money. 'Quarter' means a period of three months [*IHTA 1984, s 63*].

'Potentially exempt transfer'

[8.32] A 'potentially exempt transfer' is *now* a transfer of value made by an individual which is a gift to another individual or to a disabled trust and is not an exempt transfer [*IHTA 1984, s 3A*]. Should the individual survive the transfer by at least seven years it will become exempt; otherwise it is chargeable. The transfer is assumed to be exempt unless it becomes chargeable (and see **8.34**). A termination of a qualifying interest in possession can also produce a potentially exempt transfer. Prior to 22 March 2006, gifts to interest in possession and accumulation and maintenance trusts were also potentially exempt transfers. A gift to a disabled trust (or, before 22 March 2006, to an accumulation and maintenance settlement) must become settled property in order to qualify.

[8.33] FA 2006 introduced two further categories of potentially exempt transfer, from 22 March 2006. These are:

(a) the payment of premiums on or after 22 March 2006 to trustees of life assurance policies settled on life interest or accumulation and maintenance trusts before that date; and
(b) a lifetime termination of an IPDI in favour of a bereaved minors trust.

[IHTA 1984, s 46A–46B, s 3A (1A)(c)(iii)]

[8.34] If the donor outlives the gift by seven years, the transfer becomes exempt. If he dies during the seven years, it is chargeable. If death occurs within three years of the gift, the full rate of tax is paid. Tapering relief is given in the fourth, fifth, sixth and seventh years. The relief is against tax and does not alter the amount of the transfer which has become chargeable by reason of the premature death. It follows that tapering relief achieves nothing if the transfer is within the nil-rate band. Tapering relief works by reducing the tax charged on the value transferred as follows:

Length of Time Before Death	*Reduction in Tax Charged*
More than 3 but no more than 4 years	20%
More than 4 but no more than 5 years	40%
More than 5 but no more than 6 years	60%
More than 6 but no more than 7 years	80%

[IHTA 1984, s 7(4)]

[8.35] There are a number of transfers which might be thought to be, but which are not, potentially exempt, eg:

(a) a policy on the settlor's own life is settled on accumulation and maintenance trusts (before 22 March 2006). The payment of the premium does not create settled property and the gift does not qualify [IHTA 1984, s 3A(3)]. A payment of cash to the trustees to permit payment of the premium does qualify;
(b) grandfather pays school fees direct to his grandson's school. This is not a gift to an individual etc and does not qualify. If the money is given to the father and he pays the fees, there is then a potentially exempt transfer;
(c) the transfer of woodlands where there has been an estate duty deferment cannot be a potentially exempt transfer. However, business property relief should be available.

[IHTA 1984, s 3A; FA 1986, Sch 19, para 46]

'Gift with reservation'

[8.36] 'Gift with reservation' means any gift made by an individual on or after 18 March 1986 where the donee has not assumed possession and enjoyment at or before the beginning of the 'relevant period', or where throughout the 'relevant period' the donee does not enjoy the gift to the entire exclusion or virtually the entire exclusion of the donor and of any benefit to him by contract or otherwise [FA 1986, s 102]. The 'relevant period' is the seven-year period ending with the donor's death or, if shorter, the period commencing with the gift and ending with the death. There are therefore three tests:

(i)   the donee must take possession and must have the enjoyment of his gift;
(ii) the donor must be excluded (or virtually so) from the asset which he has given away;
(iii) the donor's exclusion must extend to any arrangement whereby he might benefit from the asset or from the gift.

HMRC's Inheritance Tax Manual at IHTM14333 explains their view of 'virtual exclusion' through seven examples, largely in relation to a gift of the family home.

[8.37] In addition, from 22 March 2006, the reservation of benefit regime was extended by treating certain beneficiaries of an interest in possession trust as having made a disposal of the trust property by way of gift where the interest in possession comes to an end during the beneficiary's life. These cases are where the interest in possession arises before 22 March 2006 or, where on or after 22 March 2006, the interest is an immediate post-death interest, a disabled person's interest or a transitional serial interest. Where in such case the beneficiary continues to benefit from the trust property after his interest has come to an end, the provisions of *FA 1986, s 102* and *Sch 20* (but not sections *102A, 102B* and *102C* introduced in 1999) are expressed to apply [*FA 1986, s 102ZA*].

[8.38] The pre-owned assets rules, introduced by *FA 2004* from 2005/06 to counter arrangements made to avoid the reservation of benefit regime, are described at **4.39–4.49**.

[8.39] It will be appreciated that a gift made on or after 18 March 1986 and more than seven years before the donor's death will be caught by the reservation of benefit regime, if within the 'relevant period' one or more of the three tests summarised at 8.36 is not satisfied. If the reservation ends during the relevant period, there is a deemed potentially exempt transfer at that point [*FA 1986, s 102(4)*].

[8.40] If the gift was made during the relevant period and a benefit was reserved, whether or not subsisting at death, there will also be a failed potentially exempt transfer (or indeed an immediately chargeable transfer if the gift was to a relevant property trust). There is therefore the potential for a double charge to inheritance tax which, however, should be relieved by the *Inheritance Tax (Double Charges Relief) Regulations, SI 1987/1130*: typically, the charge which produces the higher amount of tax is retained and the other is disapplied.

Protective trusts

[8.41] The standard definition of the protective trust is in *Trustee Act 1925, s 33* (see APPENDIX D). It is traditionally a trust for a spendthrift life tenant. If he takes any steps to sell, mortgage or anticipate his rights, those rights are brought to an end (as, indeed, if he becomes bankrupt) and the trust becomes discretionary. He and his family are the objects of the discretion. These trusts were popular in Victorian times. More recently they enjoyed a brief spell of popularity when it was found that some inheritance tax schemes could be based upon them. This popularity came to an end on 12 April 1978 when new tax rules took effect.

[8.42] Such trusts made before 22 March 2006 were treated for inheritance tax as interest in possession settlements, the principal beneficiary being the individual with the deemed interest in possession [*IHTA 1984, s 88*]. This analysis continued for inheritance tax (but not for capital gains tax, income tax or general law) purposes even after the trust had become discretionary. As such, however, a protective trust made on or after 22 March 2006 will fall within the 'relevant property' regime.

Chapter 9

Inheritance Tax: Relevant Property Settlements — The Ten-Year Charge

Overview

[9.1] The inheritance tax regime for discretionary (or relevant property) settlements was introduced by *FA 1975*. The ten-year charge is the principal charge to inheritance tax for discretionary settlements. The charge at other times is based on the ten-year charge, but is scaled down to allow for the fact that ten years will not have elapsed. That is the proportionate or 'exit' charge (described in CHAPTER 10).

[9.2] The rules for inheritance tax on discretionary settlements created before 27 March 1974 were slightly different. These are explained at 10.2.

[9.3] Historically, many practitioners have been put off by the complexity of the sections dealing with relevant property settlements. In fact, the statutory provisions which apply to a simple case are themselves simple. The rates of tax are low – a maximum of 6% every ten years – and most modern discretionary settlements (or, since 22 March 2006, lifetime settlements more generally) are modest in size to begin with and the capital very often remains undisturbed. Much of the legislation is about events which will not often happen in practice, such as settlements which are only partly within the relevant property regime, or where there are related settlements, added property and so on.

[9.4] Budget 2012 suggested that the inheritance tax charging regime for relevant property settlements could be usefully simplified in a way which would be revenue neutral. Three Consultation Documents have since been published on the subject. The first *Inheritance Tax: Simplifying Charges on Trusts*, published in July 2012, was a very generic document seeking practitioners' general views on the simplification of relevant property taxation. The second *Inheritance Tax: Simplifying Charges on Trusts – the next stage*, published on 31 May 2013, set out a number of specific proposals. Following much criticism from professionals, proposed new rules for limiting the nil-rate band available to trustees were deferred (until 2015/16 and after further consultation) whereas other changes (concerning income retained but not accumulated (see 9.33–9.36)) and reporting and payment time limits (see 21.2–21.6) were confirmed in Budget 2014, with specific legislation included in Finance Act 2014.

[9.5] On 6 June 2014, HMRC published the third Consultation Document in relation to the items deferred from the second consultation: *Inheritance Tax: A Fairer Way of Calculating Trust Charges* and this set out the idea for a 'Settlement Nil Rate Band' (SNRB) available to each individual to allocate between his or her trusts. The consultation included much detail and worked examples. It was stated that the new rules would apply from 6 June 2014. All the indications were that this was going to become law, and much professional time was spent studying the proposed changes and explaining them to clients. Paragraphs **10.79–10.88** of the 24th edition of this book describe how it was suggested that the SNRB would work.

[9.6] As it turned out, the SNRB idea was dropped in the Chancellor's Autumn Statement of 2014. Instead, an entirely new approach was adopted – without, thankfully, a fourth consultation – and draft legislation was published in December 2014. These changes were not included in the coalition's final *Finance Act 2015*, so there was a further unsatisfactory period of limbo, and the changes were finally adopted as part of *Finance (No 2) Act 2015* which received Royal Assent on 18 November 2015.

[9.7] These changes comprised two main elements:

- *anti-avoidance* rules targeting the use of 'pilot trusts' (see **9.44–9.48**); and
- changes specifically designed to *simplify* the taxation of relevant property trusts (see **9.55–9.56**).

In addition, they also include three miscellaneous 'tidying up' provisions in relation to heritage property, *IHTA, s 144* and *IHTA s 80* and these are detailed at, respectively, paragraphs **9.22**, **10.13** and **9.76**.

The ten-year anniversary

[9.8] In order to discover when the ten-year charge is due, the date of the ten-year anniversary must be ascertained. It is any tenth anniversary of the date of commencement of the settlement [*IHTA 1984, s 61(1)*]. The commencement of a settlement is the date when property is first settled [*IHTA 1984, s 60*]. It is not uncommon to form a settlement with a nominal trust fund of £10 or £100 and to add property later. It is the settling of the initial capital which is the commencement of the settlement and it is this date which will determine the ten-year anniversary. The way in which the legislation allows for added property is by an adjustment which affects the rate of tax rather than by an attempt to tax it as if it were a separate settlement. The adjustments for added property are explained in **9.57–9.64**. No date before 1 April 1983 could have been a ten-year anniversary. In certain cases, where a chargeable event occurred during the year to 31 March 1984 as a result of court proceedings, the first ten-year anniversary could be deferred until 1 April 1984. This does not affect the dates of later anniversaries [*IHTA 1984, s 61(3),(4)*].

[9.9] *IHTA 1984, s 80* could cause a difficulty in deciding the proper ten-year anniversary. *Section 80* deals with the case where a modern settlement (ie one made after 26 March 1974) has become discretionary (or otherwise relevant property) on the termination of a qualifying interest in possession to which the settlor or his spouse/civil partner, widow or widower or surviving civil partner was entitled. This could happen where a man died leaving his estate to his widow for life with remainder over on relevant property trusts for other members of his family. In such a case, *section 80* treats the entry into the discretionary regime as if it were a separate settlement made by the deceased life tenant. Despite this provision, the ten-year anniversaries of the settlement will be determined by reference to the original date of commencement and not to the date on which the interest in possession ceased [*IHTA 1984, s 61(2)*]. This rule in *section 80* was due to be repealed by the original version of *Finance (No 2) Bill 2006*, but was reinstated at Committee Stage. (A drafting error in relation to *section 80* was corrected in *Summer Finance Act 2015* – see **9.76**. This point corrected is somewhat obscure and should be relevant only in a very limited number of unusual cases.)

[9.10] Property can be left on relevant property trusts by a Will. In that case, the settlor's death is the commencement of the settlement and the ten-year anniversaries are determined accordingly [*IHTA 1984, s 83*]. One does not have to consider the administration period, since death is the commencement. Where a relevant property settlement is established by a post-death deed of variation which attracts the relief under *IHTA 1984, s 142(2)*, it is the date of death which constitutes commencement of the settlement (and not the date of the deed). For income tax the position is different. For the period during which the estate administration is in progress, there is no settlement for income tax. The settlement commences when (and to the extent that) the administration period comes to an end – see **2.7–2.12**.

[9.11] One impact of the current regime for trusts introduced by *FA 2006* is that the relevant property regime will apply to many more settlements than it had before Budget Day 2006, particularly to:

- non-qualifying interest in possession trusts (ie all those not listed at **12.1**); and
- accumulation and maintenance settlements in being at 22 March 2006 which were not 'converted' before 6 April 2008 as described at **13.2–13.3**.

In relation to such settlements new to the relevant property regime, the principles for establishing the commencement date of the settlement and the ten-year anniversaries are as found above: there are no special rules. A similar point applies in relation to establishing the settlor's cumulative total of chargeable transfers in the seven year period prior to the making of the settlement (see **9.25–9.26**) and indeed in the case where there are related settlements (see **9.37–9.42**).

EXAMPLE

Reginald made an accumulation and maintenance settlement with £300,000 for his three children on 1 April 1995. The terms of the trust were: entitlement to income to arise on the later of expiry of the 21-year accumulation period from the date of making the settlement and any child's attaining the age 18, with capital deferred until his grandchildren attained 18, with wide powers of advancing capital meanwhile. Reginald had on 1 December 1988 made a discretionary settlement of £100,000 for a wide class of beneficiaries (not including his wife or himself, however). Reginald was aware on 1 April 1995 that were he to die before 1 April 2002 the potentially exempt transfer constituted by £300,000 worth of stocks and shares would have become a chargeable transfer and that the £100,000 put into the 1988 discretionary settlement would have had 'first call' on his nil-rate band (whereas, had he waited until 2 December 1995 to make the accumulation and maintenance settlement, death within seven years would not have had the same effect in terms of accumulation of the discretionary trust transfer). Indeed, on surviving until 1 April 2002, a bottle of champagne was duly enjoyed.

[9.11] Relevant Property Settlements — The Ten-Year Charge

More recently, however, and following professional advice Reginald and his wife Alicia did not wish to change the terms of the accumulation and maintenance settlement to provide either for capital to vest at age 18 or for an 'age 18-to-25' trust (see **8.13–8.15**) and so the trust property entered the relevant property regime on 6 April 2008. The first ten-year charge under the *FA 2006* regime will arise on 1 April 2015 when the relevant property then in the settlement will fall into charge. However, the rate of tax to be applied will take into account the £100,000 settled on discretionary trusts in 1988. There was no way that Reginald or his advisers could have known in 1995 that a completely separate trust would under a new inheritance tax regime affect inheritance tax liabilities and actions taken years later in relation to his accumulation and maintenance settlement.

The amount which is chargeable

Relevant property

[9.12] The amount which will bear the ten-year charge is the value of all 'relevant property' (see **2.34**) contained in the settlement immediately before the anniversary [*IHTA 1984, s 64*]. The words 'immediately before' are taken to require the valuation of shares by reference to prices on the day before the anniversary. Excluded from the charge, from 6 April 2009, is a foreign-owned work of art which is situated in the UK for one or more of the purposes of public display, cleaning and restoration [*IHTA 1984, s 64(2)*].

Accumulations of income

[9.13] Accumulations are brought in as part of the capital at the ten-year anniversary. Therefore, they affect the rate and the amount which is chargeable. The impact of their not having been part of the settled property throughout the period is discussed at **9.30–9.33**. It should be stressed that 'accumulated' in this context has the strict meaning of income having been allocated to capital for trust law purposes eg by trustees exercising a specific power (statutory or express) to accumulate. 'Accumulated income' therefore has to be contrasted to 'undistributed income': income which has been received by the trustees not yet distributed to any beneficiary but not formally allocated to capital. As the relevant property is all the settled property in which there is no qualifying interest in possession, when these rules first appeared it was originally thought that undistributed income was caught too. Happily, however, HMRC take the view that, while accumulations are caught, undistributed income is not (Inland Revenue Statement of Practice SP 8/86, see APPENDIX A). That said, from 2014/15 a new statutory rule brought income which has remained undistributed for five years or more into charge. The provisions of this new rule are detailed at **9.34–9.36**.

Expenses

[9.14] Expenses of valuation for the ten-year charge may not be deducted because they will not have become a liability at the anniversary. The valuation principles which apply are those of *IHTA 1984, s 160* (market value) and *s 162* (liabilities). Where trustees hold property which is expensive to value, such as a landed estate or a holding of shares in a private company, they might commission a valuation shortly before the ten-year anniversary and update it at the anniversary. Alternatively, they might make progress payments against bills rendered before the ten-year anniversary. Anything which lessens the total of the relevant property may be good planning although, given that the tax rate is so low, such planning may not be worth the trouble.

Latent capital gains tax

[9.15] If settled property has increased in value, there may appear to be an anomaly in that the potential liability to capital gains tax cannot be deducted. If there is no expectation of a sale this seems fair. However, if the sale of a holding, say two years after a ten-year anniversary, causes a substantial payment of capital gains tax, the settled capital might well be less than that assessed to the ten-year charge. No relief is available in these circumstances.

[9.16] This point should not be so important in a standard managed portfolio of investments, given the current 20% rate of capital gains tax. As the ten-year charge will not collect tax on shares, etc attracting 100% business property relief or agricultural property relief, holdings in family trading companies should not be at risk.

Business and agricultural property reliefs

[9.17] Business property relief and agricultural property relief are available to relevant property settlements [*IHTA 1984, ss 103(1), 115(1)*]. These are valuation reliefs and, therefore, only affect the amount which is brought into charge.

Valuation principles: liabilities

[9.18] The normal valuation principles of *IHTA 1984, Pt VI* apply. These include a provision directing that a liability secured on a property reduces the value of that property [*IHTA 1984, s 162(4) subject to s 162A inserted by FA 2013, Sch 36*]. Therefore, prior to 17 July 2013, to mortgage agricultural or business property when there are other assets available as security was inheritance tax inefficient (at least in the context of charging relevant property settlements). The contrary position is possible, namely that trustees borrow on the security of assets with no relief, in order to invest in assets attracting the relief. Before 17 July 2013, *section 162(4)* would then cause the debt to be deducted from the assets on which it is secured (so long as, for purposes of business property relief, a liability secured on a non-business asset cannot be regarded as 'incurred' for the purposes of the business: see **9.19**). As a consequence, a settlement which is half invested in assets attracting no relief and half in qualifying agricultural property which is financed by debt secured on the first half could be treated as wholly invested in agricultural property when it came to charging inheritance tax.

[9.18] Relevant Property Settlements — The Ten-Year Charge

EXAMPLE

	£ '000
As viewed for IHT	
Government securities	500
Less: borrowing secured thereon	(500)
	Nil
Agricultural property purchased with above borrowing, attracting APR	500
APR at 100% (assuming requirements are met)	(500)
	Nil
As viewed for commercial purposes	
Government securities	500
Agricultural property	500
Chargeable value	1,000
Less: borrowing	(500)
Net capital	£500

[9.19] It was not possible to activate a reduction in the value of the business for business property relief purposes to the extent that there are liabilities incurred for the purposes of the business (even if either unsecured or secured on non-business assets). These had to be deducted [*IHTA 1984, s 110(b)*].

[9.20] Since 17 July 2013 this planning idea has been rendered ineffective by IHTA 1984, s 162A in respect of liabilities incurred on or after 6 April 2013. For liabilities already in place before that date, the above analysis still stands (but see further **18.71**, particularly in relation to the care required to maintain the beneficial status of pre-6 April 2013 liabilities).

Heritage property

[9.21] Settled heritage property which is the subject of conditional exemption is excluded from the ten-year charge, but it is not possible for trustees to lessen the charge on other property by purchasing such property, as the cost of the property is added to the deemed cumulative total when calculating the next ten-year charge on other property in the settlement [*IHTA 1984, s 79(8), (9)*].

[9.22] *Finance (No 2) Act 2015* amended *IHTA 1984, s 79* to enable claims for conditional exemption to be made within two years of a ten-yearly charge, for charges arising on or after 18 November 2015. For ten yearly charges before this date, a claim had to be made and accepted prior to the anniversary.

The calculation of the tax

[9.23] Having discovered the amount on which tax is chargeable, the rate of tax must be ascertained. This will be 30% of the effective rate (see **9.28**) applicable to a lifetime charge (which is of course half the death rates). The 'effective rate' is determined by reference to a deemed chargeable transfer and a deemed cumulative total. There were different rules for settlements created before 27 March 1974 from those applying to settlements created on or after that date. The rules for pre-27 March 1974 settlements are dealt with at 10.2. The cumulative total of a settlement made after 26 March 1974 includes the settlor's cumulative total of chargeable transfers for the seven years ending with the making of the settlement. There are special rules where property is added (see 9.57–9.64). The rules are explained below, taking the simplest and likeliest situations first and the more complicated ones later [*IHTA 1984, s 66*].

The ten-year charge (simple case)

The deemed chargeable transfer

[9.24] The simplest case is a discretionary settlement with no related settlements, no non-relevant property, no added property, no accumulations of income, and from Royal Assent of the *Summer Finance Bill 2015*, no same-day additions. In such a case there will be only one component in the deemed chargeable transfer, namely the value immediately before the ten-year anniversary of the relevant property contained in the settlement. This will be all the assets within the settlement except for any income arising in the previous five years which remains undistributed.

The deemed cumulative total

[9.25] The cumulative total which will determine the starting point on the rate scale is found by adding:

(a) the settlor's cumulative total of chargeable lifetime transfers in the period of seven years prior to the making of the settlement (ie excluding all transactions on the day when the settlement commenced). Before 18 March 1986, the settlor's cumulative total during the previous ten years was used, but that is irrelevant to any current calculation [*IHTA 1984, s 66(5), (6)*]; and

(b) the amounts assessed to a charge (see CHAPTER 10) during the ten-year period prior to the ten-year anniversary, including amounts charged at the nil rate.

[9.26] Note that, whatever the anniversary, the settlor's 'cumulative total' is always the same, because it is always the seven years ending with the making of the settlement which counts (subject to adjustment where the added property rules apply: see 9.57–9.64). This may be viewed as an anomaly because, while the individual can shake off his old seven-year cumulation with the passage of time, the trustees never can. However, the difference in treatment does seem reasonable. A moment's thought as to the likely number of tax saving discretionary settlements which would spring up were they permitted their second, third etc ten-year charges without any deemed cumulative total will illustrate the point. Note too that all transfers on the day of the settlement are ignored in discovering the cumulative total. However, these transfers will be brought in as related settlements if they are transfers into settlement (see **9.37–9.41**).

[9.27] In calculating the settlor's deemed cumulative total, where the settlement was made before 10 March 1982, distribution payments used to be included. Before 9 March 1982, there was no exit charge. The removal of capital from discretionary settlements was still taxed, but the charge was on 'distribution payments' [*IHTA 1984, s 66(6)*].

The effective rate

[9.28] Having calculated the deemed chargeable transfer and the deemed cumulative total, the lifetime scale (ie the half rate [*IHTA 1984, s 7(2)*] is used to discover the tax appropriate to the deemed chargeable transfer. The tax divided by the deemed chargeable transfer and expressed as a percentage gives the effective (ie average) rate [*IHTA 1984, s 66(1)*].

The rate of ten-year charge

[9.29] The rate of tax actually charged is 30% of the effective rate (see **9.28**). This is applied to the value of the relevant property immediately before the ten-year anniversary to discover the tax payable [*IHTA 1984, ss 64, 66(1)*].

EXAMPLE

Robert, a generous man, used all his annual exemptions up to and including 2004/05 and, by the end of August 2004, had a cumulative total of £263,000 of chargeable transfers over seven years. On 1 September 2004, he settled £75,000 on discretionary trusts. He paid inheritance tax of £18,750 (on the grossed up amount of the gift). He lived for more than seven years. His trustees invested the £75,000 and distributed income regularly. By 1 September 2014, their investments were worth £300,000. The inheritance tax rates in 2014/15 are the same as in 2004/05, but the nil-rate threshold has been increased to £325,000.

The ten-year charge is therefore calculated as follows:

	£	£
Deemed chargeable transfer (ie the value of the relevant property immediately before 1 September 2014)		300,000
Nil-rate band in 2014/15	325,000	
Settlor's cumulative seven year total	(263,000)	
Balance of nil-rate band		62,000
Inheritance tax on lifetime scale (half rate, ie 20% of £238,000)		47,600
Effective rate: £47,600 divided by £300,000 = 15.87%		
Rate of ten-year charge = 30% of 15.87% = 4.76%		
Ten-year charge £300,000 @ 4.76%		£14,280

Note that in such a simple example, the calculation of the effective rate is an unnecessary step; the tax has to be 30% of the charge which would have been due on the lifetime scale.

In a case (unlike the above) where the deemed cumulative total exceeds the nil-rate band in the relevant year, the effective rate can never be more than 20% and so the rate of the ten-year charge never more than 6%.

Accumulations of income

[9.30] Accumulations of income do form part of the total of relevant property: see **9.13** [*IHTA 1984, s 64*]. Therefore, they affect the rate. However, they are not taxed at the same rate as other relevant property because they have not been comprised in the settlement for the whole ten years. That part of the relevant property at the ten-year anniversary which represents accumulations must be taxed at a proportion of the rate, calculated on a time basis [*IHTA 1984, s 66(2)*].

[9.31] The rate on each accumulation is reduced by one fortieth for each successive quarter before that accumulation became relevant property. In other words, if an accumulation took place $2\frac{1}{2}$ years (ie 10 quarters) after the last ten-year anniversary it will be taxed at $^{30}/_{40}$ of the rate suffered by ordinary relevant property. If there are many investments, sales, payments of expenses, reinvestments and so on, it is impossible to point to any particular asset held at the ten-year anniversary and say that that is an accumulation made on a particular date. HMRC Trusts and Estates have an actuarial formula which can deal with this sort of case. It assumes even growth over the ten years. Fortunately, many settlements contain only a few holdings, so that the origin of capital at the ten-year anniversary can be traced back. This leads to the question of when, as a matter of general law, undistributed income becomes an accumulation. Sometimes, the investment of the income demonstrates accumulation. In many cases it will be related to the date when the trustees consider the accounts for the year. See **6.80–6.85** for the income tax analysis of whether a payment constitutes income or capital for the recipient.

[9.32] Decided cases have considered this issue, eg *Gulbenkian's Settlement Trusts (No 2), Re, Stevens v Maun* [1970] Ch 408, [1969] 2 All ER 1173, Ch D. That case related to two settlements made in 1929 and 1938 by Calouste Sarkis Gulbenkian. He died domiciled in Portugal in 1955 but the proper law of the settlements was that of England. The trustees doubted their powers and made no decision as to income. There was a possibility of the settlements being void for uncertainty. The point was resolved in the House of Lords in 1968. The income not distributed dated back to 1957 when the doubts first arose. It was found to have been reasonable for the trustees to have left matters undecided for so long, and their power to accumulate the income of past years could still be exercised.

Undistributed income

[9.33] In cases where trustees have no doubts about the extent of their power to accumulate there will nevertheless inevitably be a time gap between the receipt of trust income and the trustees' decision to either distribute it to a beneficiary or accumulate it to capital. When, as a matter of general law, does undistributed income become an accumulation in these circumstances? There seems to have been a rule of thumb within HMRC Trusts and Estates to treat undistributed income as becoming capital for purposes of the ten-year charge once two years have passed since it arose unless there was evidence to the contrary; however, it was pointed out by Chris Whitehouse at the Chartered

[9.33] Relevant Property Settlements — The Ten-Year Charge

Institute of Taxation's Residential Conference in September 2012 that there is no basis for this two-year time limit applied by HMRC. HMRC acknowledged the legal uncertainty in the 'Summary of Responses' document to the second consultation (*Inheritance Tax: Simplification of trust charges – the next stage*) published in December 2013 and concluded that a specific deeming rule is required. Paragraph 3.52 reads:

> 'Often the income is retained for many years and reinvested within the income account but when the 10 year anniversary arrives the trustees will maintain (where there is a mere power to accumulate) that the power still exists but they have not yet decided whether to accumulate. HMRC sometimes challenge this sort of analysis and in effect argues that if the power has expired but the income has been retained there has been a de facto accumulation – but without recourse to litigation it is not clear what the true legal position is. Similarly where there is a trust to accumulate and a power to distribute, trustees will argue that even where income has been retained for long periods and reinvested, they still have the power to distribute it. HMRC therefore considered a deeming rule would provide certainty about the IHT position in these situations and avoid long running disputes between the taxpayer and HMRC.'

The deeming rule is now contained in *IHTA 1984, s 64(1A), (1B), (1C) and (2A)* (and as introduced by *Finance Act 2014*), the details of which are explained at **9.34–9.36**.

[9.34] Undistributed income of a settlement will (subject to the two caveats outlined at **9.35**), in relation to any ten-year anniversary charge arising on or after 6 April 2014, be deemed to be relevant property comprised in the settlement in the following circumstances [*IHTA 1984, s 64(1A)*]:

- the income arose before the start of the five years ending immediately before the ten-year anniversary. HMRC had originally proposed a two year period but this was extended following the consultation;
- the income arose (directly or indirectly) from property comprised in the settlement that, when the income arose, was relevant property; and
- when the income arose, no person was beneficially entitled to an interest in possession in the property from which the income arose.

[9.35] There are two caveats to the general rule – both relating to 'excluded property'. First, income arising in an 'excluded property settlement' (see **8.24–8.25**) will not be deemed to be relevant property where it is situated outside the United Kingdom, or is represented by a holding in an authorised unit trust or a share in an open-ended investment company [*IHTA 1984, s 64(1B)*]. Secondly, income of a settlement will not be deemed to be relevant property where that income is represented by FOTRA securities held for a qualifying beneficiary (see **8.26–8.27**) [*IHTA 1984, s 64(1C)*].

[9.36] There are three final observations to make in relation to this new deeming rule:

- First, there is no requirement that the five year 'retention' period needs to have arisen post-6 April 2014. Income which had been retained for five years or more as at that date became immediately liable to charge in relation to any ten-year anniversary charge after that date.

- Secondly, where undistributed income does become liable to charge, the time apportionment rules which would ordinarily apply to accumulations (see 9.30) are disapplied [IHTA 1984, s 64(2A)]. In effect, the undistributed income is treated as having been relevant property for the whole of the ten-year period.
- Thirdly, the rules apply only to ten-year anniversary charges. Specifically, they do not apply to exit charges (detailed in CHAPTER 10). This is helpful because it means that when distributing income, trustees do not have to consider the possibility that an exit charge might arise – ie as would otherwise have been the case whenever they were distributing income retained for more than five years.

Where the amounts involved are significant enough, the second and third points above will provide a motive for trustees to consider either formally accumulating (to get the benefit of time apportionment) or distributing (to avoid a relevant property charge completely) retained income before a ten yearly anniversary.

Related settlements

[9.37] The first complication which can affect the calculation of the ten-year charge, but which will not often be seen in practice, is the related settlement. Settlements are related if the settlor is the same and they commence on the same day. There is an exception for charitable settlements (but not temporary ones) [IHTA 1984, s 62]. There is no exception for any other type of settlement, so that if a discretionary settlement and a qualifying disabled trust were made on the same day, the discretionary settlement would have a related settlement. (Given the terms of the new rules for mixed trusts introduced by *Finance (No 2) Act 2015* – which, broadly, excludes non-relevant property from a calculation of the rate of charge – this is now something of an anomaly – see 9.55–9.56). In a lifetime situation, a related settlement could be an avoidance device because the deemed cumulative total does not include transfers made on the day on which the settlement commences. Therefore, were the related settlement not brought into account, there might be occasions when a settlor could have a number of small settlements all made on the same day with the intention of producing a lower rate. Ten settlements each with £10,000, all sharing the same deemed cumulative total, would obviously be more inheritance tax efficient looking forward than one with £100,000, were it not for the aggregation of related settlements. If the property will grow substantially in value, several settlements on the same day may be acceptable, as the related settlement is brought into the calculation at its value at commencement. Historically, a better result could be achieved by a series of small settlements made on separate days, followed up by a substantial gift on one day. The result is a series of settlements each with a different commencement date, not being related settlements. There would, of course, be tax on the substantial gift. See 9.39 for a decided case on the point. The new rules for 'same-day additions' introduced by *Finance (No 2) Act 2015* mean that since 10 December 2014 such planning has no longer been effective – see 9.44–9.48.

[9.38] The potentially adverse impact of related settlements is to be found in *IHTA 1984, s 66(4)(c)*. The deemed chargeable transfer mentioned in 9.24 is increased by the value of the related settlement at the time it was set up. Note that this value is not itself charged to tax, unless it is chargeable in its own right (ie the related settlement is itself within the relevant property regime); it is brought into account in order to fix the rate applicable to the main settlement. As has been said, the value of the related settlement which has to be brought into the deemed chargeable transfer is the value of the property comprised in it at the time it was set up. Once ascertained, this figure will recur on every ten-year anniversary. Changes in the related settlement once it has been set up have no consequence. It can have been distributed but the figure will still recur as part of the deemed chargeable transfer. The proposed new rules for 'same-day additions' will operate in a similar way – see 9.44–9.48).

[9.39] HMRC Trusts and Estates have traditionally challenged both a series of settlements made on successive days and a group of nominal settlements made by the one person on the same day, where further substantial capital is added on a subsequent day, even in cases where there are only three or four settlements, on the basis of the associated operations rules [*IHTA 1984, s 268*]. There has been a case on this point: *Rysaffe Trustee Co (CI) Ltd v IRC* [2003] EWCA Civ 356, [2003] STC 536, 5 ITELR 706. The Special Commissioner decided in favour of HMRC, but her decision was reversed in the High Court. Put simply, Park J said that there had been five settlements in this case as a matter of trust law, each executed on successive days and that they could not be treated otherwise for inheritance tax purposes under *IHTA 1984, s 43* or indeed under the associated operations provisions of *section 268*. In particular, the judge held that *section 268* was not an anti-avoidance provision, but rather a rule of construction. The High Court decision was upheld by the Court of Appeal.

[9.40] The issue of related settlements can occur also following a death. A fairly common formula is for a legacy equal to the nil-rate band to be settled by the Will on discretionary terms and for the residue to be settled on the widow/surviving civil partner for life. The widow's/surviving civil partner's fund would not be a related settlement when calculating a ten-year charge on the nil-rate band settlement because of the exception provided by *IHTA 1984, s 80*. If, after the widow's/civil partner's death, the residuary estate remained settled for the benefit of the children of the marriage, then it would still not 'relate' to the nil-rate band legacy given by their father, as the section deems the children's interest to have been settled by their mother (and, accordingly, perhaps oddly, could be related to another relevant property settlement made under the widow's/surviving civil partner's Will). However, if the Will did not benefit the surviving spouse/civil partner, *section 80* has no relevance. Therefore, if the Will set up a nil-rate band discretionary settlement and a residuary settlement for children, the residuary settlement would be 'related' to the other. Before 10 December 2014 (see 9.43), this issue could also be avoided by the use of 'pilot' settlements. For example, if the testator had on the day on which he made his Will established a £10 'pilot' settlement and then under his Will directed the transfer of the nil-rate band amount to the lifetime settlement, there would not have been a related settlement issue arising out of the residuary settlement for his children. This was because, under *IHTA 1984*, s 62, the discretionary settlement would be treated as having been made on the date of the pilot settlement.

[9.41] The significance of the related settlements rule was extended by the present inheritance tax regime for trusts introduced by *FA 2006*. Settlements which, when made, were potentially exempt transfers became in certain cases brought into the relevant property regime for the first time. So when, for example, a person made, say, an accumulation and maintenance settlement in 1991, wanting also to make an interest in possession settlement at around that time, he would have had no reason to consider the related settlements rules. Indeed, there might have been a very good reason for making both settlements on the same day. This is that, in the event of death within seven years, both settlements would share rateably in the nil-rate band. Unfortunately that became something of a disadvantage. This is because, once *s 49(1)* ceases to apply to the interest in possession settlement, and assume that following 5 April 2008 the accumulation and maintenance settlement enters the relevant property regime, the initial value of each settlement was taken into account in computing the ten-year anniversary charge in the other.

EXAMPLE

Developing the example at **9.11**, on 1 April 1995 Reginald also made an interest in possession settlement in the sum of £125,000 for his spendthrift sister Ruth. Again, this was a potentially exempt transfer. However, Reginald now finds, for reasons explained above, that the £125,000 initial value is brought into account as a related settlement in computing the first ten-year anniversary charge on the settlement for his children (but not likely subsequent charges), which expressly had been kept outside the relevant property regime in 1995 when Reginald set up the trust for his sister.

[9.42] The inheritance tax planning suggestion of a series of pilot trusts to take advantage of what might be called 'the *Rysaffe* principle' was expressly approved by HMRC, for purposes of the General Anti-Abuse rule which applies from 2013/14. This may be seen by example 26 in the guidance where HMRC comment on the example that 'the arrangements accord with established practice accepted by HMRC and are accordingly not regarded as abusive'.

[9.43] Thus, although from 10 December 2014, it has to be assumed that such planning will no longer be effective (because of the introduction of a new rule for same-day additions), planning completed before that date is 'grandfathered' and should remain effective (see **9.44–9.48**).

Same-day additions

[9.44] To block the use of 'pilot trusts' to maximise the nil-rate bands available when calculating relevant property charges, as described at **9.39–9.43**, *Finance (No 2) Act 2015* introduced new provisions for 'same-day additions' (now contained in *IHTA 1984, ss 62A–62C*). The planning was simple enough, with a series of settlements being created on separate days with nominal amounts, and then additions made to all those settlements on the same day. Had all the settlements been created on the same day, they would

[9.44] Relevant Property Settlements — The Ten-Year Charge

have been 'related settlements' for inheritance tax purposes and the total value of all of them would have been taken into account when calculating the rate of a tax on a ten-yearly or exit charge for each of them. However, *additions* made to other settlements on the same day were not brought into account in the same way, thus effectively enabling each settlement to benefit from a much larger nil-rate band. The new rules treat 'same-day additions' in broadly the same way as related settlements (see **9.38**) and 'same-day additions' to other settlements (together with the initial value in those settlements) will have to be brought into account when calculating the rate of tax.

[9.45] The final legislation differed in some significant respects from that originally published in draft in December 2014:

- It is now a requirement [*IHTA 1984, ss 62A(1)(d), (e)*, and *62A(3)*] that for a least some part of the period up to the addition, the settlement added to has to be a 'relevant property' settlement. This brings these rules into line with the simplification change set out below.
- *De minimis* additions of up to £5,000 [IHTA 1984, s 62B(3) and (4)] can also now be ignored.

[9.46] There are specific exceptions [*IHTA 1984, s 62B(1)*] allowing additions to charitable settlements and the lifetime payment of certain life insurance premiums to be ignored.

[9.47] Finally, there is some element of grandfathering in relation to 'Protected settlements' [*IHTA 1984, s 62C*]:

- where a settlement was created before 10 December 2014 (the date of the original draft legislation is still the cut off date) and the settlor has made no additions to it after that date, any 'same-day additions' relevant to it before that date will not be taken into account; and
- where there is an addition after that date which is made under the terms of the settlor's Will which was also made before that date (but see further below), that too will not be taken into account provided the addition is made before 6 April 2017.

This, of course, means that the settlor has to die before 6 April 2017 to take advantage of this provision. (The original date proposed in the December 2014 draft was 6 April 2016.)

[9.48] It is also not strictly necessary that the Will was in place before 10 December 2014, as the legislation talks only of a 'protected testamentary disposition'. This is defined [*IHTA 1984, s 62C(4)*] as being 'a disposition effected by the provisions of the settlor's Will that at the settlor's death are, in substance, the same as they were immediately before 10 December 2014'. HMRC have given little guidance on what this means; however, the use of the words 'in substance' must surely enable a settlor to create a new Will after 10 December 2014 as long as any clauses adding assets to pre-10 December 2014 settlements were in their Will before that date, and remain substantially the same in any new Will.

Relevant and non-relevant property combined

[9.49] To date, the next complication which could affect the calculation has been an adjustment which is necessary if there are assets within the settlement which have never been within the relevant property regime. This is something of a parallel to the idea of related settlements and, in the same way, the deemed chargeable transfer is increased by the value of the non-relevant property immediately after the capital was settled (and which has not subsequently become relevant property, while remaining comprised in the settlement) [*IHTA 1984, s 66(4)(b)*]. The one element of true simplification introduced by *Finance (No 2) Act 2015* was a change to these rules (see **9.55–9.56**). These new rules have effect only for events on or after 18 November 2015, and the rules set out below will still apply to earlier events.

[9.50] It was considered necessary to bring in these assets because of the possibility of siphoning value between parts of the same settlement. The likeliest situation in which this might emerge is a settlement where some members of a family have been given fixed interests (ie qualifying interests in possession) and there is some fund within the settlement where others are to benefit from a discretionary power. This must be something of a rarity, especially since 22 March 2006. In such a case the value of the assets which have never been relevant property (ie never within the relevant property regime) is brought into the deemed chargeable transfer to fix the rate, but is not itself charged to tax. These assets are not part of the cumulative total because the cumulative total does not include transactions effected on the day on which the discretionary settlement commenced.

[9.51] As a variation of the above, property could have changed in character, having been non-relevant for part of the ten-year period whilst being relevant immediately before the ten-year anniversary. This is dealt with by an adjustment to the rate and not to the deemed chargeable transfer. For instance, the trustees of a discretionary settlement might purchase a house for the beneficiary and (HMRC applying Statement of Practice SP 10/79) create a qualifying interest in possession, before 22 March 2006. In due course, the beneficiary leaves and the property reverts to being relevant property. The rate applicable to such property is reduced by one-fortieth for each successive complete quarter before it became or last became relevant property [*IHTA 1984, s 66(2)*]. See **9.31** for the application of this principle to accumulations of income; and see also **9.65** for an additional example of the alteration to the deemed cumulative total which is necessary when, within the ten-year period, relevant property became non-relevant and relevant again before the ten-year anniversary.

EXAMPLE 1

Rachel's case is identical to that of Robert in the example in **9.29**, except that her settlement was discretionary as to one half and there was a qualifying disabled trust of the other half. The ten-year charge is calculated as follows:

[9.51] Relevant Property Settlements — The Ten-Year Charge

	£
Deemed chargeable transfer	
Value of relevant property immediately before 1 September 2014	150,000
Value of non-relevant property on 1 September 2004 (*not* 2014)	37,500
	187,500
Deemed cumulative total (ie the settlor's chargeable transfers before commencement)	263,000
	450,500
Nil-rate band	(325,000)
Value charged to IHT	125,500
IHT on lifetime scale (half rate, ie £125,500 @ 20%)	25,100
Effective rate: £25,100 divided by £187,500 = 13.39%	
Rate of ten-year charge = 30% of 13.39% = 4.02%	
Ten-year charge on £150,000 @ 4.02%	£6,030

EXAMPLE 2

Ros' case was identical to that of Rachel in Example 1 above except that the disabled trust lasted only two years. The disabled trust comes to an end on 1 September 2006 and is succeeded by a non-qualifying interest in possession. On 1 September 2014, the settled funds are worth £300,000. The ten-year charge is calculated thus:

	£
Deemed chargeable transfer	
Value of relevant property immediately before 1 September 2014	300,000
Deemed cumulative total (ie the settlor's chargeable transfers before commencement)	263,000
Value charged to tax (£238,000 being in excess of the nil-rate band of £325,000, so that only this amount attracts tax at a positive rate)	563,000
Inheritance tax on lifetime scale (half rate, ie £238,000 @ 20%)	47,600
Effective rate: £47,600 divided by £300,000 = 15.87%	
Rate of ten-year charge = 30% of 15.87% = 4.76%	
Ten-year charge:	
4.76% on one half (£150,000)	7,140
32/40ths of 4.76% on other half (£150,000)	5,712
	£12,852

[9.52] The opposite case, where the capital is all discretionary at the commencement but is appointed away from the discretionary regime before the ten-year anniversary and remains outside that regime, is taxed by an exit charge (see CHAPTER 10). In the alternative case, that is where property comprised in the settlement was not relevant property immediately before the ten-year anniversary but was relevant property at some time during the ten-year period, there will have been an exit charge on the property ceasing to be relevant property: see Example 1 at **10.25**.

[9.53] It is not unknown for settlements to have a life tenant (ie with a qualifying interest in possession) and for discretionary trusts to emerge on the death of the life tenant. This could most easily happen in a settlement made by a Will, where with a death on or after 22 March 2006 the life tenant would have an immediate post-death interest. If the settlement is an inter vivos settlement then the question of avoidance arises under *IHTA 1984, ss 54A, 54B*. Those provisions are aimed at the use of potentially exempt transfers as a cheap method of creating discretionary settlements (though since 22 March 2006 have become largely redundant, except where a qualifying disabled trust is set up). Once interest in possession settlements became potentially exempt transfers, the way was open to settle capital on someone who had not yet used his nil-rate band and after a short period arrange for the termination of his interest. If the result of the termination was that the capital was held on discretionary trusts, the result was a discretionary settlement sheltered by the former life tenant's nil-rate band. This device became impossible on 17 March 1987 when *IHTA 1984, ss 54A* and *54B* became effective. It could (before 22 March 2006) have been used on a longer term basis where the termination was not to take place within the next seven years nor at a time when the settlor was still alive, but the creation of such a settlement seemed unlikely.

[9.54] There will be older (pre-2005) settlements where a discretionary trust arose upon the termination of a qualifying interest in possession. The most common case may be those where the income beneficiary is the settlor, his spouse, widow or widower. If the settlor is a beneficiary, then the settlement was probably made before the introduction of the gifts with reservation of benefit regime (ie before 18 March 1986). Nowadays, a settlement where there is provision for a widow/surviving civil partner, or one made by Will where the surviving spouse/civil partner has the income and discretionary trusts emerge on her/his death, are still quite common. In such a case, the property subject to the interest in possession is not brought into the calculation of the ten-year charge because the property is treated as not yet comprised in the settlement. When it does become relevant property it is treated as a separate settlement made by the deceased life tenant (see also **9.9**) [*IHTA 1984, s 80*].

Finance (No 2) Act 2015 simplification

[9.55] The one piece of true simplification resulting from the long simplification project and introduced by *Finance (No 2) Act 2015* (by way of amendments to *IHTA 1984, ss 66, 68* and *69*) is that, for events on or after 18 November 2015, when calculating the rate of any periodic charge, the historical value of any property within a settlement which has never been relevant property, will no longer be a factor. This change will be particularly helpful in two common situations:

- Many old accumulation and maintenance trusts fell into the relevant property regime from April 2008. Many such trusts had parts of the trust fund already held on qualifying interest in possession trusts (ie for older grandchildren) which were not relevant property. Going forward, the historical value of such parts can be ignored. (And there are similar new provisions for '18-25 Trusts' in *IHTA 1984, s 71F*.)
- Where an 'excluded property trust' holds some UK assets, the relevant property tax rate in relation to those assets will no longer have to be calculated by reference to any non-UK property.

[9.56] This change fits with that limiting same-day additions only to relevant property settlements; however, one anomaly remains. Related settlements (ie settlements created on the same day) continue to be counted whether or not they are relevant property settlements. A further simplification excluding such settlements from the rate calculations would be helpful and consistent.

Property is added to the settlement

[9.57] Settlors should not add to an existing relevant property settlement except, perhaps, by an exempt transfer (ie within the annual £3,000 or the normal expenditure out of income exemptions). This is because, where a chargeable transfer by the settlor increases the settled capital, the deemed cumulative total of the settlor may be recalculated [*IHTA 1984, s 67(1), (3)*]. The settlor's cumulative total before the commencement is replaced, if this is greater, by his cumulative total before the addition. The chargeable transfer could be a transfer of fresh capital or it could be a deemed disposition increasing the value rather than the amount of property within the settlement. For example, a life policy is settled on discretionary trusts and premiums continue to be paid by the settlor. The premiums are added property, unless the settlor does not make a chargeable transfer when he pays them (eg as falling within the normal expenditure out of income exemption). Note that, perhaps curiously, payments of life assurance premiums on policies settled on life interest or accumulation and maintenance trusts before 22 March 2006 continue to be potentially exempt transfers (see **8.33**).

[9.58] To prevent minor or accidental transfers from being caught, certain transfers are ignored. These are such transfers as are not primarily intended to increase the value of the settled property and do not, in fact, increase the value by more than 5% [*IHTA 1984, s 67(2)*]. In the Parliamentary debates on this provision, the example given was of a family company having financial problems which caused the family to introduce cash. If the shares were held in a discretionary settlement, the value of the trust property would be increased. The increase would be unintentional and, were it within the 5% limit, would not be within the added property provisions (see Standing Committee A's debates on the *Finance Bill 1982*, col 689, 15 June 1982). The waiver of dividends is another possibility.

[9.59] If the added property provisions do apply, the deemed cumulative total is likely to be increased. Assuming that the settlor has made only two chargeable transfers to the settlement, namely the first to set it up and a second to trigger the added property provisions, the steps are as follows:

(a) Take the original deemed cumulative total (ie the settlor's total in the seven years prior to the making of the settlement).
(b) Take the settlor's deemed cumulative total for the seven years prior to the second transfer. From this total, deduct, to the extent that they are included in the total:
   (i) the chargeable transfers made on the day when property was added to the settlement, and
   (ii) any property taken into account in determining the rate of a ten-year anniversary charge and any property suffering an exit charge in the ten years before that anniversary.
(c) Work out the deemed cumulative total on a normal basis, ie the original total plus the total of amounts subject to the exit charge.
(d) Compare this with the settlor's current cumulative total as adjusted in (*b*) above.
(e) The higher figure is the current deemed cumulative total of the settlor [*IHTA 1984, s 67*].

EXAMPLE

Ruth made a discretionary settlement of £150,000 on 1 September 2004. She was (and remains) in the habit of using her annual £3,000 exemption every year, but had not made any chargeable transfers in the seven years prior to the date of settlement, so the value fell within her nil-rate. On 1 September 2005 she gave £100,000 to each of her twin children on their 21st birthday. These were potentially exempt transfers and therefore assumed, for the time being, to be exempt. On 1 September 2007, having unexpectedly received an inheritance from a long lost cousin, she gave £125,000 to her discretionary settlement, assuming mistakenly that she was still within her nil-rate band, continuing to make use of her annual £3,000 exemptions on 1 May of each year. Unfortunately Ruth died on 1 October 2007, making the 2005 gifts subject to tax and this will affect the application of the added property provisions under *section 67* for purposes of the ten-year charge to arise on 1 September 2014.

Working through the steps above:

(a) Ruth's original deemed cumulative total was nil.
(b) Her deemed cumulative total for the seven years prior to the second transfer on 1 September 2007 was £350,000 (£150,000 settled on 1 September 2004 plus £200,000 on 1 September 2005 (the gifts to her children having now become chargeable by reason of her death within seven years). From this total a deduction of £150,000 is made on account of (ii) in (b) above reducing the total to £200,000.
(c) Ruth's deemed cumulative total on a 'normal' basis is nil.
(d) £200,000 exceeds nil.
(e) Ruth's adjusted cumulative total for purposes of calculating the ten-year anniversary charge on 1 September 2014 (at least, on the basis of the current regime) is therefore £200,000.

Separately, what is the impact of Ruth's unexpected death on both the 2005 and the 2007 gifts? The gifts of £100,000 to each of the children will, on a pro rata basis, both benefit from the balance of the nil-rate band in 2007/08 and will in part attract tax at 40%. Ruth's deemed cumulative total as at 1 September 2007 is £350,000. Because that total exceeds her nil-rate band (£300,000 for 2007/08), her gift of £125,000 to her settlement is chargeable to inheritance tax at 40%, payable by the trustees. If the tax is paid by Ruth's estate, grossing up should not apply (in the absence of a commitment by Ruth to pay any tax herself).

[9.60] There are further rules for more complex cases (eg where there have been more chargeable transfers to the settlement). However, these should never arise in practice because, once the consequences of adding property have been digested, the settlor (at least, one who is well advised) is never likely to add further property. It is, in any event, usual for the solicitor to draft a separate trust deed for each significant gift which is to be settled. It is rare to see property being added, apart from occasions when a nominal £100 is settled in order to set things going and the real gift is made a week or two later.

[9.61] The manner in which added property is dealt with is inevitably complicated. The alternative would have been even worse. It would have been necessary to treat each chargeable transfer to the trustees as a new settlement (which result has been argued to follow from the definition of 'settlement' in *IHTA 1984, s 43(2)*), though is not generally applied in practice by HMRC Trusts and Estates, at least in relation to relevant property settlements made by a UK domiciled settlor. But it will be a point taken in relation to additions to excluded property settlements (see **27.4**) where the settlor makes an addition at a time when he has become actually or deemed domiciled in the UK: see **9.64**.

[9.62] The tax consequences of added property are much worse if the addition of property to the settlement follows a significant increase in the settlor's cumulative total of transfers, so that the order of his gifts will matter. The deduction of the added property is necessary to the second calculation of the deemed cumulative total (**9.59** (b)) because that property would otherwise be counted into the total twice. It would have formed part of the second deemed cumulative total as well as being part of the relevant property brought into the deemed chargeable transfer.

[**9.63**] If there is an existing relevant property settlement and, on the settlor's death, his Will or intestacy causes property to be added to it, that property is treated as property added on the date of the death [*IHTA 1984, s 83*]. This is a sensible provision, because the general law would cause the property to vest in the settlement trustees only when appropriated or assented to by the personal representatives. The effect of the section is to ignore the administration period.

[**9.64**] Reference has been made earlier in this chapter (see **9.9** and **9.54**) to the possibility of the relevant property being added to after 26 March 1974 by the termination of an interest in possession held by the settlor or his spouse/civil partner. This is treated as a separate settlement [*IHTA 1984, s 80*] and the added property rules do not apply. There can be a rather specialised problem for the settlement which reserves a life interest to a non-UK domiciled settlor or spouse/civil partner and is held thereafter on discretionary terms. This would normally contain excluded property. However, there will be inheritance tax upon the discretionary trust coming into operation unless the former life tenant is still not domiciled in the UK at that date *and* that property (other than authorised unit trusts or shares in an open-ended investment company) remains situated outside the UK [*IHTA 1984, ss 48(3), 48(3A), 80, 82*].

Property changing character within the settlement

[**9.65**] The reduction of rates where relevant property is not relevant for the full ten years has already been explained (see **9.49** and **9.51**). Because the values caught by the exit charges are added in to the deemed cumulative total (see **9.25** (b)), there could be double counting. This would happen if property had remained within the settlement but had been subject to an exit charge in the ten years prior to the anniversary concerned. For example, a life interest might have arisen in respect of part of the property for part of the ten-year period. This would have precipitated an exit charge and yet the property, being still within the settlement at the ten-year anniversary and having become relevant property again, would form part of the deemed chargeable transfer. In order to overcome this, the deemed cumulative total is reduced by the lesser of two figures, the first being the amount charged to the exit charge and the second being the value included for that property in the deemed chargeable transfer (ie the value immediately before the ten-year anniversary of the property which had been, for a while, subject to a life interest) [*IHTA 1984, s 67(6), (7)*].

EXAMPLE

		£
1 April 2004	A discretionary settlement is made – initial capital	200,000
1 April 2006	Property is appointed to A for life with reversion to the main trusts of the settlement.	
	It is valued at	100,000
1 April 2011	A dies and the property reverts	
1 April 2014	The settled property is valued as follows:	
	The appointed property	240,000
	Other assets	150,000
	Total	£390,000

In calculating the ten-year charge on 1 April 2014, the deemed chargeable transfer is:

Per valuation	£390,000
and the deemed cumulative total is:	£
Settlor's seven-year cumulations [*IHTA 1984, s 66(5)(a)*] (say)	45,000
Amount charged to exit charge [*IHTA 1984, s 66(5)(b)*]	100,000
Adjustment per *IHTA 1984, s 67(6)*—the lesser of £100,000 and £240,000	(100,000)
Deemed cumulative total	£45,000

Settled legacies

[9.66] Property can be held on relevant property trusts by reason of a settled discretionary legacy in a Will. The property so settled is treated as being comprised in the resultant Will trust upon the death of the testator [*IHTA 1984, s 83*]. The death causes a deemed transfer of value of the deceased person's estate immediately before his death [*IHTA 1984, s 4(1)*]. The deceased is the settlor of the settled legacy and his cumulative total of chargeable lifetime transfers (including any potentially exempt transfers which become chargeable as a result of death within seven years) becomes the deemed cumulative total of the trustees. The solicitor who drafts a Will cannot guess at the chargeable transfers which the client might make in the seven years prior to death. Therefore, he should warn the client that his gifts within those seven years can substantially alter the tax position of his trustees going forward, that is even if the legacy is expressed to be free of tax on the death.

[9.67] The solicitor should also consider the effect of any other settled legacies (noting the definition of 'settlement' in *IHTA 1984, s 43(2)*), because the general rule is that they are related settlements, having the same settlor and being made on the same day (see **9.37–9.41**). A legacy settled on a surviving spouse (or civil partner) will not be a related settlement. This is the effect of *IHTA 1984, s 80*. *Section 80(2)* causes the surviving spouse/civil partner to be within the ambit of the provision. *Section 80(1)* deals with the case where the settlor, his spouse or civil partner and (by virtue of *subsection (2)*) his surviving spouse/civil partner are beneficially entitled to an interest in possession from the commencement of the settlement. *Section 80(1)* then directs that the settled property shall 'be treated as not having become comprised in the settlement on that occasion'. Therefore, the settled legacy for the widow/surviving civil partner cannot be related to another legacy for which the Will declares discretionary trusts. This section has already been addressed in **9.9** and **9.54**. However, an immediate post-death interest for a beneficiary other than a surviving spouse or civil partner, even though itself outside the scope of the relevant property regime, will be related to a discretionary trust arising under the Will.

Trusts of pension death benefits

[9.68] Property held within a registered pension scheme, a qualifying non-UK pension scheme or a *section 615(3)* scheme, is excluded from the definition of relevant property [*IHTA 1984, s 58(1)(d)*]. That protection ceases once the member's death occurs, and typically, a discretionary fund arises, to be applied according to a letter of wishes. In the past, HMRC allowed a concessionary 'grace period' of two years following the death for the freedom from the relevant property regime to continue, on the footing that the funds will be distributed during that time free of IHT. The relevant section has been withdrawn from HMRC's Inheritance Tax Manual, which at IHTM17083 now refers to *IHTA 1984, s 58(2A)*. This provides that where pension fund property is applied to pay a lump sum death benefit within *FA 2004, s 168(1)*, the property is still taken to be held for the purposes of the scheme from the date of the death until the making of the payment. Accordingly, in the case of an outright payment of capital, there would be no implications under the relevant property regime. Where, as will often happen, the payment is made to a relevant property trust, typically established by the individual during his lifetime, the payment will not be treated as entering the regime until made. Future ten-year anniversary charges will be based on the date on which the recipient settlement was made, subject to any further pronouncements from HMRC.

Anti-avoidance measures

Property moving between settlements

[9.69] Were there no check on property moving between settlements, it would be possible to move property from one rate scale to another or from one ten-year anniversary to another. Non-relevant property within a discretionary settlement is brought into the calculation of the rate. Therefore HMRC need no protection if the movement is within the settlement (eg an appointment to a sub-trust). Property is not likely to be transferred to another settlement if capital gains tax would arise (see eg *Hart (Inspector of Taxes) v Briscoe* [1979] Ch 1, [1978] 1 All ER 791, Ch D), subject to the sub-funds regime described in **7.118–7.121**. However, cash could be transferred.

[9.70] Although the modest tax rates mean that there is really little at stake, it is clear that HMRC do need protection against property moving between settlements. Therefore, in any case where tax has to be calculated on a discretionary settlement, *IHTA 1984, s 81* comes into play and the property which has moved is deemed to remain within the first settlement. There have been slightly different details in previous legislation, but the rule has been there in principle since 1975.

EXAMPLE

Grandfather left his estate to grandmother for life with remainder over to their three adult grandchildren. The grandchildren expected to inherit £750,000 after tax (ie £250,000 each). They re-settled their interests on discretionary trusts, hoping to have three nil-rate band settlements in due course. *IHTA 1984, s 81* would require the £750,000 to be treated as one settlement and not three. Had the grandchildren waited for grandmother's death and settled their inheritance, then *section 81* would have been irrelevant.

Excluded property

[9.71] *IHTA 1984, s 82* is directed at the possibility of avoidance by the use of excluded property in connection with non-UK domiciliaries. There are two situations where it can have effect:

(a) where *IHTA 1984, s 80* applies, ie where the settlor or his spouse/civil partner had an interest in possession, that interest ceased and the capital is then held on fresh trusts. The provision deems the new settlement to have been made by the last person to have had an interest in possession; and

(b) where *IHTA 1984, s 81* applies and property is deemed not to have moved from one settlement to another for inheritance tax purposes.

[9.72] The practical difficulty illustrated by the rule in *section 80* above for non-UK domiciliaries is illustrated by the example below. The problem has been exacerbated by the inheritance tax regime for trusts introduced by *FA 2006*. Under an excluded property settlement made before 22 March 2006 with an initial interest in possession to one or other of the settlor and spouse/civil partner, the trust which follows the last of these will inevitably be a relevant property settlement, even if interest in possession in form (unless it is a 'transitional serial interest': see 8.17–8.22). So if the last settlor or spouse/civil partner to enjoy an interest in possession had, on termination of that interest, (typically on death) become actually or deemed domiciled in the UK, excluded property protection is lost. By contrast, with an excluded property settlement set up on or after 22 March 2006, it would (apart from the protection of *IHTA 1984, s 48(3)*) be a relevant property settlement in any event, even if interest in possession in form and so the *section 80* rule can provide no threat. With a pre-22 March 2006 settlement which could be caught in future by the problem set out above, the answer may be to bring to an end now the interest in possession of settlor and/or spouse/civil partner (assuming that he or she is currently domiciled outside the UK for all inheritance tax purposes) and institute the relevant property regime with that protection, so preserving excluded property status for the future. Of course, registered civil partnerships came into being only on 5 December 2005, so this scenario (concerning an excluded property settlement made before 22 March 2006) is unlikely to apply to civil partnerships).

EXAMPLE

Boris, when domiciled in the Ukraine, made a settlement in January 2004. The trustee was a Jersey trust corporation and the settlement was written under Jersey law. The terms of the trust gave Boris an initial interest in possession, subject to which his wife Tatiana was to enjoy an interest in possession and on her death successive interests would arise first for their children in equal shares and then on their deaths capital would be advanced outright to Boris' grandchildren at 25. Boris and Tatiana have together set up home in London and in the ordinary course of things can expect to become deemed UK domiciled after 17 continuous years' residence under *IHTA 1984, s 267*. Assuming that Boris dies after 5 October 2008 and his wife Tatiana becomes beneficially entitled on his death, her interest will be a transitional serial interest under *IHTA 1984, s 49D* and will therefore continue to attract *s 49(1)* treatment under *IHTA 1984, s 49(1A)(c)* so that, so long as the trust fund remains situated outside the UK, it will continue to be excluded property under *IHTA 1984, s 48(3)*. However, if when Tatiana dies she is then UK domiciled (whether deemed or actually), the effect of *section 80* will be, for the purposes of inheritance tax on trusts, to treat Tatiana as making a new settlement under which she, then deemed UK domiciled, is the settlor, which could be quite expensive in inheritance tax terms as outside the protection of excluded property.

The answer may be, as suggested above, for the trustees to convert the present interest in possession structure to a discretionary structure, which should have no UK income tax impact as the trustees are non-UK resident, so prospectively 'defusing' the 'inheritance tax time bomb' which lies ahead. The only qualification to this advice is that, in the context of the anti-avoidance transfer of assets abroad regime (see **25.18–25.34**), one should bear in mind the scope of the current motive test in *ITA 2007, ss 736-742*, in the light of any 'associated operation' occurring on or after 5 December 2006.

[9.73] In the case covered by *section 81*, the excluded property remains excluded only if the settlors of both the transferor and the transferee settlements complied with the conditions at the time they made their settlements.

[9.74] Using excluded property such as FOTRA securities where dealing with non-UK residents or non-UK domiciliaries, such a person might have settled capital on himself or his wife/civil partner with remainder over on discretionary trusts, with the intention that *section 80* would give him a discretionary settlement based on excluded property, in due course. *Section 82* prevents this, unless:

(i) the original settlor complied with the conditions (see **8.26–8.27**) when the settlement was made; and

(ii) the deemed settlor under *section 80* complied with the conditions when his interest came to an end.

[9.75] Where all the potential beneficiaries of a relevant property settlement comply with the conditions (see **8.26–8.27**), FOTRA securities held by the trustees are excluded property [*IHTA 1984, s 48(4)*]. The same principle now applies, following *FA 2003, s 186(3)*, to units in authorised unit trusts and to shares in open-ended investment companies. If any such securities, units or shares are transferred between settlements, it is necessary to consider the domicile and residence of the potential beneficiaries of both settlements, because they must all qualify if the transfer is to be of excluded property

[*IHTA 1984, s 48(3A)-(3C)*]. See also **8.25** for the rule from 22 March 2012 that where there is an arrangement under which a UK domiciliary acquires or is enabled to acquire an interest in what would otherwise be excluded property with the result that there is a reduction in the value of the chargeable estate, the settled property acquired is prevented from being excluded property [*IHTA 1984, s 48(3D)-(3F)*].

[**9.76**] It should be noted, finally, that *Finance (No 2) Act 2015* made some very technical amendments to *IHTA 1984, s 80* to correct an anomaly in the legislation which allowed some interest in possession trusts to be treated as outside the life tenant's estate and yet not subject to 'relevant property' charges. The changes take effect from 19 November 2015 (the date after Royal Assent) but with some saving provisions (which are detailed not in *IHTA 1984, s 80* itself but only within *Finance (No 2) Act 2015, s 13*).

Some practical difficulties

Identification

[**9.77**] There are occasions when property has to be identified. Apart from the reduction in the rate of tax which follows where property has not been relevant property for ten years, there is a requirement to identify property for other purposes, as with added property, gifts from different settlors, value entering the relevant property regime on the termination of an interest in possession and so on. The ten-year charge (or the exit charge) may be paid either from capital or from accumulated income. Accumulated income, if still represented by relevant property at the next ten-year anniversary, requires a special calculation (see **9.30–9.33**). Therefore it is going to be necessary to know which property was used to make payments, whether to beneficiaries or for expenses. There are no special rules to show how one traces property back to its origins. The only advice which can be given is that record keeping should be impeccable and that the trust accounts should be suitably self-explanatory. There is a rule in *IHTA 1984, s 44(2)* which deals with the case where more than one person contributes to a settlement. In such case, Part III of the *IHTA 1984* (dealing with settled property) is to have effect as if the settled property were comprised in separate settlements, each made by one individual settlor, provided that 'the circumstances so require'. Specifically, however, the provisions of *section 48(4)–(6)* are outside the ambit of this rule, dealing respectively with FOTRA securities and movements between settlements between 19 April 1978 and 10 December 1981.

Failed potentially exempt transfers

[**9.78**] Problems can be caused by the settlor's premature death, that is within seven years after activating the settlement or adding to it. The trustees of a discretionary settlement may be at the greatest disadvantage to the extent that they have assets not easily converted into cash and especially if they do not know about the settlor's earlier gifts. The failed potentially exempt transfer

[9.78] Relevant Property Settlements — The Ten-Year Charge

becomes a chargeable transfer. Tapering relief applies where death occurs more than three but less than seven years after the gift. There is a difficulty with the attribution of the annual exemption in a case where a potentially exempt transfer and a chargeable transfer are made in the same year. HMRC Trusts and Estates interpret the interaction of *IHTA 1984, s 3A* and *s 19(3A)* as requiring the exemption to be allocated to the first transfer in the tax year, even if it is a potentially exempt transfer which subsequently becomes exempt. The moral in the past (pre-22 March 2006) has been, in a case where a person wishes to make both a discretionary and (say) an accumulation and maintenance settlement, to make the discretionary settlement first, to secure the annual exemption both for the current year and any balance available from the preceding year. The further reason is, of course, that this order of events would guard against the possibility of the settlor's death occurring within seven years after the potentially exempt transfer, thereby making it chargeable and causing it to fall within his cumulative total for calculating the proportionate and the ten-year anniversary charge. Now, however, with practically every lifetime settlement being a relevant property settlement, the point rather fades in significance, though it would still apply where a person wanted to make, at around the same time, both, say, a relevant property settlement and a settlement for a disabled person.

[9.79] The problems for the trustees of a discretionary settlement where the settlor dies prematurely can be illustrated as follows.

EXAMPLE

The settlor made the following gifts:

Each year on 6 April, £3,000 to use his annual exemption.
10 March 2008, to his son, £50,000
10 May 2009, to his daughter, £125,000
10 June 2010, to trustees of a discretionary settlement, £330,000
He had no history of chargeable transfers before 10 March 2008. He died on 10 April 2014.

The original inheritance tax calculations were:

10 March 2008

A potentially exempt transfer of £50,000. Ignored for the time being, as assumed to be exempt.

10 May 2009

A potentially exempt transfer of £125,000. Ignored for the time being, as assumed to be exempt.

10 June 2010

A transfer of value of £330,000, with a nil cumulative total, in 2010/11 when the nil-rate band was £325,000.

	£
Chargeable transfer (grossed-up)	331,250
Cumulative total	Nil
	331,250
Tax paid by settlor (£331,250 − £325,000 = £6,250 × 20%)	1,250

The death changes the calculations:

10 March 2008—no charge (within nil-rate band for 2014/15 ie the year of death).

10 May 2009

The transfer of value of £125,000 is the amount of the chargeable transfer given no grossing-up and is also within the 2014/15 nil-rate band.

	£
Chargeable transfer	125,000
Cumulative total	50,000
	175,000
Tax paid by daughter	Nil

10 June 2010

The chargeable transfer is not changed. However, there is now a cumulative total of £175,000.

	£
Chargeable transfer	331,250
Cumulative total	175,000
	506,250
Tax at death rate (£506,250 − 325,000 = £181,250 × 40%)	72,500
Less: paid in 2010/11	1,250
Payable by trustees	£71,250

[9.80] If there has been a potentially exempt transfer before the setting-up of a discretionary trust then it is possible, in theory at least, for the trustees to calculate their maximum risk. IHTA 1984, Sch 2 para 1A lays down that the rates of tax are those of the year of death if less than those in the year of transfer. Thus the worst which can happen is a charge at the rates used in the year of the transfer.

Gifts with reservation of benefit

[9.81] There may be inheritance tax consequences when the relevant property settlement can benefit the settlor. This will usually be due to a drafting error in the trust deed, because the result is a gift with reservation of benefit [FA 1986, s 102]. It will also be a chargeable transfer. There is nothing to prevent a gift to trustees from being both. Therefore, the death of the settlor, before any remedial action is taken, results in the settled capital being assessed as if it were part of his estate. There are provisions covering the resultant double taxation [*Inheritance Tax (Double Charges Relief) Regulations, SI 1987/1130*]. If the defect is noticed and the possibility of benefit to the settlor is removed, there is a danger period of seven years because the remedial action is a deemed potentially exempt transfer [FA 1986, s 102(4)]. There are valuation issues with this deemed potentially exempt transfer because *section 102(4)* provides that it is deemed to be made by a disposition and there must then be a question as to what is disposed of. The issue of double charges to inheritance tax has become more complex with the introduction from 2005/06 of the pre-owned assets regime (see **4.39–4.49**); see **4.52** for the double charges relief under the pre-owned assets regime.

[9.82] Relevant Property Settlements — The Ten-Year Charge

[9.82] There have been planning possibilities in this area in the past (especially with a view to securing the capital gains tax hold-over under *TCGA 1992, s 260*) through setting up a discretionary trust which is also a gift with reservation. If there is a reserved benefit, the value of the chargeable transfer may be minimal. The benefit is then released and the resultant deemed potentially exempt transfer will not be charged if the settlor lives a further seven years. See **7.78** and **7.79** for *FA 2002, s 119* following the *Melville* decision by the Court of Appeal on 31 July 2001 and for another similar arrangement which was rendered ineffective on 10 December 2003. It is quite easy and quite wrong to think that a relevant property settlement in which the settlor retains a benefit is much the same as having the settlor own the settled capital. Rather, the settlement is still relevant property, there remains a ten-year charge and it is simply that an *extra* charge will arise upon the death of the settlor too.

The impact of Finance Act 2006

[9.83] Reference has been made above to the fact that, especially on or some time after 6 April 2008 (indeed, if not before), a number of settlements made under the potentially exempt transfer regime now fall within the relevant property regime, with its system of ten-yearly and exit charges. Take for example an accumulation and maintenance settlement made on 1 April 2008 which entered the relevant property regime on 6 April 2008. (See the example at **9.11**.) On the face of it the first ten-year anniversary charge will arise on 1 April 2018. However, this will in fact be the second ten-year anniversary. So the rate of inheritance tax paid on an exit before that date will be the rate paid on the first ten-year anniversary (see **10.28**). Of course, on 1 April 2008 there was no relevant property in the settlement and so no tax was charged. However, the rate to be charged on such an exit is in fact fixed by *IHTA 1984, s 69(2)* and *(3)* by making the assumption that what has become relevant property was in fact comprised within the settlement as such at the last ten-year anniversary, at the value when it became relevant property but with an allowance for any quarters elapsing before that date (see the example below). More generally, issues such as establishing the commencement date, determining the settlor's cumulative total of chargeable transfers in the seven years before that and identifying the existence of any related settlements are all issues which may well prove troublesome, especially the second of these.

[9.84] Assume a pre-22 March 2006 accumulation and maintenance settlement which enters the mainstream trust regime on 6 April 2008. Take the Example at **9.11** as developed in the Example at **9.41** and consider an exit of property on say 31 May 2014. The chargeable amount is fixed under *IHTA 1984, s 65(2)* as that by which the relevant property in the settlement is reduced, whether in whole or in part. The rate is found under *IHTA 1984, s 69* 'rate between ten-year anniversaries' (*IHTA 1984, s 68* 'rate before first ten-year anniversary' not applying). Under *IHTA 1984, s 69(1)* this is 'the appropriate fraction' (ie depending on the number of quarters that have elapsed since the last anniversary) of the rate at which it was 'last charged under *IHTA 1984, s 64* (or would have been charged apart from *IHTA 1984, s 66(2)*)'. *IHTA 1984, s 66(2)* then applies where, as in this case, property which was comprised in the settlement immediately before the most recent ten-year anniversary (ie, in the case of the example, 1 April 2005) but was not then relevant property has become relevant property. And *IHTA 1984, s 69(3)* provides that, for purposes of the exit charge, the assumed previous ten-year anniversary charge adopts the value of the property when it became relevant property, with, however, under *IHTA 1984, s 69(4)* a discount in calculating the exit charge for the number of complete quarters since the ten-year charge during which it was not relevant property.

EXAMPLE

Assume that the value of the trust fund of Reginald's settlement (see the Example at **9.11**) on 1 April 2005 was £1.2 million. The trustees advance the whole fund (then worth £2 million) to Reginald's children in equal shares on 31 March 2014 (that is, after the settlement has been in the relevant property regime for 23 out of 40 quarters). What is the exit charge?

	£	£	£
Chargeable transfer amount			2,000,000
Deemed transfer on 1 April 2005		1,200,000	
Deemed cumulative total	100,000		
Related settlement	125,000		
		225,000	
		1,425,000	
Nil-rate band 2013/14 (*IHTA 1984, Sch 2 para 3*)		(325,000)	
		1,100,000	
IHT @ 20%		£220,000	

Effective rate: £220,000 divided by £1,325,000 = 16.60%

Appropriate fraction (expressed as a decimal): $3/10 \times 23/40$ = 0.1725

Exit charge: £2,000,000 × 16.60% × 0.1725   57,270

Note that in certain circumstances it may be cheaper to accept the next ten-year anniversary charge (eg if the nil-rate band has increased) and pay out the capital before the end of the following quarter with no further IHT liability. However, this will mean forfeiting the ability to hold over any gain under *TCGA 1992, s 260*. It may therefore be better to wait until after the first quarter to pay out the capital, accepting a small exit charge based on 1/40ths (but with the ability to hold over any gain).

Chapter 10

Inheritance Tax: Relevant Property Settlements — The Exit Charge

Introduction

[10.1] The exit charge is the charge made when property leaves a relevant property settlement regime at times other than a ten-year anniversary. It is charged at a proportion of the ten-year anniversary rate and the proportion depends upon the number of quarters during which settled property has been within the relevant property regime – each ten-year period being divided into forty periods of three months. Therefore, if a relevant property settlement were wound up at the end of its fourth year, the exit charge would be $^{16}/_{40}$ of a ten-year charge. There are other differences from the ten-year charge, particularly in the field of valuation, as the exit charge is based on the 'loss to donor' principle; however, the exit charge is essentially derived from the ten-year charge. HMRC Trusts and Estates have traditionally used the term 'proportionate charge', though this book refers to 'exit charge' as the expression most commonly used in professional practice.

[10.2] The general rules are explained below. Settlements made before 27 March 1974 were treated differently until they had been taxed on a ten-year anniversary. After that, the treatment is not dissimilar from that of settlements made after 26 March 1974. There could have been no ten-year anniversary until after 31 March 1983 (see 9.8). All pre-27 March 1974 settlements will now have had a ten-year anniversary. Readers who have to check the calculation of a charge made before the first ten-year anniversary are referred to earlier editions of this work. As for ten-year anniversary charges, the calculation of exit charges will change from Royal Assent of the *Summer Finance Act 2015* (see 9.44–9.48 for an explanation of the proposed changes); however, the majority of the 'old' rules set out below will continue to apply.

The occasions of charge

[10.3] There are two possible occasions of charge:

(a) When settled property ceases to be relevant property [*IHTA 1984, s 65(1)(a)*].
(b) When there is a fall in value of relevant property as a result of a disposition made by the trustees, and the property remains relevant property [*IHTA 1984, s 65(1)(b)*].

See 8.29 and 8.30 for the meaning of 'relevant property'.

[10.4] Property can cease to be relevant property by leaving the settlement (eg when the trustees vote a capital sum to an object of the discretion).

[10.4] The Exit Charge

Alternatively, the property may remain within the settlement. A conventional discretionary settlement gives powers of appointment in the widest terms, so that the trustees could perhaps declare charitable trusts of part of the capital, declare a life interest of part or appoint to one of the trusts mentioned in 8.29(e)–(n). Such an appointment would cause the property concerned to cease to be relevant property. In some cases, there may be no exit charge, for example on a charitable appointment (see 10.14–10.16). Most probably, the property concerned would cease to remain in the settlement. The inheritance tax implications would depend upon all the circumstances and the type of transferee trust; for example, if an excluded property trust, then it will be necessary that the transferor relevant property settlement had been made by a settlor domiciled outside the UK for all inheritance tax purposes: see 10.8–10.16 for exemptions from the exit charge, especially 10.8–10.9 for excluded property.

[10.5] The disposition in 10.3(b) which causes relevant property to fall in value is intended to bring relevant property settlements into line with individuals who are taxed on the 'loss to donor' principle [*IHTA 1984, s 3(1)*]. As with transfers of value by individuals, the disposition is not caught if it is on arm's length terms and is not intended to confer a gratuitous benefit. There is also protection for the grant of tenancies of agricultural property at a full rent [*IHTA 1984, s 65(6)*]. It is hard to imagine a transaction which causes the capital to fall in value and which is not intended to confer a gratuitous benefit. When the trustees are dealing with the objects of the discretion, they must have a gratuitous intent. Their transactions with others should not be such as to be gifts. Therefore, the practical meaning of this provision is that siphoning is caught (eg a change of rights in shares, so that the trust shares fall in value and a beneficiary's shares appreciate).

[10.6] The decided case *Macpherson v IRC*, HL [1988] STC 362, shows that there may be further point in this section. This concerned a change in arrangements for the custody, insurance etc of a collection of paintings which was settled property. Originally the collection was left at an individual's house. He paid the trustees £100 pa for the enjoyment he derived from the pictures and the arrangement could be brought to an end on three months notice. He also undertook the custody, care and insurance of the pictures. A subsequent agreement gave him the pictures for a term of years and at a reduced fee, and this reduced the value of the collection to the trustees. It was held that the subsequent agreement, together with an associated transaction, did confer a gratuitous benefit.

[10.7] Again, moving towards parity with treatment of the individual (see *IHTA 1984, s 3(3)*), the deliberate omission to exercise a right is a disposition by the trustees. The usual example is the failure to take up a rights issue in a family company. The deemed disposition is taken to be made at the latest time when the trustees could have exercised the right [*IHTA 1984, s 65(9)*].

Exemptions from the exit charge

Excluded property

[10.8] Property ceases to be relevant property upon becoming excluded property. Without specific legislation to this effect, there could have been a charge merely when trustees changed investments. Therefore, *IHTA 1984, s 65(8)* ensures that there will not be a charge when the trustees of a settlement made by a person not domiciled in the UK when the settlement was made invest in the tax-sheltered government securities mentioned in *IHTA 1984, s 6(2)* ie FOTRA securities (see **8.26–8.27**). Similarly, *IHTA 1984, s 65(7)* covers the position where such trustees move capital from the UK. That is a short-hand for the statutory expression that 'property comprised in a settlement ceases to be situated in the United Kingdom and thereby becomes excluded property . . . '. There is an interesting issue here. Clearly, to the extent that the trust fund comprises chattels, eg paintings which are physically moved out of the UK, *section 65(7)* applies. Is the same true if cash is moved from a UK bank account to, say, a Jersey bank account? While the statutory wording is not abundantly clear, it is understood that HMRC accept that the statutory protection is available in such a case too. Unfortunately, however, the sensible exclusion from the exit charge for FOTRA securities did not extend to the scenario where the trustees sell, for example, UK stocks and shares and reinvest in authorised unit trusts (AUTs) and/or open-ended investment companies (OEICs). Such an initiative could have triggered an unwelcome charge to inheritance tax. Happily, HMRC recognised the problem and *FA 2003, s 175* redresses the position with retroactive effect to 16 October 2002 (the date when the *FA 2003* changes came into effect). As a result, a change of investment by the trustees of relevant property excluded property settlements will not incur an exit charge where the trustees invest in either OEICS or AUTs.

[10.9] In deciding where the settlor was domiciled, if the capital was settled before 10 December 1974, or if the capital becomes invested in exempt gilts, only the normal tests for domicile apply. If the capital was settled on or after that date, or if property leaves the UK, then the deemed tests of domicile in *IHTA 1984, s 267* will also be used (see **27.13**).

Gratuitous transfers

[10.10] Payments which do not represent gratuitous transfers of capital are not caught. Thus the payment of costs, expenses or income does not trigger an exit charge. In case the costs or expenses relate both to relevant and non-relevant property, the exemption applies only to the amounts fairly attributable to relevant property. Dispositions which are payments of income are ignored if the payment is income of the recipient for income tax purposes or would be were he a resident of the UK [*IHTA 1984, s 65(5)*]. The work 'payment' includes a transfer of assets other than money [*IHTA 1984, s 63*].

Transfers within the first quarter

[10.11] There is an exemption if the occasion of charge happens in the first quarter of existence of a settlement or within the quarter following a ten-year anniversary [*IHTA 1984, s 65(4)*]. The word 'quarter' is defined to mean a period of three months [*IHTA 1984, s 63*]. Where property is settled on discretionary terms by Will, there is an effective two year exemption which enables property to be appointed out without incurring any additional charge to inheritance tax, with the appointment being treated as made by the testator at the time of his death. This principle was extended by *FA 2006* so that (in particular) where an appointment is made (or indeed 'any event occurring') within two years after the death which causes trusts to arise which had they been established by the Will would have resulted in an immediate post-death interest or a bereaved minors trust or an age 18-to-25 trust applying, those trusts are read back into the Will, which means for inheritance tax purposes that such trusts are treated as arising on death [*IHTA 1984, s 144*].

[10.12] Until 10 December 2014 it was important to ensure that no appointments were be made out of a discretionary Will trust within three months of the death, at least for deaths before 22 March 2006 (*Frankland v IRC* CA, [1997] STC 1450, *Harding (executor of Loveday) v IRC* [1997] STC (SCD) 321). The reason for this is that *section 144* is a relieving section and, for reasons mentioned in the previous paragraph, there would have been no exit charge on capital leaving the discretionary regime within the first three months of the existence of the settlement. A significant change was made to *section 144* by *FA 2006*, inserting (in particular) *subsection 144(3)(c)*. The effect is to disapply the *Frankland* trap, where the appointment creates either an immediate post-death interest, a bereaved minor's trust, or an age 18-to-25 trust. But the trap does remain for absolute appointments.

[10.13] Changes to *section 144(1)(b)* in the *Finance (No 2) Act 2015* are effective for deaths on or after 10 December 2014. These remove the *Frankland* trap for Will Trusts completely. It should be noted, however, that a trap will remain for the trustees of inter vivos trusts. Because any appointment from a relevant property trust within three months of its commencement (or of a ten-yearly anniversary) will not give rise to an exit charge, capital gains tax 'hold over' relief under TCGA 1992, s 260 will not be available (although it could still be available under TCGA 1992, s 165) – see 9.44–9.48.

Other exemptions

[10.14] Other exemptions cover property which becomes held on certain trusts which are themselves sheltered from the tax, namely:

(a) employee trusts [*IHTA 1984, s 75*];
(b) maintenance funds for historic buildings [*IHTA 1984, Sch 4 para 16*];
(c) permanent charities [*IHTA 1984, s 76(1)(a)*];
(d) political parties qualifying for exemption under *IHTA 1984, s 24* [*IHTA 1984, s 76(1)(b)*]; and
(e) national heritage bodies as in *IHTA 1984, Sch 3* [*IHTA 1984, s 76(1)(c)*].

[10.15] Until 17 March 1998 there was also an exemption for non-profit-making bodies approved by the Treasury and holding heritage property. For practical purposes the general exemption for charities will serve just as well.

[10.16] There is a restriction on the exemption for the last three types of beneficiary (ie those mentioned in *IHTA 1984, s 76(1)*). If the value of the property going to them is one figure in the hands of the relevant property settlement's trustees and a lower amount in the hands of the body which is the beneficiary, then it is the lesser amount which is exempt. In making this comparison, the value of the property to the trustees making the transfer is not reduced by agricultural or business property relief, and it is not grossed up [*IHTA 1984, s 76(3)(4)*]. The logic behind this can be seen where there is a controlling interest in a company, say 51%, and the trustees planned to give 2% to a charity before appointing 49% to an individual. In practice the strict letter of the law is not enforced (see HMRC Statement of Practice E13 in APPENDIX A). Further anti-avoidance legislation prevents the exemption applying where the disposition is defeasible; where the asset can be deflected to some other person; and, where interests under the relevant property settlement have been purchased by certain exempt bodies [*IHTA 1984, s 76(5)–(8)*].

The amount chargeable

[10.17] The amount subject to the exit charge is the fall in value of the relevant property, and if the tax is paid out of the remaining relevant property, the amount is grossed up [*IHTA 1984, s 65(2)*]. The rate of tax on exit charges before the first ten-year anniversary is explained in *IHTA 1984, s 68*. Section 68(1) sets the rate by reference to 'the value transferred' by a deemed chargeable transfer, the amount of which is 'equal to . . . the value, immediately after the settlement commenced, of the property then comprised in it' [*Section 68(5)(a)*]. There are provisions to bring in related settlements etc. There is no reduction of these values by reason of business property relief/agricultural property relief, because the reference in *section 68(5)(a)* is to the gross unrelieved value of the property. (The value chargeable, however, may attract business property relief or agricultural property relief even before the first ten-year anniversary, see **10.18**.) The rate is calculated not by reference to the amount charged to tax, but by reference to an artificial deemed chargeable transfer and a valuation relief can operate only by reducing an amount which is to be taxed.

[10.18] Bearing in mind the nature of relevant property settlements, there should not be too many cases where relevant business property or agricultural property is removed before the first ten-year anniversary. The likeliest is where an asset has appreciated very considerably and, shortly before the ten years have elapsed, some restructuring is desired. For instance if a nil-rate discretionary settlement contained shares in a family trading company which has since become an investment company, the gross value of which was within the nil rate on settlement, it is possible that after nine years those shares are worth, say, £750,000. That, in itself, might have been (before 22 March 2006) a reason to create a sub-trust on accumulation and maintenance trusts. Because it started as a nil-rate settlement, the appointment to the sub-trust could be made at a nil rate and the absence of business property relief is of no consequence. It is only where the shares do not qualify for 100% relief that tax planning considerations may suggest an appointment shortly before the ten-year anniversary. And now that practically every lifetime settlement will fall within the relevant property regime, the point made above remains good in such a case. Similarly, if, for example, it were desired to make outright appointments of capital to various members of the family so as to prevent the first ten-year anniversary charge. The key thing of course is that the initial gross value of the property settled (together with the initial gross value of any related settlements) was within the then nil-rate band, given the settlor's seven year cumulative total of chargeable transfers.

[10.19] The legislation for the ten-year charge is worded differently and the two valuation reliefs are available against the charge on the relevant property at the ten-year anniversary. Accordingly, the valuation reliefs are available on an exit charge between ten-year anniversaries, in that (as explained at 10.28) the rate of inheritance tax is related to that charged on the last ten-year anniversary, duly scaled down as there explained. The rate calculation requires the trustees to bring in non-relevant property which has remained non-relevant and the value of related settlements when they commenced [*IHTA 1984, s 66(4)(b)(c)*] and no valuation reliefs can be deducted from these two components of the deemed chargeable transfer. The valuation reliefs cannot reduce the value of something not being charged to tax.

The rate of charge

[10.20] An exit charge requires ascertainment of a deemed chargeable transfer and a deemed cumulative total. The deemed chargeable transfer has nothing to do with the amount which is chargeable. This is because the scheme of the exit charge is to use the rate which was charged on the last ten-year anniversary. Therefore, the deemed chargeable transfer is that which was calculated for the last ten-year charge or a substitute for it where no ten-year charge has been made so far. The rate of tax can be varied retrospectively if the settlor dies within seven years of making the settlement and there are prior potentially exempt transfers. Those transfers are made chargeable by the death and alter the charge on making the relevant property settlement. If the result is a higher rate of tax, subsequent exit charges due before the settlor's death will be reworked and the trustees will have to reclaim the extra tax from the recipient of the capital which they released. This subject was discussed in 9.78–9.80.

Exit charge before first ten-year anniversary

The deemed chargeable transfer

[10.21] The deemed chargeable transfer before the first ten-year anniversary comprises:

(a) the value of the settled property on commencement;
(b) the value of any related settlement (see **9.37–9.41**) upon its commencement; and
(c) the value of added property at the time of its addition, where added before the event giving rise to the exit charge.

[*IHTA 1984, s 68(5)*] In relation to (a) above, for events after 18 November 2015, (as provided by *Finance (No 2) Act 2015*), settled property which has never been relevant property will be ignored. Likewise in relation to (b) the value of 'same-day additions' will also need to be included. (See **9.44–9.48** and **9.55–9.56**.)

[10.22] Thus no new valuation of the settled property is necessary, save to discover the chargeable amount by reference to the fall in value of the relevant property (see **10.5**). The usual scheme for payment of tax over ten years is available either where instalment assets are subject to the charge (see **21.19–21.25**), which might be interest-free so long as each instalment is paid on time, or more generally if the beneficiary pays the tax [*IHTA 1984, s 227(1)(b)*].

[10.23] Business property relief or agricultural property relief may, depending upon the circumstances (ie if the trustees themselves qualify), apply to reduce the value chargeable by either 100% or 50%. This is a separate point from that made at **10.17**.

The deemed cumulative total

[10.24] The deemed cumulative total is the cumulative total of the settlor in the seven years ending on the day the settlement commenced but excluding transfers made on that day [*IHTA 1984, s 68(4)(b)*].

Rate of charge

[10.25] Once the deemed chargeable transfer and deemed cumulative total have been ascertained, the current lifetime rates (ie the half rates) are used to discover the effective rate (ie the average rate on the deemed chargeable transfer). Next, 30% of the effective rate is calculated. So far, the calculation is similar to that of a ten-year charge. However, this is an exit charge and the proportion is calculated by reference to complete quarters ended before the occasion of charge. Therefore, the 30% of the effective rate is reduced in proportion to the number of complete successive quarters which have elapsed since the commencement of the settlement. The quarter within which the occasion of charge occurs is ignored. This fraction of the 30% of the effective rate is then applied to the amount which is chargeable (see **10.17–10.19**) [*IHTA 1984, s 68(1), (2)*].

EXAMPLE 1—WITH A SUBSTANTIAL CUMULATIVE TOTAL (NOT AT ALL USUAL)

Sarah settled £115,000 on discretionary trusts on 1 May 2008. At that time she had used her annual exemptions and had a cumulative seven year total of chargeable transfers of £312,000. There were no related settlements. The trustees paid the inheritance tax on the lifetime transfer of

[10.25] The Exit Charge

£115,000. No further property was added. By 10 May 2014, when the trustees made their first disposition, the capital had quadrupled in value and the £115,000 had become £460,000. They appointed £150,000 on disabled person's trusts on 10 May 2014.

The exit charge is calculated as follows:

			£
Amount of original settlement of capital (s 68(5)(a))			115,000
Deemed cumulative total (ie settlor's total down to 30.4.08, s 68(4)(b))			312,000
Total to determine rate (deemed chargeable transfer)			£427,000
	£	£	£
Inheritance tax, lifetime rate			
	325,000	@ nil	
	102,000	@ 20%	20,400
	427,000		£20,400
Effective rate	20,400	= 17.74%	
	115,000		
30% of effective rate		= 5.32%	

There are 24 complete quarters between 1 May 2008 and 10 May 2014. The charge is:

$^{24}/_{40}$ of 5.32% of £150,000 = £4,788

The point of this example is to show how a calculation in 2014/15 depends on figures possibly dating back to May 2001 (7 years before 1 May 2008).

EXAMPLE 2—WITH NO CUMULATIVE TOTAL (MUCH MORE USUAL).

Everything is as in Example 1 but Sarah made no chargeable transfers before 1 May 2008. The figures then become:

	£
Original amount settled	115,000
Deemed cumulative total	0
Total to determine rate (deemed chargeable transfer)	£115,000

The rate is nil.

EXAMPLE 3

Immediately following the appointment of 10 May 2014 in Example 1 the trustees appointed the remaining £310,000 to Sarah's son Rupert. The effective rate, etc is as in Example 1 so that the tax on the appointment to Rupert is:

$^{24}/_{40}$ of 5.32% of £310,000 = £9,895

[10.26] Because the rate of tax is effectively always an historic one, ie either the rate at the commencement of the settlement or the rate at the commencement of the ten-year period, it is essential that, several months before any ten-year anniversary, the trustees consider their position. If the assets have grown fast, then the wisdom of some appointment etc is clearly indicated, as in the example above where £460,000 with a deemed cumulative total of £300,000 could be moved at the rate applicable to £115,000 with a deemed cumulative total of £300,000. This has been touched upon in **10.18**. Any such planning must allow for capital gains tax. The rate of capital gains tax is presently either 20% or 28% for trustees (depending upon the asset concerned). The availability of hold-over relief was significantly reduced on

10 December 2003 (see **7.81–7.82**). However, note that, where settlor-interested trusts are concerned, it is only transfers to and not transfers out of such trusts where hold-over is precluded (*TCGA 1992, s 169B*). However, the *section 169B* rule would prevent hold-over of a gain on an asset coming out of one trust (whether or not settlor-interested) to another trust which is settlor-interested (if, indeed, hold-over relief would have been available at all in these circumstances – for example, if *IHTA 194, s 81* applies on a transfer between settlements, *section 260* hold-over would not be available because there could be no exit charge arising). Apart from this, there is the general hold-over to defer gains on assets coming out of a relevant property trust and, if the trust is not of a relevant property description, business assets hold-over may be available under *section 165*. Note that where business assets leave a relevant property trust, *section 260* hold-over takes priority [*TCGA 1992, s 165(3)(d)*].

[10.27] The exit charge on a relevant property settlement before its first ten-year anniversary is not too clouded by problems arising from added property, as that is included in the deemed chargeable transfer (see **10.21**(*c*)). Nevertheless, because the number of quarters used in the first exit charge depends on the date of commencement of the settlement, there could be an anomaly if the property charged were property which had only recently been added. Similarly, property could have changed its character and been relevant property for only part of the period. If such property is to be taxed, then the quarters before it became relevant property or before it was added are ignored [*IHTA 1984, s 68(3)*]. One would hope that this problem would be rare in practice because it is normally inadvisable to add to an existing settlement – see **9.57–9.64**.

Exit charge between ten-year anniversaries

[10.28] In a simple case, the rate between ten-year anniversaries is the rate charged on the last ten-year anniversary, scaled down by reference to the number of quarters which have elapsed since then, but see **10.30** for interim reductions in rate [*IHTA 1984, s 69(1)(4)*].

EXAMPLE

Susan's discretionary settlement was made on 25 February 2004 and the first ten-year charge is assessed on 25 February 2014. There is no added property.

On 25 February 2014 the settled property is valued at	£500,000
On 25 February 2004 Susan's cumulative total was	£125,000
The ten-year charge is:	£
Value at 25 May 2014	500,000
Deemed cumulative total	125,000
Total for rate (deemed chargeable transfer)	£625,000
325,000 @ nil	–
300,000 @ 20%	60,000

[10.28] The Exit Charge

Tax on lifetime scale £60,000

$$\text{Effective rate} = \frac{60,000}{500,000} = 12\%$$

Rate of ten-year charge = 30% of 12% = 3.6%
Ten-year charge = 3.6% of £500,000 = £18,000

On 26 May 2014 (ie just after one complete quarter has passed) the value of the investments is £550,000 (ie a 10% increase since the 10-year anniversary) and half is appointed to Susan's son Tim absolutely. The exit charge is:

$1/40$ of 3.6% of £275,000 = £247.50

The tax is paid from the capital subject to the life interest, so that grossing-up is unnecessary.

[10.29] The rate of the ten-year charge may have been reduced because there was added property, or because property was not relevant property for the whole period etc. These reductions are ignored in calculating a subsequent exit charge [IHTA 1984, s 69(1)].

[10.30] Where the table of rates is less at the date of the exit charge than it was at the date of the preceding ten-year charge, then the effective rate is re-worked on the new scale [IHTA 1984, Sch 2 para 3].

EXAMPLE

Susan's trustees in the example in **10.28** incur an exit charge on 26 May 2014, on appointing capital of £275,000. If in that year's Budget, the nil-rate band had been increased to £350,000 for 2014/15 this would have affected the calculation of the exit charge.

There would still have been only one complete quarter, so that the rate of the exit charge would become:

	£
The (re-worked) ten-year charge is:	
Value at 25 May 2023	500,000
Deemed cumulative total	125,000
Total for rate (deemed chargeable transfer)	£625,000
350,000 @ nil	–
275,000 @ 20%	55,000
Tax on lifetime scale	£55,000

$$\text{Effective rate} = \frac{55,000}{500,000} = 11\%$$

Rate of reworked ten-year charge = 30% of 11% = 3.3%

Hence the rate of exit charge is: $1/40$th of 3.3% = 0.0825%, producing an exit charge of £226.88 on the £275,000 capital appointment.

[10.31] Complications arise where property has been added since the last ten-year anniversary or property which was then non-relevant property has since become relevant property (eg as a result of a life interest coming to an end, property has reverted to the relevant property regime). In such a case, the rate of the last ten-year charge is adjusted to what it would have been had the new property or newly relevant property been included in the ten-year charge. The value used where property has been added is the value immediately after it was added to the settlement. If the capital was within the settlement at the ten-year anniversary but was then non-relevant property, it is valued at the date when it became relevant property. This fits the philosophy of the exit charge in that the only valuations which are required at the time of the charge are those for the property which ceases to be relevant property [*IHTA 1984, s 69(2)(3)*].

The 'age 18-to-25 trust' charge

[10.32] As discussed at 8.13–8.15, the 2006 trust changes introduced the new category of 'age 18-to-25 trust'. In very broad terms, such trusts enjoy a favoured treatment akin to an accumulation and maintenance trust while the beneficiary is under the age of 18 [*IHTA 1984, s 71E(2)(3)*]. There could be no ten-yearly charge between the age of 18 and 25; however, any capital payment or appointment in favour of a beneficiary absolutely (or to an interest in possession in their favour) gives rise to a charge (as does a depreciatory transaction) [*IHTA 1984, ss 71E(1)(5), 71F(2)*].

[10.33] The charge arising can be thought of as a quasi-exit charge, calculated as follows [*IHTA 1984, s 71F*]:

Chargeable amount x Relevant fraction x Settlement rate = Tax due

Where:

- *Chargeable amount* is the amount by which the value of the property in the trust reduces as a result of the transfer. This needs to be grossed up where the trustees bear the tax
- *Relevant fraction* is three-tenths multiplied by so many fortieths that have elapsed since the beneficiary attained 18 (or, if later, when the trust property became subject to the 'age 18-to-25 trust'); and
- *Settlement rate* is the effective rate at which tax would be charged on the value transferred by a chargeable transfer of the aggregate value of:
  - the settlement immediately after commencement;
  - any related settlement; and
  - any additions.

[10.34] For events after 18 November 2015, non-relevant property contained in a settlement is excluded from the tax calculation (see **9.55–9.56**).

EXAMPLE (TO ILLUSTRATE THE EXIT CHARGE FROM AN AGE 18-TO-25 TRUST)

Harold made a settlement for his children on 1 January 1984. Under the terms of the settlement there was a direction to accumulate income for 21 years (now therefore expired) with children becoming entitled to income at age 18 and capital deferred broadly until grandchildren attained 18, with wide powers of advancement of capital before that age. Harold has three children: Arabella, Bertha and Charles. Each of Arabella and Bertha is in line for substantial inheritances from godparents and so before either attained an interest in possession under the settlement they were effectively excluded, leaving Charles as the sole prospective beneficiary. Charles becomes 18 on 1 January 2014. Before 6 April 2008 the terms of the trust were changed to become compliant with *section 71D*.

[10.34] The Exit Charge

In the seven years before he made the settlement Harold had cumulative chargeable transfers of £100,000 and there were no related settlements. The initial value of the settlement was £200,000. The trust assets are now worth £500,000. When Charles becomes 25 on 1 January 2021 when, let us suppose, the fund is worth £1 million and that the rates of tax are as in 2007/08 but with a nil-rate band of £450,000, the calculation under *section 71F* of the *section 71E* exit charge proceeds as follows. No part of the trust fund attracts business or agricultural property relief.

The tax is: chargeable amount × relevant fraction × settlement rate (*section 71F(3)*).

The 'chargeable amount' is £1 million (assuming that any tax is paid out of it and not out of any property remaining subject to *section 71D* trusts, in which case there would be grossing up (*section 71F(4)*). The 'relevant fraction' is 3/10 × 28/40 (the number of complete successive quarters in the period, ie 0.21 (*section 71F(5)*). The 'settlement rate' is the effective rate found under *section 71F(7)–(9)* as follows:

	£
Deemed chargeable transfer (s 71F(9))	200,000
Add: settlor's chargeable transfer total (s 71F(8)(b))	100,000
	300,000
Less: nil-rate band	(450,000)
Deemed taxable amount	0

Therefore the settlement rate is 0%.

So, in this case, the IHT is zero: £1,000,000 × 0.21 × 0.

Suppose that Charles had a brother, David, whom the trustees also wanted to benefit. David was born two years after Charles and so the capital of around £1 million is divided between them, David inheriting his share on 1 January 2026. The calculation of the rate of tax applicable on the exit would be exactly the same for David as it is for Charles.

Chapter 11

Inheritance Tax: Accumulation and Maintenance Settlements

Historical background

[11.1] When, in 2006, the then Chancellor Gordon Brown, announced in his Budget Statement his radical reform of the inheritance taxation of trust one of the principal casualties was the accumulation and maintenance trust. Such trusts had been introduced by a Labour Government some 31 years earlier, and although transitional rules enabled some accumulation and maintenance trusts to continue to have favoured treatment beyond this date (see **11.2** and **11.3**), no new trusts within that favoured regime can have been created after 21 March 2006.

[11.2] In the Court of Session case of *Marquess of Linlithgow v Revenue and Customs Comrs* [2010] CSIH 19, [2010] STC 1563, 2010 SC 391, the Court had to consider the effective date of an accumulation and trust. The transfers in land were made on 15 March 2006, but were not recorded in the Register of Sasines until 10 October and 16 November 2006 respectively. The Court held (unsurprisingly) that a transfer of value occurred when the gratuitous disposition of heritable subjects in Scotland was delivered to the transferee rather than when it was recorded in the Register of Sasines.

[11.3] Although accumulation and maintenance trusts are principally of historical significance, many such trusts remain in existence. A very limited class of these continue to attract a favoured trust status; others have lost that status but practitioners need to understand how they are now taxed (the various regimes are described at **11.4–11.28**). Finally, an understanding of the options available in relation to such trusts in the transitional period between 22 March 2006 and 5 April 2005 will be helpful in understanding the historical background to such trusts (see **11.31**).

What is an accumulation and maintenance trust?

The historical position

[11.4] Accumulation and maintenance settlements are defined for inheritance tax purposes in *IHTA 1984, s 71(1),(2)*. The definition follows closely the statutory trusts for infants in *Trustee Act 1925, s 31* (see APPENDIX D). However, whereas *Trustee Act 1925, s 31* applies to the income from funds held prospectively for those under the age of 18, the inheritance tax favoured regime for accumulation and maintenance trusts originally provided for beneficiaries to be denied a vested interest up to the age of 25.

[11.5] The general scheme was that under the age of 25 the trustees managed the beneficiaries' capital, spending income upon them if it was desirable and saving it for them (ie accumulating) if there was no reason to spend it. However, once a beneficiary attained 25 he or she acquired a right either to a share of the income from the trust or to a share in the capital itself. There was therefore a form of discretionary trust under the age of 25, and either an interest in possession or an absolute interest thereafter.

Two sets of statutory conditions

[11.6] The first set of conditions which had to be fulfilled for a trust to be within the protection of *IHTA 1984, s 71* were that under the age of 25:

(a) there was no interest in possession in the trust;
(b) the income from the trust had to be accumulated so far as not applied for the maintenance, education, or benefit of a beneficiary; and
(c) one or more persons had to become beneficially entitled to the settled property or to an interest in possession in it before attaining a specified age not exceeding 25 years.

[*IHTA 1984, s 71(1)*]

[11.7] In most cases, it was obvious whether condition (a) above was satisfied. Condition (b) required a trust to accumulate. A mere power to accumulate was not enough. A trust would be within this condition if the trusts of income required either the whole of the income to be disbursed or, alternatively, the whole income to be accumulated. An accumulation trust with power to maintain could also satisfy the test. The words 'maintenance, education or benefit' are lifted from *Trustee Act 1925, s 31* (see Appendix **D**) and are used in the same sense as in that Act. 'Maintenance' and 'education' also appear in *IHTA 1984, s 11* (dispositions for maintenance of family etc) and presumably have the same meaning. There are cases on trusteeship (eg *Wilson v Turner* (1883) 22 Ch D 521, CA) which show that the automatic payment of income to the parent is not within these words. Some assessment of the situation is necessary and annual review should take place.

[11.8] 'Benefit' generally signifies the improvement of the material situation of the beneficiary. Again the trustees must consider whether a particular application of funds will benefit the beneficiary (*Moxon's Will Trusts, Re, Downey v Moxon* [1958] 1 All ER 386, [1958] 1 WLR 165, Ch D). 'Benefit' is also given a wide meaning and has been found to include resettlement (*Pilkington v IRC* [1964] AC 612, [1962] 3 All ER 622, HL) and the making of a charitable donation (*Clore's Settlement Trusts, Re, Sainer v Clore* [1966] 2 All ER 272, [1966] 1 WLR 955, Ch D) where that was expected of the beneficiary, by way of moral obligation. More recently, in *Hampden Settlement Trust, Re*, [1977] TR 177, [2001] WTLR 195 an advance by trustees on accumulation and maintenance trusts for the children of the beneficiary was held to be for his benefit, but on the grounds that he had sufficient money in his own right to have been able to make such a trust for his children. That there is some limitation on the concept of 'benefit' in the context of a settled advance can be seen from the High Court case *X v A* [2005] EWHC 2706 (Ch), [2006] 1 All ER 952, [2006] 1 WLR 741. In this case the Court considered that a revocation and appointment sought to redirect property both to charities and to non-beneficiaries was not for the benefit of the life tenant (the wife of the settlor). This was because (within *Clore*) she had no moral obligation to make payments to the charities and (within *Hampden*) the amount of the payment for the non-beneficiaries was greater than her personal financial resources: her motivation was simply that in her view the beneficiaries who would take after her life interest were sufficiently well provided for without further money coming to them from the trust. The standard administrative powers would take a settlement outside *IHTA 1984, s 71* if they could divert income. The most obvious is a power to insure lives out of income. This is not maintenance or education etc, and it is not accumulation. Therefore this power would prevent condition (b) being certain and the settlement would be outside *section 71*.

[11.9] Condition (c) above contains an imperative. Provisions which could defeat the beneficiaries from obtaining an interest in possession, etc, on attaining the specified age meant that a trust would fail the test (see *Inglewood (Lord) v IRC* [1983] 1 WLR 366, [1983] STC 133, CA). Put another way, the only thing which the beneficiaries have to do to qualify is to survive to the specified age (apart from the prior exercise by the trustees of a power varying the presumptive shares). Provided they reach that age, nothing should disqualify them. HMRC have stated:

> 'Also, a trust which otherwise satisfies the requirement of *section 71(1)(a)* would not be disqualified by the existence of a power to vary or determine the respective shares of members of the class (even to the extent of excluding some members altogether) provided the power is exercisable only in favour of a person under 25 who is a member of the class.'

See also ESC F8 (reproduced in Appendix B).

[11.10] If the trust instrument is silent, it is likely that *Trustee Act 1925, s 31* would apply and that the age at which the beneficiaries would be entitled to an interest in possession would be 18. This would save the status of the settlement.

[11.11] Having satisfied all three of the conditions mentioned above, a second test had to be passed – one of the following conditions had to be satisfied:

(a) not more than 25 years have elapsed since the creation of the trust or, if it has been some other sort of trust and has been converted into an accumulation and maintenance settlement, not more than 25 years have elapsed since it became such a trust; or
(b) all the persons who were beneficiaries, were grandchildren of a common grandparent. But where a grandchild had died before attaining a vested interest, then his children, widows or widowers or surviving civil partners could take his place as beneficiaries.

[*IHTA 1984, s 71(2)*]

[11.12] One problem with condition (a) (the 25-year test) was ascertaining the day on which the 25 years started to run. This had to be a particular day and, bearing in mind that one could have been dealing with a trust which commenced a long time ago, considerable research into family histories was sometimes needed. Thankfully, reliance on this test was rare.

[11.13] Another problem with relying on the 25-year test was that, if before the expiry of that period the trusts have not been converted into either interest in possession or absolute form, there was an automatic charge to inheritance tax on the property then in the settlement at a rate of 21%, with no allowance for the nil-rate band (see **11.24–11.26**).

[11.14] Condition (b) (the one generation test) had other issues. If the trust instrument mentioned as beneficiaries 'children or remoter issue of X', then it failed the condition even though only grandchildren of a common grandparent do, in fact, benefit. The section is, however, quite generous in that illegitimate children, adopted children and stepchildren are treated in the same way as legitimate children of the full blood [*IHTA 1984, s 71(8)*].

[11.15] Questions have arisen as to whether the mere existence of a power to appoint income or capital (which power does not itself offend the conditions of *IHTA 1984, s 71(1)(a)*) in favour of beneficiaries who are not grandchildren of a common grandparent would take a trust outside the common grandparent rule. *Inland Revenue Tax Bulletin* Issue 55 October 2001 confirmed the HMRC view that the mere existence of a power, as opposed to its actual exercise, does not take a trust outside the common grandparent category.

The inheritance tax consequences

[11.16] There were typically three inheritance tax consequences to note in relation to an accumulation and maintenance trust before 22 March 2006:

- Any lifetime gift to an accumulation and maintenance settlement was a potentially exempt transfer [*IHTA 1984, s 3A(1)(c)*].
- The pre-age 25 trusts had 'favoured' status and were outside the relevant property regime.
- Any interest in possession trusts arising after the age of 25 would be what are now (post-2006) referred to as 'qualifying' interests in possession. In other words, they would remain outside the relevant property regime but a beneficiary over the age of 25 would be treated as owning the assets in which his interest subsisted.

[11.17] In combination, these rules provided for a very attractive regime. There was no ten-year charge because the settled property was not relevant property. Nor was there a charge when, on a beneficiary attaining the specified age, property became subject to an interest in possession. Nor was there a charge on the death of a beneficiary before attaining a specified age [*IHTA 1984, s 71(4)*].

[11.18] The next occasion of possible inheritance tax charge after a beneficiary had attained the specified age would thus be when he made a transfer of the capital he had received from the settlement (assuming he had taken an absolute interest) or when his interest in possession terminated. Death was the most obvious termination which was an occasion of charge. Another was a resettlement on discretionary trusts. Most other terminations would themselves have been potentially exempt transfers.

The 2006 changes

The main changes

[11.19] The key consequence of the 2006 changes for accumulation and maintenance trusts were as follows:

- It was not possible to create a new accumulation and maintenance settlement (nor indeed to add property to an earlier one) after 22 March 2006. (This was achieved by amendments made by *FA 2006* to *IHTA 1984, s 71*.)
- Until 5 April 2008, the favoured treatment of *all* accumulation and maintenance trusts (ie the exclusion from the relevant property regime while a beneficiary was under the specified age) continued.
- Beyond 2008:
    - the favoured treatment of any accumulation and maintenance trust in which the specified age was 18 (or younger) *and the beneficiary took an absolute interest* continued;
    - any accumulation and maintenance trust in which the specified age was between 18 and 25 *and the beneficiary took an absolute interest* fell into a new regime for an 'age 18-to-25' trusts; and
    - all other accumulation and maintenance trusts – particularly any trust in which a beneficiary took an *interest in possession* at the specified age, rather than an absolute interest, fell into the relevant property regime.

[11.20] The position for any accumulation and maintenance trust in which a beneficiary took an interest in possession at the specified age became particularly complex after 22 April 2006 because any interests in possession arising in the trust before that date were 'qualifying' interests in possession, in which the trust's assets were treated as forming part of the life tenant's estates, but interests in possession arising after 22 April 2006 fell within the relevant property regime (ie if a beneficiary attained the specified age between 22 April 2006 and 5 April 2008). For trusts with a large class of beneficiaries of widely differing ages, this could lead to a very complex tax position.

The options in the transitional period

[11.21] The trustees of an accumulation and maintenance trust had from 22 March 2006 to 6 April 2008 to decide what if any action to take, no doubt in consultation with the settlor and the family's professional advisers. Where capital already vested absolutely at 18, no action was required. Where capital vested absolutely at between 18 and 25, action was required only if it was desired to avoid the 'age 18 to 25 trust' provisions. The main category of trust where change did need to be considered was where the beneficiaries attained only an interest in possession at the specified age. For such trusts there were four distinct options:

(a)   To bring the trust to an end before 6 April 2008.

[11.21] Inheritance Tax: Accumulation and Maintenance Settlements

(b) To alter the terms of the trust, so as to provide for capital to vest absolutely at or before age 18 – in which case the favoured status simply continued.
(c) To alter the terms of the trust, so as to provide for capital to vest absolutely at or before age 25 – in which case the favoured status continued until the age of 18 and the 'age 18-to-25 trust' provisions applied from there.
(d) To take no action and allow relevant property regime to apply from 6 April 2008.

By 6 April 2008, and depending upon the original terms of the trust and the options taken by the trustees in the transitional period, an accumulation and maintenance trust would take one of the following three forms.

The 'continuing' accumulation and maintenance trust

[11.22] As is hopefully clear from the above commentary, for any accumulation and maintenance trust in which capital vested absolutely at 18 (whether because those were its original terms or because such terms were adopted within the transitional period), the favoured regime simply continued. Such trusts, with such treatment, could be around for some time yet. An accumulation and maintenance trust set up (let's assume on the same day!) for triplets born on 21 March 2006 and which was subsequently varied so that capital vested at 18 will continue to be taxed under the favoured A & M regime until 21 March 2024.

The 'age 18 to 25 trust' accumulation and maintenance trust

[11.23] Where capital vests absolutely between 18 and 25, the special 'age 18 to 25 trust' regime applies. The essence of this regime is that:

- the trust's favoured status continues for beneficiaries while under the age of 18;
- once a beneficiary reaches the age of 18, any capital transferred to him beyond that date is subject to special inheritance tax charge – including when capital vests at the specified age; but
- in the meantime, there is no charge on the ten-yearly anniversaries of the trust.

[11.24] Further commentary on 'age 18 to 25 trusts' can be found at 8.13. The charge which arises on the payment of capital to a beneficiary between the ages of 18 and 25 can be thought of as a quasi-'exit charge' and a description of how the charge works in practise can therefore be found in CHAPTER 10 at 10.32.

The 'relevant property' accumulation and maintenance trust

[11.25] In the most typical type of accumulation and maintenance trust beneficiaries would become entitled to an interest in possession in a share of the trust fund at the age of 25. As from 6 April 2008, any trusts still with this form will have entered the 'relevant property' regime. Therefore, for these trusts it became material to know all of the information necessary to calculate a 'relevant property' charge (see CHAPTERS 9 and 10), ie:

(a) when the settlement commenced, that is when property first became comprised in the settlement;
(b) what was the settlor's cumulative total of chargeable transfers in the period of seven years prior to that date;
(c) whether any other non-charitable settlements were made by that settlor on the same day as related settlements; and
(d) whether there have been any additions to the settlement.

Any of these things may not be at all easy to ascertain and the avoidance of the administrative difficulties inherent in collating this information was one of the principal drivers behind the proposals for the simplification of the relevant property regime (see 9.44–9.48).

Deciding between these options

[11.26] Of course, 5 April 2008 having long passed, the trustees of accumulation and maintenance trusts not longer have any decisions to make. Nevertheless, a brief understanding of the thought processes undertaken by trustees at that time may be helpful.

[11.27] The simplest option was, of course, to either wind up the trust or convert it to ones in which capital vested absolutely at 18, but the difficulty with these option was that the beneficiaries then took the assets at ages earlier than those originally intended by the settlor. Denying beneficiaries the right to capital at too young an age is, of course, one of the main reasons why any trust is established. Conversely, allowing a trust to fall into the relevant property regime, enabled the trust to continue, with the assets kept out of the hands of the beneficiaries, but with the trustees then having the headache of having to fund relevant property charges which had not been anticipated. Conversion to an 'age 18-to-25 trust' offered something of a compromise, deferring capital vesting until 25 but avoiding any ten-yearly charges in the meantime. Additionally, the retention by the trustees of a power of advancement did not undermine the 'age 18-to-25 trust' status and, thus, many trustees ensured that such a power was in place so that a settled advance might be made in favour of, for example, a beneficiary for whom an outright payment of capital might not be appropriate, even at 25. And the decision on this could then be deferred until the cusp of the 25th birthday.

[11.28] In cases where there was a large class of beneficiaries of widely differing ages, one of the practical difficulties for trustees was that some beneficiaries would be over 25 with interests in possession already (and with a share of the trust therefore deemed to be owned by them, and outside the relevant property regime), others were under 18 with the full range of options therefore available, others still were aged between 18 and 25 with therefore fewer choices. Trying to maintain a balance between the beneficiaries in these circumstances was far from easy.

The charge to tax on failure

[11.29] In the unlikely event of an accumulation and maintenance settlement failing, a separate regime imposed, in effect, a penal inheritance tax charge. The likeliest occasion of charge was where a settlement with no common grandparent subsisted for more than 25 years. There could before 6 April 2008 be no charge:

(a) on a beneficiary becoming entitled to the settled property or to an interest in possession in it by reaching the age of 25 or any earlier qualifying age specified in the trust instrument; nor
(b) on the death of a beneficiary before reaching the qualifying age. It would seem that, even if all the beneficiaries died, and as a consequence the settlement ceased to fall within the general qualifying conditions, IHTA 1984, s 71(4) would prevent a charge to inheritance tax. And the same principles continue to apply since 6 April 2008, with the substitution of age 18 for age 25 [*IHTA 1984, s 71(4)*].

[11.30] Where there is a charge, the rate of tax increases quarter by quarter for the period during which the settlement has existed, as follows:

	Maximum %
0.25% per quarter for 40 quarters	10
0.20% per quarter for 40 quarters	8
0.15% per quarter for 40 quarters	6
0.10% per quarter for 40 quarters	4
0.05% per quarter for 40 quarters	2
Maximum charge after 50 years	30%

[11.31] It is hard to see how an accumulation and maintenance settlement could continue for so many quarters and, in fact, this table is a standard table applied to a number of sheltered types of settlement when their shelter fails. The first quarter which could be caught, where the settlement dates back so far, is that commencing on 13 March 1975. For a quarter to be caught, it must be a complete quarter ended before the occasion of charge [*IHTA 1984, ss 70(6), (8), 71(3), (5)*].

EXAMPLE

There is only one beneficiary of an accumulation and maintenance settlement. Accumulation and maintenance can continue until he is aged 25. At the age of 22 (and before 22 March 2006), he assigns all his interest in the settlement to his girlfriend, then aged 26. The settled property is worth £60,000 at the date of the assignment and the settlement has been in existence for 15 years and a day. There will be a charge of £8,400 calculated as follows:

	%
0.25% per quarter for 40 quarters	10
0.20% per quarter for 20 quarters	4
	14%
14% of £60,000	£8,400

Note that, had the beneficiary waited until age 25, when he would have obtained either an interest in possession or an absolute interest in the capital, or if the trustees had exercised powers in the settlement to accelerate the interest in possession before the assignment, the gift would have been a potentially exempt transfer, with no immediate charge to tax under the accumulation and maintenance regime.

Chapter 12

Inheritance Tax: Qualifying Interest in Possession Trusts

[12.1] As previously explained (at **8.7**) qualifying interest in possession trusts are interest in possession trusts which fall outside the relevant property regime. The practitioner will, in most cases, meet only six types, namely:

- an interest in possession in being at 22 March 2006;
- an annuity created before 22 March 2006;
- a transitional serial interest (see **8.17–8.22**);
- an immediate post-death interest (see **8.8**);
- a bereaved minors trust (see **8.9–8.12**); and
- a disabled person's interest (see **8.16**).

For the inheritance tax treatment of all other interest in possession settlements, the reader should refer to CHAPTERS **9** and **10** for the relevant property regime.

[12.2] Property subject to a qualifying interest in possession is taxed almost as if it belonged to the income beneficiary. This is made clear in *IHTA 1984, s 49(1)* which provides that a person beneficially entitled to a qualifying interest in possession shall be treated as beneficially entitled to the property in which the interest subsists. The inheritance tax consequences then follow in the way that might be imagined. If the individual is still entitled to the qualifying interest on death, there is a charge to inheritance tax (subject to available reliefs) at 40%. Likewise, if the individual's interest comes to end during his lifetime, the treatment is akin to the individual having made a lifetime transfer of the property.

The charge on death

[12.3] On the death of an individual with a qualifying interest in possession, the value of the trust property in which the interest subsists is subject to inheritance tax, together with any assets owned in the individual's 'free' estate. Taking a very simple example, a widow might be entitled to an interest in possession in her late husband's Will Trust worth £500,000 and have assets in her own name worth £1,000,000. On her death, the total aggregate value of the assets to which she is 'beneficially entitled' is £1,500,000 and, assuming that she has a full transferable nil rate band available to her as well as her own, the inheritance tax liability (assuming no special reliefs) would be £1,500,000 less £650,000 = £850,000 @ 40% = £340,000. This liability would then be apportioned pro rata between her late husband's trustees and her executors, with the trustees being liable for one-third (£113,333) and the executors two-thirds (£226,667).

[12.4] There is a planning point to note here about the burden of tax, being that the nil rate band is allocated first against lifetime transfers. Thus, if the

[12.4] Qualifying Interest in Possession Settlements

widow's life interest was terminated the day before her death the trustees would have no inheritance tax liability on her death because the available nil rate band of £650,000 would cover the value of the Will Trust – and the executors would be left with a nil rate band of only £150,000 to offset against their £1,000,000, and their inheritance tax liability would increase to the full £340,000. Likewise, if the widow made a gift to her daughter of £650,000 the day before her death, that gift would be inheritance tax free and the inheritance tax on death would then have to be apportioned between trustees and executors in the ratio 500:350 or 10:7 – the trustees would be liable for £200,000 and the executors £140,000. Where the beneficiaries entitled to the widow's estate and the Will Trust property after her death are the same, the point is somewhat academic. Where they are different (eg the children from his first marriage, and the children from hers) all this will can have a significant impact.

[12.5] Where, on death, interests in the same property have to be aggregated – for example, because the trustees and executors hold shares in the same private company, or interests in the same residential property – the so called 'estate principle' applies. The two interests have to be valued as if they would be sold together and the value again apportioned between the trustees and the executors. This contrasts with the position on the lifetime termination of a qualifying interest in possession, when the trustees' assets can be valued in isolation (see **12.9–12.11**).

[12.6] Where the qualifying interest in possession extends to only a part of an undivided fund, the 'property in which his interest subsisted' [*IHTA 1984, s 52(1)*] is his fraction of the whole fund [*IHTA 1984, s 50(1)*]. There are also provisions [*IHTA 1984, s 50(3)*] to prevent trustees from arguing that all the high-yielding investments support one beneficiary's interest whilst the low-yielding ones benefit another where tax is chargeable by reference to the value of part of a property producing a specified amount (eg an annuity) or by reference to the value of the remainder.

[12.7] In the following cases, the death of the life tenant will not give rise to an charge on death:

(a) the termination is prevented from becoming a chargeable transfer because of an exemption, perhaps because it goes to the income beneficiary's spouse/civil partner absolutely [*IHTA 1984, s 53(4)(a)*]; perhaps because it is succeeded by a transitional serial interest in favour of the life tenant's spouse (this can now be the case only where the life tenant's interest subsists in a pre-22 March 2006 interest in possession trust); or perhaps because the trust owns relievable business or agricultural assets;

(b) where the 'reverter to settlor' exemption applies operates – see **12.13–12.16**; and

(c) where the settled property was within the old estate duty surviving spouse exemption which is preserved by *IHTA 1984, Sch 6, para 2*. For that exemption to apply, the settled property must have been liable to estate duty on the death of the first spouse (ie the first spouse died before 13 November 1974) and the second spouse must have had a life interest. There must have been no right for the surviving spouse to draw on the capital. The protection of this rule is obtained if there would have been a liability to estate duty on the first death but for either the threshold or the relief for agricultural or business property.

The charge on lifetime termination

[12.8] There are many reasons why a qualifying interest in possession might come to an end during the life tenant's lifetime, for example:

- because the trustees exercise a power of appointment or advancement to terminate it;
- because the life tenant surrenders it; or
- because it is automatically terminates after a fixed period; on the happening of certain events (eg the remarriage of a surviving spouse) or, in the case of an interest autre vie, the death of someone else.

[12.9] Where a qualifying interest comes to an end during lifetime, tax is then charged as if the life tenant had made a transfer of value equal to the value of the property in which his interest subsisted [*IHTA 1984, s 52(1)*]. The transfer of value could escape a charge to inheritance for one of the reasons set out at (a) and (b) at **12.7**, or because the capital has been advanced to the income beneficiary [*IHTA 1984, s 53(2)*](and therefore remains in his estate). Alternatively, the transfer of value could constitute a potentially exempt transfer because:

- the termination constitutes an outright transfer to an individual or to a disabled trust; or
- in the case of a lifetime termination of an immediate post-death interest only, gives rise to, a bereaved minors trust.

Otherwise, the lifetime termination of a qualifying interest in possession will be a chargeable transfer.

[12.10] As is indicated above, the valuation rules on a lifetime termination are not the same as on death, and tend to ignore *IHTA 1984, s 49(1)* to the extent that they do not operate as if the trust property truly belonged to the income beneficiary. Instead any charge is restricted to '... the value of the property in which his interest subsisted' [*IHTA 1984, s 52(1)*].

[12.11] A transfer by the beneficiary from his free estate would be calculated as the fall in value of his estate for inheritance tax purposes. Originally it was thought that *section 49(1)* had an effect for valuation purposes in that the holding of an income beneficiary was plainly part of his estate but shares settled on him were deemed to be his as well. Therefore if there were 20 shares settled and 60 owned outright, the valuation of the 20 shares was thought to be 20/80ths of the value of 80 shares. However, on 21 March 1990 a new view was communicated to the professional bodies by HMRC (see Appendix A). This now requires the settled property to be valued in isolation (subject, however, in appropriate cases to the application of the *Ramsay* principle or the associated operations provisions of *IHTA 1984, s 268*) or, indeed, from 2013/14 the General Anti-Abuse Rule or GAAR (see Chapter 23).

EXAMPLES

Shares in an investment company are valued at £1,000 each in parcels of 200 and £5,000 each in parcels of 800. The total issued capital is 1,000 shares.

EXAMPLE 1

The income beneficiary has an interest in possession in 200 shares and has 600 shares in his own name. His interest in possession terminates. There is a transfer of value of £200,000 (200 x £1,000).

EXAMPLE 2

The income beneficiary has an interest in possession in 800 shares. His interest terminates in 200 shares. There is a transfer of value of £1,000,000 (200 x £5,000).

EXAMPLE 3

The income beneficiary has an interest in possession in 200 shares. He owns 600 shares himself. He dies. There is a transfer of value of £4,000,000 (subject to the availability of business property relief @ 100%). This is because there is a single transfer of value ((200 + 600) x £5,000).

[12.12] On the inter vivos termination of a qualifying interest in possession, just as on a beneficial gift, there are available the annual £3,000 exemption and the marriage exemption. However, both of these depend upon the giving of notice by the beneficiary to the trustees as to the availability of the exemption and confirming the extent to which it is available [*IHTA 1984, s 57*]. The notice must be given within six months of the event on what used to be Revenue Form 222, though this has now been withdrawn and the notice is given simply by a letter from the beneficiary to the trustees.

Reverter to settlor

[12.13] As mentioned above, there is no charge to inheritance tax when a qualifying interest in possession comes to an end either on the death of the life tenant [*IHTA 1984, s 54*] or during his lifetime [*IHTA 1984, s 53(3)–(8)*] if the property reverts to:

- the settlor; or
- the settlor's spouse or civil partner or, where the settlor has died less than two years earlier, the widow or widower of the settlor or his surviving civil partner, providing that the spouse, civil partner widow or widower is domiciled in the UK. (There is no requirement that the settlor be UK domiciled.)

[12.14] Prior to 22 March 2006, these exemptions would also apply if the assets reverted to an interest in possession for the settlor or his spouse etc because back then any interest in possession trust would effectively place the beneficial ownership of the trust assets with the new life tenant, given the fiction in *section 49(1)*. Of course – since that date - this will apply now only where the subsequent interest in possession interest in possession is also a qualifying interest in possession. This would have been the case for a 'reverter to settlor trust' made before 22 March 2006, if the life tenant died before

6 October 2008 because a continuing life interest for the settlor would have been a transitional serial interest. Now, the only trust would could conceivably qualify would be a disable trust.

[12.15] On death, there is a huge advantage in providing for property to revert to a trust for the settlor rather than to him absolutely because the former enables a capital gains tax uplift to be obtained whereas for the latter, the property reverts to the settlor at his original base cost for capital gains tax purposes (see **7.26**). Now, given the limited opportunity to attract the inheritance tax exemption while still using a trust (see above), in most cases a choice needs to be made between using a trust which provides for a capital gains uplift but no inheritance exemption, and using an outright reversion where the inheritance tax exemption will apply but where there is no uplift. In most cases, the inheritance tax exemption will be more valuable; however, where, for example, inheritance tax reliefs are likely to apply, taking the uplift may be the better option. The terms of any pre-22 March 2006 reverter to settlor trust should be reviewed in this respect.

[12.16] There are a number of very technical exemptions to the reverter to settlor rules which apply in relation to certain very old trusts and where the reversionary interests have been acquired for consideration. These will not apply in the majority of common situations [*IHTA 1984, s 53(5)-(8), 54(3)*].

Reversionary interests

[12.17] Where there is a qualifying interest in possession then the reversionary interest is excluded property (except where, in particular, owned by settlor or spouse/civil partner) [*IHTA 1984, s 48(1)*]. The reversioner can therefore pass on his interest with no inheritance tax repercussions at all and no capital gains tax implications (assuming that he has not acquired his interest for value), even were he to die the following day. See **3.3**.

[12.18] The interest of a remainderman is typically excluded property for inheritance tax purposes. In those few occasions provided by *IHTA 1984, s 48(1), (2)* where excluded property treatment is denied, this will not apply if the remainderman is not domiciled in the UK (see **24.13–24.14**). The disposal of a reversionary interest is (usually) exempt from capital gains tax under *TCGA 1992, s 76*, provided that it is original to the settlement and has not been acquired for a consideration. The capital gains tax exemption depends upon the trustees never having been resident outside the UK [*TCGA 1992, ss 76(1A), (1B), 85* and see **7.134**]. This provides a painless route for the son whose inheritance from his father is subject to his mother's life interest to resettle his interest for the benefit of his children.

Reservation of benefit

[12.19] Historically, interest in possession settlements could be used to overcome the reservation of benefit provisions. This was on the basis that the termination of the interest by the trustees did not constitute a 'gift' by the life

[12.19] Qualifying Interest in Possession Settlements

tenant and therefore – although it was a transfer of value – the gift with reservation of benefit provisions could not apply. This enabled, for example, residential property to be left upon life interest trusts for a widow, the trustees could appoint the interest away from the widow as a potentially exempt and the widow could remain in the property without any 'reservation of benefit' consequences. Now, following 22 March 2006, such a termination of a qualifying interest in possession will give rise to a disposition by way of gift on the part of the beneficiary, and therefore the operation of the reservation of benefit rules [FA 1986, s 102ZA].

[12.20] The earlier rule was also an essential part of what became known as the *Eversden* planning scheme. There is a rule in FA 1986, s 102(5) that a disposition which is protected by a number of specified exemptions from inheritance tax, including the spouse/civil partner exemption in paragraph (a), cannot be caught by the reservation of benefit rules. The High Court refused HMRC's appeal from a decision of the Special Commissioner in favour of the taxpayer using such a ploy *IRC v Eversden* [2002] EWHC 1360 (Ch), [2002] STC 1109, 75 TC 340). In this case, it was held that a transfer by a wife of a majority share in the matrimonial home to a life interest settlement on her husband which after the husband's death reverted into discretionary trusts, the wife being one of the discretionary beneficiaries, was not treated as part of her estate on her death, some ten years after the original gift. Lightman J held that any initial interest in possession given to the settlor's spouse under a settlement, whether or not of short duration, obviates the operation of the gift with reservation provisions in respect to that settlement.

[12.21] Tax planning opportunists were able to take advantage of this decision (following HMRC's further appeal which was refused by the Court of Appeal in May 2003 ([2003] STC 822)) only up to 19 June 2003, as anti-avoidance measures were announced on 20 June for gifts into settlement on or after that day [FA 2003, s 185].

[12.22] For other purposes, the termination of a qualifying interest in possession may still not be a 'gift, ie:

(a) the erstwhile life tenant is not a settlor for the purposes of *ITTOIA 2005, s 629(1)* (settlements on own infant children); and
(b) the erstwhile life tenant is not a settlor for the purposes of *TCGA 1992, s 77* (before 2008/09: see **4.33**) or *TCGA 1992, s 86* (see **26.17–26.32**: capital gains tax and settlor with an interest in a settlement).

Disguised interests in possession

[12.23] It should be remembered that there can be cases where a settlement which is ostensibly discretionary in form may for inheritance tax purposes be treated as an interest in possession. Where this applies in a case where the interest in possession would be a qualifying interest in possession the result would be to unexpectedly take the assets into the estate of the life tenant. All the cases described below pre-date the 2006 trust changes but the point is still relevant to the extent that an 'unexpected' immediate post-death interest could arise.

[12.24] Such cases typically involve Will trusts of the family home, usually made under the Will of the first to die of a married couple (or civil partnership) who have held their home as tenants in common in equal shares. The aim was to make use of the nil-rate band available on the first death and, in the absence of other assets, an attempt was made to employ the share in the family home, subject, however, to maintaining the surviving spouse's/civil partner's security of tenure. Quite apart from that, an unsuccessful attempt was made in *IRC v Lloyds Private Banking Ltd* [1998] STC 559, [1998] 2 FCR 41 to give the daughter an immediate absolute interest in the house subject only to a requirement on the trustees to allow the husband to continue occupying the deceased's wife's half share, subject to conditions as to insurance etc, for so long as he wanted to do so. The High Court held that, on the wording of the Will, the husband had been given an interest in possession.

[12.25] In another decided case, each of three children was under their father's Will entitled to occupy the family home for as long as he or she wished to live there. First, the daughter died. Then, on the death of one of the sons, he but not his brother was in occupation. It was held that the deceased's son had enjoyed an interest in possession, since there was a requirement on the trustees to permit occupation, but that that interest in possession had been in one half only of the house (*Woodhall (Personal Representative of Woodhall) v IRC* [2000] STC (SCD) 558). An interest in possession analysis was also applied in *Faulkner (Trustee of Adams) v IRC* SpC 278 [2001] STC (SCD) 112, against the executors who had argued that the Will trust was discretionary.

[12.26] More generally, with an express discretionary trust, HMRC Trusts and Estates may take the view that the exercise of the trusts is such as to give the surviving spouse/civil partner an interest in possession within principles set out in Statement of Practice 10/79 (SP 10/79) reproduced in APPENDIX A. This would apply where there is a power sufficiently wide to 'cover the creation of an exclusive or joint right of residence, albeit revocable, for a definite or indefinite period, and is exercised with the intention of providing a particular beneficiary with a permanent home', when HMRC will regard such an exercise as creating an interest in possession. This view has not yet been tested in the courts. This is not the place to go into such issues, though see also **12.27**. However, it should be noted that it is conceivable that the terms of occupation of the matrimonial home (or share therein), by the surviving spouse/civil partner might immediately after the death be discretionary (or at least not an interest in possession) in nature but might become interest in possession within two years after the death (and whether or not under Statement of Practice SP 10/79). In that event, the 'reading back' provisions of *IHTA 1984, s 144(4)(a)* would apply to treat the interest in possession as having arisen on death and therefore to be an immediate post-death interest. However, if, on HMRC's view, an interest in possession for the surviving spouse were to arise on these principles following the expiry of the two-year period after death, this would have no inheritance tax implications: a trust which on death fell within the relevant property regime would continue to be so. That said, of course, given now the transferable nil-rate band introduced by *IHTA 1984, s 8A*, the fiscal incentive will be to avoid any chargeable transfers on the first death and to maximise the benefit of the spouse exemption, whether through an immediate post-death interest or by an absolute gift. See also the end of

APPENDIX E for the exchange of correspondence between STEP/CIOT and HMRC with regard to SP 10/79 in the context of transitional serial interests.

[12.27] A more helpful case for the taxpayer again concerned the issue of whether an apparently discretionary trust could be construed for inheritance tax purposes as an interest in possession trust was decided by the Special Commissioner (Dr Nuala Brice) in *Judge and another v HMRC* [2005] STC (SCD) 863 on 5 October 2005. In that case the late Mr Walden had owned the whole of the house in London which was left under his Will to a discretionary trust. Mrs Walden had a power of veto over the trustees' power of sale but otherwise the trustees had a full discretion to allow her to occupy the house for the rest of her life, though with no right for Mrs Walden to do so. As a matter of interest, both the corporate trustee of Mr Walden's Will and HMRC took the view that on Mr Walden's death the clause in his Will gave his widow an interest in possession. But that view was challenged following Mrs Walden's death, with Dr Brice deciding that there was a discretionary trust, and therefore a chargeable transfer on the first death, but no aggregation with Mrs Walden's estate on the second. Statement of Practice 10/79 was not mentioned. Dr Brice expressly disapproved HMRC's argument that in substance the discretionary trust in fact gave an interest in possession to Mrs Walden such that she could, if she so chose, occupy the house for the rest of her life.

Miscellaneous anti-avoidance

[12.28] The making of a qualifying interest in possession settlement before 22 March 1986 was almost always a potentially exempt transfer. There could still be complexities for the draftsman to address in relation to various anti-avoidance legislation, rules, for example if the settlor might benefit (in which case there would be 'gift with reservation of benefit' issues) or:

(a) where the settlement was initially for life or some shorter period and on termination of the interest in possession, the capital was held on relevant property trusts;
(b) where there is a lifetime termination of a non-qualifying interest in possession, the restriction which catches interests acquired on or after 9 December 2009 if the beneficiary entitled to it *acquired* it when he was UK domiciled and by virtue of a disposition made without gratuitous benefit. This has the general effect of treating the settled property in which the new *IHTA 1984, s 5(1B)* interest subsists as part of the estate of the person entitled to the interest, and thereby of treating it as part of that person's estate on death [*FA 2010, s 53 (3)(b)*].

[12.29] There was a period when the device in (a) above was used with the settlor's spouse as the life tenant and the short period was one month. The idea was to use the spouse exemption to exempt the making of the settlement and then to use the spouse's nil-rate band etc, if this was tax-efficient, to cover the transfer to discretionary trusts. This scheme was used when potentially exempt transfer treatment was extended to interest in possession settlements in 1987, and *IHTA 1984, ss 54A, 54B* were introduced specifically to block this possible loophole. The countering of the device in (b) above was introduced by *FA 2010, s 53(3)* to correct a possible drafting anomaly and seeks to cover an unlikely case where, say, one individual (Alan) makes a settlement which confers an interest in possession on another (Bill) where Bill pays full value. This is therefore a commercial transaction which *IHTA 1984, s 10* exempts from being a transfer of value by either Alan or Bill. Accordingly, the settled property falls out of Bill's estate (in the absence of the *FA 2010* provision), because *IHTA 1984, s 5(1A)* as inserted by *FA 2006*, has the effect that an interest in possession (other than a disabled person's interest) which is acquired under a new lifetime settlement made after 21 March 2006 does not for inheritance tax purposes form part of the estate of the person entitled to the interest in possession.

Chapter 13

Stamp Taxes: Liability and Compliance

Summary

[13.1] Stamp duty has since 1 December 2003 been restricted to documents transferring stocks or marketable securities. From that date stamp duty land tax (SDLT) has applied to transactions in land and it is with that tax that this chapter principally deals. It is an error to refer to 'stamp duty' being charged on the acquisition of a building or land, as the newspapers and even certain official documents do. *Finance Act 2003, s 105* and *Sch 16* contain the SDLT provisions which relate to trust interests and the responsibilities of trustees in relation to SDLT. The legislation defines two types of trust for stamp duty land tax purposes, namely 'bare trusts' and 'settlements' (see **13.5** and **13.10**). This chapter deals principally with the specific legislative provisions applying SDLT to trusts. Specifically, this chapter does not deal with the SDLT regime in general, nor in particular with the *sections 75A, B and C* introduced by *Finance Act 2007* into *Finance Act 2003*, incorporating very extensive anti-avoidance measures which must be considered by all purchasers of land, not just trustees.

[13.2] While not of direct relevance to trusts, this book needs to draw attention to the three limbed anti-avoidance regime introduced in 2012 and 2013 to discourage the ownership of high value houses by a 'non-natural person' (typically a corporate vehicle but not necessarily so). First, 2012 saw the introduction of a 15% SDLT entry charge into such a structure (see **13.34**) and then *Finance Act 2013* introduced both the so called ATED ('Annual Tax on Enveloped Dwellings') charge (see **13.40–13.45**), *and* a new capital gains tax charge (see **7.126**). Originally, 'high value' in this context meant a house worth more than £2 million; however, *Finance Act 2014* has reduced the threshold to £500,000 (with effect from 30 March 2014 in relation to the 15% entry charge, but otherwise phased in by 1 April 2016 – see relevant sections below). A trust is not a 'non-natural person' but can, of course, holds shares or an interest in the same.

[13.3] Practitioners should note that from 1 April 2015, SDLT was replaced in Scotland by a new *Land and Buildings Transaction Tax* (LBTT). See 13.37–13.39.

[13.4] The government announced at Autumn Statement 2015 that it would reduce the SDLT filing and payment window from 30 days to 14 days in 2017–18 and would consult on changes to the SDLT filing and payment process in 2016. A consultation document *Stamp duty land tax: changes to the filing and payment process* was published on 10 August 2016, with the closing date for comments of 7 October 2016.

Stamp Duty Land Tax

Bare trusts

[13.5] A 'bare trust' is defined as a 'trust under which property is held by a person as trustee:

(a) for a person absolutely entitled as against the trustee, or who would be so entitled but for being a minor or other person or other person under a disability, or
(b) for two or more persons who are or would be jointly so entitled'.

[FA 2003, Sch 16, para 1(2)]

[13.6] That definition is obviously based on the capital gains tax provisions of *TCGA 1992, s 60*.

[13.7] A bare trust includes the case in which a person holds property as nominee for another. In Scotland, a bare trust is known as a 'simple trust'.

[13.8] 'Absolutely entitled' as against the trustee means the situation where the person has the exclusive right, subject only to satisfying any outstanding charge, lien or other right of the trustee, to resort to the property for payment of duty, taxes, costs or other outgoings or to direct how the property is to be dealt with. In the Stamp Duty Land Tax Manual at SDLTM31710 HMRC refer users to the more detailed explanation given in the Capital Gains Manual (at paras CG34320–34352). The definition in *FA 2003, Sch 16, para 1(1)* is wide enough to include one or more sub-funds of what would be a single settlement for capital gains tax purposes. That has in the past been thought to cause a problem in a case where there is an exchange of interests in land or an acquisition of land as between sub-funds of a single settlement, at least where the trustees of each sub-fund comprised different individuals, albeit with no implications for capital gains tax purposes. In such circumstances it is arguable that each set of trustees would be a purchaser and liable to SDLT accordingly. If there is no 'purchaser' (as defined: see below), the compliance obligations under *FA 2003, s 76* fall away. The perceived problem, where there are different individuals constituting the trustees of each sub-fund, could therefore be avoided by ensuring that, before the land transaction, the two or more sets of trustees comprise the same individuals. HMRC Stamp Taxes, however, have in the past taken the view, somewhat surprisingly, that in such a case it is not the trustees, but the relevant beneficiary/beneficiaries who is or are the purchaser (even though, within the definition of 'purchaser' in *FA 2003, s 43(4)* a person cannot be a purchaser if he is neither a party to the transaction nor gives consideration for it, typically the case here). Furthermore, the chargeable consideration was said not to relate to the value of the land but to the actuarial value of the relevant life interest! The point was vigorously disputed with Stamp Taxes and the somewhat surprising outcome, announced at Budget 2006, is first that HMRC Stamp Taxes concede that there never has been an issue as to there being chargeable consideration for SDLT purposes in such circumstances in principle. Second, in the case where specifically there might be thought to be a problem where the reallocation of trust property as between funds required the consent of one or more beneficiaries, *FA 2003, Sch*

16, para 8 (inserted by FA 2006, s 165) expressly confirms that the giving of consent does not mean that there is chargeable consideration for the acquisition.

[13.9] Where a trustee acquires a chargeable interest as a bare trustee, the acquisition is deemed to be an acquisition by the beneficiary [FA 2003, Sch 16, para 3].

Settlement

[13.10] A 'settlement' is defined as a trust which is not a bare trust [FA 2003, Sch 16, para 1(1)]. A 'settlement' therefore will include interest in possession trusts, discretionary trusts (including accumulation and maintenance trusts) and mixed trusts.

[13.11] Where a person acquires a chargeable interest or an interest in a partnership as trustees of a settlement, the trustees are deemed to acquire the interest acquired including the beneficial interest [FA 2003, Sch 16, para 4]. Accordingly, the trustee is the purchaser. The legislation makes no distinction between a person acquiring a chargeable interest in a beneficial capacity and one who does so as a fiduciary, that is a trustee. There might therefore seem to be a technical problem for an incoming trustee of a settlement where the trust fund includes land which is subject to a mortgage – or indeed a retiring trustee of such a settlement. A specific rule in FA 2003, Sch 4, para 8(1), (1A), (1B) ensures that in such a case (whatever the identity of the purchaser) the amount of the liability is pro-rated between the number of co-owners. Thus an unforeseen liability might arise insofar as the share of the liability assumed by an incoming trustee exceeded £150,000 (in the case of, typically, non-residential property) or indeed for each of the continuing trustees on the retirement of a trustee. The point applies not just to trustees of family settlements, but also to trustees of unit trusts, pension funds and charities. Notwithstanding the above technical concern, however, HMRC Stamp Taxes have confirmed that the FA 2003, Sch 16 regime implies that trustees are a single continuing body of persons, as they are for capital gains tax. See HMRC's Stamp Duty Land Tax Manual at SDLTM31745. Accordingly, there are no SDLT implications on appointments and retirements of trustees. While hard to follow, this interpretation provides welcome relief to many professional advisers who had been concerned about the problem.

Trustees' responsibilities

General

[13.12] As the purchaser of a chargeable interest is deemed to be the trustee, the responsible trustees (see **13.13**) will have all the statutory obligations of a purchaser such as payment of the tax and submitting a land transaction return or self-certificate.

Who are the 'responsible trustees?'

[13.13] The 'responsible trustees' in relation to a land transaction are defined as the persons who are trustees at the effective date of the transaction and any person who subsequently becomes a trustee [*FA 2003, Sch 16, para 5(3)*].

Recovery of tax from trustees

[13.14] Where the trustees are liable to pay the tax, interest on unpaid tax, a penalty or interest on the penalty or to make a payment because of an excessive repayment, moneys can be recovered from any one or more of the responsible trustees [*FA 2003, Sch 16, para 5(1)*]. Such moneys can be recovered only once. No penalty or interest on a penalty can be recovered from a person who did not become a responsible trustee until after the relevant time [*FA 2003, Sch 16, para 5(2)*].

[13.15] The 'relevant time', in relation to a daily penalty, is defined as the beginning of that day and, in relation to any other penalty or interest on that penalty, is the time when the act or omission occurred which caused the penalty to become payable [*FA 2003, Sch 16, para 5(4)*].

Filling in the land transaction return or self-certificate: the 'relevant trustees'

[13.16] A land transaction return or (prior to 12 March 2008) a self-certification to the Land Registry may be made or given by any one or more of the trustees who are responsible trustees in relation to the transaction [*FA 2003, Sch 16, para 6(1)*]. The requirement for self-certificates (on form SDLT 60) has generally been removed by *FA 2008* from Budget Day, 12 March 2008. The trustees who make the return or self-certificate are defined as the 'relevant trustees'. The declaration confirming that the land transaction return or self-certificate is complete and true must be signed by all the relevant trustees [*FA 2003, Sch 16, para 6(2)*].

Enquiry

[13.17] HMRC must give notice of an enquiry to each of the relevant trustees [*FA 2003, Sch 16, para 6(3)*]. HMRC's powers relating to the provision of information and production of documents are exercisable separately for each trustee [*FA 2003, Sch 16, para 6(3)*]. Although any relevant trustee can apply for a closure notice to be given, the closure notice must be given to each relevant trustee. An enquiry notice or closure notice will not be effective unless notice is given to all the relevant trustees whose identity is known to HMRC.

[13.18] A determination or discovery assessment must be made against all the relevant trustees. It is not effective against any of them unless notice is given to all the relevant trustees whose identity is known to HMRC [*FA 2003, Sch 16, para 6(4)*].

Chargeable consideration [13.24]

Appeals

[13.19] Any of the relevant trustees may bring an appeal, but notice of the appeal must be given to any of the trustees who did not bring the appeal [*FA 2003, Sch 16, para 6(5)*]. The agreement of an appeal requires agreement of all the relevant trustees.

Scottish trusts and offshore trusts

[13.20] Property held in trust under Scottish law or under the law of a country outside the United Kingdom on such terms that under the laws of England and Wales a beneficiary would be treated as having an equitable interest in the trust property, will be deemed as having such an equitable interest, even though such an interest is not recognised under the law governing that trust [*FA 2003, Sch 16, para 2(a)*].

[13.21] An acquisition of a beneficiary's interest under the trust is deemed to involve the acquisition of an interest in the trust property [*FA 2003, Sch 16, para 2(b)*].

Exercise of power of appointment or discretion

[13.22] Any consideration given for a person in whose favour an appointment was made or discretion exercised becoming an object of the power or discretion, is treated as consideration for the acquisition of the chargeable interest in the case where the interest is acquired by the exercise of a power of appointment or exercise of a discretion vested in the trustees of a settlement [*FA 2003, Sch 16, para 7*].

Chargeable consideration

[13.23] Until 3 December 2014, SDLT operated universally on the basis of a 'slab system', ie with a single rate of charge applying to the entire consideration and with that rate determined by size of the consideration (*FA 2003, s 55(2)*). Different thresholds applied for residential and for non-residential or mixed use land. On 3 December 2014, the date of the Chancellor's Autumn Statement, it was announced that an entirely new system would apply *from 4 December 2014*, but only for residential land. Thus, for a while, there were two entirely separate and very different sets of rules. The position has become more consistent since Budget 2016 when it was announced that the 'slab' system would be abolished for non-residential or mixed use land too (*from 17 March 2016*). For completeness, both the old and current rules are also set out below. Each set of rules includes a nil-rate threshold below which no SDLT is chargeable.

[13.24] The Autumn Statement 2015 also announced the introduction (from 1 April 2016) of an additional SDLT charge on the purchase of, essentially, second homes, and the provisions to effect this were included in *Finance Bill 2016* by way of the introduction of new *Finance Act 2003, Sch 4ZA*. Because

[13.24] Stamp Taxes: Liability and Compliance

of the way these rules are drafted, they can apply to trustees even where they own only one property. These rules are explained at **13.29–13.33**. Practitioners also need to be aware of the possible application of the special 'ATED' SDLT charge outlined at **13.34**.

Non-residential or mixed use land

[13.25] For non-residential or mixed use land, prior to 17 March 2016 the slab system applied and the rates were as follows for the following overall level of consideration:

£0–£150,000	0%
£150,001– £250,000	1%
£250,001–£500,000	3%
Above £500,000	4%

[13.26] For non-residential or mixed use land transactions on or after 17 March 2016, the slab system has been abandoned and instead SDLT is charged at the following rates on the portion of the consideration which falls within the following bands:

£0–£150,000	0%
£150,001– £250,000	2%
Above £250,000	5%

Residential land

[13.27] For residential land prior to 3 December 2014, the slab system applied and the rates were as follows:

£0–£125,000	0%
£125,001– £250,000	1%
£250,001–£500,000	3%
Above £500,000	4%
Above £1 million	5% (from 6 April 2011 only)
Above £2 million	7% (from 6 April 2011 only)

[13.28] For residential land transactions on or after 4 December 2014, the slab system has been abandoned and instead SDLT is charged at the following rates on the portion of the consideration which falls within the following bands:

£0–£125,000	0%
£125,001–£250,000	2%
£250,001–£925,000	5%

£925,001–£1,500,000   10%
Over 1,500,000   12%

Additional Residential Properties

[13.29] Budget 2016 announced the introduction of an additional rate of SDLT on the purchase of 'additional residential properties' of an extra 3% in respect of each of the 'consideration' bands in excess of £40,000. Thus, the effective rates where this additional rate applies are, *from 1 April 2016*:

£0–£40,000	0%
£40,001–£125,000	3%
£125,001–£250,000	5%
£250,001–£925,000	8%
£925,001–£1,500,000	13%
Over 1,500,000	15%

[13.30] The new rules are set out in *Finance Act 2003, Sch 4ZA*. They do not apply in Scotland which operates a separate *Land and Buildings Transaction Tax* ('LBTT' see 13.37–13.38); however, there are similar provisions operate in relation to LBTT (see 13.39). In very broad terms – and subject, of course, to a number of specific technical provisions the detail of which is beyond the scope of this book – the main body of these rules operate so that the increased rates set out above apply whenever an individual is purchasing a new interest in a 'dwelling' where he or she already owns another such interest, and where the new dwelling does not replace the purchaser's 'only or main residence'. Thus, the additional rate will not apply if the purchase is of the individual's *only* residential property or if the individual does own more than one but where the purchase is replacing his or her only or main residence (in other words, the purchase is maintaining the status quo for the individual rather than adding additional let properties to his or her portfolio).

[13.31] The rules for trusts are contained in *Sch 4ZA, paras 10–13* and can be summarised as follows:

- For bare trusts, one looks at the circumstances of the beneficiary when determining whether the new rate applies (ie how many residential properties does he or she own etc?).
- For *interest in possession* trusts (where either the beneficiary has a right of occupation or a right to income), again it will be the circumstances of the income beneficiary which will determine whether or not the new rates apply. There is no requirement in this context that the interest in possession needs to be a 'qualifying interest in possession' within the terms of the inheritance tax legislation (see **8.7**).
- For all other trusts – particularly discretionary trusts – the new rates will always apply.

[13.32] It should be remembered, of course, that these additional rates apply only to residential property purchases but in these circumstances they will nevertheless impose an additional tax burden on the trustees of, particularly, all discretionary trusts. The trustees of interest in possession trusts will not be liable for the additional rates when purchasing residential property for a life tenant who owns no other dwelling. Nor will they be so liable if they are replacing a life tenant's main residence. In all other circumstances, however, they too will be subject to the additional rates.

[13.33] For further information see www.gov.uk/government/consultations/consultation-on-higher-rates-of-stamp-duty-land-tax-sdlt-on-purchases-of-additional-residential-properties.

The 'ATED' SDLT charge

[13.34] A 15% rate of stamp duty land tax will continue to apply where certain types of 'non-natural persons' (including companies, collective investment schemes and partnerships in which a non-natural person is a partner) acquire a dwelling for a chargeable consideration of more than £500,000 on or after 20 March 2014 (or £2 million between 21 March 2012 and that date) [*FA 2012, s 214, Sch 35*]. This constitutes a one off 'entry charge' for UK residential property into typically an offshore corporate structure. Exempted from this charge are also those situations mentioned at **13.44** in connection with the 'Annual Tax on Enveloped Dwellings' or ATED. This charge does not apply in Scotland.

Other points

[13.35] Where land is charged with a liability, typically a mortgage, and the transferee accepts liability for the mortgage: the amount of the mortgage constitutes consideration paid by them (*FA 2003 Sch 4, para 8(1)*). If the amount of the mortgage does not exceed the appropriate nil-rate threshold there will still be no positive SDLT liability. However (assuming the mortgage is £40,000 or more or, before 12 March 2008, £1,000 or more) the document cannot be self-certified and the trustees must, within 30 days of the gift, complete form SDLT 1 and send it to the Stamp Office at Netherton, from whom they will receive Certificate SDLT 5, which is sent to the Land Registry to procure registration.

[13.36] Except where trustees purchase land (when the SDLT implications will be as for any other type of purchaser), land transactions involving trustees, whether transfers to or transfers by trustees, will often be for no consideration and hence exempt from SDLT under *FA 2003, Sch 3, para 1*. Among the four categories of case where the *Stamp Duty Land Tax (Amendment to the Finance Act 2003) Regulations 2006, SI 2006/875*, inserting *FA 2003, Sch 4, paras 16A and 16B*) confirm that there is no chargeable consideration for Stamp Duty Land Tax purposes, with effect from 12 April 2006 (but, informally, from the introduction of the tax on 1 December 2003) are two circumstances which touch directly on trusts and deceased estates. First, the transfer of property to a person as a gift, or under a Will or intestacy, may result in that person having a liability or potential liability, or agreeing, to pay inheritance tax. The regulations provide that this liability or agreement is not chargeable consideration. Second, the transfer of property to a person as a gift, or in other circumstances which do not amount to a bargain made at arm's length, may result in that person having a liability or potential liability, or agreeing, to pay capital gains tax. Again, the regulations provide that this liability or agreement is not chargeable consideration (though the exclusion does not apply if there is any other chargeable consideration).

Land and Buildings Transaction Tax

[13.37] From 1 April 2015, SDLT was replaced in Scotland by *Land and Buildings Transaction Tax* (LBTT). A full discussion of this tax is beyond the scope of this book; however, LBTT also abandons the 'slab system' (see **13.28**) and applies the following rates on the *portion* of the consideration which falls within the following bands for both residential and non-residential property.

For *residential* property
£0–£145,000	0%
£145,001–£250,000	2%
£250,001–£325,000	5%
£325,001–£750,000	10%
Above £750,000	12%

For *non-residential* property
£0–£150,000	0%
£150,001–£350,000	3%
Above £350,000	4.5%

[13.38] Further information on the LBTT can be found here: www.revenue.scot/land-buildings-transaction-tax. It should be noted that although the main ATED charge (see immediately below) continues to apply in Scotland, the 15% ATED stamp tax charge (see **13.34**) does not.

[13.39] *Land and Buildings Transaction Tax (Amendment) (Scotland) Act 2016* also introduced an effective 3% surcharge on the purchases of second homes from 1 April 2016 the provisions of which are broadly similar to those for SDLT (see **13.29–13.33**). (See www.legislation.gov.uk/asp/2016/11/contents/enacted.)

The Annual Tax on Enveloped Dwellings (ATED)

[13.40] As announced at Budget 2012 an annual charge applies from 2013/14 in the case where a UK residential property worth at least £2 million is owned by a 'non-natural person' (*FA 2013 ss 94–174, Schs 33–35*). This is called the 'Annual Tax on Enveloped Dwellings' (or ATED). The annual charges for the first two years was as follows:

| *Property Value* | *2013/14 Charge* | *2014/15 Charge* |

[13.40] Stamp Taxes: Liability and Compliance

£2 million to £5 million	£15,000	£15,400
£5 million to £10 million	£35,000	£35,900
£10 million to £20 million	£70,000	£71,850
More than £20 million	£140,000	£143,750

[13.41] Budget 2014 announced, and *Finance Act 2014* enacted two additional ATED bands from 2015/16 and 2016/17 for properties worth in excess of, respectively, £1 million and £500,000, as follows:

Property Value	*2015/16 Charge*	*2016/17 Charge*
£500,000 to £1 million	N/A	£3,500
£1 million to £2 million	£7,000	£7,000

[13.42] In his Autumn Statement of 3 December 2014, George Osbourne announced an approximate 50% increase in the ATED charges for properties worth £2 million and above from 2015/16. There was no increase in the proposed new charge for properties worth £1 million to £2 million and there was also no increase in rates for 2016/17. Thus, the rates of charge for 2015/16 and 2016/17 are as follows:

Property Value	*2015/16 Charge*	*2016/17 Charge*
£500,000 to £1 million	N/A	£3,500
£1 million to £2 million	£7,000	£7,000
£2 million to £5 million	£23,350	£23,350
£5 million to £10 million	£54,450	£54,450
£10 million to £20 million	£109,050	£109,050
More than £20 million	£218,200	£218,200

[13.43] The annual charges are levied on 15 April each tax year by reference to property values on 1 April in the preceding tax year (except that for 2013/14 when the return and payment were due on 1 October 2013, and for properties coming within the new lower bands commencing in 2015/16 and 2016/17, the return deadline will also be 1 October following the introduction, and the payment date 31 October). Where the taxpayer considers that the value of the property is within 10% of any one of these thresholds, the value can be confirmed with HMRC through a 'pre-return banding check'. While the expression 'non-natural person' does not include trustees, trustees may well be indirectly affected by these new charges, insofar as they hold shares in such a non-natural person (typically where the trustees are non-UK resident).

[13.44] Excluded from the scope of the new entry and annual charges (as well as the charge to capital gains tax) outlined at **7.126** are the following (inter alia): property development, property rental and property trading businesses, where in each case the property is not occupied by a connected person, properties open to the public for at least 28 days a year and run as a business; employee accommodation, provided the employer is not too closely connected with the company; most dwellings owned by charities; farmhouses occupied by a working farmer, properties which are occupied by diplomats and are publicly owned; and property which is conditionally exempt from inheritance tax.

[13.45] For the latest guidance on completing an ATED return, which was updated on 27 April 2016, see www.gov.uk/government/publications/stld-annual-tax-on-enveloped-dwellings-ated.

Stamp duty

[13.46] Stamp duty remains payable on the transfer of stock and marketable securities. Therefore stamp duty (at 0.5%) needs to be considered in relation to acquisitions by trustees in cases where the consideration exceeds £1,000. *FA 2008, s 98* provides an exemption from Stamp Duty, subject to certification, where the consideration does not exceed £1,000 (*FA 1999, Sch 13, para 1(3A)*). The transfer of shares to trustees by a settlor will be exempt under category L of *The Stamp Duty (Exempt Instruments) Regulations 1987, SI 1987/516*. And an advance of shares by the trustees to a beneficiary entitled under the settlement will be exempt under category F. The exemption depends upon certification. Among various repeals of Stamp Duty by *FA 2008, Sch 32* is the £5 fixed duty on declarations of trust of shares and securities, with effect from 13 March 2008.

[13.47] *Finance Act 2014, Sch 24* provided an exemption, with effect from 28 April 2014, for SDRT and stamp duty on 'recognised growth markets'. Currently these include the following markets:

- Alternative Investment Market (AIM);
- Enterprise Securities Market;
- GXG markets A/S;
- High Growth Sector; and
- ICAP Securities and Derivatives Exchange Ltd.

Application of the disclosure regime to SDLT

[13.48] See CHAPTER 23 for details of the statutory disclosure regime applicable to SDLT.

Chapter 14

Charitable Trusts

Introduction

[14.1] A charity is generally exempt from taxes and so are transfers to a charity. After considering what is meant by a charity (see **14.4–14.9**) this chapter contains a brief outline of the main taxation provisions concerning charities. Charities are of importance in any trust and estate practice. Traditionally, the UK exemptions for gifts to, and income and gains of a charity depend upon its establishment in the UK and its supervision by the Charity Commission. In a case emanating from Germany, the European Court of Justice ruled that German legislation which accorded an income tax deduction for a gift of assets to a German charity which was denied for a gift to a Portuguese charity contravened the free movement of capital article 56 in the European Union Treaty (*Hein Persche v Finanzamt Lüdenscheid*) C–318/07) [2009] STC 586 ECJ. The UK subsequently received from the European Commission a notice requesting the amendment of UK legislation so as to make it compatible with the European Treaty.

[14.2] *FA 2010, s 30* and *Sch 6, Pt 1* extend UK charitable tax reliefs to certain organisations equivalent to UK charities and community amateur sports clubs (CASCs) in the EU and in the European Economic Area (EEA) countries of Norway and Iceland, following the judgment by the European Court of Justice in the *Persche* case. As announced by Budget Notice 32 on 24 March 2010, a number of changes to the law and processes were introduced at the same time. These:

- align the definition of a charity across all charity tax reliefs and charity exemptions administered by HMRC;
- limit the scope for fraudulent claims to charitable tax reliefs;
- remove inconsistencies in the current rules; and
- ensure that HMRC can maintain a cost efficient service to charities.

Norway and Iceland were confirmed as 'relevant territories' with effect from 20 August 2010 (*The Taxes Definition of Charity) (Relevant Territories) Regulations 2010, SI 2010/1904*). Otherwise, for effective dates:

- the restrictions on the payment of charitable funds outside the UK have effect on and after 24 March 2010 (*FA 2010, Sch 8, para 8(3)*);
- changing the nature of payroll giving income, such that it needs to be put to charitable purposes to qualify for exemption, has effect on and after 24 March 2010 (*FA 2010, Sch 8, para 8(1), (2)*); and
- the new definition of a charity applies to donations by individuals to charities under Gift Aid on or after 6 April 2010; and

- the *FA 2010* definitions apply to all other UK charity tax reliefs and exemptions from 1 April 2012 onwards (*Finance Act 2010 Sch 6 Part 2 (Commencement) Order 2012, SI 2012/735* and *Finance Act 2010 Sch 6 Part 1 (Further Consequential and Incidental Provisions etc) Order 2012, SI 2012/736*).

Claims to inheritance tax relief in respect of donations to organisations equivalent to UK charities in the EU, Norway or Iceland after the date of the ECJ judgment on 27 January 2009 and before 1 April 2010 (it appears) are being considered on a case by case basis, as a matter of concession. New procedures for dealing with Gift Aid repayment claims were introduced later in 2010 following discussions with charities on the proposals.

[14.3] An alternative legal structure to a charitable trust has long been a charitable company. Although this brings with it additional compliance obligations, as for any company, it offers the protection of limited liability. A third possibility, discussed for some years, is now on offer: a charitable incorporated organisation, which is something of a hybrid between a company and a trust offering the protection of legal liability but with a lesser degree of compliance obligations. The Charity Commission announced in March 2013 that unincorporated charities can apply to convert into a charitable incorporated organisation and transfer their assets in to it, with a timescale which incorporates a sliding scale of gradually reducing annual incomes over the course of 2013, presumably to avoid a flood of applications all at the same time. From 2014 it has been possible for charitable companies to apply for conversion into charitable incorporated organisations.

Definition of a charity

[14.4] A charity is, for many practitioners, a trust which is registered under the *Charities Act 1993*, the *Charities Act 2006* or, now, the *Charities Act 2011* (see **14.8**). The *Charities Acts* have very limited application outside England and Wales and not all charities are registered anyway. However, registration is *prima facie* evidence that the trust is charitable. HMRC will apply their own tests and decide separately whether to accord charitable status. The historic tests were laid down in the *Pemsel* case (*Income Tax Special Purposes Comrs v Pemsel* [1891] AC 531, HL) as follows:

(a) *The relief of poverty.* This need not be general and the beneficiaries may come from a designated class.

(b) *The advancement of religion.* This need not be for the public benefit in layman's English. Those who fashioned the law believed that it is good for mankind to have and practise a religion. Therefore sects which demand absolute obedience from their adherents and shut out strangers will qualify. A contemplative order does not advance religion and so is not charitable. However, if there is an element of its work which is for the public benefit, it may qualify (see Decisions of the Charity Commissioners vol 3, *The Society of the Precious Blood*).

(c) *Education.* Virtually all independent schools are charities. So are youth organisations such as the Boy Scouts. Museums and libraries come under this heading.

(d) *Other purposes beneficial to the community.* These must not benefit a clique or class. Many worthy causes fail because they are too narrowly based to benefit an important part of the community. A sports club which qualifies as a 'community amateur sports club' under *FA 2002, Sch 18* will (whether or not it is charitable) enjoy a number of tax reliefs and donors to such a club will have tax incentives to support it. Some sports clubs have historically been registered charities, but on the footing that they exist not simply to promote sport but for other purposes which are charitable in law. In November 2001 the Charity Commission said that it would recognise as charitable:
- 'The promotion of community participation in healthy recreation by the provision of facilities for the playing of particular sports'; and
- 'The advancement of the physical education of young people not undergoing formal education'.

Amended guidance was issued by the Commission on these two new purposes on 18 April 2002 and the legislation was enacted in *FA 2002, Sch 18*, although now repealed and found in *CTA 2010, Pt 13, Ch 9*. Satisfaction by a community amateur sports club of the following four conditions will enable it to apply for charitable status: the club is open to the whole community; it is organised on an amateur basis; it meets the location condition (broadly, being established within the EU, Norway, Iceland and, from 31 July 2014, Liechtenstein); and it meets the management condition (that the managers are 'fit and proper persons to be managers of the club'): *CTA 2010, s 658(1)* as amended by *FA 2012, s 52*. As explained at **14.6**, the CASC exemption now applies to sports clubs within EU member states from 6 April 2010 providing they conform with the requirements [*FA 2010, Sch 6, paras 30, 32*]. (See **14.8** for changes made by *Charities Act 2006* to these historic categories.)

[14.5] For the purpose of applying tax exemptions, *FA 2010, Sch 6, Pt 1* introduced a new definition of 'charity' for tax purposes. The new definition applies to either a charitable company or a charitable trust which:

(a) is established for charitable purposes only;
(b) meets the jurisdiction condition, ie it is subject to the control of a court in the UK or within the European Economic Area (the EU plus Norway, Iceland and, from 31 July 2014, Liechtenstein);
(c) meets the registration condition, in terms of compliance with any requirement to be registered in the register of charities kept in England and Wales or, where in a territory outside England and Wales, in a corresponding register; and
(d) meets the management condition, that is that 'its managers are fit and proper persons to be managers of the body or trust', where the managers are 'the persons having the general control and management of the administration of the body or trust'.

This definition applies for Gift Aid from 2010/11 [*ITTOIA 2005, s 878(1); IHTA 1984, s 272* amended by *FA 2010, Sch 6, para 10*]. For all other personal tax purposes it applies from 6 April 2012 onwards (1 April 2012 for corporation tax and value added tax purposes) [*Finance Act 2010 Schedule 6 Part 1 (Further Consequential and Incidental Provisions etc) Order 2012/735* and *Finance Act 2010 Schedule 6 Part 2 Commencement Order 2012 SI 2012/736*, both made on 8 March 2012].

[14.6] Prior to *FA 2010, Sch 6*, it was necessary that the charity be founded in the UK. It could benefit people overseas but, to benefit from the UK's tax exemptions, it had to be founded here. (*Dreyfus (Camille and Henry) Foundation Inc v IRC*, [1956] AC 39, [1955] 3 All ER 97, HL). That said, the law has now been changed so that the UK's tax exemptions are extended in favour of a charity based anywhere in the European Economic Area (following the ECJ decision in *Persche (Hein) v Finanzamt Ludenscheid* C-318/07 [2009] ECR I-359, [2009] All ER (EC) 673, ECJ and a formal request from the European Union to the UK to widen the territorial scope of its tax exemptions for charities). For the effective dates of the *Finance Act 2010* new definitions, see 14.5. That said, however, it appears that claims to inheritance tax relief in respect of donations at any time from the date of the ECJ judgment on 27 January 2009 have been considered (and approved) on a case by case basis.

[14.7] A charity will normally exist in perpetuity, ie it is not required to be wound up after any specific period, although the trustees may effectively wind it up by distributing the whole of the trust fund. However, it is possible to have a charity which has a definite life, say 10 years. Such a trust is known as a 'time charity'. The author is not sure whether any exist, but the draftsman of the *IHTA 1984* had to contemplate the possibility. Had he not done so, there would have been a considerable loophole. Hence *IHTA 1984, s 70* applies an inheritance tax charge upon property leaving a temporary charitable trust.

[14.8] Substantial changes to charity law were made by the *Charities Act 2006*, though these do not affect taxation to a great degree, and a new *Charities Act 2011* (into which the *Charities Act 2006* has been largely consolidated) has been enacted. The position on implementation of the various 2006 Act provisions may be summarised as follows:

(a) Most (but not all) of the *Charities Act 2006* has been consolidated into the *Charities Act 2011*, with effect from 14 March 2012. (The *Charities Act 1993* was also consolidated into the 2011 Act.)

(b) The provisions relating to charitable incorporated organisations (CIOs) were consolidated and now form *Part 11* of the *Charities Act 2011, ss 204–250*. Most of the provisions were brought into effect from 2 January 2013. However, *sections 228–234* have not yet been brought into effect, as dealing with conversion to a CIO by other corporate entities. Those provisions are expected to be brought into effect in 2014. So, registration as a CIO is currently open only to new charities and to existing unincorporated charities wishing to convert to a CIO. However, as it was unclear how much demand there would be to register such existing charities as CIOs, the Charity Commission has been staggering CIO registration of existing charities according to annual income.

(c) The provisions relating to the licensing and regulation of public charitable collections were not consolidated into the 2011 Act and so still reside in the *Charities Act 2006*. (The reason given for their non-consolidation is that the provisions are not restricted purely to charities). The provisions have still not been implemented. It remains unclear when, or whether, the provisions may be implemented. Paragraph 8.58 of the Hodgson Review Report refers to the provisions as being 'unaffordable, and also may not be effective'. Instead, the Report recommends more effective regulation at a local level (see recommendations at pp 103–104 of the Report).

(d) The Review of the operation of the *Charities Act 2006* has now happened. Lord Hodgson of Astley Abbotts was appointed on 8 November 2011 to conduct the Review. He reported on 16 July 2012 in his report 'Trusted and Independent: Giving Charity back to Charities'. The Report made a number of recommendations, and the Law Commission subsequently issued a consultation *Technical Issues in Charity Law*, which ran from 20 March to 3 July 2015. At the time of writing the Law Commission is still considering the responses to the consultation.

[14.9] A set of '13 descriptions of purposes' has now been enacted, to replace the historic categorisation summarised at **14.4**. The emphasis is on the public benefit requirement in every case, together with the removal of the presumption of public benefit from organisations for the relief of poverty, the advancement of religion and the promotion of education. The 13 'descriptions of purposes' listed at section 3 of the 2011 Act are as follows:

- the prevention or relief of poverty;
- the advancement of education;
- the advancement of religion;
- the advancement of health or the saving of lives;
- the advancement of citizenship or community development;
- the advancement of the arts, culture, heritage or science;
- the advancement of amateur sports;
- the advancement of human rights, conflict resolution or reconciliation or the promotion of religious or racial harmony or equality and diversity;
- the advancement of environmental protection or improvement;
- the relief of those in need by reason of youth, age, ill health, disability, financial hardship or other disadvantage
- the advancement of animal welfare;
- the promotion of the efficiency of the armed forces of the Crown or of the efficiency of the police, fire and rescue services or ambulance services;
- any other purposes recognised as charitable purposes under existing charity law or analogous to or within the spirit of those purposes or the purposes listed above.

Exemptions on setting up or giving to charities

Stamp duty and stamp duty land tax

[14.10] No duty was charged on conveyances or other transfers to a charity before 1 December 2003. The document of transfer had to be adjudicated for stamp duty purposes [*FA 1982, s 129*]. Exemption continues for transfers of interests in UK land and buildings under stamp duty land tax from 1 December 2003 [*FA 2003, s 68* and *Sch 8*] and, indeed under *FA 2004, s 302*, for charitable trusts which did not qualify for the *FA 2003* exemption. This exemption applies whether or not there is consideration for the transfer. That is, if for example the transferee charity assumes liability for a mortgage debt secured on the land, the normal rule that the amount of the debt assumed constitutes chargeable consideration does not apply. HMRC Stamp Taxes have published a four page leaflet (SO 11). Note that the charities relief will be clawed back, with implications for both compliance and repayment of the tax relieved (with interest), if a disqualifying event occurs within three years, eg the land ceasing to be held for charitable purposes.

[14.11] The exemption from stamp duty land tax also applies where the charity is a joint purchaser, relief being given to the extent of the charity's share of the purchase price. This was confirmed in the case of *Pollen Estate Trustee Company* [2013] EWCA Civ 753, [2013] 3 All ER 742 which was heard in the Court of Appeal. Following this case *FA 2003, Sch 8* has been amended by *FA 2004* to reflect the decision.

Inheritance tax

[14.12] Gifts and legacies to charities are exempt transfers [*IHTA 1984, s 23*]. This extends to transfers from discretionary settlements [*IHTA 1984, s 76*]. There are anti-avoidance provisions.

[14.13] While not directly relevant to the scope of this book, some reference should be made to the provisions of *Finance Act 2012, s 209, Sch 33*. For deaths on or after 6 April 2012, the rate of inheritance tax on the chargeable estate is reduced from 40% to 36% where (in broad terms) at least 10% of the 'baseline amount' of one or more components of the estate goes to charity. The scheme of the legislation is to split the estate into three components, ie property which passes by survivorship, settled property and the free estate. The new reduced rate is applied to each component separately, or by election to any two or all three of the components, after applicable reliefs (other than gifts to charity) are deducted. A pro rata share of the available nil-rate band (whether or not including an element of the transferable nil-rate band available from the prior death of a spouse or civil partner) is applied to the property in each component. Although the new relief applies only to assets on hand at death (ie does not extend to potentially exempt transfers which become chargeable by reason of death within seven years), assets which are taxed as gifts with reservation of benefit at death may also attract tax at the 36% rate, subject to an election for merger with one or more of the three components. HMRC have published a reduced rate calculator which can be used to work out whether an estate qualifies for the reduced rate. Extended, and useful, guidance on the regime may be found in HMRC's Inheritance Tax Manual at IHTM45001 to IHTM45051.

Capital gains tax

[14.14] A gift to a charity which involves a disposal of a chargeable asset is exempt [*TCGA 1992, s 257*].

Income tax

[14.15] Settlements of income (eg deeds of covenant) generate a tax recovery for the charity. Payroll giving [*ITEPA 2003, ss 713–715*] is not counted as taxable income of the individual and therefore reaches the charity as a gross sum, with no limit. *FA 2000, s 38* increased the benefit of certain payroll giving schemes through a 10% supplement paid by the Treasury. Gift Aid was introduced with effect from 1 October 1990 for one-off gifts of £600 or more [*ITA 2007, Pt 8, Ch 2*]. As from 6 April 2000, there is no minimum: the Gift Aid Declaration (which covers all gifts by an individual to a charity) simply acknowledges that the donor has sufficient liability to income tax or capital gains tax to frank the gift(s). In the event that in the year of the gift to charity the donor has insufficient liability to income tax or capital gains tax, to cover all gifts to charity in that year, it is the donor and not the charity/charities which suffer(s). A recipient charity is able to recover the basic rate tax subject to which the gift is treated as made. The donor will receive an assessment for the tax underpaid.

[14.16] Gift Aid relief is not given if any benefits are 'associated' with the gift [*ITA 2007, s 417 and s 416(7); CTA 2010, s 196 and s 191(7)*]. The expression 'associated benefits' is defined in terms of monetary value, as extended by *Finance Act 2011* [*ITA 2007, ss 418–419; CTA 2010, ss 197–198*] and is subject to the disregard of certain admission rights [*ITA 2007, ss 420–421*]. A Special Commissioner held in *St Dunstan's v Major* (SpC 217) [1997] STC (SCD) 212 that the reduction in inheritance tax under a deed of variation directing part of an inheritance to charity was such a disqualifying benefit. This decision has been widely criticised in that it is commonly thought that only a benefit which flows from the charity should be able to disapply Gift Aid relief. However, the *St Dunstan's* principle has been followed in 2010 by the First-tier Tribunal in *Harris (trustee of Harris Family Charitable Trust) v Revenue and Customs Comrs* [2010] UKFTT 385 (TC), [2010] SFTD 1159, which is now final, the taxpayers having withdrawn their appeal to the Upper Tribunal. Note that the *St Dunstan's* principle does not apply to the separate relief for gifts of shares or land mentioned at 14.26.

[14.17] On 18 February 2016, the government issued the consultation document *Simplifying the Gift Aid donor benefits* rules with responses required before 12 May 2016. At the time of writing the responses are still being considered.

[14.18] Following a Budget 2011 proposal and separate consultations in 2011 and 2012, charities and CASCs which receive small donations of £20 or less are able to apply for a Gift Aid style repayment without the need to obtain Gift Aid declarations for those donations. The *Small Charitable Donations Act 2012* was passed on 19 December 2012, to give effect to the proposal from 2013/14 and the *Small Charitable Donations Regulations 2013, SI 2013/938*, which set out the administrative framework, came into force on 19 April 2013.

[14.19] The amount of small donations on which the new repayment can be claimed was originally capped at £5,000 per year, per charity, but this was increased to £8,000 with effect from 6 April 2016 by the *Small Charitable Donations Act (Amendment) Order 2015*. The government has also been consulting more widely on the operation of the small donations scheme and their response to the consultation *Gift Aid Small* Donations Scheme was published on 10 August 2016.

[14.20] The government issued a new shorter Gift Aid declaration on 21 October 2015 and, further guidance, last updated on 20 January 2016, is available here: www.gov.uk/guidance/gift-aid-declarations-claiming-tax-back-on-donations.

[14.21] The government announced at Autumn Statement 2013 that it would give intermediaries, operating within the charity sector, a greater role in administering Gift Aid. Since then, the government has published provisions in *Finance Bill 2015* and *2016* to support this aim. On 10 August 2016, the technical consultation *Gift Aid and Intermediaries* was published, with comments requested before 5 October 2016. This consultation sets out those draft Regulations and asks for comments to ensure they achieve the desired outcome.

[14.22] Generally, Gift Aid made the deposited deed of covenant redundant. The donor is treated as having deducted basic rate tax which the charity recovers. The gift is relieved against the donor's higher rate tax. Gift Aid is also available to companies supporting charity. Non-close companies do not have a minimum restriction.

[14.23] *F(No 2)A 1992, s 27* used to permit deeds of covenant to be drafted which run for a minimum of four years and continue thereafter until cancelled. Payments under a deed of covenant which commenced before 6 April 2000 may continue without the Gift Aid Declaration. While there is no tax reason for making a deed of covenant now, such deeds will be welcomed by charities as ensuring some continuity in giving. If a deed of covenant is made on or after 6 April 2000, the donor must still complete the relative Gift Aid Declaration to enable recovery of tax by the charity.

[14.24] The reduction of the tax credit on dividends from 20% to 10% in 1999/2000 was a serious blow to charities. Therefore compensation was given by payments of 21% of dividends received in 1999/2000 reducing to 17%, 13%, 8% and 4% over the following years, ie 4% in 2003/04, with no compensation after 5 April 2004. A further blow occurred from tax year 2008/09 with the reduction in the basic rate from 22% to 20%. This produced a loss of some £3.20 in recovery of income tax for every £100 given net under Gift Aid (or old deed of covenant). However, there was transitional relief for 2008/09, 2009/10 and 2010/11. As from 2011/12 the reduction in basic rate recovery for charities has become permanent, subject to any change in the basic rate or in the rules [FA 2008, Sch 19, para 3].

[14.25] It was possible for a higher rate donor to direct to any charity the benefit of the higher rate relief, or indeed any tax repayment from HMRC eg through loss relief. This could be done simply through the self assessment return, most easily by reference to a code for participating charities which enabled HMRC to pay the charity direct. However, it was announced at Budget 2011 that this scheme (called 'SA Donate') would be withdrawn in relation to tax repayments for: tax returns for 2011/12 onwards; and tax returns up to and including 2010/11 where the repayment is made on or after 6 April 2012. *ITA 2007, s 429* was repealed by *FA 2012, s 50*.

[14.26] Since 6 April 2000, a person has been able to obtain income tax relief on the disposal of a 'qualifying investment' to a charity [*ITA 2007, ss 431–434*]. This expression is defined to mean shares or securities listed or dealt in on a recognised stock exchange, units in an authorised unit trust, shares in an open-ended investment company and an interest in an offshore fund. Similar relief is also given to a company for corporation tax purposes since 1 April 2000. For an individual, the market value of the qualifying investment is taken off his taxable income. If the disposal was made at an undervalue, the reduction for income tax purposes is the difference between the market value and the consideration given. If the person making the disposal (or someone connected with him) receives a benefit in consequence of the disposal, the value of the benefit is reduced from the amount attracting tax relief. *FA 2002, s 97* added to the list of qualifying investments a freehold or leasehold interest in UK land. Note that this income tax relief for qualifying investments is not Gift Aid, which is restricted to transfers of cash.

[14.27] Companies making a cash donation to charity are given tax relief by *CTA 2010, Pt 6; ITA 2007, s 522*. Subject to certain de minimis monetary limits, no relief is available for close companies where the company receives benefits in consequence of making the gift. Also, relief is not available if a gift is made subject to a condition as to repayment or is made as part of an arrangement for the acquisition of property from the company or connected persons otherwise than at arm's length. A new rule applying from 1 April 2006 extended these restrictions and this limit on benefits received in consequence of a gift to companies which are not close companies.

Transfer of family shareholdings to charities

[14.28] As outlined above, there are no tax costs in setting up a charity. Further, the income of a charity will normally be exempt. So will its capital gains. Therefore, a benevolent family with a family company could easily use a charity as the vehicle for ownership of an important minority holding in the company. The trustees would be drawn from the family. It is hard to envisage circumstances in which the trustees would need to vote in opposition to the rest of the family. Of course, this can happen now and again and some years ago the trustees of just such a charity had to seek a takeover bid for a family company (a plc) because it made losses. In that case, the block of shares held by the charity was influential. The gift of a holding of shares would satisfy the charitable instincts of the family, particularly if there were dividends which could fund annual donations. There will be some compliance costs if income is taken from the company because the *Charities Act 2011* requires an audit or similar if the charity has a substantial income.

[14.29] Bearing in mind the difference between the valuation of shares in, for instance, a 51% holding and those in a 49% holding, HMRC Trusts and

Estates need protection for inheritance tax purposes. As a generalisation this is still true, despite the generous business and agricultural property reliefs introduced in *F(No 2)A 1992* and subsequently further extended. Hence assets transferred to a charity are within the 'related property' provisions. This does not affect the trustees, but it does affect the estate planning of the donor. In a case where the shares would be valued at a higher figure if the holdings of the charity and the donor were aggregated, then that is done for the calculation of any inheritance tax on the donor's estate. Therefore, if the donor had 49% and the charity 2%, the donor's shares would be valued as if they formed part of a 51% holding (ie 49/51 × 51%). Transfers to charities before 16 April 1976 are ignored. This 'relating' of the two holdings is applied not only to shares transferred by the donor but also by his spouse. If the trustees dispose of the shares they remain 'related property' so far as the donor is concerned for a further five years [*IHTA 1984, s 161*].

[14.30] There is no parallel legislation for capital gains tax. The application of that tax depends upon the size of the holding which is disposed of rather than the 'loss to donor' principle which is behind much of inheritance tax. Any protection needed against breaking shareholdings down is contained in *TCGA 1992, s 19* (assets disposed of in a series of transactions).

Tax exemptions for charities

[14.31] Once set up, the tax exemptions which can be claimed by the trustees of a charity on money received by them depend upon it having being spent or accumulated for charitable purposes. The exemptions include the following:

(i) Rents and anything else received from properties which would otherwise be assessed as property income or trading income [*CTA 2010, s 485; ITA 2007, s 531*].
(ii) Savings and investment income [*CTA 2010, s 486; ITA 2007, s 532*].
(iii) Covenanted payments.
(iv) The trading profits of the charity if either:
  (a) that trade is part of a primary purpose of the charity, eg running a school; or
  (b) the work in connection with the trade is carried out wholly or mainly by beneficiaries, eg work for disabled people.
  Finance Act 2006, s 56 codified a previous practice of HMRC Charities (which they had been advised was not legitimate). In either of the above cases, where only partial relief would have been obtained (that is, where the trade might be only in part but not in whole a primary purpose trade or the work is carried out only partly but not mainly by beneficiaries of the charity), the trade is split notionally into two separate parts, with tax relief given only to the profits of the primary purpose part or on the profits of the part carried out by the beneficiaries of the charity [*CTA 2010, ss 478–479; ITA 2007, ss 524–526*]. See also 14.34–14.35.
(v) Donations from another charity [*CTA 2010, s 474; ITA 2007, s 523*].
(vi) Single gifts by companies from which tax has been deducted [*CTA 2010, s 473; ITA 2007, s 522*].

Tax exemptions for charities [14.37]

(vii)   Chargeable gains [*TCGA 1992, s 256*].

[**14.32**] Obviously a key question is: what are charitable purposes? There should be no problem about payments which are charged against income. They will be proper administrative expenses, grants to other charities or money expended on the work for the charity. This leaves what one may describe as capital payments. It is quite possible to apply funds to building projects which will appear in the trust Balance Sheet (eg a charity may build new classrooms or buy playing fields if it is a school). Saving up for a few years for some charitable project which requires a lump sum, or paying off a loan incurred for such a project, are charitable purposes. Therefore, there are times when HMRC will, quite correctly, take a long view and there will be times when they will view a capital project as completely charitable.

[**14.33**] Trading income derived by a charity from, for example, the sale of Christmas cards is not exempt. The traditional structure for trustees wanting to trade is to establish their own subsidiary company to carry on such a trade, with the company then Gift Aiding its income back to the charity (but see **14.35**). Statute allows the company to donate its profits by Gift Aid to the charity up to nine months following the end of the accounting period [*CTA 2010, s 199*]. The charity should not, in principle, then hand back to the company the Gift-Aided profits to enhance the company's trade. Although a Special Commissioner's case was lost by HMRC on this issue (*Nightingale Ltd v Price (Inspector of Taxes)* (SpC 66) [1996] STC (SCD) 116), a charity should beware of engaging in a simple circularity of payments. That case was decided before the enactment of *ICTA 1988, Sch 20* [now *CTA 2010, Pt 11. Ch 4*] and the rules about 'non-qualifying expenditure' (see **14.53**), though the new rules are not thought to have affected the principle.

[**14.34**] If the finance required to set up a trading subsidiary could be a drain on the charity's finances, the Charity Commission might object. They would suggest that the investment is inappropriate and damaging to charitable status. An alternative to the subsidiary route could be for the charity to enter into a franchising arrangement rather than to trade itself. Another entity would be permitted under licence by the charity to use the charity's name, for which the charity would receive royalty payments within *ITTOIA 2005, Pt 5, Ch 2*, attracting tax relief for the payer. Any agreement between the charity and the independent trading entity would require very careful consideration.

[**14.35**] *Finance Act 2000, s 46* removed the need for small charities to have set up a subsidiary company to run their fund raising trade. There is now a tax exemption for all trading by a charity with a turnover of less than £5,000 or, where the trading turnover represents 25% of the charity's total income, up to a maximum of £50,000 [*CTA 2010, ss 480 and 482; ITA 2007, ss 526, 528*].

[**14.36**] A technical problem where a lottery is promoted for a charity came to light in July 1994 with the discovery that the profits were taxable. Relief was first given by extra-statutory concession and amending legislation was enacted by *FA 1995, s 138(1)* which introduced what are now *CTA 2010, s 484* and *ITA 2007, s 530*).

[**14.37**] By concession, subject to certain conditions, assessments are not raised on the profits of bazaars, jumble sales, gymkhanas and the like

223

[14.37] Charitable Trusts

(Extra-statutory Concession C4). For relief in respect of charitable donations to qualifying Community Amateur Sports Clubs (CASCs) see **14.4**(d).

[14.38] There have been difficulties in obtaining refunds of tax when discretionary payments of income have been made to charities by personal representatives. This was cleared up by SP 4/93 (see APPENDIX A). It is to be noted that claims previously refused will now be repaid. A minor technical amendment was made to the concession in March 1994.

[14.39] The Charity Commission have issued a free booklet CC 20 'Charities and Fundraising' (now available as a pdf document at www.gov.uk/government/publications/charities-and-fundraising-cc20), which has a section on fundraising events and tax.

[14.40] VAT must not be overlooked, as there is no automatic exemption for charities. VAT is a tax on goods and services supplied by a taxable person. A taxable person must account to HMRC for tax on their 'outputs', that is, supplies of goods and services, if VAT registered. The person can offset against that liability the input tax that is on goods and services bought in for the business, referable to the business. Very often, the problem for a charity is that there is a shortage of input tax, which can be related to the taxable activity. Subject to the turnover level (£82,000 from 1 April 2015), a charity whose taxable supplies exceed this must register, assuming that the taxable supplies are standard-rated. Examples might be:

- first aid classes where fees are taken;
- food provided to employees in a canteen;
- sales of second-hand goods.

Transactions in property will not necessarily be exempt and can result in a VAT liability. Charities do benefit to some extent from reliefs, in that a number of different supplies to them are zero-rated. To the extent that charities are concerned with listed buildings there are concessions in respect of building works.

[14.41] The following ameliorating VAT changes for charities were *inter alia* made by *FA 2000*:

(a) an extension and alignment of the income tax and VAT exemptions for charity fundraising events;
(b) a significant extension to the VAT zero rating of advertisements bought by charities;
(c) raising from £250 to £1,000 the de minimis limit below which charities and other businesses do not have to account for VAT when they de-register.

[14.42] From 1 April 2015, *FA 2015, s 66* introduced new rules allowing medical courier and palliative care charities to reclaim VAT.

Charities: the 'fit and proper persons' test in FA 2010

[14.43] *Finance Act 2010, Sch 6, Pt 1* introduced a new definition for tax purposes of charities and other organisations entitled to UK charity tax reliefs (ie 'a charity' or 'charities', 'charitable company' or 'charitable trust'). The new definition includes a requirement that to be a charity an organisation must satisfy: the jurisdiction condition (see **14.1** and **14.2**); the registration condition; and the management condition. The management condition requires the managers of the charity to be 'fit and proper persons to be managers of the body or trust'. And 'managers' are 'the persons having the general control and management of the administration of the body or trust' (*FA 2010 Sch 6, paras 1–4*).

[14.44] HMRC guidance on this test is available at www.gov.uk/government/publications/charities-fit-and-proper-persons-test/guidance-on-the-fit-and-proper-persons-test and was last updated on 3 May 2016. It explains how HMRC will apply this test to those who have the general control and management of the administration of the charity. HMRC assume that all people appointed by charities are fit and proper persons unless they hold information to show otherwise. Provided charities take appropriate steps on appointing personnel then they may assume that they meet the management condition at all times unless, exceptionally, they are challenged by HMRC. Where HMRC find that a manager of a charity is not a fit and proper person, a charity will not necessarily lose entitlement to the charity tax reliefs. As they explain, HMRC are able to treat a charity as having met the management condition where either the manager has no ability to influence the charitable purposes of the charity or the application of its funds, or the circumstances are such that it is just and reasonable to treat the charity as having met the management conditions throughout the period the manager has been in office. The guidance suggests that anyone who (inter alia):

- has used a tax avoidance scheme featuring charitable reliefs or using a charity to facilitate the avoidance; or
- has been involved in designing and/or promoting tax avoidance schemes

will not be considered by HMRC as a fit and proper person.

[14.45] A template for a 'fit and proper person declaration' (which charities should ask personnel to sign) is also available at www.gov.uk/government/uploads/system/uploads/attachment_data/file/392977/model-dec-ff-persons.pdf.

[14.46] The fit and proper persons test makes it harder for sham charities and fraudsters working within a charity, or targeting a charity from outside, to abuse charity tax reliefs. It is not intended as something to deny tax reliefs to charities who make a genuine mistake, say HMRC.

Anti-avoidance

[14.47] Those who set up charities must ensure that the trustees know what they are about. The Charity Commissioners, having been vastly under-resourced, are making an effort to enforce the law. The results include inquiries which have looked at national charities such as War on Want, Oxfam and the Royal British Legion. The inquirers were critical but no punishments were made. The *Charities Act 2011* (and before it the *Charities Act 2006*) contains a volume of legislation relating to administrative, financial and accounting.

[14.48] The fact that charities are generally tax exempt has always attracted tax planners: see **14.63–14.65** for recent examples. By 1986 the then Inland Revenue found themselves in a position where protection was needed. By way of illustration, at least one of the Rossminster schemes required a charity as one of the players and other scheme advisers followed suit. The *Helen Slater* case (*IRC v Helen Slater Charitable Trust Ltd*, [1982] Ch 49, [1981] 3 All ER 98, CA) had gone against HMRC. That case showed that if one 'family charity' paid income to another or made a donation to another, that satisfied the requirement to apply income to charitable purposes. The donee charity could then use the donation to invest in some family venture, perhaps even by way of loan to an overseas company and so on. The consequence of such ingenious tax planning was a substantial body of anti-avoidance legislation in *FA 1986*. This is now incorporated in *CTA 2010, ss 492 to 501* and *ITA 2007, ss 539 to 548*.

[14.49] More recently, a variety of avoidance arrangements led to the introduction of Spotlights 7 and 9 respectively (see **14.63** and **14.64**). The Cup Trust (which reportedly spent just £55,000 on donations to beneficiaries despite receiving £176 million in donations and received adverse publicity in the newspapers in January 2013) was on the face of it based on the blatantly ineffective device highlighted by HMRC in Spotlight 9, which was re-issued on 12 June 2013.

[14.50] A further avoidance case has been ruled on by the First-tier Tribunal in HMRC's favour: *Ferguson v Revenue and Customs Comrs* [2014] UKFTT 433 (TC), [2014] SFTD 934. In this case the taxpayer transferred bonds to a charity trust which sold them before transferring around 99% of the proceeds to a private trust for the taxpayer. The taxpayer claimed tax relief on the transfer of the bonds but it was held that relief was not available. The transfer did not meet the purposive test of the legislation, to encourage charitable giving, as the overall effect of the transaction transferred the value to a trust for the taxpayer.

Charities: the 'purpose of establishment condition'

[14.51] The increase in avoidance schemes to exploit Gift Aid led HMRC to publish on 20 March 2014 (seeking comments by 11 April 2014): *Discussion paper – approaches to preventing charities being set up to avoid tax*, and seeking views on introducing a new 'purpose of establishment condition' to stop charities being established to abuse charity tax reliefs. Two approaches were suggested; both to catch (and prohibit) cases where a charity is established to 'secure a tax advantage'. The first involved a wide test: where securing a tax advantage was one of the main purposes, while the second involved a narrower test of whether it was the main purpose.

[14.52] Responses to the paper were that the first approach was too strict and could catch genuine charities ie on the basis that obtaining a tax advantage is very often one of the main purposes behind the establishment of charity – eg to provide a vehicle for gift aid payments. On the other hand, the second was considered too weak as an apparent alternative 'main' purpose could often be found. Following these responses HMRC announced on 30 June 2014 'that changing the law is not justified at this point', citing a 'disproportionate and unacceptable effect upon the charity sector and legitimate donors' as a key reason for their decision. They added that they already have sufficient tools to enable them to tackle avoidance, eg recent changes to the General Anti-Abuse Rule, while recent success in the courts will also help. They confirmed that they will continue to monitor the situation and will act where they consider more controls are needed. This quick volte-face is welcome. The two options put forward in the original discussion document were extraordinarily crude and neither offered a workable solution to the perceived problem.

Non-qualifying expenditure

[14.53] This regime has its own definitions:

(i) 'Attributable income and gains' is income which is taxable or would be taxable were it not for the exemptions in *CTA 2010, ss 471–491; ITA 2007, ss 521–542* (see **14.31**) and capital gains, whether relieved by *TCGA 1992, s 256* or not [*ITA 2007, s 540(3); CTA 2010 s 493(3)*].

(ii) 'Non-charitable expenditure' is that which is not for charitable purposes only, and, what is more, money invested in investments which are not qualifying investments. Payments to overseas bodies are non-qualifying expenditure unless it is reasonably certain that they will be used for charitable purposes [*ITA 2007, s 543; CTA 2010 s 496*].

(iii) 'Chargeable period' is an accounting period if the charity is a company. Otherwise it is the fiscal year [*CTA 2010, s 1119; ITA 2007, s 989*].

[14.54] There used to be a de minimis provision in that a charity with less than £10,000 by way of relevant income and gains in the chargeable period is not within the anti-avoidance legislation. It still has to apply its receipts to charitable purposes if it is to claim exemption. The £10,000 threshold was removed by *FA 2006, s 55* in relation to transactions which take place on or after 22 March 2006.

[14.55] Having eliminated small cases, the legislation goes on to attack any 'relevant income and gains' which is in excess of the 'qualifying expenditure' and is expended on 'non-qualifying expenditure'. There are provisions to catch teeming and lading between different years. This should be enough to prevent charities from investing money in family companies or projects more beneficial to the sponsors than to a charitable purpose. *FA 2006, s 55* reverses the order in which charitable and non-charitable expenditure is set against the charity's tax-relieved income and gains. This means that, for every £1 of non-charitable expenditure incurred by the charity, there will be a corresponding restriction of the income and gains which attract tax exemption. [Generally, *CTA 2010, ss 492–501; ITA 2007, ss 543–548*.]

[14.56] A further part of the anti-avoidance legislation relates to grants made by one charity to another. Such grants are chargeable to tax on the charity which receives them, unless used for charitable purposes.

Substantial donors (before 1 April 2011)

[14.57] Further anti-avoidance measures introduced by *FA 2006* are as follows. Additional restrictions are placed on transactions which can take place between a charity and its 'substantial donors' without a restriction of the charity's tax relief. An individual or a company is a 'substantial donor' if they give to the charity £25,000 or more in any twelve-month period or £150,000 or more over a six-year period (increased from £100,000 with effect from 23 April 2009, following Budget 2009: *SI 2009/1029*). The donor is a substantial donor for the chargeable period in which they exceed these limits and the following five chargeable periods. The rule applies to certain specified transactions unless the transaction is otherwise exempt, ie those in which HMRC are satisfied that a charity engages for genuine commercial reasons, on terms which are no less beneficial to the charity than those that might be expected on an identical arms-length transaction, so long as the transaction is not part of an arrangement for the avoidance of tax [*CTA 2010, ss 502–510; ITA 2007, ss 549–557*].

Tainted donations (after 31 March 2011)

[14.58] A new regime took effect from April 1 2011, for both income tax and corporation tax purposes [*ITA 2007, ss 809ZH–809ZR and CTA 2010, ss 939A–939I, inserted by FA 2011, Sch 3*]. In broad terms, a relievable charity donation is a tainted donation if Conditions A, B and C are met. Condition A is that a linked person enters into arrangements and it is reasonable to assume that the donation would not have been made and the arrangements would not have been entered into independently of one another. A 'linked person' is the donor or a person connected to the donor at a relevant time. Condition B is that the main purpose or one of the main purposes of the linked person is to obtain a financial advantage, whether from the donee charity or a connected charity or from one or more non-charitable linked persons. Condition C is that the donor is not a 'qualifying charity-owned company' or a 'relevant housing provider' linked with the donee charity. The meaning of 'financial advantage' is spelled out, as indeed are the effects of a tainted donation in terms of removal of reliefs and imposition of a charge to tax where Gift Aid is withdrawn. For capital gains tax purposes relief is not given to a tainted donation or any associated donation [*TCGA 1992, s 257A, inserted by FA 2011, Sch 3, para 3*].

[14.59] One significant difference between the old substantial donors rule and the present tainted donations regime is that under the latter it is the donor who is principally affected by losing any tax relief he would have received on the donation. He will also face an income tax assessment for the basic rate income tax recovered by the charity on the gift. Only if the charity is aware of or is a party to the arrangements does the charity lose out. By contrast, under the previous substantial donor rules, the charity had to monitor the donations and run the risk of forfeiting tax relief where HMRC considered the donation to be abusive.

Abnormal dividends

[14.60] Several sections are aimed at stratagems which could involve any gross fund. *ITA 2007, Pt 13, Ch 1* deal with abnormal dividends which follow a transaction in securities and where there is a tax advantage. The problem is illustrated by the case of *Sheppard (Trustees of the Woodland Trust) v IRC (No 2) Ch D*, [1993] STC 240, 65 TC 724, Ch D. The Woodland Trust is a charity. The Sheppard family had a prosperous family company. A bonus issue was renounced in favour of the charity, dividend waivers were lodged by the family and a substantial dividend was paid to the charity so that it could reclaim tax. Plainly the profits out of which the dividend came had been earned to a large extent prior to the charity becoming a shareholder. Aldous J did not see a tax advantage within the meaning of what is now ITA 2007, s 683 (which is restricted) and so the appeal by the charity succeeded. There had been a transaction in securities. *ICTA 1988, s 235* (repealed from 1999/2000) ensured that no refund could be claimed in respect of the pre-acquisition profits paid up by way of dividend. HMRC have said that, but for a technical point relating to the assessment, they would have appealed. In their *Tax Bulletin* of August 1993, at page 90, the Inland Revenue warned that they would continue to reject claims in similar circumstances. One of the claims rejected was discussed in *IRC v Universities Superannuation Scheme Ltd*, [1997] STC 1, 70 TC 193, Ch D when a decision by the Special Commissioners favourable to the taxpayer was referred back to a tribunal under what is now *ITA 2007, s 705*.

[14.61] The *Charities Act 2011*, as did the *Charities Act 2006*, provides for the disclosure of information to the Charity Commissioners by HMRC. This provision applies only to charities in England and Wales.

Spotlights

[14.62] 'Spotlights' were introduced in April 2009 as a means of alerting taxpayers and agents to arrangements of which HMRC have become aware in the market place which do not, in their view, deliver the fiscal benefits anticipated by their promoters. In Spotlights HMRC say that they will:

- Provide some advice on tax planning to be wary of, listing some indicators that HMRC see as suggesting that a scheme may involve tax avoidance and which they are likely to investigate.
- Identify specific schemes which, in their view, are not likely to deliver the tax savings advertised. Where HMRC see such schemes being used, subject to the particular facts, they will make a challenge and seek to ensure full payment of the right tax on the right due date.

[14.63] Spotlight 7 was issued on 6 January 2010 as follows:

'HMRC are aware of schemes that seek to generate Gift Aid and Gift of Shares tax relief claims. A cash donation to a nominated charity is required and in return shares are received from an unnamed non-UK "philanthropist". These shares are claimed to be worth up to eight times the amount of the cash donation and are in companies listed on a stock exchange that is not recognised by HMRC, for example The Open Market of The Frankfurt Stock Exchange. The scheme anticipates that the shares will be donated to the nominated charity. There is also strong evidence that these schemes have links to share scams such as "boiler rooms". They usually involve a high level of upfront "fee", paid to the scheme promoters, which is concealed within the original cash "donation" given to the charity. HMRC's view is that no Gift Aid is due on the cash donation because the donor receives a benefit (the shares) that is in excess of the donation. HMRC also consider that no Gift of Shares relief is due because the requirement that the shares are listed on a stock exchange recognised by HMRC is not met.'

[14.64] Spotlight 9 (which was re-issued on 12 June 2013) addresses an avoidance scheme disclosed to HMRC which exploits the Gift Aid provisions:

'The scheme seeks to exploit the rules which enable a charity to claim a repayment of tax at the basic rate on a qualifying donation by an individual. The individual may claim relief for the donation on the difference between the higher and the basic rates of tax. The scheme depends upon a circular series of payments. It starts with the charity purchasing, say, gilts of £100,000 which pass through a third party to an individual taxpayer for perhaps £10. The taxpayer is expected to make a sale for £100,000 and pass the money to the charity. There is an option that ensures that the gilts will be returned to the charity if it does not receive a cash gift of £100,000 within one or two days. HMRC do not accept that the charity is entitled to a repayment of tax or that Gift Aid relief is due to the individual. In their view a gift has not been made to the charity as it is no better off than before entering the arrangements. Therefore Gift Aid is not due. HMRC will challenge the reliefs claimed in any instances where this scheme has been used and will litigate where appropriate.'

Gift of qualifying investments: avoidance arrangement blocked by statute

[14.65] An avoidance arrangement was blocked with effect from 15 December 2009 [*FA 2010, s 31* and *Sch 7*]. The avoidance and the effect of the new rule was explained by HMRC on their website on 15 December 2009 as follows. The avoidance depended on the donor receiving tax relief at their highest marginal rate of tax (then 40% where the donor is a higher rate taxpayer) on the full market value of the qualifying investments at the date of the gift where:

- the donor acquired the investments at below market value as part of a scheme or arrangement, or
- the market value of the investment is artificially inflated at the date of the gift to charity.

The new rules adjust the amount of relief to the donor to the economic cost of acquisition of the gift to the donor where:

- the qualifying investment given to the charity (or anything from which the investment derives) was acquired within four years of the date of disposal; and

- where the main purpose, or one of the main purposes, of acquiring the qualifying investment was to dispose of it to a charity and claim the tax relief.

A number of examples were given by HMRC to illustrate cases where the new restriction would and where it would not apply.

Latest developments

[14.66] The *Charities (Protection and Social Investment) Act 2016* gave the Charity Commission new powers to regulate charities. Two of these have been the subject of recent consultations: *Disqualification of trustees* (the closing deadline for which was 22 August 2016) and *Official warnings to trustees or charities* (the closing deadline for which was 23 September 2016). In addition, the House of Lords Select Committee on Charities was established on 25 May 2016 and on 20 July 2016 it issued a call for written evidence on a range of subjects with a view to understanding the pressures faced by charities, and to improve charity governance, transparency and accountability. The Committee is expected to report before 31 March 2017. (For further information see commentary at www.wilsonslaw.com/news/charity-commission-consultations.)

Time charities

[14.67] Time charities have been mentioned (see **14.7**). These should be able to claim income tax relief and should be free from the ten-year charge etc for inheritance tax. However, they lack inheritance tax exemptions when they are set up and they pay a special inheritance tax charge [*IHTA 1984, s 70*] when they come to an end.

HMRC administration

[14.68] HMRC have two offices designated to attend to the income tax of charities. These are HMRC Charities based at Bootle and at Edinburgh. These used to be the Financial Intermediaries and Claims Offices (FICO). District Inspectors are involved, to a very limited extent, because, if a charity ceased to be charitable or carried on non-exempt activity, the District would be involved. HMRC recognise that a new appeal fund may be set up for a specific disaster (TSEM1471). If an appeal fund trust claims charitable status, the papers should be submitted to HMRC Charities in Bootle. Alternatively, if the appeal fund trust does not claim charitable status, the normal treatment for a new trust should be followed (see **17.6–17.8**).

[14.69] HMRC have published on their website new procedures and forms, ie CHA1, to apply for recognition as a charity for tax purposes. The application is sent to HMRC Charities, St Johns House, Merton Road, Liverpool, L75 1BB. Once HMRC Charities recognises you as a charity for tax purposes, they will set up a record so that any repayment claims you make can be processed. They will then send you:

- your reference number for use on all claims and correspondence;
- all the forms needed for your first repayment claim; and
- the date from which your charitable status is effective.

For more help you can contact the Charities Helpline on tel 0845 302 0203 (open from 8.00am to 5.00pm, Monday to Friday). Select option two for registering a charity for Gift Aid or charitable status.

[14.70] It used to be the case that charities sent their accounts to FICO as a matter of routine so that it could be seen that their income was being used for charitable purposes. From 4 March 1998 this is not necessary. HMRC Charities will ask for accounts when they want to see them. By contrast, as part of their ongoing supervision of charities, the Charity Commission will request accounts, with an examiner's report, for any year in which the income received or payments made by a charity exceed £25,000.

[14.71] UK charities were able to raise funds from 31 July 1998 under the millennium Gift Aid scheme, with a view to giving support to anti-poverty or educational projects in one or more of eighty poor countries. They had to register with HMRC Charities at Bootle or at Edinburgh who would send a guidance pack. It was announced at Budget 2011 that millennium Gift Aid would be repealed from 2011/12. The repeal was effected by *FA 2011, Sch 26, para 2*.

[14.72] It was announced at Budget 2011 that in 2012/13 HMRC would introduce a new online system for charities to register their details for Gift Aid and to make Gift Aid claims. As a first step towards this, HMRC published four new 'intelligent' forms for charities to use, including the standard tax repayment claim form. The forms contain automatic checks to improve the accuracy of information and reduce administrative burdens. HMRC have worked with the charity sector to develop both the new forms and new online system, which in the event came into operation on 22 April 2013. HMRC have also worked with the charity sector to develop a supporting electronic Gift Aid database for Gift Aid declarations.

[14.73] On 16 February 2015, a new *Charities Digital Service* went live for the online registration of new charities' details with HMRC. The service has in-built checks and guidance to help organisations provide the right information and supporting documentation to enable HMRC to confirm their tax status.

Disaster funds

[14.74] Public appeals following some tragedy attracting immediate sympathy may or may not be charitable. Those which are charitable can offer tax savings to donors and have tax exemptions themselves. However, they are subject to the scrutiny of the Charity Commission and cannot give money to an individual without limit. Any grant in excess of that which an individual needs must be non-charitable. An appeal fund which is not charitable escapes this restriction. However, the disposal of any surplus funds becomes a problem – they belong to the donors. There is also the question of inheritance tax because the appeal fund which is not charitable will be a trust of some sort and it will now fall within the relevant property regime. (See CHAPTERS 9 and CHAPTER 10).

[14.75] The Inland Revenue and Customs and Excise jointly issued, in November 1989, a free leaflet giving guidelines on the tax treatment of disaster funds (see Inland Revenue Press Release 23 November 1989). Most recently, HMRC published on their website on 17 May 2001 guidance notes on the tax treatment of appeal funds. The Charity Commission issued a helpful leaflet CC40 'Disaster Appeals—Attorney General's Guidelines' (now available as a pdf document at www.gov.uk/government/uploads/system/uploads/attachment_data/file/359658/CC40text.pdf). It would be very easy to set up a charitable disaster fund and then, in ignorance, contravene *Charities Acts 2006/2011* in relation to collections.

Miscellaneous

Some background to the 2006 and 2011 reforms

[14.76] Most of the *Charities Act 1992* was consolidated into the *Charities Act 1993*. At the end of September 2002 the Cabinet Office Strategy Unit (formerly known as the Performance and Innovation Unit) published its long-awaited Review of Charities. This led to a new *Charities Act*, which received Royal Assent on 8 November 2006, including a new statutory definition of charity (see **14.43** and **14.77**) and giving increased powers and greater flexibility to charity trustees. The *Charities Act 2006* has been introduced in stages.

[14.77] Following the *Charities Act 2006*, the *Charities Act 2011* represents a comprehensive updating of the legislative framework for charities (see **14.6**). Among the current framework and definitions, 'charitable purpose' is a purpose which falls within any of the thirteen descriptions of purposes as set out in the Act and which is for the public benefit. The thirteen purposes are essentially the four historic heads (relief of poverty, advancement of education, advancement of religion and other purposes beneficial to the community) plus the major purposes which have been recognised by the Charity Commission as charitable over recent years (and which would previously have fallen within the fourth head – other purposes etc) which are now set out separately (see **14.4**). The question of whether or not there ever was a presumption of public benefit in the case of some charities (ie those for the relief of poverty, advancement of education or advancement of religion), and if so what effect it had, is open to some debate. Accordingly, the effect of what is now *Charities Act 2011, s 4(2)* is not certain. What is clear is the statutory provision that it is not to be presumed that a purpose of any particular description is for the public benefit. There is still no definition of 'public benefit', however, and guidance has been given by the Charity Commission. Application to the Charity Commission for charitable status has to be made on the merits of each case.

Cessation of charitable use

[14.78] There can be problems when land given for educational or other charitable purposes ceases to be so used. The land could then revert under the *Reverter of Sites Act 1987* or pursuant to the *Education Act 1973, s 2* or under some other provision. The result would be a chargeable gain under *TCGA 1992, s 256(2)*. However, where, within six years, the land is again held for charitable purposes income tax and capital gains tax will be discharged. Apparently, there were benefactors in early Victorian times who would give land and buildings for educational purposes but would want them back if the education ceased. If the revertee cannot be identified tax may be postponed until he is identified (press release 9.3.94).

Schools

[14.79] School fee payment plans arranged with educational trusts suffered a reverse in 1996. Their charitable status was removed. In a written Parliamentary answer on 29 October 1996 it was said that there would be no change with regard to payments made in plans in existence on 20 June 1996. Charitable donations to schools themselves (provided they have charitable status) still qualify, so long as the donor receives no personal benefit from the donation. That said, independent schools in particular are under some pressure to be able to demonstrate their public benefit.

The Trust (Capital and Income) Act 2013

[14.80] This Act, enacted on 31 January 2013, is of particular interest to charitable trusts. Such a trust with a permanent endowment can now resolve to opt for an investment policy of total return in line with new Charity Commission regulations, without the need to have separate regard to income and capital respectively. Accordingly, a charity with permanent endowment is enabled to treat capital appreciation on its endowment assets in the same way as income without the need to make express application to the Charity Commission. Two further changes are made by the Act. First, the statutory rule requiring time apportionment of income and certain case law rules of apportionment are disapplied, for trusts coming into existence after commencement (unless those rules are expressly applied by the trust deed). Second, corporate receipts from all tax exempt de-mergers are classified as capital rather than as income.

Chapter 15

Trusts for Disabled or Vulnerable Persons

Overview

[15.1] The UK tax legislation does not include a completely coordinated set of rules for trusts for disabled or vulnerable beneficiaries. The inheritance tax legislation includes rules providing a 'favoured trust' status (ie outside the scope of the relevant property regime) for certain 'trusts for disabled persons' (also referred to in this book and elsewhere as 'Disabled Trusts') (see **15.7–15.13**). The income and capital gains tax include special rules for certain 'trusts for vulnerable beneficiaries' (see **15.14–15.18**). Finally, there is a special regime for certain 'trusts compensating asbestos victims' (see **15.19**).

[15.2] Since 2013/14 there has been some simplification in this area, to the extent that the same definition of 'disabled person' now applies for all taxes. Practitioners should nevertheless be aware that there remain significant differences between the different sets of rules.

Disabled person

[15.3] The definition of a 'disabled person' was changed by *FA 2013, Sch 44, para 19*, inserting into *FA 2005* new *Schedule 1A*, with effect from 2013/14, for purposes of the inheritance tax regime (see new *IHTA 1984, s 89 (4) and (4A), s 89B(2)*) as well as the special regime for trusts for vulnerable persons: see **15.14–15.18**). The *FA 2005, Sch 1A*, was then itself amended by *FA 2014, s 291*. The meaning of 'disabled person' now means (for the purposes of *IHTA 1984, ss 89, 89A and 89B* in relation to property transferred into settlement on or after 6 April 2014, and for all other purposes, from 2013/14 on):

(a) a person who by reason of mental disorder within the meaning of the *Mental Health Act 1983* is incapable of administering his or her property or managing his or her affairs;
(b) a person in receipt of attendance allowance;
(c) a person in receipt of a disability living allowance by virtue of entitlement to—
  (i) the care component at the highest or middle rate, or
  (ii) the mobility component at the higher rate;
(d) a person in receipt of personal independence payment;
(e) a person in receipt of an increased disablement pension;
(f) a person in receipt of constant attendance allowance; or
(g) a person in receipt of armed forces independence payment.

The meaning of these expressions is detailed in the *Schedule 1A*.

[15.4] Before 2013/14 a 'disabled person' for purposes of inheritance tax was one:

[15.4] Trusts for Disabled or Vulnerable Persons

(a) incapable of looking after their own affairs by reason of a mental disorder within the *Mental Health Act 1983* as amended by the *Mental Health Act 2007*; or

(b) in receipt of an attendance allowance or (noting **15.5**) a disability living allowance by virtue of entitlement to the care component at the highest or middle rate, under the *Social Security Contributions and Benefits Act 1992* (subject to certain relaxations from 22 March 2006 – see (d) below). For an attendance allowance the disability has to be such as to require supervision or attention in connection with the person's bodily functions. It is not enough to qualify for either allowance – the disabled person must actually receive it. Incapacity benefit was introduced by the *Social Security (Incapacity for Work) Act 1994*. However, the attendance allowance continues. The principal difference is that attendance allowance is paid only to those aged 65 or more;

(c) from 22 March 2006, who would have been in receipt of attendance allowance had the restriction under the *Social Security Contributions and Benefits Act 1992* or the *Social Securities Contributions and Benefits (Northern Ireland) Act 1992* as to non-satisfaction of conditions for attendance allowance where the person is undergoing treatment for renal failure in a hospital or is provided with certain accommodation been ignored;

(d) from 22 March 2006 (noting **15.5**), in receipt of disability living allowance by virtue of entitlement to the care component at the highest or middle rate, had the qualification under either of the 1992 Acts (no payment of disability living allowance for persons for whom certain accommodation is provided) been ignored.

[15.5] Under the *Welfare Reform Act 2012* (which received Royal Assent on 8 March 2012), the disability living allowance was replaced by a personal independence payment from 8 April 2013. At that point, whether a person was a 'disabled person' depended on whether they were in receipt of the daily living component of the personal independence payment at a rate to be determined by the Secretary of State for Work and Pensions. There are two such rates under *section 78* of the Act:

(a) the standard rate, payable to a person whose 'ability to carry out daily living activities is limited by [their] physical or mental condition'; and

(b) the enhanced rate, payable where 'the person's ability to carry out daily living activities is severely limited by [their] physical or mental condition'.

Careful attention was therefore needed in any particular case as to whether, under the revised definition, an individual who previously qualified as a disabled person continued to do so after the change, even if their condition remained unaltered (see *TAXline* September 2011 p 11, contribution by Robin Williamson).

[15.6] Between 2004/05 and 2013/14 a 'disabled person' for the purposes of the 'trusts for vulnerable beneficiaries' regime (see **15.14–15.18**) was as set out at **15.3** but not including the criteria at (d) and (e).

Inheritance tax

[15.7] For inheritance tax purposes, certain trusts for 'disabled persons' fall outside the relevant property regime and are instead, in essence, treated in the same way as qualifying interest in possession trusts ie the assets are deemed to be owned by the disabled beneficiary. As a consequence, a transfer to such a trust is also a potentially exempt transfer for inheritance tax purposes, even after 21 March 2006 (and see **15.13** for the possibility that the creation of the trust might include no transfer of value at all).

[15.8] Prior to 22 March 2006, a trust for a disabled person attracted a favoured status only if it was a discretionary trust conforming to the requirements of *IHTA 1984, s 89* being, broadly, that at least half the benefits arising in the trust are used to benefit the disabled person. The type of trust which could qualify was, however, helpfully extended by *Finance Act 2006* and, since 22 March 2006 now includes both interest in possession trusts and a new category of disabled trust where a person who expects to become disabled in the future establishes a trust to provide for his or her future needs, whether discretionary or interest in possession in form [*IHTA 1984, s 89A* and *s 89B(1)(d)*].

[15.9] Accordingly, the expression 'disabled person's interest' is now defined for inheritance tax purposes by *IHTA 1984, s 89B* as follows:

(a) a discretionary trust in which there is a deemed interest in possession (the traditional disabled person's trust found in *section 89*);
(b) a discretionary trust made on or after 22 March 2006 at a time when the settlor had a condition reasonably expected to lead to his disability which in broad terms secures that:
 (i) if any of the settled property is applied during his lifetime it is applied for his benefit; and
 (ii) if the trusts are brought to an end during the settlor's lifetime the capital will be owned either by the settlor or by some other person beneficially or be held on a disabled person's interest within (c) or (d) below (*section 89A(4)*, that is the *Finance Act 2006* equivalent of the traditional type);
(c) an express interest in possession trust made for a disabled person on or after 22 March 2006 (new category *section 89B(1)(c)*); and
(d) an interest in possession trust made on or after 22 March 2006 at a time when the settlor had a condition reasonably expected to lead to his disability (new *section 89B(1)(d)*).

[15.10] The scope of a qualifying disabled trust has also been extended by *FA 2013, Sch 44*. Such a trust made on or after 8 April 2013 may provide for the payment of small amounts of income or capital to beneficiaries other than the principal beneficiary, without prejudicing its favoured status. That small amount (or 'annual limit') is the lower of £3,000 and 3% of the maximum value of the settled property during the period in question. The same power to apply small amounts for other beneficiaries is added to the special income tax and capital gains tax regime for vulnerable beneficiary trusts under *Finance Act 2005* by amendments to *section 34* (disabled persons) and *section 35* (relevant minors): see **15.14–15.18**. This concessionary power in relation to

[15.10] Trusts for Disabled or Vulnerable Persons

property transferred into settlement on or after 8 April 2013 also applies to 'bereaved minor trusts' and 'age 18-to-25 trusts' (see **8.9–8.12** and **8.13–8.15** respectively). However, the effective date for purposes of new *IHTA 1984, s 89C* (disabled person's interest: powers of advancement etc) is 17 July 2013. Where property is transferred into a 'relevant settlement' on or after 8 April 2013, none of these amendments will prevent that property from being property to which *IHTA 1984, s 89* or *s 89A* applies. The definition of 'relevant settlement' is:

(a)   one created before 8 April 2013, the trusts of which have not been altered on or after that date; or
(b)   a settlement arising after 8 April 2013 under a Will executed for that date which has not been altered on or after that date.

The amendments to *FA 2005* have effect for tax year 2013/14 and subsequent tax years.

[15.11] Because of the restrictive nature of the *IHTA 1984, s 89* regime, trusts for the disabled have been something of a rarity in practice and the new regime has certainly increased the usefulness of such trusts. This is particularly important given that the creation of a qualifying trust for a disabled person is now the only lifetime non-charitable trust which still counts as a potentially exempt transfer. Care must always be taken, of course, to consider the effect on a disabled person's state benefits of becoming the beneficiary of trust. Although a wider discussion of this area is beyond the scope of this book, it is likely that receiving an income as of right would be more problematic that receiving only a discretionary benefit.

A capital gains tax uplift?

[15.12] There is one particular type of settlement, ie for a qualifying disabled person, where there is no actual interest in possession and yet there is a deemed interest in possession, under *IHTA 1984, s 89(2)*. Such a settlement is expressly excluded from the relevant property regime and because there is no actual interest in possession, on the death of the disabled life tenant before 5 December 2013 there was no uplift to market value of the trust property for capital gains tax purposes. This was an anomaly and could have resulted in inheritance tax being charged on death and capital gains tax being charged on the same value on a subsequent sale. Thankfully, the anomaly has been removed by *Finance Act 2014* in relation to all deaths on or after 5 December 2013 (the date of the Chancellor's Autumn Statement when this changed was first announced) and all settlements for disabled persons where there is a deemed interest in possession now qualify for an uplift on death.

No transfer of value?

[15.13] There may also be cases where the lifetime creation of a trust for a disabled person is a disposition for maintenance of the family and, as a consequence, not a transfer of value at all [*IHTA 1984, s 11*]. There is therefore an interesting, and maybe significant, distinction between lifetime transfers into a disabled trust which are sufficiently 'reasonable' in amount to gain the protection of the *section 11* provision and transfers of the same amount into a trust for the disabled person on death, which will necessarily be a chargeable transfer. The 2008 case of *McKelvey (personal representative of McKelvey, dec'd) v Revenue and Customs Comrs* (SpC 694) [2008] STC (SCD) 944 confirmed, albeit not involving a trust, that *section 11* could extend to the transfer of capital. (One technical issue with *section 11* when a transfer to a trust is made is to ensure that the trust is for the benefit of only the disabled beneficiary.)

Income and capital gains tax

[15.14] A rather complex set of rules applies from 2004/05 [*FA 2005, ss 23–45* and *Sch 1*]. They enable a discretionary or accumulation trust (which would otherwise be taxed at the special rates described in Chapter 6), to be taxed according to the personal financial circumstances of one or more beneficiaries, so long as they are qualifying 'vulnerable persons', as defined. 'Vulnerable persons' include 'disabled persons' (see **15.3** and **15.6**) and 'relevant minors'. A 'relevant minor' is simply a person under 18 with at least one parent having died. The trust must also be a 'qualifying trust', as defined. In the case of a disabled person, that means that where any trust property is applied for the benefit of a beneficiary it must be applied for the benefit of that disabled person. In the case of a relevant minor, a qualifying trust may be (a) a trust arising by statute on intestacy; or (b) a Will trust; or (c) a trust established under the Criminal Injuries Compensation Scheme or (from 8 April 2010) the Victims of Overseas Terrorism Compensation Scheme, which, in each case, ensures that the minor receives capital and income and accumulations absolutely at age 18. This last condition is likely to make the regime unattractive to many people (who wish to see benefits deferred beyond the age of 18) from choosing to create such a trust. See also **15.10** for the ability of the trustees to apply small amounts of income and capital to other than the principal beneficiary, from 8 April 2013.

[15.15] The thinking behind the regime is to make the vulnerable person's personal allowances and lower rate bands available to the trustees. This treatment must be claimed for each tax year and does not apply where the trust income is taxed on the settlor as a settlor-interested trust (see **4.3–4.13**). *FA 2005* provides a series of steps to compute what is known as the 'vulnerable person's liability' and then to ascertain the reduction in the income tax liability of the trustees [*FA 2005, s 28*]. Somewhat curiously, the income of an accumulation or discretionary trust for which the vulnerable person's election is made is not on distribution precluded from the *ITA 2007, s 493* mechanism (see **6.65–6.67**). That is, the trustees must still be able to certify that on making a payment of income in 2015/16 or 2016/17 that income has borne income tax at 45% or in the case of dividend income, the appropriate rate for the year. *ITTOIA 2005, s 629(8)*, applying *FA 2005, s 28A*, provides, sensibly, that income of a vulnerable person's trust for which election has been made cannot also be assessed on the settlor under *ITTOIA 2005, s 629(1)*.

[15.16] As with income tax, the capital gains tax relief must be claimed and the applicable provisions vary according to whether the vulnerable person is

UK resident or non-UK resident. Before 23 June 2010 there was a single rate of capital gains tax, for both individuals and trustees, so that the vulnerable persons election might seem unnecessary to that extent. However, the availability of the annual exemption (or, perhaps rather more materially, allowable losses) might make a difference to the tax charged. And, for disposals between 22 June 2010 and 5 April 2016, the difference between 18% for individuals (to the extent that the chargeable gain when added to their taxable income would not exceed the basic rate band) and 28% for trustees may well make a vulnerable persons election a worthwhile thing to make for capital gains tax purposes. Beyond 6 April 2016, the rate of tax for most trustee gains (see Chapter 7) has reduced to 20%, reducing the marginal advantage. Although there is a separate set of capital gains tax rules in cases where the beneficiary is non-UK resident (which are extremely complex), the basic scheme of the regime is to compare (a) the chargeable gains as if they had arisen to the vulnerable person beneficially and (b) the chargeable gains computed as arising to the trustees on the ordinary basis. The difference between the two amounts may be the subject of a claim. (Note that HMRC will look to the trustees to pay the tax even where a valid vulnerable person's election has been made: it is the trustees, after all, who have made the disposal.)

Electing for special treatment

[15.17] The election must be made on or before the 31 January in the tax year following that where the regime is to apply. Therefore, to adopt the regime for 2015/16 the election must be made on or before 31 January 2017. The election must be made both by the trustees and the vulnerable person – or someone on his behalf. The election is irrevocable. The election will cease to have effect when the person ceases to be vulnerable or the trust is no longer qualifying or comes to an end, in which event the trustees must inform HMRC within 90 days.

Administration

[15.18] HMRC are empowered to confirm that the beneficiary is indeed vulnerable and that the settlement is a qualifying trust, subject to giving a minimum of 60 days' notice. If HMRC find that the statutory requirements are not met (or that since the effective date of the election there has been an event which terminates the validity of the election), they can give notice that the election never had or has ceased to have effect.

EXAMPLE

Both Debbie's parents were killed in a car crash in 2006, neither having made a Will. Under the intestacy rules, a trust has been established for Debbie aged 10 which for 2013/14 produces gross dividend income of £15,000 and gross interest income of £15,000 and makes chargeable gains of £12,000. Debbie has no other income.

Assuming that the trustees and Debbie (or rather her guardian) made the necessary election on or before 31 January 2015, the effect of the regime is as follows:

TLV1 (see below) = (£1,969)
TLV2 (see below) = £0 (Debbie's other income)
TQTI (see below) = £9,459
VQT1: Reduction in the trustees' tax liability on a claim is £11,428 (£9,459 + £1,969), which will lead to a repayment of tax by HMRC.

	Debbie's assumed tax liability		Trustees' actual tax liability	
	£	£	£	£
Income tax	15,000		15,000	
Dividend income (including tax credits £1,500)				
Interest income (before tax deducted £3,000)	15,000		15,000	
	30,000		30,000	
Personal allowance	(9,440)			
Taxable	20,560		30,000	
£2,790 @ 10%		279		
Next £2,770 (interest at 20%)		554		
15,000 (dividends at 10%)		1,500		
		2,333		
Trust, first slice (£1,000 at 20%)				200
Next £14,000 (interest at 45%)				6,300
£15,000 (dividends at 27.5%)				5,625
				12,125
Less:				
Dividend tax credits		(1,500)		(1,500)
Tax deducted from interest		(3,000)		(3,000)
Income tax repayable/payable		(£2,167)		£7,625

	Debbie	Trustees
Capital gains tax		
Gains arising	12,000	12,000
Less annual exemption	(10,900)	(5,450)
Gain charged at 18%/28%	1,100	6,550
Tax payable	198	1,834
SUMMARY		
Income Tax repayable/payable	(2,167)	7,625
+ CGT	198	1,834
	(1,969)	9,459
	(TLV1)	(TQT1)

Trusts compensating asbestos victims

[15.19] The first 2010 Budget on 24 March 2010 proposed a measure to exempt trustees of certain trusts from capital gains tax, inheritance tax and income tax. The legislation was enacted in *Finance (No 3) Act 2010, Sch 14, paras 1–3*, and the trusts that benefit are those set up on or before 23 March 2010 as part of an arrangement made by a company with its creditors and specifically to pay compensation to, or in respect of, individuals with asbestos-related conditions. Previously (and in broad terms), trustees have been subject to inheritance tax charges every ten years on the value of property held in such trusts above the IHT nil-rate band and also on exit charges. Trustees had also been liable to income tax on income arising to the trust, and to capital gains tax on disposals of certain trust assets. The new measure provides for exemptions from those tax charges on the trustees of these types of trust, with effect from 6 April 2006.

Chapter 16

Trusts for Employees

Overview

[16.1] There are number of reasons why – usually a company – would want to establish a trust for the benefit of employees: to facilitate employee share ownership, retirement benefit or share schemes; or, simply – and particularly in the recent past – as a means of providing tax-efficient benefits for employees. Likewise, such trusts can take a variety of different forms. It is beyond the scope of this short chapter to cover the subject in detail and readers are referred, for example, to *Chapter 14* of *Tolley's Tax Planning* for a wider discussion of the subject – particularly in the context of tax planning. What is intended here is an overview of the key differences in the tax rules applying to trusts for the benefit of employees, as opposed to 'standard' discretionary trusts (as almost all trusts for the benefit of employees would be in discretionary form).

[16.2] Two types of trust are considered below. *Employee Benefit Trusts* (see **16.3–16.35**) have been used extensively for a variety of tax planning purposes, which planning has, in turn, prompted considerable anti-avoidance in recent years. By contrast, *Employee Ownership Trusts* (see **16.36–16.43**) were introduced only in 2014.

Employee Benefit Trusts (EBTs)

[16.3] 'EBT' is not a term of art and is rather a catch all term describing any trust established for the benefit of employees over the last twenty years or so; and while the uses for and types of EBT have been many and varied, they have also been used extensively as a tax avoidance vehicle – particularly as a vehicle for minimising the tax on employee remuneration. In the late 1990s and early 2000s, for example, many EBTs were established on the back of advice that:

(a) the company's contribution to the EBT would be deductible for corporation tax purposes;
(b) there would be no inheritance tax on the EBT's establishment;
(c) the EBT could make tax efficient payments to employees, typically through loans; and
(d) that the burden of those loans would constitute a deduction for inheritance tax purposes in the hands of the employee.

Quite a nice package of tax benefits! Not surprising HMRC and the Treasury have found such planning problematic (see, for example, HMRC 'Spotlights' 5, 6 and 17) and over the years each of these benefits has been chipped away.

A corporation tax deduction?

[16.4] In his Autumn Statement on 27 November 2002, the Chancellor announced, for accounting periods starting on or after 1 January 2003, a statutory deduction for the cost of providing shares for employee share schemes, now found in *ITTOIA 2005, ss 38–44; CTA 2009, ss 1290–1297*. A deduction will be given where the employees are subject to UK tax on the awarded shares (or would be but for the fact that shares are obtained under an HMRC approved scheme or enterprise management incentives). Thus, since then, there has been no automatic corporation tax deduction when funds are added to an EBT and a deduction arises only when an employee receives a taxable benefit. This has implications for inheritance tax and the availability of relief under *IHTA 1984, s 12* (see **16.8**).

[16.5] The statutory rules mentioned above announced by the Chancellor on 27 November 2002 were a direct response to the decision of the Special Commissioners in favour of the taxpayer in *Dextra Accessories Ltd v MacDonald (Inspector of Taxes)* [2002] STC (SCD) 413. In that case the trustee of an employee benefit trust made revocable deeds of appointment which created sub-funds for each of six employees. Loans were made to those employees out of their respective sub-trusts. The Special Commissioners found both that the contributions made by the company were deductible for corporation tax purposes and that loans out of the sub-trusts did not constitute either taxable emoluments or benefits in kind. A crucial finding of fact was that the sub-trusts could not be treated as a moneybox for the individuals because the trustee was not in a commercial sense inevitably compelled to comply with their wishes. HMRC appealed unsuccessfully to the High Court (see [2003] STC 749), though HMRC's further appeal was upheld by the Court of Appeal on the grounds that the payments by the company did constitute 'potential emoluments' for the employees within *FA 1989, s 43* ([2004] STC 339). In 2005, the House of Lords rejected the taxpayer's final appeal: [2005] UKHL 47, [2005] STC 1111.

Inheritance tax

[16.6] An EBT will typically be a discretionary trust; however, most EBT's have a 'favoured' status – and therefore fall outside the relevant property regime – thus avoiding ongoing ten-yearly or exit charges. This arises as a result of the specific exemption contained in *IHTA 1984, s 86* which applies whenever none of the settled property can be applied other than for the benefit of:

(a) persons of a class defined by reference to employment in a particular trade or profession, or employment by, or office with, a body carrying on a trade, profession or undertaking; or
(b) persons defined by reference to marriage/civil partnership or relationship to, or dependants of, persons of a class defined as mentioned in (*a*).

Section 86 allows the application of trust property for charitable purposes and also interests in possession to be held by individual employees amounting to not more than 5% of the trust fund.

[16.7] Even where *section 86* applies, there may be potential exit charges under *IHTA 1984, s 72*. In the normal case, however, *section 72* will not bite as it applies only in the case of payments to a limited class of persons. There is a further exemption where the payment out of the trust constitutes income of anyone for income tax purposes (or would do so but for the fact that he is non-UK resident).

[16.8] The inheritance tax position in relation to the transfer *to* an EBT is more complicated. The starting point is that any transfer of value made by a close company (as defined in *IHTA 1984, s 102(1)*) is treated as a transfer of value by the participators in the company [*IHTA 1984, s 94*]. In the circumstances of a transfer to an EBT, any transfer of value would *not* be a potentially exempt transfer. Thus, in the absence of any other relieving provision, a chargeable transfer could arise. There, are, however, three specific provisions which could (but which will not necessarily) assist the taxpayer:

- *IHTA 1984, s 10* applies in relation to essentially commercial transactions, where there is no intention to confer any gratuitous benefit.
- *IHTA 1984, s 12* applies if the payment is deductible for corporation tax purposes.
- Finally, *IHTA 1984, s 13* applies if the trust satisfies the definition in *IHTA 1984, s 86* and no participator in the company with an interest of more than 5% or a person connected with him can benefit under the trust.

[16.9] In August 2009 HMRC set out their view on the application of these provisions (*Revenue and Customs Brief 49/09 11 August 2009*). The Brief covered a lot of ground, but in broad terms HMRC were arguing that in the usual case (where the contribution is to a trust which satisfies *IHTA 1984, s 86*) the contribution will be a transfer of value because it is not protected by *section 10* as being made in an arm's length transaction not intended to confer a gratuitous benefit. That statement was then been superseded and amplified by *Revenue & Customs Brief 18/11 of 4 April 2011*, dealing in addition with income tax. HMRC maintained their stance that *section 10* protection will not be available 'if there is the slightest possibility of gratuitous intent at the date the contribution is made'. Similarly, in discussing the case where the payment is not a transfer of value because it is deductible for corporation tax purposes under *section 12*, HMRC say that *section 12* applies only to the extent that a deduction is allowed to the company for the tax year in which the contribution is made (again, which is more restrictive than *section 12* actually provides). At least, which was not admitted in the 2009 statement, HMRC admit the possibility that business property relief may apply to reduce the chargeable transfer. This follows a suggestion made by the author in an article *Gift with strings attached* in *Taxation* (1 October 2009). On the basis of the High Court decision in *Revenue and Customs Comrs v Trustees of the Nelson Dance Family* [2009] EWHC 71 (Ch), [2009] STC 802, 79 TC 605, see **18.40**, a cash contribution by a trading close company to an EBT which would be apportioned to the participators under *IHTA 1984, s 94* can be reduced by 100% business property relief. Although cash is not itself 'relevant business property' as defined in *IHTA 1984, s 105(1)*, the estate of the company has been reduced, on an 'estate before less estate after' basis. It is this argument that is accepted in principle by HMRC. For a further discussion of the inheritance tax issues, readers are referred to the author's previously mentioned *Taxation* article.

[16.10] Where an individual rather than a company makes a transfer to an employee trust there is a separate exemption under *IHTA 1984, s 28*, ie provided that the trust satisfies the *section 86* conditions, the beneficiaries include all or most of the employees and the trust controls the company.

Income tax

[16.11] Given that the EBT is discretionary, payments made by the company to the trustees will not attract income tax for the employees. This is on the basis that no employee has a right to receive payments from the trust fund (see *Edwards (Inspector of Taxes) v Roberts* (1935) 19 TC 618, CA). Historically, the taxation of distributions from the trust would depend upon how they were made. The payment of cash attracts income tax as employment income. If the employees receive shares from the trust they will be assessed to income tax on the value of the shares when distributed (see *Weight v Salmon* (1935) 19 TC 174, HL). However, if loans were made to a beneficiary only a beneficial loan charge under *ITEPA 2003, Pt 3, Ch 7, ss 173–191* would be triggered. Likewise, more complex planning involved the use of other structures intended to produce a beneficial result. Many of these structures have been the subject of recent cases.

[16.12] Payments made via an EBT to 'money box companies' were held to be taxable under PAYE on the employees who held shares in the companies (*Aberdeen Asset Management plc v Revenue and Customs Comrs* [2013] CSIH 84, [2014] STC 438, 2014 SC 271). The key point was that each company's only asset was cash, and so the employees' ownership of the companies gave them unfettered access to the cash.

[16.13] In the recent well-publicised case involving Glasgow Rangers Football Club, the First-tier Tribunal held that payments from a sub-trust for the families of each employee did not give rise to income tax and national insurance liabilities. By a 2:1 majority the Tribunal found that the principal trust and the sub-trust were 'genuine legal events with real legal effects'. The cash loans made to the players were discretionary and could be recovered and so did not represent taxable earnings (*Murray Group Holdings v Revenue and Customs Comrs* [2012] UKFTT 692 (TC), [2013] SFTD 149, [2013] SWTI 492). The Upper Tribunal largely upheld the decision of the First-tier Tribunal ([2014] UKUT 0292 (TCC)); however, the decision was overturned by the Court of Session (*Murray Group Holdings v HMRC* [2015] CSIH 77) on 4 November 2015.

[16.14] Under the Murray Group scheme, a group company made a cash payment to a principal trust, which would then resettle the amount to a sub-trust for the income and capital to be applied according to the wishes of the employee (Rangers' executives and players). The monies would then be lent by the sub-trust to the employee. The Court of Session found that monies paid via trusts were taxable as earnings and that 'the critical feature of an emolument and of earnings as so defined is that it represents the product of the employee's work', even if the income was paid to a third party or via a trust. The Court of Session has granted the taxpayer leave to appeal, so we can expect a final decision from the Supreme Court in time for the next edition of this book!

[16.15] From 2011/12, avoiding tax by channelling funds from an EBT via loans and other complex structures has become considerably more difficult. This is as a result of *FA 2011, s 26, Sch 2*, which introduced a new *Part 7A* into *ITEPA 2003*. HMRC's thinking behind the new regime was the introduction of a charge to income tax (and national insurance contributions) in the case of arrangements for deferred remuneration where a third party (typically an Employee Benefit Trust or an Employer-Financed Retirement Benefit Scheme (EFRBS)) is used to channel what is described as 'disguised remuneration' to an employee or a member of the employee's family in such a way as so to avoid both income tax and national insurance contributions. The new regime applies from 6 April 2011, with transitional provisions from 9 December 2010, and catches the earmarking of income or gains for the future benefit of an individual, including benefits provided through loans and beneficial occupation of accommodation.

[16.16] HMRC have emphasised their view that the 'disguised remuneration' rules will now catch most relevant EBT avoidance arrangements. On 3 March 2011 HMRC issued Spotlight 11 'Avoiding Income Tax on Pay' aimed to forestall the use of products designed to shelter funds in earlier schemes from the effect on the new *Part 7A*. Such arrangements were said to rely on the availability of credit for loan repayments made before 6 April 2012. In HMRC's view, such convoluted arrangements did not succeed in their aim of weaving a way through the legal changes – and even if they did HMRC would still challenge them as delivering remuneration which should have been subject to PAYE on first principles.

[16.17] HMRC issued Spotlight 12 on 23 August 2011, as 'Ineffective Schemes to Avoid the Disguised Remuneration Rules'. The targeted arrangements are said to 'involve payments passing through a series of companies, loans from a third party or an offshore alleged employer, a deed of covenant, secondments from one employer company to another or claims of self-employment, etc'. HMRC warn that they 'will challenge these arrangements and litigate where necessary to recover unpaid tax and National Insurance contributions.

[16.18] Likewise, revised guidance on the operation of the GAAR (see CHAPTER 23) was approved by the Advisory Panel with effect from 30 January 2015 and includes a specific example involving planning designed to side-step the 'Disguised Remuneration' rules – involving the use of 'money-box' companies and 'loan cleansing' – and concludes that such planning would be abusive as it is designed to frustrate the specific purpose of the rules.

[16.19] In Budget 2016 the government announced a further package of measures to tackle the current and historic use of disguised remuneration schemes. Legislation included in *Finance Bill 2016* prevents a relief in the existing legislation from applying where it is used as part of a tax avoidance scheme from Budget Day (16 March 2016). HMRC published a technical note

[16.19] Trusts for Employees

– *Tackling disguised remuneration avoidance schemes overview of changes* – explaining these changes alongside the Budget, which is available here: www.gov.uk/government/publications/tackling-disguised-remuneration-avoidance-schemes-overview-of-changes-and-technical-note. On 10 August 2016, the government issued a further technical consultation – *Tackling Disguised Remuneration* – which details (with draft legislation) further changes to be included in *Finance Bill 2017* (and which is available here: www.gov.uk/government/consultations/tackling-disguised-remuneration-technical-consultation).

[16.20] A more technical point arises in relation to distributions out of discretionary trusts under *ITA 2007, Pt 9, Ch 7, ss 493–498*. *Sections 496A and 496B* (which have enacted Inland Revenue Extra-statutory Concession A68) apply to payments out of a discretionary trust which are taxable as employment income (to which the discretionary payment regime does not strictly apply). While in such a case the employee will not be entitled to his usual tax credit under that regime, the trustees can claim a payment from HMRC subject to conditions. For this the trustees must be UK resident. Where the trustees are non-UK resident they may apply for a payment under *section 496B*, provided that the payments are made out of income: often, of course, they will be made out of capital. The advantage of a trust which is non-UK resident for tax purposes (within *ITA 2007, ss 475–476*) is that it achieves a tax-free roll up on non-UK source income.

[16.21] Trustees of UK resident EBTs may claim compensation payments under *section 496B* in order to alleviate the effect of a double charge to tax on trust income. The double charge would otherwise arise because discretionary payments to employees as beneficiaries are employment income and as a result they are not grossed up and do not carry the normal credit for the tax paid by the trustees. In the absence of the concession tax would be suffered twice, firstly in the hands of the trustees on trust income and again in the hands of the employee/beneficiary where the discretionary payment made out of that trust income is taxed as employment income. The legislation has been drafted to provide a new statutory entitlement to income tax relief for trustees of EBTs in these circumstances. It goes a little further than the previous concession, as explained by HMRC Inheritance Tax and Trusts Newsletter – August 2009, in that:

- relief is also available where some or all of the trust capital of the EBT has been provided by someone other than the employer (for example by a shareholder),
- the claim process has been brought into the self assessment system so claims can be made in the Trust & Estate Tax Return, and
- the repayment will be of income tax (as opposed to a payment of compensation) and repayment supplement will therefore be available, where appropriate.

[16.22] Assuming that the trust was established for bona fide commercial reasons, there will not be a settlement for purposes of the anti-avoidance income tax provisions of *ITTOIA 2005, Pt 5, Ch 5, ss 619–648*. (Contributions by an employer to an employee trust should not attract a liability to national insurance. However, distributions from the trust may attract such a liability as constituting earnings for these purposes.)

Capital gains tax

[16.23] If the trustees are non-UK resident for tax purposes (within *TCGA 1992, s 69*), they will not be liable to capital gains tax on their disposals. Given that the arrangement was established on a commercial rather than a gratuitous basis, the anti-avoidance provisions of *sections 86* and *87* of *TCGA 1992* should not apply (see **26.17–26.51**). Where the trustees are non-UK resident, then, if the arrangement has not been a bona fide commercial one and there is an element of bounty in the establishment of the trust, there could be a liability to capital gains tax on advances out of the trust to beneficiaries under *TCGA 1992, s 87*. If, of course, the trustees are UK resident, they will be chargeable on their gains at 28% on disposals in 2015/16 and 20% on (most) disposals in 2016/17, in the usual way.

[16.24] Note that where *section 13* or *28* of *IHTA 1984* applies to prevent a transfer of value for inheritance tax purposes, a corresponding relief from capital gains tax is provided by *TCGA 1992, s 239*. Any gain arising on the disposal is held over, so that the base cost for the assets in the hands of the trustees is reduced by the held-over gain.

[16.25] If the distribution of shares from an EBT occurs through an unapproved option scheme there will be an income tax liability under *ITEPA 2003, Pt 7, Ch 5, ss 471–484* when the options are exercised, on broadly the excess of the market value of the shares over the sum of the exercise price and any consideration given for the options. The distribution of shares to employees through an approved share option scheme will, however, usually escape an income tax liability on the recipient. Instead, if on subsequent disposal by the employee a gain arises, this will be subject to capital gains tax. In such circumstances, what is his base cost? Traditionally HMRC argued that it was the market value of the option when granted plus any consideration given by the employee on exercise. However, the Court of Appeal, affirming the High Court, decided otherwise in *Mansworth (Inspector or Taxes) v Jelley* [2002] EWCA Civ 1829, [2003] STC 53, 75 TC 1. The asset sold is the shares. Any consideration contributable to the option is irrelevant: *TCGA 1992, s 144(3)* merges the grant of the option into the acquisition of the asset where the option is exercised. Accordingly, since the market value rule under *TCGA 1992, s 17(1)* applies – both because the option was granted at other than arm's length and because it was granted to an employee – it is the market value of the shares when the option was exercised which forms the base cost. It is unclear how *Mansworth v Jelley* interacts with *TCGA 1992, s 149A* which prevents the application of *section 17(1)* where options are granted to employees by trustees. Many employees have benefited from the decision in claiming repayments of tax, subject to the time limits for self assessment. As widely predicted, the decision in *Mansworth v Jelley* was statutorily reversed by *FA 2003, s 158* in relation to the exercise of options on or after 10 April 2003, by introducing into *TCGA 1992* new *section 144ZA*. The new rule was itself exploited after 9 April 2003, by carefully constructed option arrangements designed to ensure that the actual consideration rather than the market

[16.25] Trusts for Employees

value of the underlying asset was the value taken into account for capital gains tax purposes. However, *F(No 2)A 2005, Sch 5* then introduced into *TCGA 1992 ss 144ZB, ZC* and *ZD* in relation to options exercised on or after 2 December 2004 to block the opportunity which was left open following 9 April 2003. On 12 May 2009 HMRC published revised guidance on allowable deductions following the sale of shares acquired by exercising employee share options (see *Revenue & Customs Brief 30/09*).

[16.26] There has been an (interesting) postscript to the *Mansworth v Jelley* decision in the Court of Appeal, but of more general application. A taxpayer, Mr Monro wanted to amend his self assessment out of time, following the Court of Appeal decision, to take advantage of it. However, his application was refused by both the High Court and the Court of Appeal, on the grounds that the self assessment was made in accordance with the practice generally prevailing at the time and therefore no error or mistake claim could be made under what was then *TMA 1970, s 33* (*Monro v Revenue and Customs Comrs* [2008] EWCA Civ 306, [2009] Ch 69, [2008] 3 WLR 734).

[16.27] Most recently, there remain a number of outstanding *Mansworth v Jelley* capital loss claims. HMRC were writing to all affected taxpayers in February 2012 inviting them to withdraw their claims and, if a taxpayer would not do so, undertaking to review the case on an individual basis. However, in particular, for those taxpayers who adopted the latter course, evidence suggests that HMRC simply sent out a standard letter in response. In that letter they rejected any basis of a 'legitimate expectation' argument on the part of the taxpayer, saying that, notwithstanding any action taken following the date of the Court of Appeal judgment in December 2002, the taxpayer remains in the same position as they were when they undertook the initial transaction which gave rise to the loss (which, apart from the Court of Appeal decision, they did not know they had). To say that the taxpayer necessarily remains in the same position seems disingenuous. In particular, a taxpayer may well have triggered a disposal of the gain in reliance on HMRC's statement following the Court of Appeal judgment, purely in order to be able to use the loss, quite apart from any other action taken in reliance on HMRC's various statements. Generally, see *Revenue and Customs Briefs 30/09* (Shares acquired before 10 April 2003 by exercising employee share options – allowable deductions) and *60/09* (HMRC's responses to questions raised on *Brief 30/9*).

[16.28] It was reported in *Taxation* on 10 June 2014 that a department body for advising on tax dispute policy has noted that it would be appropriate for the HMRC to allow the taxpayers' claims for *Mansworth v Jelley* losses in certain cases. The announcement follows an HMRC CGT liaison group meeting at which representatives requested an update of the status of such cases under enquiry.

[16.29] The personal tax contentious issues panel considered whether tax officials could use their collection and management powers to give taxpayers the benefit of incorrect guidance when they could realistically show they relied on the information to their detriment. HMRC's legal advice was that the taxpayers did not have sufficient evidence to support their claims and would not succeed at judicial review – but the lapse of time since the guidance was published in 2003 makes evidence difficult to locate.

[16.30] The panel agreed that, in certain cases, it would be appropriate for the HMRC to allow claims for losses. The cases would be those in which:

- Taxpayers can make a realistic case that they relied on incorrect guidance;
- The taxpayer would suffer detriment if the losses were denied; and
- There would have been a legitimate expectation except that the tax department's delay in working the enquiry means that the level of evidence officials are able to provide is limited.

HMRC have to date agreed three claims that fell within the criteria.

[16.31] More recently, in *The Queen on the application of Ralph Hely-Hutchinson v HMRC* [2015] EWHC 3261 the taxpayer won an application for Judicial Review of HMRC's handling of his *Mansworth v Jelley* loss claims. The High Court found that the taxpayer had relied upon clear HMRC guidance and that he had a legitimate expectation that his loss claims would be allowed, notwithstanding that HMRC had later changed its view. HMRC should also have taken into account the fact that other taxpayers in an identical position were treated differently, and that this created an intrinsic unfairness. It is understood that HMRC intends to appeal the decision.

The deductibility of a loan from an EBT

[16.32] As described above, EBTs were frequently used to provide benefit to employees in the form of loans (interest free or otherwise). One of the 'advertised' benefits of such loans was that they would constitute a deductible liability in the estate of the employee in the event of his or her death (and with, in some cases, an implicit assumption that the trustees might not seek repayment or might, as long as it is could be done without any further income tax charge, write off the loan post-death). The author has always been sceptical about the idea that such loans were *necessarily* deductible – his concern being that in some circumstances HMRC might invoke *FA 1986, s 103* (which denies deductible to certain 'circular' loans). In any event, radical changes to the inheritance tax rules for the deduction of liabilities have significantly undermined the effectiveness of such planning.

[16.33] With effect from 17 July 2013, *IHTA 1984, s 175A* provides that a liability will be deductible on death only to the extent that it is repaid. There is an exemption where there is a real commercial reason for non-payment *and* non-repayment is not part of any arrangements the main purpose of which is securing a tax advantage. There is also *deemed* to be a 'real commercial reason' where the debt is due to someone dealing at arm's length (eg a standard bank loan) or that if it were to such a person, they would not require repayment; however, it seems clear that this exemption would not apply to a debt due to an EBT. Indeed, it is thought that countering the use of non-discharged EBT loans was one of the reasons for the change in the legislation (which, given the wide exemption for 'third party' loans, is narrowly targeted).

[16.34] The new legislation applies to all loans in existence at 17 July 2013, and thus in addition to deterring (alongside the 'Disguised Remuneration' legislation) the use of loans from new EBTs, it creates problems for existing structures. Anyone dying now owing money to an EBT, faces a difficult choice. Unless the funds are repaid, there will be no IHT deduction; however, if the funds *are* repaid, the 'Disguised Remuneration' legislation will make it extremely difficult to get the funds out of the EBT again without a large tax charge.

Settlement opportunity

[16.35] On 20 April 2011, HMRC offered an opportunity to employers who have used EBTs (and similar arrangements) to resolve outstanding enquiries without recourse to litigation, on the basis of the existing law. HMRC wrote to all employers or companies who had open EBT enquiries before the end of August 2011 to invite discussion about potential settlements. If no response was received by 31 December 2011 HMRC would assume that the employer or company was not interested in engaging in the settlement offer and would look to progress enquiries formally. HMRC subsequently waived that deadline and continue to invite employers to contact them in relation to their EBT settlement offer. This settlement offer was withdrawn from 31 March 2015.

Employee Ownership Trusts (EOTs)

[16.36] One might have imagined, given the considerable history of avoidance and anti-avoidance associated with EBTs, that the government would hesitate to introduce any new reliefs in relation to employee trusts; however, the objective of increased employee involvement appears to remain a strong one because *Finance Act 2014, Sch 37* introduced a new category of employee trust – the Employee Ownership Trust, or EOT, which, in HMRC's words (see IHTM42995) is a trust 'designed to encourage employee ownership of the company they work for'. The qualification conditions for an EOT are strict (see **16.37**); however, EOTs attract new (and in the case of the first, highly significant) capital gains tax (see **16.38–16.40**) and income tax (see **16.41**) benefits, as well as many of the same inheritance tax benefits associated with EBTs.

Qualification conditions

[16.37] The EOT qualification conditions, now contained in clauses *TCGA 1992, ss 236H-236U*, comprise (broadly):

- The '*trading*' requirement [*TCGA 1992, s 236I*]– the shares held by the EOT have to be of a single trading company or of the principal company of a trading group.
- The '*all-employee benefit*' requirement [*TCGA 1992, s 236J – 236L*]– the EOT deed must ensure that property can be applied only for the benefit of all eligible employees *on the same terms* (referred to as 'the equality requirement'). Employees and office holders otherwise holding (by themselves or with connected persons) 5% or more of the com-

pany's shares are excluded from the class of eligible employees. There are also restrictions on the use of sub-trusts, loans to employees and transfers to other trusts.

- The *'controlling interest'* requirement [TCGA 1992, s 236M]– the trustees must hold more than 50% of the company's share capital and exercise a majority of the votes. Given that one of key EOT benefits relates to the disposal of shares to it (see below), this condition needs to be met only at the end of the year in which a disposal takes place (ie the disposal itself can contribute to this condition being met).
- The 'limited participation' requirement [TCGA 1992, s 236N]– The number of continuing 5% participators who are directors or employees (and connected parties) must not exceed 40% of the total number of employees.

Capital gains tax

[16.38] The key capital gains tax benefit of an EOT is that, on or after 6 April 2014, where a person (other than a company) disposes of ordinary shares in the company to the EOT, the transaction takes place on a no gain, no loss basis (*TCGA 1992, s 236H*), and this is whether or not the disposal is for consideration, full or otherwise.

[16.39] It should be noted, however, that 'clawback' rules can apply if certain 'disqualifying events' occur. As might be imagined, this involves a breach of one or more of the requirements outlined at **16.37**. If a disqualifying event occurs in the tax year following that of the disposal, *the disposing shareholder* cannot claim the relief or, if it has already been claimed, it must be revoked [*TCGA 1992, s 236O*]. In subsequent years, a disqualifying event results in a deemed disposal of shares by the trustees of the EOT [*TCGA 1992, s 236P*].

[16.40] Otherwise, there are no specific capital gains tax reliefs applying to the disposal of shares by the trustees of an EOT, the treatment being the same as for an EBT (see **16.23–16.31**).

Income tax

[16.41] The key income tax benefit is that, on or after 1 October 2014, bonus payments made by a company owned by an EOT to qualifying employees on a 'same terms' basis are exempt from income tax up to £3,600 per tax year [*ITEPA 2003, ss 312A-312I*].

Inheritance tax

[16.42] Because is it conceivable that a trust could qualify as an EOT while not qualifying as an EBT for the purposes of *IHTA 1984, s 86* (see IHTM42996) *Finance Act 2014, Sch 37* introduced a number of amendments to the inheritance tax legislation – effective for transfers on or after 6 April 2014 – to ensure, broadly, that an EOT would attract a similar treatment to an EBT, ie:

[16.42] Trusts for Employees

- *IHTA 1984, s 86(3)(d)* provides that an EOT that meets the trading, controlling interest and all-employee benefit requirements (see **16.37**) qualifies as a '*s 86*' trust for inheritance tax purposes;
- *IHTA 1984, s 13A* provides that the transfer by a close company to such a trust is not a transfer of value;
- *IHTA 1984, s 28A* mirrors this position in the case of a transfer by an individual; and
- *IHTA 1984, ss 72(3A)* and *75A* provides exemptions to certain exit and '*s 72*' type charges.

[16.43] The *s 13A* provision is worth noting. In the right circumstances, it provides a mechanism by which an EOT can be funded by a company, potentially then enabling the EOT to acquire a controlling interest in the company from a majority shareholder for full consideration.

Chapter 17

Starting a Trust: Tax and Tax Planning

Overview

[17.1] Transfers of property, whether cash, shares, land or anything else, to trustees will move the ownership of that property from the settlor to the trustees. This may occur both on setting up the trust and when property is added to a trust. This chapter considers the tax implications of transfers to a trust.

[17.2] Ideally, any one settlement will have just one settlor. From time to time one comes across husband and wife settlements, that is the one settlement made by both spouses, which the author dislikes in principle, as account must be kept not only at outset but during the currency of the trust of the tax implications of property deriving from each settlor. Similarly, and worse, is the case where an individual contributes to a settlement made by someone other than his spouse or civil partner: it is best avoided as tax law, though not trust law (in general terms) will regard there as being within the one formal settlement two or more settlements for tax purposes.

[17.3] The only income tax point to consider is that following the transfer, income will start to arise for both substantive and compliance purposes to the transferee trustees in place of the transferor settlor. That said, there are anti-avoidance rules outlined in CHAPTER 4 which may, for tax purposes, treat income or indeed capital (and before 2008/09 chargeable gains) as remaining with the settlor.

[17.4] More interesting are the capital gains tax, inheritance tax and stamp duties implications of a gift to the trustees, each of which is examined in this chapter. They will not apply to gifts to charitable trusts which will be broadly exempt from such taxes, as explained at 14.10–14.14.

[17.5] One other point should be appreciated. It is likely that the fiscal thinking behind the settlement of an asset is the inheritance tax mitigation motive for getting the asset out of the settlor's chargeable estate. Had the asset remained in the estate until death, its then value would have attracted inheritance tax on death at up to 40% (at current rates and subject to any available exemptions); however, for capital gains tax purposes there would, at that point, also have been the familiar tax-free uplift to market value provided by *TCGA 1992, s 62* (under which no chargeable gain accrues and the recipient beneficiary takes the asset at its then market value). If the asset is settled, the inherent gain is at best (following a hold-over relief election) preserved within the trust with the potential for a chargeable gain to arise in the future on a disposal by the trustees (subject to the possibility of deferral by a further hold-over should that occur by way of advance to a beneficiary). Although, a deferral of capital gains is to be preferred to an immediate charge (and incurring an immediate capital gains tax charge so as to achieve a future inheritance tax saving is only rarely sensible); it needs to be remembered that this is still not as good as a full 'uplift'. There is then usually an inherent capital gains tax downside in the transfer of chargeable assets into trust.

Compliance on setting up a trust

[17.6] The requirements to notify HMRC for each of capital gains tax, inheritance tax and stamp taxes purposes have their own rules and time limits, as explained below. For ongoing income tax and capital gains tax purposes, HMRC Trusts and Estates (whether at Nottingham, Edinburgh or Truro) need to be given details of the new settlement, so that they can establish a tax record and issue a unique tax reference. While that information can be given to HMRC in any form, it is convenient and recognised good practice for the non-statutory Form 41G (Trust) to be completed and submitted to HMRC Trusts. As for personal representatives, the Edinburgh Office of HMRC Trusts deals with large estates in administration. Relatively small estates are left with the districts of the deceased.

[17.7] A new rebranded and resigned Form 41G (Trust) was published in 2015 and is available at www.gov.uk/government/publications/trusts-and-estates-trust-details-41g-trust. The content has not changed apart from 2 additions which HMRC hope customers will find helpful:

- a request to complete authorisation form 64-8 if a professional agent is acting together with a link to a copy of form 64-8 and supporting guidance.
- a link to guidance on trusts for vulnerable people.

Form 41G (Trust)

[17.8] The information requested on the form is as follows, divided into five parts, to which the author has added numbering below. The form largely speaks for itself, though reference will be made to various issues that arise, in what follows.

Part A—Complete for each new trust created, whether by living settlor, Will or intestacy, deed of variation or family arrangement

Trust

(1)   Full title of the trust.

Trustees

(2)   Full names and addresses (including postcodes) of the trustees. *State first the trustee to whom return forms should normally be sent. Continue on a separate sheet if necessary.*

(3)   Contact details of any professional agent acting. If no professional agent acting, give trustee's telephone number in the space below. Where a professional is acting, there is a request for a form 64-8 to be completed and attached.

(4)   Is the trust governed by the law of a country outside the UK? Is the trust's general administration carried on outside the UK? Is the trust established under Scots law? Is the trust employment-related? Is this a trust for a vulnerable beneficiary?

Part B—Complete if the trust is established by a Will or intestacy.

The deceased

(5)   Full name and last address of the deceased.
(6)   Date of death.
(7)   Date trust commenced.
(8)   HMRC office that dealt with the deceased's last Tax Return or received the probate, letters of administration, etc.
(9)   Reference in that office **or** National Insurance number.

Administration period

(10) Has the administration period ended and if so when? If yes, the date it ended.

Part C—Complete if the trust was established by deed of variation or family arrangement.

Boxes to be ticked only if the trust established by the deed of variation or family arrangement is one of the following:

(11) Additional to the Will trust? If so, complete part B and also give details at part A.
(12) A replacement for the Will trust? If so, do not complete part B but give details at part A.

In either case, complete Part D to give details of each person who took less under the deed than they would have done under the Will – each person is a settlor of the amount given up.

Part D—Complete if the trust was established in the settlor's lifetime.

(13) Date trust established (if under a deed of variation, etc, this is the date of the deed).

Settlor

(14) Full name and address of settlor. Where there is more than one settlor you should give details for each, using a separate sheet if necessary.
(15) HMRC office that deals with the settlor's tax affairs.
(16) Reference in that office **or** National Insurance number.

Part E—Complete for all trusts

Assets settled

(17) Give details of the assets settled by each settlor, including values. Use a separate sheet if necessary. *If land or buildings, state the address. If shares, state number, class and Company Registration Number.*
(18) The form must be signed and dated, with a note of the capacity in which the form is signed, eg whether settlor, trustee, solicitor, etc.

Capital gains tax

[17.9] The transfer of sterling cash does not trigger a chargeable gain [*TCGA 1992, s 251(1)*]. However, a transfer of currency other than sterling may produce a chargeable gain, at least before 6 April 2012 [*TCGA 1992, s 252*]. The only exception, unlikely to apply in the present context, is the extent to which a sum in the foreign currency bank account represents currency acquired by the holder for the personal expenditure outside the UK of himself or his family or dependants (including expenditure on the provision or maintenance of any residence outside the UK). There is an equivalent exemption for foreign currency cash in *section 269*.

[17.10] As from 6 April 2012, gains arising on all sums within a foreign currency bank account have been removed from the scope of capital gains tax. This let-out applies only to an individual, trustees and personal representatives [*TCGA 1992, s 252* as amended by *FA 2012, s 35*].

[17.11] There is a variety of other reliefs and exemptions such as on the disposal of private main residences [*TCGA 1992, ss 222–226B*] discussed at 7.51–7.57 and so on, though generally beyond the scope of this book. Subject thereto, the transfer of any other asset will be a chargeable disposal which may give rise to either a chargeable gain or an allowable loss, though the latter may be subject to restriction in its use.

[17.12] An individual's capital gains tax position is determined for the tax year. So, for 2014/15 and 2015/16, any chargeable gains made during the tax year are netted off against any allowable losses. To the extent that the net total does not exceed the annual exempt amount for the year, £11,100 for 2015/16 and 2016/17, there is no capital gains tax liability, though (depending on the details) individual disposals may have to be recorded on the self assessment return. If the total exceeds the year's annual exemption, use may be made of any brought forward losses to bring the total down to the threshold. Otherwise there will be a positive liability, except to the extent that it can be reduced or eliminated by hold-over relief: see below. As to losses, there is a restriction which applies both to current year and to brought forward losses. Because the settlor is a 'connected person' with the trustees, (*TCGA 1992, s 286(3)(a)*), a loss which accrues on a disposal by settlor to trustees will be a restricted connected party loss, deductible only from a chargeable gain accruing on a disposal by him to the same set of trustees, whether in that or in a subsequent year [*TCGA 1992, s 18(3)*].

Hold-over relief

[17.13] This relief can apply just as much to gains accruing on an advancement of capital by the trustees to a beneficiary as on the transfer of assets by the settlor to the trustees and, as such, is dealt with in more detail in CHAPTER 7 on capital gains tax at 7.60–7.82. The effect of a valid election to hold-over relief, which must be made on an asset by asset basis, is to reduce the acquisition cost of the trustees by the amount of the 'held over' gain. This is the chargeable gain which would have accrued to the settlor but for the election, so in effect causing the trust to inherit the settlor's own base cost, preserving the accrued gain in the hands of the trustees until such time as they come to dispose of the asset.

The two categories

[17.14] There are two separate heads of hold-over relief: (a) chargeable transfers for inheritance tax purposes and (b) defined business assets [*TCGA 1992, s 260 and s 165* respectively]. Transfers to almost all lifetime trusts will fall within *section 260*, whether or not business assets are concerned – and it will only be where a lifetime settlement is made to a qualifying interest in possession trusts (which, in terms of lifetime trust, will now include only disabled trusts) that *s 260* hold-over will not be possible.

[17.15] However, neither head of hold-over can apply where the transferee settlement is 'settlor-interested' see **7.81** generally where the settlor, spouse/civil partner or minor child (including a step child) could benefit). This is provided by *section 169B*. Further, even if at the time of settlement the trust is not settlor-interested and hold-over relief is given, there can be a claw-back of relief under *section 169C* if the settlement becomes settlor-interested within six years after the end of the year of assessment in which the disposal was made. Interestingly, despite the general reduction from five years and ten months to four years after the end of the tax year for making claims to relief, this period has not been reduced. And it is worth noting that the conditions for claw-back of relief to apply include not just the case where within that period the settlement becomes settlor-interested, but also if within that period 'an arrangement subsists under which such an interest will or may be acquired by a settlor'. This is an anti-avoidance provision to prevent availability of hold-over where a settlor might acquire an interest in a settlement after expiry of the six year period, however improbable.

Claiming hold-over relief

[17.16] The claim is made, typically though not necessarily within a self assessment return, on HMRC Helpsheet HS 295. On 1 April 2010 the time limit for making the claim was reduced to four years after the end of the tax year in which the disposal was made, having previously been five years and ten months from that time (the *Finance Act 2008 Schedule 39 (Appointed Day, Transitional Provisions and Savings) Order 2009, SI 2009/403*, pursuant to *FA 2008, s 188 and Sch 39, para 12*). The settlor must indicate on HS 295 whether the claim is made under *section 260* or under *section 165*. Statement of Practice SP 8/92 confirms that, while it may be usual for the claim to include a computation of the gain, that is not necessary for the claim to be valid.

[17.17] Of course, it should also be remembered that in some circumstances – for example, where capital gains tax Entrepreneurs' Relief is available in full (see **7.102–7.106**) – it may be preferable to trigger an immediate capital gains tax charge which is eligible for relief, rather than to hold over gains which might become chargeable without relief in the short to medium term (eg on an early disposal by the trustees).

Payment of tax

[17.18] Any capital gains tax payable for a tax year is due on or before the 31 January following the end of the tax year, so in relation to 2015/16, or on before 31 January 2017 and in relation to 2017/18 on or before 31 January 2018. The rate of tax for disposals by an individual between 23 June 2010 and 5 April 2016 is either 18% or, to the extent that when the taxable gain is added to the taxpayer's taxable income would if income attract the higher rates, 28%. From 6 April 2016, these rates remain for disposal of residential property (not covered by main residence relief) and 'carried interest', but reduce to 10% and 20% respectively for all other disposals (see CHAPTER 7 for further details).

[17.19] It may be that the parties intend to submit a hold-over claim, which in the case of a disposal in 2015/16 must be made before 6 April 2020, but if not done before the due payment date tax must be paid and (if a hold-over claim is made later) subsequently reclaimed with the benefit of repayment interest currently running at a rate of 0.5% [*Taxes and Duties, etc (Interest Rate) Regulations 2011, SI 2011/2446* with effect from 31 October 2011, replacing the *Taxes and Duties (Interest Rate) Regulations 2010, SI 2010/1879*].

Inheritance tax

[17.20] The 'alignment of inheritance tax for trusts' with effect from 22 March 2006 has at least simplified the inheritance tax implications of making a trust, even if the position has become rather worse for settlors who wish to achieve the protection of a settled structure for assets which exceed the nil-rate band in value and which attract neither agricultural nor business property relief. The gift into settlement will be a transfer of value, in reducing the value of the settlor's estate [*IHTA 1984, s 3*] by way of a chargeable transfer. Only if the gift is to a qualifying disabled trust (see **15.7–15.11**), will the transfer of value be a potentially exempt transfer within *IHTA 1984, s 3A*. In that event whatever the amount of the transfer of value the gift will be exempt except in the case where the settlor dies within seven years.

The small exemptions

[17.21] Either of the annual £3,000 exemption or the 'normal expenditure out of income' exemption may apply to reduce the chargeable transfer [*IHTA 1984, s 19* and *s 21* respectively]. If, for 2016/17 say the full £3,000 is given away any remaining part of the 2015/16 exemption may be used in that year (though cannot be carried forward further). For the normal expenditure exemption to apply it must be shown that the gift forms part of a series, not necessarily of the same amount each time or indeed to the same donee, made by the donor out of his post-tax income which can be shown to be part of his normal expenditure, ie not made out of capital.

Compliance issues

[17.22] The detail of Form IHT100 for reporting the chargeable transfer subject to *de minimis* limits and the time for payment of tax are discussed at CHAPTER 21.

[17.23] The date on which a trust is made and property is transferred to the trustees is determined by the passing of a beneficial rather than a legal interest in the property. In a 2010 case the Court of Session unanimously accepted that the transfers of value had been made before 22 March 2006 so as to constitute a valid accumulation and maintenance trust (and not, as HMRC argued, after that date, so that they would have been chargeable transfers). Holding that the transfers were potentially exempt, the Court allowed the appeals, applying the principles laid down in the estate duty case of *Thomas v Lord Advocate* (1953) 32 ATC 18, [1953] TR 19. The gratuitous dispositions of land were executed and delivered to the trustees on 15 March 2006, but they were not registered in the Register of Sasines until 10 October and 16 October 2006 respectively. The Court of Session held that the transfers of value occurred when the gratuitous disposition of heritable subjects in Scotland was delivered to the transferee rather than when it was recorded in the register of Sasines. Further, HMRC's argument that there was no completed gift until registration had occurred was mistaken (*Marquess of Linlithgow v HMRC (and related appeal)* CS [2010] STC 1563). HMRC's arguments seem very odd (although perhaps the amounts at stake might have been large), certainly in the context of clear findings by the Court in eg *Re Rose* [1949] Ch 78 with share transfers that it was the date of the transfer form not the date of registration in the company's books which determined the date of transfer. There is a clear distinction between the legal and (as relevant for tax purposes) the beneficial interest. That said, there may be cases, typically involving private companies, where the transfer of value will take place after the date of the transfer form, for example where there are pre-emption rights (when it will not be until all potential purchasers of the shares have been eliminated) or perhaps where certain transfers of shares require board approval: even so, in either case, this may be before the date of registration. The point might also be relevant more generally in terms of determining the date of the transfer of value which constitutes a potentially exempt transfer under the current regime, in terms of starting the seven year risk period.

DOTAS

[17.24] Anyone transferring property to a trust will need to consider the Disclosure of Tax Avoidance Schemes legislation as it applies to inheritance tax. This is dealt with at 23.17–23.23. In the majority of cases, these rules will not be in point but it is nevertheless important to check.

Stamp taxes

[17.25] There are three forms of stamp tax:

[17.25] Starting a Trust: Tax and Tax Planning

(1) Stamp duty – now limited to paper transfers of shares and marketable securities;
(2) Stamp duty reserve tax (SDRT) – on agreements to transfer marketable securities for a consideration; and
(3) Stamp duty land tax (SDLT) – on transfers of UK land (outside Scotland).
(4) Land and buildings transaction tax (LBTT) – on transfers of land in Scotland.

The rates of stamp duty and SDRT are standardly 0.5% (though a rate of 1.5% applies to the issue of a depository receipt for chargeable securities or the entry of chargeable securities into a clearance system). LBTT is charged at rates of up to 15%, and with very different rates applying for residential and non-residential property, and where land is acquired by a 'non-natural person'. The rules are set out in detail in Chapter 13.

[17.26] For all types of stamp tax, there is an exception for gifts. The only catch, with all types of property though most particularly likely to apply to land, is that the transfer of property subject to a liability or in consideration of the discharge of a liability is treated as being for a consideration equal to the amount of the liability concerned. This is discussed in more detail at **13.35**. In the case of land it may well be that the amount of the liability is within the nil-rate threshold although there may still be compliance implications as discussed at **13.35**.

Charities

[17.27] Gifts to charitable trusts are generally exempt from all of capital gains tax, inheritance tax and stamp taxes and are discussed in **14.2–14.14**.

Tax planning

[17.28] Before the terms of the trust are finalised, consider how the various tax regimes might impact upon the drafting. For example, it is almost axiomatic that both settlor and spouse/civil partner should be irrevocably excluded from benefit, to avoid assessment of the trustees' income on the settlor (see **4.3**) and to prevent the trust property being treated as included within the settlor's estate on death under the reservation of benefit regime (see **8.36–8.40**).

[17.29] The advantage for capital gains tax purposes is that, excluding settlor and spouse/civil partner (together with their minor children) will mean that any gains arising on the transfer into trust will be capable of hold-over (see **17.16** and **7.81**).

[17.30] There are two principal types of income structure: (a) one or more fixed interests where under the beneficiary/beneficiaries is/are entitled to the income as it arises, net of proper trustee expenses (called an interest in possession); and (b) a discretionary trust where the trustees have a discretion to distribute income among a class of beneficiaries.

[17.31] For trusts made now this distinction is immaterial for both capital gains tax and inheritance tax purposes, though it was at one time relevant for each of those taxes in its own way. However, there are two income tax points, both going to the rate of tax payable. First, trustees of a discretionary (or accumulation) trust must, subject to income falling within the £1,000 standard rate band, pay tax at a maximum rate of 45% (with slightly lower rates for dividends) in 2015/16 and 2016/17, and, as explained at **5.13**, such tax is payable by the trustees even in cases where the trust is settlor-interested; the settlor is credited with the tax paid by the trustees in his own self assessment. By contrast, to the extent that the income arises to one or more beneficiaries as of right (ie under the terms of an interest in possession trust), the trustees cannot be liable to tax at more than the basic 20% rate, as appropriate; albeit that (subject to the tax credit provided by the trustees) any beneficiary will be taxed at his or her marginal rates on the income. (For details of trustees' income tax rates see **6.45–6.58**).

[17.32] Secondly, as illustrated by the Example at **6.73**, a beneficiary who receives a distribution of dividend income from a discretionary trust will suffer a much greater effective rate of income tax than had he received it as of right via an interest in possession trust. Similarly, the new (from 2016/17) *personal savings* and *dividend* allowances can only be available to beneficiaries receiving savings or dividend income from an interest in possession. Income received from a discretionary trust loses its income 'character' for these purposes.

The nil-rate band trust: inheritance tax planning

[17.33] The level of the nil-rate band threshold has not increased substantively in recent years. Frozen at £325,000 since 2010/11 (previously until the end of 2017/18), the first Conservative 2015 Summer Budget has announced a further freezing to the end of 2021/22. The threshold stood at £255,000 in 2003/04 and at £150,000 in 1993/94. The Conservative Party had promised that if elected it would introduce a nil-rate band of £1m. Under the Coalition Government such a policy was not implemented; however, David Cameron confirmed in early 2014 that this remained the aspiration of the Conservative Party. As it has turned out, this policy commitment was fulfilled by the announcement in the 2015 Summer Budget of an additional nil-rate band for family homes of £175,000 (which when added to the main nil-rate band produces £1m per couple). This, however, will be phased in (£100,000 in 2017/18; £125,000 in 2018/19; £150,000 in 2019/20) and will not reach £175,000 until 2020/21. (See further CHAPTER 18).

[17.34] Consider a married couple starting to consider inheritance tax mitigation seriously (in their late 50s, say?) and making a nil-rate band trust every seven years. Assume survival until age 80 or thereabouts. This might enable three exempt 'bites at the cherry'. Assuming a constant nil-rate band of £325,000 this would get just £1.95m out of the combined estates, so prospectively saving some £780,000 in inheritance tax. By contrast, if they were wealthy enough to give away £6m between them over that period, the saving increases to £2.4m, always assuming non-relievable property. As the major concern for the older generation is often the possible vulnerability of their children (matrimonial entanglements or personal insolvency), the use of a trust carries a potent incentive. Interestingly, research initiated by the last Government in mid-2004 and published in January 2007 reported that in general terms the reason why people made trusts was not so much as to avoid tax as to retain control over assets which they wanted to give away to their children or other relatives (see HMRC news release 4 January 2007).

[17.35] For the income tax reasons explained in CHAPTER 6 a lifetime nil-rate band trust is likely to be interest in possession in form subject to overriding powers of appointment. It goes without saying that under this and all succeeding suggestions the settlor and spouse/civil partner should be irrevocably excluded from benefit, to ensure no reservation of benefit for inheritance tax purposes – and to prevent any income tax liability for the settlor.

Agricultural and business property

[17.36] The conditions for the reliefs for such property may be found at **18.28–18.75**. In summary, they go (separately for each relief) to the type of property and the period of ownership. But suppose that the intending settlor has such property in his beneficial ownership. He can settle any amount as a chargeable transfer but reduced to zero (in the case of 100% relieved property) or otherwise 50% of its value, for inheritance tax purposes.

[17.37] Against the risk of the settlor's death within the following seven years, steps should be taken to ensure that the negative claw-back conditions discussed at **18.66–18.70** do not apply retrospectively to deny relief. In particular, the trustees should take care to ensure that they continue to hold the original property given away or, if sold in an arm's length sale, qualifying replacement property up to the full value net of incidental costs of disposal and acquisition and that it continues to qualify for relief in their hands. There is one perhaps surprising exception: where it is shares in a trading company which are given away and the settlor dies within seven years, it does not matter if the company has then become an investment company not attracting business property relief [*IHTA 1984, s 113A(3A)(b)*].

[17.38] Interestingly, in this case, should the settlor reserve a benefit, there may still be relief on death in the case of agricultural property where the benefit is reserved because of occupation (given the two year occupation test in *IHTA 1984, s 117(a)*) or, more generally, for both business and agricultural property because of the very useful deeming provisions of *FA 1986, Sch 20, para 8*. That said, one would ordinarily plan to avoid any reservation of benefit from the outset.

[17.39] As with the other lifetime trusts made now, the trust fund will enter the relevant property regime, with its system of ten-year and exit charges, which should not be of concern, subject to the rate of business or agricultural property relief in force remaining at 100% at the relevant time. The well-known exit charge trap should be mentioned. That is, merely because no inheritance tax is payable on entry, this does not mean that whatever the value on exit within the first ten years there will necessarily be no tax to pay. In computing the exit charge, *IHTA 1984, s 68(5)(a)* assumes the *gross* not the *net* value of the gift in calculating the rate. This is because the settled property has to be valued immediately after the settlement commences and at this time, because the trustees could not yet meet the two-year ownership condition, no business or agricultural property relief could be available to them. The fact that there may be a positive rate will be academic if the chargeable property qualifies for relief in the hands of the trustees at the time of the relevant property charge. However, if, for example, the original property had been sold and re-invested in non-qualifying property, it could well lead to an actual charge to tax.

Bare trusts

[17.40] These are worth a mention, though unlikely to be hugely attractive, in that we are assuming an amount settled in excess of the nil-rate band (see also 2.44–2.48). There will be no substantive protection against claims in matrimonial proceedings or by a trustee in bankruptcy, so far as the donee is concerned. (By contrast, had the property been settled, and the trustees are not directed to maintain the bankrupt beneficiary of a discretionary trust but are merely empowered to do so (ie a 'true' discretionary trust), the beneficiary is entitled only to require the trustee(s) to consider from time to time whether or not to make a distribution in his/her favour.) Unless and until such distribution is made, his creditors are not entitled to any part of the trust fund. Notwithstanding the breadth of definition of a bankrupt's property under the *Insolvency Act 1986, s 283*, his interest under a discretionary trust is a mere hope ('*spes*')). However, it may be thought that, especially where the trustees are a couple of hardened professional advisers (as opposed to parents or family members), a bare trust may prove to be one line of protection in practice. The beneficiary is going to receive the income as of right and the trustees may be favourably disposed to requests from the beneficial owner of the capital from time to time, eg in relatively modest amounts to finance a new business venture, although the trustees have no right to refuse a direction from the beneficial adult owner to transfer the capital to him. For all of inheritance tax, capital gains tax and income tax purposes the settlement is treated as if it were absolute ownership: the compliance implications for trust returns were highlighted in HMRC's Inheritance Tax & Trusts Newsletter of June 2010. And so for inheritance tax purposes there is simply a potentially exempt transfer to an individual.

Defeasible absolute interests: 'non-settlements'?

[17.41] The definition of 'settlement' for inheritance tax purposes in *IHTA 1984, s 43(2)* includes the cases where the property is held (a) in trust for persons in succession or for any person subject to a contingency; or (b) on accumulation or discretionary trusts; or (c) so that property is charged with the payment of an annuity. The question then is this: is the transfer of property to trustees for an individual absolutely subject to a power for the trustees to be able to defeat that interest (eg by appointing the property to other individuals whether named or within a class) a 'settlement' as defined? The suggestion was being made on the lecture circuit in around 2007/08 that it is not (it being hard to see that such a structure fits happily into any of the definitions under section 43(2)), but the better view is that such a structure is indeed caught as a statutory settlement. Of course, were HMRC, somewhat improbably, to agree that such an interest was not a settlement, it would carry the inheritance tax advantage of being treated as an outright gift, ie a potentially exempt transfer (albeit for property for capital gains tax purposes) while carrying the protection of ownership by the trustees. For income tax purposes the beneficiary would be entitled to the income as it arose.

Sales at an under-value

[17.42] Suppose that the settlor wants to settle property in excess of the nil-rate band. He might make a sale of that property to the trustees for a consideration equal to the excess over the nil-rate band. Thus property worth £1 million would be sold for £700,000, reducing the transfer of value to £300,000 which would be left outstanding on loan account, non-interest bearing and repayable on demand. This would limit the chargeable transfer to £300,000, but would ensure that any growth in value accrued to the trust. Typically the loan would be repaid on sale of the trust asset if not on death of the principal beneficiary. If the trust asset is land or shares, stamp duty land tax or stamp duty would be payable by the trustees on the consideration.

[17.43] Hold-over relief from capital gains tax under *TCGA 1992, s 260* would be available (to the extent that the consideration exceeds the allowable expenditure: *TCGA 1992, s 260(5)*). For income tax it has been thought important that it is a life interest and not a discretionary settlement, given the provisions of *ITTOIA 2005, ss 633–642* imposing an income tax charge on the settlor in the event that the loan is repaid at some stage, if there were undistributed income in the structure, however unlikely. However, for the reasons mentioned at 4.30, this is now seen to be a 'non-point' (except possibly in the case of dividend income).

[17.44] The only caution to be expressed with this suggestion is the argument that a loan by the settlor to the trustees on beneficial terms gives the settlor an interest in the income of the trust (following cases such as *Jenkins v IRC* [1944] 2 All ER 491, (1944) 26 TC 265, CA. The author is not aware of what view HMRC take. However, if the settlement were settlor-interested there would be unwelcome income tax and capital gains tax implications (see CHAPTER 4 generally).

Exceeding the nil-rate band

[17.45] It may be thought improbable that an intending settlor would be content for the transfer into settlement to attract lifetime inheritance tax at 20% (with a further 20% payable should death follow within seven years). But the author has come across one or two cases where that is so. One of the reasons for the scenario might be that there is the prospect of substantial appreciation in future which the settlor wishes to keep outside his chargeable estate. And it may be that the above idea of a sale at an under-value is thought to be over-complex (though in principle is to be preferred to this suggestion). Remember that the inheritance tax must be paid by the trustees, as if paid by the settlor there will be grossing up as constituting a further gift. But at least the tax can be paid by interest-bearing instalments over a ten-year period, which may soften the burden.

[17.46] Overall, however, it needs to be remembered that the 'net present value' of a 40% charge at some point in the future will be less than 40% now – with the longer the future deferral, the larger the discount. A comparison of 20% as against 40% is not therefore the correct measure.

Life assurance trusts and IHT mitigation

[17.47] The trust has long been a key element in products marketed by the life assurance industry with a view to mitigating inheritance tax. As with any such aim it is essential to avoid both the reservation of benefit and the pre-owned assets regimes and (being the main point of a trust) to achieve some form of security for the beneficiaries. The principal marketed advantage of these arrangements is securing growth in an asset for the beneficiaries (subject always to investment performance), but retaining an element of benefit for the settlor in a tax-efficient way.

[17.48] As with any arrangement involving trusts, the restriction of the potentially exempt transfer regime from 22 March 2006 has hit hard, so that to avoid inheritance tax on entry the chargeable transfer must not exceed the nil-rate band (of £325,000 for 2015/16 and 2016/17). However, in particular in the case of the discounted gift trust described below, this may be seen to present a marketing advantage.

[17.49] Against this background, the two principal schemes on offer at present are the discounted gift trust and gift and loan arrangements each of which is described below. There is also a third, less popular and to the author's mind more vulnerable, arrangement called the flexible reversionary trust, also described. The key feature of all these structures, certainly in HMRC's view, which enables them to escape both the reservation of benefit and the pre-owned assets regimes, is that there is a separation of rights, ie the rights for the settlor which he has retained, as quite distinct from the rights he has given away and from which he can enjoy no benefit. This is specifically confirmed, at least in relation to discounted gift trusts in HMRC's guidance on income tax and pre-owned assets which is now contained in CHAPTER 44 of the Inheritance Tax Manual where they say at IHTM44112:

> In the straightforward case where the settlor has retained the right to an annual income or to a reversion under arrangements which are not subject to the reservation of benefit legislation, that right is property within [paragraph 8 of Schedule 15 to Finance Act 2004] as the trustees hold it on bare trusts for the settlor. A bare trust is not a settlement for inheritance tax purposes (IHTM16030). The settlor is excluded from other benefits under the policy and so the POA charge does not apply.

[17.50] While not specifically germane to trusts of non-qualifying life assurance policies, it might be worth noting one point illustrated by two recent First-tier Tribunal cases. Both the discounted gift trusts and the gift and loan arrangement described below depend on the '5% withdrawal rule'. Amounts drawn from the policy or policies not exceeding 5% of the original premium on a cumulative annual basis do not involve an immediate charge to tax. Rather, there is a deferral of tax at the higher of the additional rates (for a UK policy) or at the total combined rate (for an offshore policy) on the happening of a chargeable event, typically the surrender of all the rights under the policy or contract (see *ITTOIA 2005, s 484*, subject to certain exclusions, and *ss 485, 487* and *488*), subject to top-slicing relief. In the case where more than 5% is drawn there can be a counter-intuitively substantial charge to income tax, as was found recently by Messrs Lobler and Anderson, in the latter case involving an additional penal charge as a personal portfolio bond within *ITTOIA 2005, ss 515–526*) (*Lobler (Joost) v Revenue and Customs Comrs* [2013] UKFTT 141 (TC), [2013] SWTI 1777) and *Anderson (R) v Revenue and Customs Comrs* [2013] UKFTT 126 (TC), [2013] SWTI 1812).

The discounted gift trust

[17.51] The asset which the settlor or (with the settled cash) the trustees acquire is a life assurance bond, whether issued by a UK or by a non-UK insurance company. The lives assured would be the settlor and/or spouse/civil partner or, sometimes, other individuals. The bond has two distinct sets of rights: the one arising under a retained fund (entirely for the benefit of the settlor) and the other under a settled fund (from which the settlor and spouse/civil partner are excluded). The rights under the retained fund are (typically) to annual 5% withdrawals, the value of which depends upon the settlor's age and state of health when he makes the arrangement. The value of these rights has the effect of reducing the amount of the initial chargeable transfer. An example provided to the previous author, Matthew Hutton, by Colin Jelley of Skandia UK is as follows:

> A male settlor who is a non-smoker and in good health aged 60 at his next birthday could invest as much as £803,700 in a discounted gift trust and take 5% withdrawals a year (monthly in arrears) without incurring an IHT charge (in 2013/14). This assumes that he has made no chargeable gifts within the previous seven years. The value of the settlor's fund would be £478,700 and the discounted gift value would be £325,000. If the settlor were to die within the following seven years, his beneficiaries would inherit the whole amount IHT-free because the value of £478,700 which is subject to an absolute or bare trust arrangement for the settlor is extinguished on his death, and the £325,000 falls within the nil-rate band for IHT purposes.

This illustration emphasises the inheritance tax attraction of the arrangement, that is the settlor can ensure that, while for inheritance tax purposes the chargeable transfer is limited to the available balance of the nil-rate band, a much greater gross value is extracted from his chargeable estate. If he survives the seven-year period, the whole of that gross value is inheritance tax free so far as his estate is concerned. Any of the 5% withdrawals which remain in his estate unspent will of course form part of the chargeable estate on death, subject to the spouse/civil partner exemption.

[17.52] A continuing eye should be had to the value in the trust, especially while the settlor remains alive, but also after his death if following encashment of the bond the trust continues. At the first ten-year anniversary the value of the settled fund will be that much greater as the remaining retained fund will have fallen in value. Consider the following example based on Colin Jelley's illustration.

EXAMPLE

Bruce aged 60 and is single. He has a chargeable estate of £3 million. He has made no previous chargeable lifetime transfers. With the nil-rate band of £325,000, his family would face an inheritance charge of £1.07 million on death. Within that estate he has cash of £1 million currently producing income of only £10,000 a year.

In 2014/15 he decides to put £803,700 into a discounted gift trust taking 5% withdrawals per annum. That causes him to make a chargeable transfer of £325,000, leaving him with the retained fund worth say £478,700, although this value would disappear on death and so fall outside the chargeable estate.

On death in say seven years and six months after the settlement, assuming that the nil-rate band and rates of inheritance tax stay the same, Bruce's chargeable estate will be some £2.196 million less the nil-rate band of £325,000, giving £1.871 million taxed at 40% to produce a tax bill of £748,520, a saving in inheritance tax of £321,480 or 30%. Meanwhile, Bruce is receiving £40,185 each year, significantly increasing his spendable resources (and he might choose to use some of that in taking out a life policy written in trust to help pay some of the inheritance tax arising on death). There will be a chargeable event gain on his death. Suppose that the value of the children's fund and the amount paid out is £600,000. How is this taxed at the higher rates, on the trustees?

Policy proceeds	£600,000
Add: withdrawals	£300,000
	£900,000
Less: premium paid	(£803,700)
Subject to income tax	£96,300

Further, his death occurring more than seven years after the gift, Bruce's estate has a fresh nil-rate band.

[17.53] The inheritance tax attraction of the arrangement assumes that the retained rights have a sufficiently attractive value to involve a significant discount for inheritance tax purposes on the gross value of the sum contributed. HMRC have historically taken the view that the open market value of those retained rights depends upon an hypothetical open market purchaser being able to take out life assurance on the life of the settlor which requires him to be aged less than 90 (whether male or female). The point is that without life cover the whole investment will fail should the settlor die shortly after the purchase. This view has been confirmed by the High Court in *Revenue and Customs Comrs v Bower (executors of Bower (decd))* [2008] EWHC 3105 (Ch), [2009] STC 510, 79 TC 544, which has been followed by the First-tier Tribunal in *Watkins (D M) & Harvey (C J) (Mrs K M Watkins' Executors) v Revenue and Customs Comrs* (TC01582) [2011] UKFTT 745 (TC), [2012] SWTI 38. HMRC published a Technical Note on 1 May 2007 about the methodology they would adopt in valuing lifetime transfers and, in particular, where spouses (or civil partners) took out a discounted gift arrangement that transfer of value would be calculated separately for each spouse/civil partner depending on their respective ages and states of health. HMRC have warned that if, following the *Test-Achats* case market practice changes so that unisex tables are introduced by the insurance industry, HMRC will discuss with insurers and representative bodies how best to incorporate that change into their practice (*HMRC Trusts & Estates Newsletter April 2011*). As at 31 July 2013, HMRC's practice and guidance had not changed, though they issued further guidance on 6 August 2013 (Revenue and Customs Brief 22/13) with further clarification following in HMRC Trusts and Estates Newsletter, December 2013.

[17.54] For purposes of the General Anti Abuse Rule (GAAR) – see 23.11 – HMRC's example D27 in their GAAR guidance confirms that the discounted gift trust 'arrangements accord with established practice and so are not within the scope of the GAAR'. While not expressly treated in the examples, it should be assumed that the gift and loan arrangement described below would be similarly regarded.

The gift and loan arrangement

[17.55] The principal inheritance tax aspect of this arrangement is that there is no chargeable transfer at outset, but that capital growth in the subject-matter of the gift accrues outside the taxpayer's estate for the benefit of, say, his children. The trust itself is established with a nominal amount of say £10. The beneficiaries are, say, children and remoter issue. The settlor and spouse/civil partner are irrevocably excluded from benefit. The settlor then lends a substantive sum, say £250,000 on terms that no interest is payable and that it is repayable on demand which it is thought prevents the loan from being a transfer of value.

[17.56] The trustees invest the cash in a non-qualifying life assurance policy which may be written on the lives of one or more named children, on a joint lives and survivor basis, so that the bond will pay out after the settlor's death. Repayment of the loan typically takes place at 5% per annum, that is within the threshold of the income tax chargeable event regime for non-qualifying policies. To this end the bond itself might comprise 20 different segments, with the trustees surrendering one each year. There will be a higher rate income tax liability at any time when the total amounts withdrawn exceed the cumulative 5% withdrawals or on the death of the settlor or on the expiry of 20 years. The rate of tax will be up to 25% if a UK policy (that is, given payment of basic rate within the bond) or up to 45% if non-UK, for 2015/16 and 2016/17. These marginal rates may be reduced by top-slicing relief (*ITTOIA 2005, ss 535–537*). This works by dividing the chargeable gain on maturity by the number of complete tax years it has been in force. The resulting 'slice' is added to the taxpayer's other income for the relevant tax year, so as to form the highest part of his income. The resulting tax on the slice is multiplied by the number of complete tax years to produce the tax payable on the chargeable event gain. However, where a chargeable event occurs with a policy of substantial value which has been in place for one year or less, any top-slicing relief may be worthless in practice. Income tax takes priority over capital gains tax. To the extent that there is any amount of the loan remaining repayable at the date of the taxpayer's death that will form part of his chargeable estate.

EXAMPLE

In 2014/15 Bertie invests £300,000 in a gift and loan scheme for the benefit of his children, making the settlement with a nominal £100 trust fund. Assume that the trustees repay Bertie at 5% per annum and that the balance of the bond grows also at 5% per annum. Repayment each year is effected by surrender of one of 20 segments in the bond.

Year	Loan outstanding	Repaid to Bertie	Illustrative investment growth outside Bertie's estate
	£	£	£
0	300,000		
5	225,000	75,000	70,200
10	150,000	150,000	143,100
15	75,000	225,000	215,400
20	0	300,000	286,500

The longer that the taxpayer survives, the greater the benefit. However, note that top slicing relief is given only to individuals, so that if the chargeable event gain is assessed on the trustees after the taxpayer's death the whole gain will be taxed at 25% (on a UK policy). Accordingly, in the above example a gain of £215,400 at year 15 will attract an income tax charge on the trustees as follows (assuming continuation of current rates):

Policy proceeds	£215,400
Add: withdrawals	£225,000
Less: premium paid	(£300,000)
Gain	£140,400
Income tax @ 25%	£35,100

The flexible reversionary trust

[17.57] The flexible reversionary trust appears to be of far less widespread use than the discounted gift trust. This may be because in particular of one perceived technical disadvantage. The settlor arranges a series of qualifying life policies, each with a single premium and with a term so as to mature in successive year: that is, Policy A matures in year 2, Policy B in year 3 and so on. The rights under the policies are then transferred to a trust from which both settlor and spouse/civil partner are irrevocably excluded from benefit. There is therefore no discount and the chargeable value is the value of the policies. Should the settlor survive the maturity of any policy, the proceeds will be paid to him. However, the trustees are given power to defeat that interest before it matures, for example by appointing capital to one or more of the beneficiaries, and they also have the option to extend the maturity date. It is these powers which effectively ensure that the initial transfer of value is the full value of the initial investment.

[17.58] The arrangement is therefore more flexible than the discounted gift trust. It would be up to the settlor to write to the trustees in the event of his needing proceeds of any cash. The problem, however, is surely this. Given that the settlor is not a beneficiary, are not the trustees bound to have regard to the needs only of the beneficiaries in exercising their discretions and so would they not feel bound to defeat the settlor's interests in all the policies before maturity and/or extend the maturity dates? The argument against this proposition is that in exercising their discretion trustees should have regard to all the circumstances including the wishes of the settlor, but this seems very doubtful to the author.

Avoidance

[17.59] The line between avoidance, which according to HMRC is unacceptable, and mitigation, which HMRC accept, is not always easy to draw – and commentators will not necessarily agree with HMRC's categories and distinctions. Certainly, there are principles established both by statute and case law which affect all taxpayers, though not necessarily specifically involving trustees. Inheritance tax trust-based avoidance schemes were added to the statutory regime for the disclosure of tax avoidance schemes with effect from 6 April 2011 and a more general DOTAS rule is in the process of being finalised: see **17.24**.

[17.60] With effect from 2013/14, practitioners involved in anything other than 'vanilla' planning will need to ensure that their planning is not caught by the General Anti-Abuse Rule (GAAR): see **23.11–23.14**.

Chapter 18

Running a Trust: Tax Planning

General principles and overview of the chapter

[18.1] The trustees and those advising them will be seeking to manage the trust fund in a tax-efficient way. CHAPTER 17 considered some tax planning principles which might be taken into account in starting a trust, whether inheritance tax, capital gains tax or stamp taxes and, in the context of inheritance tax, maximising the opportunities presented by the nil-rate band. The fundamental distinction in analysing a trust, assuming always that it is neither a charitable trust (see CHAPTER 14) nor an excluded property trust (see 27.2–27.6), is between one with a qualifying interest in possession and a relevant property settlement. Of course, since 22 March 2006 every new non-charitable lifetime trust, except a qualifying trust for a disabled person (see **15.7–15.11**) will be a relevant property trust. There will, however, continue to be qualifying interest in possession trusts, whether lifetime trusts made before 22 March 2006 or Will trusts with an immediate interest in possession, and consideration should be given to those, typically in relation to the inheritance tax planning of the life tenant: this generally is the subject of CHAPTER 12. The principal inheritance tax mitigation opportunity which will apply to both types of trust, but of special significance in relation to the relevant property trust with its regime of ten-year and exit charges, is of course the availability of business and agricultural property relief (see **18.28–18.74**). It is relevant in this chapter to mention planning arrangements which no longer work, for example to do with mitigating capital gains tax on the second home (see **18.85–18.89**). Other taxes must not be forgotten: capital gains tax with the ability to hold over gains on entry to a relevant property trust (assuming that it is not settlor-interested – see **7.82–7.83**) or indeed income tax with the opportunity to create revocable interest in possession so as to avoid the special rates of income tax for the trustees.

Avoiding aggregation

[18.2] Avoiding the aggregation of two funds intended to benefit members of the same family must always be beneficial. The present nil-rate band of £325,000 is hardly a significant sum nowadays (eg a modest house outside London with the mortgage paid off). Consider the effect of a legacy of £325,000 to someone who either has £325,000 already or will have that sum in his estate on death. Ignoring the use of the spouse/civil partner exemption (and assuming no chargeable lifetime transfers in the seven years before death), the inheritance tax on the death of someone:

- with £325,000 is nil;
- with £650,000 is £130,000.

Thus, ensuring that the legacy is left to a trust for the benefit of, but outside the estate of, the transferee can save £130,000 on the transferee's death.

[18.3] Where the legatee knows in advance that he will receive something, he might persuade the testator to amend his Will. Sometimes, however, the legacy will come out of the blue or the testator may have already lost the necessary capacity to be able to amend his Will. In such circumstances the use of a post-death deed of variation (within the provisions of *IHTA 1984, s 142*) could be considered to achieve the same objective. Typically the variation would redirect the legacy to a discretionary trust. In these circumstances, the original legatee can remain as a beneficiary of the trust without triggering a gift with reservation of benefit because it is the testator who is considered to have created the trust for inheritance tax purposes.

The age of the donee

[18.4] The advantage in keeping assets out of a donee's estate is particularly marked in the case of an elderly person. This is simply because the prospect of an inheritance tax charge on the donee's death is so much more likely. Where a wealthy young person is to inherit, the prospect of a 40% inheritance tax charge at some distant point needs to be weighed against the potential relevant property charges over his lifetime. It might be thought that one would need to incur seven ten-yearly charges (7 x 6% = 42%) to be worse off than paying a 40% charge on death, but this is to ignore the cost of money – the 'net present value' of a 40% charge deferred for, say, 45 years (ie the donee's likely life expectancy) will be significantly less than 40%.

Married couples and registered civil partners

[18.5] Prior to the introduction of the transferable nil-rate band on the second death of a married couple or registered civil partnership, discretionary settlements were commonly used in the planning of Wills – and in some cases even since 9 October 2007, they continue to be so used. The couple who make full use of the spouse/civil partner exemption on the first death (ie by having reciprocal Wills leaving everything to each other) do not use that spouse's or civil partner's nil-rate band. For each to leave £325,000 to the children may be good tax planning, but it will leave the survivor exposed unless the couple are quite well off. The standard solution was to incorporate a nil-rate band legacy on discretionary terms in each Will, with the surviving spouse/civil partner as one of the trustees and, also, an object of the trustees' discretion.

[18.6] However, conventional thinking has changed somewhat with the introduction of the transferable nil-rate band on a second death on or after 9 October 2007 [*IHTA 1984, s 8A*]. It is now generally thought sensible to maximise (where possible) the nil-rate band available on the first death, so as to carry forward the unused proportion to the second death, enhancing the nil-rate band available in the survivor's estate by up to 100%. Furthermore, such a carry forward is possible even where the chargeable value of the estate of the first to die is below the then nil-rate band. Nonetheless, even with spouses or civil partners there may be circumstances where it may be sensible (perhaps for non-tax reasons) to use the nil-rate band on the first death, in which event the following example is interesting. With the current expectation of only modest increases (if any) in the nil-rate band from 2021/2022 (given the 'freezing' of the nil-rate band at £325,000 until 2020/21) and in the hope of more substantial capital appreciation in property, it may turn out to be worthwhile in many cases to have made full use of the nil-rate band on the first death.

EXAMPLE 1

H1 (husband) and W1 (wife) have estates as follows:

	H1 £	W1 £
House (tenants in common)	500,000	500,000
Less: mortgage	(25,000)	(25,000)
	475,000	475,000
Maturity value of mortgage protection policy	25,000	25,000
Chattels	100,000	75,000
National Savings, bank balance etc	25,000	75,000
Investments	500,000	
Life policy (maturity value, not written in trust))	30,000	
Death in service benefit from employer (not written in trust)	100,000	
	£1,255,000	£650,000

H1 dies in 2014/15. His Will includes a nil-rate band legacy on discretionary terms. Residue of £930,000 (£1,255,000 less £325,000) to be left to W1. There is no tax on H1's death. On the death of W1 eight years later, the position is as follows:

Her estate – as above (£650,000 plus £930,000)	£1,580,000
A discretionary Will trust of	£325,000

Suppose that when W1 dies there is a nil-rate band of £400,000, leaving, £1,180,000 chargeable at 40%, producing a tax liability of £472,000. The death of a beneficiary is not an occasion of charge for a discretionary trust. (For the sake of illustration, this and the following examples ignore the possible availability of a 'residence nil rate band' from 2017/18 (see 18.11–18.16).)

EXAMPLE 2

H2 and W2 are in the same position and die in the same order (in the same tax years) but H2's Will leaves his entire estate to W2 and the spouse/civil partner exemption prevents a tax charge. Indeed, H2 has not used his nil-rate band at all, having made no chargeable lifetime transfers within the seven years before death and there being no other circumstances which trigger inheritance tax. This means that when W2 dies her executors can claim a nil-rate band in her estate enhanced by 100%. The total chargeable value in her estate of £1,905,000 therefore attracts an enhanced nil-rate band of £800,000, with an inheritance tax liability of £442,000. H2 and W2 save £30,000 in inheritance tax.

EXAMPLE 3

The circumstances (and dates and order of deaths) of H3 and W3 are the same as those of H2 and W2. However, immediately after the death of H3, W3 makes a lifetime relevant property trust within her nil-rate band of £325,000, which she survives by at least seven years. W3 dies in the same tax year as W2, when there is a nil-rate band of £400,000 which, as with W2, is enhanced by 100% in W3's estate. Given the lifetime trust the taxable value of W3's estate after the enhanced nil-rate band of £800,000 is £780,000 which attracts inheritance tax of £312,000, representing an inheritance tax saving of £130,000 on H2 and W2's combined estates (and £160,000 over the joint estates of H1 and W1).

[18.7] Moving from the thought of Will trusts to lifetime trusts, assume that there is within the estate of each spouse surplus assets to the tune of the nil-rate band. Such couples might set up two discretionary settlements now, each of £325,000 with the intention of removing assets from their estates. Doing so would mean that on their deaths within seven years there would be no nil-rate band available; however, once they had survived for seven years their nil-rate bands could again be used. Indeed, for wealthy enough individuals such nil-rate band trusts could be established every seven years.

[18.8] Taking all taxes together, it is highly unlikely that either spouse/civil partner would be an object of discretion in the other's settlement during his or her lifetime. This is because the anti-avoidance regime would subject the settlor to income tax on the income of the trustees – and before 2008/09 to capital gains tax on the trustees' gains (see 4.33). Therefore it would be important to know that these sums could be spared without risk of discomfort to the couple. One thing which might make it easier would be to allow the wife to benefit from the husband's settlement after his death and vice versa. One would expect the income of the household to be adequate whilst both were alive but there would be a fall (eg loss of one pension) when the first spouse died. Hence the desirability of allowing the surviving spouse/civil partner some help from the discretionary settlement of the first to die.

[18.9] Where a couple have conventional Wills, each leaving his or her estate for the benefit of the other, it is still possible following the first death to establish a discretionary settlement of £325,000. This would again be done within the provisions of *IHTA 1984, s 142* which allows for deeds of variation and disclaimers. There has been one attempt to have *section 142* repealed, in 1989. However, the facility remains for the moment. 'Double death' variations are possible: if within a short space of time both spouses/civil partners die and the second inherits the whole of the estate of the first, the executors (and, probably, the beneficiaries) of the second can vary the Will of the first (within two years after the first death). This will maximise use of the nil-rate band in the estate of the first. This mechanism is (rather surprisingly) accepted by HMRC Trusts and Estates, even if the assets concerned end up in exactly the same hands, albeit by a different route. If effecting a so-called double death variation, the detail of the documentation is important; in particular, the deed of variation should recite that the estate of the second to die is able to meet all the deceased's debts and liabilities, without resort to the assets of the first to die.

[18.10] In the final Coalition Budget of 2015 the government announced a general review of the uses of Deeds of Variation, and the consultation *Review looking at the use of Deeds of Variation (DoV) for tax purposes* launched a formal call for evidence on 15 July 2015, to be submitted by 7 October 2015. The review was perhaps prompted by political mischief making – Ed Miliband having been revealed to have used a Deed of Variation in relation to his father's estate – and, perhaps not surprisingly it resulted in no change. The government's response in December 2015 was that: "The Government will not introduce new restrictions on how DoVs can be used for tax purposes but will continue to monitor their use."

Residence nil rate band

[18.11] From 6 April 2017, for inheritance tax purposes, an additional "residential nil-rate band" ("RNRB") may be available against the value of a residential property on a person's death. The RNRB will start at £100,000 in 2017 and will increase by £25,000 a year until 2020/21 when it will reach £175,000. There are strict conditions on the availability of the relief (including restrictions where an estate exceeds £2 million) and these are summarised below. The relief will, however, be available in relation to certain trust interests (see **18.13**). The rules are contained in *IHTA 1984, ss 8D – 8M*, the majority of which were introduced by *Finance (No 2) Act 2015*. The rules in relation to 'downsizing' are introduced by *Finance Act 2016, Schedule 15*.

[18.12] The two main conditions for the relief to apply are that (1) there is a 'residential property interest' in a person's estate which is (2) 'closely inherited'. A 'residential property interest' is an interest in a dwelling house which has been the individual's residence (and the various capital gains tax cases on main residence relief will likely inform what constitutes a 'residence'). Special rules will, however, allow an individual to claim the RNRB (up to the value of the previous residence) if they had previously owned a residential property but no longer own it at death i.e. if they have 'downsized' or moved into residential care.

[18.13] For a residence to be 'closely inherited' it must pass on death to the deceased's children or grandchildren (including step-children, adopted children and foster children) or a spouse of the same. Where the residence was held *in trust* for the deceased or is held, post-death, for the children or grandchildren etc. this condition will still be met as long as, broadly, the trust is such that the residence forms part of the estate of the deceased and/or inheritor – in other words was held in one of the various 'qualifying interest in possession' trusts.

[18.14] The RNRB will be available in full only for estates under £2,000,000. For those in excess of this amount, it will reduce at a rate of £1 for every £2 by which the value of the net estate exceeds £2,000,000. By 2021, when the relief is available at £175,000, estates over £2.35 million will not benefit.

[18.15] Married couples and civil partners are able to transfer any unused RNRB to the survivor. The RNRB transfers even if the first spouse owns no 'residential property interest'; however, the ability to transfer relief *is* restricted where the first spouse has an estate in excess of £2 million.

[18.16] Given the relatively small additional inheritance tax benefit that this new exemption will provide, it is not going too far to say that it is *ridiculously* complicated and, particularly, where there is value in an estate in excess of £2 million, great care will be required. Whereas, following the ability to transfer the main nil rate band, we have got used to ignoring the precise split of assets between spouses or civil partners, going forward it may be necessary to 'equalise' estates to ensure that on the first death the £2 million limit is not breached (i.e. so that the RNRB can transfer). Likewise, the making of lifetime gifts to reduce an estate below £2 million will also become important, and trusts will have a role to play here. More specifically, where residential property interests are held in qualifying interest in possession trusts, it will be important to check that those interests will be 'closely inherited' on the death of the life tenant. Wherever there are post-death trusts which are not 'qualifying' interest in possession trusts, the RNRB will not be available, and planning may be needed to improve the position.

'Having your cake': pre-March 1986 settlements

[18.17] Before 18 March 1986, it was possible for the settlor to be the beneficiary of a discretionary trust established during his lifetime. The *FA 1986, s 102* (gifts with reservation) applies only where the settlement was made on or after 18 March 1986. Therefore, these older settlements still work as intended but they must not receive further capital from the settlor etc. (For all other tax purposes such trusts *are* settlor interested.)

Family companies

[18.18] There are now three categories of family company so far as trustees and their liability to inheritance tax is concerned. There are those where the shares qualify for 100% business property relief (or agricultural property relief), those where (exceptionally) business property relief is only 50%, and those which are not, or are not wholly, eligible for these valuation reliefs. The shares which do not qualify in full could still be shares in a trading or farming company but either:

(a) they do not qualify as relevant business property or as agricultural property (eg they fail the two-year ownership test or the two-year occupation or seven-year ownership tests for agricultural property); or
(b) some of their assets are 'excepted assets', eg cash surplus to business requirements: see **18.48** [*IHTA 1984, s 112*].

[18.19] Valuation is always important in relation to company shares and the principles of valuation for them are of long standing. They date back to the introduction of estate duty in 1894 and have remained virtually unchanged since. Therefore, it would seem reasonable to expect these rules to be the basis of fiscal valuation for some time to come. Apart from 100% business property relief, these rules favour small minority holdings, each owned by a different taxpayer as compared with influential holdings. Between 6 April 1998 and 5 April 2000, the taper relief from capital gains tax encouraged the ownership by trustees of at least 25% of a trading company, so as to qualify for the higher rate of business taper. Alternatively, within an interest in possession trust where the life tenant was a full-time working officer or employee, the trustees could hold just 5%. Up to the repeal of taper relief on 6 April 2008 and with the new improved regime of business taper from 6 April 2000, it did not matter how many shares the trustees owned in a qualifying trading company. From 6 April 2000 to 5 April 2008, a shareholding by life interest trustees of no more than 10% in a non-trading company attracted business assets taper if the life tenant was an employee of the company. Similarly, to secure entrepreneurs' relief from 2008/09, it matters not how many shares the *trustees* own, however, the qualifying conditions must be met by a qualifying beneficiary and this involves the beneficiary in having an interest in possession and holding not less than 5% of the voting shares (see 7.104). There is no minimum shareholding for the new investors' relief where the qualifying conditions must similarly be met by an 'eligible beneficiary' (see 7.110–7.111).

[18.20] The next example is one where the valuation reliefs are not important but the valuation rules are. The example could relate to a successful investor in property.

EXAMPLE (AND SUBJECT TO THE REVISED REGIME FROM 2015/16)

An entrepreneur aged 30 feels that he has financial responsibility not only for his wife and one-year old child but also for his parents who live on social security and on gifts from him. He wishes to start a new company with £3,000. He has made no previous chargeable transfers and can give away £3,000 within his annual exemption. He makes six settlements each of £500 on discretionary trusts for his father, mother, his present child and any further children born in the next 30 years. After his death, his widow can benefit. The trustees of the settlements subscribe for the entire £3,000 share capital of his new company (which is denominated into 3,000 £1 nominal value shares). The company is an investment company and so the shares do not attract business property relief. He dies at the age of 60 when inheritance tax nil-rate band is £325,000. The company could be worth, say, £3,000,000 on a takeover. One-sixth of its shares put on the market as a single parcel would be worth, say, £300,000 (ie the pro rata value would be £500,000 but this would be subject to discount for a minority holding). Therefore the total settled shares are:

(a) worth £3,000,000, and
(b) valued at £1,800,000 (= £300,000 × 6) for inheritance tax purposes

and each settlement can distribute its holdings without tax, as follows:

	£
Valuation of 500 shares	300,000
5 related settlements valued at commencement	2,500
Chargeable to inheritance tax	£302,500

Inheritance tax is nil.

There will, in the meantime, have been three ten-year charges but there will have been no tax unless the valuations on those occasions exceeded the then nil-rate band (£325,000). If the company were one whose shares were relevant business property there would be no tax (whatever the number of shares and whether or not there were several settlements, for so long as the present rules subsist).

[18.21] Where there are management reasons for keeping a block of shares intact but there are several people who should benefit, a discretionary trust is the obvious solution. Perhaps a testator owns such a block of shares and has several children. His Will could dispose of them by way of a settled legacy on discretionary terms to benefit his issue. Alternatively, if there are no strong capital gains tax reasons for his retention of the shares, he could settle them now. There is an income tax disincentive for the use of a discretionary structure (see 6.73) due to the special rates of tax that apply and the fact that dividend income does not retain its character when received via such a trust. Subject to the circumstances, an interest in possession structure (albeit non-qualifying for inheritance tax purposes) is likely to prove preferable.

[18.22] It might be sensible for the settlor to be a trustee. This would permit him to be involved in the management of the trusts and so in the exercise of the voting rights. Unless the Articles of Association of the company are most unusual, the votes of shares which are jointly held are exercised by the first-named. This means that the company secretary does not have to consider the form of ownership of the shares and, if he were to discover that they were held within a trust, he does not have to enquire whether the vote is exercised in the manner laid down by the trust instrument. However, this is simply a matter of company law. As a matter of trust law, the trustees should normally discuss how their vote is to be used and, once they have reached unanimity (subject to any provision to the contrary in the trust instrument), the first-named would be instructed as to how their vote should be exercised. Therefore, the second or third-named trustee has just as much influence over the way in which the vote is cast as does the first-named. Although it is difficult to say why the settlor should not be the first-named trustee, many draftsmen feel happier if he is not. As it is only the question of casting a vote and receiving circulars, notices etc which turns on this, it is often easier to have the trust instrument show someone other than the settlor as the first-named. Once the settlor has some way of influencing the vote, he will normally raise little objection to very substantial holdings being put in trust if his professional advisers can find sound reasons for so doing. After all, to the extent that the company is successful, he should be able to achieve reasonable remuneration and perhaps a substantial retirement scheme, and so should not need the shares.

[18.23] The UK *Small Business, Enterprise and Employment Act* received Royal Assent on 26 March 2015 and introduced a central registry of company ownership, principally to address the use of corporate directors and 'front' directors, from 6 April 2016. The register is available for public scrutiny and lists those persons who have 'significant influence or control' over a company being anyone in the company who:

- owns more than 25% of the company's shares;
- holds more than 25% of the company's voting rights;
- holds the right to appoint or remove the majority of directors;
- has the right to, or actually exercises significant influence or control; or
- holds the right to exercise or actually exercises significant control over a trust or company that meets any of the other 4 conditions (see www.gov.uk/government/news/keeping-your-people-with-significant-control-psc-register).

[18.24] The legislation seeks to identify the 'people with significant control' (PSC) in relation to each company and companies will be required to collect information about their PSCs, and impose corresponding duties on others to supply it. Essentially, the company must write to anyone whom it thinks may qualify as a PSC or who may know someone who qualifies, asking if the person agrees. The person must reply and give appropriate identification details.

Public companies will have to maintain this information themselves in their own private registry, available to the public on request. Private companies can report their PSC information to a central registry maintained by an official registrar or keep their own registry. There are provisions for the exclusion of certain material, including the PSCs' residential addresses and a PSC can apply to the registrar to have any other details withheld on specified grounds. (For a recent update about the register see: https://companieshouse.blog.gov.uk/2016/04/13/the-new-people-with-significant-control-register/.

[18.25] The question of trusteeship is important in relation to remuneration. As a general rule and in the absence of any special clause in the trust instrument, if the settlor needs the votes of the settled shares to secure his remuneration, it must belong to the trust (see eg *re Gee, Wood v Staples* Ch D, [1948] 1 All ER 498). Incidentally, the question whether the directorship causes there to be a gift with reservation is usually covered by *IHTA 1984, s 90* which permits reasonable remuneration.

[18.26] HMRC may try to argue that a gift of shares by a shareholder-director can be a gift with reservation of benefit where the directorship continues. However, if the remuneration package is that which an outsider would have had, the point is not raised. If the remuneration is really excessive, then the gift could be caught; however, if the remuneration contract is in place prior to the gift, a 'carve out' argument may be possible. Remuneration received by trustees is always a difficult area. There is the general rule that trustees may not profit from their trusteeship, which gave rise to the *Gee, Wood* case mentioned immediately above. Modern trust deeds are generously worded so as to allow remuneration. However, cases do turn up where the remuneration is clearly unearned. In *re Keeler's Settled Trusts*, Ch D, [1981] 1 All ER 888 there was a charging clause and power to appoint trustees to be directors but no clause authorising those people to retain fees. The court allowed remuneration appropriate to their efforts. Anything else had to be handed over to the trust. This included all the emoluments of the settlor's wife.

[18.27] Where shares in a family company are settled, readers should note the 'loss to donor' principle for inheritance tax. The next example shows one pitfall, in that the trustees cannot divide their holding of shares into two halves unless the division is done on the same day. There would be no problem were the shares to qualify for a 100% valuation relief.

EXAMPLE

	£
Value of trust property	
$66^2/_3$% of the capital of a family company	1,000,000
Liquid assets	500,000
	£1,500,000

The trustees appoint half their holding of shares for the adult children of brother A. A similar appointment of the rest of the shares will be made when brother B's family is of age.

	£
Fall in value of the holding	

From 66²/₃% worth	1,000,000
To 33¹/₃% worth (say)	(400,000)
Fall in value (chargeable to inheritance tax)	£600,000

In a year's time, brother B's family takes the rest and the remaining half of the original holding is appointed. Values have not changed.

33¹/₃% holding worth (being the amount chargeable to inheritance tax)	£400,000

The division must take place on the same day if the inheritance tax on each half of the fund is to be equal. In that event, it becomes unnecessary to show the calculation of the tax with grossing-up and the depletion of the £500,000 liquid assets.

Business property relief

[18.28] Business property relief may apply to reduce the value transferred by a transfer of value or a deemed transfer of value. The termination of an interest in possession is a deemed transfer. So is a ten-year charge or an exit charge. Secondly, some or all of the value transferred has to be attributable to 'relevant business property'. It is not necessary for that property to be transferred. All that is required is for part of the value of the transfer, etc to be attributable to the value of 'relevant business property' (see **18.40**). Therefore trustees will normally be given business property relief if they hold the right category of asset (see **18.29–18.33**) and the underlying business is of a particularly sort – very broadly, it must be 'trading', but with some trades excluded (see **18.34–18.47**).

Relevant business property

[18.29] As from 6 April 1996 the commonest forms of relevant business property fall into two categories.

First group

(a) A business or an interest in a business (which must be the interest of a proprietor so that, for example, mere loan account balances do not qualify, see: *Beckman v IRC* [2000] STC (SCD) 59).
(b) Unquoted (ie unlisted) securities of a company which (whether by themselves or together with other such securities and any unquoted shares) gave control. In this context, it is important that the securities contribute towards control. Where, for example, trustees hold unquoted shares which already give them control of a company, any securities held by them, even if carrying a right to vote, would not qualify.
(c) Unquoted shares in a company.

Second group

(d) Quoted (ie listed) shares or securities giving control.

(e) Land or buildings, machinery or plant used for the business of a company controlled by the transferor or by a partnership to which he belongs. It was held in *Walker's Executors v IRC* [2001] STC (SCD) 86 that a 50% shareholding plus a casting vote as chairman was sufficient to confer control for these purposes.

(f) Land or buildings, machinery or plant owned by trustees of an interest in possession settlement and used by the life tenant for his business.

[18.30] The first group of relevant business property can attract 100% relief, whilst a transfer within the second group can qualify for only 50% relief. The relief is given by a reduction in the value for tax purposes.

[18.31] The relief is intended to benefit trades and professions, so that there are rules designed to exclude property not really likely to be used for trade, etc and to exclude recently acquired property and property in the course of sale or winding up. There are 'see through' provisions in *IHTA 1984, ss 107* and *108* which protect the relief for company reconstructions, inheritance and so on.

AIM shares

[18.32] There are two definitions of unlisted shares for inheritance tax. The term 'unlisted' is now generally used instead of 'unquoted' [*FA 1996, s 199* and *Sch 38*]. *IHTA 1984, s 272* is the definition section. It defines 'quoted' as meaning 'listed on a recognised stock exchange or dealt in on the USM'. However, for the business property relief a different definition is used. This is in *s 105(1ZA)* which says that 'quoted' means listed on a recognised stock exchange. The AIM was introduced on 19 June 1995. The Inland Revenue press release of 20 February 1995 gave advance notice that, for the purpose of business property relief, AIM investments would be treated as unlisted. This point was effectively confirmed at Budget 2007. HMRC have been given power (by *FA 2007, s 109* and *Sch 26*) to designate any market of a recognised investment exchange as a recognised stock exchange (RSE). AIM is a market platform of the London stock exchange and the London stock exchange is a RSE, so AIM shares are already traded on a RSE. What differentiates them from the main market for most tax purposes is that they are not included in the official UK list maintained by the Financial Services Authority as the UK listing authority and therefore (for the time being, at least) are unaffected by the changed boundaries of the rules under *FA 2007, s 109* and *Sch 26*. BES shares are unlisted, although these will not normally appear in settlements (and in any case there are not many such shares left). Unlisted shares for the purposes of inheritance tax would also include OFEX shares (see Inheritance Tax Manual at IHTM 18337).

[18.33] The introduction of the AIM has increased the range of companies in which to invest for inheritance tax mitigation. Trustees do not have such a wide range of tax saving investments as do individuals. They cannot claim losses under *ITA 2007, ss 131–151*. In other directions there are worthwhile inheritance tax and capital gains tax savings. Firstly, there is business property relief, as mentioned above. This is 50% for a control holding in a listed company but is 100% for holdings in AIM and unlisted companies engaged in trading, rather than in property or investments. For capital gains tax there is hold-over relief for gifts of business assets (*TCGA 1992, s 165* and 7.60–7.74) where shares are listed on the AIM or are unlisted. Further, trustees can defer a capital gains tax liability by subscribing for EIS shares from 6 April 1998 [*TCGA 1992, Sch 5B, para 17*], but, note, not by investing in a venture capital trust.

Disqualified and qualifying businesses

[18.34] Section 105(3) of IHTA 1984 excludes from relevant business property an interest in a business or shares in a company where the business concerned consists wholly or mainly of:

(a) dealing in securities, stocks or shares, land or buildings; or
(b) making or holding investments (with an exception for shares in the holding company of, broadly, a trading group (*s 105(4)(b)*) see 18.51–18.53.

Identifying what constitutes a business of 'holding investments' has been the subject matter of many tribunal and court decisions over the last twenty years. Some of the more important are explained in 18.35–18.46.

[18.35] Following two Special Commissioners' cases in 1995 and a further two in 1997, 1999 saw four cases in relation to caravan parks and properties which, despite taking up much of their time in management, had the occupation of land by third parties as central to the business. Of these, most significant were the two caravan cases, *Furness v IRC* [1999] STC (SCD) 232 and *Weston v IRC* [2000] STC (SCD) 30, together with *Farmer v IRC* [1999] STC (SCD) 321. *Furness* and *Weston* were caravan park cases, won by the taxpayer and by HMRC respectively. (The decision in *Weston* was upheld in the High Court on 17 November 2000: [2000] STC 1064.) *Farmer*, won by the taxpayer, concerned the letting by a farmer of property in the centre of the farm surplus to agricultural requirements. What emerges from these cases is that, in applying the *IHTA 1984, s 105(3)* rule, there is no single test. Rather, the matter must be considered 'in the round', with regard not just to the profitability and turnover of the trading and investment sides of the business respectively, but also to the overall context of the business, the capital employed and the time spent in the various sides of the business by the proprietors and the employees. Critical to the taxpayer's success in *Farmer* was the fact that there was a single set of accounts for the whole business and that there was unified management of the whole business.

[18.36] In another caravan park case, *Stedman's Executors v IRC* [2002] STC (SCD) 358, the Special Commissioner found that the business of the company did not consist mainly of making or holding investments. This conclusion was reached by analysing each of the company's activities, leading to the conclusion that in the relevant year, 1998, 40% of the turnover, 20% of the gross profit and 16% of the net profit (before the directors' fees) were referable to holding investments, that is less than 50% in each case. HMRC appealed successfully to the High Court under the name of *IRC v George* [2003] STC 468. The High Court agreed with HMRC that the Special Commissioner had erred in applying the *'Farmer'* test at too low a level, ie that it was incorrect to look separately at each of the company's activities. Rather, having separated the investment from the non-investment activities (and in so doing those which were incidental to investment were not separable from it), the 'wholly or mainly' test of *section 105(3)* should be applied through the eyes of a reasonable businessman to determine whether or not the particular business consisted wholly or mainly of making or holding investments.

[18.37] However, the Court of Appeal reversed the High Court decision, in finding for the taxpayers and confirming that the overall approach of the Special Commissioner was correct in law. *Section 105(3)* does not require the opening of an investment 'bag', into which are placed all the activities linked to the caravan park, simply on the basis that they were 'ancillary' to that investment business. Moreover, it is not necessary to determine whether or not investment was 'the very business' of the company. The statutory language does not require such a definitive categorisation. In the present context, this gave insufficient weight to the hybrid nature of the caravan site business. The holding of property as an investment was only one component of the business, and on the findings of the Commissioner it was not the main component. It was difficult to see why an active family business, such as that in the present case, should be excluded from business property relief merely because a necessary component of its profit-making activity was the use of land ([2004] STC 147).

[18.38] A case decided by the Special Commissioner on 27 September 2005 concerned the status of shares in a family company (*Clark and another (Executors of Clark deceased) v HMRC* [2005] STC (SCD) 823 SpC 502). The company, originally founded as a partnership in 1895, had a large portfolio of properties (holding investments) but also a rental activity in relation both to its own properties and third party properties. On the facts, and looking at the matter 'in the round', the Special Commissioner found that the shares were not 'relevant business property'. By contrast, in *Phillips and others (Executors of Phillips deceased) v HMRC* [2006] STC (SCD) 639 SpC 555, the company concerned had previously been an investment company but had, by the time of the death of the main shareholder, changed its business to that of lending money, largely to associated companies. The Special Commissioner held that, looking at all the facts in the round, the business carried on by the company at the date of the death did not consist only or mainly of making or holding investments – and so business property relief was available. *Clark* is the more typical of the two decisions – it being inconceivable, particularly in the light of subsequent decisions (see below), that any property investment business could qualify for relief. Likewise, the decision in *Phillips* may not be repeated if similar facts came before another tribunal.

[18.39] Four further cases on business property relief were heard in 2008 and 2009. The first (*McCall and another as personal representatives of Eileen McClean v HMRC* [2008] STC 752 SpC 678) concerned farmland occupied under arrangements particular to Northern Ireland called agistment. The principal issue was whether *IHTA 1984, s 105(3)* denied relief on the grounds that, while Mrs McClean was running a grazing business through the agency of her son-in-law, that business was little other than holding an investment. All that the son-in-law did, ie inspecting and repairing fencing, attending to the drains, the weed control and finding the grazier were all management activities directly related to letting the land. There was only an activity of providing water which was distinct from this and which was not so substantial as to tip the balance. The taxpayers' appeal was dismissed by the Court of Appeal in Northern Ireland (*McCall and another (personal representatives of McClean deceased) v RCC* [2009] NICA 12. The Court found unsustainable the argument for the taxpayers that Mrs McClean, through her son-in-law, had been growing a crop of grass for consumption by the animals of the grazier. The Court affirmed the analysis of the Special Commissioner. The taxpayers' application to the House of Lords for leave to appeal was refused and so the decision is final.

[18.40] The second case concerned the definition of 'relevant business property' in *IHTA 1984, s 105(3)* which does not include land or buildings (or machinery or plant) as distinct from 'an interest in a business' in the case where the business structure is a sole trade rather than a partnership or a company. However, Special Commissioner Dr John Avery Jones found that the transfer of land (with development value) by a farmer to the trustees of a family discretionary trust did attract relief (*Trustees of Nelson Dance Family Settlement v HMRC* [2008] STC 792 (SpC 682)). The reason is that the structure of business property relief is much more concerned with values than with property. While the relief is attributed to the net value of the business as a whole, this does not imply that the value transferred had to relate to the whole business. And so it did not matter that the remainder, indeed the majority of the business, remained in the hands of the settlor. The High Court upheld the decision (*RCC v The Trustees of the Nelson Dance Family Settlement* [2009] EWCA 71 Ch; [2009] STC 802). Among the specific reasons given by Sales J was the fact that the general principle governing the operation of *Inheritance Tax Act 1984 (IHTA 1984)* is the 'loss to donor' principle and the construction of *IHTA 1984, s 104* put forward on behalf of the taxpayers provided for an application of business property relief which was more in harmony with the other instances contemplated by the other categories of relevant business property than did HMRC's construction.

[18.41] Third, in *Executors of Piercey deceased v HMRC* [2008] STC (SCD) 858 SpC 687, business property relief was allowed on shares in a company which carried on property development, notwithstanding significant land values in the company at the shareholder's death; that land remained stock and had not been appropriated as an investment.

[18.42] Finally, in a landed estate case emanating from Scotland with somewhat complex facts, the First-tier Tribunal held that there was a single business not disqualified from relief by *section 105(3)* and protected by the replacement property provisions of *section 107* (*Brander (as personal representative of Balfour) v RCC* (2009) TC 69)). The deceased's interest in a farming partnership on a landed estate was *relevant business property* within IHTA 1984, s 105(1)(a) and so attracted business property relief under *section 104(1)(a)*. On the facts, the estate management and farming activities had been managed as a single composite business prior to the setting up of the partnership, the partnership replaced those activities, the disputed assets of the estate were used in that business and all the property replaced by the capital of the partnership was *relevant business property* immediately before it was so replaced. Moreover, the business activities carried on at the estate did not consist wholly or mainly of making or holding investments and *section 105(3)* was not engaged. *Section 107* was at issue because, within two years before his death (the relevant period of ownership qualification provided by *section 106*) the late Earl had inherited the property from the trustees of a *Settled Land Act 1925* settlement and had transferred it to a partnership with his nephew. HMRC's appeal was rejected by the Upper Tribunal (UT) on 17 August 2010. The UT was satisfied that, on the evidence before it, the FTT had not erred in law in holding that Lord Balfour, operated a single composite business. Going on to apply the well-established *Farmer* criteria – namely context, turnover, net profit, time spent and capital value – the FTT had reached the correct conclusion in deciding that Lord Balfour's business was not mainly one of holding investments. In fact, the only factor which pointed to investment was that of capital value (where the let properties exceeded the value of the other properties in the ratio of 1.88:1); however, the FTT had been entitled to attach little weight to capital value, as the long-term policy of the Estate had been to retain land, so that market values were generally immaterial to Lord Balfour's business decisions. All the other factors supported the conclusion that this was mainly a trading business ([2010] UKUT 307 (TCC)).

[18.43] Historically, HMRC Trusts and Estates accepted in principle that one or more properties run as *furnished holiday accommodation* could attract business property relief (quite apart from the specific statutory reliefs for income tax and capital gains tax purposes given to furnished holiday accommodation by *ITTOIA 2005, Pt 3, Ch 6, ss 322–328B* and *TCGA 1992, s 241*). However, HMRC changed their instructions to their officers in 2008 (see Inheritance Tax Manual IHTM 25278) – making it clear that in the future the relief would be less generously granted. The issue was tested in the case of *Pawson v CRC* [2012] UKFTT 51 (TC), TC01748 where the First-tier Tribunal ruled in favour of the taxpayer. A cottage on the Suffolk coast had been run by the deceased, producing profits in three out of the four years ending with the tax year of death and the Tribunal found that 'the operation of the property as a holiday cottage for letting to holiday makers was a serious undertaking earnestly pursued', adopting the six indicia of a business established in the VAT case *CIR v Lord Fisher* [1981] STC 238. Applying the test established by the Court of Appeal in *George* (see **18.36–18.37**), the Tribunal said that they had:

> 'no doubt that an intelligent businessman would not regard the ownership of a holiday letting property as an investment as such and would regard it as involving far too active an operation for it to come under that heading. The need constantly to find new occupants and to provide services unconnected with and over and above those needed for the bare upkeep of the property as a property lead us to conclude that no postulated intelligent businessman would conclude such a property as Fairhaven to be correctly characterised as an investment. He would consider it to be a business asset to be exploited as part of the provision of services going well beyond an investment as such'.

[18.44] HMRC's appeal in *Pawson* was decisively upheld in the Upper Tribunal by Henderson J (*Revenue and Customs Comrs v Lockyer and Robertson (personal representatives of Pawson, dec'd)* [2013] UKUT 50 (TCC), [2013] STC 976, [2013] NLJR 291). Henderson J found that, on the basis of its findings of fact, the First-tier Tribunal made an error of law. Henderson J took as his starting point 'the proposition that the owning and holding of land in order to obtain an income from it is generally to be characterised as an investment activity'. He drew heavily upon the judgment of Carnwath LJ in *George*, in particular to characterise the particular nature of the letting in *Pawson* as no different from a 'normal' property letting. Drawing on Carnwath LJ's judgment, Henderson J said that property management forms part of the business of holding property as an investment and that in 'any normal property letting business, the provision of additional services or facilities of a non-investment nature will either be incidental to the business of holding the property as an investment, or at least will not predominate to such an extent that the business ceases to be mainly one of holding the property as an investment'. That was the case in *Pawson* where the services provided 'were all of a relatively standard nature, and they were all aimed at maximising the income which the family could obtain from the short-term holiday letting of the property. Looking at the business in the round, there was in my view nothing to distinguish it from any other actively managed furnished letting business of a holiday property, and certainly no basis for concluding that the services comprised in the total package preponderated to such an extent that the business ceased to be one which was mainly of an investment nature'. Specifically, Henderson J did not accept the submission for the taxpayers that 'a holiday letting business is inherently of such a nature that it falls outside the scope of a "normal" property letting business'. Applications by the executors for leave to appeal were rejected by both the Upper Tribunal and the Court of Appeal, so the Upper Tribunal decision is final.

[18.45] HMRC's victory in *Pawson* has been followed by three further First-tier Tribunal decisions in favour of HMRC. All involve businesses where income is received from land being provided to third party occupiers. In *The Trustees of David Zetland Settlement* [2013] UKFTT 284 (TC) the FTT rejected a claim for business property relief in the case of a business providing serviced offices. In *John Best (Executor of the Estate of Alfred William Buller deceased)* [2014] UKFTT 077 (TC), the FTT rejected a claim for business property relief in the case of business which operated a trading estate. Most recently in *Green (Anne Christine Curtis) v Revenue and Customs Comrs* [2015] UKFTT 236 (TC), [2015] SWTI 2486 relief was denied to a business which let *five* units of self-contained holiday accommodation.

[18.46] In the author's experience, HMRC have become emboldened by their victories in *Pawson, Zetland Best* and *Green*, and it is now HMRC's working rule of thumb that any business which derives an income from the provision of land to third party occupiers should be assumed to be considered to be investment businesses which should not attract business property. In the author's view, this view is an oversimplification and fails to acknowledge why it should be the case that a hotel would qualify for business property relief. The correct test is the 'intelligent businessman' test and it is unfortunate that the FTT is not applying it with any conviction (in *Best*, for example, the test was mentioned but not applied!). For the author's views on the 'intelligent businessman' test and some of the difficulties inherent in applying it, see his joint article, with Priya Dutta, *A Line in the Sand* in *Taxation*, 14 November 2013.

[18.47] If at the date of the chargeable transfer the company has sold its business for cash, HMRC Trusts and Estates are likely to contend that the company has become an investment company, precluding relief under *section 105(3)*. There has been a case involving a company which had just sold its nightclub and was looking for another which went the other way. At the time of death of the principal shareholder (22 months after the sale) the company's main asset was cash on short-term deposit. The activities of the company showed that it was not in the business of making investments because it was looking for a replacement nightclub and maintained an administrative office. Therefore, business property relief was available (*Brown's Executors v IRC* (SpC 83) [1996] STC (SCD) 277).

Excepted assets

[18.48] Relief is denied to the extent that the assets of the business constitute 'excepted assets' defined in *IHTA 1984, s 112* as (broadly) not used in the business or required for future business purposes. Cash surplus to reasonable business requirements will typically be an excepted asset. In *Barclay's Bank Trust Co Ltd v IRC* (SpC 158) [1998] STC (SCD), £300,000 out of £450,000 (on a turnover of £600,000) was found to be an excepted asset in that it was not needed for the future purposes of the business at the date of the shareholder's death. Evidence is all-important and in the *Barclays Bank* case very little contemporaneous evidence was produced to support the claim that the £300,000 (which was very clearly not required for day to day business purposes) was required for future projects. The key in the case of most businesses is for contemporaneous minutes to be kept detailing why the business requires its cash.

[18.49] In an interesting, but unhelpful, development in this area, the following question was put to HMRC as part of the ICAEW Technical Release: *IHT Business Property Relief – Interests in Partnerships/LLPs and Surplus Cash Holdings* (Taxguide 1/14 (Tech 01/14 Tax)):

> ' . . . in the light of the current economic climate and in order to weather the financial adversity faced by many businesses within the UK, it is widely recognised that businesses are retaining increased cash buffers in case of any further downturn in their trade . . . In this regard, confirmation from HMRC that they are aware of this change in mind-set of business owners and company directors, and look favourably on surplus cash held in this regard, would be extremely useful to our members.'

HMRC replied:

> 'We understand that due to the financial circumstances in which business find themselves, they may choose to hold more cash in case of a potential downturn in trade . . . However, our guidance remains the same, and unless there is evidence which directs us to the fact that the cash is held for an identifiable future purpose, then it is likely it will be treated as an excepted asset. Therefore the holding of funds as an 'excess buffer' to weather the economic climate is not a sufficient reason for it not to be classed as an excepted asset.'

In the author's view, HMRC's view is wrong. There is no statutory requirement that the future purpose has to be as narrow and specific as this answer would suggest.

[18.50] One final point to note is that in a 1979 case (*American Leaf Blending Co Sdn Bhd v Director General of Inland Revenue (Malaysia)*

[1979] AC 676, [1978] 3 All ER 1185) the Privy Council decided in broad terms that the business of a company is whatever the company does. On that basis, therefore, provided a company is not wholly or mainly an investment company, the fact that alongside its trade it may own an investment property has no adverse effect on the availability of business property relief for the shares. Indeed, this is the principle on which the *Farmer* case was won by the taxpayers (see 18.34). Accordingly, there could also be an argument open to the taxpayer that what might appear to be a cash surplus to business requirements is, by being put on deposit earning interest, used for the purposes of the business, within the *American Leaf* case. The argument might also be strengthened by investing the cash in other 'investment' assets – this is on the basis that it is usually 'cash at bank' (rather than 'investments') on the balance sheet which catches HMRC's eye.

Groups

[18.51] As explained at 18.34, a company which is the holding company of a 'wholly or mainly' trading group will, although the company is itself one of holding investments, qualify for business property relief [*IHTA 1984, s 105(4)(b)*]. An exchange of correspondence between HMRC and the Chartered Institute of Taxation published on the STEP website on 4 April 2011 clarifies the meaning of 'holding company' for this purpose, with reference to the *Companies Act 2006* definition. Specifically, HMRC confirm that the fact that the holding company does more than merely hold the shares in its subsidiaries, ie provides loan and other finance, co-ordinates the activities of the subsidiaries and monitors their financial performance etc does not prejudice its status as a 'holding company'.

[18.52] The simplest group is a parent company and its subsidiaries. However, there can be sub-subsidiaries which can also attract relief: it does not matter how many tiers of holding company there are. It should be noted, however, that any subsidiary (or sub-subsidiary etc) which is itself wholly or mainly in the business of holding investments will be denied relief [*IHTA 1984, s 111*].

[18.53] Finally, great care is required where the 'holding' entity is a partnership of LLP rather than a company. In a series of replies to questions and examples provided as part of ICAEW Technical Release: *IHT Business Property Relief – Interests in Partnerships/LLPs and Surplus Cash Holdings* (Taxguide 1/14 (Tech 01/14 Tax)), HMRC make it clear that in the majority of such cases, they do not consider that business property relief is available. This is on the basis that neither a partnership nor an LLP is 'transparent' for inheritance tax purposes (ie it is not possible to simply 'look through' to any underlying 'trading' entities) and the rule in *IHTA 1984, s 105(4)(b)* applies only to companies. A contrary view was put forward by James Kessler QC and Oliver Marre in their article *A merry dance* in *Taxation* (20 March 2014).

Minimum period of ownership

[18.54] Relevant business property must generally have been held for at least two years [*IHTA 1984, s 106*]. However, note that there is no express statutory requirement that the property must have been 'relevant business property' for throughout that two-year period. There are also express exemptions to the two-year rule in *sections 108* and *109*, together with 'see through' provisions to protect company reconstructions, replacement property and so on in *section 107*.

Sales and liquidations

[18.55] Business property relief ceases to be available where an unconditional contract for sale has been concluded [*IHTA 1984, s 113*]. Relief is likewise denied in relation to a company in the process of a winding-up or liquidation, unless this is part of a reconstruction or amalgamation [*IHTA 1984, s 105(5)*].

Agricultural property relief

[18.56] Agricultural property relief was substantially improved in 1992, in line with business property relief. From 10 March 1992 agricultural property with vacant possession (or the right to it within 12 or by concession 24 months) has qualified for 100% relief. Other agricultural properties attracted 50% relief, except where they are the reversion to a tenancy commencing before 10 March 1981 and remain protected by the transitional 'working farmer' provision. However, where the tenancy starts after 31 August 1995 the 50% relief becomes 100%. This has increased the number of tenancies being granted because the 1992 rates of relief did work against tenanted structures. From 6 April 1995 the cultivation of short rotation coppice qualifies as an agricultural purpose. Previously this was forestry. These changes stem from *FA 1995, ss 154, 155*. The *Finance Act 1997, s 94* enacted a new *section 124C* for the *Inheritance Tax Act 1984*. As a result, from 26 November 1996 land taken out of agricultural use and dedicated as a wildlife habitat can qualify as agricultural property.

Agricultural property

[18.57] The expression 'agricultural property' is defined by dividing it into three limbs: limb 1 is 'agricultural land or pasture'; limb 2 is 'woodland and any building used in connection with the intensive rearing of livestock or fish if the woodland or building is occupied with agricultural land or pasture and the occupation is ancillary to that of the agricultural land or pasture'; and limb 3 is 'such cottages, farm buildings and farmhouses, together with the land occupied with them, as are of a character appropriate to the property' [*IHTA 1984, s 115(2)*]. The expression in limb 1 'agricultural land or pasture' means bare land and does not include buildings, as held by the Court of Appeal in *Starke v IRC* [1996] 1 All ER 622, [1995] 1 WLR 1439. The court in that case also held that 'the property' in limb 3 refers to the bare land or pasture in limb 1 and that the cottages, farm buildings and farmhouses must be in the same ownership as that of the bare land or pasture, the so-called 'nexus test'. Morritt LJ in *Starke* suggested that the nexus might be common occupation rather than common ownership, but in *Rosser*, a 2003 Special Commissioner's case (see **18.60**), the decision followed the *ownership* nexus established by *Starke*. Most recently, the First-tier Tribunal has decided that the proper nexus is that of *occupation* (*Joseph Nicholas Hanson v RCC* [2012] UKFTT 95 (TC)). The decision has been upheld by the Upper Tribunal. Warren J said that there had to be some nexus to establish that the agricultural land in limb 1 of the definition of 'agricultural property' was connected in a relevant way with the limb 3 property. However, the *ownership* nexus propounded by HMRC was not an essential condition for the relief and on the present facts, where both the land and the farmhouse were *occupied* by the son of the settlor, there was a sufficient functional connection between the land and the farmhouse (*Joseph Nicholas Hanson as Trustee of the William Hanson 1957 Settlement v Revenue and Customs Comrs* [2012] UKFTT 95 (TC), [2012] SFTD 705, [2012] SWTI 1388).

Farmhouses

[18.58] The definition of 'agricultural property' in *IHTA 1984, s 115(2)* includes 'such cottages, farm buildings and farm houses, together with the land occupied with them, as are of a character appropriate to the property'. There can be difficulties in claiming relief for farmhouses which are over-large or over-luxurious for the farm of which they are part. The farmhouse must be 'of a character appropriate' to bare agricultural land in the same ownership. Decisions in two Special Commissioners cases on this issue were released on 17 October 2002. In the *Higginson's Executors v IRC* [2002] STC (SCD) 483, a 'charming family home' in Northern Ireland was held not to be 'of a character appropriate' to a landed estate of 134 acres: indeed, Ballywood Lodge was not even a 'farmhouse'. By contrast, in *Lloyd's TSB (personal representative of Antrobus, dec'd) v IRC* [2002] STC (SCD) 468, a listed 16th century house, in poor condition, was held to be a farmhouse which was of a character appropriate to the 126 acres of freehold land which had been actively farmed by the deceased. As in all such cases, the facts (and indeed the expert evidence) were fundamental to the decisions made.

[18.59] The *Antrobus* case was referred to the Lands Tribunal for a decision on the 'agricultural value' of the farmhouse. Whereas business property relief is given on market value, agricultural property relief is given on only 'agricultural value', defined by *IHTA 1984, s 115(3)* as the value 'if the property was subject to a perpetual covenant prohibiting its use otherwise than as agricultural property'. In finding for a 30% discount from market value for the agricultural value of the house in question (Cookhill Priory) the Lands Tribunal also found, somewhat controversially, that a residence cannot be a farmhouse for purposes of agricultural property relief unless it is occupied by the person who 'farms the land on a day-to-day basis'. This is rather more restrictive than what HMRC Trusts and Estates say in their Inheritance Tax Manual as revised in 2009. For example, at IHTM24036, they say ' . . . the key factor is to identify if the occupant of the house has a significant role in the management, or actual operations, of the farming activity being carried out on the land involved'. The Lands Tribunal said that if they were incorrect on this particular point (the so-called 'lifestyle buyer' issue), then the discount would be 15%. The decision was not appealed but is generally thought to be questionable (see, for example, *Lloyd's TSB Private Banking plc v Revenue and Customs Comrs* DET/47/2005 (10 October 2005, unreported)).

[18.60] In *Rosser v IRC* (SpC 368) [2003] STC (SCD) 311 relief was given on a barn but denied on the house which had ceased to be a farmhouse following the retirement of the taxpayer wife and her husband five years before she died. In any event, however, following a gift to their daughter of 39 out of 41 acres, the house was not 'of a character appropriate' to the two acres retained.

[18.61] In *Arnander (executors of McKenna, decd) v Revenue and Customs Comrs* (SpC 565) [2006] STC (SCD) 800, [2007] RVR 208, it was held that the house in question was not a farmhouse for purposes of agricultural property relief. This is because at the date of the taxpayer's death, it was found on the facts that the house was not the main dwelling from which the agricultural operations over the land were conducted and managed. The day-to-day management and all acts of farm husbandry over the land were solely the responsibility of the contractors who were managed by an independent agent. The engagement of an agent to manage the land meant that the use of the house for farming matters was very much reduced. The purpose of Mr McKenna's occupation of the house was not to undertake the day-to-day farming activities (nor indeed the management). It remains the official HMRC position that a house can be a farmhouse where occupied by the landowner, or a partner in the landowning partnership, under a contract farming structure. However, for that to be the case that partner must be a de facto manager and management must take place at the farmhouse, which manifestly did not happen in *Arnander*. Indeed, the questions posed in schedule IHT 414 to the Inheritance Tax account form IHT400 suggest that HMRC will make very careful scrutiny, especially in contract farming arrangements, of the degree of time and expertise devoted to the partnership business by the partner occupying the farmhouse.

[18.62] One of the distinctions between agricultural property relief and business property relief is that unlike the latter, the farming business does not have to be run 'for gain' (see *IHTA 1984, s 103(3)*). Indeed, in *Antrobus* (see 18.58) the taxpayer had made losses in 15 out of the last 18 years before she died. In *Golding v RCC* [2011] UKFTT 351 (TC) the First-tier Tribunal held that the sale of a few eggs from about 70 hens at the farm gate making an annual taxable profit ranging from £1,047 to £1,600 in the four years before death was a sufficient agricultural activity for a farmer in his 80's who had carried on the business for nearly 70 years from the same house. Specifically, in answer to the question 'was the deceased farming?', the Tribunal said that ' . . . at 80 years of age, it would be unreasonable to expect that to be an extensive activity. In fact if one did, there would be very few farms which would qualify as 'character appropriate' . . . ' and the Tribunal said specifically 'we do not accept that the lack of a substantial property is detrimental to a decision that the farmhouse is 'character appropriate'. The decision is final. Following *Golding*, HMRC have added new guidance to their Inheritance Tax Manual at IHTM 24050 (' . . . each case must be determined as a matter of fact and degree, having regard to all relevant material considerations'), emphasising that each case should be judged on its own particular facts.

[18.63] A valuation point which might be of passing interest to trustees, mentioned principally because it has been explored only in the 1990s, is the value to the tenant of a non-assignable agricultural tenancy. There is value in such a tenancy but there is no market. A market has therefore to be hypothesised, for purposes of reaching a market value in accordance with IHTA 1984, s 160. See *IRC v Gray (surviving exor of Lady Fox)* CA, [1994] STC 360 and *Baird's executors v IRC*, Lands Tribunal for Scotland 1990 [1991] 1 EGLR 201, [1991] 09 EG 129, and also *Walton (Executor of Walton) v IRC* CA, [1996] STC 68.

The alternative occupation and ownership tests

[18.64] The agricultural property must have been either occupied by the taxpayer for agricultural purposes for at least two years or owned for at least seven years and occupied throughout that period by someone for agricultural purposes [*IHTA 1984, s 117*]. Note that trustees of a life interest trust cannot rely on the two-year occupation test unless the life tenant himself occupies, for example, as a partner in his own right, although in such a case it is likely that business property relief would be given.

[18.65] The requirement for occupation throughout the two year and seven year periods respectively before, typically, death or other chargeable transfer is strictly interpreted by HMRC, although in their Manual they have conceded that in certain circumstances where the relevant taxpayer is out of occupation of the farmhouse at the date of death because he is in a hospital or nursing home (with every expectation of returning) the test can still be treated as satisfied on the basis of 'functional occupation': see IHTM 24083. In *Atkinson* the senior partner of a family farming partnership, having run the farm for many years from the bungalow in which he lived, was taken ill and after a stay in hospital spent the last four years of his life in a nursing home. His partners continued to maintain the bungalow, visiting it a few times a week, although it was effectively empty and exempt from council tax on that basis. Although the First-tier Tribunal held that it was the partnership who continued to occupy the property ie satisfying the seven year test for the purposes of agriculture, for agricultural purposes (*Atkinson and Smith (executors of the Will of William Atkinson dec'd) v Revenue and Customs Comrs* [2010] UKFTT 108 (TC), [2010] SWTI 2123), this was overturned by the Upper Tribunal on the basis that the First-tier Tribunal had made an error of law. The correct approach in a case such as this is 'to identify what does and what does not amount to a sufficient connection between the use and occupation of the property in question (the bungalow in the present case) and the agricultural activities being carried on the agricultural property (the farm in the present case); and to ask whether the facts give rise to a sufficient connection'. On that basis the only possible conclusion was that the bungalow had not been occupied for the purposes of agriculture since it had become apparent that Mr Atkinson would never be able to return there to live (*Revenue and Customs Comrs v Atkinson and Smith (executors of the Will of William Atkinson dec'd)* (FTC/61/2010) [2011] UKUT 506 (TCC), [2012] STC 289).

Claw-back of business and agricultural property reliefs

[18.66] It is to be expected that families owning a family company or a landed estate will use settlements. If there is a settlement of such assets, the valuation reliefs are extremely important and the trustees should exercise great care during the first seven years of their ownership to avoid the operation of the notorious claw-back rules. There are sections [*IHTA 1984, ss 113A, 113B, 124A, 124B*] dealing with the position where:

(a) there has been a transfer, whether potentially exempt or immediately chargeable;
(b) at the time of the transfer a valuation relief was available;
(c) the transferor had died before the seven years has expired; and
(d) the property transferred has been sold.

Unless the property has been replaced (within 12 months before or 3 years after the sale) by other property qualifying for a valuation relief, the tax on death is calculated as if no relief was due. The provisions relating to replacement property are not straightforward. Where a company changes character between the gift and the death (eg from being trading to investment in character) that is ignored [*IHTA 1984, s 113A(3)(b), (3A)*].

[18.67] The above said, however, there is an interesting distinction in the operation of the claw-back between the case where the original transfer was potentially exempt on the one hand and immediately chargeable on the other. In the former, potentially exempt, case the effect of the claw-back is to cause the unrelieved value to be applied for all inheritance tax purposes [*IHTA 1984, s 113A(1) and s 124A(1)*]. However, where, as will inevitably be the case now with a new relevant property settlement, the transfer was immediately chargeable, it is only for purposes of calculating the additional tax due by reason of the death that the unrelieved value is used [*IHTA 1984 (s 113A(2) and s 124A(2)*]. This has the effect that, as accepted by HMRC, if the initial gross value of the transfer was within the nil-rate band at death (not, at the time of the transfer) the claw-back has no impact on a gift to a relevant property trust. And, indeed, to the extent that the initial gross value of the transfer exceeds the available nil-rate band at death, only the excess will be affected by a charge to inheritance tax at 40%. This point would assume added significance in the event of a future substantial increase to the nil-rate band threshold.

[18.68] There was a concern that, where business property replaced agricultural property (or vice versa) within the seven-year period, there would necessarily be a claw-back problem on the donor's death within that period. However, publication of an article in *Inland Revenue Tax Bulletin, Issue 14*, December 1994, indicates that 'mix and match' may be allowed, subject to satisfying certain conditions. However, the position is not completely straightforward and, if trustees are given property which attracts either of the valuation reliefs and they wish to reinvest or change the use of the property, they should first look carefully at the replacement provisions as amplified by the *Tax Bulletin* article; let agricultural land, for example, cannot be relevant business property.

[18.69] Running a Trust: Tax Planning

[18.69] There used to be a trap to catch out the unwary where a potentially exempt transfer was made to an accumulation and maintenance settlement (before 22 March 2006) for older children and the settlor dies within seven years. If by then the settled shares etc have vested in the children, whether on interests in possession or on absolute interests, by reason of their having attained the age of 25 etc, there has been a change of ownership. Because the donee is required to be the same, both when the gift is made and when the premature death occurs, business or agricultural property relief is lost by reason of the death. In such a case the original gift should have been made on life interest trusts, to avoid the claw-back of relief.

[18.70] The consequences of premature death causing a loss of business property relief can be serious. The more complex case is where there has been a gift of business or agricultural property to a relevant property trust, no tax being paid on commencement and tax falling due on the premature death of the settlor.

EXAMPLE

		£
(a) May 2014	Settlement of shares	450,000
	Less: 100% business property relief	(450,000)
	Transfer of value	NIL
	NB: Assume that no capital gains tax hold-over election is made.	
(b) July 2014	Following a bid for the company the shares are sold for £450,000 (ie the same figure as in May of the same year). The cash remains on deposit.	
(c) Sept 2014	The settlor dies. Therefore, there is an additional charge upon the trustees [*IHTA 1984, s 7(4)*]. The business property relief is no longer available [*IHTA 1984, s 113A(2)*].	
	The tax is calculated as follows:	£
	Original chargeable transfer net of business property relief	NIL
	Add back amount of business property relief	450,000
	Chargeable value	450,000
		£
	£325,000 @ nil	–
	£125,000 @ 40%	50,000
		50,000
	Extra tax	50,000
	The cumulative total of chargeable transfers of the deceased is not affected.	

It seems clear that, in July, the trustees should have considered term assurance unless they were going to invest in business property. What is more, a very different result arises if the company sells the business and retains the cash whilst looking for another business (*Brown's executors* case at 18.47).

Treatment of liabilities for financing relievable property: anti-avoidance rules

[18.71] In the ordinary course a liability secured on any asset has the effect of reducing its chargeable value for inheritance tax purposes [*IHTA 1984, s 162(4)*]. It had always made sense, where the liability is incurred to acquire property which attracts either business or agricultural property relief, for the liability to be secured on non-relievable property. HMRC consider this to be unacceptable avoidance and so have introduced new rules with effect from Royal Assent to Finance Bill 2013 (17 July 2013), which form a package of measures introduced by *FA 2013, s 176, Sch 36*. New *sections 162B* and *162C* introduced into *IHTA 1984* have the general effect of requiring liabilities incurred to finance either the acquisition or the maintenance or an enhancement of the value of relievable property to be taken as reducing the chargeable value of that property (rather than property on which it may be secured). Happily, by an amendment introduced at Report Stage of the Parliamentary debates, the new rule applies only in respect of liabilities incurred on or after 6 April 2013, so that liabilities in place before that day are unaffected. Because of the importance now attached to identifying the date on which a liability was incurred, HMRC have now provided specific guidance (see IHTM 28011):

> 'In most cases, the terms for repaying borrowed money will be recorded by a written loan agreement. FA13/Sch36/Para5(3)(b) says that a liability is to be treated as incurred on the date the agreement was made. So the date of an agreement will determine whether or not the liability is affected by the restrictions contained in IHTA84/S162B (IHTM28019). Where a loan is refinanced, resulting in a new loan agreement being made, the date the liability was incurred is the date that the new loan agreement was made.
>
> Without specific provisions to stop it happening, it would be possible to avoid the restrictions by arranging further loans to be made after 6 April 2013 under a pre-existing loan agreement. So, if an existing loan agreement is varied so that additional funds can be made available, the additional liability is treated as having been incurred on the date the agreement was varied, FA13/Sch36/Para5(3)(a).
>
> If there is no written agreement recording the terms of the loan, the liability should be treated as incurred on the date the money is paid to the borrower.'

Given the terms of the above, great care is required when re-financing or varying an existing loan. In the worst case, this could cost 40% of the value of the loan in terms of its future non-deductibility for inheritance tax purposes.

Hold-over relief for capital gains tax

[18.72] There is also a risk for capital gains tax. So long as the trustees have property which attracts a valuation relief or which produces an exit charge if passed to a beneficiary, they will almost always have the right to hold over a capital gain under *TCGA 1992, ss 165* or *260* (see 7.60–7.74). They must be careful not to lose this privilege without being aware of it. If the disposal is a chargeable transfer for inheritance tax as well as a disposal for capital gains tax, capital gains tax hold-over relief should be available under *TCGA 1992, s 260* (which takes priority over *section 165* hold-over: *section 165(3)(d)*).

One exception, in the case of *section 260* hold-over, is where the advance of capital occurs in a quarter beginning with the date of the settlement or a 10-year anniversary (see *IHTA 1984, s 65(4)*).

Planning considerations

[18.73] The fact that a settlement does not contain relevant business property or agricultural property does not prevent its trustees grooming it, as it were, so that it does contain such property in time for the ten-year anniversary. Theoretically, they could go in and out of qualifying business etc property so as to get the best yields or capital appreciation and the best tax treatment. However, for all but the most sophisticated taxpayers this is likely to be an impractical scenario. Further, one should seriously consider whether such a stratagem would be subject to the General Anti-Abuse Rule which applies to arrangements entered into after 17 July 2013 (see **23.11**).

[18.74] Until the 100% business property relief was introduced, it was standard estate planning to split large holdings so that the valuations were always valuations of tiny minority holdings. Then it became better to have larger holdings because the 100% relief was given on holdings larger than 25% and the smaller holdings attracted just 50%. Now that, from 6 April 1996, any size of holding attracts 100% relief, tax strategies do not touch on the issue at all.

Future considerations

[18.75] One of the biggest problems in using relevant property settlements where one strays outside the nil-rate band is the question of funding the ten-year charge. The cash which will be needed to pay the inheritance tax is capital. Most settlements are fully invested and if the assets are dear to the family as with the holding of shares in a family company, the power to accumulate is essential in order to provide cash. However, this power will run for only 21 years in most cases (excepting settlements made on or after 1 April 2010, following enactment of the *Perpetuities and Accumulations Act 2009*). Perhaps by then some other means will have been found of providing cash. The solution is not likely to be for the company to buy its own shares. Much more probable would be finding some other person within the family who would buy a few shares from time to time. This could, however, lead to problems. *IHTA 1984, s 65(1)(b)* ensures that a disposition by the trustees which lessens the value of property within the discretionary regime is itself an occasion of charge. The sale of a few shares would normally take place at a value appropriate to a minority holding. However, if the shares came from an influential holding, the fall in value would exceed the price. In order to avoid the resultant charge to inheritance tax, the trustees might attempt to sell at the price appropriate to a substantial holding. In that case, the purchaser may be making a chargeable transfer himself insofar as he pays more than the market value.

[18.76] Since 2008/09 trustees have paid capital gains tax at the maximum rate for individuals (ie 18% until 22 June 2010, 28% until 5 April 2016 and 20% or 28% (depending on the asset) from 6 April 2016). Likewise, an effective rate of capital gains tax at 10% may be available to both trustees and individuals under entrepreneurs' relief (see **7.93–7.96**) or investors' relief (see 7.107–7.111). Therefore any possible capital gains tax advantage of holding appreciating assets within a settlement has now gone.

Income tax planning

[18.77] The possibility of using a settlement as a reservoir for income, leaking it out as is convenient has already been explained (see **6.77**). Stripping old settlements is explained in **6.78**. Apart from these possibilities, in a very wealthy family, accumulation may be acceptable even when taxed at the higher special rates for trustees. If recourse is had to accumulations and the numbers are particularly large, it would be prudent to take expert opinion as to whether the payments could be income in the hands of the beneficiary (see **6.80–6.85**).

[18.78] The tax system for 1999/2000 and later years has proved a disincentive for deriving income from discretionary settlements because, even where trustees have received dividend income, the trustees have to deduct 45% from gross payments of income to beneficiaries (see **6.73**). Perhaps companies may consider interest-bearing loan stocks as an alternative to ordinary shares, in some contexts.

[18.79] Unless the beneficiaries of actual distributions from a discretionary or accumulation settlement are themselves paying tax at the additional rate, there will be a cash-flow disadvantage of making income distributions to non-taxpaying or basic rate taxpaying beneficiaries, as well as the 'dividend trap' illustrated at **6.73**, which applies even with a non-taxpaying or basic rate beneficiary. It is much better therefore, if there is likely to be a reasonable continuity for the time being in the desire to income beneficiaries for the trustees to make a revocable appointment of income in the trust onto interest in possession trusts for the intended beneficiaries. Since 22 March 2006, this has no inheritance tax implications and effectively creates a 'see through' situation for income tax purposes, bypassing the trustees for all compliance and substantive purposes.

[18.80] Historically, a settlement (relevant property or otherwise) could normally run for 80 years in England, although different periods were possible in other parts of the UK: there is no perpetuity limit for a Scottish discretionary settlement. The power to accumulate income can normally be exercised for the first 21 years. However, both these limitations have gone for new settlements following enactment of the Perpetuities and Accumulations Act 2009, with provision for the trustees of existing settlements to elect for the extension of the perpetuity period to 125 years from the date of the settlement and repeal of the restriction on accumulating income.

[18.81] It may not be straightforward for trustees to re-settle trust property. The new trustees could be irresponsible and this could render the original trustees susceptible to action by the beneficiaries. However, in a discretionary settlement, there are usually powers to appoint property in the form of a sub-trust. This is done by a clause empowering the trustees to declare trusts of all or part of the settled property provided those trusts are for the benefit of objects of the discretion. Such appointments are made by deed. They may be revocable or irrevocable. See 7.118–7.121 for the special capital gains tax and income tax regime for sub-funds.

[18.82] Provided the appointment can be regarded as the trustees 'filling in blanks' in the instructions given to them by their trust instrument, then the sub-trust is not a new trust. The importance of this distinction was illustrated in the case of *Hart v Briscoe* Ch D 1977 [1978] STC 89. In that case, there were two completely separate settlements, one made in 1955, another in 1972. The trustees were the same. As trustees of the 1955 settlement, they declared that certain assets in the 1955 settlement would thenceforth be held on the trusts of the 1972 settlement. The result was an argument about capital gains tax which went in favour of HMRC. The two settlements were separate and there had been an occasion of charge because assets had left the 1955 settlement and gone into the 1972 settlement [*TCGA 1992, s 71(1)*]. As a consequence, HMRC issued a Statement of Practice SP 9/81 on 23 September 1981. This has been superseded by SP 7/84 (see APPENDIX A), following *Bond v Pickford* CA [1983] STC 517, explaining how the Board would distinguish between appointments that created sub-trusts and those transactions where there had been a transfer to a new settlement.

[18.83] A standard use of powers of appointment before 22 March 2006 was to create an 'accumulation and maintenance settlement' out of a settlement which originally was completely discretionary. Given modern precedents and good draftsmanship, it was standard practice to use a power to declare fresh trusts of property within the discretionary regime so as to take the capital into a different regime, and to be able to revoke those trusts and redirect the property without capital ever leaving the main settlement. Now, however, that practically every new lifetime settlement following 21 March 2006 enters the relevant property regime (apart from a trust for a disabled person), the main distinction is between the trust remaining subject to that regime (with its system of ten-year and exit charges) and capital vesting outright, with inheritance tax at up to 40% chargeable on every death (subject to quick succession relief if the same property is charged as a result of successive deaths within a five-year period.) The relevant property regime is not necessarily more expensive in inheritance tax terms in the long run (again, the age of the intended absolute beneficiary is the important factor – see **18.4**) and it gives what to many settlors is more important, namely security over the trust assets.

Own share purchases

[18.84] Sometimes it may be desired to extract surplus cash from a family company and yet not to have the cash spread around the family. In such a case it might be possible for the company to buy back its own shares, the only shareholders selling shares being trustees. Whether the trust is interest in possession or discretionary/accumulation for income tax purposes, the special rates of income tax will apply (*ITA 2007, s 482 Type 1*) where the payment by the company is treated as a qualifying distribution. If on the other hand capital treatment applies under *CTA 2010, ss 1033–1048* (formerly *ICTA 1988, ss 219–229*), the trustees will pay capital gains tax on the gain: between 22 June 2010 and 5 April 2016 the rate was 28%; since 6 April 2016 it is 20%. In either case the proceeds of sale will be treated as capital for trust law purposes. For more details see **6.60(a)**.

The second home: washing the gain?

[18.85] It is possible to hold over a gain on a non-business asset which enters a discretionary trust, even when the value of the gift is within the settlor's nil-rate band and no inheritance tax charge arises [*TCGA 1992, s 260*]. The 1991 HMRC Consultative Document on the Income Tax and Capital Gains Tax Treatment of UK Resident Trusts (which was withdrawn in 1993) postulated the possible restriction of this relief to the case where and to the extent that the transfer caused the settlor to exceed his nil-rate band, thus producing an inheritance tax liability at 20%. To date, no such legislation has been introduced. In the past, this relief could be used with a discretionary trust, to shelter an accrued gain on a home which did not benefit from main residence relief. Assume, for example, that an individual owned a second home worth £250,000, with an indexed base cost of £100,000. The property was used for occasional holidays by various members of the family. The taxpayer settled the house in a new discretionary trust, holding over the gain. After an interval of a few months the house became, pursuant to the exercise by the trustees of powers in the settlement, the only or main residence of one of the beneficiaries, typically an adult child of the settlor: if that child had more than one residence he could have elected in favour of the trust property, together with the trustees, under *section 222(5)(a)* as applied by *section 225*. How long the house was retained by the trustees (and indeed occupied by the beneficiary) would depend upon the circumstances. However, the house might have been sold by the trustees within three years of acquisition and provided that for a reasonable period (let us say at least six if not twelve, months) during that time the house was occupied by the beneficiary as his only or main residence, the whole of the gain held over would have been exempt, by virtue of *section 223(1)*. Of course, the settlor could be a beneficiary, though any gain assessed on him under *section 77(1)* would be reduced by *section 225* relief. To avoid any argument of circularity, the net proceeds of sale should (obviously) not have simply been advanced back to the settlor.

[18.86] The arrangement described at **18.85** was made impossible from 10 December 2003 by what is now *FA 2004, Sch 22* (see **7.82**). If, prior to 10 December 2003, the property had been advanced to a discretionary trust under hold-over election, any qualifying period of occupation by a beneficiary before 10 December 2003 is exempt from gain under *TCGA 1992, s 225* on ultimate disposal by the trustees (see the example at **7.82**). However, any period of occupation after 9 December 2003, even if within the last 18 months of ownership, cannot attract relief under *section 225*.

[18.87] What is interesting about *FA 2004, Sch 22* is that it is only the combination of *section 260* hold-over and *section 225* relief which has been barred. That is, it remained open (but only until 21 March 2006) to employ the combination of *section 165* hold-over (business assets) and *section 225*. Among qualifying business assets for this purpose is furnished holiday accommodation (FHA) as defined in *ITTOIA 2005, s 325* and following. It would be pretty unlikely (although possible) that a second property had throughout the period of ownership been used as FHA, so as to qualify for complete hold-over under *section 165*. Of course, if the property had been used as such for only part of the period, the amount of the gain which can be held over is cut down under *Pt II* of *Sch 7 of TCGA 1992*. Because the hold-over needed to be under *section 165* and not under *section 260*, a life interest (rather than a discretionary) settlement would be used, ie the value did not have to be within the settlor's nil-rate band to avoid an immediate charge to inheritance tax on transfer to the trustees. The gain was held over under *section 165*. The trustees then allowed one of the children to occupy under the terms of the settlement and on subsequent disposal the whole of the gain, including that arising before the date of settlement, was effectively 'washed' under *section 225*.

[18.88] Unfortunately, the advent of the current inheritance tax regime for trusts on 22 March 2006 has effectively rendered the suggestion made at **18.87** impossible. The reason is that any non-charitable lifetime settlement now (with one exception, ie trusts for a disabled person) will be an immediately chargeable transfer and thus a gain capable of hold-over under *section 260*. In such a case, it is not open to claim *section 165* relief [*TCGA 1992, s 165(3)(d)*].

[18.89] That said, however, it would still be possible to use the suggestion of FHA so as to secure unrestricted hold-over under *section 165*, if the parents were prepared for one or more of the children to own the holiday home outright. In that event, following the gift to one or more children under *section 165* hold-over, he or they would occupy the property as their only or main residence and claim relief on disposal under *section 223(1)*, washing the whole of the gain. It seemed from Budget 2009 that such an arrangement would become impossible from 2010/11, with the repeal of deemed trading treatment for FHA for both income tax and capital gains tax purposes. Only if on general principles the running of the particular FHA could be said to be a trade would this hold-over suggestion continue to be possible However, following a consultation in 2010 the deemed trading treatment was not repealed. Instead the main qualifying conditions were increased by *FA 2011, Sch 14, para 2*, effective from 2012/13. The new conditions are that in the relevant 12-month period the property needs to be available for letting for 30 weeks and actually let for 15 weeks (a 50% increase in the previous 20 weeksand 10 weeks respectively). As from 2011/12 losses are relievable only from profits from that qualifying furnished holiday lettings business (a UK business being separate from a non-UK EU business). Accordingly, for the time being at least, such treatment remains and so the planning suggestion, albeit not involving trusts, holds good.

The family home: 'double trust' arrangement rendered ineffective

[18.90] Among the schemes for mitigating inheritance tax on the family home adopted in the early 2000's was the 'lifetime loan' or 'double trust' scheme. In very simple terms the taxpayer would contract to sell his house to the trustees of Trust One (giving him a life interest) for its market value, on terms that the matter would be left to 'rest in contract', so deferring any stamp duty until completion. The advent of stamp duty land tax on 1 December 2003 put paid to the attractiveness of these schemes, since under the contract there would be 'substantial performance' through payment by the trustees for the property by an unsecured loan note carrying the right for the holder to call for interest at a commercial rate and redeemable typically after the taxpayer's death. The taxpayer would then settle the loan note on life interest trusts (Trust Two) for the children, from which the taxpayer and his spouse were excluded from benefit. The purpose of the arrangement was to ensure that on the taxpayer's death only any subsequent appreciation in value of the property would fall within his chargeable estate, as the value charged (under *IHTA 1984, s 49(1)*) would be offset by the debt owed by Trust One to Trust Two. Payment of full value was thought to put paid to any reservation of benefit problem. Quite apart from the stamp duty land tax point, the introduction of the pre-owned assets code (see **4.39–4.51**) created an immediate annual charge as the taxpayer continued to occupy the property. While HMRC have pronounced their views on the scheme, which takes a multiplicity of forms, there has as yet been no case in the Courts.

[18.91] However, specifically in their Income Tax and Pre-owned Assets guidance at section 5, HMRC changed their view in October 2010 to advise that reservation of benefit would apply in the case where the loan was repayable only after the death of the taxpayer/life tenant of Trust One (which in the original version they had confirmed would apply only in the case where the debt was repayable on demand). Further, HMRC state that there is double taxation in that the reservation of benefit lies in the loan not the house and the pre-owned assets charge continues to apply in relation to the house. Most recently, a 'test case' which was to have come to the Tribunal (involving a scheme where the debt was repayable only after the death of the taxpayer(s)) was settled and so it is understood that HMRC are now looking for a new test case. Importantly, HMRC did not accept the merits of the taxpayer's argument in the now withdrawn test case which was settled on the basis of 'reasonable expectation'. However, as a severe limitation of this possible argument, namely that between 2005 and October 2011 the taxpayer relied on HMRC's then guidance that only a home loan scheme where the debt was repayable on demand was caught by reservation of benefit, HMRC have stated that the argument is not of general validity. HMRC say that they will accept the reasonable expectation argument only where there has been an enquiry into the pre-owned assets charge and HMRC have accepted that the charge applies. Where however, pre-owned assets tax has been paid and the case has not been the subject of an enquiry, HMRC maintain that they are entitled to argue for reservation of benefit on death, albeit that they will set off income tax already paid against the inheritance tax liability. This stance is not necessarily accepted by professional advisers, given the clear terms of HMRC's guidance issued before October 2010. Meanwhile, we await the advent (and outcome) of a test case on the issue.

Avoidance of double charges

[18.92] There are regulations in force for the avoidance of double charges. This is because the same property could be charged twice, once as a chargeable transfer and once as a gift with a reservation of benefit. The regulations are in SI 1987/1130. They cover situations where:

(a) a potentially exempt transfer has become chargeable and the estate of the deceased includes property given to him by the recipient of the original transfer; or
(b) there is both a chargeable transfer and a gift with reservation in respect of the same property; or
(c) the deceased owed money to a former donee, the debt is abated by *FA 1986, s 103* and the deceased had made a transfer of value to his creditor; or
(d) the deceased died within seven years of making a chargeable transfer and the property had returned to him, during his lifetime and other than for full consideration, so as to form part of his estate on death.

[18.93] More recently, double charges regulations have been made, specifically in relation to the pre-owned assets regime, in March 2005. In the narrow circumstance where a taxpayer has entered into a double trust (but no other type) of arrangement and has elected into reservation of benefit under *FA 2004, Sch 15, para 21*, any double charge to inheritance tax that might arise through the taxpayer's dying within seven years after the gift of the debt to the second trust is effectively cancelled. As with the scheme of the 1987 regulations, HMRC take whatever produces the higher amount of inheritance tax, whether under the reservation of benefit regime or under the failed potentially exempt transfer [*FA 1986, s 104; Charge to Income Tax by Reference to Enjoyment of Property Previously Owned Regulations 2005, SI 2005/724, reg 6*]. A second set of regulations [*Inheritance Tax (Double Charges Relief) Regulations 2005, SI 2005/3441*] apply from 4 January 2006 in the case where a double trust scheme is unscrambled within the terms of the trust.

Chapter 19

Ending a Trust: Tax Planning

Overview

[19.1] There are broadly two types of scenario for the ending of a trust:

(a) where the trustees will have no control over when the event will occur, eg on a beneficiary attaining a particular age, say 25 for an 'age 18-to-25 trust', or on the death of the beneficiary; or
(b) where they make an active decision to bring a trust to an end eg using one of their power to appoint or advance capital to beneficiaries.

In both cases, the tax position will the same, albeit that when the trustees make an active decision to end a trust they are, of course, in a better to position to manage the process and, particularly, the timing, to make sure that any tax is mitigated or avoided as far as possible.

[19.2] The key taxes that will need to be considered are:

- *Inheritance tax* – there could be an 'exit charge' or a life tenant could be deemed to make a chargeable or potentially exempt transfer.
- *Capital gains tax* – the ending of a trust can constitute a deemed disposal by the trustees and consideration will need to be given to whether this could trigger a chargeable gain and/or whether the gain can be held-over.

The taxation principles which apply in these cases are set out in CHAPTERS 7 to 12 (and should be referred to for the detailed commentary). The following is intended as an overview to show how those principles apply in the particular context of a trust's termination.

Inheritance tax

[19.3] Where the trust is a relevant property trust, there is likely to be an *exit* charge when property leaves the trusts (see CHAPTER 10). Under the current rules for 2016/17, there will be no exit charge if the exit occurs within three months of either the settlement being made (unlikely) or a ten-year anniversary [*IHTA 1984, s 65(4)* (see 10.11–10.12)]. The regime is designed to ensure that a 'fair' exit charge is levied according to the length of time that has elapsed since the date of settlement or the last ten-year anniversary and the value of the asset concerned on exit. Where the event occurs following a ten-year anniversary there is a proportionate charge fixed to the rate applying at the last ten-year anniversary subject to any interim increases in the nil-rate band. On the other hand, where the exit occurs within the first ten years there is no exit charge, whatever the value of the asset or trust on exit, if the making of the trust was within the settlor's nil-rate band (and, importantly, ignoring any agricultural and business property that might have been available at the settlement date). For this reason, the trustees of a nil-rate band settlement should always be reviewing the situation once, say, nine years have elapsed to see whether it is sensible to engineer an exit or whether instead they should wait and accept a first ten-year anniversary charge.

[19.4] Because of the operation of *IHTA 1984, s 81* there is no exit charge when property moves from one relevant property trust to another.

[19.5] Where there is a 'qualifying interest in possession', the life tenant is treated as owning the trust property and the inheritance tax treatment is akin to the position had the life tenant simple given the assets away (see CHAPTER 12). The precise inheritance tax position will be determined by the timing of the termination and the position following the termination, as the following paragraphs describe.

[19.6] A trust may come to an end, for example, on the *death* of a beneficiary with a qualifying interest in possession. The terms of such a trust may be, in very simple terms, 'to pay the income to Betty for her lifetime and on her death to hold the capital for such of Betty's children as may then be alive and have attained the age of 18'. When Betty dies, the assets of the trust will be treated as forming part of Betty's estate.

[19.7] If, however, Betty's interest comes to her end *during her lifetime*, then:

- there could be no inheritance tax consequence if the assets pass to Betty absolutely or outright to Betty's spouse;
- there could be a potentially exempt transfer if the assets pass to other beneficiaries outright or become held upon further qualifying interests in possession in their favour (although the latter will now rarely occur);
- there could be a chargeable transfer if assets become held upon relevant property trusts; and
- specific exemptions could apply in some cases – eg where there is an old 'Estate Duty' trust, or a 'revertor to settlor' trust.

[19.8] Outside the realm of straightforward relevant property and qualifying interest in possession trusts, it is difficult to generalise. Some 'favoured trusts' can be outside inheritance tax completely – eg Employee Trusts (see CHAPTER 16) – for others different provisions with apply – eg the quasi-exit charge for 'age 18-to-25 trusts' (see **10.32–10.34**).

[19.9] In all cases, business or agricultural property relief, could be available to mitigate any inheritance tax charge.

Capital gains tax

[19.10] Of course, when a trust ends this often happens alongside a sale of trust assets. Assets actually disposed of by trustees are, of course, subject to capital gains tax subject to the normal reliefs and exemptions. We are not considering that situation here. Rather we are considering the position where either:

- the *terms* of a settlement have been changed (most likely by the trustees exercising a power of appointment); or

- assets have been distributed from a trust – either to beneficiaries absolutely or to other trusts for their benefit.

[19.11] The general rule is that if the capital remains subject to the trusts of the settlement – albeit that the trusts might have been changed – there is no occasion of charge for capital gains tax. However, if capital leaves the settlement, there is a chargeable event because someone – the beneficiaries or the trustees of a new trust – have become 'absolutely entitled as against the trustees' and the trustees are therefore deemed to have disposed of the assets. Determining whether a settlement continues or whether a new settlement has been created by the actions of the trustees is not always straightforward. A well-drafted deed of appointment or advancement will make it clear whether the power exercised by the trustees is revocable or irrevocable. If it is irrevocable, then for capital gains tax purposes the property concerned has indeed left the settlement. If, on the other hand it is revocable, then the property remains subject to the trusts of the settlement even if for the time being the legal ownership of the property has changed.

[19.12] When appointing only part of a trust onto new trusts, the regime for sub-funds found in *TCGA 1992, Sch 4ZA* should also be considered (see 7.118–7.122). In broad terms, the sub-fund election allows the future gains accruing to the trustees of an identified sub-settlement to be assessed on those persons and not on the trustees of the principal settlement, that is overriding the principle set out in Statement of Practice 7/84 reproduced in APPENDIX A. Because the election also triggers a capital gains tax liability for the trustees, in the author's experience, such elections are relatively rare in a planning context.

[19.13] Where there is a deemed disposal by trustees, the following may be in point:
- On the death of the life tenant of a qualifying life interest trust, the familiar 'uplift' to market value will usually apply. *TCGA 1992, s 71(1)* deems there to be a disposal for all the settled property by the trustees and reacquisition at market value and *TCGA 1992, s 73(1)(a)* excludes a chargeable gain, subject to two exemptions:
  - if on the death, the trust property reverts to the settlor, there would be no capital gains tax free uplift to market value, but rather the settlor would instead acquire the trust property at the trustees' acquisition cost [*TCGA 1992, s 73(1)(b)*]; and
  - to the extent that any of the trust property was acquired by the trustees with gains held-over (whether under *section 165* for business assets or *section 260* for chargeable transfers), the held-over gain is crystallised by *section 74* – albeit that in some circumstances it may be open to defer the gain further by another hold-over election.
- Where capital leaves a relevant property settlement, because there is usually (but not always – see above) an exit charge, hold-over relief would ordinarily be available under *TCGA 1992, s 260*.
- *Section 260* hold-over relief would not ordinarily be available when property leaves a qualifying interest in possession trust; however, business asset hold-over relief may be available under *TCGA 1992, s 165*.

[19.14] Ending a Trust: Tax Planning

Other taxes

Income tax

[19.14] The subject-matter of this chapter is the exit of capital rather than income from a trust. The payment of income by trustees, whether as of right under a fixed or on exercising their discretion under a discretionary trust, is dealt with in CHAPTER 6. The obvious income tax implication of capital leaving a trust is that income from that capital will no longer arise to the trustees. Even where that capital has been subject to an interest in possession, the trustees had liability to pay tax at basic rate as described in CHAPTER 6 and that liability will fall away for the future. Having said that, two questions in the Trust and Estate Return deal with the payment of capital by trustees to beneficiaries as described below.

[19.15] Question 15 asks 'Have the trustees made any capital payments to, or for the benefit of, relevant children of the settlor during the settlor's lifetime?' If the answer is 'Yes', the total of capital payments made to relevant children is to be put in Box 15.1. The Notes to the Return observe that 'capital payments include the transfer of assets as well as payments of cash' and go on to say 'a relevant child is a minor who has never been married or in a civil partnership'.

[19.16] Question 15A asks whether there were 'capital transactions between the trustees and the settlors'. This is aimed at an anti-avoidance provision described at 4.26–4.31. HMRC's Notes to the Return state on page 25:

> 'Enter in boxes 15A.1 to 15A.12 details of any capital sums paid to the settlor or to a company connected with the settlement. If any capital sum has been paid to a company connected with the settlement, enter the name(s) of the company(ies) and its (their) registered office(s) in the appropriate box. If more than one sum has been paid, give separate details for each one.'

[19.17] A separate question, Q16, asks whether the trust has 'at any time been non-resident or received any capital from another trust which is, or at any time has been, non-resident?' and if so, whether the trustees have 'made any capital payments to, or provided any benefits for, the beneficiaries'. This question is aimed at the capital payments charge described in at 26.33–26.51, which is essentially an anti-avoidance provision. It seeks to charge UK beneficiaries, (whether or not domiciled in the UK – though if not domiciled subject to a remittance basis), on capital transferred from an offshore trust. The charge arises where there are within the trust gains which had the trustees at the time been UK resident would have attracted UK capital gains tax (and which had not previously been attributed to capital payments).

[19.18] There is an important point to note in the case of a trust which may currently be UK resident but which has in the past been non-UK resident, during which period the trustees made gains which had they then been UK resident would have attracted UK tax. This is that the potential for a tax charge on recipient beneficiaries who are UK resident survives the immigration of a trust.

[19.19] As is explained in 26.33–26.46, under current rules, it does not matter how much time elapses between the making by the non-UK resident trustees of the gain (which had they been UK resident would have been a chargeable gain) and the receipt by the beneficiary of a 'capital payment' which can be matched to that gain. If more than one year elapses between the making of the gain and the receipt of the payment, a supplementary charge of 10% arises for each year, subject to a maximum of six [*TCGA 1992, s 91*]. Thus with a capital gains rate of 28% the maximum supplementary charge is 16.8%, making the total capital gains tax charge 44.8%. In determining chargeability to UK tax on the capital payment, what matters is the residence and domicile status of the beneficiary at the date of matching (and not at the date of either of the making of the gains or the receipt of the capital payment). If the beneficiary is domiciled outside the UK at the date of the matching and is then a remittance basis user, the remittance basis of taxation will apply to defer a gain which is not remitted. However, if by that time the beneficiary has become UK domiciled, the *section 87* charge will apply. In particular, because the beneficiary is no longer domiciled outside the UK at the date of matching, any rebasing election formerly made by the trustees to exclude from charge any part of the gain accrued prior to 6 April 2008 will be irrelevant.

Stamp taxes

[19.20] For stamp taxes purposes, again whether or not the settlement continues, it is only where land or shares are concerned that thought needs to be given. Almost inevitably in each case there will be no positive implications because the asset will leave by way of gift. The only qualification is where there is land subject to a mortgage for which the beneficiary assumes responsibility, where the position is as described at 13.35.

Planning points

[19.21] The following tax planning points could be relevant to the ending of trust:

- relevant property trusts are the 'easiest' to end as the general availability of *TCGA 1992, s 260* hold-over relief ensures that any gains can be deferred and the value of any inheritance exit charge will be relatively modest.
- For qualifying interest in possession trusts, hold-over relief will not always be available and often the prospect of a substantial capital gains tax charge will deter trustees from taking the proactive decision to end the trust. Altering the terms of the trust while not ending it – and thereby avoiding a deemed disposal by the trustees – can sometimes offer a solution.
- Converting a qualifying interest in possession trust to a relevant property trust prior to any termination, might be appropriate in some circumstances.
- Trustees should, of course, bear in mind the possibility of the held-over gain coming back to be charged on them in the event of the beneficiary's emigration within six years after the end of the tax year in which the advance occurs.

[19.21] Ending a Trust: Tax Planning

- Particularly in the case of land, the rule in *Crowe v Appleby* can offer a route whereby a trust might be terminated in part for inheritance tax purposes while remaining in place for capital gains tax purposes.
- Where the terms of a trust are such that it will end automatically on a given date, finding a way to extend the trust beyond that date – again to avoid a deemed disposal – will be the objective. The Trust Deed may include the express power to do this; alternatively, a 'settled advance' might be considered.
- Finally, and more generally, trustees should always have some idea in advance of the size of any inherent chargeable gain and whether, in the case of easily realisable assets, it may simply be worth paying it rather than deferring the gain by electing to hold-over. This will be particularly the case if reliefs are available to the trustees which are unlikely to be available to the transferee.

Chapter 20

Compliance: Income Tax and Capital Gains Tax

Returns for income tax

[20.1] Since the introduction of self assessment in 1996/97, income has been assessed on a current year basis.

[20.2] The return form for 2015/16 is 12 pages (Form SA900, see APPENDIX F) and the guide to filling it in runs to another 31 pages. The tax calculation form takes 16 pages. Supplementary schedules add to the number. The simplification of the self assessment literature for individual taxpayers from 2007/08 has not been adopted for trustees. Because taxpayers are required to self assess, the forms must be filled in correctly to avoid the risk of becoming a back duty case by accident. If there is no tax to collect, the return is simple. So, if the trust is an interest in possession trust of which the income is mandated to the life tenant, or all the income is taxed at source, etc the form requires only a few ticks and a signature. If there is tax to collect then details of income are required. If there are capital gains and losses these will usually have to be reported. The losses will have to be calculated whether there is any chance of using them or not. The reporting of a loss on the capital gains supplementary pages SA905 would satisfy the requirement of *TCGA 1992, s 16(2A)* that notice be given.

[20.3] Although the trustees are not asked to forward vouchers or other supporting documentation, they will have to retain them. If, in the course of a year, an estate is administered by personal representatives and then becomes a trust, two returns are needed.

[20.4] The income tax rules for what under *ITTOIA 2005* are from 2005/06 'property income' and 'trading income' (previously Sch A and Sch D respectively) are general and not specific to trusts. Where income arises from let property, the whole of a landlord's income is treated as if his holdings were a business. The property business will usually be that of the trustees, unless in the case of an interest in possession trust they have delegated their powers of management to the life tenant (in which event it will be his).

[20.5] The completion of Form SA900 is straightforward but does require care and attention. The tax computation is difficult and, at current charge-out rates, might be expensive to complete. This in itself is a good enough reason to file all returns for 2015/16 on or before 31 October 2016, the first send back date. It will then be HMRC's job to calculate the tax which the practitioner can check. In any event the beneficiaries will want their tax vouchers early so that they, too, can file their returns in time. If there is any obvious error in the return or anything incomplete, it will be returned and treated as if it had not been sent. This will mean that some taxpayers filing returns at the last minute will be caught out and will have to compute their own tax. The second (and last) send back date is 31 January 2016 and anybody using that date has to calculate their own tax. The filing date of 31 January is, from 2007/08, intended only for e-filing, with, from 2010/11, the prospect of a penalty for any paper return submitted after the following 31 October.

[20.6] Up to and including 2009/10, provided that all the tax due was paid on or before 31 January 2010, there was no penalty for a late submission of a return. The £100 penalty for late filing was mitigated to the extent of the tax outstanding after 31 January. However, as from 2010/11, the automatic penalty applies for paper returns filed after 31 October, even if no tax remains outstanding after the following 31 January [*SI 2011/702, para 2*]. Trustees who want to file electronically must incur the expense of acquiring commercial software, as it is not produced by HMRC as it is for individuals. There was an interesting First-tier Tribunal decision in a partnership case (*Paul and Annette Galbraith (t/a Galbraith Ceramics) v Revenue and Customs Comrs* (TC02639) [2013] UKFTT 225 (TC), [2013] SFTD 857, [2013] SWTI 2221). There the partnership successfully contested a late penalty notice for filing their 2010/11 return in paper form after 31 October (but before 31 January 2012). Their case was that they needed longer than 31 October provided in order to file the return and it was 'unfair, unreasonable and discriminatory' to require taxpayers to spend money in order to satisfy a statutory obligation. The opposite result was achieved for trustees in the First-tier Tribunal case of *Trustee of the Georgia Vickery, Franki and Mia Settlement v Revenue and Customs Comrs* (TC02688) [2013] UKFTT 282 (TC). There the Tribunal upheld the view of HMRC that it was not unreasonable to expect the trustee to obtain the requisite software to enable him to submit the outstanding return for 2010/11 online.

[20.7] The practitioner has to work out the beneficiaries' income on his own forms, the old Inland Revenue form R59 having been discontinued. The tax voucher for beneficiaries is form R185 (Trust Income). A photocopied form is acceptable.

[20.8] If the trustee has arranged matters so that the calculation of the tax is done for him, he will want to check it. This could be much quicker if he uses the traditional method of calculation as in APPENDIX C.

Notification of liability

[20.9] Taxpayers must notify liability to HMRC within six months of the end of the year of assessment, if they have not received a notice requiring a return to be made (*TMA 1970, s 7*). Up to 2008/09 this notice used to take the form of a paper SA 900 issued shortly after 6 April. Now that electronic filing is encouraged, a one page notice SA 316 is issued instead.

[20.10] As has been mentioned, the last send back date is normally 31 January. If the return is late then an alternative period is three months from the date of issue. In that case, if the return is filed within two months of issue HMRC will calculate the tax.

[20.11] HMRC can correct obvious errors in the taxpayer's calculations within nine months of filing. Taxpayers have twelve months to make a correction (*TMA 1970, ss 9ZA* and *9ZB*).

Trusts with no income

[20.12] In an attempt to eliminate the issue of unnecessary annual self assessment returns to trusts with no income (and no likelihood of income or gains):

(a) trustees of a trust with no income or gains do not have to notify the Trust District of the existence of a trust; and
(b) for existing trusts, the trustees may request either that the record for the trust should be closed by the Trust District or that tax returns shall not be issued annually. As a result annual returns would not normally be issued but the position may be reviewed periodically. If, exceptionally, a return is issued it must be completed.

In their Trusts, Settlements and Estates Manual, HMRC give to their officers the following instructions at TSEM3014:

> 'Trustees whose income year on year does not exceed the standard rate band and whose liability is covered in full by tax deducted at source or non-payable tax credits are not usually required to make a return every year. This will mostly affect those trustees whose income is within the £1000 limit . . . and is made up of net interest and UK dividends, as they will have no additional liability.
>
> Where such cases are identified and there is no open enquiry set the 'Last SA Return' year to that of the most recently filed Trust & Estate Tax Return, for example if this was for 2009/10, set this as '10' and send the 'SRB/TAS dormancy' letter to the trustees and copy to the agent where appropriate (see TSEM3015). If a return has already been selected for issue for the following year, the dormancy procedure does not apply and no further action is required.'

[20.13] New trusts are notified to HMRC on Form 41G(Trust). Submission of the form for those trusts which are not expected to receive income or have chargeable gains can lead to unnecessary self assessment returns being issued. To avoid this HMRC have advised that they would only expect to be notified of a new trust where it is expected to:

(i) receive income; and/or
(ii) have chargeable gains.

See HMRC Trusts and Estates Newsletter, August 2013.

[20.14] HMRC have been given new powers by *FA 2013, s 233, Sch 51* to withdraw notices issued under *Taxes Management Act 1970, ss 8, 8A* or *12AA* to file a self assessment return for 2012/13 onwards and also to cancel late filing penalties. For years before that legislation came into force HMRC have said that they will consider withdrawing such notices in cases where a return is not needed for example because all income has ceased. This, however, is a discretionary power.

[20.15] Compliance: Income Tax and Capital Gains Tax

[20.15] The trustees, of course, still have a legal responsibility to notify the Trust District of chargeable income and/or capital gains for any year for which no return is issued (*IR Working Together*, Issue 3, December 2000, p 4).

[20.16] *TMA 1970, s 8A* imposes a duty on the trustees to make a return when required and to provide supporting information, etc as may be required. Although one of the trustees will normally be treated as principal acting trustee and be issued with the return, the 'relevant trustee' legislation makes it possible for any trustee to be involved. This commenced in 1996/97 [*TMA 1970, s 107A*]. The change may seem trifling but under the old rules if the responsibility had to be transferred to a different trustee, a new return form had to be issued in the new name, etc. The trustees must now be more self-reliant. They must decide matters for themselves as they fill in the return. For instance they will decide what their country of residence is and whether they are liable to the additional rate or simply basic rate taxation. There will be decisions to take as to the acquisition value for capital gains tax and whether exemptions such as main residence relief will apply. *TMA 1970, s 42* explains how reliefs are to be claimed. Where effect will be given to a relief by carrying it back to an earlier year, a freestanding claim can be made, or else the claim can be included in the next return. Thus the self assessment for the prior year need not be disturbed, the relief being given by adjusting the balancing payment of tax due for the year when the relief is claimed. Claims must be made on prescribed forms. Interest calculations are related to the normal filing date of the later year. If a claim involves a repayment of tax then the taxpayer has to have documentary proof of payment of tax (ie the official record of payment).

Payment of tax

[20.17] There are two dates for payment of tax, namely 31 January and 31 July. Interest in possession settlements are unlikely to be involved because their income is generally taxed at source. Discretionary and accumulation settlements are certain to have a liability. Late paid tax will attract interest and maybe also penalties (see **22.3–22.7** and **22.22**).

[20.18] The payment dates for 2015/16 and 2016/17 are:

- 31 January 2016: first payment of income tax for 2015/16.
- 31 July 2016: second payment of income tax for 2015/16.
- 31 January 2017: capital gains tax for 2015/16, any balance of income tax for 2015/16, first payment of income tax for 2016/17.
- 31 July 2017: second payment of income tax for 2016/17.
- 31 January 2018: capital gains tax for 2016/17, any balance of income tax for 2016/17, first payment of income tax for 2017/18.

The payments on account are fixed at 50% of the prior year's income tax liability, subject to the de minimis provision mentioned at **20.19**.

[20.19] There are de minimis rules so that where the tax is £1,000 or less or if 80% of the income is taxed at source, no payments on account are required. See HMRC Trusts & Estates Newsletter, June 2010.

Estimates

[20.20] The Return specifically asks (Question 21.5 – see APPENDIX F) whether any provisional figures have been used. When a settlement includes unquoted investments or land and a disposal takes place it is highly likely that a provisional figure for the acquisition cost will be used. The provisional figure can be checked by application on form CG34. This form is available at district offices. It should be submitted after the disposal but before filing the Return. The tax office will refer matters to Shares Valuation Division or to the District Valuer as may be appropriate. We are told that a minimum of 56 days is necessary for an official view of the provisional figure to be available. In fact it could easily be longer. It must be to the taxpayer's advantage to submit the form at the earliest moment with every detail, plan, etc which might speed things up. This service is known as the 'pre-filing date valuation service'. As something of a last resort, an appeal may be made to the First-tier Tribunal (or, for matters concerning land, to the Lands Tribunal).

Finality for deceased estates

[20.21] If HMRC find it necessary, they will formally notify the taxpayer that they are commencing an enquiry. They can do so only in the twelve months following the actual date of filing. In the absence of any such notification the self assessment is final and can be disturbed only if there is an inaccuracy resulting from lack of reasonable care (previously negligence) or fraud. Plainly personal representatives and trustees having wound up an estate will not want to wait for the tax return to be issued after the end of the tax year and then wait for twelve months from the filing date. In April 1996 HMRC announced that they would issue returns early in such cases and would confirm that they do not seek to enquire into the return (see Inland Revenue press release of 4 April 1996). Current practice is that HMRC will normally allow this 'informal payment procedure' (ie without completion of a self assessment return) so long as the estate is not regarded as 'complex' (see below) and the liability for the whole of the administration is met fully by one payment and the payment is accompanied by a simple calculation showing details of the charge (see TSEM7410). An estate will be regarded as 'complex' where: the total tax liability of the estate is in excess of £10,000; the value exceeds £2.5 million; or the proceeds of sale of chargeable assets in any one tax year exceed £250,000. However, if a self assessment return has been issued it must be completed. The author understands also that, where the income does not exceed £100, personal representatives are being encouraged not to deal with HMRC at all, but rather to make the payment gross and to leave the tax liability to be returned and paid by the beneficiary.

Clearance

[20.22] If no enquiry is raised within 12 months of the statutory filing date, clearance is automatically given, although HMRC have power to raise a 'discovery assessment' in the case of an inaccuracy resulting from lack of reasonable care or deliberate error within six years after the end of the tax year in question (*TMA 1970, s 36*) (see **20.25–20.29**). If the return is filed late, the 12 months runs from the end of the quarter in which filing takes place. If earlier clearance is desired (eg to assist in winding up a trust) it will be available.

Policy for trustees

[20.23] Trustees must look carefully at their programmes for filing returns and for quality control. A statutory requirement for the retention of records is to be found in *TMA 1970, s 12B*. This is a general provision and although there may be cases where trustees have to keep tax records for some six years the period will be shorter in most cases. This is purely to do with tax and there can, of course, be good non-tax reasons for keeping trust papers for long periods.

[20.24] HMRC recognise that the return may not be enough for them to be aware of any underassessment or excessive relief. It is open to the taxpayer to file additional documents so that adequate disclosure is made. Separate accounts are not expected where accounts are the basis of the assessment. Instead the standard accounts information will be appropriate. Provided the return and any supporting materials amount to full disclosure then the file for the year will be closed at the usual time (see **20.22**, also *TMA 1970, ss 9A, 19A, 28A, 29*). This was confirmed in an Inland Revenue press release dated 31 May 1996.

Discovery

[20.25] Once the so-called 'enquiry window' has closed, a self assessment will be final unless an HMRC officer makes a 'discovery assessment' under *TMA 1970, s 29*. This requires the discovery that:

(a)   any income or chargeable gains have not been properly assessed;
(b)   an assessment is or has become insufficient; or
(c)   any relief given is or has become excessive.

One of two conditions must then be satisfied: either, first, the taxpayer or his agent has acted carelessly or deliberately; or, second, at the time when the enquiry window closed, whether by elapse of the 12 months or by express notice by the HMRC officer that he had completed his enquiries,

> 'the officer could not have been reasonably expected, on the basis of the information made available to him before that time, to be aware of the situation mentioned in [(a), (b) or (c) above]'.

[20.26] The time limits for an assessment are, in the case of action by the taxpayer or agent, six years for lack of reasonable care or 20 years for deliberate action (what used to be called 'fraud') and, in the case of a discovery assessment, four years, after the end of the relevant year of assessment (*TMA 1970 s 36 and s 34* respectively).

[20.27] A number of recent cases have concerned the issue of what the officer concerned should have reasonably been aware of, in particular in terms of what the taxpayer has disclosed on the 'white space' box in the return for any further information. To preclude the possibility of a discovery assessment, the taxpayer must give a full and detailed disclosure of the events which have occurred to support his analysis of the tax implications. In the CA decision in *Veltema v Langham* [2004] STC 544, Auld LJ, speaking of the discovery regime, said that:

> 'the key to the scheme is that the inspector is shut out from making a discovery assessment under [s 29] only where the taxpayer or his representatives, in making an honest and accurate return or in responding to a section 9(A) enquiry, have clearly alerted him to the insufficiency of the assessment, not where the inspector may have some other information, not normally part of his checks, but might put the sufficiency of the assessment in question'.

[20.28] In *Revenue and Customs Comrs v Lansdowne Partners Ltd Partnership* [2011] EWCA Civ 1578, [2012] STC 544, 81 TC 318, the taxpayer claimed in their self assessment return a deduction for an expense which was inadmissible. Being outside the enquiry window, HMRC raised a discovery assessment, to which the Court of Appeal held they were not entitled. The Court held that an officer of the Board could have been reasonably expected, on the basis of information disclosed in correspondence following a meeting with HMRC, to be aware that an amount of profits included in the partnership statement was insufficient, by the expiry of the time for opening an enquiry. The hypothetical inspector having before him the relevant documents and the note of the meeting would have been aware of an actual insufficiency in the declared profit.

[20.29] The more recent cases of *Sanderson v Revenue and Customs Comrs* [2016] EWCA Civ 19 (in the Court of Appeal) and *Smith v HMRC* (TC02768) [2013] UKFTT 368 (TC) both involved marketed avoidance schemes which were disclosed in the 'white space' of the tax return. It was held in both that HMRC were entitled to make a discovery assessment despite the disclosure on the return. However, in *Revenue and Customs Comrs v Charlton* [2012] UKUT 770 (TCC) it was held that the information provided with the return was sufficient such that 'no officer could have missed the point that an artificial tax avoidance scheme had been implemented' and that 'on the basis of the information made available to him before the closure of the enquiry window, an officer would have been reasonably expected to have been aware of the insufficiency of tax such as to justify an assessment'. Accordingly, a discovery assessment was not possible – it was not necessary that a hypothetical officer should have a full understanding of the scheme or be able to form a reasoned view of it.

[20.30] Of course, HMRC would prefer to have the flexibility of raising assessments without too much restriction and this will no doubt continue to be an area of dispute and litigation for some years to come. One recent decision of general help to taxpayers is that of *Burgess v Revenue and Customs Commissioners* [2015] UKUT 578 (TCC), [2016] STC 579, [2015] All ER (D) 209 (Nov), where the Upper Tribunal held that the burden of proof always rests with HMRC in demonstrating the validity of any discovery assessment.

The beneficiaries

[20.31] The beneficiaries have their own self assessment returns and the same timetable as the trustees. Therefore the beneficiaries have to know the amount of trust income, whether from an interest in possession or discretionary/accumulation trust, in each tax year.

Deceased estates

[20.32] Personal representatives will be dealt with by the deceased's tax district for the first year or so of the administration, though see **17.6**.

[20.33] Under the self assessment regime figures have to be certain. The income paid out by the personal representatives is the income of the beneficiary in the year of receipt. All this is a complete contrast to the calculation of the income of a beneficiary of a fixed interest trust which is done on a 'see through' basis, that is to say that the income of a particular tax year when received by the trustees remains income of that year in the beneficiary's computations whenever it is paid out. Whatever balance of income is outstanding at the end of the administration period will be the income of the year in which the end of that period falls, regardless of when the income was assessed upon the personal representatives. Given the width of the tax rate bands of individuals there may not be a lot of planning to do, but where there are beneficiaries who might recover tax or might be liable at 45% (for 2014/15), the personal representatives should pass on the income regularly so as to avoid any bunching. The 'applicable rate' (in *ITTOIA 2005, s 663(1)*) enables income to retain its character through the estate into the hands of the income beneficiary (now *ITTOIA 2005, s 656*).

[20.34] Similar rules apply where there is an 'absolute interest' in an estate. That is to say that the beneficiary is entitled to income and capital. He, too, is treated as receiving income in the year it is paid to him, regardless of the year of receipt by the personal representatives. Running totals have to be kept totalling the estate income and the payments to him, so that he is taxed on the lesser of the cumulative estate income or the amounts actually paid. Again, whatever income is due at the close of the administration will be the income of the beneficiary for the year when the administration comes to an end. Again, the 'applicable rate' is used to track the income's character to the beneficiary.

[20.35] Personal representatives have to recognise an unexpected rule in certifying the income of a beneficiary for a particular year. The payment of capital or (albeit unlikely) the release of a debt, although capital in nature, might trigger an income tax liability on the beneficiary to the extent that there is during that tax year, or a previous tax year of the estate, undistributed income [*ITTOIA 2005, s 681*]. Accordingly, a distribution of chattels to beneficiaries may trigger income tax liabilities. The beneficiary is treated as having received a gross amount of income equal to the greater of the value of the chattel and the amount of undistributed income in that or previous years, from which tax has been deducted at the applicable rate. The gross and the net amounts will be recorded on the form R185 (Estate Income) which the personal representatives will give to the beneficiary to enable completion of the personal return.

[20.36] ITTOIA 2005, s 682A places a duty on the personal representatives to provide a tax voucher to the beneficiary, distinguishing the different types of income received. Form R185 (Estate Income) is designed to enable this to be done.

Completing the Trust and Estate Tax Return — SA900

[20.37] This commentary should be taken as a summary guide only and should be used in conjunction with the booklet SA950 'Trust and Estate Tax Return Guide'. The notes on the front cover of the return (Form SA900 – see APPENDIX F) should be read before starting to complete the return.

Page 2

[20.38] *Step 1*—These boxes are very important because if any one applies, you do not need to complete the income boxes but merely consider pages 10 to 12. *The questions relate only to bare trusts, interest in possession settlements and personal representatives.* Only one box should be ticked.

[20.39] Bare Trusts—HMRC accept that bare trustees can submit a Trust Return, settle the liability and vouch the income to the beneficiaries in the normal way. It must be stressed, however, that any capital gains/losses arising must be entered on the personal tax returns of the beneficiaries and not on the trust return.

Pages 2–3

[20.40] *Step 2*—Questions 1–7 and 23—If the trustees receive income which needs to be returned on one or more of the supplementary pages, then the appropriate box/es must be ticked and the supplementary pages completed. The supplementary pages are as follows: Trade, Partnership, UK Property, Foreign, Capital Gains, Non-Residence, Charities and Estate Pension Charges etc. This chapter makes no particular comment on these except at 20.71 in relation to foreign dividends to be entered on the foreign supplementary pages.

[20.41] Question 8—These boxes are important because they determine the rate at which the trust/estate will be charged to tax. If you get it wrong it could have serious consequences in the future.

Pages 4–5

[20.42] Question 9—Whether the income needs to be entered will depend on the type of trust. For interest in possession settlements the notes should be read carefully. It may not be necessary to record all the income (eg where mandated to the life tenant). However, where you wish to claim accrued income relief

[20.42] Compliance: Income Tax and Capital Gains Tax

then the appropriate boxes must be completed. If for example the relief is from a 'gilt' then boxes 9.12 to 9.14 must be completed. The relief is obtained by reducing the gross interest in box 9.14 by the amount of the allowance.

[20.43] For accumulation or discretionary settlements the whole of the income must be declared in the appropriate boxes. The boxes are self-explanatory.

[20.44] If trustees receive any income which does not fall to be entered in boxes 9.1 to 9.31 inclusive and which is not to be included in any of the supplementary pages, then boxes 9.32 to 9.40 inclusive should be used. (Pages 18 to 20 of the Guide explain in detail the type of income which qualifies under this section.)

[20.45] The treatment of accrued income allowances has been dealt with earlier. Accrued income charges should be entered in box 9.37A. This applies to both interest in possession and discretionary trusts as the liability on such charges is the rate applicable to trusts regardless of the type of trust. This box should also be used for relevant discounted securities which have replaced those types of securities previously termed deep discount securities and deep gain securities.

[20.46] Box 9.40 should be used in cases where trustees receive a qualifying distribution following the re-purchase by a company of its own shares. In such cases box 9.39 should be used to enter the notional tax at the special rates attached to the distribution.

[20.47] Question 9A, at box 9A.1, requests the amount of the standard rate band (see **6.52–6.54**) which will be somewhere between £1,000 and £200, depending upon the number of settlements made by the same settlor.

Page 6

[20.48] Question 10A—Do you want to claim any reliefs or have you made any annual payments? Where an annuity is paid to a beneficiary, the tax to be deducted is at the basic rate. This means that if the trustees receive only dividend income, then there is a shortfall, on 2015/16 tax rates, of 10% which must be paid by virtue of *ITA 2007, s 964*. In interest in possession cases sufficient income must be included in the boxes on pages 3 and 4 to cover the amount of the annuity. If this is not done the tax calculation will claw back the full amount of tax deducted from the annuity. The amount of the annuity to be included under this heading is an amount equal to the total income received by the trustees. If the annuity exceeds the total income and the trustees have to revert to capital to make up the annuity, then the excess must be entered at boxes 11.1 to 11.3.

[20.49] Question 10B—Do you want to claim special income tax treatment where a valid vulnerable beneficiary election has effect? For this see **15.14–15.18** and specifically **15.17** for the election.

[20.50] Question 12—Have any assets or funds been put into the trust in year 2015/16? There has been a change in the formulation of the question since 2002. The question is no longer directed only to additions to existing trusts, but in the case of a new trust the answer 'yes' has to be given, with details of the assets settled.

Page 7

[20.51] Question 13—This section of the form starts with the question 'Is any part of the trust income not liable to tax at the special trust rates?' There are three categories: income paid to beneficiaries whose entitlement is not subject to the trustees' (or any other person's) discretion; income allocated to specific purposes; and trust management expenses. If the answer is yes, boxes 13.7 to 13.21 must be completed; if no, only boxes 13.19 to 13.21. This question has been somewhat modified in the last four tax years, helpfully one must say, in referring to specific amounts rather than (as it first did) to percentages of income and the return for 2006/07 expressly distinguishes between the three categories of income. The various sub-questions distinguish between income chargeable at the 10% rate and at the basic rate and to trust management expenses applicable to each tranche of income. First boxes 13.7 to 13.12 require details of income which is not subject to the 'trustees' discretion (and applicable expenses). Next boxes 13.13 to 13.18 request details of income allocated to specific purposes and their relative trust management expenses. This might include income applied towards redeeming a lease or a mortgage (but not income applied for the maintenance, education or benefit of minor beneficiaries). Box 13.19 requests the total amount of deductible trust management expenses, which is clarified by page 22 of the Guide, with a reference to *Help Sheet 392* (discussed at **6.40**) *Trust Management Expenses*. See also **6.34–6.35** for the *Peter Clay Discretionary Trust* litigation. Box 13.20 is for the total expenses set against income not liable at the special trust rates. Box 13.21 is for non-UK resident trusts only, asking for the total income not liable to UK income tax which is not included elsewhere on the self assessment return. Page 24 of the Guide incorporates a Working Sheet for Question 13.

[20.52] Question 13A—The question here is 'is this a settlor-interested trust where part of the income is not settlor-interested?' If the answer is yes, box 13A.1 requires the amount of the tax pool applicable to income which is not settlor-interested.

Page 8

[20.53] Question 14—The boxes should be completed only for discretionary payments. They must not be completed for payments made to beneficiaries who are absolutely entitled to the income as it arises.

[20.54] The amount to be entered is the net payment. If the distribution is to the minor or unmarried child of the settlor and the settlor is alive, then the appropriate box must be ticked. This is because under the provisions of (*ITTOIA 2005 ss 622, 629(1), (2)*) the distributed income will be treated as that of the settlor for that year of assessment and not as the income of any other person.

[20.55] *Box 14.15*—It is important that the 'tax pool' is computed each year and the amount entered in the box. The 'tax pool' is calculated at stage 9 on pages 16 and 17 of the *Tax Calculation Guide For Trusts and Estates* under boxes T9.1 to T9.27 inclusive.

[20.56] If you make no entry and discretionary payments are made to beneficiaries, a charge under *ITA 2007, Pt 9, Ch 7, ss 493–498* will be payable, at 45% of the gross payments (except to the extent that the charge is covered by any balance in the tax pool as at the end of 2014/15 as supplemented by tax paid by the trustees in 2015/16 other than the 10% non-recoverable tax credit on dividends). See **6.68–6.79**.

[20.57] Question 15 asks whether the trustees have made any capital payments to or for the benefit of, relevant [ie minor, unmarried] children of the settlor during the settlor's lifetime. If so, there will again be implications for the settlor under *ITTOIA 2005, ss 622, 629(1), (2)*. Question 15A asks whether there have been any capital transactions between the trustees and the settlor: the tax significance is explained on page 25 of the Guide.

Page 9

[20.58] Question 16 asks whether the trust has at any time been non-UK resident or received any capital from another trust, which is or at any time has been non-UK resident. If it has, details of capital payments made by the trustees to, or any benefits provided for, beneficiaries are required. If so, this may have capital gains tax implications under *TCGA 1992, s 87* (see **26.33–26.52**).

Page 10

[20.59] Question 17—When you reach this point of the return it is decision time. If you decide not to self-calculate then the return (for 2015/16) must be submitted to HMRC on or before 31 October 2016. If this is done then HMRC guarantee to calculate the liability in time for the correct payments to be made by 31 January 2017. This follows from the requirement that a paper return must be submitted on or before the 31 October after the end of the year of assessment to which it refers. Submission of an electronic return on or before the following 31 January will automatically calculate the tax due on 31 January.

[20.60] If you decide to compute the liability then all the appropriate boxes must be completed. This is so that HMRC can check to see whether the calculation is correct.

[20.61] Box 17.2 is marked 'tax due for earlier years'. Where returns for a number of years are being submitted at the same time, this box should not be completed with the amounts of tax due to some of the earlier years. This is because the box is intended for use where, eg the rules for farmers' averaging, for the carry-back of post-cessation receipts or for the spreading of copyright income apply. The box should not be used to cover liabilities outstanding as shown on previous returns.

[20.62] If you wish to reduce the payment on account tick box 17.5 and explain why in the 'Additional Information' box on page 12.

[20.63] If the liability is under £1,000 in 2015/16, you will not have to make payments on account on 31 January and 31 July 2017 towards your 2016/17 liability, but will instead make a single payment of tax for that year on 31 January 2018.

[20.64] If a repayment arises (eg because all the income is taxed at source and there is an accrued income allowance for the year) then the amount of the repayment will have been entered in box 17.1, in brackets.

[20.65] If you wish to claim the repayment then boxes 18.1 to boxes 18.12 must be completed, including a signature at 18.12. HMRC will not repay if question 18 has been ignored. In such cases the repayment will be allocated against the next tax bill.

Page 11

[20.66] Question 19 asks for details of the trustee/personal representative (and of his adviser) who completes and signs the form.

Question 20—It is important to complete the appropriate boxes where there has been either a change of trustee or merely a change of address. It is advisable to notify the relevant Trusts Office by letter as soon as the event takes place so that correspondence such as statements can be sent to the new trustee during the year. The boxes on the return must still be completed even though the information has already been sent to HMRC.

Page 12

[20.67] Question 21—Boxes 21.2 and 21.4 are important. If the trust or administration has ceased, enter the date. This will stop the issue of any further returns and unnecessary correspondence by HMRC.

[20.68] Question 22—Tick the appropriate box for the return. If supplementary pages have been completed then tick those boxes also. When you are satisfied sign the declaration. If you fail to do so or you have failed to include the supplementary pages, HMRC will send the return back to you with a covering letter.

[20.69] The relevant Trusts Office will assist the taxpayer or his agent with any difficulties which may arise.

Toolkit

[20.70] For further help in completing the return, the document *2015–16 Trusts and Estates Toolkit* is available from HMRC's website.

The foreign supplementary pages: dividends from non-UK companies

[20.71] Prior to 2008/09 the non-repayable tax credit was available only in respect of UK dividends. From 2008/09 it was extended to benefit an individual who receives or is taxed on dividends from non-UK resident companies provided that his interest is in less than 10% of the shares of the company. The tax credit is one ninth of the dividend [*ITTOIA 2005, s 397A*, inserted by *FA 2008, Sch 12, para 4*]. A double grossing up exercise is required by section 398. The 10% restriction has been removed from 2009/10, though the tax credit will not be available if the country in which the distributing companies resident does not levy a tax on corporate profits similar to corporation tax. UK resident UK domiciled individuals are taxed at 32.5% on the non-UK dividend income in 2009/10 at 42.5% in 2010/11, 2011/12 and 2012/13 and 37.5% in 2013/14, 2014/15, and 2015/16. This applies also to UK resident non-UK domiciliaries who are not remittance basis users (see *ITA 2007, s 19(2)(b)*, subject to *sections 13(1)(c)* and *14(1)(c)*). By contrast, the rate is 40% for 2009/10 and 50% for 2010/11, 2011/12 and 2012/13 for non-UK domiciled individuals who are remittance basis users, falling to 45% for 2013/14, 2014/15 and 2015/16.

[20.72] HMRC's original guidance for 2008/09 stated that tax credit was not available either to settlors of settlor-interested trusts or to beneficiaries of interest in possession trusts. However, that is clearly not correct and HMRC admitted as much in the summer of 2009. Some issues can arise in relation to the completion of form R185 (Trust Income), in relation to which HMRC said the following in their inheritance tax and trusts newsletter – August 2009 on 27 August 2009. HMRC Trusts are also aware that there may be some confusion regarding the completion of section 7 (foreign income) on the form R185 (Trust Income). The taxable amount is the total of the net amount plus the UK tax paid plus the foreign tax paid and any foreign tax credit that may be due. On a separate sheet, the trustees should tell the beneficiary what type of income this is, so they can complete the Foreign pages (SA 904) on the Tax Return which have recently been altered. See HMRC Trusts & Estates Newsletter, June 2010.

The non-residence etc supplementary pages: statutory residence test

[20.73] Following the introduction of the Statutory Residence Test (SRT) from 2013/14 assessing the trustees' residence status is now a two stage process. First deciding the residence of the persons who are actually trustees (using the SRT where appropriate) and then determining the residence of the trustees as a whole. The notes to Questions 1—3 on page 1 of the Notes on Trust and Estate Non-Residence will assist in finding the residence of the trustees as a whole.

Trust and Estate capital gains

[20.74] Trustees should complete the eight page SA 905 if:

- they disposed of chargeable assets in 2014/15 for a consideration of more than £44,400 (four times the individual's annual exemption); or
- they made losses and their chargeable gains before losses total more than their applicable annual exemption; or
- having deducted no losses, the trustees' taxable gains exceed their annual exemption; or
- the trustees want to claim an allowable loss or make any other capital gains tax claim or election for the year.

If the trust is a bare trust, any gains should be returned by the beneficiaries on their personal tax returns and not by the trustees (see **2.44**). For the applicable annual exemption see **7.36–7.39**. As does the individual self assessment return the Trusts and Estates capital gains form distinguishes between quoted securities, unquoted securities, land and other assets.

Chapter 21

Compliance: Inheritance Tax

[21.1] Most of the administrative provisions which relate to inheritance tax and settlements are to be found in *IHTA 1984, Pt VIII (ss 215–261)*. In many of the paragraphs of those provisions references to chargeable transfers appear. *IHTA 1984, s 2(3)* ensures that references to chargeable transfers can be construed as references to occasions of charge on relevant property settlements, whether they be ten-year charges or exit charges.

[21.2] *Finance Act 2014* includes (*Schedule 25, paragraph 5*) amendments to *IHTA 1984* to synchronise the dates for the delivery of accounts and the payment of tax; however, perversely, this aspect of the 'simplification' project applies only to chargeable transfers made by trustees (ie ten-year and exit charges) and the pre-5 April 2014 rules will continue to apply to any chargeable transfer arising on a settlor's transfers to a trust' (see **21.4–21.7**).

Determination of tax chargeable

The Inheritance Tax Account (other than on death)

[21.3] The first administrative step will be the rendering of an Inheritance Tax Account on form IHT 100. This form must be used to inform HMRC Trusts and Estates about all events which give rise to inheritance tax, other than death, and is the lead form in a set of forms dealing with a full range of matters to be returned and calculations based thereon. An account is the equivalent in inheritance tax terms of a return for other taxes.

[21.4] The time limits for the delivery of an account for chargeable transfers by trustees (ie for ten-year and exit charges) were changed by *Finance Act 2014*. For chargeable transfers by trustees made on or before 5 April 2014, the due date for delivery to HMRC Trusts and Estates is twelve months after the end of the month in which the occasion of charge took place. Alternatively, the due date is three months after the trustees first become liable for tax if that is later than the normal due date [*IHTA 1984, s 216(6)*]. There can be different dates where heritage property is concerned [*IHTA 1984, s 216(7)*]. For chargeable transfers by trustees on or after 6 April 2014, the due date for delivery is now six months from the end of the month in which the occasion of charge occurs. For penalties for failure to deliver an account, see **22.19**.

[21.5] For chargeable transfers by a settlor (ie on creation of a trust), the time limits for the delivery of an account are the same as those set out in **21.4** for chargeable transfers by trustees prior to 6 April 2014. That is to say, these time limits are unaffected by the *Finance Act 2014* changes.

Payment of tax

[21.6] The payment dates for inheritance tax payable in relation to chargeable transfers by trustees (ie for ten-year and exit charges) were also changed by *Finance Act 2014*. For chargeable transfers by trustees made on or before 5 April 2014, the tax fell due six months after the end of the month in which the chargeable transfer took place or, in the case of a transfer after 5 April and before 6 October in any year, on the following 30 April, ie before the deadline for delivery of the account [*IHTA 1984, s 226(1)*]. For chargeable transfers by trustees on or after 6 April 2014, the payment date is now six months from the end of the month in which the occasion of charge occurs regardless of when it occurs. For penalties and interest for late payment of inheritance tax, see **22.6** and **22.22**.

[21.7] For chargeable transfers by a settlor (ie on creation of a trust), the payment dates for inheritance tax payable are again the same as those set out in **21.6** for chargeable transfers by trustees prior to 6 April 2014.

De minimis provisions: excepted transfers and excepted settlements

[21.8] The obligation to report is removed by the *de minimis* provisions, which have been substantially increased with effect from 2007/08. Following the enactment of the *Finance Act 2006* regime for trusts, it was recognised that many more lifetime settlements would fall within the relevant property regime and that the thresholds for reporting then applying seemed absurdly low (that is, under the *Inheritance Tax (Delivery of Accounts) (Excepted Transfers and Excepted Terminations) Regulations 2002, SI 2002/1731*: only if either the total of chargeable transfers (including the one in question) made in the present tax year exceeded £10,000 *or* the total of all transfers made in the previous ten years (including the transfer in question) exceeded £40,000, an account had to be delivered). Two sets of regulations were passed in late January 2008, with effect from 2007/08, one dealing with excepted transfers and the other with excepted settlements.

[21.9] An excepted transfer is an actual (not a deemed) chargeable transfer made by an individual on or after 6 April 2007, where one of two circumstances apply:

(1) Where the value transferred is attributable to either cash or quoted shares or securities and that value, together with the transferor's chargeable transfers in the previous seven years, does not exceed the threshold for payment of inheritance tax for the year in which the transfer was made ('the IHT threshold'); or
(2) Where the amount of the chargeable transfer, together with the transferor's chargeable transfers in the previous seven years, does not exceed 80% of the IHT threshold, and the amount of the transfer of value does not exceed that threshold less the amount of the transferor's chargeable transfers in the previous seven years.

[*Inheritance Tax (Delivery of Accounts) (Excepted Transfers and Excepted Terminations) Regulations 2008, SI 2008/605*]

[21.10] An excepted termination means the termination of an interest in possession in the settled property of a specified trust (separately defined) in one of three circumstances:

(1) Where the termination is wholly covered by an exemption made available to the trustees; or
(2) Where the value in which the interest subsisted is attributable to either cash or quoted shares or securities, and the value transferred by the termination together with the amount of the transferor's chargeable transfers in the previous seven years does not exceed the IHT threshold; or
(3) Where the value transferred by the termination, together with the transferor's chargeable transfers in the previous seven years, does not exceed 80% of the IHT threshold, and the amount of the transfer of value does not exceed that threshold less the amount of the transferor's chargeable transfers in the previous seven years.

[21.11] The second set of regulations built on the *Inheritance Tax (Delivery of Accounts) (Excepted Settlements) Regulations 2002, SI 2002/1732*, which repealed the requirement for discretionary trusts to report chargeable transfers where the funds may be far too small to give rise to any liability, eg 'pilot trusts' (settlements set up with a nominal cash fund in the expectation that more substantial property would be added later but which as yet have not received such property). The 2008 regulations provide that a person is not required to deliver an account for inheritance tax purposes where property is comprised in one of a class of trusts where a chargeable event occurs on or after 6 April 2007. There are five categories of excepted settlement, all requiring there to be no qualifying interest in possession subsisting in the settled property. The rules are complicated but the following points can should be noted:

- The first category is a settlement where the settled property can comprise only cash, the trustees must be UK resident, the settlor must not have provided any additions to the settled property following the commencement of the settlement or have created any other settlements on the same day and the value of the settled property at the time of the chargeable event must not exceed £1,000.
- In relation to the other categories there are general requirements applying to all categories and a specific requirement ('the condition').
- The general requirements are that the settlor is UK domiciled at the commencement of the settlement and thereafter until the chargeable event (or his death, if earlier), the trustees must be UK resident throughout the existence of the settlement and there must be no related settlements.
- The specific requirement is that the value transferred by the relevant notional chargeable transfer under the 1984 Act does not exceed 80% of the IHT threshold for the year in which the chargeable event occurs, ignoring for the purpose of determining the value any liabilities, exemptions or reliefs that would otherwise be deductible under the 1984 Act. These other categories are: the ten-year anniversary charge, an exit charge before the first ten-year anniversary, an exit charge

between ten-year anniversaries and a chargeable event in an age 18-to-25 trust [*Inheritance Tax (Delivery of Accounts) (Excepted Settlements) Regulations 2008, SI 2008/606*].

Note that, in relation to both the second circumstance under the excepted transfers regulations and the specific requirement in relation to the second to fifth categories of excepted settlements, the value in point is the gross value ie before any agricultural or business property relief. That is, where the trust holds such property, HMRC want an opportunity to test any claim to relief.

The settlor's chargeable gifts history

[21.12] The trustees of any family settlement must find some way of being informed of the settlor's death should that occur within seven years of the gift(s) into settlement. If their settlement is an accumulation and maintenance settlement, then, if it was set up after 17 March 1986 and before 22 March 2006, it will have been a potentially exempt transfer. The same is true of an interest in possession settlement made after 16 March 1987 and before 22 March 2006. The death of the settlor within seven years after the gift(s) moves these transfers from the 'potentially exempt' to the 'chargeable' category [*IHTA 1984, s 3A(4)*] and they will not have been reported [*IHTA 1984, s 3A(5)*]. The trustees will be expected to pay the tax, but the personal representatives of the deceased settlor can also be liable, subject to limitation, if the tax remains unpaid [*IHTA 1984, ss 199(1)(a), (2), 204(5)–(8)*]. As a matter of prudence, trustees who receive transfers of value (whether PETs, rather less likely since 22 March 2006, or immediately chargeable transfers) should enquire as to the settlor's history of transfers. The need to know about chargeable transfers is obvious. However, the settlor's potentially exempt transfers can turn into chargeable transfers and this upsets the arithmetic of subsequent transfers which were chargeable during his lifetime. If the gift is of shares in a private company, the trustees might ask for recent published accounts and generally assemble a file so that, in the event of the settlor's premature death, they have the material from which a valuation can be made. This assumes that no valuation reliefs are available at 100% (remembering also the claw-back rules under *IHTA 1984, s 113A* and *124A* which can retrospectively withdraw the relief from a lifetime transfer (see 18.66–18.70)). The trustees of a discretionary settlement or of a settlement made prior to 18 March 1986 will not have received potentially exempt transfers, but the passage of the seven years will now have freed them from any possibility of a charge under *IHTA 1984, s 7(4)*. Where a potentially exempt transfer to trustees has become chargeable, an account is required from the trustees [*IHTA 1984, s 216(1)(bc)(bd)*]. The time limit for delivery of these accounts is twelve months after the month of death, but the due date for tax is six months after the end of the month of death [*IHTA 1984, ss 216(6), 226(3)(3A)(3B)*].

[21.13] Although the income beneficiary of a qualifying interest in possession trust is the deemed owner of the settled property, the trustees have primary liability for the inheritance tax. The personal representatives of the life tenant are also liable (see *IHTA 1984, s 201(1)(a), (b)*), and, in either case, the limitations against double charges set out in *IHTA 1984, s 104* apply. Early in

1991 the then Inland Revenue wrote to the Law Society to give some reassurance to personal representatives liable for inheritance tax under *section 199(2)* on lifetime transfers made by their deceased during the seven years prior to his death. Personal representatives 'should not usually' be pursued where they have distributed the estate before a chargeable lifetime transfer comes to light, having:

(a) made the fullest enquiries that are reasonably practicable to discover lifetime transfers; and
(b) made full disclosure of everything known to them; and
(c) obtained a certificate of discharge.

Although not directly referring to the liabilities of trustees, this letter must give some comfort. See now IHTM30044 of HMRC's Inheritance Tax Manual for the present terms of the reassurance (replacing 'should not usually' with 'will not actually'). The First-tier Tribunal decision in the case of *Hutchings (Timothy Clayton) v Revenue and Customs Comrs* [2015] UKFTT 9 (TC), although not directly relevant to this particular tax point (see **22.18**), provides some useful guidance on the extent to which personal representatives need to investigate the lifetime transfers of the deceased.

Late payment of tax

[21.14] Tax paid late is subject to interest and the interest is not deductible for income tax purposes, so that it can be expensive to delay filing the account, even though the account may not be due [*IHTA 1984, s 233*]. Where there is certain to be a valuation argument (eg about land or shares in a family company), it will be difficult to avoid paying interest unless one overpays. Trustees would not normally overpay. However, there is provision for them to receive interest on tax overpaid [*IHTA 1984, s 235*]. There is an anomaly in that repayment is necessary to produce the interest. If there were instalment assets (see below) then it is possible for a generous deposit and a leisurely agreement of the tax to produce a repayment equal to the excess of the deposit over the tax due on non-instalment assets and, say, the first two instalments on the instalment assets. HMRC will not allow interest on that proportion of the deposit used to discharge the instalments, because it is never repaid. It is also possible to buy certificates of tax deposit (see **21.27**). The certificates can pay tax but not interest on tax. Interest on certificates will, in effect, offset the interest on the tax. One circumstance in which HMRC may at their discretion defer the liability to interest on late paid tax is where there has been a disaster or emergency of national significance [*FA 2008, s 135*]. The penalty for late paid tax under *FA 2009, Sch 56* has yet to be applied to inheritance tax (see **22.19–22.20**).

Reporting requirements

[21.15] HMRC Trusts and Estates can call for information about settlements simply by giving written notice. The notice need not be to the trustees; it may go to any person, eg the bank, a stockbroker etc. The consent of the First-tier Tribunal (previously, a Special Commissioner) is required for such a notice. A response is required within thirty days. Barristers and solicitors can claim professional privilege but, even so, a solicitor may have to disclose his client's name and address and other details. Prior to 1 April 2010, these obligations were imposed by *IHTA 1984, ss 219* and *219A*. As from 1 April 2010 HMRC are given powers to obtain information from the taxpayer or a third party by *FA 2008, Sch 36, paras 1* and *2* respectively: *para 3* requires the agreement of the taxpayer or the approval of the Tribunal to the issue of third party notices. The provisions of *Schedule 36* (information and inspection powers) are extended to inheritance tax by *FA 2009, s 96* and take effect from 1 April 2010 by *The Finance Act 2009 section 96 and Schedule 48 (Appointed Day, Savings and Consequential Amendments) Order, SI 2009/3054*.

[21.16] If a UK domiciled settlor (for which the extended definition under *IHTA, 1984, s 267* will apply) either appoints non-UK resident trustees or gives a professional person concerned with the making of a settlement cause to think that non-UK resident trustees will be appointed, then, whether requested or not, that professional person (but not a barrister) is bound to report the matter unless someone else has already done so [*IHTA 1984, s 218*]. For these purposes, the trustees are non-UK resident if the general administration of the settlement is not ordinarily carried on in the UK and if the majority of the trustees are for the time being resident outside the UK [*IHTA 1984, s 218(3)*]. This statutory reporting requirement should be taken seriously by professional firms, who should circulate their tax partners on the subject once every year.

Determination

[21.17] The Board has power to make a determination. This is the parallel of an assessment in the income tax legislation and must be appealed within thirty days if the taxpayer is to keep the position open. Late appeals are possible if there is reasonable excuse. Appeals are made to the First-tier Tribunal but it is possible for appeals to go direct to the High Court (generally by agreement, where the case is substantially confined to questions of law). Reports of cases dealt with by the Tribunal are published and, in particular, there have already been reports on valuation cases. The Tribunal deal with valuation disputes relating to shares but disputes on the value of land in the UK have to be referred to the appropriate tribunal. For land in England or Wales this is the Upper Tribunal while for land in Scotland or Northern Ireland it is the respective Lands Tribunal. Determinations are relatively rare. In most cases the account will be completed so that a determination is unnecessary and all that the Board have to do to collect the tax will be to assess it on forms 301 and 302 (for individuals) or 303 and 304 (for trustees) [*IHTA 1984, ss 221–223*]. In this connection the Royal Institute of Chartered Surveyors (RICS) have issued guidelines in GN21 regarding valuations for capital gains tax and inheritance tax on a basis that is acceptable to the Valuations Office Agency (VOA). It would be appropriate for valuation matters to encompass a review of GN21 in the current version of the Appraisal and Valuation Manual ('The Red Book').

Quick succession relief

[21.18] There can be no quick succession relief so far as trustees of relevant property settlements (as against settlements with a qualifying interest in possession) are concerned. However, if the exit charge is paid when property leaves the settlement and vests in an individual, then a second charge by reason of the deemed transfer on his death can attract quick succession relief if it happens within five years of the transfer from the relevant property settlement [*IHTA 1984, ss 2(3), 141*].

Payment of tax by instalments

[21.19] A useful relief is that of payment of tax by instalments which applies to the categories of assets set out in **21.20**. Where inheritance tax has been charged on instalment assets, tax may be paid by ten equal annual instalments [*IHTA 1984, ss 227*]. Where the premature death of the settlor causes a charge on assets contained in a potentially exempt transfer to a settlement, then the transfer must have been of instalment assets still held by the trustees at the death (ie the property is tested twice, once on the gift and again on the death). In general, no interest is charged on the outstanding instalments unless they are paid late, though see **21.20** and **21.22** for exceptions to this rule [*IHTA 1984, ss 227, 234*].

[21.20] Instalment assets are as follows:

(a) Land of any description and in any country.
(b) A controlling holding in a company. This could be a public company, but it is unlikely that many trustees could control a listed company. An AIM company might be so controlled. Note that the related property provisions of *IHTA 1984, s 161* work in one direction, so as to relate property contained in certain favoured trusts to that contained in an individual's estate, not to relate his property to that contained in one of those trusts. However, the deemed ownership accorded, by *IHTA 1984, s 49(1)*, to an income beneficiary of an interest in possession settlement counts as ownership for this purpose. Of course, this rule will operate only where the interest in possession falls under *section 49(1)* and, specifically, is not relevant property following the new regime introduced by *Finance Act 2006*.
(c) Shares or securities of a company which is not controlled by the trustees and which is not listed, where:
   (i) HMRC accept that payment in one sum would cause undue hardship; or
   (ii) the value of the shares transferred exceeds £20,000 and the shareholding is at least 10% of the nominal share capital of the company or, if the shares are ordinary shares, it is at least 10% of the ordinary share capital.
(d) The net value of a business or of an interest in a business. This is the interest of a proprietor rather than that of a creditor. The question whether it is a business is decided without reference to income tax legislation and therefore the fact that it produces 'unearned' income is

not decisive. The classic example unfortunately has little to do with settlements. It is that of the Lloyd's underwriter who, although not in any way concerned with the work of the syndicate, is nevertheless a proprietor. Therefore he has an interest in a business although it produces 'unearned' income.

(e) Land on which agricultural property relief is due.
(f) Standing timber, in certain circumstances.

[IHTA 1984, ss 227–229]

[21.21] The general rule is that interest is charged on outstanding instalments [IHTA 1984, 234]. There are exceptions to this where interest is only charged if instalments are paid late. The exceptions are assets within the following categories given in **21.20**:

(i) certain shares within categories (b) and (c)– those in companies other than those mentioned in **21.23**;
(ii) businesses or interests in businesses under category (d);
(iii) certain agricultural land under category (e); and
(iv) certain standing timber under category (f).

Land will only carry interest relief if it can be included under one of the other heads (ie (d) or (e)).

[21.22] Shares quoted on the AIM are unlisted for this purpose (see **18.32** and **18.33**).

[21.23] The interest relief (see **21.21**) for categories (*b*) and (*c*) above does not apply to shares and securities of every company. Shares etc in a company dealing in securities, stocks, shares, land or buildings and one making or holding investments will not qualify, unless either the company's business is holding land which qualifies for agricultural property relief or the company is a holding company for one or more ordinary trading companies or it is a UK market maker or discount house. The words 'market maker' were introduced by *FA 1986*. They mean a dealer in Stock Exchange securities and apply from the date when one person can be both a broker and a jobber. Until that date, jobbers qualified [*IHTA 1984, s 234*]. There is some similarity with the valuation reliefs. However, the privilege of paying by instalments is for a different reason. These are cases where money to pay the tax cannot be found quickly. Note, however, that there is no similar restriction for an 'interest in a business' under category (d). Thus, an interest free instalment option should be available for an investment business.

[21.24] Where the instalment property is sold while instalments are still outstanding, the balance of the tax together with any accrued interest is payable immediately [*IHTA 1984, s 227(4)*].

[21.25] The facility to pay tax by instalments is available for the ten-year charge on relevant property settlements as well as for the exit charge. To qualify, either the instalment assets must continue to be comprised in the settlement or the beneficiary must pay the tax. The person paying the tax must give notice in writing to the Board that he wishes to pay by instalments [*IHTA 1984, s 227(1)*]. There is a space for this in the Inheritance Tax Account. The first instalment is normally due six months after the end of the month in which the chargeable event occurs [IHTA 1984, s 227(3)]. As the interest relief on outstanding instalments does not apply to land unless it forms part of a business, relevant property trustees who are in business have an advantage. Farmland where the trustees are in possession and land on which commercial woodlands stand are examples of land forming part of a business. They would be eligible for the interest relief under 21.20(a), as also being within 21.20(d) and so would be instalment assets *with* the interest relief.

Liability for tax

[21.26] A complex web is created by seven statutory sections (*IHTA 1984, ss 199–205*) as to persons liable to pay the tax in various specific circumstances and in some cases limiting their liability. While generally in any particular case (eg *section 199* for dispositions by transferor, *section 200* for transfer on death and *section 201* for settled property) there is a list of persons liable, the statute does not provide an order of priority. HMRC do not much mind who pays the tax and will leave it to one taxpayer to seek recovery from another if he is able, whether by statute or by any agreement. The one exception is where there is a lifetime chargeable transfer and the transferor pays the tax. In this case grossing up must be applied so HMRC will usually take an interest to ensure that the correct amount of tax is paid: see the Inheritance Tax Manual at IHTM14541, which states that:

> 'You should gross up the value transferred if:
> - the account or correspondence states that the transferor is to bear the tax;
> - at the time of the transfer the transferor enters into a binding agreement to pay the tax;
> - after the transfer, the transferor pays tax (even an instalment) direct to HMRC, or
> - the tax is paid from the transferor's death estate (IHTM14543).'

Generally, grossing up applies only to immediately chargeable transfers and not to failed PETs. The Manual also deals separately with priority as between persons liable on failed potentially exempt transfers (IHTM30042) on the one hand on and immediately chargeable lifetime transfers (IHTM30062) on the other. Only in the former case is someone said to be primarily liable, ie the transferee or, where the property was settled by the transfer, the trustees. Where property leaves a relevant property settlement, the individual who benefits can be liable if the trustees do not pay [*IHTA 1984, s 201(1)(c)*]. The Inland Revenue [sic] charge applies, so that HMRC can have recourse to the property [*IHTA 1984, s 237*].

[21.27] Certificates of discharge can be obtained [*IHTA 1984, s 239*]. The first discharges the property from tax, the second discharges the taxpayer. Applications are made on Form IHT 30 and, bearing in mind that trustees must act with extreme caution, it must be recommended that certificates of discharge are obtained. Even though a discharge has been obtained, that is not the end of the matter if some failure to disclose material facts is discovered [*IHTA 1984, s 239(4)*]. The obvious danger is a failed potentially exempt transfer not reported by the family. (There was a somewhat puzzling article in

HMRC's *Inheritance Tax Newsletter* of April 2007 attempting to discourage agents from submitting applications for a certificate of discharge in deceased estates on the grounds that such certificates 'add no value' to the matter. Of course this disregards the degree of protection which such certificates give to both the agent and the personal representatives – and this article makes no mention of the HMRC assurance given in 1991: see **21.13**.)

[21.28] Certificates of tax deposit can be used by trustees. If surrendered in payment of inheritance tax, the interest on the certificate and any interest on unpaid tax cancel each other out. If encashed, interest is paid which is chargeable to income tax. Therefore it is possible to buy certificates for an amount exceeding the first estimate of tax, in the knowledge that there can be no interest on the likely amount of tax and that (subject to the period and the amount of the deposit) interest will usually be received on any balance from the certificates. The interest rates change from time to time.

[21.29] Deposits on account of tax due can be made by direct payment. In this case interest will be received on any overpayment (see **22.6**) and it will be tax exempt [*IHTA 1984, s 235*].

National heritage property

[21.30] National heritage property is a specialised subject. For many years the HMRC Library at Somerset House sold a very useful guide. This is obsolete from 17 March 1998 as regards gifts to charities and conditional exemptions (*FA 1998, s 143, Sch 25*). A memorandum was published online in September 2011, as an annex to the Inheritance Tax Manual, which covers the matters covered in the obsolete IR 67 (last updated 1986) and titled 'Capital Taxation and the National Heritage'. (See www.gov.uk/government/publications/capital-taxation-and-tax-exempt-heritage-assets.)

Self assessment and electronic delivery

[21.31] One of the ideas raised as part of the recent project to simplify the taxation of trusts (see **9.4–9.5**) was that a system for the self assessment of trust inheritance tax charges would be introduced. On 6 July 2015, the *Inheritance Tax (Electronic Communications) Regulations 2015, SI 2015/1378*, come into force and this provides the legal framework for a new inheritance tax online service, which will include the electronic delivery of returns. This service itself is being introduced in phases from Autumn 2015, and in May 2015 revised statutory directions under the 2015 regulations updated the approved method for authenticating the identity of persons using the online service, demonstrating that the project is progressing.

Chapter 22

Compliance: The Interest and Penalty Regimes

[22.1] A unified interest regime for both underpaid and overpaid tax was introduced for all the taxes from 29 September 2009 and from 2009/10 the legislation brings together all the taxes under a unified penalty regime, at least for incorrect returns, though not for late filing and late payment. It is convenient therefore to deal with this subject within the one chapter, although different treatment applied before those dates, as explained below.

[22.2] In the last 12 months there have also been a considerable number of new policy initiatives announced in relation to, particularly, the penalties for offshore evasion and these are discussed at **22.31**.

Interest

[22.3] Each of the taxes has a due date for payment and, which may be different, for filing of a return. Under the self assessment regime for income tax, the general rule is that tax is payable by two payments on account, on 31 January in and 31 July following the tax year, with a final balancing payment due on 31 January following the end of the tax year. Capital gains tax for the year is also payable on 31 January following the end of the tax year. SDLT currently falls due 30 days after the effective date of the land transaction (but there is currently a consultation about reducing this period). For inheritance tax payable on death, the due date for payment is six months after the end of the month in which death occurred. With a chargeable lifetime transfer, inheritance tax must be paid on or before the end of six months following the end of the month of transfer, except where the transfer was made after 5 April but before 1 October in any year, in which case the tax falls due on the following 30 April [*IHTA 1984, s 226*]. As from 2014/15 the due date for inheritance tax on chargeable transfers relating to relevant property settlements is six months following the end of the month of chargeable event. Prior to 2014/15 the due date was the same as that for chargeable lifetime transfers (see **21.6**).

[22.4] Tax due but unpaid on and from 29 September 2009 is payable on the basis of a formula. This is Bank of England base rate plus 2.5% for underpayments and (subject to a minimum of 0.5%) Bank of England base rate less 1% for overpayments. So the rates at the time of writing are 2.75% for underpayments and 0.5% for overpayments of tax. For tax due but unpaid before 23 August 2016 the separate tables, in the case of each of income tax, capital gains tax and stamp taxes on the one hand underpaid and overpaid tax treated separately and for inheritance tax on the other hand are as follows.

[22.5] The rates of interest for underpayments and overpayments of tax are as follows:

[22.5] Compliance: The Interest and Penalty Regimes

Underpayments

Income tax, capital gains tax and SDLT
From 23 August 2016	2.75%
From 29 September 2009 to 22 August 2016	3.0%
From 24 March 2009 to 28 September 2009	2.5%
From 27 January to 23 March 2009	3.5%
From 6 January 2009 to 26 January 2009	4.5%
From 6 December 2008 to 5 January 2009	5.5%
From 6 November 2008 to 5 December 2008	6.5%
From 6 January 2008 to 5 November 2008	7.5%
From 6 August 2007 to 5 January 2008	8.5%
From 6 September 2006 to 5 August 2007	7.5%

Overpayments

Overpaid income tax, capital gains tax and SDLT repayment supplement
From 29 September 2009	0.5%
From 27 January 2009 to 28 September 2009	0%
From 6 January 2009 to 26 January 2009	0.75%
From 6 December 2008 to 5 January 2009	1.5%
From 6 November 2008 to 5 December 2008	2.25%
From 6 January 2008 to 5 November 2008	3.00%
From 6 August 2007 to 5 January 2008	4.00%
From 6 September 2006 to 5 August 2007	3.00%

Inheritance tax

[22.6] The rates for both underpayments and overpayments of inheritance tax were as detailed in the table below up until 28 September 2009. However, since 29 September 2009 the rates have aligned with those for other taxes detailed above – thus, since 23 August 2016, the rate for overpayments of tax is 0.5% and underpayments is 2.75%.

24 March 2009–28 September 2009	0%
27 January 2009–23 March 2009	1%
6 January 2009–26 January 2009	2%
6 November 2008–5 January 2009	3%
6 January 2008–5 November 2008	4%
6 August 2007–5 January 2008	5%
6 September 2006–5 August 2007	4%

Penalties

For late filed returns: income tax and capital gains tax

[22.7] There is a system of automatic penalties for late filed returns. Prior to 1 April 2011, if a return was filed after the due date the penalty was £100. If filed more than six months late then there was a further £100 [*TMA 1970, s 93*]. An appeal was, however, possible if the tax proved to be less than the penalties. The current system of penalties took effect from 1 April 2011, following the repeal of *section 93* by *Finance Act 2009, Schedules 55 and 56 (Income Tax Self Assessment and Pension Schemes) (Appointed Days and Consequential and Savings Provisions) Order 2011, SI 2011/702*. The new penalties are automatic, subject to an appeal on the grounds of reasonable excuse (see **22.16**), even if the tax outstanding is less than the penalty. If the return is late by one day to less than three months, the penalty is £100. For three months but less than six months, the penalty is £10 per day, up to a maximum of £900. Where the return is at least six months and less than 12 months overdue, the penalty is the higher of £300 and 5% of the tax due. If the return is at least 12 months late, the penalty is the higher of £300 and 5% of the tax due, subject to the proviso that in serious cases up to 100% of the tax due might be payable instead.

[22.8] Further penalties relating to tax agents include the following. Assisting in the preparation or delivery of any information, return, accounts or other information which he knows will be or is or is likely to be used for tax purposes and he knows to be incorrect is liable to a penalty not exceeding £3,000 [*TMA 1970, s 99*]. Maximum penalties under the regime before 2008/09 were subject to mitigation on various counts. Legislation regarding the dishonest conduct of tax agents is now at *FA 2012, s 223*.

Inaccuracies in a return: the FA 2007 regime

[22.9] The current penalty regime was introduced by *FA 2007, Sch 24* for income tax, capital gains tax and corporation tax which has been extended by *FA 2008, Sch 40* across the majority of taxes, including specifically inheritance tax. For income tax and capital gains tax the new regime applies to return periods beginning on or after 1 April 2008 where the return is due to be filed on or after 1 April 2009, that is to self assessment returns for 2008/09. For inheritance tax HMRC consider that the regime applies to deaths and other chargeable events occurring on or after 1 April 2009 (where the return is due on or after 1 April 2010). However, the author (along with other practitioners) takes the view that the effect of the *Finance Act 2008, Schedule 41 (Appointed Day and Transitional Provisions) Order 2009, SI 2009/511* is generally to apply the regime to inheritance tax (apart from excepted estates) from 1 April 2010 (where the return is due on or after 1 April 2011).

[22.10] Subject to the usual defence of reasonable excuse, the regime applies where there is (in broad terms) an inaccuracy in a return. Where the failure is not deliberate, the maximum penalty is 30%; where the failure is deliberate but without concealment the maximum penalty is 70%; and where it is deliberate with concealment the maximum is 100%, in each case of the 'potential lost revenue'. Instead of the previous factors for mitigation of penalties, there is now a statutory regime for disclosure, according to whether there is disclosure and whether it is prompted or unprompted. In the case of prompted disclosure the 30% penalty rate is reduced to not more than 15%; the 70% rate to not more than 35%; and the 100% rate to not more than 50%. Where the disclosure is unprompted the 30% penalty rate can be reduced to 0%; the 70% rate to not more than 20%; and the 100% rate to not more than 30%. Higher penalties can be imposed where there as an 'offshore' connection (see **22.24**).

[22.11] The legislation gives HMRC the power to reduce a penalty 'if they think it right because of special circumstances'. However, those circumstances do not include either the taxpayer's inability to pay, or the fact that a potential loss of revenue from one taxpayer is balanced by a potential overpayment by another. For a recent case in which a taxpayer was successful in arguing for 'special circumstances' see: *Seaborn (George) v Revenue and Customs Comrs* [2014] UKFTT 086 (TC). It can be noted that in the vast majority of cases where a 'special circumstances' case was put to the First-tier Tribunal in the last 12 months, it was rejected.

[22.12] Under the new regime a penalty will be charged if there is a 'relevant inaccuracy' in a return or other document which amounts to or leads to:

(a) an understatement of a liability to tax,
(b) a false or inflated statement of a loss, or
(c) a false or inflated claim to repayment of tax [*FA 2007, Sch 24, para 1A(2)*].

[22.13] The degrees of culpability which lead to the maximum penalties respectively described at **22.10** are:

(a) 'careless' if the inaccuracy is due to the taxpayer's failure to take reasonable care,
(b) 'deliberate but not concealed' if the inaccuracy is deliberate on the taxpayer's part but he has made no arrangements to conceal it, and
(c) 'deliberate and concealed' if the inaccuracy is deliberate on the taxpayer's part and he has made arrangements to conceal it (for example, by submitting false evidence in support of an inaccurate figure) [*FA 2007, Sch 24, para 3(1)*].

[22.14] So the failure to take reasonable care takes the place of the previous test of negligence, whereas 'fraud' is now represented by a deliberate inaccuracy, whether or not concealed. Experience to date suggests that HMRC are keen to raise penalty assessments where they think it appropriate. The incentive, as before, is of course to 'get to HMRC before they get to you' in terms of making an unprompted disclosure and, as is seen at para **22.10**, if the inaccuracy results from a failure to take reasonable care (only) an unprompted disclosure may even have the effect of reducing the penalty to 0%.

'Reasonable care'

[22.15] As to the concepts of 'reasonable care' and indeed a 'reasonable excuse' for not so taking, what HMRC say in their Compliance Handbook at CH 81120 may be found helpful:

'... whilst each person has a responsibility to take reasonable care, what is necessary for each person to discharge that responsibility has to be viewed in the light of that person's abilities and circumstances. For example, we do not expect the same level of knowledge or expertise from a self employed unrepresented individual as we do from a large multi-national company. We would expect a higher degree of care to be taken over large and complex matters than simple straightforward ones. HMRC expects each person to make and preserve sufficient records for them to make a correct and complete return. A person with simple, straightforward tax affairs needs only a simple regime provided they follow it carefully. But a person with larger and more complex tax affairs will need to put in place sophisticated systems and follow them equally carefully. In HMRC's view it is reasonable to expect a person who encounters a transaction or other event with which they are not familiar to take care to find out about the correct tax treatment or to seek appropriate advice.'

It is worth noting that, at the time of writing (31 July 2015), there has been a significant lack of consistency in the Tribunal and indeed higher Court decisions on the meaning of 'reasonable excuse'. This is an issue that HMRC seem to be alive to and one of the consultation documents referred to in the final section of this chapter – HMRC Penalties: a Discussion Document – is aimed, at least in part, on the need for more fairness and consistency.

'Reasonable excuse'

[22.16] HMRC state in their Compliance Handbook at CH 155600 that 'a person will not be liable to a penalty if they have a reasonable excuse for failing to pay on time and they remedy that failure without unreasonable delay after the excuse ends. There is no statutory definition of reasonable excuse ... a reasonable excuse is normally an unexpected or unusual event that is either unforeseeable or beyond the person's control, and which prevents the person from complying with an obligation to pay on time. A combination of unexpected and foreseeable events may when viewed together be a reasonable excuse. It is necessary to consider the actions of the person from the perspective of a prudent person exercising reasonable foresight and due diligence, having proper regard for their responsibilities under the Tax Acts.
... The law does specify two situations that are not reasonable excuses. These are ... shortage of funds ... and ... reliance on another person.'

[22.17] So far as concerns the application to inheritance tax of the penalty regime enacted by *FA 2007, Sch 24*, helpful information can be found in a set of 57 Frequently Asked Questions (FAQs) on the new penalties system (Revenue and Customs Brief 19 March 2009, see *Simon's Weekly Tax Intelligence*, Issue 12, 26 March 2009.

To avoid a penalty, the test is now one of 'reasonable care' rather than 'negligence'. HMRC consider that personal representatives will have taken reasonable care where they:

- follow the guidance provided about filling in forms such as the IHT 400 and IHT 205/207/C5;
- make suitable enquiries of asset holders and other people (as suggested in the guidance) to establish the extent of the deceased's estate;
- ensure correct instructions are given to valuers when valuing assets;

[22.17] Compliance: The Interest and Penalty Regimes

- seek advice about anything of which they are unsure;
- follow up inconsistencies in information they receive from asset holders, valuers and other people; and
- identify any estimated values included on the form.

The above said, in their FAQs of March 2009, HMRC ask at Q32. '*How will it affect Inheritance Tax?*' They respond: 'Like other taxes, HMRC already charge penalties for some incorrect Inheritance Tax accounts. Under the new regime if someone makes an error, despite having taken reasonable care, they will not be penalised. HMRC recognise that inheritance tax applies to a single event and concepts such as reasonable care will be somewhat different under these circumstances than for taxes where people have to make returns more regularly. HMRC also recognise that the position of personal representatives is different from other individuals and trustees who may make a transfer that is liable to inheritance tax.'

Where the personal representatives leave all this in the hands of an agent, HMRC expect them to check through the form before signing it and to question anything that does not accord with what they know about the deceased. Simply signing an account completed by an agent is not taking reasonable care. And where inheritance tax is payable other than on death, HMRC expect the transferor (or the trustees) to deliver a full and complete return of the transaction concerned, and to have sought professional advice as necessary. Again, simply signing an account completed by an agent is not taking reasonable care [*HMRC's Inheritance Tax and Trusts newsletter April 2009*].

[22.18] Penalties can be imposed where actions cause third parties to make incorrect returns. In *Hutchings (Timothy Clayton) v Revenue and Customs Comrs* [2015] UKFTT 9 (TC), Mr Hutchings failed to disclose that his father had made a significant lifetime gift to him. As a result, in addition to his own failure to pay the tax due on the gift, the personal representatives of his father *over*stated the amount of nil rate band available to his 'free estate' and therefore *under*stated their own inheritance tax liability. The Tribunal found against Mr Hutchings and upheld HMRC's 50% penalty (£87,533.80) in relation to *all* the revenue potentially lost.

Fixed penalties under inheritance tax

[22.19] Failure to deliver an inheritance tax account by the due date (see 21.6) renders the taxpayer liable to a penalty of £100 plus a further daily penalty of £60 for every day that elapses between the date of a declaration by the Court or a Tribunal and delivery of the account. A further penalty of £100 applies where court proceedings are not commenced within six months after the due date for delivery of the account. The two fixed £100 penalties are subject to a total penalty of the tax payable. If the taxpayer's failure continues beyond 12 months after the due date and the account would have shown a liability to tax, HMRC will charge an additional penalty of up to £3,000 [*IHTA 1984, s 245*]. Further penalties apply where: there is a failure to provide the information *section 245A*), incorrect information is provided (*section 247(3)*) and there is a failure to remedy errors (*section 248*). Under *section 245(5)*, these penalties cannot exceed the tax payable, so no penalty is due on late delivery of an account relating to a relevant property settlement within the nil-rate band. That said, it is a good discipline to make proper returns where required, which carries the advantage that by so doing the professional advisers are less likely to overlook the existence of a particular chargeable transfer.

[22.20] The rules at 22.19 are to be replaced by a statutory instrument (which does not yet appear to have been issued), for chargeable events on or after a prescribed date, by the new regime introduced by *FA 2009, Sch 55* (penalty for failure to make returns etc). The fixed penalty for failure to deliver an account under *section 216* will remain at £100. Where the failure continues beyond three months after the due date and HMRC decide and give notice to the taxpayer that a further penalty should be paid, £10 for each day that the failure continues becomes payable, up to a further 90 days. Continuing failure beyond six months attracts a penalty of the greater of 5% of the tax due and £300 and, if beyond 12 months and in circumstances where it is the taxpayer's deliberate withholding of information which makes HMRC unable to determine the inheritance tax due, the greater of the tax due and £300, subject to increase to up to 200% of the tax due if the tax relates to an offshore matter in a jurisdiction where there are no arrangements for the exchange of information between HMRC and the revenue authorities of that jurisdiction (*FA 2009, Sch 55, paras 3–6A*).

Unpaid tax

Fixed penalties under income tax and capital gains tax prior to 1 April 2011

[22.21] In the case of income tax and capital gains tax remaining unpaid following 28 days after the due date, which is usually the 28 February after the end of the tax year attracts a 5% surcharge. To the extent that tax still remains outstanding by 31 July after the end of the tax year an additional 5% surcharge applies [*TMA 1970, s 59C*, repealed by *SI 2011/702* from 1 April 2011]. For the position from 1 April 2011, see **22.22**.

The FA 2009 Sch 56 penalty

[22.22] A new penalty regime for unpaid tax was introduced by *FA 2009, Sch 56*. Although the regime is applied differently to individual taxes, the broad thinking is that within a period of two years three penalties at 5% of the unpaid tax may be levied. For example, unpaid inheritance tax is listed at box 7 (or, where payable by instalments, box 8) of the table at *FA 2009, Sch 56, para 1*. Subject to special provisions for instalment payments, to the extent that inheritance tax remains unpaid at the filing date of 12 months after the end of the month in which the death occurs, 5% of the unpaid tax is charged (*para 3*). To the extent that tax remains unpaid five months later there is a further 5% with tax unpaid 11 months after the penalty date attracting a third

5% charge. This regime applies *mutatis mutandis* to unpaid inheritance tax on lifetime transfers. These penalty provisions are subject to a reduction in penalty agreement with HMRC for deferred payment (para 10): in special circumstances *(para 9(1))*: and reasonable excuse *(para 16)*. This regime has been applied to PAYE and to tax due under the contractors industry scheme from 1 April 2010. Unpaid income tax and capital gains tax became subject to the *Schedule 56* regime from 1 April 2011. Replacing the 5% surcharge for income tax unpaid 28 days after the due date, unpaid income tax or capital gains tax 30 days after the due date attracts a penalty of 5% of the tax unpaid, with a further 5% penalty of any tax unpaid six months after the due date and a final 5% of the tax unpaid 12 months after the due date.

Inheritance tax

[22.23] The *FA 2009, Sch 56* regime (as outlined above) was expected to apply to inheritance tax from 1 April 2012, but the relevant statutory instrument has not yet been made.

Offshore penalties

[22.24] Penalties for unpaid tax on income or gains arising in offshore territories are levied from 2011/12 at rates of up to 200%; there are three categories of territory for this purpose: those which have agreed to exchange information with HMRC where the standard maximum of 100% continues; those that will exchange information with HMRC but only if HMRC make a request for information, where the maximum penalty is 150% of the tax; and those territories which have not agreed to share information with HMRC, where the maximum penalty is 200% of the tax.

[22.25] Legislation altering this penalty regime was included at *Finance Act 2015, s 120* to come into effect at a future date (rather than at Royal Assent). In July 2015 a further Consultation Document was issued in relation to this – *Tackling offshore tax evasion: Strengthening civil deterrents for offshore evaders* – and further legislation (which appears to supersede *section 120*) has now been included at *Finance Act 2016, s 163* and *Sch 20*. Other elements of the legislation concern the extension of the offshore penalty regime to include inheritance tax and also to non-compliance in the UK where funds are paid or moved overseas.

[22.26] Royal Assent of *Finance Act 2015* did, however, bring into force *section 121* and *Schedule 21* of the Act which impose an additional 50% penalty in relation to a 'relevant offshore asset move'. The objective behind this legislation is to penalise more harshly (if caught) those who very deliberately attempt to evade capture by, typically, moving assets to less compliant jurisdictions.

[22.27] Further penalty provisions in relation to offshore evasion and non-compliance have also been included in *Finance Act 2016*, viz:

- *Section 162* and *Schedule 20* – Penalties for the enablers of offshore tax evasion or non-compliance. (This followed the 16 July 2015 Consultation Document – *Tackling offshore tax evasion: Civil sanctions for enablers of offshore evasion.*)
- *Section 164* (amending *Finance Act 2009, s 94*) – Offshore tax errors etc: publishing details of deliberate tax defaulters.
- *Section 165* and *Schedule 22* – Asset-based penalties for offshore inaccuracies and failures.

Each of these changes will take effect from a future date by statutory instrument.

Criminal Sanctions

[22.28] The Consultation Documents *Tackling offshore tax evasion: A new criminal offence* (19 August 2014) and *Tackling offshore tax evasion: A new criminal offence for offshore evaders* (16 July 2015) raised the prospect of new criminal sanctions in relation to offshore non-disclosure, and legislation has now been included in *Finance Act 2016, s 166* to effect this. The addition of new clauses to *Taxes Management Act 1970 (TMA 1970)* created new offences in relation to:

- failing to give notice of being chargeable to tax (*TMA 1970, s 106B*);
- failing to deliver a return (*s 106C*); and
- making an inaccurate return (*s 106D*);

in each case in relation to 'offshore income, assets or activities' (which means what one would expect, as defined in *section 106F(4)*). The legislation will come into force at a future date to be specified by statutory instrument (*s 106H(4)*).

[22.29] For an offence to be committed, there has to be income or capital gains tax at stake in excess of a minimum of £25,000 (or such higher figure as is specified by regulation (*s 106F(2)*)). Trustees and personal representatives are generally excluded (*s 106E(1)*) and the Treasury has power to specify additional exclusions (*s 106E(2)*) in due course.

[22.30] When a criminal sanction was first mooted, it was presented in terms that it would be a 'strict liability' offence. In fact, each of the offences is subject to the specific defence that the taxpayer had a 'reasonable excuse' for any failure, or had taken 'reasonable care' in the case of an inaccuracy.

Policy developments

[22.31] Notwithstanding the considerable changes already enacted and referred to above, the government's offensive against avoidance and evasion continues apace, with two more Consultation Documents issued in August 2016:

- *Strengthening Tax Avoidance Sanctions and Deterrents: A discussion document* (17 August 2016) – proposes sanctions for those who *design*, *market* or *facilitate* the use of tax avoidance arrangements which are

defeated by HMRC and to change the way the existing penalty regime works for those whose tax returns are found to be inaccurate as a result of using such arrangements.
- *Tackling offshore tax evasion: A Requirement to Correct* (24 August 2016) – proposes new rules requiring a person who has undeclared UK tax liabilities in respect of an offshore interest to declare them before September 2018, or face specific sanctions.

Chapter 23

Anti-avoidance

Overview

[23.1] In previous editions of this book, the subject of anti-avoidance has been distributed between different chapters; however, the subject is getting bigger and bigger as governments compete to crackdown harder on evasion and avoidance. The author therefore thought it useful to pull the different strands together. For most of the taxpayers and advisers reading this book, there will absolutely no desire to become involved in anything that could be considered 'aggressive' and the intention here is therefore to provide simply a summary of the main provisions relevant to trust practitioners. Thus, there is also a greater focus on inheritance tax than other taxes.

[23.2] Historically, the main distinction that tax advisers needed to understand was between illegal tax evasion and acceptable (if begrudged by the then Inland Revenue) tax avoidance. Times have changed. A second distinction is now drawn between acceptable tax mitigation and unacceptable tax avoidance. This is based on HMRC's interpretation of the dictum of Lord Nolan in *IRC v Willoughby* [1997] 4 All ER 65, [1997] 1 WLR 1071, HL, 'the hallmark of tax avoidance is that the taxpayer reduces his liability to tax without incurring the economic consequences that the Parliament intended to be suffered by any taxpayer qualifying for such reduction in his tax liabilities. The hallmark of tax mitigation, on the other hand, is that the taxpayer takes advantage of a fiscally attractive option afforded to him by the tax legislation, and genuinely suffers the economic consequences that Parliament intended to be suffered by those taking advantage of the option'.

[23.3] For many years – aside from anti-avoidance rules targeted at specific taxes, reliefs and exemptions (see **23.4–23.10**) – the courts alone were relied upon to define the boundary between acceptable and unacceptable tax planning and previous editions of this book outlined the tortuous and complex route taken by them – beginning, of course, the iconic House of Lords decision in *W T Ramsay Ltd v IRC* [1982] AC 300, [1981] 1 All ER 865. However, the last 10 years have seen a decided shift towards a more statutory approach. We now have four separate disclosure regimes for: direct taxes, introduced in 2004 and extended in 2006; VAT introduced in 2004; stamp duty land tax in 2005 (extended in 2009 and 2010) (see **23.24–23.26**); and finally for inheritance tax from 6 April 2011 (see **23.17–23.23**). Since 17 July 2013, advisers have also had to reckon with the General Anti-Abuse Rule (see **23.11–23.12**) and from 2014 the introduction of regimes targeting 'high-risk promoters', and new 'follower' and 'accelerated payment' notices (see **23.27–23.33**).

Inheritance tax anti-avoidance

[23.4] The legislation includes (a) the catch-all of 'associated operations' (defined in *IHTA 1984, s 268* and (b) the *FA 1986* reservation of benefit regime by *FA 1986, Sch 20, para 6(1)(c)*). The former is a powerful deterrent to artificiality. HMRC Trusts and Estates may regard the making of a loan followed by annual write-offs within the annual exemption as being associated operations, although this should be in order provided that the annual releases are effected by deed. If a family settlement contains significant assets and is intended to be an enduring part of the family's planning the risk of using sophisticated schemes which could turn out to be associated operations is obvious. Therefore, the estate planner using settlements will usually prefer a solution unlikely to be attacked by HMRC under present legislation or anything likely to be used as a weapon by them in the foreseeable future. At least, following the 2002 Court of Appeal decision in *Rysaffe Trustee Co (CI) Ltd v IRC* (see **9.39**), the scope of the associated operations doctrine under *IHTA 1984, s 268* has been very significantly restricted – subject of course, in the case of a series of pilot settlements, to the new relevant property settlement charging regime from 2015/16 (see **9.44–9.48**).

[23.5] The *Finance Act 1986* reintroduced the concept of gifts with reservation of benefit [*FA 1986, s 102*]. This was part of the anti-avoidance legislation of estate duty. It is interesting to see that the phrase 'to the entire exclusion of the donor' in *FA 1986, s 102(1)(b)* derives from the *Customs and Inland Revenue Act, 1881, s 38(2)(A)*. Because the gift with reservation of benefit was part of the UK tax system until the repeal of estate duty, there is a body of case law and the concept is well understood. Obviously, nobody will knowingly create a settlement now where there is a benefit reserved. That said, there could be a case for settled gifts with reservation of benefit because (somewhat curiously, even within a relevant property settlement) the ending of the benefit counts as a potentially exempt transfer.

[23.6] The slimming down of estates with properties in them which owners still want to occupy has occupied estate planners for many years. A case on these lines completed its passage through the Courts in December 1998 (*Ingram (executors of Lady Ingram) v IRC*, [2000] 1 AC 293, [1999] 1 All ER 297, HL). In March 1987 Lady Ingram transferred property to a nominee. That nominee purported to grant her two leases giving her the property rent-free for 20 years. He then transferred the property subject to the leases to a settlement of which Lady Ingram was not a beneficiary. She died in February 1989. The High Court found in favour of the taxpayer on the grounds that valid leases had been made in equity subject to which the reversionary interest had been given away from which Lady Ingram was excluded from benefit. That decision was reversed by the Court of Appeal. However, the House of Lords decided in favour of the taxpayer on 10 December 1998, finding both that the leases to a nominee were effective and also that the subject matter of the gift made by Lady Ingram, namely the reversions, was enjoyed to her entire exclusion. The effect of that decision was reversed, substantially at least, by *FA 1999, s 104* which introduced ss 102A to 102C into the FA 1986 reservation of benefit code. Notwithstanding the statutory reversal of *Ingram* schemes, and the introduction of the pre-owned assets regime from 2005/06 (see

4.39–4.40), it is clear from HMRC's guidance on the General Anti-Abuse Rule that they accept the effectiveness in principle of a carve-out of a legal interest, as pronounced to be valid by the House of Lords in *Ingram*, where HMRC say '[a]lthough artificial, such transactions have genuine economic consequences in that the donor no longer has the valuable asset to sell; the donee acquires the asset for low cost and it is the donee's asset to do with as he pleases. Moreover the donor will have to pay pre-owned assets income tax instead of inheritance tax and therefore has accepted the penalty for carrying out such tax planning. Such transactions may therefore fall on the right side of the "abusive" line despite their apparent artificiality.' HMRC give as an example the creation and gift of reversionary leases.

[23.7] HMRC were unsuccessful in the Court of Appeal in arguing for reservation of benefit in a reversionary lease scheme (*Buzzoni (M) (Kamhi's Executor) v Revenue and Customs Comrs* [2013] EWCA Civ 1684, [2014] 1 WLR 3040, [2014] 1 EGLR 181). Out of a 100-year lease of a flat in London the taxpayer granted an under-lease commencing 10 years hence to the trustees of a new settlement. The terms of the under-lease included a covenant to pay to the grantor an amount equal to the service charge which she had to pay under the head lease, which in 2008 amounted to some £9,000 per annum, (although there was no requirement on the sub-lessee to pay rent). Equally, there were covenants for the repair of the flat. The First-tier Tribunal (Judge Barbara Mosedale) held that the reservation of covenants (to pay the service charge and to repair the flat) had to be a benefit to the deceased taxpayer, which was not protected by the 'de minimis' provisions. Likewise, The Upper Tribunal turned down the taxpayers' appeal, Proudman J holding that there had been a benefit to Mrs Kamhi 'by transferring to the trustee of her settlement a liability which she would otherwise have borne'. However, in the Court of Appeal, Moses LJ found that it was necessary for any benefit to 'trench' on the gifted property and, as the covenants in favour of Mrs Kamhi mirrored those to which the donees were already bound in favour of the landlord of the property, the covenants in favour of Mrs Kamhi did not undermine the donees' enjoyment of the property – therefore the statutory provisions were not met. HMRC do not intend to appeal the Court of Appeal decision.

[23.8] This remains, however, a complex area where much turns on the facts. In *Viscount Hood, executor of the estate of Lady Diana Hood v HMRC* [2016] UKFTT 59, the First-tier Tribunal found that a gifted sub-lease was subject to a reservation of benefit for the donor. The author understands that the taxpayer is appealing this decision.

[23.9] A history of successful attempts by taxpayers to set up arrangements which enable them to enjoy the benefits of assets given away, yet without the scope of the reservation of benefit regime, led to the introduction of the pre-owned assets rules, applying from 2005/06 (see **4.39–4.51**) and these, of course, remain the biggest deterrent to any future tax planning involving carve outs.

[23.10] A number of other, more targeted, inheritance tax anti-avoidance measures have also been introduced since in recent years:

[23.10] Anti-avoidance

(1) *FA 2010* introduced *IHTA 1984, s 81A* from 9 December 2009 to block the use of a so-called 'Melville Mark 3'.

(2) *FA 2010* also introduced legislation from 9 December 2009 to block inheritance tax trust arrangements aimed at reducing inheritance tax. Broadly an interest under a trust was acquired at full market value. This resulted in property being added to the trust without a chargeable transfer but with a reduction in the chargeable estate (as the trust interest would not form part of it).

(3) *FA 2012* further penalised any attempt by a UK domiciliary to mitigate the potential inheritance tax liability on death through the use of excluded property settlements: see **27.26**.

(4) *FA 2013* has introduced three inheritance tax anti-avoidance measures relating to deductions for liabilities. The first two are aimed at preventing relief on borrowing on chargeable assets to finance excluded property *(IHTA 1984 s 162A* – see **27.9**) or relievable property *(IHTA 1984 s 162B* – see **18.71**. The third measure *(IHTA 1984 s 175A)* broadly denies an inheritance deduction for a liability incurred by the deceased at his death except to the extent that it is actually paid by the personal representatives out of the estate. The measures were extended by *FA 2014* to deny a deduction for a liability incurred by the deceased at his death which was used to finance foreign currency bank accounts. Such accounts are not 'excluded property' (so do not fall within the first restriction above) but are nonetheless not taken into account for inheritance tax on death.

The General Anti-Abuse Rule

[23.11] Trustees, and indeed settlors, like any other taxpayer must bear in mind the general anti-abuse rule introduced from 2013/14 by *FA 2013, Part 5, ss 206–215*. It is not appropriate, in a book of this nature to go in any detail into the General Anti-Abuse Rule (GAAR). Certainly, the existing and extensive body of anti-avoidance rules remains, whether enacted by legislation or to be found in case law, which is a point emphasised by the guidance. The GAAR will not apply to cases where a taxpayer is given a straightforward legislative choice between different courses of action or indeed to what might be described as 'long established practice', into which category falls, for example, gift and loan trusts (discussed at **17.55–17.56**). Equally, situations where the law deliberately sets out precise rules or boundaries creates an entitlement for taxpayers to assume that they are on the right side of the line if they have satisfied the statutory conditions. That said, HMRC warn that once an element of contrivance or artificiality is introduced into a standard arrangement, the GAAR might well apply. And here they acknowledge that in the context of inheritance tax and trusts generally the position can be particularly difficult to determine.

[23.12] In general terms the purpose of the GAAR is to act as a kind of 'keep off the grass' warning as to particular types of transaction which HMRC consider abusive and will pursue through the courts if entered into. In the context of trusts, two examples are given at D20 and D21 of capital gains tax where arrangements for 'washing out gains' are found respectively to be non-abusive and abusive. In the context of inheritance tax, pilot trusts at D26 receive official approval given the Court of Appeal's decision in *Rysaffe* (see 9.39). However, the relevant property regime blocks this type of planning (see 9.44–9.48). Like gift and loan trusts, and, discounted gift schemes (see 17.51–17.55) are approved, as accepted by long established practice. By contrast, somewhat provocative death-bed schemes involving excluded property trusts and debt and bypassing the charge on death with an employee benefit trust (examples D.23 and D.29 respectively) areas are seen to be abusive. The difficulty, looking forward, is that in the absence of an advance clearance procedure, taxpayers and their advisers are left to take their own counsel, perhaps using the white space in a relevant self assessment form or other tax return to draw the transaction to the attention of HMRC in the hope of achieving HMRC's agreement to their own analysis that GAAR does not apply.

[23.13] The latest version of the GAAR guidance, which is updated regularly and approved by the independent GAAR advisory panel is available here: www.gov.uk/government/publications/tax-avoidance-general-anti-abus e-rules. It was last updated on 18 January 2016. In this context it is important to note that the guidance's function is explicitly recognised by the GAAR legislation and any court or tribunal which is considering the application of the GAAR must take it into account.

[23.14] Following two consultations in 2015, *Finance Act 2016, s 158* (which introduces new *section 212A* and *Schedule 43C* into *FA 2013, Part 5*) provides for a specific 60% GAAR penalty to apply in relation to tax arrangements entered into after Royal Assent of *Finance Bill 2016* which fall foul of the GAAR.

DOTAS

[23.15] The recent history of a far more proactive HMRC approach to anti-avoidance can be traced back to the introduction of the *Disclosure of Tax Avoidance Schemes* (DOTAS) rules in 2004. Designed as an 'early warning system' to enable HMRC to know about schemes at a very early stage of their implementation, DOTAS originally applied only to direct taxes: income tax, corporation tax and capital gains tax from employment or financial products. They were then extended, with effect from 1 August 2006, so that they applied to the whole of income tax, corporation tax and capital gains tax if any one of specified 'hallmarks' applied.

[23.16] On 31 July 2014 HMRC opened a new consultation *Strengthening the Tax Avoidance Disclosure Regimes* which ran until 23 October 2014. In their response to the consultation, published on 10 December 2014, the Government announced that they would be taking forward a number of changes. Facilitating legislation was included in *Finance Act 2015, s 117* and *Sch 17* and draft new 'hallmark' regulations were published on 16 July 2015, for consultation until 10 September 2015. The *Tax Avoidance Schemes (Prescribed Descriptions of Arrangements) (Amendment) Regulations 2016* were subsequently published and are effective from 23 February 2016. New DOTAS rules for inheritance tax were also promised in December 2014 and draft regulations published on 16 July 2015; however, these were subject to further amendment and consultation and the final regulations are still awaited (see **23.18–23.23**).

Inheritance tax

[23.17] The DOTAS regime was first extended to inheritance tax in 2011. The *Inheritance Tax Avoidance Schemes (Prescribed Descriptions of Arrangements) Regulations 2011, SI 2011/170* took effect from 6 April 2011, requiring the disclosure of arrangements which seek to avoid inheritance tax charges associated with transfers of property into trust (only). This followed a 12 week consultation which closed on 20 October 2010. Disclosure is limited to situations where:

- there are arrangements or proposals for arrangements which result in property becoming 'relevant property';
- those arrangements or proposals for arrangements are such that they enable a 'relevant property entry charge' advantage; and
- the tax advantage is a main benefit of the arrangements (within *FA 2004, s 306(1)(c)*).

Excepted from disclosure are arrangements:

(a) which were first made available for implementation before 6 April 2011; or
(b) in relation to which the date of any transaction forming part of the arrangements falls before 6 April 2011; or
(c) in relation to which a promoter made a firm approach to another person before 6 April 2011.

Certain arrangements are taken out of the regime by 'grandfathering', as follows:

A: Arrangements where property does not become relevant property.

B: Arrangements that qualify for relief/exemptions.

C: The purchase of business assets with a view to transferring the assets into a relevant property trust after two years.

D: The purchase of agricultural assets with a view to transferring the assets into a relevant property trust after the appropriate period.

E: Pilot Settlements.

F: Discounted Gift Trusts/Schemes.

G: Excluded property trusts; disabled trusts; employee benefit trusts which satisfy *IHTA 1984, s 86*; and a qualifying interest in possession trust.

H: Transfers on death into relevant property trusts.

I: Changes in distribution of deceased's estates.

J: Transfers of the nil-rate band every seven years.

K: Loan trusts.

L: Insurance Policy trusts.

M: Making a chargeable transfer followed by a potentially exempt transfer.

N: Deferred shares.

O: Items of national importance.

P: Pension death benefits.

Q: Reversionary interests.

R: Transfers of value.

S: Gifts to Companies.

However, the above list is qualified in a way which is not altogether transparent. For example disclosure will be required 'where an individual makes a potentially exempt transfer to another person and the arrangements are such that the subject-matter of the transfer becomes relevant property, unless the arrangements are covered by the grandfathering rule'. Clearly HMRC did not want to be inundated by unnecessary disclosures.

[23.18] The DOTAS rules for inheritance tax are currently being extended. The idea was first announced in the consultation *Strengthening the Tax Avoidance Disclosure Regimes* (referred to at **23.16**) and facilitating legislation was included in *Finance Act 2015, s 117* and *Sch 17*. A first draft of the regulations for the new rules – *Inheritance Tax Avoidance Schemes (Prescribed Descriptions of Arrangements) Regulations 2015* – was published on 16 July 2015 for consultation until 10 September 2015.

[23.19] Any new regulations are intended to replace the existing ones, and that first draft applied a very wide and much more general test, requiring disclosure of any arrangement if 'an informed observer, having studied the arrangements and having regard to all the relevant circumstances, could reasonably be expected to conclude that':

- one of the main purposes of the arrangements is that a person might reasonably be expected to obtain an advantage in relation to inheritance tax ('the tax advantage'); and
- either:
  - one or more elements of the arrangements would be unlikely to have been entered into but for the obtaining of the tax advantage; or
  - the arrangements involve one or more contrived or abnormal steps without which the tax advantage could not be obtained;

and with only limited exemptions for inheritance tax planning involving the making of a will or codicil; the use of fixed term life assurance; and the use of loans to trustees.

[23.20] There was a general feeling amongst commentators that the scope of the first draft regulations were too widely drawn, and that as well as capturing avoidance arrangements, they would also catch legitimate and non-abusive use of reliefs. In their response to the original consultation (published on 2 February 2016) the government acknowledged these concerns and revised draft regulations were subsequently published on 20 April 2016 as part of a second Consultation Document – *Strengthening the Tax Avoidance Disclosure Regimes for Indirect Taxes and Inheritance Tax* (the closing date for comment for which was 13 July 2016).

[23.21] The overall approach of the revised regulations is similar to the original, with arrangements having to be notified if it would be reasonable to expect an informed observer to conclude that two conditions are met. However, the hallmark has been simplified. The revised conditions, both of which need to be met, are that:

- the main purpose, or one of the main purposes, of the arrangements is to enable a person to obtain a tax advantage; and
- the arrangements are contrived or abnormal or involve one or more contrived or abnormal steps without which a tax advantage could not be obtained.

[23.22] In the commentary which supported the revised regulations the government makes it clear that the revised approach is intended to ' . . . link the tax advantage much more clearly to arrangements which are abnormal or contrived. Consequently ordinary tax planning arrangements which result in a tax advantage yet are not contrived or abnormal are not caught by the revised hallmark'.

[23.23] At the time of writing, the government was still considering its response to the latest consultation. Many commentators believe that the simplified conditions are still too wide but it remains to be seen whether there will be any further amendment or simplification. Clearly, given the much wider scope of the proposed new regulations – when compared to those existing from 2011 – practitioners will need to consider their application in many more cases of inheritance tax planning in the future, than previously.

SDLT

[23.24] Tax avoidance arrangements in relation to SDLT were brought within the scope of the regime from 1 August 2005. There are only limited exceptions to the scope of the regime.

The main differences compared to the disclosure regime for income tax, corporation tax and capital gains tax are:

(a) the hallmarks are not applied to limit what is required to be disclosed. However, there is a 'white list' of arrangements that are not required to be disclosed and from 1 April 2010 schemes that have been disclosed by any person before that date are exempted from disclosure;
(b) promoters are not obliged to provide reference numbers to scheme users before 1 April 2010; and
(c) there are some minor differences in the time limits for making disclosure.

'Grandfathering' applies to certain pre-1 April 2010 arrangements (but see 23.25).

[23.25] HMRC extended the disclosure regime for SDLT from 1 November 2012 (*SIs 2012/2395* and *2012/2396*). The first set of regulations (regarding the 'Prescribed Descriptions of Arrangements'):

- removed the transaction-value thresholds (see 23.26);
- removed the *'grandfathering'* rule for certain arrangements involving the 'transfer of rights' legislation; and
- updated the list of excluded arrangements.

The second set of regulations (regarding 'Specified Proposals or Arrangements') has modified how *FA 2004, s 308* applies in certain circumstances. This means that if a promoter made a disclosure before April 2010 of certain arrangements involving the 'transfer of rights' legislation, they will have to make one further disclosure if they are still making those arrangements available. (*HMRC website What's New? 17.07.12.*)

[23.26] When SDLT was brought within the scope of the regime a transaction-value threshold applied to restrict the regime to transactions in relation to non-residential UK transactions for a consideration of at least £5million. This was then extended from 1 April 2010 to cover transactions where the subject-matter is:

(a) non-residential property with a market value of at least £5 million;
(b) mixed use property where the subject-matter of the arrangements contains non-residential property with a market value of at least £5 million and/or residential property with a market value of at least £1 million; and/or
(c) residential property with a market value of at least £1 million.

High risk promoters, follower and accelerated payment notices

[23.27] Following a period of consultation, *FA 2014* introduced a number of new powers for HMRC relating to marketed tax avoidance schemes. These gave HMRC new information and penalty powers relating to those considered to be 'high-risk' promoters and the right to issue 'follower' and 'accelerated payment' notices. These powers will operate separately from any obligation to provide information under the existing DOTAS (Disclosure of Tax Avoidance Schemes) rules.

[23.28] The measures are aimed at those who have used marketed tax avoidance schemes still under open investigation or litigation. In particular, HMRC dislikes the fact that such taxpayers can hold on to the disputed tax even after the schemes have been investigated and challenged in court.

[23.29] Broadly, the new information powers relating to high-risk promoters allow HMRC:

- To issue conduct notices to promoters that meet a threshold condition in the previous three years.

- To monitor promoters who breach a condition of a conduct notice. A monitored promoter:
  (i) will be subject to new disclosure obligations;
  (ii) may be named by HMRC; and
  (iii) will be required to inform clients that they are monitored and of their promoter reference number.

[23.30] *Follower notices* are aimed at encouraging users of avoidance schemes to settle with HMRC after similar schemes have been defeated in court or Tribunal. Under the new procedure, HMRC will issue a notice to taxpayers involved in schemes where there has been a final judicial decision in another case involving the same or similar arrangements. The notice requires the taxpayer either to amend his tax return or agree to settle the dispute, depending on how far the case has gone. A First-tier Tribunal decision that is not going to be appealed can form the basis for a follower notice. Those presented with a follower notice but who choose not to amend their return (but to continue to fight their case through the courts) will face a penalty if they fight on and ultimately lose. The maximum penalty will be 50% of the disputed tax but this can reduce to 10% if the taxpayer 'cooperates' with HMRC. It is possible to appeal the penalty on the grounds that a case does not 'follow' the decision identified by HMRC. The penalty can also be appealed on the grounds that it was 'reasonable in all the circumstances' for the taxpayer to continue to fight on.

[23.31] Finally, accelerated payment notices, require taxpayers to pay tax upfront in certain cases – ie prior to the resolution of any dispute as to the tax due. This issue of such notices is intended to negate the cash-flow advantages which otherwise arise from the deferral of a tax charge while a case is being litigated and David Richardson, Director of HMRC's Counter Avoidance Directorate justified the new rule as follows:

> 'The policy reflects the Government's view that, during investigations and litigation into avoidance, the tax should sit with the Exchequer not the taxpayer. This approach will not change the underlying rules and the taxpayer will be free to continue to make his case to the tribunal or court. If the taxpayer is successful, the money will be returned with interest.
>
> Changing the economics in this way, so that HMRC hold on to the disputed tax rather than the taxpayer, reflects the reality that most avoidance schemes do not work as shown by the department's litigation success rate.'

[23.32] An accelerated payment notice can be issued to taxpayers who:

- have received a Follower Notice;
- are subject to a GAAR counteraction; or
- have used a DOTAS notifiable arrangement;

and it is this last trigger condition which has proved most controversial because, of course, previously it was not understood that making a DOTAS disclosure would accelerate the payment of tax.

[23.33] The rules in relation to follower notices and accelerated payment notices are complex and extremely draconian, with tight deadlines and very limited grounds for appeal. HMRC issued extensive guidance on both on

17 July 2014 and this is available here: www.gov.uk/government/publications/follower-notices-and-accelerated-payments. In September 2016 HMRC announced that it had issued 60,000 accelerated payment notices which had collected £3 billion in tax.

[23.34] To summarise the general anti-avoidance position now:

- Much tax planning is now the subject of disclosure under the DOTAS regulations;
- Anything disclosed could trigger an upfront tax payment;
- Anything which is 'abusive' will not work and could be subject to a 60% penalty;
- Any 'final' court decision in favour of HMRC can be applied to similar cases, with potential penalties for those who chose to fight on, and an upfront payment required.

Part II:

Non-UK Resident Trusts

Chapter 24

Residence and Domicile

Introduction

[24.1] The use of trusts in tax planning in England goes back to their origins in medieval times. Their use in an international context is more recent, deriving from the period after the First World War when levels of tax on income and estates reached punitive proportions. The introduction of capital gains tax in 1965, levied for many years on largely inflationary gains, provided a new incentive to ensure that such gains accrued outside the UK tax net.

[24.2] For their part, the authorities have sought over the years to prevent tax avoidance through the use of offshore structures, most of which have involved trusts at some stage. The legislation has tended to be highly draconian in character, catching the unaware as well as those who harboured an intent to avoid tax. Trustees as well as beneficiaries may be penalised as a result, so that it behoves anyone who may be involved in whatever capacity with an offshore trust to be aware of the pitfalls.

Basic concepts

[24.3] There are now two important concepts in the UK tax code relating to liability for UK tax on income or capital arising outside the UK. These are residence and domicile. Prior to 2013/14 there was a third concept, ordinary residence, but this is now of historical interest only and is covered separately in APPENDIX G. In the context of trusts these concepts may be relevant in relation to settlors, beneficiaries or trustees. A trustee is personally at risk for the liabilities of the trust, including tax, though this may be mitigated by indemnities given to him under the trust deed or, on retirement, by the continuing trustees. The residence of a trust, that is more particularly of a particular set of trustees from time to time, depends upon the individual residence status of each of the trustees, as explained below. Domicile is a concept relevant to settlors and beneficiaries but not, in their capacity as such, to trustees. This chapter proceeds to examine the concept of residence, focusing particularly, in paragraphs 24.9–24.10, on the new comprehensive statutory test for residence which has applied since 2013/14. The residence of trustees is discussed at 24.22–24.25 and the concept of domicile at 24.26–24.35. After a look at some historical policy developments, at paragraphs 24.39–24.40, the chapter considers the FA 2008 revisions for non-UK domiciliaries, together with the new rules proposed in the Summer Budget of 2015 to introduce a new 'deemed domicile' rule for income and capital gains tax, see **24.46–24.50**, before two final paragraphs on the residence of companies at 24.51–24.52. The reason why it is necessary to give, in a book on trusts, so much attention to the residence of individuals is of course that trustees insofar as they are (usually) individuals have their residence as a body determined by the residence of the individual trustees, as explained at 24.22.

Residence of individuals (before 2013/14)

[24.4] Before 2013/14, there was no statutory definition of residence but rather residence was largely a question of fact based on factors determined by the Courts in numerous decisions over the years. Given the variety of the facts in each cases, it was often difficult to know with any certainty whether or not an individual was resident in the UK. Broadly speaking, in order to break residence from the UK an individual had to:

- Leave the UK for a complete tax year under a full time contract of employment with minimal visits to the UK;
- Leave the UK permanently or indefinitely for a settled purpose and demonstrate a clean and distinct break from the UK; or
- Leave the UK for a settled purpose and not set foot in the UK for a complete tax year.

[24.5] A comprehensive background to some of the historically important cases and issues is included in APPENDIX G; however two contrasting First-tier Tribunal decisions from November 2013 illustrate the uncertainties in establishing a non-UK residence before 2013/14.

[24.6] In the case of *James Glyn* [2013] UKFTT 645 (TC), Mr Glyn moved to Monaco and subsequently received a sizeable dividend of £29 million. HMRC contended that Mr Glyn had remained UK resident during the period so that the dividend was subject to UK tax, arguing that Mr Glyn had not shown a 'distinct break' from the UK because he had not shown a sufficient loosening of his family and social ties. These arguments centred on the fact that Mr Glyn retained a six bedroomed family home in North London to which he returned frequently to observe Friday night family dinners and certain other Jewish holidays with his wife and UK resident adult children. Against this, Mr Glyn had severed his UK business ties; taken up 'quality' residence in Monaco; saw very little of his friends in the UK; and had only 44 days of UK presence (excluding travel days) during the tax year in question. He was also meticulous in his record keeping. The Tribunal found in favour of Mr Glyn and that he had made a 'distinct break' and was not resident in the UK.

[24.7] In the second case, *Stephen Norman Rumbelow* [2013] UKFTT 637 (TC), the decision went the other way. Mr and Mrs Rumbelow left their home in the UK, moving first to Belgium but later to Portugal. Their links to their home in Cheshire also remained strong, particularly because the couple's 15-year-old daughter remained there. Significantly, however, they did not forge strong ties in Belgium and their record keeping was not as good as Mr Glyn's. The Tribunal were not ultimately satisfied that they had made a clean break.

[24.8] To further illustrate the profound difficulties in interpreting the pre-2013/14 rules, the Upper Tribunal in *Glyn v Revenue and Customs Comrs* [2015] UKUT 551, following an appeal by HMRC, determined that the First-tier Tribunal had based its decision in some irrelevant factors and had also failed to take into consideration certain relevant factors. The Upper Tribunal determined that the decision could not stand and the case has been referred back to the First-tier Tribunal for a re-hearing.

The comprehensive statutory test for residence (from 2013/14)

[24.9] *FA 2013, s 218, Sch 45* introduced a statutory residence test for 2013/14 and future years by *FA 2013, s 218, Sch 45*. The test applies for all of income tax, capital gains tax and (so far as the residence status of individuals is relevant) inheritance tax and corporation tax. The schedule is arranged logically: *Part 1* embracing what are called 'The Rules', *Part 2* 'Key Concepts', *Part 3* 'Dealing with Split Year Treatment', *Part 4* 'Covering Anti-avoidance' and *Part 5* 'Miscellaneous'. The new regime is generally to be welcomed as offering a greater degree of certainty than was the case up to and including 2012/13 (see above). That said, however, the new regime is complex and not always straightforward in its operation. While generally there will be far fewer individuals for whom their residence status is uncertain, uncertainty will undoubtedly remain for a few. Even though HMRC have introduced a tax residence indicator designed to enable an individual to see where he/she is resident, that of course will depend upon feeding in the correct information (for example, as to the location of one or more 'homes'), where the definitions can bring counter-intuitive results and so could well lead an individual astray. Unfortunately, there can be no substitute in difficult cases for clear professional advice. Guidance is available on the HMRC website (*RDR1: Guidance Note on Residence, Domicile and the Remittance Basis* (updated in June 2016) and *RDR3: Guidance note on the Statutory Residence Test* (updated in August 2016)).

The rules

[24.10] An individual will be UK resident for a tax year if either 'the automatic residence test' is met or 'the sufficient ties test' is met. If neither such test is met, the individual (called 'P' in the legislation) is not UK resident for that year. The automatic residence test is met if P satisfies at least one of 'the automatic UK tests' and none of the 'automatic overseas tests'.

[24.11] There are five 'automatic overseas' tests. The first test is that P was UK resident for one or more of the three immediately preceding tax years; the number of days in year X which he spends in the UK is less than 16; and he does not die in the year. The second automatic overseas test is that P was resident in the UK for none of the three preceding tax years and the number of days spent in the UK in year X is less than 46. The third automatic overseas test is that in year X P works 'sufficient hours overseas' (for which there is a five-step test); during year X there are no 'significant breaks from overseas work', the number of days in year X on which P does more than three hours work in the UK is less than 31, and the number of days spent by him in the UK in year X is less than 91 – subject to the deeming rule that, once he has spent 30 qualifying days in the UK in year X (ie present at midnight), each subsequent 'qualifying day' in the tax year (on which he is present in the UK at some point in the day, though not at the end of the day) is to be treated as a day he spends in the UK. The fourth automatic overseas test is that P dies in year X, he was UK resident for neither of the two immediately preceding tax years; or the year before the preceding year was a split year on certain grounds and he spends less than 46 days in the UK in year X. The fifth automatic overseas test is that P dies in the year; he was resident in the UK for neither of the two tax years preceding year X because either he met the third automatic overseas test for each of those years or alternatively a split year condition is satisfied for the year before the immediately preceding year and a further condition satisfying a modification of the third automatic overseas test is satisfied.

[24.12] There are four 'automatic UK' tests. The first test is that P spends at least 183 days in the UK in the year ('year X'). The second test is that P has a home in the UK during all or part of year X; that home is one where he spends a sufficient amount of time in the year; and there is at least one period of 91 consecutive days in respect of which he has that home, at least 30 days of that period fall within year X and throughout that 91-day period either or both of Condition A or Condition B is met. Condition A is that he has no home overseas. Condition B is that he has one or more homes overseas, but spends no more than 'a permitted amount of time' there. The expression 'a sufficient amount of time' means at least 30 days in the year, no matter how short a time on each day. The third test is that P works 'sufficient hours' in the UK; there are no 'significant breaks' from UK work during that period; all or part of that period falls within year X; more than 75% of the total number of days in the 365-day period on which he does more than three hours work are days on which he does more than three hours work in the UK; and at least one day in the year is a day on which he does more than three hours work in the UK. There is a five-step process to work out whether P works 'sufficient hours in the UK' for any given period of 365 days. The fourth automatic UK test is that P dies in year X; for each of the three previous tax years he was UK resident on account of meeting the automatic residence test; even assuming he were not resident in the UK for the year, the tax year immediately preceding it would not be a split year; and, at the date of death, either P's home was in the UK or he had more than one home at least one of which was in the UK (unless he spends 'sufficient time' in an overseas home).

[24.13] The 'sufficient ties' test is met for year X if P meets none of the automatic UK tests and none of the automatic overseas tests, but he has sufficient UK ties for that year. 'UK ties' is defined in *Part 2*. The number of UK ties required depends upon whether (broadly) P may be described as a 'leaver' or an 'arriver' (convenient, albeit not statutory, expressions). Not surprisingly, fewer ties have to be satisfied for a long-term UK resident effectively to leave the UK than are required for an arriver to be treated as UK resident. A leaver is someone who is UK resident for one or more of the three tax years preceding year X. If he spends more than 15 but no more than 45 days in the UK in year X, four ties are required to make him UK resident: more than 45 but no more than 90 days, three days are required; more than 90 but no more than 120 days in UK, at least two ties are required; and more than 120 days, only one tie is required. For an arriver (someone who has been UK resident for none of the

The comprehensive statutory test for residence (from 2013/14) [24.15]

three tax years preceding year X); where he spends more than 45 but no more than 90 days in the UK, all four ties are required to make him UK resident; with more than 90 but no more than 120 days, at least three ties; and more than 120 days, at least two days are required.

[24.14] As to UK ties, in relation to a leaver, there are five types of tie: a family tie, an accommodation tie, a work tie, a 90-day tie and a country tie. For an arriver there are four ties: a family tie, an accommodation tie, a work tie and a 90-day tie. P will have a family tie if in that year there is 'a relevant relationship' between him and another person and that other person is UK resident for that year. There will be a relevant relationship with a spouse or civil partner (from whom he is not separated) if P and the other person are living together as (or as if they were) husband and wife or civil partners or that other person is a minor child of P's. Further provisions fill out these definitions. There is an accommodation tie if P has 'a place to live' in the UK which is available to him for a continuous period of at least 91 days and he spends at least one night there in the year. If there is a gap of fewer than 16 days between periods in the year when a particular place is available to P, that place is treated as continuing to be available to him during the gap. A place to live is wider than a home, in that it includes a holiday home or a temporary retreat. Again, there are further provisions. P will have a 'work tie' for the year if he works in the UK for at least 40 days (whether continuously or intermittently) in the year. P works for a day if he does more than three hours work in the UK on that day. Again, there are supplementary provisions. P has a 90 day tie for year X if he has spent more than 90 days in the UK in either or both of the year preceding year X and the tax year preceding that tax year. Finally, P has a 'country tie' for year X if the country in which P meets 'the midnight test' for the greatest number of days in the year is the UK. The 'midnight test' is satisfied for a country if P is present in that country at the end of the day. There is a tie breaker rule.

[24.15] As to the 'key concepts' in *Part 2*, it is beyond the scope of this book to go into these in any detail except to make two observations. The first is the definition is 'days spent', where the regime continues the previous system of counting as a day spent in the UK one where he is present in the UK at the end of a day, subject to a let-out for 'transit passengers' or where he is in the UK only for exceptional circumstances beyond his control which prevent him from leaving the UK and he intends to leave the UK as soon as those circumstances permit. A transit passenger assumes that he arrives in the UK on that day, that he leaves the UK the following day and between arrival and departure he does not engage in activities 'that are to a substantial extent unrelated to' his passage through the UK. Second, an individual's 'home' is defined (inclusively) as one which 'could be a building or part of a building or, for example, a vehicle, vessel or structure of any kind'. Whether there is a sufficient degree of permanence or stability for the place to count as one or a number of P's homes will depend on all the circumstances of the case. Somewhere used as nothing more than a holiday home or temporary retreat does not count as a home. A place may be a home whether or not P holds any estate or interest in it. Further, there are detailed definitions of 'work', 'location of work', 'significant breaks from UK or overseas work' and 'relevant jobs on board vehicles, aircraft or ships'. The concept of work embraces both an employment and a trade (whether a sole trade or a partnership). Travelling time counts as time spent working if the cost of the journey is or could be deductible for income tax purposes or whether something else is done during the journey which would itself count as work. A voluntary position with no contract of service does not count as an employment. There is a 'significant break from UK work' if at least 31 days go by and not one of those days is a day on which he does more than three hours' work in the UK or is a day on which he would have done more than three hours' work in the UK but for being on annual leave, sick leave or parenting leave. There is a corresponding definition of 'significant break from overseas work'.

[24.16] The general rule is that an individual is either resident for the whole tax year or for none of it. In special circumstances, however, the year may be split. *Part 3* contains detailed rules for splitting the tax year so that an individual is resident for part of the year but not all of it. The rules will apply where the individual satisfies one or more of eight specified cases being.

- Case 1: starting full time work overseas
- Case 2: the partner of someone starting full time work overseas
- Case 3: ceasing to have a home in the UK
- Case 4 starting to have a home in the UK only
- Case 5: starting full time work in the UK
- Case 6: starting full time work overseas
- Case 7: the partner of someone starting full time work overseas
- Case 8: starting to have a home in the UK

[24.17] In order for the split year treatment to be available in a particular tax year, the individual has to be resident under the SRT in either the preceding or following full tax year. In the event of split year treatment there are special charging rules for, respectively, employment income, pension income, PAYE income, trading income, property income, savings and investment income, miscellaneous income, relevant foreign income charged on the remittance basis and capital gains. There are also special rules for trustees, inserting new provisions into *TCGA 1992, s 69* and *ITA 2007, s 475*, in the case where an individual ceases to be a trustee of the settlement in the course of a split year. The split year rules, are extremely complicated and readers are referred to the excellent two part article 'The Reality' by Anne Redston in *Taxation* on 12 and 19 September 2013 for further details.

[24.18] *Part 4* of *Sch 43* deals with various anti-avoidance rules, relating to 'temporary non-residents' as defined, for purposes of all of: *ITEPA 2003*, capital gains tax [*TCGA 1992, s 10A* and *s 86A*], lump sum payments under pension schemes, distributions to participators in close companies, dividends from non-UK resident companies and chargeable event gains from non-qualifying life assurance contracts.

[24.19] *Part 5* has miscellaneous provisions including definitions and consequential amendments. There is an interesting transitional provision where it becomes necessary to determine for 2013/14, 2014/15 or 2015/16 whether an individual was UK resident or non-UK resident for a tax year before 2013/14. P may give notice to HMRC for his residence status to be determined in accordance with the statutory residence test rather than the pre-2013/14 regime.

[24.20] *Finance Act 2013 s 219, Sch 46* effectively repeals the concept of ordinary residence from 2013/14. So, for example, a claim for the remittance basis is now restricted to a non-UK domiciliary, having previously been open to a UK domiciliary who was not ordinarily UK resident in the tax year. The income tax advantage of being not ordinarily resident in the case of receipt of 'relevant foreign earnings' under *ITEPA 2003*, is retained, however, substituting a definition in *ITEPA 2003, s 26A* which is intended to give statutory effect to the concept of being non-ordinarily resident over a three year period. The remainder of the *Schedule* makes consequential amendments throughout the *Taxes Acts* to remove references to the concept of ordinary residence.

Temporary non-residence

[24.21] There are special anti-avoidance rules for both income tax (see 25.53–25.57) and capital gains tax (see 26.57–26.58) for taxpayers who are resident outside the UK for only a temporary period. FA 2013 introduced a single definition of temporary non-residence for these purposes, which can apply to an individual who, broadly speaking, has:

- been resident in the UK for four out of the preceding seven tax years; and who
- becomes resident outside the UK for less than five years (calculated as anniversaries from the date of departure).

Residence of trustees

[24.22] Where trustees are resident in the UK they are chargeable on the receipt of income, profits or gains. The trustees of a settlement are treated as being a single and continuing body of persons, distinct from the persons who may from time to time be trustees. The rule for residence is that where the settlor was resident, ordinarily resident or domiciled in the UK at any relevant time, then if at least one trustee is resident in the UK, they are all treated as so resident. The rule is in fact a bit more complex than as is straightforwardly stated in the previous sentence. In broad terms the legislation regards the status of the settlor at all times until he 'ceases to be a settlor' and deals with three separate situations: a life-time settlement, a Will trust and the transfer of property from settlement one to settlement two (when the residence status of settlement two depends on the circumstances of settlement one). A person ceases to be a settlor when no property of which he is the settlor is comprised in the settlement, he has not undertaken to provide property directly or indirectly for the purposes of the settlement in the future and he has not made reciprocal arrangements with someone else for that other person to enter into the settlement in the future. It is understood that the significance of this rule is to cater for situations where more than one person has contributed bounty to a settlement and thus it is necessary to identify the property which is taken into account for purposes of ascertaining the residence status of the trustees. A trustee who is non-UK resident is nevertheless treated as UK resident at any time when he is acting as trustee in the course of a business that he carries on

[24.22] Residence and Domicile

in the UK through a branch, agency or permanent establishment there [*ITA 2007, s 475(6)*]. See HMRC guidance on this at www.gov.uk/guidance/non-resident-trusts and the joint guidance note published as Trustee Residence Taxguide 06/15 (Updating Taxguide 3/10) by the ICAEW Tax Faculty, CIOT and STEP on 2 September 2015. Subject to the application of these deeming rules, if all the trustees are personally UK resident, then the trustees as a body are UK resident; if they are all personally non-UK resident, then the trustees as a whole are non-UK resident [*ITA 2007, ss 474–476*]. Amendments made by FA 2013, Sch 45 remove the references to 'ordinarily resident'.

[24.23] For capital gains tax there was a special rule up to and including 2006/07 [*TCGA 1992, s 69*]. The body of trustees was treated as being resident and ordinarily resident in the UK unless:

- the general administration of the trusts was ordinarily carried on outside the UK; and
- the trustees or a majority of them for the time being are not resident or not ordinarily resident in the UK.

A further useful rule provided that, in the case of a trust made by someone not domiciled, resident or ordinarily resident in the UK, a person acting as a trustee would, notwithstanding their personal UK residence, be treated as not UK resident if they carried on a business which consists of or includes the management of trusts and they acted as trustee of the trust in the course of that business. If in such a case all or a majority of the trustees were or were treated in relation to that trust as not UK resident, the general administration of the trust was treated as ordinarily carried on outside the UK. However, under the current statutory rule which takes effect from 2007/08, this favourable 'professional trustee' rule was repealed and new *section 69* inserted by FA 2006, Sch 12, *para* 2 into TCGA 1992 provides, in effect, the rule described at **24.22** for income tax purposes. The capital gains tax rules are expressed in slightly different terms reflecting the fact that the income tax legislation was drafted under the tax law re-write project.

[24.24] It remains important to know whether there is a single settlement perhaps divided into a number of different funds for which a sub-fund election has not been made as opposed to two or more different settlements. The trap is illustrated by the decision in *Roome and Denne v Edwards (Inspector of Taxes)* [1982] AC 279, [1981] 1 All ER 736, HL. In that case a settlement which had been divided into two funds was held to constitute still a single settlement and the trustees, resident and non-UK resident, to constitute a single body, so that gains which in fact accrued to Cayman Island trustees could be assessed on UK trustees. The case highlights the extreme care that must be taken if trustees wish to carve a completely separate new settlement out of an existing one. It is likely to be a matter of general trust law, as applied to the specific terms of the deeds in question, as to whether this is in fact possible. See Inland Revenue Statement of Practice SP 7/84 for the HMRC view on this matter (APPENDIX A).

[24.25] *Section 83A* of *TCGA 1992* (which has been amended by *FA 2013, Sch 46* to remove references to ordinarily resident) is an anti-avoidance section which applies to disposals on or after 16 March 2005. The provision addresses the situation where trustees realise a gain at a time when they are either non-UK resident under UK domestic law or, while UK resident under such law, non-UK resident under the tie-breaker clause in an applicable double tax treaty. This clause prevents the treaty from applying to the gain if at any time in the tax year in which the gain is realised the trustees are 'within the charge to capital gains tax'. *Section 83A* defines this expression to mean resident in the UK under UK domestic law and not (if the treaty is then applicable) non-UK resident under the tie-breaker clause in the treaty. The avoidance schemes blocked by this section involved changes of trustee residence at some point during the tax year. The High Court overturned the Special Commissioner in a test case on the issue (*Smallwood v Revenue and Customs Comrs* [2009] EWHC 777 (Ch), [2009] STC 1222, 11 ITLR 943). In the tax year of the disposal the trustees had been resident in all of Jersey, Mauritius and the UK, but at the time of the disposal were resident in Mauritius. This, according to the High Court, was critical for purposes of applying the then UK-Mauritius Treaty Article 13(4). The Special Commissioners had erred in creating a simultaneous residence for the trustees spanning the Mauritius period. The treaty gave the right to tax capital gains to the state in which there was residence at the time of the disposition – and the fact that there was no Mauritius tax on chargeable gains did not affect the issue. However, the CA reversed this decision (by a 2-1 majority, Patten LJ dissenting). Hughes LJ held that the Commissioners had been entitled to find that the place of effective management of the trust was in the UK. He observed that 'it was integral to the scheme that the trust should be exported to Mauritius for a brief temporary period only and then be returned, within the fiscal year, to the United Kingdom, which occurred. Mr Smallwood remained throughout in the UK. There was a scheme of management of this trust which went above and beyond the day to day management exercised by the trustees for the time being, and the control of it was located in the United Kingdom.' (*Trevor Smallwood Trust, Re; Smallwood v Revenue and Customs Comrs* [2010] EWCA Civ 778, [2010] STC 2045, 80 TC 536.) This decision is now final, the Supreme Court having refused the taxpayers leave to appeal.

Domicile

[24.26] In contrast to residence, which is largely a question of fact and UK domestic law, domicile (or domicil) is a highly technical matter of private international law, or conflict of laws, rather than English common law. Within the United Kingdom, an individual is domiciled in England and Wales, Scotland or Northern Ireland under the general law, albeit within the UK for tax purposes; similarly with individual states within say the US or Australia. The fiscal importance of domicile is immense, since non-UK domiciled individuals are taxed only on a remittance basis on their offshore income [*ITTOIA 2005, s 832*] and capital gains [*TCGA 1992, s 12*], both provisions as amended by *FA 2013, Sch 45*, while their offshore property is excluded from inheritance tax [*IHTA 1984, s 6*] (subject to the deemed domicile rules of *IHTA 1984, s 267*). Such remittance basis treatment for non-UK income and gains, as from 2008/09, is summarised at **24.42** [*ITA 2007, ss 809C, 809D* as inserted by *FA 2008, Sch 7*].

[24.27] Residence and Domicile

[24.27] Each individual must have a domicile, but only one domicile at any time, whereas multiple residence or ordinary residence (or even no residence at all) is possible. Everyone starts life with a *domicile of origin*, which will derive from that of his parent, usually the father. This is also known as a *domicile of dependency*. At one time a married woman acquired her husband's domicile as a domicile of dependency, but this relic of the subordination of women was swept away by the *Domicile and Matrimonial Proceedings Act 1973*, which provided that a married woman who had a domicile of dependency based on her husband's domicile was to be treated on the coming into force of the Act as having a domicile of choice in the relevant jurisdiction. The consequences which flowed from this rule were confirmed in *IRC v Duchess of Portland* [1982] Ch 314, [1982] 1 All ER 784, Ch D where it was held that, where a wife had acquired her husband's domicile under the previous rules, this subsisted until she changed her domicile in accordance with general principles.

[24.28] Each individual, on attaining the age of sixteen, can acquire a *domicile of choice*. The classic formulation of what is required to constitute a domicile of choice was made by Lord Westbury in *Udny v Udny* HL (1869) 1 LR Sc & Div 441 at p 458:

> 'Domicil of choice is a conclusion or inference which the law derives from the fact of a man fixing voluntarily his sole or chief residence in a particular place, with an intention of continuing to reside there for an unlimited time. This is a description of the circumstances which create or constitute a domicil, and not a definition of the term. There must be a residence freely chosen, and not prescribed or dictated by any external necessity, such as the duties of office, the demands of creditors, or the relief from illness; and it must be residence fixed not for a limited period or particular purpose, but general and indefinite in its future contemplation.'

[24.29] It will be seen that the onus of proving that an individual has acquired a domicile of choice is a heavy one and there is a line of cases in which individuals who have lived in England for long periods have nonetheless retained their domicile of origin. For example, in *Ramsay v Liverpool Royal Infirmary* [1930] AC 588, 99 LJPC 134, HL a Scot who had lived in England continuously for 35 years was held to have retained nevertheless his Scottish domicile of origin. There were similar facts and outcome in a more recent case, *Civil Engineer v IRC* (SpC 299) [2002] STC (SCD) 72, [2002] WTLR 491. The taxpayer who had a domicile of origin in England, had lived and worked in Hong Kong for 29 years before returning to the UK in 1989. The Special Commissioner found on the evidence that the taxpayer had never established a domicile of choice in Hong Kong. If a domicile of choice is established but later abandoned (by actual action, not by intention or declaration only: see *Faye v IRC* (1961) 40 TC 103, 40 ATC 304, Ch D) reversion to domicile of origin is automatic as confirmed by the Court of Appeal in *Barlow Clowes International Ltd v Henwood* [2008] EWCA Civ 577, (2008) Times, 18 June, [2008] BPIR 778.

[24.30] This principle is similarly illustrated by the earlier case of *IRC v Bullock* [1976] 3 All ER 353, [1976] 1 WLR 1178, CA. Group Captain Bullock was a Canadian, born in 1910, who served in the Royal Air Force from 1932 to 1959 and then retired in England. His wife refused to live in Canada, but he retained the intention of returning there in the event of his surviving her. Along with other indications such as his maintenance of

Canadian citizenship, this was held to be enough to rebut the contention that he had acquired a domicile of choice in England.

[24.31] For trusts the significance of domicile is that a trust created by a non-UK domiciled individual will always retain that character. Equally, a trust created by a UK domiciled individual will also retain that character. The residence of a settlement can change, but not its domicile, which remains that of the settlor. That said, however, it must be remembered that the addition of property to a settlement may create a separate settlement or, if not, then within an offshore context, produce a single settlement for inheritance tax purposes, part of which is protected as excluded property and part of which (added after the settlor has become actually or deemed domiciled in the UK) is not (see 27.7 and 9.57–9.64).

[24.32] In order to agree domicile status for UK tax purposes, traditionally a taxpayer has completed and submitted form DOM 1 for assessment by HMRC, typically on the basis that he or she retains a domicile outside the UK. In any event HMRC would only consider a particular form if a UK tax issue hung on it, for example where a purported non-UK domiciliary was making an excluded property settlement which had he been UK domiciled would trigger a chargeable transfer attracting inheritance tax at 20%.

[24.33] In more recent years HMRC have been more and more disinclined to entertain applications for domicile rulings and, from 25 March 2009, the DOM1 facility was withdrawn altogether. HMRC said in their Brief 17/09 of 25 March 2009 that the procedure would be replaced by the new comprehensive guidance on domicile in the new Residence, Domicile and Remittances Manual which is intended to enable the vast majority of taxpayers to self assess their own domicile status. While largely for income tax and capital gains tax purposes, the point also applies to inheritance tax. Specifically, interestingly in relation to inheritance tax HMRC stated 'an individual setting up a non-resident trust who, having taken account of the new HMRC guidance, considers they are non-UK domiciled is not obliged to submit an inheritance tax account to HMRC. If the settlor is non-UK domiciled then no inheritance tax is due.' But if an inheritance tax account is submitted in these circumstances, HMRC would continue their existing practice and only open an enquiry into the return if the amounts of inheritance tax at stake make such an enquiry cost effective to carry out. That limit was £10,000 (ie involving a chargeable transfer, above the nil-rate band, of £25,000 or more).

[24.34] However, on 24 August 2010 HMRC announced in Revenue & Customs HMRC Brief 34/10 that what they had said in March 2009 would no longer apply. In future HMRC would consider opening an enquiry where domicile could be an issue, or making a determination of inheritance tax in such cases, only where there was a significant risk of loss of UK tax. The significance of the risk will be assessed by HMRC using a wide range of factors. The factors will depend very much on the individual case but will include for example: a review of the information available to HMRC about the individual on HMRC databases; and whether there is a significant amount of tax (all taxes and duties, not just inheritance tax) at risk. In particular, HMRC do not consider it appropriate to state an amount of tax that would be considered significant, as the amount of tax at stake is only one factor. It

[24.35] One anxiety felt by expatriates in relation to domicile was removed by *FA 1996, s 200*. This provides that in determining a person's domicile for tax purposes no regard shall be had to any action taken by him to register as an overseas elector or to vote in an election. There is a proviso that the action can be taken into account for determining any person's liability to tax if that person so wishes. The domicile so ascertained applies only for that purpose.

[24.36] HMRC have over the last few years or so been attacking the domicile status of foreigners after they have resided in the UK for more than a decade. Basing themselves on the *Bullock* case (see **24.30**), they have been known to ask for a specific event that would cause the foreign resident to return home. This line of reasoning is fallacious and should be resisted. The test to be applied was stated as follows by the Earl of Halsbury LC in *Winans v A-G* [1904] AC 287, HL:

> 'Now the law is plain, that where a domicil of origin is proved it lies upon the person who asserts a change of domicil to establish it and it is necessary to prove that the person who is alleged to have changed his domicil had a fixed and determined purpose to make the place of his new domicil his permanent home.'

[24.37] Naturally the longer an individual resides here the easier it becomes to prove that point, and if he dies here, then it may be hard to resist the inference that the UK had become his permanent home. For example, in *Furse, Re, Furse v IRC* [1980] 3 All ER 838, [1980] STC 596, Ch D, a case which is an instructive contrast to *Bullock*, an American who came to England at the age of four and died here at the age of 80, having spent 58 out of the intervening 76 years here, was held to have died domiciled in England, despite a vaguely expressed intention to return to the United States when he was no longer able to live an active physical life on his farm. Compare this decision, on the other hand, with that in *Civil Engineer* (see **24.29**) where residence in Hong Kong for 30 years was on the facts held insufficient to establish an independent domicile of choice there.

[24.38] For those seeking to lose a domicile of origin within the UK and acquire a foreign domicile of choice the law imposes a three-year quarantine period for inheritance tax purposes [*IHTA 1984, s 267*]. That is, notwithstanding the acquisition of an independent domicile of choice in another jurisdiction to which the individual moves, he will be treated as continuing to be domiciled in the UK for a period of three calendar years. Accordingly, death within that period would trigger chargeability to inheritance tax on a worldwide assets basis, even if he then had no UK situs property. And the making of a settlement, whether within or outside the UK, would mean a chargeable transfer, triggering a positive liability to inheritance tax at 20% to the extent that he exceeded his available nil-rate band. In view of the adhesive quality of the domicile of origin, the acquisition of a domicile of choice requires careful forethought and planning. The problems which can arise where this is not done is illustrated by the case of Sir Charles Clore (see *Clore (No 2), Re, Official Solicitor v Clore* [1984] STC 609, Ch D on the domicile point) which generated extensive litigation.

Non-UK domiciliaries: policy developments

[24.39] HMRC are naturally unappreciative of the fact that wealthy foreigners have been able to live in the UK for decades but shelter much of their income and assets from UK tax, and it is worth reflecting on the various policy statements made about domicile over the last thirty years or so:

- In 1991 the then Conservative Government announced that it proposed to implement the Law Commissioners' joint report on the law of domicile (Cm 200). This would have replaced the concepts of domicile of origin and domicile of choice with a new rule that a child should be domiciled in the country with which he is for the time being most closely connected and that for the acquisition of a new domicile by an adult it should be sufficient to show that he intended to settle in the country in question for an indefinite period.
- However, by 1993, in a Parliamentary written answer on 26 May (HC Debs, Vol 225, Col 600), the Prime Minister stated that the Government had no immediate plans to introduce legislation on this subject. Concern had been expressed on the damage that the proposed change might cause and this obviously had an effect on official thinking.
- The was no indication that this policy would be changed during the first term of the new Labour Government, and the matter might perhaps have been regarded as settled. However, in his 2002 Budget speech, the then Chancellor Gordon Brown announced that he was '...reviewing the complex rules on residence and domicile' (HC Debs, Vol 383, Col 584).
- Budget 2003 saw the publication of a joint Inland Revenue and HM Treasury background paper, 'Reviewing the Residence and Domicile Rules as they Affect the Taxation of Individuals', reviewing residence and domicile; however, Budgets 2006 and 2007 merely confirmed the ongoing review.

[24.40] What was puzzling about the background paper was its apparent pre-occupation with foreign domiciliaries in receipt of employment income. High net worth individuals resident but not domiciled in the UK may not pay much in the way of direct tax, but they do spend money in the UK and thereby boost the UK economy. This is the continuing issue of what has traditionally been known as 'the Greek ship-owners' lobby'. If the historically generous income tax and capital gains tax rules based on the definition of domicile under the general law were to be changed, the additional tax revenues for the UK might well be less than the consequent economic downside of driving such people abroad. The prospect of such a fiscal own goal may well have proved to be a significant factor in the very substantial watering down of the October 2007 pre-Budget Report proposals before they found their way onto the statute book in 2008 in the form outlined below.

The FA 2008 revisions

[24.41] What has been said above illustrates the point that for at least a generation the preferential treatment given by the UK tax system to those who are resident in but domiciled outside the UK under the general law means that

[24.41] Residence and Domicile

they have been able to regard the UK to all intents and purposes as a tax haven, so long as they have played their cards correctly to take full advantage of the remittance basis for both income tax and capital gains tax. This is subject only to the qualification presented by the deemed domicile rule for inheritance tax under *IHTA 1984, s 267* (see **27.13–27.14** and that itself can be effectively sidestepped by the making of an excluded property settlement before deemed UK domicile kicks in typically after 17 continuous tax years). The nettle of that privileged position enjoyed by non-UK domiciliaries was finally grasped in the pre-Budget Report of 9 October 2007, though what were seen as clearly very draconian proposals, especially with their retroactive effect, were in the event very considerably watered down in the Budget Statement of 12 March 2008 and in the legislation which finally appeared. The effect of this is very briefly summarised at **24.42** and, for offshore trusts and companies, at **26.47–26.51**.

[24.42] The rule from 2008/09 is (in broad terms) that an adult non-UK domiciliary who has been resident here in at least seven out of the previous nine years (and with additional 'qualification' periods introduced from 2012/13 – see **24.44**) and who has unremitted income and gains of at least £2,000 must pay an annual tax – the 'remittance basis charge' or 'RBC' – if he wishes to enjoy the benefit of the remittance basis for income tax and capital gains tax, and which he must expressly claim (see **24.44** for the quantum of the RBC charge). The RBC is a tax on unremitted income and gains, presenting quite complex identification issues, especially for purposes of claiming a credit against non-UK tax on that income or gains under an applicable double tax treaty. Payment of the tax direct to HMRC does not itself trigger a remittance. The 2008 changes also codified the rules for determining what is a remittance, tightening them up and removing a number of well-established avoidance routes, though there are some useful exceptions. *Finance Act 2009* introduced minor changes to these new rules, and *Finance Act 2012* introduced a significant exemption: permitting non-UK domiciliaries to make tax-free remittances for investment in companies carrying on a trade or undertaking the development or letting of commercial property (the so called 'Business Investment Relief' now contained in *ITA 2007, s 809VA*).

[24.43] In relation to the anti-avoidance regime for trusts, the settlor charge under *TCGA 1992, s 86* continues to be limited to UK domiciled settlors (see **26.17–26.32**). The capital payments charge under *section 87* is extended to payments received by non-UK domiciled UK resident beneficiaries, though only in respect of capital payments made on or after 6 April 2008 and with the option for the trustees to elect for rebasing of assets at 5 April 2008, so as in effect to protect from charge for non-UK domiciled beneficiaries any gain accrued up to that date (including gains accrued within underlying companies) (see **26.33–26.51**). Such a beneficiary who has elected for the remittance basis in the relevant year enjoys the remittance basis for the capital payments charge. Similar rules, but without the ability to elect for rebasing where shares or other financial instruments are held by an individual, are introduced for offshore income gains and indeed also for the apportionment provision for gains made by non-UK resident companies which if UK resident would be close where the participator with his associates has an interest of more than 10%, under *TCGA 1992, s 13*. No longer, from 2008/09, does the UK resident participator need to be UK domiciled to be caught by *section 13*. A new *section 14A* applies the remittance basis to non-UK domiciled participators where the asset disposed of was situated outside the UK. Note, however, that it is a remittance by the company and not by the participator which triggers the capital gains tax liability on the foreign chargeable gain.

The quantum of the RBC charge

[24.44] It has been fascinating to watch how the RBC charge has 'mushroomed' over the last seven years. When it was originally introduced from 2008/09, it comprised a single charge of £30,000 for any non-UK domiciliary who had been resident in the UK for seven out of the previous nine years. This remains the starting point for the charge, but from 2012/13 the annual charge increased to £50,000 for those who had been resident in the UK for at least 12 out of the preceding 14 years.

[24.45] The taxation of non-UK domiciliaries again became a political 'hot potato' in the final Autumn Statement of the Coalition Government in December 2014 and, with an election looming and the Labour Party increasingly using the taxation of non-UK domiciliaries as an example of 'unfair' taxation, the final Budget of the Coalition Government in March 2015 announced that from 2015/16 (and which changes were included in *Finance Act 2015*):

(a) The '12 out of 14 year' RBC charge would increase to £60,000; and
(b) There would be a new RBC charge rate of £90,000 for any non-UK domiciliary resident in the UK for 17 out of 20 tax years.

For 2014/15 there are therefore two rates: £30,000 for 7/9 years; and £50,000 for 12/14 years. For 2015/16 there are three rates: £30,000 for 7/9 years; £60,000 for 12/14 years and £90,000 for 17/20 years. Things, however, are currently moving very quickly in this area of taxation and, as explained in the following paragraph, the £90,000 is unlikely to remain relevant beyond 2016/17. Proposals to impose a minimum claim period for the RBC – ie removing the option for non-UK domiciliaries to claim it on a year by year basis based on their tax liability for that particularly tax year – were announced in the March 2015 but withdrawn, following consultation, on 17 July 2015.

The Summer Budget 2015 proposals

[24.46] In a somewhat surprising move, in the Summer Budget of 2015 following the election of a Conservative majority government, Chancellor George Osborne announced an end to the 'tinkering' with the RBC charge. Instead, from 2017/18 onwards, it proposed that:

> ' . . . those who have been resident in the UK for more than 15 out of the past 20 tax years will . . . be treated as deemed UK domiciled for all tax purposes. This will mean that they will no longer be able to use the remittance basis and they will be deemed domiciled for inheritance tax purposes.'

Thus, the third '£90,000' RBC charge will become redundant (having only been in place for 2015/16 and 2016/17), and the 'deemed domicile' position for inheritance tax will also change.

[24.47] Also announced was a proposed new rule for '*the returning UK dom*':

> 'In addition, those who had a domicile in the UK at the date of their birth will revert to having a UK domicile for tax purposes whenever they are resident in the UK, even if under general law they have acquired a domicile in another country.'

In theory, this represents a significant change. However, where someone with a UK domicile of origin acquires a domicile of choice overseas and then returns to the UK, there is always the possibility that they will be considered by HMRC to have abandoned that domicile of choice or, indeed, HMRC may argue that the fact of their return demonstrated that they had never changed domicile at all. It is thought that this change has been prompted specifically by the publicity surrounding the appearance in March 2015 before the Public Accounts Committee of the Chief Executive of HSBC, Stuart Gulliver. Born and educated in the UK, and then living in the UK, Mr Gulliver was, nevertheless, apparently claiming a non-UK domiciled status as a result of a move to Hong Kong some years previously.

[24.48] On 30 September 2015, the government published a formal consultation document in relation to these proposals – *Reforms to the taxation of non-domiciles* – with the consultation running for six weeks. On 9 December 2015 and 2 February 2016, draft legislation was published. Progress stalled during the early part of 2016 – not least, it is assumed, due to the government's attention being focused on Brexit – but a further consultation document – *Reforms to the taxation of non-domiciles: further consultation* – was published on 19 August 2016, together with 16 pages of draft legislation setting out the main elements of the proposed reforms. This consultation runs until 20 October 2016 and it is intended that the whole package of reforms will be formally legislated in Finance Bill 2017.

[24.49] Further commentary on the proposed changes appears in the relevant paragraphs of CHAPTERS 25, 26 and 27 which follow and more detailed commentary will appear in next year's edition once the current consultation has completed and the rules are finalised; however, the key points confirmed in the latest consultation are as follows:

- The two main changes to the deemed domiciled rules – the '15/20 year' rule and the 'returning UK doms' rule will go ahead broadly as originally proposed. (The detail in relation to these rules is set out at 27.15–27.16.)
- When considering years of residence prior to 2013/14, the pre-Statutory Residence Test rules (see **24.4–24.7**) will need to be used and the proposal (by some respondents to the consultation) that the Statutory Residence Test could be used has been rejected by the government.
- Years spent in the UK during an individual's childhood (ie under the age of 18) will be counted, as will years where an individual was able to claim a split year treatment.
- For inheritance tax purposes only, there will be a 'grace period' for 'returning UK doms'. Whereas for other taxes, a deemed UK domicile will be re-acquired in the year of return. For inheritance tax, it will be necessary for the individual to have been resident in at least one of the

two previous tax years. Someone arriving in the UK shortly after 6 April will therefore have a grace period of one year. For others, arriving later in the tax year, the grace period may amount to only a few months.
- For inheritance tax purposes only, a 17/20 year rule will continue to apply for those leaving the UK.
- For the '15/20 year' rule, only those gains arising from 2017/18 should be subject to capital gains tax and, to achieve this, rebasing to 5 April 2017 will be possible. Rebasing will not be available to those deemed domiciled under the 'returning UK dom' provisions.
- There will be some specifically targeted transitional provisions to protect the position of some 'temporary non-residents' who made disposals prior to the announcement of the new rules and who return to the UK.
- There will also be a temporary window during the tax year 2017/18 for individuals holding (some) mixed funds overseas to separate those into their constituent parts to enable 'clean capital' to be remitted in years of future deemed domicile. Again, this facility will not be available to those becoming deemed domiciled under the 'returning UK dom' provisions.
- The £2,000 de minimis will continue.

[24.50] The possibility of an individual becoming deemed domiciled under the new rules, raised the issue of how non-UK resident trusts created by such individuals prior to them achieving that status should be taxed. One option was simply to tax them in the same way as individuals who are domiciled in the UK as a matter of general law; however, the government wished to provide some form of special treatment for some such trusts and the original consultation document proposed that such individuals would not be treated in the same way as 'ordinary' UK domiciliaries but would instead be subject to a new system of taxing the value of the *benefits* they received once they had become deemed domiciled. This threated to create a very complex system of different rules for different types of domiciliary and the government has now announced in the latest consultation document that they will not be proceeding with this idea. Instead, specific protections will be included within the existing anti-avoidance legislation for income tax and capital gains tax, and the 'excluded property' status of some settlements will be maintained for inheritance tax purposes. Interestingly, those who become deemed domiciled under the 'returning UK dom' rules will not get any special treatment, and their trusts will also lose their 'excluded property' status. The specific proposals for each tax are outlined in the relevant paragraphs of CHAPTERS 25, 26 and 27 which follow.

Companies

[24.51] Trustees will need to consider the residence of companies on two counts. Firstly, where the trustee is a company, that company's residence will need to be considered to establish the tax treatment of the trust. Secondly, the trustees may hold shares in a company and the tax treatment of dividends and

[24.51] Residence and Domicile

disposals may rest on the residence position of the underlying company. Under the authority of a body of UK case law, a company is resident for UK tax purposes where the central management and control of its business is carried on (see Statement of Practice 1/90). This is subject to the overriding rules that a company incorporated within any part of the UK is resident here for tax purposes [*CTA 2009, s 14*, formerly *FA 1988, s 66*]. The issue has been the subject of recent legislation, *Wood v Holden (Inspector of Taxes)* [2006] EWCA Civ 26, [2006] 1 WLR 1393, [2006] STC 443, the Court of Appeal upholding the High Court in favour of the taxpayer and disagreeing with the Special Commissioner. This was a capital gains tax avoidance case involving disposals between companies owned by a non-UK resident trust made by a person, Mr Wood, resident and domiciled in the UK. The Court upheld the traditional case law definition of a company's residence, which gave the same result as the application of the UK/Netherlands treaty test of effective management. That is, disapproving the approach taken by the Special Commissioners, the fact that the directors took decisions which were consonant with the wishes of the UK resident settlor of the trust which owned them did not of itself indicate that Mr Wood was a shadow director and that the central management and control of the company was being exercised in the UK. This was not a case where the functions of the board of directors had been usurped by someone outside their number.

[24.52] Unlike the case of *Wood v Holden*, in *Laerstate BV v Revenue and Customs Comrs (TC00162)* [2009] UKFTT 209 (TC), [2009] SFTD 551, [2009] SWTI 2669 an individual was held to have usurped the functions of the board, both while he was an actual director and after he had ceased to be a director. Although formal board meetings were held in the Netherlands, the personal residence of the dominant individual in the UK meant that both (a) for domestic UK purposes the central management and control of the company's business and (b) for purposes of the UK/Netherlands double tax convention the place of effective management of the company's business, were situated in the UK. The taxpayer's appeal the Upper Tribunal was struck out on 1 March 2011, following the failure to comply with directions.

Chapter 25

Income Tax

Liability to UK tax

[25.1] The fundamental rule governing the liability of non-UK residents to income tax was stated as follows by Lord Wrenbury in *Whitney v IRC* HL (1925) 10 TC 88 at p 112:

> 'The policy of the Act is to tax the person resident in the United Kingdom upon all his income wheresoever derived, and to tax the person not resident in the United Kingdom upon all income derived from property in the United Kingdom.'

[25.2] Trustees resident in the UK are accordingly taxable on the worldwide income of the trust, while non-UK resident trustees are taxable only on income arising in the UK.

[25.3] The question of what is the trustees' income for this purpose came up for consideration in *Williams v Singer and others* HL (1920) 7 TC 387. A number of shares in the Singer Company of New Jersey were held by UK resident trustees for a beneficiary who was neither resident nor domiciled in the UK. The dividends on the shares were paid under mandate to a New York bank. The Inland Revenue assessed the trustees on the dividends. At first instance Sankey J confessed that he appreciated the position of those persons who 'found no end in wandering mazes lost', but his decision against the Revenue was upheld in both the Court of Appeal and the House of Lords. Viscount Cave founded his reasoning on what is now *ITTOIA 2005, s 8* in relation to trade profits (with corresponding provisions in relation to different categories of income), charging income tax under what was then Schedule D on the persons 'receiving or entitled to the income'.

> 'The fact is that, if the Income Tax Acts are examined, it will be found that the person charged with tax is neither the trustee nor the beneficiary as such, but the person in actual receipt and control of the income which it is sought to reach.'

Identifying the income of the beneficiary

[25.4] A converse point arose in *Archer-Shee v Baker* HL (1927) 11 TC 749. Lady Archer-Shee was the UK resident beneficiary under an American Will trust. The assets consisted of foreign property the income from which was paid by the trustees to Lady Archer-Shee's order at a New York bank. At that time there was a distinction between Case IV and Case V of Schedule D [*ICTA 1988, s 18*], tax under Case IV on foreign securities being charged on an arising basis, and tax under Case V on foreign possessions being charged on a remittance basis. The case was decided against the appellant on the basis that English law applied. A second appeal was commenced for later years of assessment and expert evidence was led regarding the New York law which

[25.4] Income Tax

was applicable (*Garland v Archer-Shee* HL (1930) 15 TC 693). This evidence was that Lady Archer-Shee's life interest gave her no proprietary interest in the income arising from the securities, stocks and shares constituting the trust fund, but rather a right of action against the trustees if they failed to carry out their duties. The case was finally decided by the House of Lords in favour of the appellant on the grounds that this right, technically a chose in action, was a possession.

[25.5] The problem thrown up by the *Archer-Shee* cases remains of general significance. Although English common law has travelled widely, equity has been less successful in winning acceptance internationally. The distinction between legal and beneficial interests in property tends not to apply. Rather the property is vested in the legal owner, with the rights of the beneficial owner enforceable as a separate matter. HMRC published a useful 28 page note on 1 April 2008, providing a non-statutory outline of the UK tax liabilities that may arise in respect of income and gains arising to most non-UK resident trustees. The note ends with a helpful schedule of various overseas territories indicating how trusts governed by the law of that territory which gives an interest in possession are either 'Baker' or 'Garland' types of trust. (See now www.gov.uk/government/uploads/system/uploads/attachment_data/file/382897/Income_Tax_and_Capital_Gains_Tax_for_non-resident_trusts.pdf.)

[25.6] Beneficiaries of a '*Baker*' type trust are entitled to their appropriate share of each item of income as and when it arises to the trust. This is subject only to a deduction for trustees' expenses. Unless the remittance basis applies, the beneficiaries are chargeable on their share of the trust income, less a rateable proportion of the trust expenses. If the trust income has borne UK tax, it is taxed income of the beneficiaries. Each beneficiary's share (after a rateable proportion of trust expenses) is income which has been taxed at whatever rate of tax it has borne. Beneficiaries of a '*Baker*' type trust should make their self assessment on the Trusts etc supplementary pages.

[25.7] Beneficiaries of a '*Garland*' type trust are entitled only to their appropriate share of the net trust income remaining after the trustees have ascertained the balance available after meeting the expenses of administering the trust. Beneficiaries chargeable on the arising basis are liable by reference to the actual income receivable from the trust in the basis year. This applies whether or not it was paid out by the trustees or remitted to the UK. The nature of the income that arose to the trustees is irrelevant. Beneficiaries of a '*Garland*' type trust should enter the amount received on their self assessment tax return, on the Foreign supplementary pages. It is an untaxed source. Some of the income chargeable may be from trust income that has borne UK tax. A claim for relief in respect of the tax must be a free standing claim. It must not affect a beneficiary's self assessment. Trust income may have suffered foreign tax, for which beneficiaries can claim credit relief. This is in the same way and to the same extent as if the beneficiaries were entitled to their proportionate share of the underlying investments of the trust. A claim for credit must be a free-standing claim and must not affect a beneficiary's self assessment.

[25.8] Rather different, but equally difficult, issues were raised in *Lord Inchyra v Jennings* ChD (1965) 42 TC 388. Lady Inchyra had an interest in one quarter of the income from her mother's estate commencing in 1950 and an interest in the remainder from 1955. Additionally, from 1951 to 1970 inclusive or until her earlier death, she was to receive annually 1% of the capital value of the estate excluding real property. The Inland Revenue contended that the payments out of capital were to be treated as income and that each stream of payments was to be treated as a separate source. Under the then rules for taxing new sources of income under what were then Cases III, IV and V of Schedule D, it was advantageous to the Revenue to adopt the latter treatment.

[25.9] Although evidence was produced that the payments out of capital were treated as capital under US law, the High Court held that its character in Lady Inchyra's hands was to be determined in accordance with English law. The weight of the authorities led to the conclusion that a series of recurrent payments over a period related in some way to the life of a beneficiary must be treated as income. However, on the subsidiary issue it was held that there was a single source of income, namely Lady Inchyra's interest in her mother's estate, together with the right to have the estate applied for her benefit in accordance with the Will.

[25.10] A case which fell on the other side of the line was *Lawson v Rolfe* Ch D (1969) 46 TC 199. Mrs Lawson was entitled to a life interest in half of a trust fund. The fund was invested in US shares. In 1962, 1963 and 1964 some of the companies declared stock dividends. The rule in the US is that where such a stock dividend is paid for out of profits it does not affect the integrity of the trust fund and may be passed on to a beneficiary. The trustees did so. The Special Commissioners held that in view of this rule the stock dividends must be regarded as income. In the High Court it was common ground that under Californian law, which was applicable, Mrs Lawson had an equitable right in possession to receive during her life the proceeds of specific stocks constituting her share in the trust fund, rather than an *Archer-Shee* right to have the trusts properly administered. The judge considered the *Inchyra* decision and concluded that the stock dividends lacked the character of recurrent payments over a substantial period of time. Their issue was fortuitous and not planned so far as the trust was concerned. There was no element of recurrence so as to implant on what was capital the imprint of income when they reached Mrs Lawson's hands.

[25.11] It was established in *IRC v Regent Trust Co Ltd (Butt's 1970 Settlement Trustee)* Ch D (1979) 53 TC 54 that the additional rate tax liability (or what is now the special rates charged under *ITA 2007, Pt 9, Ch 3, ss 479–483*) applied to offshore discretionary trusts. Trust management expenses chargeable to income are apportioned pro rata between income liable to UK tax and that not so liable [*ITA 2007, s 487*]. The tax liability on any UK dividends received by offshore trustees is now computed by reference to a notional dividend ordinary rate tax credit, which is not repayable [*ITTOIA 2005, s 399*].

[25.12] A distribution by offshore trustees from such income does not strictly carry a credit under *ITA 2007, Pt 9, Ch 7, ss 493–498* (discretionary payments), but under ESC B18 (reproduced in APPENDIX B) relief will be accorded on a concessionary basis, provided the offshore trustees have

Anti-avoidance

[25.13] The decade of the *Singer* and *Archer-Shee* cases, the 1920's, also saw the beginnings of large-scale tax avoidance using offshore trusts. One of the pioneers in this field was the Vestey family, which was to have a long-running battle with the then Inland Revenue (see **25.21**).

[25.14] The Inland Revenue's difficulty arose from the fact that it is not possible for them to enforce an assessment on a non-UK resident. The decision of the government not to ratify a far-reaching OECD convention for the mutual enforcement of tax assessments indicates that this principle will continue to be observed in this country.

[25.15] Foreign tax laws are naturally considered where a double tax treaty exists between the UK and an overseas jurisdiction and unilateral relief may be available against foreign tax under *TIOPA 2010, ss 8–18* (formerly *ICTA 1988, s 790*). These provisions will usually be beneficial to the taxpayer.

The 2008/09 reforms

[25.16] Following the changes enacted by *FA 2008* for UK resident non-UK domiciliaries, corresponding changes for non-UK resident trusts mean that a non-UK domiciled UK resident beneficiary of income received outside the UK will be charged to UK tax, unless he is a remittance basis user and does not remit the income, which will include indirect remittances and remittances by a 'relevant person' [*ITA 1997, s 809M* as inserted by *FA 2008, Sch 7*]. It is beyond the scope of this book to examine in any detail the detail of the very complex regime introduced by *FA 2008, Sch 7*, beyond the briefest of summaries at **24.42–24.43**.

[25.17] Non-UK resident trustees may have an interest in a hedge fund or similar collective investment vehicle where interest is rolled up, so bringing any future gains within the offshore income gains regime. Such gains made from 2008/09 which are matched with benefits received by a non-UK domiciliary in the UK or, if not a remittance basis user, outside the UK, are assessed on the beneficiary.

Transfer of assets abroad

[25.18] The prime anti-avoidance provision is now to be found in *ITA 2007, Pt 13 Ch 2, ss 714–751*. Subject to the motive test (see **25.24–25.27**) and to the remittance basis for non-UK domiciliaries [*ITA 2007, s 726 and s 730*], the regime (which charges individuals who are ordinarily resident in the UK to income tax) falls into three parts. First, an individual who has power to enjoy the income of a non-UK resident person as a result of a relevant transfer by him is treated as if that income was his. Second, such a transferor may receive a capital sum as a result of relevant transactions and is treated as if the income arising to the non-UK resident were his. Third, a non-transferor may receive a benefit as a result of relevant transactions, in which case the relevant income within the offshore structure is assessed on him, to the extent that it has not been attributed to anyone else.

[25.19] Before amendment following the *Vestey* case (see **25.21–25.23**), its main thrust was to treat income payable to persons outside the UK as being the income of an individual ordinarily resident in the UK, where that individual had made a transfer of assets, either directly or indirectly, with a tax avoidance motive. So, in *Lord Howard de Walden v IRC* CA (1941) 25 TC 121 it was held that the income of some Canadian companies, the shares of which the taxpayer had transferred many years previously to trustees for his children, should be treated as his income.

[25.20] Shortly thereafter the House of Lords made a fateful extension of the section in *Congreve v IRC* (1948) 30 TC 163 to impose liability on individuals other than the transferor. This was used by the Inland Revenue to impose tax, for example, on Rudyard Kipling's daughter as a result of transactions carried out many years before by her parents (*Bambridge v IRC* HL (1955) 36 TC 313). Many taxpayers felt a considerable sense of grievance, in view of positive assurances that had been given when the legislation was passed. Such assurances, if given in Parliament, may now be relied on, following the decision in *Pepper v Hart* HL [1992] STC 898.

[25.21] It was the Vestey family who brought this matter to a head in *Vestey v IRC* HL (1979) 54 TC 503. The real vice of the *Congreve* decision was that the statute provided no means of apportioning foreign trust income among discretionary beneficiaries. The Inland Revenue claimed that they had a general administrative power to do this, a contention that Walton J found 'laughable'. Lord Wilberforce agreed, 'less genially', and held that the application of *Congreve* in the case of discretionary trusts produced a result which was 'arbitrary, unjust and in my opinion unconstitutional'. *Congreve* was overruled and the assessments on the Vestey family beneficiaries were quashed.

[25.22] The Inland Revenue returned to the attack in 1981 with amendments to the regime, to introduce what is now *ITA 2007, ss 731–735A*. These provisions (called in this book 'the benefits charge') impose a liability on non-transferors where they receive a benefit provided out of assets available in consequence of the transfer and referable to unmatched 'relevant income' within the trust.

[25.23] The ambit of the (original) transferor charge was extended in 1997. It was reasonably supposed that the transfer of assets triggering the operation of the section must be made by an individual ordinarily resident in the UK while so resident and that the transfer must be from the UK to an offshore jurisdiction. In *IRC v Willoughby* HL [1997] STC 995, it was held that, in view of the *Vestey* decision, the transferor charge should not apply to transfers made by non-UK residents. The expatriate planning to return to the UK, or foreigners planning to sojourn here, could therefore make arrangements prior to their arrival which would not be caught by the charge. The position was then altered to the taxpayer's disadvantage by what is now *ITA 2007, s 721(5)* and *s 723(3)*.

The 'motive test'

[25.24] There is a statutory exemption in *ITA 2007, ss 736–742* where it can be shown that the transfer had no tax avoidance purpose or was a bona fide commercial transaction (the so-called 'purpose (or motive) defence'). However, this may well be difficult to demonstrate. In the *Willoughby* case, it was held that the roll-over of offshore insurance policies after the return of the expatriate did not constitute tax avoidance at all, but was rather acceptable tax mitigation following the analysis of Lord Templeman in *IRC v Challenge Corpn Ltd* PC [1986] STC 548.

[25.25] A high profile decided case on the *transferor charge* is *IRC v Botnar* CA, [1999] STC 711. The taxpayer transferred shares to a trust established in Liechtenstein. The Special Commissioners held that the section did not apply since Mr Botnar and his family were excluded from benefit under the trust. However, the Revenue's appeal was allowed in the High Court on the grounds that the assets could be transferred to another trust from which Mr Botnar and his family might benefit. Mr Botnar was not represented at the appeal and died shortly thereafter. An appeal to the Court of Appeal by Mr Botnar's Swiss lawyer, at which full argument was heard, was dismissed.

[25.26] A Special Commissioner decided against the taxpayers early in 2009 in *Burns v HMRC* [2009] STC (SCD) 165 SpC 728. Assignments of their interests in an industrial estate settled by their grandfather were made by the taxpayers on their 18th birthdays while resident in Jersey. Subsequently they became UK resident and were assessed to income tax under the transferor provisions in respect of income arising to the assignee Jersey companies. They pleaded the purpose defence unsuccessfully. The argument was that the main purpose of the assignments was to divorce ownership from management and to put the management responsibility in relation to the properties into the hands of the taxpayers' parents who were the directors of both companies. The Special Commissioner found that the purposes underlying the transactions, which were clearly implemented very deliberately, were those influencing the parents rather than the taxpayers themselves. The Special Commissioner was unable to accept that the transactions were designed to separate ownership from management and that that was a bona fide commercial purpose. The transfers had no effect on the continuing management of the estate by the grandfather and his UK agents. And it was not established that UK tax avoidance was absent from the purposes for which the transfers were made.

[25.27] An intriguing argument on the motive test was raised before the Upper Tribunal in *Anson v CIR* [2012] UKUT 59 (TCC). Mr Anson is a UK resident non-UK domiciled individual taxable on the remittance basis. He remitted to the UK income from a Delaware limited liability corporation (LLC). He sought to set off against his UK income tax liability the US tax paid by the Delaware corporation on his share of the profits. That he could not do, because a Delaware LLC is 'opaque' rather than 'transparent' (although treated as such by the US), rather like a company in the UK as opposed to a partnership. Mr Anson then tried to argue that, as the transferor of assets abroad, he had 'power to enjoy' the income of the non-UK resident corporation and therefore should be taxed as if the Delaware LLC's income was his. HMRC countered by contending that the motive test took Mr Anson out of the regime, on the grounds that the arrangements were made for bona fide commercial purposes. Mr Anson's response was that the motive test applied only if 'the individual shows in writing or otherwise to the satisfaction of the Board' that there was no tax avoidance purpose and this of course Mr Anson had not done. However, the Upper Tribunal resolved the issue simply by ruling that anti-avoidance legislation can have no application in analysing a transaction for tax purposes where no avoidance of taxation was intended or indeed had occurred.

The 2005 revision

[25.28] The loss by the Inland Revenue before the Special Commissioners of a number of cases involving the purpose defence led to a replacement statutory regime, from 5 December 2005 in what is now *ITA 2007, ss 736–742*. (Specifically, in *A Beneficiary v IRC* [1999] STC (SCD) 134 SpC 190, the Special Commissioner held that the test in the purpose defence is subjective). Under the present rule the anti-avoidance regime will not apply to post-4 December 2005 transactions if the taxpayer satisfies HMRC:

(a) that Condition A is met; or
(b) in a case where Condition A is not met, that Condition B is met.

Condition A is that it would not be reasonable to draw the conclusion, from all the circumstances of the case, that the purpose of avoiding liability to taxation was the purpose, or one of the purposes, for which the relevant transactions or any of them were effected.

Condition B is that:

(a) all the relevant transactions were genuine commercial transactions, and
(b) it would not be reasonable to draw the conclusion, from all the circumstances of the case, that any one or more of those transactions was more than incidentally designed for the purpose of avoiding liability to taxation.

[25.29] A relevant transaction is a commercial transaction only if it is effected:

(a) in the course of a trade or business; or
(b) with a view to setting up and commencing a trade or business,

and, in either case, for the purposes of that trade or business (*ITA 2007, s 738(1), (2), (4)*). The making and managing of investments, or the making or managing of investments, is provided to be not a trade or business except to the extent that:

(a) the person by whom it is done, and
(b) the person for whom it is done,

are unconnected persons dealing at arm's length.

[25.30] A 'commercial transaction' does not include:

(a) a transaction on terms other than those that would have been made between persons not connected with each other dealing at arm's length, or
(b) a transaction that would not have been entered into between such persons so dealing [ITA 2007, s 738(3)].

[25.31] The legislation deals with the case where there are transactions or part of transactions which fall both before 5 December and after 4 December 2005, by applying a just and reasonable apportionment test [ITA 2007, ss 740–742].

[25.32] The regime as revised in December 2005 allows HMRC to have regard to all operations which are associated. The definition is extremely wide as including a benefit provided out of assets which are available for the purpose as a result of either the transfer or one or more associated operations [ITA 2007, s 732(1)(c)]. Although, under the transitional rules, pre-5 December 2005 structures protected by the purpose test remain protected, once tainted the *whole* trust falls outside the purpose test, with the consequent danger of tax liability for any beneficiary who becomes UK resident and enjoys benefits from the structure.

[25.33] Once an operation occurs which breaches the revised purpose test, protection is lost and the risks for UK ordinarily resident beneficiaries who receive benefits are that:

(a) the transferor regime applies to all the income from 5 December 2005 or from the beginning of the tax year of the offending operation (regardless how small is the impact of the operation);
(b) the benefits regime applies to benefits received from the beginning of that year (by reference to relevant income whenever it accrued). All associated operations since 5 December 2005 must be considered. If any of these is tainted by tax avoidance, so is the whole structure. If the structure is caught, one must then go back to 1981 to identify the relevant income within the structure; and
(c) the apportionment allowed for the purposes of the transferor regime where the commercial limb (only) of the defence is in point is very limited.

The FA 2013 amendments

[25.34] Prompted by the EU Commission, on the grounds that the transfer of assets abroad code reaches EU Treaty freedoms, FA 2013, s 26, Sch 10, has made a number of changes). In particular there is a new exemption from the tax charge for 'genuine transactions' that is transactions effected on or after 6 April 2012 where conditions A and B are met. Condition A is that '(a) were, viewed objectively, the transaction to be considered to be a genuine transaction having regard to any arrangements under which it is effected and any other relevant circumstances and (b) were the individual to be liable to tax under this chapter by reference to the transaction, the individual's liability to tax would, in contravention of a relevant treaty provision, constitute an unjustified and disproportionate restriction on a freedom protected under that relevant treaty provision.' Condition B is 'that the individual satisfies an officer of Revenue and Customs that, viewed objectively, the transaction must be considered to be a genuine transaction having regard to any arrangements under which it is effected and any other relevant circumstances.' Other changes generally provide greater certainty to how the regime will operate.

[25.35] In April 2013 the concept of ordinary residence was removed from the UK tax legislation (see 24.3). Since this date, whether an individual is subject to a transfer of assets abroad charge, will turn on whether or not they are resident (not ordinarily resident) in the UK. Where an individual arrives or leaves the UK part way through a tax year the split year rules may be in point in determining whether a charge arises (see 24.16).

[25.36] The government published the first version of draft legislation for *FA 2013* as part of a consultation opened on 30 July 2012 asking for views on whether it was necessary to have new rules for matching benefits received by non-transferors with income arising to the person abroad.

[25.37] The 2012 response document indicated overwhelming favour for having new matching rules. At the same time, HMRC published draft rules intended to replace the current rules (in ITA, ss 733 to 735A) with effect from 2013/14. However, in the 2013 Budget, the government announced that the new matching rules would not be included in *FA 2013*, but would be the subject of a further consultation with a view to legislating in *FA 2014*.

[25.38] On 18 July 2013, HMRC published a further consultation document with a request for views on matching rules for the non-transferor charge. The 2013 consultation did not propose any specific amendments to the draft matching rules published in December 2012, but summarised the perceived problems with the current rules and listed high-level options for reform.

[25.39] On 20 December 2013, HMRC published a response to the 2013 consultation. This announces that the government will not implement any changes to the matching rules at present. It does not give any reasons why the government has decided not to amend the matching rules, stating simply that it has considered the views put forward in the consultation and the working group.

[25.40] According to the consultation response, there was support for improving the clarity and certainty of the matching rules by improving HMRC guidance, however, the draft matching rules guidance did not reflect HMRC practice and some issues might be difficult to resolve through guidance.

Proposed changes from 2017/18

[25.41] As set out at 24.50, the proposed new deemed domicile rules for income and capital gains tax to be introduced from 2017/18 will have an impact on the settlors and beneficiaries of non-UK resident trusts who become deemed domiciled.

[25.42] Where an individual becomes deemed domiciled under the 'returning UK dom' rule, it is proposed that there will be no protection in relation to trusts established prior to that event – and the individual will simply be taxed as an ordinary UK domiciled settlor in relation to the income of the trust. Where, however, an individual becomes deemed domiciled under the '15/20 year' rule, it is proposed that any trusts settled by him or her prior to that event should be given protection in the form of an exemption from some of the rules which would otherwise apply – which protection will last until (if ever) the trust becomes 'tainted' (see below). The proposed exemptions for income tax are that:

- the settlor should not become subject to income tax in relation to non-UK source income on an arising basis; and
- the transfer of assets abroad regime will not apply to attribute non-UK source trust income to the individual. The rules in relation to non-trust income (ie the income of an underlying company) are not yet entirely clear but it is understood that there will be some protection there too.

[25.43] A trust will become tainted if funds are added to it after a settlor has become deemed domiciled, and what constitutes an 'addition' is likely to be drawn or interpreted widely. Thus, while an arm's length sale at full market value will not be an addition, a sale at any undervalue is likely to be caught.

[25.44] The corresponding rules for capital gains tax (see **26.53–26.56**) provide that a trust will also be tainted where capital or income is applied for the benefit of the settlor, his or her spouse or civil partner, or minor children. At present, there is no proposal for such an event to trigger tainting for income tax purposes. Instead, it would appear that this would trigger a settlor charge in the relevant year only. Indications at this stage suggest that the rules in this area will be complex.

[25.45] One interesting consequence of the current proposal is that (assuming that a trust had not become 'tainted') a settlor who has been paying the remittance basis charge (following seven years residence in the UK) to avoid being taxed on non-UK trust income on an arising basis, will still not be taxed but will no longer have to pay the remittance basis charge once he or she becomes deemed domiciled.

Transactions in land

[25.46] An attack on artificial transactions in land is made by what is now *ITA 2007, Pt 13 Ch 3, ss 752–772*. The regime applies when:

(a) land is acquired with the object of realising a gain from its disposal; or
(b) land is held as trading stock; or
(c) land is developed with the object of realising a gain from its disposal when developed;

and a gain of a capital nature is obtained from the disposal of the land directly or indirectly. Such a gain is brought into charge to income tax as miscellaneous income (see **6.96–6.98**).

[25.47] There is an express exception from the regime for a gain accruing to an individual (note, not trustees) if the gain is exempt from capital gains tax by reason of the main residence relief in *TCGA 1992, ss 222 to 226* [which, interestingly, includes the trustee relief under *section 225*] or the gain would be exempt but for the anti-avoidance provisions of *section 224(3)*, residences acquired partly with a view to making a gain [*ITA 2007, s 767*].

[25.48] Although the transactions in land regime, unlike the transfer of assets abroad regime, is not exclusively aimed at offshore structures, it has been used extensively in this connection. The leading example of the section in this context is provided by *Yuill v Wilson (Inspector of Taxes)* [1980] 3 All ER 7, [1980] 1 WLR 910, HL and *Yuill v Fletcher (Inspector of Taxes)* [1984] STC 401, 58 TC 145, CA. Mr Yuill was a builder whose family company owned some land with valuable development potential. The beneficial ownership of this land found its way into the hands of trustees of Guernsey discretionary settlements. There was never much doubt in the course of prolonged litigation that Mr Yuill had incurred a charge to income tax by transmitting the opportunity of making a gain to the trustees under what is now *ITA 2007, s 756(5)*, the only real issue being the point at which the charge crystallised.

[25.49] It has become clear that the transactions in land regime can be used to penalise perfectly normal transactions in land entered into with no tax avoidance motive. In *Page (Inspector of Taxes) v Lowther* [1983] STC 799, 57 TC 199, CA, a wholly commercial arrangement whereby the trustees of the Holland Park Estate were to participate in the premiums realised on a development was caught by the regime. To emphasise the point, the rubric 'artificial transactions in land', which had been carried by the original legislation in 1969 and the consolidation in 1970 was dropped in the 1988 consolidation.

[25.50] There is a statutory clearance procedure under *ITA 2007, s 770*. As with all clearance procedures the person submitting the application must make a full and accurate disclosure of all material facts and considerations. HMRC must respond within 30 days as to whether the anti-avoidance regime would in their view apply. The traditional thinking on such a clearance application is that except in a case where the regime would clearly not apply, making the application puts one as something of a hostage to fortune in that HMRC may well decide to refuse the application on the grounds that there is evident concern that the regime might apply; it is perhaps better therefore not to raise the point at all. This can be something of a dangerous course to adopt, especially when the strict obligations under self assessment are considered and the potential liability to interest and penalties should those obligations not be fulfilled. Furthermore, there are provisions enabling HMRC to recover tax chargeable under the regime where the consideration is receivable by a person who is not the taxpayer, with a statutory right of recovery by the person assessed against the taxpayer (*ITA 2007, s 768*). There is therefore an incentive on any such person receiving the consideration to be sure that the regime does not apply.

Deduction of tax

[25.51] From 2016/17, all bank and building society interest is paid gross. Prior to this, under arrangements effective from 6 April 1996 [*ITA 2007, ss 853–857; Income Tax (Deposit-Takers and Building Societies) (Interest*

Payments) Regulations 2008, SI 2008/2682], bank and building society interest has been payable without deduction of tax to the trustees of offshore discretionary trusts. This is subject to completion of a declaration in approved form that the trustees are not resident in the UK and do not have any reasonable grounds for believing that any of the beneficiaries of the trust is an individual who is ordinarily resident in the UK or a company which is resident in the UK.

[25.52] Provisions found at *ITA 2007*, *ss 499–503* apply to trust management expenses incurred by the trustees where a beneficiary has an interest in possession but is not liable to tax on an amount of that income by reason of being non-UK resident in the UK for tax purposes. In such a case *section 501* provides that a proportion of the expenses is disregarded in computing the income of the beneficiary equal to the proportion which the untaxed income bears to all the income arising to the trustees to which the beneficiary is entitled. The disallowance is computed on the basis of income arising to the trustees net of any tax chargeable on them. 'Disregarded income' (defined in *ITA 2007*, *s 813*) on which the beneficiary pays no tax because no tax is deducted at source, is to be treated as income on which the beneficiary is not liable to tax by reason of being non-UK resident in the UK for tax purposes.

Temporary non-residents

[25.53] In *FA 2013* new anti-avoidance rules were introduced for 'temporary non-residents'. This rule was introduced in response to a perceived mischief – individuals avoiding income tax by temporarily becoming non-resident (see 24.18). By way of example, before the introduction of this rule the majority shareholder of a company could become non-resident for a single complete tax year and take out substantial tax free dividends relating to profits made whilst he was previously resident in the UK.

[25.54] A similar temporary non-resident rule was previously introduced by *FA 2008* in relation to remittance basis users. Prior to *FA 2008*, a non-domiciliary could use a short period of non-residence to remit relevant income and gains from prior years without attracting a tax charge.

[25.55] Since April 2013 certain types of income received or remitted during a period of temporary non-residence will become chargeable to UK income tax if the individual returns to the UK after a period of temporary non-residence.

[25.56] This anti-avoidance rule only applies to certain types of income, namely:

- Dividends and other distributions from closely controlled companies
- Remitted foreign income
- Certain pension payments
- Income taxable under the disguised remuneration rules (see CHAPTER 6)
- Loans to participators written off or released
- Chargeable event gains (on a life insurance, life annuity or capital redemption policy)
- Offshore income gains

[25.57] The first two – close company dividends and remitted foreign income – are particularly relevant to trustees. It is not unusual for an offshore trust to hold shares in an offshore 'closely controlled' company. An issue arises where that company pays a dividend to the trustees. Is such a dividend treated as a dividend paid to the beneficiary and so caught by the temporary non-residence rules? The answer will depend on type of trust in question. Beneficiaries of a 'Baker' type trust are entitled to their appropriate share of the dividend as and when it arises to the trust (see **25.5–25.6**) and so the beneficiary may be treated as a participator and subject to the temporary non-residence rules. In contrast, in relation to a 'Garland' type trust the nature of the income that arises to the trustees is irrelevant (see **25.7**). The beneficiary receives a trust distribution and not a company dividend and so the temporary non-residence rules ought not to apply.

[25.58] There is a limited exception from the charge where for example, it can be shown that the dividend relates to trading profits accruing during a period when the beneficiary was non-resident. Similarly, broadly speaking, remittances of income made in relation to income earned during a non-resident period will not be subject to charge.

Chapter 26

Capital Gains Tax

Introduction

[26.1] The application of capital gains tax to non-UK resident trusts has been a developing saga, stemming from just one anti-avoidance provision built into the original legislation in 1965. This related to non-UK resident trusts where the settlor was domiciled and either resident or (before the concept was abolished by *FA 2013, Sch 46* from 2013/14 onwards) ordinarily resident in the UK or had that status when he made the settlement. In such a case, any beneficiary with the same status could have the gains of the trust apportioned to him on a 'just and reasonable' basis, according to the respective value of his interest [*FA 1965, s 42*]. It took the 1982 House of Lords decision in *Leedale v Lewis* [1982] STC 835 to show quite how unfairly this rule could impact and this is why the capital payments charge in *TCGA 1992, s 87* was introduced in 1991 (see **26.33–26.52**). Following *FA 2008*, there is a significant distinction in applying the capital payments charge in 2008/09 and subsequent years from the rule which applied up to and including 2007/08. In broad terms gains made by non-UK resident trustees can now be assessed on UK resident non-UK domiciliaries receiving a capital payment on or after 6 April 2008, subject to the remittance basis of taxation and to the ability of the trustees to elect that only post-5 April 2008 accrual of gains can be so taken into account. This change in approach is a reflection of the present regime applying from 2008/09 for applying the remittance basis of taxation for income tax and capital gains tax purposes to such individuals outlined at **24.41**, but that is beyond the scope of this book.

It should be noted that numerous provisions cited in this chapter have been amended by *FA 2013, Sch 46* to remove the concept of ordinary residence from 2013/14 onwards.

[26.2] The legislation continues to restrict the primary charge to capital gains tax to UK resident persons, whether individuals, trustees or personal representatives. That is, gains on disposals of UK situs assets are free from capital gains tax except where used for a trade carried on in the UK through a branch or agency (*TCGA 1992, s 10*) or, from 6 April 2015, when disposing of UK residential property (see **26.66–26.68**). The rule before 2013/14 is that 'a person shall be chargeable to capital gains tax in respect of chargeable gains accruing to him in a year of assessment during any part of which he is resident in the United Kingdom, or during which he is ordinarily resident in the United Kingdom' [*TCGA 1992, s 2(1)*]. From 2013/14 liability to capital gains tax depends upon satisfaction of 'the residence condition' in new *section 2(1A)*. The residence test for trustees for capital gains tax (and, indeed, also for income tax) purposes is set out at **24.22**. There was a significant change from 2007/08, aligning the residence rules for trustees for capital gains tax purposes to those which already existed for income tax. In particular, this involved abolition of the favourable 'professional trustee' rule applying up to and including 2006/07 (see **24.23**). Anti-avoidance legislation, of some sophistication, was required to prevent in broad terms the enjoyment of gains accruing to non-UK resident trustees (and indeed companies) which could be enjoyed by UK resident individuals. Under each of three heads of charge outlined at **26.4**, the chapter summarises how the constituent parts of the charge have developed over the years, so as to apply (in this book) to 2014/15 for compliance purposes and for 2015/16 for planning (and also future compliance) purposes. Avoidance techniques which have been blocked (ie disposals of interests in non-UK trusts and so-called 'flip-flop' schemes) are discussed at **26.59–26.61**.

[26.3] The capital gains tax charge on the disposal after 6 April 2012 of UK residential property for more than £500,000 by 'non-natural persons', whether or not UK resident can be found at **7.126**.

Three heads of charge

[26.4] In outline, the three main occasions of charge are as follows:

(a) an exit charge when a trust becomes non-UK resident after 18 March 1991 [*TCGA 1992, ss 80–84*];

(b) a charge on the settlor on the gains of a non-UK resident trust created after 18 March 1991 where he or his family retain an interest in the trust [*TCGA 1992, s 86, Sch 5*];

(c) a charge on capital payments made to beneficiaries of non-UK resident trusts in which the gains are not taxable on the settlor, to the extent that those payments are referable to gains made by the trustees [*TCGA 1992, s 91*]. (Further matching rules under *TCGA 1992, ss 92–95* applied before 2008/09, though these were repealed by *FA 2008, Sch 7, para 113*.) To this is added a supplementary charge on payments after 5 April 1992 where more than 12 months elapse from making of the gain by the trustees to the making of the payment to the beneficiary, up to a maximum of 6 years.

The exit charge

[26.5] *Section 80* provides that where after 18 March 1991 the trustees of a settlement become neither resident nor (before 2013/14) ordinarily resident in the UK, they are deemed to have disposed of all the assets of the settlement immediately prior to that time and to have reacquired them at market value. There are two exceptions to a *section 80* charge:

(i) where the assets are used or held for the purposes of a trade carried on by the trustees in the UK through a branch or agency (where there is a continuing liability to capital gains tax under *TCGA 1992, s 10* – and it should be noted that there is no corresponding exception for UK residential property even though there is, from 6 April 2015, a continuing liability there too);

(ii) where the trustees are protected by a double tax treaty (although in such a case they may be liable to charge under *TCGA 1992, s 83*. See **26.9** and **24.9**).

Roll-over relief under *TCGA 1992, s 152* is not available where the old assets are disposed of prior to the emigration of trustees and the new assets are acquired afterwards, unless the assets are used for a trade which the trustees are carrying on a trade in the UK.

[26.6] An exit charge can occur inadvertently. Consider a settlement made by a non-UK domiciled UK resident individual. There are three individual trustees, two resident outside the UK and one resident in the UK. Under the tests set out at **24.22**, the trustees as a body are UK resident. However, if the UK resident trustee emigrates to (say) Spain (or retires as a trustee), the trustees will automatically become non-UK resident, triggering an exit charge. The only exception to this principle is where the change of residence is caused by the death of a trustee, as described at **26.7**. To protect against the danger presented by the situation above, one might consider appointing a UK trust company as a trustee, if not the appointment of more UK resident individuals.

Death of a trustee

[26.7] A settlement may become non-UK resident through the death of a trustee. If in such a case the majority of the trustees become non-UK resident, it would be unjust in such a case for an adventitious charge to arise. Accordingly, *TCGA 1992, s 81* provides a period of grace of six months during which the trustees can take steps to become UK resident again. For temporarily non-UK resident trustees the relief does not apply to assets disposed of during the period of non-UK residence (although the trustees would almost certainly be chargeable in any case) nor to assets protected by a double tax treaty, because this would open the door to tax avoidance. In the case of re-emigrating trustees, relief is denied where assets are acquired during the period of non-UK residence to which *TCGA 1992, s 165* (relief for gifts of business assets) or *TCGA 1992, s 260(3)* (gifts on which inheritance tax is chargeable) applies.

Past trustees: liability for tax

[26.8] It is one thing to impose a tax charge on non-UK residents, quite another to collect it. *TCGA 1992, s 82* attempts to give the charge some extra teeth by imposing a liability in certain circumstances on retired trustees. Where the exit charge is not paid within six months of the time when it becomes payable, HMRC have three years from the time the amount of tax is determined to have recourse to anyone who was a trustee within the period of twelve months (but after 18 March 1991) before the emigration. A past trustee is exempt from charge where he can show that when he ceased to be a trustee there was no proposal that the trust might emigrate. It is difficult to prove a negative, and a trustee in circumstances where this provision might apply would naturally require a full indemnity. In view of the fact that the right of recovery he is given against the migrating trustees may be of limited value, he would be well advised to have documentary evidence showing that he did make the necessary enquiries at the time of his retirement.

Exit charge on trustees becoming dual resident

[26.9] *TCGA 1992, s 83* is the provision directed against the use of double tax treaties to avoid a capital gains tax charge. In cases where trustees continue to be resident and (before 2013/14) ordinarily resident in the UK under UK domestic law but become exempt from capital gains tax on the disposal of assets because of the residence provisions of a double tax treaty, they are deemed immediately before the point of becoming dual resident to have disposed of the assets and reacquired them at market value. The charge applies where trustees become dual resident after 18 March 1991. It is unclear how far this has been a loophole in practice as the UK does not have double tax treaties dealing with capital gains tax with most of the territories which are usually regarded as tax havens. The basis of HMRC's concern is *TIOPA 2010, s 6(3)* (formerly *ICTA 1988, s 733(3)*) which gives tax treaties primacy over 'anything in any enactment', even anti-avoidance provisions. This has been confirmed by decisions in *Lord Strathalmond v IRC* Ch D (1972), 48 TC 537 and *Padmore v IRC* CA [1989] STC 493.

Hold-over restriction

[26.10] *TCGA 1992, s 169* was introduced to block avoidance by dual resident trusts. A trust might attain this status if a majority of the trustees were resident in the UK but its general administration was carried on elsewhere. The trust would be resident in the UK under UK law [*TCGA 1992, s 69*], but a double tax treaty might provide that the trust would be treated as resident where the general administration was carried on. Use of the then existing general relief for gifts or the other roll-over reliefs available allowed assets to be transferred into such trusts without tax. They could then be disposed of without triggering a charge under the shelter of the double tax treaty. *Section 169* strikes at this by denying hold-over relief on the transfer.

Charging gains realised by disposing of interests in settlements

[26.11] Under *TCGA 1992, s 76* the disposal of an interest in a settlement (which has only ever been UK resident) is exempted from capital gains tax except where the interest has been acquired for value. This protection is withdrawn in the case of non-UK resident trusts *(TCGA 1992, s 85)*. Where a disposal takes place, that is protected by *section 76* and the trust subsequently emigrates, the gain is chargeable on the trustees, unless they have disposed of all the assets in the settlement before it emigrates. Tax not paid by the trustees can be charged on the disponor of the interest.

[26.12] *TCGA 1992, s 85(2)–(9)* provides a relief from the charge under *TCGA 1992, s 85(1)* where an interest in a non-UK resident settlement is disposed of. In cases where there has already been a charge under *TCGA 1992, s 80*, the base value of the interest concerned is increased to its market value at the time of migration, ie when the previous charge arose, so preventing the same gain from being taxed twice. This relief is modified where the trustees become dual resident in circumstances such that a charge under *TCGA 1992, s 83* was incurred before the *section 80* exit charge on emigration. If the interest disposed of was created for or acquired by the beneficiary only after the trustees became dual resident, there is no relief at all, ie no uplift in base cost to market value at the time of migration. If the interest disposed of was created or acquired before the dates of becoming dual resident and becoming non-UK resident, there is partial relief, with the beneficiary's base cost being uplifted to market value at the date the trust became dual resident.

[26.13] This anti-avoidance provision noted at 26.11 and 26.12 was regarded as so urgent that it came into effect ahead of Budget Day, on 6 March 1998. The exemption under *TCGA 1992, s 76* is disapplied for gains made on the disposal of an interest by a beneficiary in a trust where the interest disposed of is in, or originates from, a trust which has ever been an offshore trust. The provision covers cases where an interest in an offshore trust, which has been transferred to the UK, is subsequently moved to another trust which has always been resident in the UK prior to disposal [*TCGA 1992, s 76* as amended by *FA 1998, s 128*]. This prevents a beneficiary in an offshore trust pregnant with capital gains from realising these gains tax-free by disposing of his interest in the trust after it has been transferred to the UK.

Acquisition by dual resident trustees

[26.14] *TCGA 1992, s 84* continues on the theme of dual resident trusts by denying roll-over relief under *TCGA 1992, s 152* where the new assets are acquired by such trustees after 18 March 1991. This mirrors the treatment under *TCGA 1992, s 80* where the new assets are acquired after the emigration of the trust.

The immigration emigration route blocked

[26.15] A device whereby a trust is brought onshore and then exported again was blocked in 2000. The gains on the trust property escaped charge because they were realised while the trust was offshore, whereas the beneficiary paid little or no tax on the sale of an interest in the trust because of the rule providing for its value to be uplifted on the trust's emigration from the UK. The amendments provide that there will be no uplift where the trust is pregnant with gains not attributed to beneficiaries or the trust has gains which are caught under the measures against flip-flop schemes in *FA 2000, Schs 25 and 26* [*TCGA 1992, s 85*].

The 30 day rule for share identification

[26.16] A successful attempt to avoid the emigration charge was made in *Davies v Hicks* [2005] EWHC 847(Ch), [2005] STC 850. The retiring UK trustees took advantage of the 30-day share identification rule in *TCGA 1992, s 106A* (introduced in 1998 to counter the traditional practice of 'bed and breakfasting' in order to uplift base costs at the end of the tax year). Shares realising a gain were sold, the UK trustees retired and new trustees resident in Mauritius were appointed. The Mauritius trustees then, within 30 days of the disposal, bought back shares of the same class and description as had been sold by the former UK trustees. The effect of *section 106A* was to identify the shares sold with the shares acquired, thus eliminating the gain. At the date of immigration the only assets held by the trustees were non-chargeable sterling cash. The effect of this decision was reversed by *FA 2006, s 74*, disapplying the *section 106A* rule where the person acquiring the shares is not UK resident.

The settlor charge

[26.17] The detailed provisions in connection with the charge are contained in *TCGA 1992, s 86, Sch 5*. The charging section is *section 86(4)* as amended by *FA 2013, Sch 45*, which provides in effect that the chargeable gains of a qualifying settlement shall be treated as accruing to the settlor if he has an interest in it.

[26.18] There are two provisions dealing with the interaction between the settlor charge and, first, the capital payments charge described below and, second, the corresponding settlor charge for UK resident trusts (which has been repealed from 2008/09). These are as follows:

(a) the first is *TCGA 1992, s 87(3)* to make it clear that gains deemed to accrue to the settlor under *TCGA 1992, s 86(4)* cannot also be trust gains (or, from 2008/09, 'section 2(2) amounts') chargeable on the beneficiaries for the purposes of *TCGA 1992, s 87(2)*;

(b) the second deals with the situation where gains are treated as accruing to a settlor under both *TCGA 1992, s 86(4)* and (prior to 2008/09) *TCGA 1992, s 77(2)* (gains of UK resident trust chargeable on settlor – see **4.33**). Under *TCGA 1992, s 78* (before its repeal by *FA 2008, Sch 2, para 5*) the settlor had a right of recovery for any tax paid by him. *TCGA 1992, s 78(3)*, in conjunction with *TCGA 1992, s 86(4)(b)*, provides that the gains deemed to be those of the settlor as the highest part of the amount on which he is chargeable are those accruing under *TCGA 1992, s 86*, in priority to those under *TCGA 1992, s 77*: the need for this ordering rule ceases to apply from 2008/09 with the repeal of *section 77* (by *FA 2008, Sch 2, para 5*).

[26.19] Where a charge under these provisions arises on a temporarily non-UK resident settlor (under *TCGA 1992, s 10A*, inserted by *FA 1998, s 127* and then substituted by *FA 2013, Sch 45*), this is reduced by the amount of the gains charged on UK-resident beneficiaries of the settlement during the non-UK resident period [*TCGA 1992, s 86A*].

Meaning of settlor with 'an interest in the settlement'

[26.20] A settlor is chargeable if he has an 'interest in the settlement' [*TCGA 1992, Sch 5, para 2*] and if the trust's disposals consist of or include those of property 'originating' from him [*TCGA 1992, Sch 5, para 8*]. However, the charge does not apply if the settlor is not domiciled in the UK during the year of assessment concerned [*TCGA 1992, s 86(1)(c)*]. HMRC failed in their attempt to raise a *section 86* charge on a rich man who provided most of the cash to enable an Isle of Man company to buy some land in Cornwall which it sold at a 200% profit. The shares were subsequently transferred to an Isle of Man settlement of which the individual and his wife were the only beneficiaries. However, he successfully argued that he was not a 'settlor' for these purposes, the High Court accepting that the land sold by the company was not 'settled property' because it had never been held in trust for the settlement (*Coombes v HMRC* [2008] STC 2984).

[26.21] The test whether the settlor has an interest turns on whether property or income in the trust originating from him can be applied for his benefit or for the benefit of the same range of persons as in the qualifying settlements provision [*TCGA 1992, Sch 5, para 2(3)*]. There are exceptions to this similar to those in *ITTOIA 2005, s 625(2),(3)*). These deal with circumstances where the settlor's interest is contingent on the death or bankruptcy of someone else in specified circumstances [*TCGA 1992, Sch 5, para 2(4)–(6)*].

[26.22] The charge is also excluded where the settlor dies during the year and where the life or marriage/civil partnership of some other person by reason of which the settlor is treated as having an interest ends during the year [*TCGA 1992, Sch 5, paras 3–5*].

[26.23] There are extensive provisions [*TCGA 1992, Sch 5, para 8*] expanding on the term 'originating' in relation to property or income in the trust. They are designed to prevent avoidance through the provision of funds under reciprocal arrangements or through a closely controlled private company (subject to a 5% *de minimis* rule for any participator) or otherwise indirectly.

[26.24] The settlor is given a right of recovery against the trustees for any amount charged on him [*TCGA 1992, Sch 5, para 6*]. Even if the trustees have the power under the trust deed to make such a payment, they will need to consider whether it is a proper thing for them to exercise it. On the authorities it is unlikely that he could enforce such a right against non-UK resident trustees and if he did perhaps such a payment could constitute a capital payment chargeable under *TCGA 1992, s 87*.

[26.25] Is the definition of 'settlor' overridden by *TCGA 1992, s 62(6)* in the case of a post-death deed of variation? This was broadly the question for the House of Lords in *Marshall v Kerr* HL, [1994] STC 638 (see **7.113–7.116**). In the context of the 1981 provisions, it was held that a UK resident and domiciled beneficiary who executed a deed of variation altering the provisions of her non-UK resident and non-UK domiciled father's Will did become a settlor of the trust created by the deed.

Qualifying settlements

[26.26] 'Qualifying settlements', ie those which are potentially caught, are defined in *TCGA 1992, Sch 5, para 9*. Every settlement created on or after 19 March 1991 is a qualifying settlement. Settlements created earlier may also come within the qualifying settlement net if one of four conditions is satisfied.

(a) Property or income is provided directly or indirectly for the purposes of the settlement otherwise than under a transaction entered into at arm's length, and otherwise than in pursuance of a liability incurred by any person before 19 March 1991. However, payments towards meeting the trust's expenses relating to administration and taxation are ignored to the extent that these exceed its income.

(b) The trustees either become neither resident nor (before 2013/14) ordinarily resident in the UK or become dual resident for the purposes of a double tax treaty.

(c) The terms of the trust are varied so that any one of a range of persons becomes for the first time a person who will or might benefit from the trust. The persons include settlors, their spouses/civil partners, children and stepchildren, and (from 17 March 1998) grandchildren, *their* spouses/civil partners, any company controlled by them and any associated company. 'Control' and 'associated company' are construed in accordance with *CTA 2010, s 450 and s 449*, but in deciding questions of control or whether companies are associated, no rights or powers of an associate of a person are to be attributed to him if he is not a participator in the company. 'Associate' and 'participator' are defined in *CTA 2010, s 448 and s 454*. This goes some way to prevent, say, a member of a family who is in the position of an innocent bystander from being sucked into charge by having shareholdings of relatives attributed to him when he himself has no personal interest in the company.

(d)   One of the persons mentioned under condition *(c)* enjoys a benefit for the first time and is not one who, looking at the terms of the trust before 19 March 1991, would be capable of enjoying a benefit thereafter. This appears designed to catch what are sometimes known as 'limbo trusts', where perhaps the apparent ultimate beneficiary is a charity, behind wide discretionary trusts, but some operation takes place not amounting to a variation whereby benefits flow to the settlor or his family.

[26.27] The distinction between pre-1991 trusts and post-1991 trusts was prospectively abolished at Budget 1998 [*FA 1998, s 132* amending *TCGA 1992, Sch 5, para 9*]. This does not apply to 'protected settlements', defined as pre-1991 trusts where the beneficiaries are confined to children under 18, or future children; the future spouse of any child or the settlor; and persons who are not the settlor, his immediate family, or companies they control. A protected settlement will lose its exemption if any of the circumstances bringing a pre-1991 trust into charge previously is fulfilled (see **26.26**).

Transitional provisions 1998/99

[26.28] The 1998 charge on settlements for grandchildren exempts trusts set up before 17 March 1998, unless funds are added or the trust migrates [*FA 1998, Sch 22*].

[26.29] The 1998 charge on pre-1991 trusts applied to gains made after 5 April 1999. This allowed a transitional period for those affected to re-organise their affairs if they so wished: for example, for the settlor, his immediate family and companies they control to exclude themselves as beneficiaries; or for the trust to be wound up or become resident in the UK. There were rules to prevent exploitation of the transitional period. Gains made during that period were chargeable on the settlor in 1999/2000 where the trust did not fall within the charge on the settlor until the end of the transitional period. Gains would also be chargeable on the settlor where the trust assets were transferred to another settlement from which, at the end of the transitional period, the settlor, his immediate family, or companies they controlled, could benefit. It also applied where the trust assets were transferred in similar circumstances to a 'foreign institution', defined as any company or other institution resident outside the UK. There were exceptions where the only members of the settlor's family who could benefit are children under eighteen, future children and future spouses, or where the settlor was dead or where a beneficiary died or ceased to be married. There were rules to prevent double charges from arising under these provisions [*FA 1998, Sch 23*].

Application

[26.30] The Inland Revenue issued a Statement of Practice (SP 5/92) on 21 May 1992 indicating how they would apply the 1991 provisions, particularly in relation to the charge on settlors. On the same date they issued ESC D40, relaxing the definition of 'participator' in a company to exclude individuals whose connection is only that they are beneficiaries of a settlement with an interest in the company. It should be borne in mind, however, that HMRC will not permit a concession to be used for what they consider to be tax avoidance. HMRC announced in February 2013 that they were informally consulting practitioners about ESC D40, seeking to know whether the concession was widely used, so that they could consider whether to withdraw it or to provide for it in legislation. Subsequently, draft legislation was published for consultation in October 2014 and, at the time of writing and the consultation having closed on 27 November 2014, the responses to the draft legislation are still being considered.

[26.31] Further clarification on the interpretation of SP 5/92 was given by the Inland Revenue in Issue 8, page 82 and Issue 16, page 204 of their *Tax Bulletin* see Revenue Interpretation RI 198 (December 1998). There are a number of events that HMRC may regard as 'tainting' a pre-1991 trust, and it is critical to ensure competent administration for an offshore trust so that the rules are not contravened.

[26.32] The 1998 measures prospectively closed the gap between trusts created before 19 March 1991 and those created after 18 March 1991, save in the case of 'protected settlements'. During the transitional period, thought had to be given to appropriate action to keep pre-March 1991 trusts outside the ambit of the new charge. This required careful consideration and expert advice so that the action taken did not itself trigger a charge to tax (see 26.28).

The capital payments charge

[26.33] Introduced in 1981, this charge applies to trusts with non-UK resident trustees where (before 1997/98) the settlor had been, when he made the settlement or during any year in which the trustees are at no time resident or (before 2013/14) ordinarily resident in the UK, domiciled and either resident or (before 2013/14) ordinarily resident in the UK. For gains and capital payments made on or after 17 March 1998, the residence and domicile status of the settlor is irrelevant. In such a case trust gains are to be treated as accruing to the beneficiaries, but only to the extent to which they receive capital payments (see 26.41) from the trustees. The attribution of gains to beneficiaries is not to exceed the amount actually received by them [*TCGA 1992, s 87*].

[26.34] The charge was extended in 1998/89 to trusts set up by non-UK domiciled and non-UK resident settlors, but a non-UK domiciled beneficiary was protected from charge by *TCGA 1992, s 87(7)*, before 2008/09. A settlement arising under a Will or intestacy is to be treated as made by the testator or intestate at the time of his death [*TCGA 1992, s 87(6)*, as substituted by *FA 2008, Sch 7, para 108*].

Anti-avoidance provisions

[26.35] There is a raft of supplementary provisions, as follows.

[26.36] *TCGA 1992, s 88* was inserted to apply the charge on beneficiaries under the 1981 code not only to non-UK resident settlements but also to resident settlements which are treated as non-UK resident because of the application of a double tax treaty.

[26.37] *TCGA 1992, s 89* deals with the position of 'migrant settlements', ie settlements which move in and out of the UK. A capital payment made to a beneficiary during a time when the trust was resident in the UK can be apportioned if it was made in anticipation of a disposal made by the trustees later when non-UK resident. Similarly, outstanding gains from the last year of a non-UK resident period can be attributed to capital payments made when the trust moves back to the UK.

[26.38] *TCGA 1992, s 90* is designed to prevent avoidance by transferring assets from one trust to another.

[26.39] Payments received by beneficiaries for the purposes of *TCGA 1992, s 87* are extended by *TCGA 1992, s 96* to include:

(i) payments from a company controlled by the trustees either alone or together with the settlor and persons connected with the settlor; and
(ii) payments to a non-UK resident company controlled by beneficiaries.

These new provisions run very much in tandem with the other 1991 changes. They were given some mitigating treatment in Committee as regards the definition of 'control' (see **26.26**(c)).

[26.40] *TCGA 1992, s 96(5)* was amended in 2000 to eliminate the requirement that each of the persons controlling an offshore company to which payments are made by offshore trustees must be resident or (now, before 2013/14) ordinarily resident in the UK. The interposition of non-UK resident persons in the control of the offshore company had been used to frustrate the operation of *TCGA 1992, s 96*.

[26.41] *TCGA 1992, s 97* provides a wide definition of 'capital payment', to include any payment not chargeable to income tax, or, in the case of a non-UK resident, received otherwise than as income. The conferring of any benefit, including loans on favourable terms, is included in the charge to the value of the benefit. However, by way of distinction from the pre-1981 provisions, losses are permitted to be deducted from gains [*TCGA 1992, s 97(6)*]. 'Capital payment' now does not include a payment under a transaction entered into at arm's length [*TCGA 1992, s 97(1)(b)*]. It was held in *Billingham v Cooper* Ch D [2000] STC 122; CA [2001] STC 1177 that an interest-free on demand loan was caught by *section 97*. Similarly, HMRC contend that beneficial (typically rent-free) accommodation constitutes a capital payment.

[26.42] *TCGA 1992, s 98* confers on HMRC the same wide information-gathering powers for the purposes of *sections 87–90* that they have under the transfer of assets abroad regime (now in *ITA 2007, ss 748–750*). A limited amount of protection is given to solicitors and banks, but the details which may be required from the latter trench deeply into traditional banking confidentiality (see *Royal Bank of Canada v IRC* Ch D 1971, 47 TC 565 and *Clinch v IRC* QB [1973] STC 155, concerning transactions with the Bahamas and Bermuda respectively).

[26.43] *TCGA 1992, s 13(10)* extends to non-UK resident trustees the provisions attributing gains made by non-UK resident close companies to shareholders (or rather, 'participators', with an interest in the company of more than 25%) resident or (before 2013/14) ordinarily resident (and in the case of individuals, domiciled) in the UK. From 2008/09, it matters not where the participator is domiciled, though a remittance basis of taxation has been introduced for non-UK domiciled participators (by new *section 14A*). Such gains realised by non-UK resident trusts are accordingly brought with the ambit of *section 87*. This provision is of some importance since a very common offshore structure is to hold assets in a company that is owned by a trust. Double tax treaties cannot be used to shelter gains realised by offshore companies owned by a trust. Such gains may be attributed to resident or non-UK resident trustees as participators in those companies [*TCGA 1992, Sch 5, para 1(3)*].

[26.44] In response to a 'request' from the EU Commission (on the grounds that the provisions of *TCGA 1992, ss 13* and *14A* breach EU Treaty freedoms, *FA 2013, s 62* has with retroactive effect from 2012/13 significantly cut down the scope of the regime. The threshold above which apportioned gains are subject to capital gains tax is increased from 10% to 25%. Gains will not be attributed where the chargeable gain accrues from the disposal of an asset used only for the purposes of economically significant activities carried on by the company wholly or mainly outside the UK. Nor will attribution occur where it is shown that neither the disposal of the asset by the company nor the acquisition or holding of the asset of the company form part of a scheme or arrangements of which the main purpose, or one of the main purposes, was avoidance of liability to capital gains tax or corporation tax. Confirmation that the pre-amended rules were in breach of the free movement of capital came on 13 November 2014 in a decision of the European Court of Justice in the case of *European Commission v United Kingdom: C-112/14 (2014) ECLI:EU:C:2014:2369* [2015] 1 CMLR 1515, [2015] STC 591. This decision opens the possibility of tax repayment claims where *section 13* has been illegally applied in the past.

The supplementary charge

[26.45] A new concept was introduced in UK tax law in 1991, in effect charging interest on beneficiaries who receive capital payments from offshore trusts. The idea appears to have been borrowed from the US tax code. The basic principle is that a 10% per annum surcharge on the capital gains tax due under *TCGA 1992, s 87* will be charged in addition on delayed capital payments to beneficiaries, up to a maximum of six years. Thus, where trustees are paying capital gains at 28%, the maximum is 44.8% (28% plus 10% of 28% × 6) and where trustees are paying at 20%, the maximum is 32% (20% plus 10% of 20% × 6). An outline of the provisions, contained in *TCGA 1992, s 91*, is as follows:

[26.45] Capital Gains Tax

(a) where a capital payment is made on or after 6 April 1992 by trustees of a settlement to which *TCGA 1992, s 87* applies and the payment is matched with a gain of the trust for a previous year of assessment, then the tax payable by the beneficiary under *TCGA 1992, s 87* is increased by 10% per annum for the 'chargeable period';

(b) the 'chargeable period' is the period beginning on 1 December in the year of assessment following that in which the 'qualifying amount' is realised by the trust and ending on 30 November in the year of assessment following that in which the capital payment is made;

(c) capital payments are matched with gains on a first-in, first-out basis (reversed from 2008/09: see **26.48**); and

(d) gains made before 6 April 1990 are treated as accruing in the 1990/91 year of assessment.

Under these rules, no charge could arise before 6 April 1992, nor on a distribution made in the year of assessment following that in which a qualifying amount is realised. The Treasury is given power to vary by statutory instrument the percentage currently fixed at 10%. See **26.48** for the changes to the supplementary charge from 2008/09.

[26.46] The determining factor for a CGT liability to arise is UK residence, with the well-known protection of the remittance basis where the taxpayer is non-UK domiciled and claims the remittance basis. So, while the loss of a non-UK domicile will cause a forfeiture of the remittance basis for the future, the following trap in relation to non-UK resident trusts can easily go unnoticed. That is, unmatched capital payments made to the foreign domiciliary when he was foreign domiciled or non-UK resident can subsequently be charged on him if the capital payments are matched to trust gains realised at a time when he has acquired a UK domicile and UK residence. Moreover none of the transitional reliefs such as rebasing will then apply. The critical date for charging to UK tax is the date of matching and not the date of the capital payment or the date the gains are realised.

The 2008/09 changes

[26.47] The changes made by *FA 2008* to the offshore trust regime may be taken as the other side of the coin of the changes for UK resident and non-UK domiciliaries. Those changes were extensive, but might perhaps be summarised simply by the proposition that such individuals became taxable on income and gains on a worldwide arising basis unless they elected for a remittance basis. An adult who did this having been resident in the UK for at least 7 out of the preceding 9 tax years must pay the Remittance Basis Charge at one of its various levels explained at **24.44–24.45**, though no claim is needed where those income and gains are less than £2,000. A claim to the remittance basis will forfeit the right to income tax personal allowances or to the capital gains tax annual exemption. A raft of new rules has been enacted to block arrangements perceived by HMRC as avoidance, for example involving source ceasing or alienation of assets. New statutory rules determine the identification of pure capital, income and gains within a mixed fund.

[26.48] As to trusts, there was no change to the settlor rule, so a settlor domiciled outside the UK will not be taxed on gains made by the trustees (except as a beneficiary under the capital payments charge). From 2008/09 the capital payments charge is extended to receipts by a non-UK domiciliary, worldwide or, if a remittance basis user, in the UK. The supplementary charge continues, as outlined at 26.46.

[26.49] Importantly, the *FA 2008* changes were not intended to be retrospective (as they would have been had the original proposals in the October 2007 Pre-Budget Report been enacted). Accordingly, gains accruing to non-UK resident trustees before 2008/09 can be preserved from a capital gains tax liability on a non-UK domiciliary receiving a capital payment on or after 6 April 2008. This will require the trustees to make a re-basing election treating all the assets held by the trustees and by any underlying companies as disposed of and reacquired at market value on 6 April 2008. The election, which is irrevocable, must be made on or before the 31 January following the tax year during which a capital payment is first made to a UK resident beneficiary or part of a trust fund is transferred to a new trust. The effect of the election will be that when an asset held at 6 April 2008 is sold, the element of the gain which arose before 6 April 2008 will not be a trust gain for taxation on a non-UK domiciled beneficiary (whether or not a remittance basis user and/or he benefits in the UK). The re-basing election applies only to trust assets and to assets held within companies which are themselves owned by trustees. That is, the re-basing election cannot be made for assets within companies held directly by individuals.

[26.50] It seems generally to be agreed that there is no downside of making the election, on special form RBE1, which requires the disclosure of no significant details whether about the trust or the settlor or the beneficiaries.

[26.51] Changes to the trustee borrowing legislation in *TCGA 1992, Schedule 4C* caused it to apply from 2008/09 to a non-UK resident trust which has exclusively non-UK domiciled beneficiaries. If the legislation applies, any deemed gains are chargeable on a non-UK domiciled beneficiary who benefits in the UK or if not a remittance basis user.

[26.52] The *F(No 2)A 2010* regime, increasing the marginal rate of capital gains tax to 28%, comprised some transitional rules in Schedule 1 which determined whether, depending on the circumstances, the beneficiary of a capital payment was treated as accruing before 23 June or after 22 June 2010.

Proposed changes from 2017/18

[26.53] As set out at 24.50, the proposed new deemed domicile rules for income and capital gains tax to be introduced from 2017/18 will have an impact on the settlors and beneficiaries of non-UK resident trusts who become deemed domiciled.

[26.54] Where an individual becomes deemed domiciled under the 'returning UK dom' rule, it is proposed that there will be no protection in relation to trusts established prior to that event – and the individual will simply be taxed as an ordinary UK domiciled settlor in relation to the capital gains of the trust. Where, however, an individual becomes deemed domiciled under the '15/20 year' rule, it is proposed that any trusts settled by him or her prior to that event should be given protection in the form of an exemption from some of the rules which would otherwise apply – which protection will last until (if ever) the trust becomes 'tainted' (see below). The proposed exemption for capital gains tax is that the settlor will not be subject to tax on an arising basis under *TCGA 1992, s 86* in respect of gains realised by the trustees or attributed to them in relation to underlying companies. For deemed domiciled beneficiaries, is it proposed that *TCGA 1992, s 87* will apply to them in the same way as if they were domiciled in the UK as a matter of general law; however, the possibility that a trust may become 'tainted' by the distribution of capital should also be noted (see **26.56**).

[26.55] A trust will become tainted if funds are added to it after a settlor has become deemed domiciled, and what constitutes an 'addition' is likely to be drawn or interpreted widely. Thus, while an arms length sale at full market value will not be an addition, a sale at any undervalue is likely to be caught.

[26.56] The rules for capital gains tax (which are not the same as for income tax see **25.41–25.45**) provide that a trust will also be tainted where capital or income is applied for the benefit of the settlor, his/her spouse or civil partner, or minor children. The impossibility of either adding to or taking from a settlement without tainting it, will impose a heavy burden on those wishing to preserve a trust's capital gains tax protection.

Temporary non-residents

[26.57] Special rules apply to an individual who is temporarily non-resident (see **24.21**). For capital gains tax purposes, gains and losses which accrue to him during a period of non-residence – except in relation to assets acquired while abroad – are treated as accruing to him in the tax year of return to the UK [*TCGA 1992, s 10A*].

[26.58] Such a rule has been in force since 1998; however, prior to 6 April 2013, to avoid temporary non-residence, it was necessary to be out of the UK for more than five *tax* years whereas now the five years is measured in *normal* years starting from the date of departure.

The 'flip-flop' schemes

[26.59] The *FA 2000, Sch 26* dealt with offshore aspects of the device known as a 'flip-flop', whereby gains are extracted from a trust tax-free, or with a significant tax saving, using borrowed money: see **4.34–4.35** for the onshore variant. *Schedule 25* deals with the flip-flop in relation to a UK-resident trust. *Schedule 26* extends the anti-avoidance provision to offshore trusts by inserting *TCGA 1992, Schedule 4C*. The flip-flop worked by the trustees borrowing money on the security of assets in the trust and advancing the money to another trust. The settlor then severed his interest in the first trust. In the following tax year the trustees of the first trust sold the assets and used the proceeds to repay the debt. Capital payments could then be made to UK-resident beneficiaries from the second trust without charge to tax. *TCGA*

1992, Schedule 4C charges beneficiaries in respect of gains accruing to offshore trustees by virtue of a transfer of value made by them which falls within *Schedule 4B*, inserted by *FA 2000, Schedule 25* (as amended by *FA 2013, Sch 45* to take account of changes to *section 10A*).

[26.60] The *FA 2000* amendments effectively counteracted what was known as the 'mark 1 flip-flop', as explained at **26.59**. However, *section 90(5)* inserted into *TCGA 1992* by *FA 2000* (before its substitution by *FA 2008, Sch 7, para 111*) paved the way for mark 2 flip-flop schemes designed for cases where there were pre-existing stockpiled gains. Although the settlement concerned had already disposed of all or most of its assets, the gains had not yet been attributed to beneficiaries. The transfer of value to another settlement triggered a deemed disposal of the settlement's assets, but the settlement had few if any unrealised assets, so there were few if any gains to go into the *Schedule 4C* gains pool. Since the legislation required only gains created by the deemed disposal to go into the pool, any existing unattributed gains remained in the transferor settlement and it was claimed that the capital from the transfer of value could then be paid out to beneficiaries by the trustees of a transferee settlement without triggering a charge to capital gains tax. In the first case to come before the courts, the Special Commissioner ruled that the scheme was ineffective (*Herman v Revenue and Customs Comrs* (SpC 609) [2007] STC (SCD) 571). In that case the trustees of the transferee settlement made payments to a UK settlement which then advanced capital to the original settlor beneficiaries of the offshore settlement. Although the Special Commissioner was not able to find that the outcome was pre-ordained, he felt that it had been intended and so the amounts received by the beneficiaries were capital payments within *TCGA 1992, s 97(5)*.

[26.61] Further amendments were made by *FA 2003, s 163* and *Sch 29* to prevent the continued use of 'flip-flop' schemes by offshore trusts.

Situs of assets

[26.62] Generally, the rules relating to situs of assets are not as significant for capital gains tax as they are for inheritance tax (see **27.21**). They are material in relation to disposals of assets outside the UK where the proceeds are not remitted to the UK, to take advantage of the additional freedom from capital gains tax provided to an individual resident but not domiciled in the UK by *TCGA 1992, s 12*. That said, specific rules in relation to certain intangible assets were inserted by *F(No 2)A 2005* into *TCGA 1992 as section 275A*.

Information powers and requirements

[26.63] It is one thing to create an elaborate structure for charging the gains of non-UK resident trusts, it is quite another to gather the information necessary to raise an assessment. In many cases property in the UK may be held, say, by a Cayman Islands trust through a British Virgin Islands company. And, in a case where any of the UK's anti-avoidance provisions applies, whether for income tax or for capital gains tax purposes, it may not always be easy to apply the UK's statutory provisions to local accounting records, sometimes going back over many years.

[26.64] To counter this, *FA 2008, Sch 36, Pt 1* (which replaced *TCGA 1992, Sch 5, para 10* from 2009/10) gives HMRC officers powers to demand such information from trustees, beneficiaries and settlors as they think necessary for the purposes of *TCGA 1992, s 86* and *Sch 5*. *TCGA 1992, Sch 5A* imposes reporting requirements for relevant occurrences in relation to the migration of trusts or the creation of non-UK resident trusts or the return to UK residence and domicile of a previously offshore settlor. These powers and requirements are backed by the penalty provision of *TMA 1970, s 98* (£300 initial penalty, plus £60 per day for continued non-compliance).

[26.65] Obviously no professional person will want to run the risk of falling foul of these requirements. Even if he is non-UK resident, there is always the risk of harassment by HMRC should he ever visit the UK. The parameters of HMRC's powers in this area have been examined in *Clore (No 3), Re, IRC v Stype Trustees (Jersey) Ltd* [1985] 2 All ER 819, [1985] STC 394, Ch D and *Tucker (a bankrupt), Re, ex p Tucker* [1990] Ch 148, [1988] 1 All ER 603, CA.

Capital gains tax for non-residents holding UK residential property

[26.66] In the December 2013 Autumn Statement, the Coalition Government announced that they would be introducing a special CGT charge for non-residents holding UK residential property and, following a formal consultation between 28 March and 21 June 2014, legislation was included in *Finance Act 2015, Sch 7* making consequential amendments to *TCGA 1992* and other relevant statutes.

[26.67] The changes take effect from 2015/16 onwards in relation to gains on disposals of interests in UK residential property by a non-resident persons (as so called 'NRCGT gain') and subject to the following key provisions:

- Individuals are charged to capital gains tax at either 18% or 28% depending on the level of their taxable income.
- Trustees and personal representatives are charged at 28%.
- Companies are charged at 20%, and with special rules for certain group disposals.
- The annual exempt amount is available in the normal way and losses on disposals of UK residential property interests can be used to offset gains, including brought forward losses. There are complex rules for carrying forward losses on NRCGT disposals.
- Only gains post-5 April 2015 are taxable. There is a special rule to allow for time apportionment where is it desired not to obtain a 5 April 2015 valuation.
- There are rules to avoid double charges where any gain is also taxable under the ATED-related CGT rules (see **7.126–7.128**).

- An NRCGT disposal must be reported to HMRC on a special return within 30 days. Likewise, tax is due at the same time unless the disposer is within the self-assessment regime, when the normal rules apply.

[26.68] When this change was initially announced in December 2013, it was made clear that there would need to be amendments to the capital gains tax exemption for private residences, the concern being that a non-domiciled person with only one such residence in the UK could simply elect for that property to be their main residence and thereby avoid any charge. One early suggestion was that private residence relief elections might be abolished completely – ie even for UK residents – and, thankfully, this idea was not adopted. Instead, for disposals on or after 6 April 2015, the private residence rules now include a concept of a 'non-qualifying tax year' being any year in which the taxpayer *or his spouse or civil partner* is not tax resident where the property is located *and* where they stay overnight in the property for less than 90 days during the tax year. Thus, for a non-UK resident person disposing of a UK residential property, occupation in the property for at least 90 'nights' is needed in order to claim the relief (either on the basis that the property is their main residence as a matter of fact, or by election) [*TCGA 1992, ss 222B, C*]. For a discussion of the practical impact of these rules see the 8 January 2015 *Taxation* article *90 Midnight Feasts* by Tina Riches.

Chapter 27

Inheritance Tax

Domicile the determining factor

[27.1] The defining factor for offshore trusts in relation to inheritance tax is not residence or ordinary residence, but rather the domicile of the settlor. The trustees of an excluded property settlement (see 27.4) can be UK resident without prejudicing its inheritance tax efficiency. Accordingly, a UK domiciled beneficiary under a Will of a non-UK domiciled testator can effectively vary for inheritance tax purposes his inheritance into an excluded property settlement (under *IHTA 1984, s 142*). This will have the effect of preserving the non-UK assets held by the trustees from inheritance tax for so long as the settlement continues. Because, typically, the settlement will be settlor-interested, the settlor for income tax and capital gains tax purposes will be the original beneficiary and so the trustees might as well be UK resident, which should have the advantage also of reducing start-up and ongoing administration costs.

Excluded property

[27.2] 'Excluded property' is property excluded from the scope of an inheritance tax charge either for a lifetime disposition or for a deemed transfer on death. In relation to trusts, if the excluded property is settled property, the termination of an interest in possession in it is not taxable, nor is it relevant property for the purposes of the inheritance tax regime applied to discretionary trusts [*IHTA 1984, ss 3(1), (2), 5(1)(b), 53(1), 58(1)(f)*].

[27.3] The main provisions relating to excluded property and trusts are to be found in *IHTA 1984, s 48*, which makes certain interests in trusts and certain assets held in some trusts excluded property.

Settled property situated outside the UK

[27.4] Under *IHTA 1984, s 48(3)(a)*, where property in a trust is situated outside the UK (but not a reversionary interest in the property – see 27.27) it is excluded property unless the settlor was domiciled in the UK at the time the settlement was made. This is a provision of the highest importance, since it confers (in most cases) a permanent exemption from inheritance tax irrespective of the subsequent history of the trust, provided the property itself is situated outside the UK. Of particular importance is the fact that this exemption extends to situations where the settlor retains an interest in the trust – in other words, even where one might expect the 'gift with reservation of benefit' provisions to be in point. Even in the case of a settlor who – subsequent to the establishment of the trust – acquires a UK domicile, the excluded property status will continue to outflank the reservation of benefit provisions.

411

The one proposed exception to the rule that the excluded property exemption remains permanent is where a settlor becomes deemed domiciled under the 'returning UK dom' rules (see 27.20). In these cases, it is proposed that the 'excluded property' status should be lost during the period of deemed domicile.

[27.5] Because the 'excluded property' status of a trust is determined (by reference to the settlor's domicile) at the time it is made *and* the inheritance tax legislation for trusts contemplates that there can be additions to them at a later date, it has always been something of a debatable point as to whether the addition of property to a settlement *after* a settlor has become UK domiciled or deemed domiciled, should taint its status. This question now appears to have been resolved by the case of *Barclays Wealth Trustees (Jersey) Ltd v HMRC* [2015] EWHC 2878 (Ch) where a non-domiciled settlor created a Jersey settlement but then later transferred assets to it (assets which had in fact been transferred from it to another settlement) *after* having become deemed domiciled. The court found that Parliament had not intended to allow a trust's 'excluded property' status to continue simply because, when the settlement was created, the settlor was non-UK domiciled. It found that the time the settlement was 'made' must refer to the time when property was transferred to it and if, by that time, the settlor had lost his non-domiciled status, the trust's 'excluded property' status would no longer apply.

[27.6] There had been a trap with excluded property settlements in the case where the non-UK domiciled settlor had a qualifying interest in possession which terminated during his lifetime (and where he was effectively excluded from all future benefit under the settlement). That termination is a deemed potentially exempt transfer (PET) under the reservation of benefit code (*FA 1986, s 102(4)*) and for many years it was thought that – for certain technical reasons – that PET was *not* trumped by the excluded property status of the trust. Thus, the PET would become chargeable if the beneficiary died within seven years. Happily, however, some years ago HMRC changed their Inheritance Tax Manual at IHTM14396 which now reads as follows:

> 'Where the settlor was domiciled outside the UK at the time a settlement was made, any foreign property in the settlement is excluded property and is not brought into charge for inheritance tax purposes (IHTM27220). This rule applies where property is subject to a reservation of benefit even though the settlor may have acquired a domicile of choice in the UK, or be deemed to be domiciled in the UK, at the time the GWR charge arises (IHTM04071) . . . At the material date *FA 1986, s 102(3)* deems the donor to be beneficially entitled to property that is, at that time, settled property. As the property in which the reservation subsisted is 'property comprised in a settlement', it is the provisions of *IHTA 1984, s 48(3)* that are in point. It is the domicile of the settlor at the time the settlement was made that is relevant in deciding whether foreign property in which the reservation subsisted is excluded property.'

Note that HMRC go on to warn that this analysis will not apply:

- 'If the trustees had sold the foreign assets so that at the date of death the settled property was invested in UK assets, the exclusion would not apply as the property comprised in the settlement was not situated outside the UK, so *IHTA 1984, s 48(3)* cannot apply.

- If the donor has acquired a domicile of choice (or is deemed domiciled) in the UK and adds other property to the settlement (irrespective of the situs (IHTM27071) of the property), we regard the donor as creating a separate settlement (IHTM04272). All the trust assets will be property subject to a reservation, but the foreign assets settled when the donor was domiciled outside the UK will be excluded property, whereas the assets settled when the donor was domiciled in the UK will be subject to IHT.
- And in the reverse situation, if a donor who is domiciled (or deemed domiciled) in the UK creates a settlement with foreign assets and the settled property remains subject to a reservation at death, the trust assets will be subject to IHT under *FA 1986, s 102(3)* even if the settlor dies domiciled outside the UK as *IHTA 1984, s 48(3)* does not apply – as well as being subject to relevant property trust charges (IHTM42000).'

While some doubt has been cast on the technical accuracy of HMRC's stance (see for example *Trusts Discussion Forum* 31 January 2001, posting by Ray Magill), it is of course welcome.

The settlor

[27.7] It should be noted that *IHTA 1984, s 44(1)* provides a wide definition of 'settlor' to include 'any person by whom the settlement was made directly or indirectly, and in particular (but without prejudice to the generality of the preceding words) includes any person who has provided funds directly or indirectly for the purpose of or in connection with the settlement or has made with any other person a reciprocal arrangement for that other person to make the settlement'. Where this definition produces more than one settlor, the part provided by each can be treated as a separate trust [*IHTA 1984, s 44(2)*]. This will catch arrangements where there is a dummy settlor and subsequently other property finds its way into the trust. Accordingly, if a UK domiciled husband makes a potentially exempt transfer of assets to his non-UK domiciled wife (which he survives by seven years and so the potentially exempt transfer becomes exempt, given only the limited spouse exemption provided by *IHTA 1984, s 18(2)*), there may be a risk depending on all the circumstances if the wife subsequently settles those assets. The question is whether the husband can be regarded as the real settlor, so precluding excluded property settlement status. HMRC's Inheritance Tax Manual states at IHTM 14833 'where property given unconditionally by one spouse or civil partner to the other is subsequently transferred by the latter to a third party, you cannot use the associated operations provisions to attribute the transfer to the first spouse or civil partner.' The question begged is of course the application of the word 'unconditionally' to the facts of the case.

[27.8] Following a consultation, *FA 2013, s 178* has from 2013/14 increased the threshold of the spouse/civil partner exemption for a transfer from a UK domiciliary to a non-UK domiciliary under *IHTA 1984, s 18(2)*, from £55,000 to the prevailing nil-rate band threshold (currently £325,000). Further, *FA 2013, s 177* inserts into *IHTA 1984* new *sections 267ZA* and *267ZB* enabling a non-UK domiciliary to elect to be treated as UK domiciled for inheritance tax purposes, subject to various details. While this obviously removes the downside of *section 18(2)* for example on the first death, there would be the corresponding disadvantage of bringing, on the second death, the whole of the survivor's worldwide estate into the inheritance tax net. While an election, whether made in relation to, and within seven years after, a lifetime transfer (which typically the transferor has failed to survive for seven years) or a death transfer, made within two years after the death, cannot be revoked, it will cease to have effect once the elector has become non-UK resident for at least four successive tax years.)

Liabilities and excluded property

[27.9] An anti-avoidance provision which takes effect from 17 July 2013 (Royal Assent to *Finance Bill 2013*) disallows a deduction for a liability which is 'attributable to financing (directly or indirectly)—

(a) the acquisition of any excluded property, or
(b) the maintenance, or an enhancement, of the value of any such property'.

[*IHTA 1984, s 162A inserted by FA 2013, s 176, Sch 36, para 3*]

In the case where there has been a disposal of the acquired property for consideration or where the liability exceeds the value of the excluded property, a deduction may be allowed, subject to the satisfaction of certain conditions. The typical ('unacceptable') scenario at which the provision is aimed is a non-UK domiciliary who owns a valuable UK residential property borrowing money by way of loan secured on the property and then using the borrowed money to acquire assets situated outside the UK, so relieving the chargeable value of the UK property for inheritance purposes. A similar example could involving an excluded property settlement. On the other hand, the new rule would have no application to a straightforward purchase of a UK property, using (substantially) borrowed money which is secured on the UK property.

[27.10] Following the enactment of *FA 2013, Sch 36* it was believed that foreign currency accounts could be used to sidestep restrictions introduced by *FA 2013*, which disallow the deduction of certain liabilities for inheritance tax purposes. The rationale was that the provisions disallow a deduction for liabilities used to acquire 'excluded property' (broadly, non-UK property owned by a non-UK domicile). Although foreign currency bank accounts situated in the UK are not 'excluded property', they were not taken into account for inheritance tax on the death of a person who is both non-UK domiciled and non-UK resident immediately before their death. As the accounts were not excluded property there was no restriction on the deduction of liabilities used to fund such an account.

[27.11] An anti-avoidance provision takes effect from Royal Assent of *FA 2014* so that no deduction is also now allowed for liabilities incurred to fund foreign currency bank accounts. It does not matter when the liability was incurred.

[27.12] This change affects non-UK resident and non-UK domiciled individuals with foreign currency bank accounts funded by borrowed funds, particularly arrangements made to sidestep the changes introduced by *FA 2013*.

Deemed domicile

The current rules (to 2016/17)

[27.13] In addition to the general law of domicile mentioned at 24.26–24.37, an individual may be treated under *IHTA 1984, s 267 for the purposes of inheritance tax only* as 'deemed' domiciled in the UK at a time (the 'relevant time') when he is domiciled elsewhere under general law. This applies where:

- he was domiciled (under general law) in the UK at any time during the 36-month period immediately preceding the relevant time (ie one works backwards for three years from the actual date rather than counting tax years); or
- he was resident in the UK in not less than 17 of the 20 tax years of assessment (ie ending on 5 April) *ending with the year of assessment in which the relevant time falls*. The income tax rules for determining residence apply (see 24.4–24.7).

[27.14] This deemed domicile rule does not apply in the following circumstances [*IHTA 1984, s 267(2), (3)*]:

(a) in determining whether exempt gilts which are in the beneficial ownership of a non-UK domiciled person (or are settled property to which such a person is entitled to a qualifying interest in possession) are excluded property;
(b) in determining whether certain savings to which persons domiciled in the Channel Islands or Isle of Man are beneficially entitled are excluded property;
(c) where the domicile of a person is determined under a double tax treaty having inheritance tax effect;
(d) in determining whether settled property which became comprised in a settlement before 10 December 1974 is excluded property; and
(e) in determining the settlor's domicile for the purposes of *IHTA 1984, s 65(8)* in relation to property held on discretionary trusts which became comprised in the settlement before 10 December 1974.

Domicile for inheritance tax purposes is to be determined apart from new *sections 267ZA* and *267ZB* enabling a non-UK domiciliary to elect to be treated as UK domiciled for inheritance tax purposes [new *IHTA 1984, s 267(5)*, introduced by *FA 2013, s 177(2)*].

Proposed new rules (from 2017/18)

[27.15] As set out at 24.50, proposed new deemed domicile rules are to be introduced from 2017/18 onwards, vis:

- A new 15 out of 20 year 'deemed domicile' rule for all taxes.
- A new rule for 'the returning UK dom', deeming anyone with a UK domicile of origin who was born in the UK to be deemed domiciled in the UK whenever resident here (ie even if they have acquired a domicile of choice overseas).

Draft legislation has been published (for consultation until 20 October 2016) in relation to some of the new rules; however, they will not be finally legislated until *Finance Bill 2017*. The following commentary sets out the position as currently understood but the reader should be aware that further changes may be forthcoming. Readers should also note that slightly different rules apply for inheritance tax, as is explained in the paragraphs below.

The 15/20 year rule

[27.16] The proposal that will apply for income tax, capital gains tax *and* inheritance tax is that once an individual has been resident in the UK in 15 out of the previous 20 tax years, he or she will become deemed domiciled in the UK. As the current inheritance tax rule is based on a 17 out of 20 year test, but counting backwards from the *current* year, the proposal represents only a modest change for those coming to the UK. That is to say that they will become deemed domiciled at the beginning of the sixteenth year after arrival, rather than the seventeenth.

[27.17] For those leaving the UK, however, a 15 out of 20 year rule would represent a significant change. Under the current rules one has to be non-resident for four years to escape the 17/20 year test. Under a 15/20 year test, one would need to be non-resident for six years. In its most recent consultation document, the government has indicated that there was no policy intention to extend the required period of non-residence in this way, and the latest draft legislation indicates that, for those leaving the UK, and for inheritance tax purposes only (as this concession does not apply for income and capital gains tax), an individual's deemed domiciled status will fall away once he or she has been non-resident for four years. Thus, whereas currently, it is possible to be deemed domiciled for inheritance tax purposes but not for income or capital gains tax purposes, going forward there will be instances where someone has left the UK for four years and therefore remains deemed domiciled for income and capital gains tax purposes, but not for inheritance tax purposes.

The 'returning UK dom' rule

[27.18] The rules in relation to a 'returning UK dom' are also proposed to be different for inheritance tax and income and capital gains tax purposes. For income and capital gains tax purposes, a 'returning UK dom' will become deemed domiciled in the tax year he or she becomes resident in the UK. However, for inheritance tax purposes there is a short 'grace period' in that it will be necessary for the individual to have been resident in at least one of the two previous tax years before becoming deemed domiciled. The latest consultation documents makes clear that most respondents to the original consultation thought that the 'grace period' should extend to all taxes and should last for two to three years, but the government has stated specifically that it does not believe that there is a compelling case to 'soften the effect of these reforms further'.

[27.19] It should be noted that to be a 'returning UK dom' it is not sufficient to have UK domicile of origin, one also needs to have been born in the UK. The latest consultation document confirms that:

> Many of those who responded . . . thought the policy of treating those who were born in the UK with a UK domicile of origin as being UK domiciled was unfair, as an individual's place of birth is beyond their control. A number of respondents said that the policy shouldn't apply if the individual had left the UK during their childhood or by the time they finished full-time education.

but again the government has stated explicitly that it does not intend to change the policy. The introduction of the 'born in the UK' requirement is indeed very strange as it *excludes* from the new rules all those with a UK domicile of origin who were not born in the UK, even if, for example, they returned to the UK shortly after their birth, and the author cannot see the policy reason for not simply using a UK domicile of origin as the criterion.

The status of 'excluded property trusts'

[27.20] The proposed inheritance tax rules for trusts where a settlor becomes deemed domiciled are simple enough. Acquiring a deemed domicile status under the '15/20 year' rules will *not* taint a trust's 'excluded property' status. However, a trust established by a 'returning UK dom' (ie established while they were non-UK domiciled) will lose its 'excluded property' status as soon as the settlor becomes deemed domiciled (and subject, of course, to the period of grace referred to above).

Situs of property

[27.21] The situation, or 'situs', of property is, like the domicile of an individual, a question governed by private international law. In many cases there will be no real doubt regarding the situation of property. Land is obviously situated where it is located and shares in a company are situated where the register is kept (albeit see **27.39–27.52** for details of a proposed new rule to 'look through' non-UK companies (and other vehicles) which hold UK residential property). Sometimes points of greater complication arise, requiring reference to the general law, or to a double tax treaty.

[27.22] An ingenious and successful attempt to use situs rules for tax avoidance was considered in *Kwok Chi Leung Karl v Comr of Estate Duty* [1988] 1 WLR 1035, [1988] STC 728, PC. Mr Kwok, literally on his death bed, transferred shares situated in Hong Kong worth US$1.8 million to a Liberian company in consideration of a non-negotiable promissory note, payable on demand after 60 days at Monrovia. The Privy Council could see no escape from the conclusion that the chose in action represented by the promissory note was situate in Monrovia, but their Lordships issued a warning that such transactions were vulnerable on *Ramsay* principles (which had not been raised as an issue in the case).

[27.23] HMRC announced on 23 January 2013 a significant change of view in relation to the situs for inheritance tax purposes of specialty debts, that is debts made by deed. Previously their approach had been (as is still considered to be the correct position by most practitioners) that the situs depends on the location of the deed from time to time. HMRC have been advised that this approach is incorrect and they have now changed their Inheritance Tax Manual at IHTM 27079 to state that their earlier view.

> '. . . may not be the correct approach in all cases involving specialty debts; specifically that many such debts are likely to be located where the debtor resides, or where property taken as security for the debts is situated.'

The guidance goes on to state that any cases involving situs and a specialty debt must be referred to HMRC's Technical department and, of course, the use of 'may not be' in the above paragraph, leaves a taxpayer free to argue the point. Nevertheless, the change of view had immediate effect, and therefore, for chargeable transfers on or after 23 January 2013, considerable care is required. A typical scenario could be a series of loans made by an offshore trust to a non-UK domiciliary resident in the UK who uses the loans for living purposes, with the loans evidenced by specialty debts kept outside the UK. Were the individual to die UK resident, the outstanding debts at that point could now be treated by HMRC as UK situs property, so perhaps triggering a charge to inheritance tax either at that point or on a ten-yearly charge (under a qualifying interest in possession or a relevant property settlement respectively).

Avoidance blocked

[27.24] The relatively unrestricted definition of an excluded property trust (see **27.4**) led to an arrangement for mitigating inheritance tax, typically just before death. The details of the scheme were complex, though the principle may be simply stated. The UK domiciled individual would acquire with assets chargeable to inheritance tax an interest in an excluded property settlement, with a view to the trustees making available in some form the assets concerned to members of his family after his death. The effect was therefore to remove at a stroke an inheritance tax liability at 40% and for it, assuming both that the trustees did what was expected of them and that the scheme was effective, an equivalent value (less no doubt the expense or cost of entering into the scheme) would find its way to the family free of inheritance tax. Excluded property status for assets comprised in a settlement where there has been such an acquisition is denied from 5 December 2005: see **27.25**. However, where such an arrangement was adopted before 5 December 2005, it remains open to the taxpayer to argue for its effectiveness.

[27.25] Anti-avoidance measures apply from 5 December 2005 to prevent UK domiciled individuals who become entitled directly or indirectly to interests in pre-existing foreign trusts originally settled by non-UK domiciliaries which are treated as excluded property within *IHTA 1984, s 48(3)* from being treated as excluded property if they were acquired for money or money's worth. It is immaterial whether the consideration is given by the person acquiring the interest in possession in the settlement or someone else or whether the entitlement arises by way of Will or intestacy. Any inheritance tax arising as a result of this avoidance provision applying from 5 December 2005 to the day before enactment of the *Finance Act 2006* on 19 July 2006 will be due 14 days after enactment. If the acquired interest is subsequently resettled

Situs of property [27.30]

by someone who is domiciled outside the UK relief may still be available under *IHTA 1984, s 48(3)* in respect of the new settlement [*IHTA 1984, ss 48(3), (3B), (3C), 267(3); FA 2006, s 157(2), (4)–(6)*].

[**27.26**] The regime has been further tightened by *FA 2012, s 210* by amending *IHTA 1984, s 48*, inserting *subsections (3D), (3E)* and *(3F)* and by inserting *section 74A* and *section 74B*. Where a UK domiciliary acquires an interest in an excluded property settlement on or after 22 March 2012 which would reduce their estate for inheritance tax purposes, this will be treated as an immediately chargeable event causing a lifetime charge at up to 20% to arise. The relevant assets in the excluded property settlement will cease to be treated as excluded property, so becoming liable to ten-year and exit charges. Further, somewhat draconianly, where such arrangements were made before 22 March 2012, ten-year and exit charges will arise in relation to events occurring after 21 March 2012.

Reversionary interests

[**27.27**] If a reversionary interest is not already excluded property under the general rule of *IHTA 1984, s 48(1)* above (see **12.17–12.18**), it may still be excluded property if the person beneficially entitled to it is an individual domiciled outside the UK. Reversionary interests in settled property situated outside the UK are prevented from being excluded property under *IHTA 1984, s 48(3)(a)* (see **27.4**), but are brought back in as excluded property by *section 48(3)(b)* which provides that *IHTA 1984, s 6(1)* applies to a reversionary interest in the property but does not otherwise apply in relation to the property. *Section 6(1)* provides that property situated outside the UK is excluded property if the person beneficially entitled to it is an individual domiciled outside the UK. Therefore, for a reversionary interest in foreign property to be excluded property, the individual reversioner must be domiciled outside the UK.

Exempt gilts

[**27.28**] Certain UK Government securities, commonly known as exempt gilts, which are held in trust are also excluded property if certain conditions are met. The securities in question are ones issued by the Treasury on terms giving exemption from taxation so long as the securities are in the beneficial ownership of persons not domiciled or (from 1996) not ordinarily resident in the UK, at least before 2013/14 [*IHTA 1984, ss 6, 48(4)*]. From 2013/14, the condition is instead that the person is resident in the UK (*FA 2013, Sch 46, para 114*).

[**27.29**] There is an attractive range of exempt gilts available, with maturities for most years running into the third decade of this century.

[**27.30**] The conditions for exemption from inheritance tax for exempt gilts held by trusts, as set out in *IHTA 1984, s 48(4)* are as follows:

(a) no person either domiciled or ordinarily (from 2013/14 resident) in the UK is entitled to a 'qualifying interest in possession' (see **2.38** and **8.7**) in them; or

(b) there is no qualifying interest in possession in them, but it is shown that all known persons for whose benefit the trust property (or income from it) has been or might be applied, or who are or might become beneficially entitled to an interest in possession in it, are either not domiciled or not ordinarily (from 2013/14 resident) in the UK.

[27.31] To facilitate the creation of a gilt strips market, the exemption from taxation for non-UK resident holders of exempt gilts was extended from income tax to capital taxes from 1996/97. Previously the latter exemption applied only where the holder was non-UK domiciled as well as non-UK resident [*FA 1996, s 154, Sch 28, paras 7, 8*].

[27.32] Similar treatment was extended to holdings in unit trusts and OEICs from 2003/04 [*FA 2003, s 186*]. The extension of the exemption is on the face of it good news, though there is a hidden trap. Going back to the exit charge under the relevant property regime, *IHTA 1984, s 65(1)(a)* provides that 'Where the property comprised at the settlement or any part of that property ceases to be relevant property (whether because it ceases to be comprised in the settlement or otherwise)' there will be an exit charge. Happily, however, *section 65(7)* provides that 'Tax shall not be charged under this section by reason only that property comprised in a settlement ceases to be situated in the United Kingdom and thereby becomes excluded property by virtue of *section 48(3)(a)* above'. Unfortunately, this sensible exclusion from the exit charge has not extended to the possible case where the trustees sell, for example, UK stocks and shares and reinvest in authorised unit trusts and/or OEICs. This lacuna has been put right by *FA 2013, s 175*, by inserting into *IHTA 1984* new *s 65(7A)* with effect from 16 October 2002.

[27.33] There has been some litigation in connection with these provisions, not surprisingly in view of their rather convoluted nature. *Von Ernst and Cie SA v IRC* [1980] 1 All ER 677, [1980] 1 WLR 468, CA concerned a trust in what is a rather common form, with a discretionary class of individuals as primary beneficiaries and a final gift over to UK charities. Both of the individuals concerned were neither domiciled nor ordinarily resident in the UK. An interest in possession in exempt gilts was appointed to the two individuals and the trustees argued that the securities were excluded property. The transaction was charged to capital transfer tax under the provisions of *FA 1975, Sch 5, para 6(2)* as a capital distribution. The Court of Appeal held that what is now *IHTA 1984, s 48(4)(b)* did apply to exempt the securities as excluded property, since a charity, because of its fiduciary nature, could never become beneficially entitled to its property.

[27.34] A five-part scheme to use the exempt gilts provision to transfer assets tax free from a mother in the UK to her daughter abroad was ruled ineffective in *IRC v Brandenburg* [1982] STC 555, 126 Sol Jo 229, Ch D.

[27.35] In *Minden Trust (Cayman) Ltd v IRC* [1985] STC 758, CA, exempt gilts were transferred from a trust which did not qualify under *section 48(4)(b)* to one which did and then appointed on to the beneficiaries. This arrangement succeeded, but the *Minden* route has since been closed by *IHTA 1984, s 48(5)* which requires the domicile and ordinary residence (from 2013/14 residence) conditions of *IHTA 1984, s 48(4)(b)* to be satisfied by both trusts where there is a transfer of property from one trust to another.

[27.36] In *Montagu Trust Co (Jersey) Ltd v IRC* [1989] STC 477, Ch D trustees transferred exempt gilts to themselves as trustees of a second trust and then proceeded to appoint them to beneficiaries who had emigrated to Israel. This arrangement failed to meet the statutory requirements for excluded property, as it was possible that people domiciled in the UK might benefit on the technical construction of the deeds, and tax was chargeable accordingly.

[27.37] The *Von Ernst* case has supplied useful clarification on what is necessary to meet the requirements of *IHTA 1984, 48(4)*. *Minden* and *Montagu*, and the subsequent countervailing legislation in *IHTA 1984, s 48(5)*, indicate the difficulty of using the exemption through a reconstruction of existing trusts. The only really provocative attempt to utilise the exemption was in *Brandenburg* (27.34) and this failed.

[27.38] Exempt gilts provide a means for not ordinarily resident or non-UK domiciled individuals to benefit from UK gilts through a trust without incurring any charges to inheritance tax. Other uses, or abuses, of the exemption, appear decidedly risky.

A proposed 'look through' for UK residential properties

[27.39] In addition to the more general changes to the 'deemed domiciled' rules outlined at 24.49–24.50 and 27.15–27.20, Summer Budget 2015 also announced a specific change to the inheritance taxation of residential property held through an offshore holding structure, ie:

> 'The government intends to amend the rules on excluded property so that trusts or individuals owning UK residential property through an offshore company, partnership or other opaque vehicle, will pay IHT on the value of such UK property in the same way as UK domiciled individuals. The measure will apply to all UK residential property whether it is occupied or let and of whatever value.'

Thus, the fact that the situs of the holding structure might be non-UK, will not determine the UK inheritance tax exposure. It is proposed that these changes will take effect from 6 April 2017 and will be legislated in *Finance Bill 2017*.

[27.40] Following Summer Budget 2015 initial details of the proposed changes were announced in the HMRC document *Technical briefing on foreign domiciled persons/Inheritance Tax residential property changes* published on 8 July 2015; however formal consultation on the proposed changes did not begin until the publication of the latest consultation document *Reforms to the taxation of non-domiciliaries: further consultation*, on 19 August 2016 (and which runs until 20 October 2016), together with draft legislation. The key elements of the new proposals, as set out in the latest consultation document, are set out below.

Scope of the charge

[27.41] The intention is to bring residential properties in the UK within the charge to IHT where they are held within an overseas structure. The charge will apply both to individuals who are domiciled outside the UK and to trusts with settlors or beneficiaries who are non-domiciled. Such properties will be removed from the current definitions of excluded property, and shares in offshore close companies and similar entities will no longer be excluded property if, and to the extent that, the value of any interest in the entity is derived, directly or indirectly, from residential property in the UK.

[27.42] The legislation will define the types of property which will become liable to IHT and it is proposed that the definition should follow that of a 'dwelling' for the purposes of capital gains tax on disposals by non-residents of residential property in the UK, but with appropriate amendments to remove some of the exemptions which apply for capital gains tax.

[27.43] A property will be within the charge to inheritance tax where it has been wholly or partly a dwelling at any time within the two years preceding a transfer, and, if partly, it will be possible to apportion the value to reflect the extent of residential use.

[27.44] The change will be effective for all chargeable events which take place after 5 April 2017, including, for trusts, ten yearly and exit charges and charges on the death of a life tenant of a qualifying interest in possession trust.

Valuation and debts

[27.45] Valuation will follow the normal approach for inheritance tax, so that tax will be charged on the open market value of the property at the time of the relevant chargeable event; however, it will be the holding entity which will be valued (eg the shares in the company holding the property) rather than the property itself, as the example included within the consultation document makes clear.

[27.46] It will be possible to take account of relevant debts, being those which relate exclusively to the property, such as amounts outstanding on a mortgage which was taken out to purchase the property. In some cases it will be necessary to pro rata a debt which relates partly to residential property and partly to other assets. It is proposed that loans made between connected parties should be disregarded.

Anti-avoidance

[27.47] There will be targeted anti-avoidance, the effect of which will be to disregard any arrangements the whole or main purpose of which is to avoid or mitigate a charge to IHT on UK residential property.

Liability and accountability

[27.48] Because HMRC might have difficulties in identifying whether a chargeable event has taken place and hence whether a liability to inheritance tax has arisen, the government intends to extend responsibility for reporting to HMRC when chargeable events have taken place and for paying any tax which arises. HMRC will be given an expanded power to impose a charge on indirectly held UK residential property so that the property cannot be sold. In addition, a new liability will be imposed on any person who has legal ownership of the property, including any directors of the company which holds that property.

De-enveloping

[27.49] The introduction of the ATED charge of course went a long way to reducing the tax advantage of holding UK residential property in a non-UK vehicle and it is interesting that the government feels the need to go further and now address this issue more directly. There is no suggestion that the ATED charge will be withdrawn when these new rules come into effect and, if such structures are left in place, some properties will suffer an annual ATED charge *and* be potentially subject to inheritance tax too. In many cases there will be a clear advantage in removing a residential property from an offshore holding entity – so-called 'de-enveloping'.

[27.50] Unfortunately, there are often potential tax costs associated with de-enveloping (typically SDLT and/or capital gains tax) and the original technical note was alive to this issue and hinted at possible transitional provisions to encourage de-enveloping:

> The proposed changes to the IHT rules will change the IHT treatment, so some non-doms and trusts may wish to remove the envelope and move into a simpler more straightforward structure outside the scope of future ATED charges, ATED reporting or ATED-related CGT. If the property is mortgaged or has increased in value since 2013 there may however, be significant costs in de-enveloping . . . The government will consider the costs associated with de-enveloping and any other concerns stakeholders may have during the course of the consultation regarding de-enveloping.

[27.51] In the previous edition of this book, the author commented as follows on this:

> *A system whereby holding structures could be unravelled without a tax charge would certainly help taxpayers simplify existing structures; however, the author's impression is that, to date, the Treasury has been reluctant to forego the potential tax (typically CGT and SDLT) that might otherwise be triggered by de-enveloping. Taxpayers wishing to de-envelope and currently facing a tax charge to do so, may now wonder whether they should delay in the hope of more helpful rules to come. However, any delay may simply increase their future charges if no relieving provisions materialise. Hopefully, clarity will be forthcoming relatively quickly in this respect because the uncertainty simply leaves taxpayers in limbo.*

[27.52] Well the 'limbo' is now at an end, as the latest consultation document states:

> At the 2015 Summer Budget, the government said that it would consider the cost associated with de-enveloping of properties. However, while the government can see there might be a case for encouraging de-enveloping, it does not think it would be appropriate to provide any incentive to encourage individuals to exit from their enveloped structures at this time.

We will presumably never know whether dangling this particular carrot was a cynical ploy to encourage potential de-envelopers to delay. Either way, there is now nothing really to be gained from further delay, if de-enveloping is the most sensible response to the proposed new rules.

Double tax treaties

[27.53] The total number of double tax treaties covering inheritance tax has remained small in comparison with the treaties dealing with income tax, corporation tax and capital gains tax. Only ten treaties relevant to inheritance tax remain in force and three of these (Sweden, India and Pakistan) have abolished the tax! The remaining seven treaties with France, Italy, Ireland, South Africa, the USA, the Netherlands and Switzerland are, however, of practical significance whenever one is dealing with individuals resident in those jurisdictions. Five of them – the treaties with Ireland, the Netherlands, South Africa, Sweden and the USA – also contain specific provisions dealing with settled property.

[27.54] Although India and Pakistan have abolished estate duty, there remains an interesting point in relation to the person who has his domicile under the general law in India or Pakistan (and it is important to establish the position under both UK law *and* the law of those countries) but who is deemed domiciled in the UK for inheritance tax purposes. The treaties with both countries displace the deemed domicile rules on death, (though not for lifetime transfers). So non-UK assets owned by such an individual will both escape inheritance tax in the UK and not be charged at all to tax in India or Pakistan, provided that the assets pass under a disposition governed by the law of a country outside the UK. It should be noted that these provisions are due to be reviewed as part of the new 'deemed domicile' rule announced at the time of Summer Budget 2015 (see **27.15**).

Reporting obligations

[27.55] HMRC Trusts and Estates are obviously faced with difficulty in obtaining information on offshore trusts. Accordingly, *IHTA 1984, s 218* imposes a liability on any person, other than a barrister, who has been concerned with the making of a trust in the course of his trade or profession, and knows or has reason to believe that the settlor was domiciled in the UK and that the trustees are not or will not be resident in the UK, to report this to HMRC within three months of the creation of the trust with the names and addresses of the settlor and the trustees.

[27.56] For the purposes of *section 218* trustees of a settlement are regarded as not resident in the UK unless the general administration of the settlement is ordinarily carried on in the UK and the trustees or a majority of them (and, where there is more than one class of trustees, a majority of each class) are for the time being resident in the UK.

[27.57] Failure to comply carries a penalty of £300 plus £60 per day if it continues after it has been declared by a court or the Tribunal. The reasonable excuse defence is provided [*IHTA 1984, s 245A*]. Note that, unlike penalties under *section 245(2)(a),(3)*, penalties under *section 245A* for continuing failure are not capped by the amount of tax on the account and are subject only to a maximum of £3,000. The requirement to provide information in this way is important in alerting HMRC to the existence of such trusts. It does not apply to Will trusts or to a trust where an account has been delivered to HMRC under *IHTA 1984, s 216*.

[27.58] The provisions of *FA 2004, Pt VII* regarding disclosure of tax avoidance schemes do not apply to inheritance tax, but could apply (however improbably) in the context of the pre-owned assets income tax charge (see

27.63). That said, of course, inheritance tax now has its own disclosure regime, from 2011/12, in respect of arrangements seeking to avoid inheritance tax charges associated with transfers of property into trust (see **17.27**).

Executors and trustees

[27.59] When an individual dies his estate vests in his personal representatives, ie his executors if he has made a Will or his administrators if he has not (for convenience it is usual to employ the term executor to connote personal representatives of either description). An executor is not exactly in the position of a trustee (although he does have fiduciary responsibilities), since his primary duty is to gather in the assets of the estate, pay off debts and liabilities (including tax) and to distribute the net estate according to the Will or the intestacy. The Will itself, however, may set up a trust and in such a case it is treated as operating from the death of a testator [*IHTA 1984, s 83*]. Where the Will provides for an interest in possession in all or part of the residue this too is treated as operating from the death [*IHTA 1984, s 91*].

[27.60] Personal representatives are defined to include any person by whom or on whose behalf an application for a grant of administration or for the resealing of a grant made outside the UK is made and also any person who takes possession or intermeddles with, or otherwise acts in relation to the property (known in Scotland as a 'vicious intromitter') [*IHTA 1984, s 272*].

[27.61] In *IRC v Stannard* [1984] 2 All ER 105, [1984] 1 WLR 1039, Ch D the executor was resident in Jersey. The Inland Revenue raised a determination against him for £60,000 and sought an order for payment out of his own assets (technically *de bonis propriis*). The court refused to do this, holding that he was liable to pay only from the deceased's assets (*de bonis testatoris*). On appeal, the order was made in the *de bonis propriis* form and Scott J held that there was no difference in this regard between the liability of executors and the liability of trustees [*IHTA 1984, s 204(1), (2)*].

Enforcement: the Clore case

[27.62] The position of executors and trustees is illustrated by the prolonged litigation in the *Clore* case. Sir Charles Clore died in July 1979, having given up residence in the UK and made moves towards establishing domicile in Monaco. The major issue was whether Sir Charles died domiciled in England or in Monaco. It took until 1984 for the court to hold that he had never abandoned his English domicile of origin (*Clore (No 2), Re, Official Solicitor v Clore* [1984] STC 609, Ch D). The case is a salutary example of how not to go about things if intending to change domicile. The other, related, litigation serves to illustrate not only that HMRC have extensive enforcement powers, from which non-UK resident executors and trustees are not exempt, but also that they will not hesitate to use those powers where there is sufficient tax at stake.

The Pre-owned Assets Regime

[27.63] See 4.39–4.51 for a broad description of the regime introduced from 2005/06 designed to counter arrangements put in place to avoid the inheritance tax reservation of benefit rules, by imposing an income tax charge in certain cases. The regime will not apply to anyone for a year of assessment during which he is not UK resident. If in any tax year a person is UK resident but non-UK domiciled, the regime cannot apply unless the property concerned is situated in the UK (*FA 2004, Sch 15, para 12*). There is a specific rule that in applying the regime to a person who has at any time been non-UK domiciled, no regard is to be had to any property which is excluded property for purposes of *IHTA 1984, s 48(3)(a)*. Domicile has of course its extended meaning for inheritance tax purposes. HMRC have confirmed that the general saving exclusions and exemptions (see **4.45** and **4.46**) apply to non-UK domiciliaries no less than to UK domiciliaries. Generally, see *para 12 of FA 2004, Sch 15*.

Chapter 28

Tax Planning Issues for Offshore Trusts: An Overview

[28.1] The *FA 1991* obviously dealt a severe blow to the emigration of trusts as a means to the avoidance or mitigation of capital gains tax. *FA 1998* extended the attack to trusts which were already non-UK resident prior to the 1991 measures. And *FA 2008, Sch 7* carried through to non-UK domiciled beneficiaries the capital payments charge, albeit with the benefit of the remittance basis (at an annual cost of between £30,000 and £90,000 as set out in 28.3 and the ability for the trustees through a rebasing election to remove from the ambit of the charge gains accrued prior to 6 April 1998 (see 26.33–26.52)) at least for the first 15 years of UK residence, until the proposed new deemed domiciled rules (see 24.48–24.50 and the relevant parts of CHAPTERS 25, 26 and 27).

[28.2] All that said, however, non-UK resident trusts will still have a part to play in tax planning in suitable cases. The trust itself remains a well-tried and flexible instrument by which an individual can make prudent and forward-looking dispositions of his property while he is still alive and retain some control over its disposal in the event of his death or incapacity.

[28.3] A foreigner coming to live in the UK will be taxed on the remittance basis on his offshore trust income, in the same way as on his personal income. From 2008/09 this comes at an annual cost of £30,000 (once he has been resident in the UK in at least seven out of the previous nine tax years and provided his unremitted non-UK income and gains are not less than £2,000), structured as a tax on unremitted income and gains and forfeiting the right to personal allowances for income tax and the annual exemption from capital gains tax [*ITA 2007, ss 809A–809Z* as inserted by *FA 2008, Sch 7*]. From 2015/16, the annual cost is £60,000 where the taxpayer has been UK resident in at least 12 out of the previous 14 tax years. For 2015/16 and 2016/17, only the annual cost is £90,000 once resident for 17 out of the previous 20 tax years. From 2017/18, for anyone resident for 15 out of the previous 20 tax years (or any 'returning UK dom') the new deemed domiciled rules will end the remittance basis and special new rules will apply (see 25.41–25.45 and 26.53–26.56).

[28.4] A trust made while he is not UK domiciled for inheritance tax purposes can also be structured so as to protect his capital indefinitely from the imposition of inheritance tax, subject to the trust fund remaining outside the UK (see 27.4–27.21). The emigrant from this country can achieve similar advantages once he has surmounted the three-year quarantine period imposed for inheritance tax under *IHTA 1984, s 267* (and even that provision can be bypassed if the trust assets are held in the form of exempt gilts). These inheritance tax rules for 'excluded property' trust largely survive the proposed introduction of new deemed domiciled rules from 2017/18, except in relation to trusts established by 'returning UK doms' (see 27.20). Domicile therefore remains of crucial importance in the use of offshore trusts.

Protection and establishment of domicile

[28.5] It is vital for the individual coming to this country and wishing to maintain his domicile of origin to maintain as close links as possible with his homeland. Circumstances may render this difficult. Many who come to this country do so because of hostile regimes in their native land. In such cases the intention to return when circumstances improve will maintain the domicile of origin. However, where residence here is voluntary, there may be more room for arguing that there is an intention to remain here permanently. HMRC now contend that this can be inferred unless there is a predictable event (other than the receipt of a massive assessment) which will cause the individual to leave this country. This contention is dubious on the decided cases and should be resisted.

[28.6] For the emigrant it is essential, given the adhesive quality of the domicile of origin, that the links with the domicile of choice should be made as firm and durable as possible and the intention to leave this country permanently evinced clearly. In this, as in so many other respects, the *Clore* case (see **27.62**) is a prime example of how *not* to manage one's affairs. Sir Charles had been given professional advice that for tax planning purposes, particularly in connection with his offshore trust, it was essential that he should establish a foreign domicile. He did in the main follow this advice. He took steps to associate himself with Monaco. Why then was he held to be still domiciled here? The reason was that four close friends provided evidence that he was profoundly unhappy in his self-imposed exile. On this basis there was not sufficient evidence to satisfy the conscience of the court that Sir Charles ever formed a settled intention to reside permanently in Monaco. Tax planning in this area can never be a mechanical exercise. The subjective intentions of an individual are all important. The more recent case of *Gaines-Cooper v HMRC* [2008] STC 1665, 23 SpC 568 concerning residence also touched on the domicile position of the appellant in circumstances that were similar to the *Clore* case. The Special Commissioners stated:

> 'We do not underestimate the part which the Seychelles plays in his thinking. Nevertheless these considerations do not outweigh the substantial and continuing part which presence in England played in his life. Our conclusion on the first issue is that the appellant has not discharged the burden of proving to us that he abandoned his domicile of origin in England and so we conclude that he was domiciled in England for the tax years from 1992/93 to 2003/04.'

See APPENDIX G for a commentary on the *Gaines-Cooper* litigation.

The trust document and its contents

[28.7] The principles of the English law of equity are so well defined in a long line of decisions that a trust deed need not be unduly complex. This is not so in other jurisdictions. Some favourite venues, such as the Cayman Islands, Jersey and Guernsey, have produced their own Trustee Acts, but for maximum flexibility the deed will usually provide for moving the trust elsewhere, particularly in case of emergency. It is also usual to spell out the powers of the trustees in some detail. Frequently the deed provides for a protector nominated by the settlor; the consent of the protector may be required for important dispositive, as distinct from administrative acts. The protector is largely unknown to English law except in the almost obsolete context of estates in tail.

[28.8] Where the trust is discretionary in form, there will usually be a letter of wishes from the settlor, not binding on the trustees, but certain to be given due weight by them.

[28.9] There may be dangers in attempting to tie things up too tightly. This was illustrated by a case in the Royal Court of Jersey, *Rahman (Abdel) v Chase Bank (CI) Trust Co Ltd* 1991 JLR 103, earlier proceedings in which are reported in 1983 JLR 1, 1984 JLR 127, 1985–86 JLR N–5, 1987–88 JLR 81 and 1990 JLR 59, 136. It concerned a Jersey trust set up by a Lebanese national. After his death his widow commenced an action against the trustees, alleging *inter alia* that the trust breached the maxim of Jersey law '*donner et retenir ne vaut*', which means, broadly, that the settlor cannot retain control of something he has given away. The court held that the maxim was applicable, but its decision on this point was overtaken by an amendment to the *Trusts (Jersey) Law 1984* providing that '*donner et retenir ne vaut*' could not be applied to invalidate a trust.

[28.10] However, the court took evidence on the actual operation of the trust and found that the settlor retained dominion and control over the trust fund during his lifetime. There were also provisions in the trust deed that aligned it more with an American grantor-controlled trust than a true discretionary trust. The court concluded that the settlement was a sham in the sense that it was made to appear what it was not.

[28.11] The obvious lesson to be drawn is that in setting up an offshore trust it is essential to be sure that it will stand up under local law as well as under English law. If the settlor is unwilling to relinquish effective personal control, it is better not to proceed. In the *Rahman* case, the trustee strongly recommended a discretionary trust with a letter of wishes, and it would have been well had this advice been heeded.

The family context

[28.12] The main purpose of an offshore trust is likely to be for benefiting the family. To achieve this purpose effectively it is important to ensure that the family is fully in sympathy with the terms and objects of the trust. This appears to have been overlooked by Mr Rahman in the case mentioned in 28.9. It was also forgotten by Sir Charles Clore (see 27.62 and 28.4). His dispositions were attacked not only by the then Inland Revenue in England, but by his son in Jersey. The result was a sorry multiplicity of proceedings. Although there were half a dozen parties to the summons in the action to determine Sir Charles' domicile, not one was prepared to make a positive case for a Monegasque domicile.

[28.13] Parallel proceedings were going on in Jersey regarding domicile, which might have reached an opposite conclusion. This was a prospect that, as the judge remarked, 'although one which may to the uninitiated seem rather odd, I have to face with equanimity'. No doubt the members of the family did not share his sang-froid.

[28.14] Where gifts to the family fail, there is sometimes a final gift over to charity. There are now few restrictions on gifts to charity for the purpose of exemption from tax, although it should be noted that:

(a) the charity must be subject to the jurisdiction of the UK courts *(Dreyfus (Camille and Henry) Foundation Inc v IRC* [1956] AC 39, [1955] 3 All ER 97, HL);
(b) it must not run foul of the anti-avoidance provisions now found in *ITA 2007, s 523; CTA 2010, s 574*, introduced to counter abuses which the Inland Revenue considered were exemplified in *IRC v Helen Slater Charitable Trust Ltd* [1982] Ch 49, [1981] 3 All ER 98, CA.

See 14.2 for the extension of the territorial limitation following a notice from the European Commission, so as to apply to charities established within the European Economic Area.

Non-UK resident children's trusts

[28.15] With a UK domiciled settlor and essentially what one might call a UK based family, one might not naturally think in terms of offshore trusts, especially in view of the vast raft of anti-avoidance legislation, not to mention the typically higher start-up and ongoing administration costs offshore. However, that said, especially in the realm of income tax mitigation, one should remember the possibility of gross roll-up. That is, given that settlor and spouse/civil partner are excluded from benefit it is only where income is paid out or benefits are provided that a tax charge will arise – and that under the transfer of assets abroad regime in *ITA 2007, Pt 13, Ch 2, ss 714–751*. Of course, even if not paid out income arising to the trustees while there is a minor child (unmarried and not in a civil partnership) of the settlor as a beneficiary will trigger an income tax liability for the settlor parent under *ITTOIA 2005, s 629*. And indeed chargeable gains will be assessed on the settlor on an arising basis under *TCGA 1992, s 86*, with perhaps little prospect of him being able successfully to exercise his statutory right of recovery. However, if this suggestion is applied to a Will trust rather than a lifetime settlement, both this point and the parental settlement issue fall away.

[28.16] In the context especially of high on-going administration costs, the typical limitation on such a trust of £325,000 as the nil-rate band to avoid a 20% entry charge to inheritance tax, certainly with lifetime trusts, might seem to rule these out of court. One might then consider whether the value of the trust fund could be enhanced using the provision in *IHTA 1984, s 11* whereby a qualifying disposition for maintenance of the family is not a transfer of value at all. It has been held that the principle applies to gifts of capital – see in particular the 2008 decision in *McKelvey (personal representative of McKelvey, dec'd) v Revenue and Customs Comrs* (SpC 694) [2008] STC (SCD) 944 and the commentary at **15.15**. The problem, however, thinking perhaps of provision for school and university fees, is that (even though say up to £15,000 per annum for prep school, £25–30,000 per annum for secondary school fees and £12,500 to £15,000 for university fees), these could be up to say £300,000 plus inflation per child. There is some limitation on what could reasonably put into trust: in particular, HMRC Trusts and Estates would surely resist an argument that *section 11* could apply to the settlement of a capital sum designed to produce income of that amount: you probably do have to show that the capital is indeed going to be spent. How is the protection of *section 11* claimed? Presumably on the transfer to a relevant property trust form IHT 100 would be submitted together with the reasoned argument as to why the chargeable transfer is within the nil-rate band, given *section 11*. Another use for *section 11* might be the transfer of property to a former spouse/civil partner while the donor is terminally ill, to minimise the possibility of a claim under the *Inheritance (Provision for Family and other Dependants) Act 1975*. Alternatively, continuing the theme of terminal illness, there might be a case for making such a transfer for the benefit of minor children or those in full-time education to mitigate IHT on death.

The location of the trust

[28.17] There are now a number of jurisdictions which actively compete for offshore trust business. In the days of the sterling area and exchange control, the Isle of Man, the Channel Islands and, to a lesser extent, Gibraltar were frequently used. More recently it has been possible to move further afield. The Cayman Islands and the Bahamas offer great expertise and a reassuring background of English law. The Channel Islands and Gibraltar among other jurisdictions have seen increased activity in this area.

[28.18] There has been a trend towards the setting up of asset protection trusts. These originated in the desire of US professionals to protect their assets from malpractice suits. In the UK such a trust would be the subject of scrutiny where there appeared to be a possibility under *Insolvency Act 1986, s 423* of an intention to defeat creditors. Some jurisdictions now have a trust ordinance that protects the trust from a creditor unless the settlor was insolvent at the time of the transfer into the trust.

[28.19] Very often an offshore structure will include companies owned by the trust and it may be desirable to incorporate these in other jurisdictions. This is also now a well-trodden route on which competent professional offshore trustees will be ready to advise.

Planning opportunities for non-UK domiciled individuals

[28.20] A non-UK domiciled or resident individual should always consider setting up an offshore trust if he intends to establish residence and more particularly domicile in the UK. It should also be remembered that the spouse/civil partner of such an individual can retain an independent foreign domicile. For the first 15 years of UK residence (if the new rules for deemed domicile come in as planned), income and gains arising on such trusts will be taxable only on a remittance basis for a non-UK domiciled individual who elects for the application of that basis, subject to the *FA 2008* regime for such a 'remittance basis user' (see **24.43**) [*TCGA 1992, s 12(1); ITTOIA 2005, s 832*]. Care must be taken not to infringe the rules regarding constructive remittances, in the light of the new regime introduced from 2008/09 [*TCGA 1992, s 12(2); ITA 2007, ss 809A–809Z6*]. Non-UK situs assets will remain outside the scope of inheritance tax (*IHTA 1984, s 48(3)*), subject, however, to the provisions of *FA 2010, s 210* (see **27.26**).

[28.21] From 2017/18, the advantages referred to in **28.20** will not be available to a 'returning UK dom' (see **24.48–24.50** and relevant sections of CHAPTERS **25**, **26** and **27**).

[28.22] A prime disadvantage is that the assets concerned will pass out of the control of the settlor to that of the trustees. The provision of a side letter indicating the settlor's wishes is frequently used in the case of a discretionary trust, but the *Rahman* case (see **28.9**) indicates the problems which may arise if the trustees are not accorded adequate discretion.

[28.23] For as long as an individual remains outside the scope of the proposed new deemed domicile rules (see **24.48–24.50**), gains made in or after 2008/09 by offshore trusts set up by non-UK resident and non-UK domiciled persons are now chargeable on UK resident beneficiaries who receive capital payments from the trust, and from 2008/09 even where non-UK domiciled, albeit subject to electing for the remittance basis on non-UK gains (see **26.47**). And the trustees can make an election to restrict such treatment to gains accrued after 5 April 2008 (see **26.49–26.50**). Happily, the *FA 2008, Sch 7* regime has its limits, not only in preserving a remittance basis for non-UK gains (albeit at an annual cost), but also allowing *section 2(2)* amounts (previously trust gains) to be 'washed' by having them attributed to capital payments made to a non-UK domiciliary in a tax year before a payment is made to a UK domiciliary. Further, as it did before 2008/09, the regime does allow tax-free advances of capital from a non-UK resident trust, whatever the domicile of settlor, to a beneficiary who is not UK resident or (before 2013/14) ordinarily resident in the year of advance (bearing in mind the extended definition of residence for capital gains tax purposes in *TCGA 1992, s 10A* as amended by *FA 2013, Sch 45*, necessitating typically five consecutive years non-UK residence).

[28.24] Finally, it should be remembered that *ITA 2007, Pt 13, Ch 2, ss 714–751* may still be deployed by HMRC to attack the best of structures. Although it was patently clear at the time of its origin that the regime meant to counter transfers of assets offshore by individuals resident in the UK at that time, and despite the savaging which the Inland Revenue received from the House of Lords in the *Vestey* case (see **25.21**) they still attempted to use the old weapon against non-UK domiciled individuals who set up offshore trusts before coming to reside in this country. See also **25.22–25.23** for the benefits charge.

[28.25] The introduction from December 2005 of the revised motive test for both the transferor charge and the benefits charge has undoubtedly strengthened the hand of HMRC (see **25.24–25.33**).

[28.26] From 2017/18, once an individual becomes deemed domiciled in the UK, the taxation of the income and gains in any non-resident trusts established by him or her before that point will depend upon whether the trust falls within the proposed 'protections' for income and capital gains tax (see 25.41–25.45 and 26.53–26.56) and, as the results of the latest consultation become clear and the terms of the legislation firm up, it will be important for the position in relation to existing trusts to be reviewed before 5 April 2017.

Information exchange

[28.27] This book is, of course, aimed at those who wish to be transparent in relation to their tax affairs and to pay any tax that is due to HMRC in relation to their offshore structures. Nevertheless, a few words are required in relation to the rapidly changing topic of information exchange.

[28.28] The powers of HMRC in relation to the enforcement of tax, including the obtaining of information which they may require, are wide (see 26.63–26.65 and 27.55–27.58) but they are not unlimited. It is beyond the scope of this book to examine them in detail and, moreover, the agreements for exchange of information with other countries under tax information agreements or double taxation agreements (introduced in *FA 2000, ss 146* and *147* and now found in *FA 2006, s 173*) and within the EU, are of equal importance, and these are many and varied.

Disclosure facilities

[28.29] Additionally, over the last few years, HMRC have adopted a 'carrot and stick' approach encouraging taxpayers to disclose their offshore structures through a number of 'disclosure facilities'.

[28.30] Things began with four 2006 Special Commissioner's decisions on *TMA 1970, s 20(8A)* (before repeal by *FA 2008, Sch 36, para 67* by virtue of *SI 2009/404, art 3*). HMRC successfully applied to a Special Commissioner for leave to serve notice on, respectively, a British Virgin Islands Company and Barclays Bank Plc to supply the details of individuals with a UK address who have income arising in accounts outside the UK which may not have been declared for UK tax purposes. Following these cases, HMRC announced an 'amnesty' called 'the Offshore Disclosure Facility' (ODF) on 17 April 2007 confirming that penalties would be capped at 10% provided that the taxpayer notified by 22 June 2007 his intention to disclose and made full disclosure and payment of all outstanding tax, interest and penalties by 26 November 2007. That initiative proved not to be as successful as HMRC had anticipated, raising by the end of 2007 just £400 million as against the £1 billion or more for which HMRC had hoped. March 2008 saw HMRC return to the fray which was quickly followed by the announcement of HMRC's intention to take proceedings against around 300 individuals whose names were provided by an informant of the Liechtenstein Bank LGT. In July 2009 HMRC were given leave by the First-tier Tribunal to obtain details of account holders from some 300 banks.

[28.31] A second initiative was announced at Budget 2009. This is 'the New Disclosure Opportunity' (NDO) for UK residents with unpaid tax connected to an offshore account. The NDO ran from 1 September 2009 to 12 March 2010 to give offshore account holders one final opportunity to disclose and to put their affairs in order. Taxpayers taking up the opportunity are expected to pay the duties owed, interest and a penalty of no more than 10%, except that a higher penalty will be imposed on those taxpayers who could have made a disclosure under the ODF. On 12 August 2009, and separately from the NDO, the *Liechtenstein Disclosure Facility* was announced (and in rather more favourable terms than the NDO). Subsequently, a *UK/Switzerland Agreement* took effect from 1 January 2013; an *Isle of Man Disclosure Facility* was announced on 19 February 2013; and *Jersey and Guernsey Disclosure Facilities* were announced the following day.

Multinational initiatives

[28.32] Separately, information disclosure has also been driven by events overseas. In 2012, France introduced a potentially punitive new tax on trusts which had either a French resident settlor or beneficiaries, or which owned assets in France, with the obligation to report and pay the special tax each calendar year. Likewise, the US *Foreign Account Tax Compliance Act* (*FATCA*) has generated a worldwide disclosure-tsunami as jurisdictions, eager to remain compliant with the IRS, have reached agreement with the US for the automatic exchange of information.

[28.33] As things have developed, *FATCA* was only a stepping stone to something much bigger and more significant. On 23 February 2014, the G20 Finance Ministers publicly endorsed the 'Common Reporting Standard for Automatic Exchange of Tax Information' (the 'CRS'). This has now been endorsed by all OECD member states, along with several non-members.

[28.34] At the time of writing, the following 54 countries will begin the automatic exchange of information in 2017:

Anguilla, Argentina, Barbados, Belgium, Bermuda, British Virgin Islands, Bulgaria, Cayman Islands, Colombia, Croatia, Curaçao, Cyprus, Czech Republic, Denmark, Estonia, Faroe Islands, Finland, France, Germany, Gibraltar, Greece, Greenland, Guernsey, Hungary, Iceland, India, Ireland, Isle of Man, Italy, Jersey, Korea, Latvia, Liechtenstein, Lithuania, Luxembourg, Malta, Mexico, Montserrat, Netherlands, Niue, Norway, Poland, Portugal, Romania, San Marino, Seychelles, Slovak Republic, Slovenia, South Africa, Spain, Sweden, Trinidad and Tobago, Turks and Caicos Islands and United Kingdom;

and the following 47 countries will begin the automatic exchange of information in 2018:

Albania, Andorra, Antigua and Barbuda, Aruba, Australia, Austria, The Bahamas, Bahrain, Belize, Brazil, Brunei Darussalam, Canada, Chile, China, Cook Islands, Costa Rica, Dominica, Ghana, Grenada, Hong Kong (China), Indonesia, Israel, Japan, Kuwait, Lebanon, Marshall Islands, Macao (China), Malaysia, Mauritius, Monaco, Nauru, New Zealand, Panama, Qatar, Russia, Saint Kitts and Nevis, Samoa, Saint Lucia, Saint Vincent and the Grenadines, Saudi Arabia, Singapore, Sint Maarten, Switzerland, Turkey, United Arab Emirates, Uruguay and Vanuatu.

[28.35] Further detailed information about the CRS can be found at www.gov.uk/guidance/automatic-exchange-of-information-introduction, which was last updated on 29 April 2016.

[28.36] The conclusion from all of the above is that attempts by dishonest taxpayers to conceal their offshore assets and trusts are significantly more likely to fail than at any point in the past.

Appendix A

Press Releases and Statements of Practice

1 NOVEMBER 1973, INLAND REVENUE STATEMENT OF PRACTICE D10
Termination of an interest in possession in settled property
(*TCGA 1992, s 71* and *TCGA 1992, s 72*)

1 Where an interest in possession in part of settled property terminates and the part can properly be identified with one or more specific assets, the Commissioners for HMRC will accept that the deemed disposals and reacquisitions under TCGA 1992 ss 71, 72 apply to those specific assets, and not to any part of the other assets comprised in the settled property. Corresponding treatment will apply where, within a reasonable period (normally three months) immediately following the termination, specific assets are appropriated by the trustees to give effect to the termination. In either case, the treatment must be consistent with that adopted for inheritance tax purposes.

2 In particular, inspectors will be prepared to agree with the trustees lists of assets properly identifiable with the termination of an interest in possession, and any such agreement will be regarded as binding on HMRC and the trustees.

3 This practice applies on any act or event which terminates an interest in possession whether voluntarily or involuntarily.

Note—The text of this statement is as it appears in IR 131 (August 2003).

15 APRIL 1976, INLAND REVENUE STATEMENT OF PRACTICE E13
Charities

1 *IHTA 1984 ss 23 and 24* exempt from IHT certain gifts to charities and political parties to the extent that the value transferred is attributable to property given to a charity etc *IHTA 1984 s 25* exempts certain gifts for national purposes and for the public benefit.

2 Where the value transferred (ie the loss to transferor's estate as a result of the disposition) exceeds the value of the gift in the hands of a charity, etc, the Commissioners for HMRC take the view that the exemption extends to the whole value transferred.

Note—This statement was amended by IR 131 Supplement (November 1998).

15 AUGUST 1979, INLAND REVENUE STATEMENT OF PRACTICE SP 10/79
Inheritance tax: power for trustees to allow a beneficiary to occupy a dwelling house

Many Wills and settlements contain a clause empowering the trustees to permit a beneficiary to occupy a dwelling house which forms part of the trust property on such terms as they think fit. The Commissioners for HMRC do not regard the existence of such a power as excluding any interest in possession in the property.

Where there is no interest in possession in the property in question the Inland Revenue do not regard the exercise of the power as creating one if the effect is merely to allow non-exclusive occupation or to create a contractual tenancy for full consideration. The Inland Revenue also take the view that no interest in possession arises on the creation of a lease for a term or a periodic tenancy for less than full consideration, though this will normally give rise to a charge for tax under [IHTA 1984, s 65(1)(b)]. On the other hand, if the power is drawn in terms wide enough to cover the creation of an exclusive or joint right of residence, albeit revocable, for a definite or indefinite period, and is exercised with the intention of providing a particular beneficiary with a permanent home, the Revenue will normally regard the exercise of the power as creating an interest in possession. And if the trustees in exercise of their powers grant a lease for life for less than full consideration, this will also be regarded as creating an interest in possession in view of [IHTA 1984, ss 43(3), 50(6)].

A similar view will be taken where the power is exercised over property in which another beneficiary had an interest in possession up to the time of the exercise.

11 OCTOBER 1984, INLAND REVENUE STATEMENT OF PRACTICE SP 7/84
Capital gains tax: exercise of a power of appointment or advancement over settled property

The Commissioners for HMRC Statement of Practice SP 9/81, which was issued on 23 September 1981 following discussions with the Law Society, set out the Revenue's views on the capital gains tax implications of the exercise of a Power of Appointment or Advancement when continuing trusts are declared, in the light of the decision of the House of Lords in *Roome & Denne v Edwards HL*, [1981] STC 96. Those views have been modified to some extent by the decision of the Court of Appeal in *Bond v Pickford CA*, [1983] STC 517.

In *Roome & Denne v Edwards* the House of Lords held that where a separate settlement is created there is a deemed disposal of the relevant assets by the old trustees for the purposes of *TCGA 1992, s 71(1)*. But the judgments emphasised that, in deciding whether or not a new settlement has been created by the exercise of a Power of Appointment or Advancement, each case must be considered on its own facts, and by applying established legal doctrine to the facts in a practical and commonsense manner. In *Bond v Pickford* the judgments in the Court of Appeal explained that the consideration of the facts must include examination of the powers which the trustees purported to exercise, and determination of the intention of the parties, viewed objectively.

It is now clear that a deemed disposal under *TCGA 1992, s 71(1)* cannot arise unless the power exercised by the trustees, or the instrument conferring the power, expressly or by necessary implication, confers on the trustees authority to remove assets from the original settlement by subjecting them to the trusts of a different settlement. Such powers (which may be powers of advancement or appointment) are referred to by the Court of Appeal as 'powers in the wider form'. However, the Commissioners for HMRC consider that a deemed disposal will not arise when such a power is exercised and trusts are declared in circumstances such that:

(a) the appointment is revocable; or
(b) the trusts declared of the advanced or appointed funds are not exhaustive so that there exists a possibility at the time when the advancement or appointment is

made that the funds covered by it will on the occasion of some event cease to be held upon such trusts and once again come to be held upon the original trusts of the settlement.

Further, when such a power is exercised the Commissioners of HMRC considers it unlikely that a deemed disposal will arise when trusts are declared if duties in regard to the appointed assets still fall to the trustees of the original settlement in their capacity as trustees of that settlement, bearing in mind the provision in *TCGA 1992, 69(1)* that the trustees of a settlement form a single and continuing body (distinct from the persons who may from time to time be the trustees).

Finally, the Commissioners for HMRC accept that a Power of Appointment or Advancement can be exercised over only part of the settled property and that the above consequences would apply to that part.

10 NOVEMBER 1986, INLAND REVENUE STATEMENT OF PRACTICE SP 8/86
Treatment of income of discretionary trusts

This statement sets out the Commissioners for HMRC's practice concerning the inheritance tax/capital transfer tax treatment of income of discretionary trusts.

The Commissioners of HMRC take the view that:

— Undistributed and unaccumulated income should not be treated as a taxable trust asset; and
— For the purposes of determining the rate of charge on accumulated income, the income should be treated as becoming a taxable asset of the trust on the date when the accumulation is made.

This practice applies from 10 November 1986 to all new cases and to existing cases where the tax liability has not been settled.

21 MARCH 1990, TEXT OF A LETTER ADDRESSED TO THE PROFESSIONAL BODIES BY THE DIRECTOR, CAPITAL AND VALUATION DIVISION OF THE INLAND REVENUE

1. SECTION 40, IHTA 1984—PARTLY EXEMPT TRANSFERS

Section 40 directs that 'where gifts taking effect on a transfer of value take effect separately out of different funds'—for example where on a death there are gifts out of the free estate and out of settlements—then each fund is to be considered separately for the purpose of the allocation of exemptions under *Chapter III* including the grossing-up of the gifts. The rate of tax used by the Capital Taxes Offices to gross up separate gifts out of different funds has until now been the rate applicable to the total value of *all* property chargeable on the testator's death. The Board now accepts that the rate of the tax to be used for grossing up should be found by looking at each fund separately and in isolation.

2. SECTION 52(1), IHTA 1984—THE COMING TO AN END OF AN INTEREST IN POSSESSION IN SETTLED PROPERTY

When an interest in possession in settled property comes to an end during the lifetime of the person entitled to it, *section 52(1)* states that the value for inheritance tax purposes is ' . . . equal to the value of the property in which his interest subsisted'. Until now this value has been determined as a rateable proportion of the aggregate value of that settled property and other property of a similar kind in the person's estate. The Board now take the view that, in these circumstances, the settled property in which the interest subsisted should be valued *in isolation* without reference to any similar property.

These statements of the Board's position are made without prejudice to the application in an appropriate case of the *Ramsay* principle or the provisions of the *Inheritance Tax Act 1984* relating to associated operations. The changes of view will be applied to all new cases and to existing cases where the tax liability has not been settled. The operation of the legislation will be kept under review.

16 MARCH 1993, INLAND REVENUE STATEMENT OF PRACTICE SP 4/93
Deceased persons' estates: discretionary interests in residue

ITTOIA 2005, ss 650(3), (4), (6), 655(1), 662 provide for discretionary payments out of the income of the residue of an estate of a deceased person, whether made directly by the personal representatives, or indirectly through a trustee or other person, to be treated as the income of the recipient for the year in which they are paid.

HMRC will apply *ITTOIA 2005 ss 650(3), (4), (6), 655(1), 662* whenever such discretionary payments are made, whether they are payments out of income of the residue as it arises or out of income arising to the personal representatives in earlier years, which has been retained pending the exercise of their discretion.

Where payments are made out of income of the residue of UK estates (as defined in *ITTOIA 2005 ss 651(1)-(3)*) they are treated for 1993–94 and later years as received after deduction of tax at the applicable rate (as defined in *ITTOIA 2005, ss 663, 679(2), (3)*).

Recipients who are not liable to income tax on the payments, including charities, are entitled to claim repayment of this tax except where the basic amount is paid from sums within *ITTOIA 2005, s 680*.

Where payments are made indirectly through trustees, the trustees may be liable to tax at the rate applicable to trusts on the payments under *TA 1988, s 686*. Beneficiaries may be treated as receiving the payments after deduction of tax at the rate applicable to trusts. This tax may be repaid or further tax charged, depending on the beneficiary's marginal rate. The trustees are not chargeable to income tax at the rate applicable to trusts, where a trust is established for charitable purposes only.

With effect from 16 March 1993 HMRC will apply *ITTOIA 2005 ss 650(3), (4), (6), 655(1), 662* in this way to all open cases whether this results in repayment of tax or an assessment to income tax at the higher rate. Claims for repayment of tax may also be made for years from 1986–87 onwards, including supplementary claims where an earlier claim was refused under previous practice.

For all payments made before 6 April 2005, the relevant provisions of *TA 1988 Part XVI* apply, and after 6 April 2005, where a company is the beneficiary of a deceased estate, the provisions of *Part XVI* continue to apply for discretionary payments to the company out of the income of the residue.

Note – The text of this statement was revised in August 2005.

6 APRIL 2004, INLAND REVENUE STATEMENT OF PRACTICE SP 2/04

Allowable expenditure: Expenses incurred by personal representatives and corporate trustees

A new Statement of Practice, SP 2/04, replaces SP 8/94 in relation to certain expenses incurred by the personal representatives of deceased persons where the death in question occurred on or after 6th April 2004, and to expenses incurred by corporate trustees in making transfers and disposals on or after 6th April 2004. The text of SP 2/04 is reproduced below.

Both Statements of Practice set out standard scales of allowable expenses which may be used for certain purposes of the Taxation of Chargeable Gains Act (TCGA) 1992 in place of the actual allowable expenditure incurred.

The main changes introduced by SP 2/04 are:

(i) an increase in the monetary values set out in the scales broadly in line with the increase in the Retail Price Index since 1994, and
(ii) the introduction of two new higher bands to cover larger estates.

In addition, there are some minor changes in wording to improve the clarity of the text.

EXPENSES INCURRED BY PERSONAL REPRESENTATIVES

1 Following consultation with representative bodies, the scale of expenses allowable under *TCGA 1992, s 38(1)(b)*, for the costs of establishing title in computing the gains or losses of personal representatives on the sale of assets comprised in a deceased person's estate, has been revised. The Commissioners for HMRC will accept computations based either on this scale or on the actual allowable expenditure incurred.

2 The revised scale is as follows—

Gross value of estate	*Allowable expenditure*
A. Not exceeding £50,000	1.8% of the probate value of the assets sold by the personal representatives.
B. Over £50,000 but not exceeding £90,000	A fixed amount of £900, to be divided between all the assets of the estate in proportion to the probate values and allowed in those proportions on assets sold by the personal representatives.
C. Over £90,000 but not exceeding £400,000	1% of the probate value of the assets sold.
D. Over £400,000 but not exceeding £500,000	A fixed amount of £4,000, to be divided as at B above.
E. Over £500,000 but not exceeding £1,000,000	0.8% of the probate value of the assets sold.
F. Over £1,000,000 but not exceeding £5,000,000	A fixed amount of £8,000, to be divided as at B above.
G Over £5,000,000	0.16 per cent of the probate value of the assets sold, subject to a maximum of £10,000.

3 The revised scale takes effect where the death in question occurred on or after 6th April 2004.

EXPENSES INCURRED BY CORPORATE TRUSTEES

4 Following consultation with representative bodies, HMRC have agreed the following scale of allowable expenditure under *TCGA 1992, ss 38 and 64(1)*, for expenses incurred by corporate trustees in the administration of estates and trusts. The Commissioners for HMRC will accept computations based either on this scale or on the actual allowable expenditure incurred.

5 The scale is as follows—

Transfers of assets to beneficiaries etc

(i) Publicly marketed shares and securities
    (A) One beneficiary—£25 per holding transferred.
    (B) Two or more beneficiaries between whom a holding must be divided— As (A), to be divided in equal shares between between the beneficiaries.
(ii) Other shares and securities—As (i) above, with the addition of any exceptional expenditure
(iii) Other assets—As (i) above, with the addition of any exceptional expenditure

For the purpose of this statement of practice, shares and securities are regarded as marketed to the general public if buying and selling prices for them are regularly published in the financial pages of a national or regional newspaper, magazine, or other journal.

Actual disposals and acquisitions

(i) Publicly marketed shares and securities—The investment fee as charged by the trustees,
(ii) Other shares and securities—As (i) above, plus actual valuation costs
(iii) Other assets—the investment fee as charged by the trustees, subject to a maximum of £75, plus actual valuation costs

Where a comprehensive annual management fee is charged, covering both the cost of administering the trust and the expenses of actual disposals and acquisitions, the investment fee for the purposes of (i), (ii) and (iii) above will be taken to be £0.25 per £100 on the sale or purchase moneys.

Deemed disposals by trustees

(i) Publicly marketed shares and securities—£8 per holding disposed of
(ii) Other shares and securities—Actual valuation costs
(iii) Other assets—Actual valuation costs

6 This scale takes effect for transfers of assets to beneficiaries, actual disposals and acquisitions, and deemed disposals by corporate trustees on or after 6th April 2004.

JUNE 2006, THE HASTINGS-BASS PRINCIPLE HMRC'S CURRENT VIEWS (HMRC TAX BULLETIN, ISSUE 83, JUNE 2006 PP 2–4)

The purpose of this article is to give an indication of HMRC's current views on some aspects of the so-called 'Hastings-Bass' principle. The principle has been applied in the context of trusts where a trustee is given a discretion as to some matter, on which he acts, but where the purported exercise of his discretion has unintended consequences.

Traditionally the courts have been reluctant to interfere in the exercise of a trustee's discretion but there is now a growing line of authority revealing the emergence of a principle whereby a court, in certain circumstances, will or may intervene. It is a principle that has been developed by the courts in England & Wales, and has been applied by the Royal Court in Jersey, although it seems that there is no equivalent principle in Scotland.

The name of the principle comes from the case of *Re Hastings-Bass deceased* [1975] Ch 25 (*'Hastings-Bass'*). In that case the Court of Appeal upheld the validity of an exercise by trustees of the statutory power of advancement, save to the extent that it was necessarily void for perpetuity, on the basis that the court should not interfere where a trustee is given a discretion as to some matter in which he acts in good faith, notwithstanding that his action does not have the full effect which he intended, unless it is clear that he would not have acted as he did

— had he not taken into account considerations which he should not have taken into account or

— had he not failed to take into account considerations which he ought to have taken into account.

The second limb of the principle was purportedly reformulated into a more readily understood, positive version by Warner J in *Mettoy Pension Trustees Ltd v Evans* [1990] 1 WLR 1587 (*'Mettoy'*) at 1621A–H as follows:

> Where a trustee acts under a discretion given to him under the terms of the trust, the court will interfere with his action if it is clear that he would not have acted as he did had he not failed to take into account considerations which he ought to have taken into account.

This reformulation in fact involved a substantial leap from the original formulation of the principle in *Hastings-Bass* itself, for two reasons. First, the word 'will' apparently denotes an obligation on the court to intervene whenever the stated conditions are satisfied. Secondly, the negative proposition that the court should not interfere unless certain conditions are fulfilled is not logically equivalent to the much wider positive proposition that the court should, or even may, interfere if those conditions are fulfilled. Nevertheless, after reviewing a number of authorities Warner J concluded in *Mettoy* that there was a principle in the positive form stated above which was separate both from the equitable remedy of rectification and from the jurisdiction of the court to set aside a written instrument for mistake.

Over the past few years there has been an increase of interest in and reliance on the principle, which has resulted in a number of decided cases at first instance, including *Abacus Trust Co Ltd v National Society for the Prevention of Cruelty to Children* [2001] STC 1344 (*'Abacus v NSPCC'*); *Breadner v Granville-Grossman* [2001] Ch 523; *Abacus Trust Co Ltd v Barr* [2003] Ch 409 (*'Abacus v Barr'*); *Burrell v Burrell* [2005] STC 569 and *Sieff v Fox* [2005] 1 WLR 3811 (*'Sieff v Fox'*) which contains a detailed and valuable review of the case law by Lloyd LJ. Apart from case law, the emerging principle has also generated a great deal of discussion and commentary by academics and practitioners alike.

An interesting, but perhaps not surprising, feature of the majority of these cases is that the unintended consequence of the mistake by the trustees was a liability to tax. For this reason HMRC have been interested in this area of the law, as it develops and is shaped by the courts. In recent years it has been the usual practice of HMRC to decline invitations to be joined as a party in cases where the court is being asked to set aside a transaction in reliance on the principle. However, in *Sieff v Fox* Lloyd LJ observed in paragraph 83 that the court's task might be easier in some cases if HMRC did not always decline the invitation to take part in cases of this kind. In the light of that observation, and our increasing concern (which is shared by many commentators) that the principle as currently formulated is too wide in its scope, HMRC will now give active consideration to participating in future cases where large amounts of tax are at stake and/or where it is felt that we could make a useful contribution to the elucidation and development of the principle. We will be particularly ready to intervene in cases where there would otherwise be no party in whose interest it would be to argue against the application of the principle.

It would be beyond the scope of this article to discuss the issues which arise in any depth, and HMRC must in any event reserve the right to advance whatever arguments appear to us appropriate in the circumstances of any given case. Subject to that caveat, however, we would make the following points in order to give an indication of our present thinking on some of the main questions which arise.

(1) In the first place, it should be noted that the principle in its present form has little or nothing to do with the type of situation which was considered by the Court of Appeal in *Hastings-Bass* itself, and that it owes its origin to the logically flawed positive reformulation of the principle in *Mettoy*. We consider that any positive formulation of the principle should state merely that the court 'may' interfere with the trustee's action, not that it 'will' do so.

(2) Secondly, and allied to point (1) above, we consider that the effect of the principle, if it applies at all, should be to make the relevant decision by the trustee voidable and not void, or at the very least should permit the court to take into account the same sort of equitable considerations that apply when it is deciding whether to grant other forms of equitable relief.

(3) Thirdly, we would tentatively suggest that the principle, as it develops, should as far as possible be assimilated with the general principles of law by reference to which (a) the exercise of a discretion by trustees may be impugned (as to which see the decision of the Court of Appeal in *Edge v Pensions Ombudsman* [2000] Ch 602, especially at 627–30 and 633), and (b) the courts will set aside voluntary transactions or written instruments for mistake. It may be the case that, properly understood, there is no room or need for a separate *Hastings-Bass* principle at all.

(4) Fourthly, in cases where the trustee acts under a discretion and is not obliged to act, we would agree with the view expressed by Lloyd LJ in *Sieff v Fox*, that the relevant test is whether the trustee 'would' have acted differently if the correct considerations had been taken into account, not whether the trustee 'might' have acted differently.

(5) Fifthly, while accepting that fiscal consequences are generally amongst the matters which a trustee should take into account when deciding how to act, we consider that a distinction needs to be drawn between cases where the trustee fails to take relevant fiscal considerations into account at all, and cases where the trustee takes steps to obtain fiscal advice but that advice turns out (for whatever reason) to be wrong. While there may be scope for the principle to apply in cases of the former type, it is felt that in cases of the latter type (which include *Sieff v Fox*) the principle should not apply.

(6) Similarly, in cases where the trustee obtains advice about the tax consequences of a proposed transaction, but then fails to implement the transaction in accordance with that advice (as in *Abacus v National Society for the Prevention of Cruelty to Children*), it is also felt that the principle should not apply. A common feature of cases like *Sieff v Fox* and *Abacus v National Society for the Prevention of Cruelty to Children* is that the trustee has sought appropriate tax advice, and in reliance on it has deliberately taken certain steps which in trust terms achieve precisely the effect which they were intended to achieve. Why then should the trustee be entitled to have the transaction set aside, in a way that would not be open to an individual taxpayer, merely because the advice which he obtained was incorrect, or because he negligently failed to follow the advice correctly? In such cases, it is suggested, the court should not interfere, tax should be paid on the basis of the transaction actually carried out, and the trust should be left to pursue whatever remedies it may have against the trustee and/or the trustee's professional advisers.

(7) Finally, despite what was said by Lightman J in *Abacus v Barr*, we are inclined to agree with Lloyd LJ in *Sieff v Fox* that a breach of duty by the trustee or the trustee's agent or advisers is not in itself a separate requirement that has to be satisfied if the principle is to apply.

In the remainder of this article, some brief comments will be made on various practical issues which have arisen from time to time.

In some instances HMRC have been asked to consent to a reversal of the tax consequences of a particular trustee decision without an order of the court, on the basis that the principle in *Hastings-Bass* applies, to save the parties the trouble and expense of going to court.

We have generally maintained that we require an order of the court before we will review the tax consequences of a decision on the basis of the *Hastings-Bass* principle, and this remains the basic position. The nature and parameters of the *Hastings-Bass* principle are still unclear in many respects and although this is something that we will consider in the context of each case as it arises, it is felt that we would not generally be entitled to agree to unwind a decision, even if we were minded to do so. Crucially, it remains to be clarified by a higher court whether the effect of an application of the principle is to make a decision void or voidable. If the decision is voidable, the question of whether it should be avoided is one for the court and cannot be resolved by consent between the parties.

At other times we have been asked to determine the tax consequences of obtaining an order, while parties consider whether or not to apply to the court. We have generally declined to do this, on the basis that the court may have a wide discretion as to the terms upon which it makes any order. Facts and circumstances in cases susceptible to consideration under the principle vary considerably and these variations may well affect the approach of the court and, in consequence, the tax treatment.

Finally, in a number of cases we have been invited to join the proceedings themselves. Some parties have complained of hardship where we have insisted on a court order before we will review the tax consequences, particularly where the parties are themselves agreed that the decision should be set aside. However, we do not consider that our insistence on a court order leads necessarily to the conclusion that we ought to be joined as parties to those proceedings, although as we have said above it is now likely that there will be cases in the future where HMRC would wish to be joined or to intervene in order to resist an application of the principle in a particular case, or to seek to influence the development of the principle in a particular direction.

This article sets out HMRC's current position on the principle in Hastings-Bass and seeks to give an indication of the type of stance we might take should we become involved in a case in the future. We are not, however, limiting ourselves to these arguments. Clearly this is a developing area of the law, certain aspects of which will require clarification by the higher courts in due course. As things evolve we will keep the principle, and our policies, under review but it is hoped that this article will assist taxpayers and practitioners in the meantime.

Appendix B

Extra-statutory Concessions

B 18 PAYMENTS OUT OF DISCRETIONARY TRUSTS (AS AMENDED BY INLAND REVENUE PRESS RELEASE ON 1 APRIL 1999)

UK RESIDENT TRUSTS

A beneficiary may receive from trustees a payment to which *TA 1988, s 687(2)* applies. Where that payment is made out of the income of the trustees in respect of which, had it been received directly, the beneficiary would have been entitled to exemption in respect of FOTRA Securities issued in accordance with *FA 1996, s 154*; or have been entitled to relief under the terms of a double taxation agreement; or not have been chargeable to UK tax because of their not resident and/or not ordinarily resident status the beneficiary may claim that exemption or relief or, where the beneficiary would not have been chargeable, repayment of the tax treated as deducted from the payment (or an appropriate proportion of it). For this purpose, the payment will be treated as having been made rateably out of all sources of income arising to the trustees on a last-in, first-out basis.

Relief or exemption, as appropriate, will be granted to the extent that the payment is out of income which arose to the trustees not earlier than six years before the end of the year of assessment in which the payment was made, provided the trustees—

— have made trust returns giving details of all sources of trust income and payments made to beneficiaries for each and every year for which they are required, and have paid all tax due, and any interest, surcharges and penalties arising, and
— keep available for inspection any relevant tax certificates.

Relief or exemption, as appropriate, will be granted to the beneficiary on a claim made within five years and ten months of the end of the year of assessment in which the beneficiary received the payment from the trustees.

NON-UK RESIDENT TRUSTS

A similar concession will operate where a beneficiary receives a payment from discretionary trustees which is not within *TA 1988, s 687(2)* (ie where non-UK resident trustees exercise their discretion outside the UK).

Where a non-UK resident beneficiary receives such a payment out of income of the trustees in respect of which, had it been received directly, it would have been chargeable to UK tax, then the beneficiary may claim relief under *TA 1988, s 278* (personal reliefs for certain non-UK residents); and may be treated as receiving that payment from a UK resident trust but claim credit only for UK tax actually paid by the trustees on income out of which the payment is made.

The beneficiary may also claim exemption from tax in respect of FOTRA securities issued in accordance with *FA 1996, s 154* to the extent that the payment is regarded as including interest from such securities.

B 18 Payments out of discretionary trusts

A UK beneficiary of a non-UK resident trust may claim appropriate credit for tax actually paid by the trustees on the income out of which the payment is made as if the payments out of UK income were from a UK resident trust and within *TA 1988, s 687(1)*.

This treatment will only be available where the trustees—

— have made trust returns giving details of all sources of trust income and payments made to beneficiaries for each and every year for which they are required, and
— have paid all tax due and any interest, surcharges and penalties arising, and
— keep available for inspection any relevant tax certificates.

Relief or exemption, as appropriate, will be granted to the beneficiary on a claim made within five years and ten months of the end of the year of assessment in which the beneficiary received the payment from the trustees.

No credit will be given for UK tax treated as paid on income received by the trustees which would not be available for set off under *TA 1988, s 687(2)* if that section applied, and that tax is not repayable (for example on dividends). However, such tax is not taken into account in calculating the gross income treated as taxable on the beneficiary under this concession.

D2 RESIDENCE IN THE UK: YEAR OF COMMENCEMENT OR CESSATION OF RESIDENCE – CAPITAL GAINS TAX

1. An individual who comes to live in the UK and is treated as resident here for any year of assessment from the date of arrival is charged to capital gains tax only in respect of chargeable gains from disposals made after arrival, provided that the individual has not been resident or ordinarily resident in the UK at any time during the five years of assessment immediately preceding the year of assessment in which he or she arrived in the UK.

2. An individual who leaves the UK and is treated on departure as not resident and not ordinarily resident here is not charged to capital gains tax on gains from disposals made after the date of departure, provided that the individual was not resident and not ordinarily resident in the UK for the whole of at least four out of the seven years of assessment immediately preceding the year of assessment in which he or she left the UK.

3. This concession does not apply to any individual in relation to gains on the disposal of assets which are situated in the UK and which, at any time between the individual's departure from the UK and the end of the year of assessment, are either –

(i) used in or for the purposes of a trade, profession or vocation carried on by that individual in the UK through a branch or agency; or
(ii) used or held for, or acquired for use by or for the purposes of, such a branch or agency.

4. This concession does not apply to the trustees of a settlement who commence or cease residence in the UK or to a settlor of a settlement in relation to gains in respect of which the settlor is chargeable under TCGA 1992 ss 77-79, or TCGA 1992 s 86, Sch 5.

5. This revised concession applies to any individual who ceases to be resident or ordinarily resident in the UK on or after 17 March 1998, or becomes resident or ordinarily resident in the UK on or after 6 April 1998.

F8 ACCUMULATION AND MAINTENANCE SETTLEMENTS

The requirement of *section 71(1)(a)* of the *IHTA 1984* is regarded as being satisfied even if no age is specified in the trust instrument, provided that it is clear that a beneficiary will in fact become entitled to the settled property (or to an interest in possession in it) by the age of 25.

Appendix C

Checking Liabilities and the Tax Pool etc in 2015/16

Basic data

The settlement was made in May 1997 for the benefit of such of the settlor's grandchildren as might attain the age of 25 (and if more than one in equal shares absolutely). The settlor has made only one settlement.

The grandchildren are:

	Date of Birth	Age in 2015/16
Alice	6 April 1989	26
Belinda	6 April 1997	18
Cathy	6 April 1998	17

The *Trustee Act 1925*, s 31 applies. This is not considered to be good drafting. As a result each presumptive share is within the accumulation and maintenance regime until income vests at age 18. Alice is entitled to her third of the capital. However, one of the assets is a property which still has to be sold and accordingly no distributions have been made so far.

This settlement had the benefit of the accumulation and maintenance regime. As at 6 April 2008 such assets as remained within the trust became subject to the relevant property regime for inheritance tax purposes. This did not include Alice's one third share in the capital mentioned above. However, for income tax purposes this change of status had no effect. So as far as Alice and Belinda are concerned, the one third share of income is hers by right. Indeed, Alice is also beneficially entitled to the shares in UK companies producing the dividends and the building society account, though not the property producing the rent because there the beneficiaries as a whole are not entitled as against the trustees. This distinction does not have any effect for income tax purposes. The other one third share of the income remains within the discretionary regime. The only distinction between Alice and Belinda is that, as noted below, there is no deduction for trust management expenses in calculating Alice's income.

In 2015/16, the trustees received:

	£
UK dividends (net)	4,500
Building society interest (net)	450
Rent (gross)	3,000
	7,950

Basic data

They paid:

	£
Professional fees for 2014/15 (chargeable against income)	940
overdraft interest	100
interest on overdue tax	20
bank charges	50
tax – as assessed to each of the beneficiaries £600 in December 2015.	1,800

In July 2016, they paid fees for 2015/16 amounting to £1,175. The rent of £3,000 was a pure profit rental.

Trustees' self assessment

On pages 4 and 5 of the return, the trustees will report:

	Gross	Tax	Net
Building society interest	563	113	450
UK dividends	5,000	500	4,500
			£4,950

The rent will be reported on the supplementary page for income from land and property.

On page 7:

(1) Alice's and Belinda's interests will be mentioned at Q.13.
(2) The total management expenses will be noted as £1,345 at Q.13.19. This comprises:

Professional fees	1,175
Overdraft interest	100
interest on tax	20
bank charges	50
	£1,345

This is in accordance with the Guide, on page 22. That tells us to deduct the expenses paid out of the income of the year. The fees were accrued at 5 April 2016 and so were paid out of 2015/16 income.

On page 8 the payment of £600 to Cathy, which was discretionary, will be reported at Q.14.

Income of the three beneficiaries

Because Alice is absolutely entitled there will be no deduction for expenses in calculating her income. There is the option for the trustees to self assess even in respect of a bare trust (see **2.43**). This they do. Expenses will be deducted from Belinda's income, however.

Alice's voucher will be based on:

	Net
10% income	1,500
20% income	950
Net share	£2,450

Belinda's income is found as follows:

Net dividends	4,500	10% income
Net interest	450	20% income
Net rent	2,400	20% income
	7,350	
Expenses	(1,345)	
Net income	£6,005	
One-third share	£2,002	

The expenses of £448 are set against the dividend income.

Therefore Belinda has:

10% income	1,052 net
20% income	950 net

and her tax voucher will be prepared accordingly.

Cathy's (only) income is the £600 paid out at Christmas and this will go on her tax voucher as:

Gross	1090.90
Tax	(490.90) (@ = 45%)
Net	£600.00

Trustees' tax liabilities

The trustees no longer have discretion over the payments to Alice and Belinda. The trustees are, therefore, liable for tax under *ITA 2007, s 479* on only one-third of the income (after expenses).

Basic data

	10%	20%
Dividends and tax credits	5,000	
Building society interest		563
Rent		3,000
2/3 children over 18	(3,333)	(2,375)
	1,667	1,188
Expenses (1,345 × 1/3 × 100/90)	(498)	(0000)
	1,169	1,188
Tax due at savings rate/ basic rate		
5,000 × 10%	500	
3,563 × 20%		712.60
Credit/paid	(500)	(112.60)
Tax payable	0	600.00

In calculating the tax pool, the only tax to be added is tax at 30.56% on one-third of the net dividends and tax charged on one-third of the other income (including that income falling within the standard rate band). The standard rate band of £1,000 covers the interest income and £812 of the rental income.

Tax at special rates
1,169 × 37.5%   438.38

188 × 45%   84.60
Less tax at savings rate /basic rate
1,169 × 10%   (116.90)

188 × 20%   (37.60)
                                 321.48   47.00

Tax at basic rate payable by trustees = £712.60 - £112.60= £600.00
Tax at special rates = £321.48 + £47.00 = £368.48
Addition to tax pool = £368.48 + £712.60 − £475.06 = £606.02

Tax pool brought forward	£2,312.22
Addition 2015/16	£606.02
	£2,918.24
Less vouched to Cathy	(490.90)
Balance 5 April 2016 ('tax pool surplus')	£2,427.34

Notes:

(1) This Schedule is not an illustration of the calculations on the form for calculating tax. It is simply a convenient check on the figures which HMRC produce, coupled with detailed workings (as for instance, Alice's income) which should be kept on file. If you are using the HMRC calculator after the end of the tax year, you should carry forward the tax pool surplus shown to the next tax year (assuming that the figures entered on the calculator match those you put on the SA900 Trust and Estate Tax Return). You should show the tax pool surplus figure on the SA900 Trust and Estate Tax Return for the following tax year at box 14.15. HMRC's tax pool calculator can also be used in-year to help trustees plan distributions to beneficiaries.

(2) Note that the 20% income has to be kept separate from the dividend income where the 10% tax is *notional*. Note the order of set off which takes the expenses from the least worthwhile income.

Appendix D

Trustee Act 1925, ss 31–33

TRUSTEE ACT 1925, SS 31–33

Some of those changes apply to all trusts whenever created – for practitioners familiar with the earlier versions, these are highlighted in **bold** below. Other changes apply only to trusts created on or after that date, or other interests under a trust resulting from powers exercised on or after that date. Text applying only to such trusts/interests is underlined below. The text applying to older trusts/interests is included in italics and within brackets in the following form: [* . . . . *]. In fact, there are only three such changes of note:

- In clause 31(1)(i) the words '*as may, in all the circumstances, be reasonable*' is replaced by 'as the trustees may think fit';
- The proviso at the end of clause 31(1) is removed; and
- In clause 32(1)(a), the words '*one-half of*' are removed.

Section 31: Power to apply income for maintenance and to accumulate surplus income during a minority
(1) Where any property is held by trustees in trust for any person for any interest whatsoever, whether vested or contingent, then, subject to any prior interests or charges affecting that property—
    (i)   during the infancy of any such person, if his interest so long continues, the trustees may, at their sole discretion, pay to his parent or guardian, if any, or otherwise apply for or towards his maintenance, education, or benefit, the whole or such part, if any, of the income of that property as the trustees may think fit [*as may, in all the circumstances, be reasonable* *] , whether or not there is—
        (a)   any other fund applicable to the same purpose; or
        (b)   any person bound by law to provide for his maintenance or education; and
    (ii)   if such person on attaining the age of [eighteen years] has not a vested interest in such income, the trustees shall thenceforth pay the income of that property and of any accretion thereto under subsection (2) of this section to him, until he either attains a vested interest therein or dies, or until failure of his interest:
[**Provided that, in deciding whether the whole or any part of the income of the property is during a minority to be paid or applied for the purposes aforesaid, the trustees shall have regard to the age of the infant and his requirements and generally to the circumstances of the case, and in particular to what other income, if any, is applicable for the same purposes; and where trustees have notice that the income of more than one fund is applicable for those purposes, then, so far as practicable, unless the entire income of the funds is paid or applied as aforesaid or the court otherwise directs, a proportionate part only of the income of each fund shall be so paid or applied.* *]

(2) During the infancy of any such person, if his interest so long continues, the trustees shall accumulate all the residue of that income by investing it, and any profits from so investing it from time to time in authorised investments, and shall hold those accumulations as follows:—

    (i)   If any such person—

        (a)   attains the age of eighteen years, or marries under that age or forms a civil partnership under that age, and his interest in such income during his infancy, or until his marriage or his formation of a civil partnership, is a vested interest; or

        (b)   on attaining the age of eighteen years or on marriage, or formation of a civil partnership, under that age becomes entitled to the property from which such income arose in fee simple, absolute or determinable, or absolutely, or for an entailed interest;

the trustees shall hold the accumulations in trust for such person absolutely, but without prejudice to any provision with respect thereto contained in any settlement by him made under any statutory powers during his infancy, and so that the receipt of such person after marriage [or formation of a civil partnership], and though still an infant, shall be a good discharge; and

    (ii)   In any other case the trustees shall, notwithstanding that such person had a vested interest in such income, hold the accumulations as an accretion to the capital of the property from which such accumulations arose, and as one fund with such capital for all purposes, and so that, if such property is settled land, such accumulations shall be held upon the same trusts as if the same were capital money arising therefrom;

but the trustees may, at any time during the infancy of such person if his interest so long continues, apply those accumulations, or any part thereof, as if they were income arising in the then current year.

(3) This section applies in the case of a contingent interest only if the limitation or trust carries the intermediate income of the property, but it applies to a future or contingent legacy by the parent of, or a person standing in loco parentis to, the legatee, if and for such period as, under the general law, the legacy carries interest for the maintenance of the legatee, and in any such case as last aforesaid the rate of interest shall (if the income available is sufficient, and subject to any rules of court to the contrary) be five pounds per centum per annum.

(4) This section applies to a vested annuity in like manner as if the annuity were the income of property held by trustees in trust to pay the income thereof to the annuitant for the same period for which the annuity is payable, save that in any case accumulations made during the infancy of the annuitant shall be held in trust for the annuitant or his personal representatives absolutely.

(5) This section does not apply where the instrument, if any, under which the interest arises came into operation before the commencement of this Act.

Section 32: Power of advancement

(1) Trustees may at any time or times pay or apply any capital money subject to a trust,**or transfer or apply any other property forming part of the capital of the trust property** for the advancement or benefit, in such manner as they may, in their absolute discretion, think fit, of any person entitled to the capital of the trust property or of any share thereof, whether absolutely or contingently on his attaining any specified age or on the occurrence of any other event, or subject to a gift over on his death under any specified age or on the occurrence of any other event, and whether in possession or in remainder or reversion, and such payment **transfer** or application may be made notwithstanding that the interest of such person is liable to be defeated by the exercise of a power of appointment or revocation, or to be diminished by the increase of the class to which he belongs:

Provided that—
- (a) property (including any money) so paid, transferred or applied for the advancement or benefit of any person must not, altogether, represent more than [*one-half of*] the presumptive or vested share or interest of that person in the trust property; and
- (b) if that person is or becomes absolutely and indefeasibly entitled to a share in the trust property **the money or other property so paid, transferred or applied** shall be brought into account as part of such share; and
- (c) no such payment, **transfer** or application shall be made so as to prejudice any person entitled to any prior life or other interest, whether vested or contingent, in the money **or other property paid, transferred** or applied unless such person is in existence and of full age and consents in writing to such payment, **transfer** or application.

(1A) In exercise of the foregoing power trustees may pay, transfer or apply money or other property on the basis (express or implied) that it shall be treated as a proportionate part of the capital out of which it was paid, transferred or applied, for the purpose of bringing it into account in accordance with proviso (b) to subsection (1) of this section.

(2) This section does not apply to capital money arising under the Settled Land Act 1925.

(3) This section does not apply to trusts constituted or created before the commencement of this Act.

Section 33: Protective trusts

(1) Where any income, including an annuity or other periodical income payment, is directed to be held on protective trusts for the benefit of any person (in this section called "the principal beneficiary") for the period of his life or for any less period, then, during that period (in this section called the "trust period") the said income shall, without prejudice to any prior interest, be held on the following trusts, namely:—
- (i) Upon trust for the principal beneficiary during the trust period or until he, whether before or after the termination of any prior interest, does or attempts to do or suffers any act or thing, or until any event happens, other than an advance under any statutory or express power, whereby, if the said income were payable during the trust period to the principal beneficiary absolutely during that period, he would be deprived of the right to receive the same or any part thereof, in any of which cases, as well as on the termination of the trust period, whichever first happens, this trust of the said income shall fail or determine;
- (ii) If the trust aforesaid fails or determines during the subsistence of the trust period, then, during the residue of that period, the said income shall be held upon trust for the application thereof for the maintenance or support, or otherwise for the benefit, of all or any one or more exclusively of the other or others of the following persons (that is to say)—
  - (a) the principal beneficiary and his or her [spouse or civil partner], if any, and his or her children or more remote issue, if any; or
  - (b) if there is no [spouse or civil partner] or issue of the principal beneficiary in existence, the principal beneficiary and the persons who would, if he were actually dead, be entitled to the trust property or the income thereof or to the annuity fund, if any, or arrears of the annuity, as the case may be;

as the trustees in their absolute discretion, without being liable to account for the exercise of such discretion, think fit.

(2) This section does not apply to trusts coming into operation before the commencement of this Act, and has effect subject to any variation of the implied trusts aforesaid contained in the instrument creating the trust.

(3) Nothing in this section operates to validate any trust which would, if contained in the instrument creating the trust, be liable to be set aside.

(4) In relation to the dispositions mentioned in section 19(1) of the Family Law Reform Act 1987, this section shall have effect as if any reference (however expressed) to any relationship between two persons were construed in accordance with section 1 of that Act.

[NB The *Trustee Act 1925* does not override the provisions of the trust instrument. It applies only to the extent that it is not excluded by the trust instrument. It has no application in Scotland.]

Appendix E

Questions by STEP/CIOT and answers from HMRC to FA 2006, Sch 20 (revised October 2008)

Index of questions and answers

Section A   Questions 1 – 10: transitional serial interests

Section B   Questions 11 – 13: administration of estates

Section C   Questions 14 – 18: immediate post death interests

Section D   Questions 19 – 32: bereaved minors trusts; 18–25 trusts, section 71A trusts

Section E   Questions 33 – 35: absolute interests, bare trusts, *Crowe v Appleby*

Section F   Question 36: disabled trusts

Section G   Questions 37 – 39: general points – additions and annuities

Section H   Questions 40 – 43 deeds of variation; section 54A

FA 2006 Sch 20: pre-existing interests in possession and related matters

Guidance on S71a, S71d and Accumulation and Maintenance Trusts

Trusts: Schedule 20 – SP 10/79 and Transitional Serial Interests

A.

Transitional serial interests (TSI)

(1)   Condition 1 contains the requirement that 'immediately before 22 March 2006, the property then comprised in the settlement was property in which B, or some other person, was beneficially entitled to an interest in possession ('the prior interest').

(2)   Can it be confirmed that this requirement will be satisfied where B, or some other person, has a beneficial interest in possession in some of the property then comprised in the settlement but not all the property so comprised.

Section A

Example 1

Under a trust there are two funds. In Fund A, Mr Smith has an interest in possession. In Fund B, Mr Jones has an interest in possession.

Question 1

Will Condition 1 be satisfied separately in relation to Fund A and/or Fund B?

HMRC Answer

We can confirm that condition 1 can be satisfied separately in relation to both funds. The new s.49C starts from the point of the view of the "current interest" – a beneficial interest in settled property. Given the wide definition of that term in s.43 IHTA, it seems that the beneficial IIP referred to in s.49C(1) can quite easily be in a fund or in property that was previously part of a larger disposition or settlement – and there is nothing to suggest that there must have been a single beneficiary.

Moreover, there is no requirement that the settlement must have been wholly IIP in nature (question 2 below) or that it must have come to an end in its entirety (question 3).

If one can then accept that the property referred to in s.49C(1) is also the property referred to in s.49C(2), and in which the "prior interest" (s.49C(2) & (3)) existed, the concerns raised in questions 1 to 4 fall away.

Question 2

Can it be confirmed that Condition 1 will be satisfied in relation to Fund A where Fund B is held not on trusts giving Mr Jones an interest in possession but on discretionary trusts? There is nothing in the wording of *section 49C* to suggest that the pre-Budget interest in possession must subsist in the entire fund.

HMRC Answer

We agree.

(3)   *Section 49C(3)* provides that Condition 2 requires the prior interest to come to an end at a time on or after 22 March 2006 but before 6 April 2008.

Question 3

Will Condition 2 be satisfied where the prior interest comes to an end in that period in part only of the settled property in which that interest subsists?

HMRC Answer

Yes – see the response to question 1 above.

Example 2

In the example given above, if Mr Smith's interest in possession in Fund A comes to an end in 60% of Fund A and is replaced by an interest in possession in favour of Mr Smith's daughter, but Mr Smith's interest in possession continues in relation to the remaining 40% of Fund A, can it be confirmed that the interest in possession in favour of the daughter will be a transitional serial interest?

HMRC Answer

We can confirm this – for the reasons given immediately below.

While it has been suggested that Condition 2 requires that the prior interest comes to an end in all the property in which the interest subsists, Condition 2 does not state this and given the definition of current interest it appears that Condition 2 must be construed as referring to the prior interest coming to an end in the settled property concerned in which B takes a current interest but not necessarily in all the settled property of a particular settlement. The 'current interest' is merely defined as an interest in possession in settled property and does not in any way require all the settled property comprised in the settlement to be a current interest.

Question 4

Please also confirm that the remaining 40% of Fund A continues to satisfy Condition 1 so that a transitional serial interest could be created in that 40% prior to 6th April 2008.

HMRC Answer

We can confirm this.

Question 5(1)

Please also confirm that in the above example if 40% of Mr Smith's pre-Budget interest in possession is ended as to half for his daughter and half for his son, both son and daughter take transitional serial interests in their respective shares.

HMRC Answer

We can confirm this.

Question 5(2)

If later the trustees wished to appropriate assets between the two funds for son and daughter and the assets were of the same value as the assets previously contained in each fund, do HMRC accept that such appropriation does not represent the termination of any qualifying interest in possession and therefore does not result in an inheritance tax charge?

HMRC Answer

We agree.

(4) We would be grateful for your views on the circumstances in which the prior interest would be considered to have come to an end and have been replaced by a current interest. This is relevant because if a prior interest is considered to have come to an end and have been replaced by a current interest (in favour of the same beneficiary) there will be no possibility of the interest being replaced by a transitional serial interest

later and the point is particularly important in relation to spousal relief because spouse exemption will not be available if a spouse of a life tenant who already has a transitional serial interest takes an interest in possession on the death of that life tenant.

Example 3

Under a pre-Budget 2006 trust a beneficiary A is entitled to the capital contingently on attaining the age of 30 years. A was 21 on 22 March 2006 and had been entitled to an interest in possession under *TA 1925 s 31* from the age of 18. The interest is therefore an interest in possession which subsisted on 22 March 2006. Before 2008 the trustees exercise their [enlarged] powers of advancement under *TA 1925 s 32* to defer the vesting of the capital from the age of 30 to the age of 45 and A's interest in possession in the fund will therefore continue until age 45. Clearly A reaches 30 after 2008 in the above example.

Question 6

There are two possible interpretations of the above and we should be grateful if HMRC could confirm which view they take.

Option 1. The exercise of the trustees' powers in this way creates a new interest in possession for A immediately on exercise of the power of advancement which therefore takes effect as the 'current interest' or 'transitional serial interest'. Any successive interest in possession after A's interest in possession has ended cannot then be a transitional serial interest. The property will be taxed as part of A's estate on his death if he dies with the transitional serial interest. He continues to have a transitional serial interest until termination at 45 or earlier death.

Option 2: A's new interest only arises when A attains the age of 30. Until then he has a pre-Budget qualifying interest in possession.

The new interest cannot take effect as a transitional serial interest at all since on the above facts it will arise after April 2008. Until 30 A will have a pre-Budget interest in possession on the basis that nothing has changed until he reaches 30. Only from 30 will he take a new non-qualifying interest so the settled property will then become relevant property. There will not be an entry charge for A at 30 of 20% due to *IHTA 1984 s 53(2)*.

If A dies before reaching 30, then on this analysis his pre-Budget interest will not previously have ended and therefore if his spouse takes an interest in possession this is a transitional serial interest or if his children take interests in possession before 2008 these will be transitional serial interests.

Does the answer to whether option 1 or option 2 applies depend on whether the advancement is drafted in such a way that it extends the interest in possession from 30 without restating A's existing interest in possession until then? Or would any variation of A's interest in possession be regarded as a transitional serial interest from the date of the variation even if the variation only took effect in the future.

HMRC Answer

We consider that A's original IIP (until 30) will have 'come to an end' when the trustees exercised their power of advancement and been replaced by a new IIP (until 45), which will therefore qualify as a TSI. A's interest is expressed as an entitlement to capital contingent on his attaining 30. It seems reasonable to regard the exercise of the *TA 1925 s 32* power as immediately bringing this interest to an end and replacing it with a new one.

NB: As regards HMRC's view on whether a charge arises on the creation of the TSI (or other interest in possession) in these circumstances see warning posted on STEP website on 24th September 2007 and see also section 140 of Finance Act 2008 which has now removed any suggestion that there could be a charge where A is given a new IIP before October 2008. Note also that there is a third view ie that no new IIP arises at all if A's entitlement to capital is deferred because his entitlement to income is not as such affected. Much may depend on how the power is exercised and whether it is an advancement or an appointment.

(5)   An interest in possession might also subsist as follows:

Example 4

Under a trust A has a life interest with remainder to his children. The trustees have a power of advancement and exercise such a power to provide that subject to A's existing life interest A's spouse takes a life interest on A's death with remainder to the children at the age of 25. A's interest in possession is not in any way altered.

Question 7

Can HMRC please confirm that the exercise of a power of advancement to create an interest in possession for the spouse, which is expressly made subject to A's existing life interest and does not in any way alter that interest but merely comes into effect on his death, will be a transitional serial interest. Similarly, if spouse predeceases A and the advancement on interest in possession trusts for A's children is made subject to A's interest and takes effect before 2008 (eg A surrenders his interest) presumably these trusts could also be transitional serial interests.

HMRC Answer

Assuming that A's present IIP existed before 22 March 2006, we can confirm that the spouse's IIP – whether or not it arises before or after 6 April 2008 – will qualify as a TSI provided that it arises on the death of A and that A is at the date of his death still entitled to a pre-budget interest in possession. Any IIP taken by A's children on the death or earlier termination of A's IIP will also be a transitional serial interest provided that this occurs before 6 April 2008. If A's pre-Budget interest in possession terminates inter vivos in favour of the spouse then the spouse will only take a TSI if this termination occurs before 6th April 2008.

If, however, A's interest was in any way amended (eg the trustees exercised powers of revocation and reappointment restating A's interest in possession

Section A

albeit in the same terms and then declaring interests in possession for A's spouse or for children if she has predeceased), presumably the interests for spouse and children could never be transitional serial interests because A's interest is a transitional serial interest?

HMRC Answer

We agree.

(6) Can it be confirmed that an interest in possession can be a transitional serial interest where the interest arises under a different settlement to that in which the original interest subsisted?

Example 5

Under Trust A Mr Smith has an interest in possession and subject to that, the capital passes to Mr Jones absolutely. Mr Jones on 30 December 2006 assigns his reversionary interest into Trust B set up in December 2006 under which his children have interests in possession. Mr Smith's interest in possession then comes to an end on 30 November 2007 at which time the settled property in Trust A passes to Trust B.

Question 8

Will the interest in possession that Mr Jones' children have following the termination of Mr Smith's interest in possession qualify as a transitional serial interest bearing in mind that the interests arise in relation to the same settled property even though not under the trusts of the original settlement? A similar situation could arise where there is technically a different settlement under which the successive life interest arises due to the exercise of the trustees' powers of appointment in the wider form (as referred to in *Bond v Pickford* [1983] (STC 517)).

HMRC Answer

Taken with question 9 below.

Question 9

If the difficulty is that Condition 1 is not satisfied because the second settlement is 'made' post Budget does it make any difference if the second settlement was made pre-Budget and the interests in the first settlement fall into the second settlement before 2008 to be held on interest in possession trusts. This is a very common situation where there are 'trusts over' and there appears nothing in the conditions to prevent this.

HMRC Answer

We do not consider that the IIPs of Mr Jones's children will qualify as TSIs whether the second settlement was made before or after Budget 2006.

As we said earlier, *section 49C* begins from the point of view of the 'current interest'. Condition 1 requires that 'the settlement' in which that interest subsists 'commenced' before 22 March 2006.

It goes on to require that, immediately before that date, the property 'then comprised' in the settlement – ie the same settlement – was subject to the 'prior interest'.

The IIPs of Mr Jones's children arise under a different settlement (albeit one which happens to hold, following Mr Smith's death, the property that comprised the earlier one) and will not, therefore, qualify as TSIs – and it will make no difference when the settlement was made.

For the same reasons, the exercise of powers of appointment in such a way that assets are removed from one settlement and subjected to the trusts of another will not give rise to TSIs.

Note: where the second settlement was set up prior to 22 March 2006 and the reversionary interest of Mr Jones was assigned into an IIP trust prior to that date STEP/CIOT do not accept that on the death of the life tenant Mr Smith the property then comprised in the second trust (formerly the reversionary interest and now the settled property originally in trust 1) is not subject to a qualifying pre March 2006 IIP. It is however accepted that a TSI cannot arise if property is appointed from one IIP trust to another whenever they were set up.

(7) Question 10

What is the position if the beneficiary holding the pre-Budget interest in possession assigns that interest in possession to another person? Does the assignee's interest qualify as a transitional serial interest? The concern here is that the original interest in possession is not 'terminated' by virtue of the assignment, and so the precise terms of the legislation do not appear to have been met.

HMRC Answer

We consider that the assignee's interest can be a TSI in this case because the assignor's IIP will have 'come to an end' for the purposes of *section 49C(3)*. (The interest will be in the original settlement, so the problem outlined in our response to question 9 will not be an issue).

B

Administration of estates

(8) Question 11

Can it be confirmed that where a will provides that a beneficiary has an interest in possession in residue, that interest in possession will be treated as commencing on the date of death of the deceased and not only when the administration of the estate is completed. This appears to be the case by virtue of *IHTA 1984 s 91*.

HMRC Answer

We can confirm this.

(9) Question 12

Can it be confirmed that the position will be the same as in Question 11 above where the interest in possession is in a settled legacy of specific assets not forming part of residue. It seems that this should be the case: *IRC v Hawley* [1929] 1 KB 578.

HMRC Answer

We agree.

This is important for two reasons:

– in order for an interest in possession to satisfy Condition 2 in *section 49A* for an Immediate Post-Death Interest (IPDI), L must have become beneficially entitled to the interest on the death of the testator or intestate;
– in determining whether an interest in possession is one which subsisted prior to 22 March 2006 where the deceased died before 22 March 2006 but the completion of the administration of the estate was on or after 22 March 2006 there would be difficulties if the pre-Budget interest in possession was not regarded as commencing on the death of the deceased.

(3) Question 13

Many wills include a provision which provides that a beneficiary will only take if he survives the testator by a period of time. Please confirm that such a provision would not by itself prevent an IPDI arising.

HMRC Answer

We can confirm this. We consider that *IHTA 1984 s 92* removes any doubt here.

C

IPDIs generally

(4) Question 14

Can it be confirmed that if on the death of X a discretionary trust set up in his Will (eg a nil-rate band legacy trust) is funded by a share in property, and the trustees allow the surviving spouse L to occupy it on an exclusive basis albeit at their discretion along the lines that occurred in *Judge & anor (Representatives of Walden deceased) Sp C 506*, this will not automatically be an IPDI but it will depend on the terms on which she occupies.

HMRC Answer

We agree.

There is a 3 month requirement for reading back under *section 144* in respect of appointments of absolute interests but this does not apply to appointments of IPDIs. Therefore if the trustees immediately on the death of X or subsequently, conferred exclusive rights of occupation on L this could indeed be an IPDI.

HMRC Answer

We agree.

It appears to us unlikely that mere exclusivity of occupation could in itself be a problem because as Judge confirms a person can occupy exclusively but not have rights which constitute an interest in possession. Indeed if the surviving spouse merely continued in occupation on the same terms as before X's death without the trustees' doing anything positive either way to affect her occupation it would appear they have not exercised their powers so as to give her any IPDI anyway.

HMRC Answer

We agree.

(Indeed it is doubtful that they have any ability under the Trusts of Land and Appointment of *Trustees Act 1996* to disturb her occupation if she already owns a half share in the property personally and therefore the trustees have not exercised any power to confer her a present right to present enjoyment which could constitute an immediate post death interest.)

It would be helpful (given how common this situation is) if HMRC could give some guidance on the various scenarios in which they would or would not regard the surviving spouse as taking an IPDI in a property left on nil-rate band discretionary trusts in the will if she is already in occupation.

HMRC Answer

This will depend on the precise terms of the testator's will or any deed of appointment exercised by the trustees after the testator's death, and we will continue to examine each case on its particular facts.

(5) **Question 15**

Can it be confirmed that where a settlement (including a settlement created by will) includes a general power of appointment and that power is exercised by will giving an immediate interest in possession, the interest created over the trust property will qualify as an IPDI?

HMRC Answer

We can confirm this.

(6) **Question 16**

Can it be confirmed that HMRC takes the view that if an individual (I) leaves by will a gift to a person's estate, when the assets in the estate are held on trusts which qualify as trusts for bereaved minors or age 18-to-25 trusts, the property added pursuant to I's will would also be treated as being held on trusts which qualify as trusts for bereaved minors or 18-to-25 trusts.

Section C

HMRC Answer

We have assumed that the scenario envisaged here is: I dies leaving a legacy in their will to P; P dies after I but before the legacy has been paid; P's estate is held on trusts that meet *section 1A* or *section 71D*. We agree that, in those circumstances, the legacy from I's estate would qualify under those provisions, also.

Example 6

I leaves his estate to his widow for life with remainder to his son S if alive at I's death. S survives I but predeceases the widow leaving a Will under which his estate passes to his children on trusts which qualify as trusts for bereaved minors. The widow dies when the children are aged 10 and 12, so that I's estate falls to be held on the trusts of S's Will. Will the property in I's estate benefit from trusts for bereaved minors status? I is the grandparent but the property is passing according to S's Will.

HMRC Answer

We consider that the property added pursuant to I's will in this example would also fall within *section 71A*.

(7) Question 17

If a property is left outright to someone by a will and they disclaim within two years of the deceased's death such that an interest in possession trust takes effect, can HMRC confirm that the trust will qualify as an IPDI?

HMRC Answer

We can confirm this.

(8) Question 18

Can it be confirmed whether, when a will leaves property to an existing settlement (whether funded or unfunded) and under that settlement a beneficiary takes an immediate interest in possession, that interest will qualify as an IPDI. Such arrangements are common for US and other foreign domiciliaries in order to avoid complex probate issues. It might be argued that the interest in possession in the existing settlement does not arise under the will of the deceased. However, there are two arguments against this.

First, HMRC's own analysis is that additions by individuals to existing settlements should be treated as new settlements. Hence the addition by will to an existing settlement is a new settlement set up by virtue of the will.

Secondly, the wording in *section 49A* Condition 1 refers to 'the settlement was effected by will or under the law of intestacy'. The question though is what 'the settlement' refers to. It would seem that it refers not as such to 'the settlement' in the sense of a document but rather to the settlement into trust of the settled property which certainly is effected by will. The same wording is used on deeds of variation under *IHTA 1984 s 142* and HMRC have always accepted that where property is added by will to a pre-existing settlement there is no reason why the beneficiary of that settlement cannot vary his entitlement.

HMRC Answer

We can confirm that the IIP in this scenario would qualify as an IPDI. We agree that 'settlement' in this context relates to the contribution of property into the settlement rather than the document under which it will become held.

D

Trusts for bereaved minors, 18–25 trusts and modified section 71 trusts: Section 71A and section 71D

(9) Question 19

Can it be confirmed that trusts otherwise satisfying the requirements of *section 71A* or *section 71D* will be regarded as satisfying those conditions where the trusts were appointed under powers contained in the will and were not provided in the will itself at the outset.

HMRC Answer

We can confirm this – where the trusts are set up as a result of the exercise of a special power of appointment. We consider the position is different with general powers, on the basis, broadly speaking, that having a general power of appointment is tantamount to owning the property.

Example 7

H dies in 2007. His Will leaves an IPDI for his surviving spouse and subject thereto on discretionary trusts for issue of H. The trustees exercise their overriding powers of appointment to create *section 71A* trusts for the children of H. It would appear that the *section 71A* provisions do not need to be incorporated within the Will Trust from the start to qualify for relief but it would be helpful to have this confirmed. Presumably the presence of overriding powers of appointment over capital in favour of surviving spouse would not be treated as breaching the *section 71A* conditions while the *section 71A* interest was a remainder interest.

HMRC Answer

We agree (subject to our comments at question 19).

(10) Question 20

Can it be further confirmed that the analysis in 16 above will apply both where the prior interest in possession is an IPDI and also where there is an interest in possession arising under the will of a person who died prior to 22 March 2006 where the interests will, by definition, not be an IPDI although in all other respects identical to an IPDI.

HMRC Answer

We can confirm this.

(11) Question 21

Can it be confirmed that, where a will contains a gift 'to such of my children as reach 18 and if more than one in equal shares' or 'to such of my children as reach 25 and if more than one in equal shares' all the interests will qualify as trusts for bereaved minors (or as age 18-to-25 trusts) even though one or more of the children might die after the testator but before the capital vests (so that their shares are divided between their siblings).

HMRC Answer

We can confirm this. We consider that each child while alive and under 18/25 has a presumptive share that is held for his or her benefit, and one can apply *section 71A* or section 71D child by child and presumptive share by presumptive share.

Question 21A

On conversion of an existing pre-Budget A & M trust to *section 71D* status does the class need to close ab initio from the date the trust was converted or is it sufficient to say that until someone else is born, the trusts for 'B' do qualify as *section 71D* trusts but not actually close the class?

HMRC answer

We consider that a trust in the position where anyone (whether unborn or not) who is not currently benefiting can nevertheless become entitled would not meet the requirements of *section 71D(6)*, since it could not be said for certain that 'B' will become absolutely entitled to the settled property etc in due course or that no income will be applied for any other person in the meantime. So we take the view that it will be necessary to close the class of beneficiaries for *section 71D* to apply.

(12) Question 22

Can it be confirmed that the answer to Question 21 is not affected by a gift over provision that substitutes the children (if any) of a deceased child who attain a certain age, so that the increase of the siblings' shares is dependent upon whether the child dies childless.

HMRC Answer

We can confirm this: the siblings' presumptive shares simply increase (or not) when one of their number dies, depending on whether or not the deceased child had any children of their own.

(13) Question 23

Can it be confirmed that agricultural property relief (apr) and business property relief (bpr) will apply to charges arising under *section 71E*. It would appear that these reliefs should be applicable as the charges under *section 71D* (by reference to *section 71E*) are charges under IHTA 1984 Chapter III or Part III and the reliefs are expressly extended to events of charge under this Chapter (*IHTA 1984 s 103(1)* in relation to bpr and *section 115(1)* in relation to apr). Further, the formula for calculating the charge under *section 71F* is similar, in principle, to the charges as calculated under *IHTA 1984 ss 65* and *68* in relation to exit charges for relevant property generally. Can HMRC confirm this analysis is agreed?

HMRC Answer

We agree – for the reasons given.

(14)   Question 24

Section 71E(4) provides that there will be no event of charge where a transaction is entered into by trustees as a result of which the assets held subject to the 18-to-25 trusts are diminished in value, where the disposition by the trustees would not have been a transfer of value under *IHTA 1984 ss 10* or *16* if they had been beneficially entitled to the trust assets. There is a further exemption in *section 71E(3)*. There are no similar provisions in relation to actions by trustees concerning assets which are held on trusts qualifying under *section 71A*. Can it be confirmed that in practice HMRC would apply similar principles in relation to events of charge under *section 71B* for *section 71A* trusts?

HMRC Answer

The provisions in *section 71E* that the question refers to are not reproduced in *section 71B* because the charge there arises under *section 70* – and *section 70* already includes identical provisions at *subsections (3)* and *(4)*. *Section 71B(3)* says:

'*Subsections (3) to (8) and (10) of section 70 apply for the purposes of this section as they apply for the purposes of that section . . .*'

(15)   Question 25

Can HMRC confirm that trusts which are held for beneficiaries as a class (eg on trust for such of my children as attain the age of 25 and if more than one in equal shares) will qualify as age 18-to-25 trusts under *section 71D(3)* and *(4)* notwithstanding that the class could be diminished by reason of the death of members of the class under the age of 25. While it might be said that the class gift does not fall within the strict wording of *section 71D(6)(a)* it might be said that nonetheless the assets are held on trust, for the time being, for each child being under the age of 25. HMRC are requested to confirm their view in relation to the continued application of *section 71D* to class gifts where a beneficiary (B) dies before reaching 25 and the assets pass to the other beneficiaries under 25 on *section 71D* trusts. (This is a separate point from the situation where in relation to existing inter vivos A & M trusts the class increases as a result of future beneficiaries being born before the eldest reaches 25.)

HMRC Answer

We can confirm this. CIOT/STEP note: further queries were raised with HMRC on the class closing rules and the application of s71D generally and these were posted on the websites separately.

Section D

(16) Question 26

HMRC is asked to confirm that *section 71A* and *section 71D* will apply to trusts for a class of children whether or not the assets have been appropriated to each child's share.

HMRC Answer

We can confirm this.

(17) Question 27

There will be a number of circumstances where different sets of beneficiaries under one accumulation and maintenance settlement may require to be treated differently (for example, a settlement for grandchildren where they differ widely in age). Can HMRC please confirm that trusts will qualify as 18–25 trusts or modified *section 71* trusts (capital vesting at age 18) if those trusts exist in only part of the settled property. Thus, a settlement might be divided into two sub-funds, one for A's children who are approaching adulthood and for whom an 18–25 trust is appropriate and another for B's children who are very young and where the trustees value retaining flexibility so that that sub-fund will be allowed to fall within the relevant property regime with effect from 6 April 2008 (or be converted into an 18 trust).

HMRC Answer

We can confirm this.

(18) Question 28

There has been some confusion about the interaction of *section 71D(3)* and *(4)* with *section 71D(1)* and *(2)*. Please confirm that existing A & M trusts set up before the Budget where the settlor may still be alive (and the beneficiary's parent has not died) can qualify for 18–25 status if converted before April 2008 if this occurs immediately after the funds cease to qualify under *section 71*.

HMRC Answer

We can confirm that *section 71D* can apply to existing A & M trusts if the conversion occurs before the funds cease to qualify under *section 71* – for the reasons set out in example 8 below.

Further that there is no inheritance tax charge on conversion of an existing accumulation and maintenance trust to a *section 71D* trust ie that *para 3(3) Schedule 20* protects all pre-Budget accumulation and maintenance trusts so that there is no inheritance tax entry charge either under *section 71* or otherwise, at the point the trust starts to qualify for *section 71D* status (or indeed enters the relevant property regime).

HMRC Answer

We can confirm this.

Example 8

U sets up an accumulation and maintenance trust for his two nieces S and T in 1999. On 22 March 2006 neither has an interest in possession. Currently the nieces take capital at 30 and income at 21. S becomes 21 in January 2007. T becomes 21 in January 2011.

The trustees exercise their powers to ensure that the trusts qualify for 18–25 status in February 2007 ie after S has attained entitlement to income (albeit this is not a qualifying interest in possession post Budget). They provide that each child takes capital outright at 25 in a fixed half share. In these circumstances it would appear that S's share cannot qualify for 18–25 status because immediately after the property ceased to be subject to *section 71* it did not then fall within *section 71D*. T's interest could however qualify under *section 71D*. There is no inheritance tax charge in February 2007 on S's part although there would be a ten-year charge in 2009 on her share because this share is now within the relevant property regime and there would be an exit charge when she reaches 25. There are no ten-year or entry or exit charges on T's interest until she reaches 25 at which point her share is subject to tax at 4.2%. (This assumes that she does not die before reaching 25).

It would be helpful if this could be spelt out in the guidance notes because trustees need to be aware of the requirement to act swiftly if beneficiaries are about to take entitlement to income. It would also be helpful if examples could be given as to how 18–25 trusts work in practice and their main advantages ie to avoid the ten-year anniversary charge.

HMRC Answer

We agree with the consequences set out in the example and will incorporate them in guidance.

(19)   Question 29

It would appear that on the death of a child before 18 on a bereaved minor trust or on an 18–25 trust there is no inheritance tax charge even if they are entitled to income (albeit there is a base cost capital gains tax uplift if they are entitled to income).

HMRC Answer

We agree – by virtue of *section 71B(2)(b)* or *section 71E(2)(b)* and new *section 5(1)(a)(i)*.

It would appear that after a child reaches 18 there is an exit charge on an 18–25 trust if the property ceases to be held on 18–25 trusts but no base cost uplift for capital gains tax purposes whether or not the child has a right to income. Please confirm.

HMRC Answer

We can confirm this.

Question 30

It would appear that, if a child reaches 18 and on his death his share of the trust fund remains on 18–25 trusts for his siblings under cross-accruer provisions, there will be no exit charge at that time. Please confirm.

Section D

HMRC Answer

We can confirm this.

(20) **Question 31**

In the HMRC Customer Guide to Inheritance Tax recently published HMRC state under the heading of 'What is an age 18–25 trust?'

> If the terms of the trust are not rewritten before 6 April 2008 and the trust has not come to an end then existing accumulation and maintenance trusts will automatically become relevant property trusts on the 18th birthday of the beneficiary.

What is the statutory justification for this view. First it is surely the case that an existing A & M trust can become subject to the relevant property regime before 6th April 2008 if a beneficiary takes a post –Budget interest in possession.

HMRC Answer

We agree and will amend the Customer Guide.

Second our understanding is that such trusts will become relevant property trusts on the 6th April 2008 or the beneficiary becoming entitled to an interest in possession before that date unless the trust meets the requirements of a *section 71D* trust. If nothing has been done by April 2008 and a beneficiary is not entitled to an interest in possession then the trust falls within the relevant property regime from that date whether or not the beneficiary is a minor. This point needs to be clarified urgently and the information amended.

HMRC Answer

We agree. *Section 71D(5)(b)* provides that *section 71D* does not apply to property to which *section 71* applies. A & M treatment will therefore continue up to an including 5 April 2008 if the trusts of the settlement meet *section 71*, and will fall away on 6 April 2008. If the trusts provide for absolute entitlement at 18 or 25, the settlement will then fall within *section 71A* or *section 71D* as appropriate; if they do not, the settlement will be 'relevant property' from that date.

(21) **Question 32**

Please also confirm whether or not hold over relief will be available if assets are distributed within 3 months of a beneficiary's 18th birthday under an 18–25 trust. There will be no inheritance tax charge as there will be no complete quarters since the 18th birthday. In these circumstances is hold over relief denied?

HMRC Answer

No. The distribution is still an occasion on which IHT is chargeable – it is just that the charge will be nil. There is no provision in *section 71F* along the lines of *section 65(4)*.

E

Absolute interests

(22) Where assets are held by a person on bare trusts for minor children *TA 1925 s 31* is implied in most cases without express reference and will apply unless expressly excluded.

(23) It might be said that the application of the section will cause the property concerned to be settled property within *section 43(2)(b)* in view of the provisions for the accumulation of income under *TA 1925 s 31(2)*. However, the contrary argument is that the accumulations of income are held for the absolute benefit for the minor concerned and would pass to his estate if he died under 18 (the minor not being able to give a good receipt) and the assets are therefore not held in any real sense subject to any contingency or provision for the diversion of income from the minor. This latter view seems to be in line with the analysis in the IHT Manual which contemplates that *section 43(2)(b)* deals with the position where there is relevant property held on discretionary trusts (paragraph 4602). The statement in the Inland Revenue letter of 12 February 1976 where, in the last sentence of the second paragraph, it is stated that a provision to accumulate income will not prevent there being an interest in possession if the accumulations are held for the absolute benefit of the beneficiary, supports the view that *TA 1925 s 31* will not in these circumstances cause the relevant property regime to apply.

(24) **Question 33**

Can HMRC confirm that the application of *TA 1925 s 31* to assets held on a bare trust for a minor will not result in the assets being settled property within the meaning of *IHTA 1984 s 43*?

HMRC Answer

We confirm that our view is that where assets are held on an absolute trust (ie a bare trust) for a minor the assets so held will not be settled property within the meaning of *IHTA 1984 s 43* and that this will be the case whether or not the provisions of *TA 1925 s 31* have been excluded.

(25) There appear to be new and unforeseen capital gains tax problems now where *Crowe v Appleby* [1975] (STC 502) applies on settled property. The position is complex albeit common and can best be illustrated by example.

Example 9

In February 2006 Andrew set up a trust for his children Charlotte and Luke. They each become entitled to one half of the income and capital on reaching 25. Charlotte becomes 25 in 2007 and Luke becomes 25 in 2009. They do not take interests in possession until reaching 25. The trust only holds one piece of land.

When Charlotte reaches 25 in 2007 she becomes absolutely entitled for inheritance tax purposes since *Crowe v Appleby* has no application for IHT purposes. The trusts over her share end for inheritance tax purposes before April 6 2008 so there is no exit charge since she is within the transitional regime. She is treated from 2007 as entitled to the half share in the property and if she died after that date it would form part of her estate for inheritance tax purposes and hence be potentially taxable.

There is a further problem. For capital gains tax purposes Charlotte does not become absolutely entitled to one half of the land. Until the land is sold or Luke reaches 25 and becomes absolutely entitled (whichever is the earlier) there is no disposal made by the trustees.

There is no inheritance tax change on 6 April 2008 but from that date Luke's share is no longer within A & M trust protection but is taxed as an 18–25 trust. There is no ten-year anniversary charge before Luke reaches 25 but if he dies before then there is an inheritance tax charge (likely to be less than 4.2%). As noted above, there is no base cost uplift for capital gains tax purposes.

On Luke reaching 25 in 2009 there is an exit charge on Luke's share of 4.2%.

HMRC Answer

(Note: we do not consider this is quite right. We assume that the 4.2% is referred to on the basis of $7/10$ths × 6%. However, the charge will not be based on the 7 years from Luke's 18th birthday. *Section 71F(5)(a)* provides that the starting date for calculating the relevant fraction is his 18th birthday 'or, if later, the day on which the property became property to which *section 71D* above applies' – in this case, 6 April 2008).

If the land has not yet been sold there will at that point be a disposal of all the land by the trustees for capital gains tax purposes because both beneficiaries become absolutely entitled. Hold over relief is available on Luke's part under *TCGA 1992 s 260* but not on Charlotte's part since there is no exit charge. In summary, the trustees will have to pay capital gains tax on any gain on Charlotte's share in 2009 and cannot hold over the gain on that share.

Question 34

Prior to the *FA 2006*, Charlotte would have been treated as having a qualifying interest in possession in her share of the trust assets. If she died before Luke reached 25, there would have been a charge to inheritance tax on her death but because she had a qualifying interest in possession, for capital gains tax purposes, there would be an uplift in base cost on her share of the land under *TCGA 1992 s 72(1)*.

Post the *FA 2006*, if Charlotte dies before Luke reaches 25 there will be a charge to inheritance tax but *TCGA 1992 s 72(1)* does not seem to be applicable because Charlotte does not appear to have a qualifying interest in possession which qualifies her for the uplift. Hence she is subject to inheritance tax on her death with no uplift for capital gains tax.

Will HMRC regard her as having a qualifying interest in possession within *section 72* for these purposes?

HMRC Answer

No – with the result, as stated, that there would be no CGT uplift under *TCGA 1992 s 72(1)*.

Question 35

If Charlotte attained 25 in say June 2015 and Luke only reached 25 in 2017 there would be an exit charge on both Luke and Charlotte's shares when each becomes 25 (rate = 4.2%) but hold over relief is only available on Luke's share when the disposal of the land takes place for capital gains tax purposes.

Prior to the *FA 2006* there would have been no exit charge when Charlotte reached 25. However, the effect of the new rules is that on reaching 25 Charlotte will now suffer an exit charge but without any entitlement to hold-over the gain which arises when the land is distributed to her when Luke reaches 25. Will HMRC in these circumstances allow hold over relief on both shares?

HMRC Answer

No – hold-over relief will be due on Luke's share only.

F

Disabled trusts

(26) *Section 89A(2)* appears to conflict with *section 89A(3)*. Condition 1 states that if any of the settled property is applied for A it is applied for the benefit of A but Condition 2 envisages that capital *could* be paid to A or another person on the termination of A's interest during his life provided that the other person became absolutely entitled.

Question 36

Is HMRC's view that capital can be appointed to someone else on the termination of the trust only if it can be demonstrated that it is for the benefit of A?

HMRC Answer

No – we do not consider that that condition is in point.

Otherwise why does *section 89A(3)* Condition 2 refer to other persons at all?

HMRC Answer

We do not agree with the proposition that there is a conflict between *section 89A(2)* and *(3)*. Condition 1 refers to the application of 'settled property' – ie to property that is held on the trusts referred to in *section 89A(1)(c)*. Condition 2, however, is applying conditions that are effective in the event of such trusts being brought to an end.

G

General points

(27) Question 37(1)

New *sections 46A(4)* and *46B(5)* provide that additions (by way of payment of further premiums) to a pre-Budget interest in possession or A & M trust which holds an insurance policy would not result either in a chargeable transfer or in any part of the trust falling within the relevant property regime.

It is understood that HMRC believe that additions of cash or other property to existing pre-Budget interest in possession settlements are subject to the new rules in Schedule 20.

There are other payments which are often made by settlors or beneficiaries on behalf of a trust. For example, buildings insurance premiums and general maintenance costs, payments to cover trust, administration and taxation expenses.

It is noted that for the purposes of *TCGA 1992 Sch 5 para 9(3)* the payment of expenses relating to administration and taxation of a trust are not be treated as the addition of property to the trust. In SP 5/92 the costs of acquiring, enhancing and disposing of a trust asset are not regarded as expenses relating to administration but other property expenses appear to fall within the definition and therefore are not treated as the addition of property to the trust. Would HMRC maintain that the addition of cash or other property to a settlement which may be used either to enhance trust property (eg payment of costs relating to the building of an extension to property) or to purchase other property will be treated as additions but accept that the payment of other trustee expenses (eg trustee fees, buildings insurance premiums and general maintenance costs) will not be treated as chargeable additions?

HMRC Answer

TCGA 1992 Sch 5 is a statutory provision relating to certain, specific circumstances. There is no legal basis on which payments of 'other trustee expenses' should not be treated as chargeable additions for IHT purposes.

Question 37(2)

If any of the additions do bring the trust within the new rules, what property within the trust will be caught and how will it be valued? For example, if an addition of cash was made which was then spent by the trustees and HMRC regard this addition as within the relevant property regime (eg an addition to pay expenses or improve properties), how would the proportion of the settled property subject to the new rules be calculated? Would a valuation be needed of the property before and after the improvement? In HMRC's view, do all subsequent post Budget additions need to be kept physically segregated?

HMRC Answer

[If a payment of cash was made and then spent immediately on, say, a tax liability or another administration expense, then that short period will be the extent of its time as "relevant property" and there will be no question of having to consider what proportion of the existing settled property represents it going forward.

If a payment was made towards the improvement of a property, then this would appear to require "with" and "without" valuations when there is a chargeable event.] Note added 6 August 2008: HMRC have indicated that they are actively reconsidering this response with a view to producing further guidance shortly.

It is clearly up to trustees to decide whether to keep post-Budget additions separate from the rest of the trust fund. We think that it may be sensible to do so – or, at least, to keep good records of additions. (The trustees of discretionary trusts already need to do this, of course, in order for the 10-year anniversary value of each addition to be identified correctly in light of the relief in s.66(2) IHTA for property that has not been "relevant property" for a full 10-year period).

(28) Question 38

It is understood that additions to a trust which fall within the normal expenditure out of income exemption will not need to be reported as and when they are made as, following the normal rules, it is not necessary to report exempt transactions? Please confirm.

HMRC Answer

We can confirm this.

(29) Question 39

It is not unknown for wills to include a gift of an annuity. Some wills give the executors sufficient powers to enable them to choose how best to satisfy the annuity. In such a case there are typically four methods which executors may use to deal with an annuity.

- Pay the annuity out of residue. In such a case the executors delay the completion of the administration of the estate until the annuitant dies.
- Create an appropriated annuity fund. In such a case the executors appropriate a capital fund of sufficient size to pay the annuity.
- Purchase an annuity. The executors purchase an annuity from an insurance office or life company.
- Commute the annuity. The executors pay the annuitant a cash sum sufficient to allow him to purchase the annuity personally.

The first two options create settled property. Will HMRC confirm that a provision in a will conferring the payment of an annuity upon a person (eg to make a gift of an annuity of £x for life) which the executors satisfy by one of the first two options outlined above will be treated as the creation of an IPDI in favour of the annuitant?

HMRC Answer

We can confirm this.

Under *section 50(2)*, where a person is entitled to a specified amount (such as an annuity) for any period his interest is taken to subsist in that part of the property that produces that amount in that period. The property in which his interest subsists may therefore vary over time.

Example 10

Say A is entitled to an annuity of £1,000 and the executors set aside a fund of £40,000 to pay this annuity. In year 1 the income from the £40,000 is £2,000 and half is paid to the annuitant. In year 2 the income from the £40,000 is £1,000 and all the income is paid to A. In year 3 (the year in which the annuitant dies) the income from the £40,000 is £4,000 and a quarter is paid to A. Please could HMRC confirm what property would fall within A's estate on his death (assuming he is treated as having an IPDI) and the basis upon which this has been calculated?

HMRC Answer

We would follow the existing principles set out in *IHTA 1984 ss 50(2)–50(5)* at the date of A's death. (As Dymond, at 16.611, points out, *section 50(2)* does not give any guidance as to the period over which the income of the settled property should be computed. But the learned authors suggest that looking at the income in the year immediately before the chargeable occasion would normally be a reasonable approach and we would agree.)

H

Deeds of variation

Questions have arisen as to the effect of deeds of variation post-Budget.

(5)   Example 11

Testator dies pre-Budget leaving everything outright to X. His will is varied by X and an election made under *section 142* to treat the variation as made by the will.

Question 40

Any trust established by the variation will be treated as having been established pre-Budget whether or not the variation is actually made pre- or post-Budget. If an interest in possession trust is established under such a variation by X, we assume it will be a qualifying interest in possession given it is deemed to be set up prior to the Budget by the deceased and not by X for inheritance tax purposes and further that it will be possible to create a transitional serial interest in relation to this trust before April 2008. Please confirm.

HMRC Answer

We can confirm this.

(6)   Example 12

Testator dies post-Budget leaving everything outright to Y. His will is varied to establish ongoing trusts and an election made under sectoin 142 to read the variation back into the will.

Question 41

Assuming that the terms of the trusts are appropriate, it is possible to establish IPDIs, 18–25 trusts and BMTs by way of such a variation made by Y. Please confirm. As in question 40 it is assumed that for inheritance tax purposes the settlor is the deceased rather than Y.

HMRC Answer

We can confirm this.

Example 13

The testator is not domiciled in the UK at his death leaving everything outright to Z. His will dealing with property outside the UK is varied to establish trusts and an election made under *section 142* to read the variation back into the will.

Question 42

Any trusts established by the variation holding non-UK property will be excluded property trusts whatever the domicile status of Z (the beneficiary making the variation) and whatever the terms of the new trusts. This will be the case whether or not the testator died pre- or post-Budget. Please confirm.

HMRC Answer

We can confirm this.

(7) *IHTA 1984 s 54A* contains certain anti-avoidance provisions that arise where a settlor settles assets into a qualifying interest in possession trust by PET and then the life interest is terminated so that discretionary trusts arise within 7 years. In effect the settlor rather than the life tenant can be treated as having made the chargeable transfer if this yields more tax. *IHTA 1984 s 54A(1A)* states that where a person becomes beneficially entitled on or after 22 March 2006 to a disabled person's interest or a TSI, *IHTA 1984 s 54(1)(b)* applies. So if the disabled person or the holder of the TSI dies and relevant property trusts arise, the anti-avoidance provision potentially applies. Nothing is said though in respect of inter vivos terminations of the TSI or disabled person's interest when relevant property trusts arise and the termination occurs within 7 years of the original PET made by the settlor.

Question 43

Is it intended that *section 54A* should only apply to interests in possession arising on or after 22 March 2006 if the disabled person's interest or TSI terminates on death rather than inter vivos?

HMRC Answer

Section 54A applies both to lifetime terminations of a TSI or disabled person's interest where the other conditions of *section 54A* are satisfied as well as a termination on the death of the life tenant. The fact that *section 54A(1)(A)* refers expressly to death and not to lifetime terminations does not mean that *section 54A* did not cover both scenarios because sectoin 54A(1) covered lifetime terminations. We believe *section 54A* can apply to both inter vivos and terminations on death because *section 54A (1)(a)* refers back to *section 52*, where *section 52 (2A)* already provides that, where the person becomes beneficially entitled to the interest in possession on or after 22 March 2006, there will only be a charge under *section 52 (1)* – and so *section 54A* will only potentially apply – if the interest is:

- an immediate post-death interes;
- a disabled person's interest; or
- a transitional serial interest.

Submitted to HMRC by The Chartered Institute of Taxation and The Society of Trust and Estate Practitioners on 7 September 2006

Response by HMRC on 3 November 2006 (as amended on 12 December 2006, January 2007 and April 2007)

Note: answer to question 33 added on 4 April 2007 based on letter from HMRC dated 23 March 2007.

Note added to response to question 37(2) on 6 August 2008 as a result of discussions with HMRC.

Updating comments also added to notes to replies to questions 6, 9 and 25 on 6 August 2008.

8 May 2007
(Response received from HMRC on 29 May which they have agreed may be publicised and this exchange represents HMRC's further views on the transitional serial interest regime).
HMRC Capital Taxes
Nottingham

FA 2006 Sch 20: pre-existing interests in possession and related matters

We are writing about a number of situations (set out in the questions below) where a person (A) was beneficially entitled to an interest in possession in settled property before 22 March 2006. Doubt has been expressed as to whether *IHTA 1984 s 49(1)* will continue to apply in the future, notwithstanding that A will throughout be entitled to the income of the settled property. We consider that, in all those situations, *section 49(1)* will continue to apply, notwithstanding *section 49(1A)* which (with exceptions) disapplies that sub-section where the interest in possession is one to which a person becomes beneficially entitled on or after 22 March 2006.

It has been suggested that A will, after that date, become entitled to a different proprietary interest in the settled property. As the Revenue argued in *Pearson v IRC* [1981] AC 753, and all the members of the House of Lords appear to have accepted, for IHT purposes the expression 'interest in possession' must be construed as a single phrase. Pearson decided that it means a present right to present enjoyment of the settled property, ie the right to the income from that property as it arises. And in each of the relevant situations, A became entitled to that right before 22 March 2006. *Section 49(1A)* does not, therefore, in our view, apply.

If we are right about this, then it means that the IHT treatment of the relevant situations will not depend on the accident of the particular drafting technique adopted, with settlements being treated differently notwithstanding that A's rights are the same and without any possible policy justification that we have been able to identify.

We would emphasise that, in each of the examples below, the trustees have not exercised any dispositive powers post-March 2006: the interest taken by A remains throughout merely an entitlement to income and, moreover, an entitlement which is defined under the terms of the settlement prior to March 2006.

We hope that you will be able to confirm that *section 49(1)* will continue to apply and, therefore, that the same pre-Budget interest in possession will continue to subsist in each of the following examples.

Example 1

(1) Settled property is held on trust to pay the income to A for life contingently on A attaining the age of 25. The trust carries the intermediate income.
(2) A attained the age of 18 on 1 January 2006 and thereupon became entitled to an interest in possession by virtue of *TA 1925 s 31*. *Section 49(1)* applies.
(3) In our view, it will continue to apply after age 25, when the express trust to pay income to him comes into effect. On any footing, A has only one interest, being the present right to present enjoyment, brought into possession earlier than would otherwise be the case by *section 31*.

Question 1 – do HMRC agree?

HMRC Answer to Question 1 – yes

Example 2

(1) Under a pre-Budget 2006 trust, A is entitled to capital contingently on attaining the age of 25 years. The clause goes on to provide that the trusts carry the intermediate income and *section 31* of the Trustee Act is to apply.
(2) The same clause provides that the capital should not vest absolutely on A attaining the age of 25 but should be retained on trust:
 (a) to pay the income to A for life, and then
 (b) for A's children after A's death,
(3) A attained the age of 18 on 1 January 2006. *Section 49(1)* applies.
(4) In our view, it will continue to apply after A attains the age of 25 on 1 January 2013, when the 'engrafted' trust to pay income to A comes into effect.

Question 2 – do HMRC agree?

HMRC Answer to Question 2 – yes

Example 3

The facts are the same as example 3, except that the engrafted trusts are contained in a separate clause. In our view, the position is the same, and *section 49(1)* will continue to apply after A attains the age of 25.

Question 3 – do HMRC agree?

HMRC Answer to Question 3 – yes

Example 4

(1) A became entitled to income at 25 in January 2006 and *section 49(1)* applies.
(2) A is contingently entitled to capital at the age of 35, but the trustees retain overriding powers of appointment exercisable during his lifetime. He therefore attains only a defeasible interest in capital in 2016, and the capital remains settled property until his death.
(3) In our view, *section 49(1)* will continue to apply after A attains the age of 35, notwithstanding that his contingent interest in capital is replaced by a vested but defeasible interest in capital.

Question 4 – do HMRC agree?

HMRC Answer to question 4 – yes

Example 5

Presumably, where a transitional serial interest (TSI) arose after 21 March 2006 but before 6 April 2008 (eg a pre-22 March 06 Budget life tenant's interest was ended in 2007 and A the new life tenant takes an immediate interest in possession and capital at 35 but that capital entitlement is defeasible being subject to any exercise of the overriding powers), HMRC would agree that *section 49C* continues to apply to A after he attains the age of 35 for the same reasons, ie that his transitional serial interest entitlement continues following his 35th birthday.

Question 5 – do HMRC agree?

HMRC Answer to Question 5 – yes

In all the above examples, A's interest arises under the terms of the Settlement, and not from the exercise of the trustees' powers. We think these examples can be distinguished from the case where a beneficiary is absolutely entitled to capital on reaching a specified age and the trustees positively exercise their powers to defer that absolute entitlement and maintain the interest in possession, where we understand that different issues may arise as set out in the previous reply to queries on *Schedule 20* – see questions revised in April 2007 and in particular Question 6

HMRC Answer – agreed

Interest in possession which continues after death of life tenant

In some circumstances, an interest in possession may continue after the death of the person entitled to the interest up until their death. HMRC have confirmed that a lifetime assignment of an interest in possession will qualify as a TSI (assuming the other requirements are satisfied – Question 10 of *Schedule 20* letter) on the basis that the interest in possession will have 'come to an end' within the meaning of *section 49C(3)*, presumably on the basis of *IHTA 1984 s 51(1)*. There is no equivalent provision to *IHTA 1984 s 51(1)* in relation to transfers on death of an autre vie, but the entitlement of the prior beneficiary who is holding an interest pur autre vie will have come to an end, even though the interest itself will not have done so. This may arise, for example, where the will of the deceased life tenant leaves their residuary estate, which would include their remaining entitlement to the interest pur autre vie, to their surviving spouse.

Question 6

Do HMRC consider that, when a pre-Budget interest in possession beneficiary who holds the pur autre vie dies, any interest in possession in such property then taken by his spouse (or any other person if that occurs before 6 April 2008) will qualify as a transitional serial interest?

HMRC Answer to Question 6 – Yes. In the circumstances outlined, it would seem that the death of the beneficiary holding a pur autre vie interest must bring 'the prior interest' within the terms of *IHTA 1984 s 49C* to an end.

IHTA 1984 s 46B

We should be grateful if you would confirm your view in relation to pre-Budget 2006 settled life policies, where a policy is held on *section 71* accumulation and maintenance trusts and the trusts are then converted into trusts within *IHTA 1984 s 71D*. Insurance premiums continue to be paid on the policy.

It is clear that the continued payment of the insurance premiums will be potentially exempt transfers under *section 46B(5)*.

Question 7

Are the added rights arising from the payment of the premiums settled property within *section 71D*, or are they separate settled property which is within the relevant property regime?

There is no equivalent provision in relation to *section 71D* trusts to *section 46B(2)*, which applies for *section 71* trusts where premiums continue to be paid on or after 22 March 2006. *Section 46B(2)* provides that the rights arising by reference to the payment of the further premiums shall also be within *section 71* if they would be but for *section71(1A)*.

The rights arising from the payment of premiums on policies held on trusts where the payments are made after such trust has been converted to *section 71D* status do not appear to be strictly within *section 71D(3)*, which is necessary for those rights to be held on trusts within *section 71D*. *Section*

46B(1) in relation to *section 71* trusts refers to *sections 46B(2)* and *(5)*, but *section 46B(3)* in relation to *section 71D* trusts only refers to *section 46B(5)*.

Do HMRC accept that the policy held on *section 71D* trusts is, in reality, the same asset as that previously held on *section 71* trusts and that, in effect, no new rights become comprised in the settlement so that all the policy and its proceeds would be within *section 71D*?

We would be grateful for HMRC's views on this.

HMRC Answer to question 7 – we do accept that any added rights from the payment of additional premiums would constitute settled property within *IHTA 1984 s 71D*. If a premium paid once the policy has become property to which *section 71D* applies gives rise to an addition to the settled property the addition will, in our view, automatically become property to which *section 71D* applies.

Section 200

Finally, we note that, under *section 200(1)(c)*, a person with a non-qualifying interest in possession can become personally liable for the tax charged on death, with his liability limited only by reference to the value of the settled property (not the value of his actuarial interest). This seems a somewhat draconian provision, given that the beneficiary is no longer treated as beneficially entitled to the capital. Surely the liability should be limited to the property or income he actually receives? Similarly, in *section 201(1)(b)*, the liability seems anomalous, given that most interests in possession will now be non-qualifying. Why should a beneficiary with a non-qualifying interest in possession have a greater personal liability than a discretionary beneficiary? Can we press for these sections to be reviewed?

HMRC Answer – we do not accept that there is an anomaly here. Although an IIP holder whose interest arose before 22 March 2006 has been regarded as owning the underlying property for inheritance tax purposes, in reality he has only ever owned a limited interest. The *FA 2006* changes do not alter the IIP owner's real position.

Emma Chamberlain	Judith Ingham
Chairman	Chairman
CIOT Capital Taxes Sub-Committee	STEP Technical

Guidance on Sections 71A, 71D and Accumulation and Maintenance Trusts

This guidance has been agreed with HMRC. It outlines the way in which HMRC interpret *section 71* (as amended by *FA 2006*), *IHTA 1984 ss 71A* and *71D–H*. **It should not be regarded as a comprehensive explanation covering all aspects of these sections.**

There are three particular areas of concern, namely:

(1) the meaning of 'B' in the legislation;
(2) the class closing rules;
(3) the scope of settled powers of advancement.

1.

The meaning of 'B' or 'bereaved minor' in the legislation

Both *section 71A* and *section 71D* are drafted by reference to a single beneficiary (in *section 71D* called 'B' and in *section 71A* called the bereaved minor). However, HMRC consider that it is possible to pluralise B or the bereaved minor to include all beneficiaries within the relevant class provided they are *alive* at the date the *section 71A* or *section 71D* trust takes effect and are under the specified age.

Accordingly a will trust in the following terms can qualify as a *section 71A* trust:

> to such of my children alive at my death as attain the age of 18 years and if more than one in such shares as the trustees shall from time to time by deed or deeds revocable or irrevocable appoint and in default of such appointment in equal shares absolutely at 18 provided that no such appointment shall be made and no such appointment shall be revoked so as to either diminish or to increase the share (or the accumulations of income forming part of the share) of or give a new share (or new accumulations of income) to a child who at the date of such appointment or revocation has reached the age of 18 nor to benefit a child who has been excluded from benefit as a result of the exercise of the power.

Note the following:

1.1 It is not necessary to fix the shares in which each child takes income and capital while they are all under 18. Hence it is possible to pay out income and capital to the minor children in unequal shares.

1.2 The power of selection must not be capable of being exercised so as to vary the share of a child who has *already* reached 18. Assume three beneficiaries B1, B2 and B3. It is possible to specify at any time before the eldest (B1) reaches 18 the share he is to take but once he reaches 18 any further power of selection can only be exercised between B2 and B3. B1 ceases to be within the definition of 'B' in these circumstances.

1.3 If the power of selection is exercised revocably then it is not possible by revoking that exercise to benefit someone who has been wholly excluded from benefit albeit revocably. If, for example, the whole relevant share is appointed revocably to B3 (but on terms that the appointment could be revoked to confer benefits on B1 or B2) then even though B1 and B2 are under 18 the trust ceases to qualify for *section 71A* status. HMRC consider that it is not possible under the *section 71A* regime for someone who is not currently benefiting to become entitled in the future. Practitioners will therefore need to be careful before exercising any power of appointment revocably.

1.4 HMRC do not consider that *section 71A* is breached merely because a power of appointment might be exercised in this way. Nor is it a problem if, in the above example, the power of appointment is exercised revocably so as to give B1 5%, B2 5% and B3 90%. Since B1 and B2 are not wholly excluded HMRC take the view that they can still benefit under a future exercise of the power since they remain within 'B'.

1.5 Nor is there a problem if a beneficiary dies under 18 leaving children in whose favour there will be incorporated substitutionary provisions. Hence if B1 dies before 18 leaving children and his presumptive or fixed share passes to those children under the terms of the Will, it is only from that point that the presumptive share of B1 will cease to qualify under *section 71A* and fall within the relevant property regime. The mere possibility that B1 could die before 18 with children taking his share does not breach the *section 71A* conditions. Any power of selection though must not be capable of varying the presumptive share of the deceased B1 once he has died – because B1's children are not within the definition of B and their share must not be increased or deceased after B1 has died.

1.6 No overriding powers of appointment can be included so that 'B's' absolute entitlement could be defeated at 18 although the legislation provides that the existence of an extended power of advancement (ie an express or statutory power of advancement that could be used to defer the beneficiary's capital entitlement by, for instance, providing that his share was to be held on life interest trusts beyond the age of 18) will not in itself cause the trust to fail to satisfy the *section 71A* conditions from the outset. However, if the settled power of advancement is exercised so as to defer vesting of capital at 18 (eg by the making of a settled advance) then although there is no charge under *section 71A* on the ending of the bereaved minor trust the relevant share from that point falls within the relevant property regime.

1.7 All the points above apply to *section 71D* trusts set up by Will and to accumulation and maintenance ('A & M') trusts which are converted to fall within *section 71D* before 6 April 2008 (or before a beneficiary has attained an interest in possession if earlier). Hence it will be necessary to ensure that any powers of appointment that are retained do not permit a beneficiary's absolute share to be altered after he has reached 25 or defeated on reaching that age and if a power of appointment is exercised revocably it must not be capable of benefiting anyone who has been wholly excluded from benefit (even if under 25 and even if the exclusion was revocable).

2.

The class closing rules

2.1 Difficult questions arise where an existing A & M trust is converted into a *section 71D* trust. Existing A & M trusts can become *section 71D* trusts provided this happens on the earlier of the beneficiary taking an entitlement to income or by 6 April 2008. (It will not be possible to convert an A & M trust into a *section 71D* trust after the beneficiary has become entitled to income on or after 22 March 2006 because once a beneficiary takes entitlement to income it no longer qualifies as an A & M trust under *section 71*. *Section 71D(3)(b)* requires conversion of the trusts immediately before the property ceases to be property to which *section 71* applies. Hence it will need to be *section 71D*-compliant by the time the beneficiary attains an interest in possession. Of course if one beneficiary becomes entitled to income from part of the trust fund the remaining part will remain within the A & M regime and so may be converted subsequently (but before 6 April 2008).)

2.2 In the case of existing A & M trusts it is possible that the class of potential beneficiaries will not yet have closed. (This is different from *section 71A* and *section 71D* trusts set up by Will where by definition the deceased parent cannot have any further children, apart from the case of a child en ventre sa mère whose father has died). In the same way that HMRC do not consider 'B' can include a beneficiary who has been excluded from benefit (albeit revocably) HMRC do not consider that B can include any unborn beneficiary, again, apart from a child en ventre sa mère.

2.3 So if, for example, an existing A & M trust in favour of the settlor's grandchildren provides that the class closes only when the eldest becomes 25 and the trust currently benefits only B1 and B2 (say grandchildren of a settlor) being the sole living beneficiaries aged 8 and 9, in order to be s71D compliant, the terms of the trust must be amended to exclude any future born beneficiaries. If B1 and B2's parent has a further child in 2009 that child *must not be capable of benefiting* from the trust fund (except in the event of the death of either B1 or B2 in which case the relevant portion of the trust will from that point fall within the relevant property regime).

2.4 Hence the power to appoint shares must only be exercisable between all or some of the beneficiaries under 25 *who are alive* at the date of conversion to *section 71D* status. HMRC consider this follows from the drafting in *section 71D(1)(a),(3)(b)(i)* and *(6)(a)* when taken together.

2.5 This is not the case if an existing A & M trust continues to satisfy the conditions in *section 71* beyond April 2008 because it falls within *FA 2006 Sch 20, para 3*. A trust which provides for all grandchildren to take outright at 18 will continue to have A & M status under *section 71*, as amended by *para 3, Sch 20*, beyond April 2008. It will be possible to pay income and capital between them in such shares as the trustees think fit and for future born children to benefit if the trust deed permits this flexibility provided that no child's share can be varied after reaching 18. The class should therefore generally be closed once the eldest child reaches 18.

3.

The scope of settled powers of advancement

3.1 HMRC accept that the mere possibility of a power of advancement being used to defer entitlement to capital at 18 or 25 does not cause the trust to fail to satisfy the requirements of *section 71A* or *section 71D* given the terms of *section 71A (4)* or *section 71D(7)* respectively. If the power of advancement is exercised in favour of that person so as to create continuing trusts under which the beneficiary's capital entitlement will be deferred beyond the age of 18 or 25 as appropriate, those trusts will fall within the relevant property regime (with either no exit charge in the case of BMTs or with the usual exit charge under *section 71E*, computed according to the provisions in *section 71F*, assuming the proper exercise of the power causes property to be 'paid or applied for the advancement or benefit of B'; otherwise, the computation would be under *section 71G*).

3.2 HMRC accept that in the case of A & M trusts (including trusts which are modified so that they satisfy the amended *section 71* definition after 6 April 2008) the mere inclusion of a wide power of advancement is unobjectionable. The exercise of such a power will not trigger an inheritance tax charge if the beneficiary takes absolutely or an interest in possession (albeit not qualifying) on or before 18 (see *IHTA 1984 s 71(4)*) and his capital entitlement is deferred beyond 18, although in the latter event, the trust for the beneficiary will thenceforth be a relevant property trust unless it can come within *section 71D*.

Emma Chamberlain/Chris Whitehouse

5 Stone Buildings

29 June 2007

This material has been reproduced here with the kind permission of the Society of Trust and Estate Practitioners and the Chartered Institute of Taxation.

Trusts: Schedule 20 – SP 10/79 and Transitional Serial Interests

Reproduced below is the fourth exchange of correspondence between STEP/CIOT and HMRC, initiated by STEP/CIOT and published with the approval of CIOT, on the practical application of the Inheritance Tax changes made by Schedule 20 to Finance Act 2006.

As the transitional serial interest period expires it is becoming more relevant to know what, if anything, trustees should do in relation to SP 10/79 type interests in possession. The following agreed exchange of correspondence between STEP/CIOT and HMRC has been released.

There have been a number of queries raised by members of the representative bodies about the longer term implications of this statement in the light of *Schedule 20*. Both STEP and the CIOT feel that it is important for these matters to be clarified, so that trustees can be made aware of the IHT implications of decisions they may make relating to property owned by the trust.

SP 10/79 says that (assuming the trustees have sufficient powers) if such a power *'is exercised with the intention of providing a particular beneficiary with a permanent home the Revenue will normally regard the exercise of the power as creating an interest in possession.'* You confirmed that it was not necessary for the trustees to have exercised their powers in writing before they could confer an interest in possession. The question of whether they have exercised their powers so as to give a beneficiary a present right to occupy is, in effect, a question of fact which has to be deduced from all the surrounding circumstances and the intentions of the trustees at the relevant time.

Question 1

When does an interest in possession not arise?

One issue that was always unclear is the use of the word *'normally'* in that SP.

In what circumstances would HMRC *not* regard the exercise of the power by trustees which gives a beneficiary an exclusive right of occupation as *not* creating an interest in possession? *Judge and Judge (Walden's Personal Representative) v HMRC* (2005) STC (SCD) 863 was a case where the trustees never positively exercised their powers because they did not know that she had, or they thought that she already had, an interest in possession.

HMRC answer

We imagine the instances where we would not regard the exercise of the power by trustees to give an exclusive right of occupation as creating an interest in possession would be rare. But such instances might be where there was no evidence of an intention by the trustees to provide a particular beneficiary with a permanent home or where significant doubt about the intentions of the trustees existed.

Question 2

When does an SP 10/79 interest arise?

It seems that the question of whether an interest in possession has been conferred comes down to whether the trustees have indeed exercised their powers in this way intending to confer exclusive occupation. While HMRC cannot give a definitive answer on a particular case without knowing the facts of that case, if there is evidence that the trustees have indeed *knowingly* exercised their powers so as to give a beneficiary exclusive [or, according to SP 10/79, joint] occupation then we assume that, as a matter of principle, HMRC would consider an interest in possession has been created and, on the same basis, that the trustees could reasonably form a view themselves on this point if the relevant facts justified this conclusion.

Do you agree?

HMRC answer

We agree.

Question 3

When does an SP 10/79 interest end – replacement properties?

Where it is clear that a beneficiary has acquired an interest in possession pursuant to SP 10/79, the question of the nature of that interest in possession then needs to be considered in the light of the transitional serial interest regime.

A beneficiary who acquires an interest in possession in line with SP 10/79 merely acquires a present right of occupation. Whether such a beneficiary acquires a right to occupy that *particular* property, or a right to occupy any house for the time being held by the trustees, would seem to depend on the facts and the trustees' intention at the relevant time.

It could be argued that the interest in possession conferred by the trustees will not also include a right to income (assuming that the trustees have merely exercised their powers to allow a beneficiary to occupy property). Hence it is possible that when the land is sold the interest in possession may cease.

Scenario 1

Trustees commonly wish to provide a home for a beneficiary in the long term, with a view to replacing the initial property with another if the beneficiary's family circumstances make this appropriate. They intend from the outset that the beneficiary should have the right to occupy any property owned by the trust, not just the property owned at the time occupation first commences.

If the original property occupied by the beneficiary is sold, in practice the sale proceeds will be held with the specific intention of providing another home for the beneficiary by purchase of a replacement property.

In our view, and we understand that this is the view that HMRC have taken in practice in the past, the beneficiary acquires an interest in possession in the property when it is first occupied, and that interest continues even though the property is sold and a replacement property is then purchased and occupied by that same beneficiary. In such cases, there can be no question of the interest in possession coming to an end when the property is sold, and a new interest in possession commencing when the replacement property has been purchased and the beneficiary enters into occupation. If, therefore, the beneficiary began occupation on or before 21 March 2006 and the property is later replaced by another property using the proceeds of sale, the pre-March 2006 interest in possession continues unchanged.

Do you agree?

HMRC answer

We agree that it is important to review the facts and the evidence of the trustees' intentions to identify the extent of the beneficiary's right of occupation. As far as Scenario 1 is concerned, we would agree with your proposition, on the basis that there is clear evidence that the trustees intended the beneficiary to have the right to occupy any property owned by the trustees for the purpose of providing a home for him.

Question 4

When does an SP 10/79 interest end – specific property?

Scenario 2

In other cases, the trustees may merely have intended to provide a specific home for the beneficiary by granting him the right to occupy a named property owned by the trust. In such circumstances, the beneficiary's interest in possession could be said to be restricted to that particular property so that, if that property is sold, even though it may be replaced in the future, the beneficiary's interest in possession would end when the first property is sold.

Do you agree?

HMRC answer

We agree.

Question 5

Transitional serial interests

In Scenario 2, the trustees may decide to exercise their dispositive powers before the property is sold, but whilst the beneficiary remains in occupation. They may decide to appoint to the beneficiary an interest in possession in the settled property for the time being, irrespective of whether it comprises a house. In a case where, on analysis, the beneficiary had, as at 21 March 2006, a right to occupy a named property only, if the trustees exercise their powers in this way before 6 April 2008, a new interest will be created which, it would seem, qualifies as a transitional serial interest.

The conditions in *section 49C* would appear to be satisfied in that, before 22 March, the property *then* comprised in the settlement (the particular house) is property in which B was beneficially entitled to an interest in possession (Condition 1). B then becomes beneficially entitled to the current interest at any time before 6 April 2008 (such interest now being different in nature). We appreciate that HMRC may take the view that *section 53(2A)* applies to impose an entry charge (a point on which we have written separately).

Do you agree?

HMRC answer

We agree with your analysis that the replacement interest in possession envisaged in Scenario 2 would qualify as a transitional serial interest.

(Queries raised by STEP and CIOT on 26 September 2007 and the responses received from HMRC in a letter dated 20 November 2007 which they have agreed can be published.)

Appendix F

Form SA900—Trust and Estate Tax Return 2015/16

Form SA900—Trust and Estate Tax Return 2015/16

HM Revenue & Customs

Trust and Estate Tax Return 2016
for the year ended 5 April 2016 (2015-16)

Tax reference

Date

Issue address

HM Revenue & Customs

For Reference

Phone

This notice requires you by law to send us a tax return giving details of income and disposals of chargeable assets, and any documents we ask for, for the year 6 April 2015 to 5 April 2016. We have sent you this paper form to fill in, but you can also file the tax return online using our internet service (you will need to buy commercial software).

Make sure the tax return, and any documents we ask for, reach us by:

- **31 October 2016** if you want **us** to calculate the trust's or estate's tax or if you file a **paper** tax return, or both, or
- **31 January 2017** if you file the return **online**

Whichever method you choose, the tax return and any documents asked for must reach us by the relevant deadline or we will charge an automatic penalty of £100.

If you file online, you have until 31 January to file the tax return and you will receive an instant on-screen acknowledgement telling you that we have received it. You can still file online even if we have sent you a paper tax return. To file online, go directly to our official website by typing www.gov.uk/file-your-self-assessment-tax-return into your internet browser address bar.
Do not use a search website to find HMRC services online.

If this return has been issued to you after 31 July 2016, then you must make sure that you fill it in and return it by the later of:

- the relevant dates above, or
- 3 months after the date of issue.

Make sure your payment of any tax the trust or estate owes reaches us by 31 January 2017. Otherwise you will have to pay interest, and possibly a late payment penalty.

We may check the Trust and Estate Tax Return. There are penalties for supplying false or incomplete information.

Calculating the trust's or estate's tax

You can choose to calculate the trust or estate's tax. But if you do not want to, and providing we receive the return by 31 October 2016, we will work out the tax for you and let you know if there is tax to pay by 31 January 2017.

However, if you file later than 31 October 2016 or 3 months after the date this notice was given, see the Trust and Estate Tax Calculation Guide (sent with this return unless we know you have a tax adviser).

The Trust and Estate Tax Return – your responsibilities

We have sent you pages 1 to 12 of the tax return.

You might need other forms – 'supplementary pages' – if the trust or estate had particular income or capital gains. Use page 3 to check.

You are responsible for sending us a complete and correct return, but we are here to help you get it right.

Ways we can help you:

- the Trust and Estate Tax Return Guide should answer most of your questions, go to www.gov.uk/self-assessment-forms-and-helpsheets, **or**
- phone us on the number above.

Form SA900—Trust and Estate Tax Return 2015/16

INCOME AND CAPITAL GAINS for the year ended 5 April 2016

Step 1

You may not have to answer all the questions in this tax return.

Tick if this applies ▼

– read the notes in the Trust and Estate Tax Return Guide

1) **If you are the trustee of a bare trust** (except an unauthorised unit trust), that is, one in which the beneficiary(ies) has/have an immediate and absolute title to both capital and income, you can go straight to Question 17 on page 10. Do not tick the box if you choose to complete the return. ☐

2) **If you are the personal representative of a deceased person** and completing this tax return for a period of administration **and all the points below apply:**

   - all the income arose in the UK
   - you do not want to claim relief (Questions 10A and 10B)
   - no annual payments have been made out of capital (Question 11)
   - all income has had tax deducted before you received it (or is UK dividends with tax credit)
   - there are no accrued income profits or losses, no income from deeply discounted securities, gilt strips, company share buy-backs, offshore income gains, or gains on life insurance policies, life annuities or capital redemption policies where no tax is treated as having been paid on the gain
   - no capital payments or benefits have been received from a non-resident, dual resident or immigrating trust

   then, if you have made no chargeable disposals, go straight to Question 17 on page 10. ☐

   If you have made chargeable disposals, answer Questions 5 and 6 at Step 2 and then Questions 17 to 22. ☐

3) **If you are the trustee of an interest in possession trust** (one which is exclusively an interest in possession trust), and:

   - no income arose to the trust, or ☐
   - you have mandated all the trust income to the beneficiary(ies), or ☐
   - all the income arose in the UK and has had tax deducted before you received it (or is UK dividends with tax credit), or ☐
   - you have mandated part of the income to the beneficiary(ies) where the part you have not mandated comprises only income arising in the UK which has had tax deducted before you received it ☐

   and all of the following points apply

   - the answer will be 'No' in box 8.13 of Question 8
   - there are no accrued income profits or losses, no income from deeply discounted securities, gilt strips, company share buy-backs, offshore income gains, or gains on life insurance policies, life annuities or capital redemption policies
   - you do not wish to claim reliefs (Questions 10A and 10B)
   - no annual payments have been made out of capital (Question 11)
   - no further capital has been added to the settlement (Question 12)
   - no capital payments have been made to, or for the benefit of, relevant children of the settlor during their lifetime (Question 15)
   - the trust has never been non-resident and has never received any capital from another trust which is, or at any time has been, non-resident (Question 16)

   then, if you have made no chargeable disposals, go straight to Question 17 on page 10. ☐

   If you have made chargeable disposals, answer Questions 5 and 6 at Step 2 and then Questions 17 to 22. ☐

4) **If you are the trustee of a charitable trust** you must complete the charity supplementary pages as well as this form:

   - If you are claiming exemption from tax on all your income and gains, you can go straight to Question 7. You should answer Questions 10 and 11, if appropriate, and complete Questions 19, 20, and 22. ☐
   - If you are claiming exemption from tax on only part of your income and gains, you must answer Questions 1 to 9 for any income for which you are not claiming exemption - you should answer Questions 10 and 11, if appropriate, and complete Questions 19, 20 and 22. ☐

5) **In any other case**, including if you are the trustee of an unauthorised unit trust, you should go to Step 2.

Step 2

Answer Questions 1 to 7 and 23 to check if you need supplementary pages to give details of particular income or gains. The notes in the Trust and Estate Tax Return Guide will help. (Ask the SA Orderline for a guide if you want one.) If you answer **'Yes'**, ask the orderline for the appropriate supplementary pages and Notes. When you have answered Questions 1 to 7 and Question 23, answer Question 8.

Go to www.gov.uk/self-assessment-forms-and-helpsheets to download any supplementary pages that you need. You can also phone the SA Orderline on 0300 200 3610 (textphone available) or fax on 0300 200 3611 (closed Christmas Day, Boxing Day and New Year's Day). Make sure you ask for the supplementary pages for the Trust and Estate Tax Return.

SA900 2016   Page 2

Form SA900—Trust and Estate Tax Return 2015/16

INCOME AND CAPITAL GAINS for the year ended 5 April 2016

Make sure you have the supplementary pages you need; tick the box below when you have got them

Q1 Did the trust or estate make any profit or loss from a sole trade? Read the note for this box in the Trust and Estate Tax Return Guide if you are the personal representative of a deceased Name at Lloyd's. Yes ☐ — Trust and estate trade ☐

Q2 Did the trust or estate make any profit or loss or have any other income from a partnership? Yes ☐ — Trust and estate partnership ☐

Q3 Did the trust or estate receive any UK property income? Yes ☐ — Trust and estate UK property ☐

Q4 Did the trust or estate receive any income from foreign companies or savings institutions, offshore funds or trusts abroad, land and property abroad, or make gains on foreign life insurance policies? Yes ☐

Is the trust or estate claiming relief for foreign tax paid on foreign income or gains, or relief from UK tax under a Double Taxation Agreement? Yes ☐ — Trust and estate foreign ☐

Q5 Capital gains
Did the trust or estate dispose of chargeable assets worth more than £44,400 in total? Yes ☐
Answer 'Yes' if:
- allowable losses are deducted from the chargeable gains made by the trust or estate, and the chargeable gains total more than the annual exempt amount before deduction of losses, **or**
- no allowable losses are deducted from the chargeable gains made by the trust or estate and the chargeable gains total more than the annual exempt amount, **or**
- you want to make a claim or election for the year.
Read the note for this box in the guide. Yes ☐ — Trust and estate capital gains ☐

Q6 Is the trust claiming to be not resident in the UK, or dual resident in the UK and another country for all or part of the year? Yes ☐ — Trust and estate non-residence ☐

Q7 Is the trust claiming total or partial exemption from tax because of its charitable status? Yes ☐ — Trust and estate charities ☐

Q23 Pensions – in the case of an estate, are there any tax charges and/or taxable lump sums? Read the note for this box in the guide. Yes ☐ — Estate pension charges etc ☐

Q8 Read the notes for this question in the guide. Answer all the questions.
Are you completing this tax return:

	No	Yes
– for a period of administration	8.1 ☐	8.2 ☐
– as the trustee of an unauthorised unit trust	8.3 ☐	8.4 ☐
– as the trustee of an employment related trust	8.5 ☐	8.6 ☐
– as the trustee of a Heritage Maintenance Fund	8.7 ☐	8.8 ☐
– as the trustee of an Employer Financed Retirement Benefit Scheme (EFRBS)? If this happened during the return year please enter the date the EFRBS first became operative in box 21.11 on page 12	8.9 ☐	8.10 ☐

If you are a trustee:

	No	Yes
– can any settlor (or living settlor's spouse or civil partner) benefit from the capital or income?	8.11 ☐	8.12 ☐
– are you a participator in an underlying non-resident company (a company that would be a close company if it were resident in the UK)?	8.13 ☐	8.14 ☐
– is the trust liable to Income Tax at the special trust rates (the trust rate of 45% or the dividend trust rate of 37.5%) on any part of the income or would it be on any income above the standard rate band (for example, you have discretion about paying income to beneficiaries)?	8.15 ☐	8.16 ☐
– has a valid vulnerable beneficiary election been made?	8.17 ☐	8.18 ☐

Step 3 Now fill in any supplementary pages BEFORE answering Questions 9 to 22, as directed.
Please use blue or black ink to fill in the Trust and Estate Tax Return.
Please do not include pence. Round down income and gains. Round up tax credits and tax deductions. Round to the nearest pound.

SA900 2016   Page 3

Form SA900—Trust and Estate Tax Return 2015/16

INCOME for the year ended 5 April 2016

Q9 Did the trust or estate receive any other income not already included on the supplementary pages? **Yes** If yes, fill in boxes 9.1 to 9.40 as appropriate.

If you wish, you may in the following circumstances leave blank some of boxes 9.1 to 9.40:
a) **if you are the trustee of an interest in possession trust** (one which is exclusively an interest in possession trust), you may exclude income which has had tax deducted before you received it (or is UK dividends with tax credit) unless
   (i) that income has not been mandated to the beneficiary and there are accrued income scheme losses to set against the interest or you are claiming losses against general income, **or**
   (ii) its exclusion would make you liable to make a payment on account which would not be due if you included it – see page 15 of the Trust and Estate Tax Calculation Guide concerning payments on account **before** following this guidance.

b) **if you are the personal representative of a deceased person** you may exclude income which has had tax deducted before you received it (or is UK dividends with tax credit) unless there are accrued income scheme losses to set against the interest. If the reliefs claimed at Question 10A on page 6 exceed untaxed income, you will need to include estate income that has had tax deducted to make sure a repayment can be calculated

Have you received any taxed income (or UK dividends with tax credit) which you are not including in this Trust and Estate Tax Return because (a) or (b) above apply? **Yes**

■ **Interest and alternative finance receipts**
● Interest and alternative finance receipts from UK banks and building societies (including UK Internet accounts)
  – if you have more than one bank or building society, etc account enter **totals** in the boxes.

  – where **no tax** has been taken off
                                                                                       Taxable amount
                                                                                       9.1 £

  – where **tax has been taken off** – there
    is a Working Sheet in the **guide** which   Amount after tax taken off   Tax taken off   Gross amount before tax
    will help you to fill in boxes 9.2 to 9.4   **9.2** £   **9.3** £   **9.4** £

● Other taxed UK interest distributions
  – read the note for this section in the   Amount after tax taken off   Tax taken off   Gross amount before tax
    guide (do not include Property   **9.5** £   **9.6** £   **9.7** £
    Income Distributions)

● National Savings & Investments (other than First Option Bonds, Guaranteed Growth Bonds
  and Guaranteed Income Bonds)   Taxable amount
                                                                                        9.8 £

● National Savings & Investments First
  Option Bonds, Guaranteed Growth   Amount after tax taken off   Tax taken off   Gross amount before tax
  Bonds and Guaranteed Income Bonds   **9.9** £   **9.10** £   **9.11** £

                                              Amount after tax taken off   Tax taken off   Gross amount before tax
● Other income from UK savings and   **9.12** £   **9.13** £   **9.14** £
  investments (except dividends)

SA900 2016   Page 4

Form SA900—Trust and Estate Tax Return 2015/16

INCOME for the year ended 5 April 2016

■ Dividends

- Dividends and other qualifying distributions from UK companies (but excluding Property Income Distributions from UK Real Estate Investment Trusts or Property Authorised Investment Funds)

  Dividend/distribution 9.15 £   Tax credit 9.16 £   Dividend/distribution plus credit 9.17 £

- Dividend distributions from UK authorised unit trusts and open-ended investment companies

  Dividend/distribution 9.18 £   Tax credit 9.19 £   Dividend/distribution plus credit 9.20 £

- Stock dividends from UK companies

  Dividend 9.21 £   Notional tax 9.22 £   Dividend plus notional tax 9.23 £

- Dividends and other qualifying distributions received by unauthorised unit trusts

  Amount of dividend only 9.24 £

- Stock dividends received by unauthorised unit trusts

  Amount of dividend only 9.25 £

- Non-qualifying distributions and loans written off

  Distribution/loan 9.26 £   Notional tax 9.27 £   Taxable amount 9.28 £

■ Gains on UK life insurance policies, life annuities and capital redemption policies

- on which **no tax** is treated as paid

  Amount of gain 9.29 £

- on which **tax is** treated as paid

  Tax treated as paid 9.30 £   Amount of gain 9.31 £

■ Other income

- Other income (including Property Income Distributions from UK Real Estate Investment Trusts or Property Authorised Investment Funds)

  Amount after tax taken off 9.32 £   Tax taken off 9.33 £   Gross amount before tax 9.34 £

  Losses brought forward 9.35 £   Losses used in 2015-16 9.36 £

  2015-16 losses carried forward 9.37 £

■ Deemed income – read the notes in the guide

- Accrued Income Scheme profits and deeply discounted securities

  Taxable amount 9.37A £

- Other deemed income etc

  Taxable amount 9.38 £

- Company purchase of its own shares

  Tax credit 9.39 £   Taxable amount 9.40 £

Q9A Standard rate band

- Amount of standard rate band – read the notes in the guide

  9A.1 £

SA900 2016   Page 5

Form SA900—Trust and Estate Tax Return 2015/16

OTHER INFORMATION for the year ended 5 April 2016

Q10A Do you want to claim any reliefs or have you made any annual payments, or patent royalty payments? **YES**

If yes, fill in boxes 10.1A to 10.7A and/or 10.1B to 10.1C as appropriate. If not applicable, go to question 11.

- Personal representatives: interest on loans and payments made under alternative finance arrangements to pay Inheritance Tax

  Amount of payment
  10.1A £

	Amount of payment	Tax taken off	Gross amount
• Trustees: annual payments	**10.2A** £	**10.3A** £	**10.4A** £
• Trustees: patent royalties	**10.5A** £	**10.6A** £	**10.7A** £

Q10B Do you want to claim special Income Tax treatment where a valid vulnerable beneficiary election has effect? **YES**

If yes, fill in box 10.1B. If not applicable, go to question 11.

- Amount of relief claimed
  10.1B £

Q10C Employee Benefit Trusts – do you want to claim relief for discretionary employment income payments? **YES**

If yes, fill in box 10.1C. If not applicable, go to question 11.

- Amount of relief claimed – read the notes in the guide
  10.1C £

Q11 Were any annual payments made out of capital or out of income not brought into charge to Income Tax? **YES**

If yes, fill in boxes 11.1 to 11.3 as appropriate. If not applicable, go to question 12.

	Amount of payment	Tax taken off	Gross amount
• Annual payments	**11.1** £	**11.2** £	**11.3** £

If you are a personal representative, go to Question 17. Do not fill in Questions 12 to 16.

Q12 Have any assets or funds been put into the trust in year 2015–16? **YES**

If yes, fill in boxes 12.1 to 12.9 as appropriate. If not applicable, go to question 13.

Settlor's name and address	Description of asset
12.1 Postcode	**12.2**

Value of asset
12.3 £

Settlor's name and address	Description of asset
12.4 Postcode	**12.5**

Value of asset
12.6 £

SA900 2016   Page 6

Form SA900—Trust and Estate Tax Return 2015/16

OTHER INFORMATION for the year ended 5 April 2016

Q12 Continued

Settlor's name and address — 12.7
Postcode

Description of asset — 12.8

Value of asset — 12.9 £

If you ticked box 8.15 in Question 8, on page 3, do not complete this page – please go to Question 16 on page 9 and carry on filling in the tax return.

If you have ticked box 8.16 in Question 8, on page 3, complete Questions 13 to 15A. Otherwise, go to Question 16.

Q13 Is any part of the trust income not liable to tax at the special trust rates?

YES

If yes, fill in boxes 13.7 to 13.21 below. Otherwise, fill in boxes 13.19 to 13.21 only.

Boxes 13.1 to 13.6, 13.9, 13.10, 13.15 and 13.16 are not being used

■ Income to beneficiaries whose entitlement is not subject to the trustees' (or any other person's) discretion

- Amount of income chargeable at the **10%** rate — 13.7 £
- Trust management expenses applicable to the income in box 13.7 — 13.8 £
- Amount of income chargeable at the **basic** rate — 13.11 £
- Trust management expenses applicable to the income in box 13.11 — 13.12 £

■ Income allocated to specific purposes

- Amount of income chargeable at the **10%** rate — 13.13 £
- Trust management expenses applicable to the income in box 13.13 — 13.14 £
- Amount of income chargeable at the **basic** rate — 13.17 £
- Trust management expenses applicable to the income in box 13.17 — 13.18 £

■ Trust management expenses

- Total amount of deductible trust management expenses – read the notes in the guide — 13.19 £
- Expenses set against income not liable at the special trust rates — total of column above — 13.20 £
- Total income not liable to UK Income Tax and not included elsewhere on this Trust and Estate Tax Return (non-resident trusts only) — 13.21 £

Q13A Is this a settlor-interested trust where part of the income is not settlor-interested?

YES

If yes, complete box 13A.1. If not applicable, go to question 14.

Complete box 13A.1 only if you have ticked both boxes 8.12 and 8.16 and part of the trust income, which is liable at the special trust rates, is not settlor-interested.

- Amount of tax pool applicable to income that is not settlor-interested – read the notes in the guide — 13A.1 £

SA900 2016   Page 7

Form SA900—Trust and Estate Tax Return 2015/16

OTHER INFORMATION for the year ended 5 April 2016

If you ticked box 8.15 in Question 8, on page 3, do not complete this page – please go to Question 16 on page 9 and carry on filling in the tax return.
If you have ticked box 8.16 in Question 8, on page 3, complete Questions 13 to 15A. Otherwise, go to Question 16.

Q14 Have discretionary payments of income been made to beneficiaries? Trustees of Heritage Maintenance Funds: do not complete these boxes for expenditure on heritage property.
Read the notes on this section in the guide before filling in these boxes.

YES

If yes, fill in boxes 14.1 to 14.15 as appropriate. Otherwise, fill in box 14.15 only.

Name of beneficiary	Net payment	Tick the box if the beneficiary was a relevant child of the settlor and the settlor was alive when payment was made.
14.1	14.2 £	
14.3	14.4 £	
14.5	14.6 £	
14.7	14.8 £	
14.9	14.10 £	
14.11	14.12 £	
14.13	14.14 £	

- Amount, if any, of unused tax pool brought forward from last year (enter '0' if appropriate)   **14.15** £

Q15 Have the trustees made any capital payments to, or for the benefit of, relevant children of the settlor during the settlor's lifetime?

YES

If yes, fill in box 15.1. If not applicable, go to question 15A.

- Total capital payments to relevant children   Amount paid **15.1** £

Q15A Were there capital transactions between the trustees and the settlors?

YES

If yes, fill in boxes 15A.1 to 15A.12 as appropriate. If not applicable, go to question 16.

■ Capital transactions between the trustees and settlors – read the notes on this section in the guide and enter the name(s) of the settlor(s) in the 'Additional information' box, box 21.11, on page 12.

Date	Amount	Name of company (if appropriate)
15A.1 / /	15A.2 £	15A.3
		Registered office
		15A.4
		Postcode
15A.5 / /	15A.6 £	15A.7
		Registered office
		15A.8
		Postcode
15A.9 / /	15A.10 £	15A.11
		Registered office
		15A.12
		Postcode

Form SA900—Trust and Estate Tax Return 2015/16

OTHER INFORMATION for the year ended 5 April 2016

Q16 Has the trust at any time been non-resident or received any capital from another trust which is, or at any time has been, non-resident? **YES**

If YES, have the trustees made any capital payments to, or provided any benefits for, the beneficiaries? **YES**

If yes, read the notes on this section in the Trust and Estate Tax Return Guide and, if appropriate, fill in box 16.1. If not applicable, go to question 17.

- Total capital payments or value of benefits provided **16.1** £

Please give details of the payments in box 16.1 in the boxes below. If there are insufficient boxes please provide the additional details on a separate sheet.

Name of beneficiary	Name of beneficiary
16.2	**16.3**
Address of beneficiary	Address of beneficiary
16.4	**16.5**
Postcode	Postcode
Amount/value of payment/benefit **16.6** £	Amount/value of payment/benefit **16.7** £
Name of beneficiary **16.8**	Name of beneficiary **16.9**
Address of beneficiary **16.10**	Address of beneficiary **16.11**
Postcode	Postcode
Amount/value of payment/benefit **16.12** £	Amount/value of payment/benefit **16.13** £
Name of beneficiary **16.14**	Name of beneficiary **16.15**
Address of beneficiary **16.16**	Address of beneficiary **16.17**
Postcode	Postcode
Amount/value of payment/benefit **16.18** £	Amount/value of payment/benefit **16.19** £

If you have received capital from any other trust which is, or at any time has been, non-resident please provide the following details.

Name of trust **16.20**	Date trust set up **16.21** / /
Address of trustee **16.22**	Amount of value received **16.23** £
Postcode	

SA900 2016   Page 9

Form SA900—Trust and Estate Tax Return 2015/16

OTHER INFORMATION for the year ended 5 April 2016

Q17 Do you want to calculate the tax? YES ☐ *If yes, do it now and then fill in boxes 17.1 to 17.10 below.*

To get the Trust and Estate Tax Calculation Guide, go to www.gov.uk/self-assessment-forms-and-helpsheets

- Total tax due for 2015–16 **before** you made any payments on account (put the amount in brackets if an overpayment) — **17.1** £
- Tax due for earlier years — **17.2** £
- Tick box 17.3 if you have calculated tax overpaid for earlier years and enter the amount in box 17.4 — **17.3** ☐ **17.4** £
- Tick box 17.5 if you are making a claim to reduce your payments on account. Enter your **reduced** payment in box 17.7 and say why in the 'Additional information' box, box 21.11, on page 12 — **17.5** ☐   Tick box 17.6 if you do not need to make payments on account **17.6** ☐
- Your first payment on account for 2016–17 (include the pence) — **17.7** £
- Tick box 17.8 if you are claiming a repayment of 2016–17 tax now and enter the amount in box 17.9 — **17.8** ☐ **17.9** £
- Pension charges due – enter the amount from box 22 of the Working Sheet in the Notes on Estate Pension Charges etc. — **17.10** £

Q18 If the trust or estate has paid too much tax do you want to claim a repayment? YES ☐ *If yes, fill in boxes 18.1 to 18.12 as appropriate. If not applicable, go to question 19.*

(If you do not tick 'Yes', or the tax overpaid is below £10, we will use the amount you are owed to reduce the next tax bill.)

If the tax has been paid by credit or debit card, we will always try to repay back to the card first before making any repayment as requested below.

Should the repayment (or payment) be sent:

- to your bank or building society account? Tick box 18.1 and fill in boxes 18.3 to 18.7 — **18.1** ☐
- If you do not have a bank or building society account, read the notes for this question in the guide, tick box 18.8A — **18.8A** ☐

or

- to your nominee's bank or building society account? Tick box 18.2 and fill in boxes 18.3 to 18.7 and boxes 18.9A to 18.12 as required — **18.2** ☐
- If you would like a cheque to be sent to your nominee, tick box 18.8B and fill in boxes 18.9A to 18.12 as required — **18.8B** ☐
- If your nominee is your adviser, tick box 18.9A — **18.9A** ☐

Name of bank or building society
18.3

Name of account holder
18.4

Branch sort code
18.5

Account number
18.6

Building society reference
18.7

Adviser's reference for you (if your nominee is your adviser)
18.9B

I authorise
Name of your nominee/adviser
18.10

Address of nominee/adviser
18.11
Postcode

to receive on my behalf the amount due

18.12 This authority must be signed by you. A photocopy of your signature will not do.

Signature

SA900 2016

Form SA900—Trust and Estate Tax Return 2015/16

OTHER INFORMATION for the year ended 5 April 2016

Q19 Trustee or personal representative details

- Your daytime phone number (including the area code) — 19.1
- Your adviser's phone number (including the area code) — 19.2
- Your adviser's name and address — 19.3

  Postcode

- Your adviser's reference for you — 19.4

Q20 Have there been any changes to the names and addresses of the trustees or personal representatives? YES

If the 'acting trustee' has changed, please give details in the 'Additional information' box, box 21.11, on page 12.

If yes, fill in boxes 20.1 to 20.12 as appropriate. If not applicable, go to question 21.

- Retiring trustees' or personal representatives' names and addresses

20.1	20.2
Postcode	Postcode
20.3	20.4
Postcode	Postcode

- New trustees' or personal representatives' names and addresses

20.5	20.6
Postcode	Postcode
20.7	20.8
Postcode	Postcode

- Existing trustees' or personal representatives' names and new addresses

20.9	20.10
Postcode	Postcode
20.11	20.12
Postcode	Postcode

SA900 2016

Form SA900—Trust and Estate Tax Return 2015/16

OTHER INFORMATION for the year ended 5 April 2016

Q21 Other information

- If you are completing this Trust and Estate Tax Return as a personal representative, please enter in box 21.1 the date of death of the deceased.

  21.1 Date / /

- If the administration period ceased in the year to 5 April 2016, please enter in box 21.2 the date of cessation.

  21.2 Date / /

- If the administration period ceased in the year to 5 April 2016 and there is a trust created by the deceased's will or the rules of intestacy that apply in England & Wales, please tick box 21.3. Read the notes in the guide. **21.3**

- If you are a trustee and the trust was terminated in the year to 5 April 2016 please enter in box 21.4 the date of termination and, in the 'Additional information' box, box 21.11 below, the reason for termination.

  21.4 Date / /

- If this Trust and Estate Tax Return contains any figures that are provisional because you do not yet have final figures, please tick box 21.5. Read the notes for this question in the guide. **21.5**

- If any 2015–16 tax was refunded directly by the HM Revenue & Customs office, or (personal representatives only) by the Jobcentre Plus (in Northern Ireland, the Social Security Agency), please enter the amount in box 21.6. Do not include any refunds of excessive payments on account or any Gift Aid repayments claimed from HMRC Charities.

  21.6 Amount £

- **Disclosure of tax avoidance schemes** – if the trust or estate is a party to one or more disclosable tax avoidance schemes you must complete boxes 21.7 and 21.8. Give details of each scheme (up to 3) on a separate line. If the trust or estate is a party to more than 3 schemes, details of the additional schemes must be reported on form AAG4.

Scheme reference number or promoter reference number	Tax year in which the expected advantage arises – year ended 5 April
21.7	**21.8**

- **Business Premises Renovation Allowance (BPRA)** Read the notes for these questions in the Trust and Estate Tax Return Guide before you fill in these boxes.

  Capital allowance **21.9** £   Balancing charge **21.10** £

21.11 Additional information

Q22 Declaration

I have filled in and am sending back to you the following Trust and Estate Tax Return pages:

- 1 to 12 of this form
- Trust and estate UK property
- Trust and estate non-residence
- Trust and estate trade
- Trust and estate foreign
- Trust and estate charities
- Trust and estate partnership
- Trust and estate capital gains
- Estate pension charges etc

Before you send the completed tax return back you must sign the statement below.

If you give false information or conceal any part of trust or estate income or chargeable gains, you may be liable to financial penalties and/or you may be prosecuted.

22.1 The information I have given in this tax return is correct and complete to the best of my knowledge and belief.

Signature   Date

- Please print your name in box 22.2
- Enter the capacity in which you are signing in box 22.3

22.2   **22.3**

SA900 2016   Page 12

Appendix G

Residence and Ordinary Residence of Individuals Before 2013/14

Residence

From 2013/14 an individual's residence position is determined by the Statutory Residence Test (SRT) (see **24.9–24.10**). Where enquiries are open into periods prior to April 2013, the old rules will still apply and an overview of these rules is therefore set out below.

Prior to 2013/14, there was limited legislation in relation to determining UK residence. Statute simply applied, rather obliquely, a 183 day test. The same test was applied respectively to foreign income and employment income of individuals who were in the UK for a temporary purpose only [ITA 2007, ss 831 and 832]. The individual was treated as non-UK resident in relation to prescribed categories of income if: (a) he was in the UK for some temporary purpose only and with no view or intention of establishing his residence in the UK and (b) in the relevant tax year he had not spent in the UK 183 days or more.

Prior to 2008/09 HMRC practice (as set out in their booklet IR20 'Residents and non-UK Residents – Liability to Tax in the United Kingdom' which from 2009/10 was superseded by HMRC6: 'Residence, Domicile and the Remittance Basis') was that days of arrival and departure were generally ignored in determining whether a day is spent in the UK. As from 2008/09 there was an express statutory rule (amending *sections 831 and 832*) that, except where present in the UK for transit travel purposes only (as defined), an individual was treated as spending a day here if he was present in the UK at midnight on that day. So, someone who arrived in the UK at midday on a Monday and remained here until departing on Thursday evening would have spent three days in the UK.

It was expressly provided that in applying the temporary purpose test any living accommodation available in the UK for the individual's use was to be ignored [*ITA 2007, s 831(1)*]. This went back to a pre-1993 rule that an individual was treated as resident in the UK in any year in which he visited the UK if he had accommodation available for his use. The legislation recognised that an individual who had been both UK resident and ordinarily UK resident may have left the UK for the purpose only of occasional residence abroad. In this case he was treated as remaining UK resident throughout any tax year during which he remained outside the UK for the purpose only of occasional residence abroad [*ITA 2007, s 829*]. This was subject to special rules for visiting forces and staff of designated allied headquarters [*ITA 2007, s 833*] and indeed for personal representatives [*ITA 2007, s 834*].

There was a technical problem on this issue, which was not addressed in the *Gaines-Cooper* decision (see below). Although the then Conservative Chancellor announced at Budget 1993 that his intention was to abolish the 'available accommodation rule', that intention was *not* reflected in the legislation. The legislation merely amended *ICTA 1988, s 336*, to the effect that accommodation should be disregarded in determining, for the purposes of that section, whether the individual was in the UK for some temporary purpose and not with a view to establishing residence.

The specific provisions about foreign income and employment income of individuals in the UK for a temporary purpose followed a general rule about residence of individuals temporarily abroad in *ITA 2007, s 829*. Someone who had been both UK resident and ordinarily UK resident and who left the UK for the purpose only of occasional residence abroad was treated as remaining UK resident.

The Inland Revenue attempted without success to use a predecessor of this section to charge a pop star who was absent in the USA for a whole tax year (*Reed (Inspector of Taxes) v Clark* [1986] Ch 1, [1985] 3 WLR 142): the Special Commissioners found that the taxpayer's presence in the US amounted to more than 'occasional residence abroad' and so that he had, for that tax year, become both not resident and not ordinarily resident in the UK. More recently, in *Shepherd v Revenue and Customs Comrs* [2006] EWHC 1512 (Ch), [2006] STC 1821 the High Court, affirming the Special Commissioner, held that a long-standing UK resident did not cease to be UK resident merely by spending less than 90 days in the tax year in the UK. Retention of a house in the UK coupled with the failure to establish residence in Cyprus (the chosen jurisdiction) meant that Mr Shepherd remained ordinarily resident in the UK within the meaning of the statutory predecessor to *section 829* and had not been in the UK for temporary purposes only.

The point, which has been reinforced in *Grace v Revenue and Customs Comrs* ([2008] STC (SCD) 531, [2008] SWTI 279, SCD) is that, if someone who has been UK resident wishes to cease to be so, there must be a 'clean break'. The Special Commissioner found that Mr Grace, unlike Mr Shepherd, managed to achieve this, even though he retained a house in the UK. He was able to show clearly that he had established residence in South Africa – and indeed the specific purpose of his UK home was to provide a base for rest and recuperation both when as an airline pilot he arrived in the country and prior to his departure. Unlike Mr Shepherd who had a domicile of origin in England, Mr Grace had the advantage of a domicile of origin, a residence and family and business connections in South Africa.

The decision was overturned on appeal (*Revenue and Customs Comrs v Grace* [2008] EWHC 2708 (Ch), [2009] STC 213, [2008] SWTI 2503). The Special Commissioner was wrong to conclude that there had been a 'distinct break' in Mr Grace's life when he set up home in Cape Town. All that happened at that point was that he acquired another home there: from being a man who resided in one place he became who resided in two. Indeed, Lewison J, noting that the phrase 'distinct break' did not feature in the legislation, said that it was not therefore helpful to attempt to define what it meant with a view to deciding whether a taxpayer was resident in the UK. In any event, however, Mr Grace's circumstances fell far short of those which in other, earlier, cases had been held to amount to a 'distinct break'. More fundamentally the Special Commissioner had made errors of law and the only possible conclusion from the primary facts was that Mr Grace remained resident in the UK in the relevant years of assessment and therefore also ordinarily resident. The reason for his remaining in the UK was neither casual nor transitory. In particular, presence in the UK to fulfil duties under a permanent or indefinite contract of employment could not be so described.

The Court of Appeal heard Mr Grace's further appeal in October 2009 and found that the Special Commissioner had misdirected herself. It remitted the case back to the FTT for reconsideration. (*Revenue and Customs Comrs v Grace* [2009] EWCA Civ 1082, [2009] STC 2707, [2009] SWTI 2834).

On 5 January 2011 the First-tier Tribunal (Judge Barbara Mosedale) confirmed that Mr Grace had continued to be UK resident during the relevant tax years, not having demonstrated a sufficient break with the UK. Taking into account all factors, but giving greatest weight to his employment and his home in the UK and the amount of time actually spent in the UK together with the frequency of his short visits, Mr Grace continued to have a settled purpose to his residence in the UK and also remained ordinarily resident (*Grace v Revenue and Customs Comrs* [2011] UKFTT 36 (TC), [2011] SFTD 669, [2011] SWTI 1581).

There was a special rule for those who work full-time outside the UK in a foreign trade and/or a foreign employment. *[ITA 2007, s 830].* HMRC6 paras 8.5 and 8.8 followed IR20 in stating that a person going abroad to an employment (for at least a whole tax year) was normally regarded as non-UK resident for income tax purposes from the day following his departure until the day preceding his return. Again available accommodation in the UK was to be disregarded. A trade was foreign if no part of it was carried on in the UK. An employment was foreign if all of its duties were performed outside the UK or if the duties were in substance performed outside the UK and the only duties performed in the UK were those which were incidental to those performed outside the UK. The latter provision was not too helpful in the light of the decision in *Robson v Dixon (Inspector of Taxes)* [1972] 3 All ER 671, [1972] 1 WLR 1493, which held that 38 landings in the UK out of 811 in a six-year period were not merely incidental to an aircraft pilot's duties. That said, however, HMRC stated at the end of March 2011 that fewer than 10 work days spent in the UK (ie on non-incidental duties) would not of itself prevent a claim that the individual has made a break with UK.. HMRC accept also that self-employment can satisfy the test. What was important was that the taxpayer was away from the UK for at least a complete tax year for reasons of full-time employment abroad (see below, where *Messrs Adams and Davies* failed the test for the relevant tax year not having left the UK before the beginning of it).

ITA 2007, s 831(1)(b) and *s 832(1)(b)* effectively laid down the rule that six months' presence in the UK for any year of assessment constituted residence for that year for income tax purposes. A long line of cases established the proposition that much shorter periods in the UK over a number of years for some continuing purpose could constitute residence. This point was made in HMRC6 at 2.2 on pages 6 and 7: 'you can also be resident in the UK if you are present here for fewer than 183 days in a tax year. This will depend on how often and how long you are here, the purpose and pattern of your presence and your connections to UK. These might include the location of your family, your property, your work life and your social connections.'

The strict rule was that an individual was resident in the UK for a tax year if he was UK resident during any part of it, though HMRC had traditionally applied a concession allowing the splitting of tax years in the cases of arrival and departure, extended to capital gains tax by ESC D2. The concession was not allowed in any case in which HMRC consider it was being used for tax avoidance purposes (*R v Inspector of Taxes, Reading, ex p Fulford-Dobson* [1987] QB 978, [1987] 3 WLR 277). For capital gains tax, the concession was also restricted by the provision in *TCGA 1992, s 10A* preserving a charge to capital gains tax on gains made by an individual who is temporarily non-resident (see **26.57–26.58**).

The statutory code was supplemented by HMRC practice, as was set out in their booklet IR20, 'Residents and Non-UK residents—Liability to Tax in the United Kingdom' (revised in December 1999 and, though only to reflect the 91-day test, HMRC Brief 1/07 – see below – in May 2008). From 2009/10 IR20 was replaced by HMRC6: Residence, Domicile and the Remittance Basis. In addition to the statutory 183 day test HMRC say that they will normally regard a person as resident in the UK for tax purposes where he visited the UK regularly and after four years the visits during those years averaged 91 days or more, so that he would be treated as resident from the fifth year (IR20 para 3.3 and HMRC6 para 7.5). The original version of para 7.5 of HMRC 6 referred to satisfaction of the test from the beginning of the fourth year after three years averaging 91 days or more; however, HMRC later confirmed that was an error and amended para 7.5 to reflect their previous practice. It is important to note that the 91 day test is relevant only to those who had been resident outside the UK and either came to the UK to establish residence or who visited the UK on a regular basis. Second, the 91 day test was relevant to those who left the UK for full-time employment abroad (see below), where the test must be satisfied during periods of absence abroad. The case of Shepherd (see above) emphasised that the test could not be used to create non-UK resident status for someone who had not 'left' the UK on a permanent basis, that was one who may have left the UK for the purpose only of occasional residence abroad within *ITA 2007, s 829*.

The 91-day test was again in issue in the Special Commissioners' decision of *Gaines-Cooper v Revenue and Customs Comrs* [2008] STC 1665, SpC 568. The facts of the case were complicated. Specifically, the Special Commissioners did not accept the taxpayer's computations of days spent in the UK, viz ignoring days of arrival and departure as found in HMRC booklet IR20. Rather, they agreed with HMRC's interpretation of the law that arrival on a Saturday and departure on the Sunday should count as one day spent in the UK. On this basis the re-written schedule of days spent in the UK took Mr Gaines-Cooper rather over the 90-day limit in each of the tax years in question. The Special Commissioners decided on the evidence that he had been both resident and ordinary resident in the UK during the relevant tax years. They found that Mr Gaines-Cooper's presence in the UK for the years under appeal was not for a temporary purpose. Further, they decided as a preliminary issue that the taxpayer had failed to establish on the balance of probabilities that he had abandoned his domicile of origin in England and acquired a domicile of choice was in the Seychelles. Mr Gaines-Cooper's application on the issue of residence was heard by the High Court in October 2008 as a matter of judicial review. That application was refused but Mr Gaines-Cooper was given permission by the Court of Appeal in July 2009 to appeal against the refusal by the High Court to grant leave to apply for judicial review: see below. His appeal on the matter of domicile, the Special Commissioners having found that he had not displaced his domicile of origin in England and Wales by acquiring an independent domicile of choice in the Seychelles, was refused by the High Court([2007] EWHC 2617 (Ch), [2008] STC 1665, 81 TC 61)).

Mr Gaines-Cooper's appeal to the Court of Appeal was heard together with the joined cases of Messrs Adams and Davies, all on the basis that HMRC had failed correctly to interpret their booklet IR20 and in particular had made unannounced alterations in that interpretation. That contention was dismissed by the court. In the cases of Adams and Davies it is clear that satisfaction of the condition that the taxpayer is away from the UK for at least a complete tax year for reasons of full-time employment abroad, he need not sever all links with the UK. Neither Messrs Davies and Adams was able to satisfy that test. (*R (on the application of Davies) v Revenue and Customs Comrs; R (on the application of Gaines-Cooper) v Revenue and Customs Comrs* [2010] EWCA Civ 83, [2010] STC 860, [2010] 09 LS Gaz R 17). A point of interest in the Court of Appeal decision was that, although earlier Courts had chosen to decide the issue on residence on the basis of the law disregarding HMRC's statement in IR20 now superseded by HMRC 6, the Court of Appeal said that HMRC were bound by the clear statements in IR20 as to how they would treat a taxpayer in particular to find circumstances, which should be applied by the Court. However, in this case it was clear that the full-time employment abroad let out did not apply to Messrs Davies and Adams and that Mr Gaines-Cooper had not been able to demonstrate that he had left the UK. In particular, the Court did not find that, as argued by the taxpayers, HMRC had changed their policy on non-UK residence. The three appellants were granted leave to appeal to the Supreme Court, which heard the case in July 2011.

The Supreme Court dismissed the appeals of all three appellants (with Lord Mance dissenting from the majority judgement of Lords Hope, Walker, Clarke and Wilson). The Court held that HMRC's guidance in IR20 did not dispense with the requirement that the taxpayer must make a 'distinct break' with the UK in order to become non-UK resident. The Court held also that there was insufficient evidence of any settled practice on HMRC's part which might give rise to a legitimate expectation that the taxpayers would be treated as non-UK resident. It had been clear since the leading case of *Levene v IRC* [1928] AC 217 (see below) that a taxpayer who had been UK resident ceased to be so resident only if he ceased to have a settled or usual abode in the UK. While the Supreme Court said that HMRC's exposition in IR20 of how one might achieve non-UK resident status should have been much clearer, overall it served to inform the ordinarily sophisticated taxpayer that he had to leave the UK, whether permanently, indefinitely or for full-time employment abroad, but he had to do more than simply take up residence abroad and that he had to relinquish his 'usual residence in the UK'. The Court of Appeal had correctly held that the taxpayers failed to establish that HMRC were departing from a settled practice such as to found a legitimate expectation. The taxpayers' evidence had failed to show that HMRC had adopted any settled practice of applying criteria different from those identified not only by the ordinary law but also in IR20 read as a whole (*R (on the application of Davies) v Revenue and Customs Comrs* [2011] UKSC 47, [2012] 1 All ER 1048, [2011] 1 WLR 2625).

In *Karim v RCC* [2010] TC 306 Ms Karim, having been born in Tanzania, completed her education and started work in the UK between 1968 and the early 2000's when having ceased to manage care homes owned by a company which she had incorporated she spent more time in Portugal and less time in the UK. Both the properties and her shares in the company were sold by Ms Karim in 2003/04 when she claimed to be not UK resident, having claimed as much in her two earlier returns. However, on the evidence the tribunal said that Ms Karim had failed to show that she was in the UK for some temporary purpose only. Indeed there was evidence of her visits to the UK were not infrequent and were not for insubstantial periods. An out of time assessment by HMRC was upheld on the basis of a discovery assessment validly made said the tribunal under *TMA 1970, s 29*.

Two cases on residence were decided against the taxpayers in the course of 2011/12. First, Dr Broome failed to satisfy the First-tier Tribunal that he had become resident in France so as to escape capital gains tax on the sale of two properties in the UK during tax year 2000/01. While the Tribunal accepted that Mr Broome had been making preparations physically to leave the UK, they did not consider that his move abroad reflected and evidenced a settled intention to become non-UK resident or that he had established a real and closer connection to France. Interestingly, it appears that Dr Broome would have become non-UK resident on the basis of the test applying from 2013/14 (see below), on the basis of a day count. However, Dr Broome may be considered to have been unfairly treated on two counts. First, the fact that he had originally not claimed non-UK resident status and then amended the return counted against him. Second, the Tribunal appears to suggest that UK residence can be lost only if residence status is established in a particular foreign jurisdiction: while persuasively helpful, that cannot be correct (*Broome v Revenue and Customs Comrs* [2011] UKFTT 760 (TC), [2012] SWTI 39). In the other case, Mr Kimber, having lived and worked in Japan from 1997 to 11 July 2005, returned to the UK on 17 July to stay with his mother in Kent until 30 July when he went to Italy on holiday until 28 August. While in Italy he sold some shares, which was held by the Tribunal to trigger a capital gains tax liability on the grounds that he had become resident in the UK at some point between 17 and 30 July during which he had agreed to lease a property in Norfolk from September and 'formed the intention to stay in the UK permanently and then become resident' (*Kimber v Revenue and Customs Comrs* [2012] UKFTT 107 (TC), [2012] SWTI 1462).

More recently two cases on residence decided in late 2013 were *Glyn v Revenue and Customs Comrs* [2013] UKFTT 645 (TC), – the first residence victory for the taxpayer since the 1970s – and *Rumbelow v Revenue and Customs Commissioners* [2013] UKFTT 637 (TC) (another failure). The cases are covered at **24.6** and **24.7**.

Ordinary Residence

Prior to April 2013, in addition to residence and domicile, an individual's tax position was determined by reference to where they were 'ordinarily resident'.

This was not a concept that had often fallen to be construed on its own apart from residence itself. One area in which it had been of importance was in connection with 'exempt gilts', which were free of income tax while in the beneficial ownership of persons not ordinarily resident in the UK. [*ITTOIA 2005 ss 713–715*]. It was *section 715* which dealt with such securities, known as securities free of tax to residents abroad or 'FOTRA securities' which were held in trust (see **8.26–8.27**). For such treatment to apply none of the beneficiaries of the trust could be ordinarily UK resident when the interest arose and this included any actual or potential beneficiary of the trust known to the trustees.

A leading case on the point is *Levene v IRC HL* [1928] AC 217, 13 TC 486. The taxpayer had admittedly spent four or five months in the UK during the relevant years and lost his appeal with regard both to residence and ordinary residence, but on the latter point the Lord Chancellor, Viscount Cave, said:

> 'The expression "ordinary residence" is found in the Income Tax Act of 1806 and occurs again and again in the later Income Tax Acts, where it is contrasted with usual or occasional or temporary residence; and I think that it connotes residence in a place with some degree of continuity and apart from accidental or temporary absences. So understood, the expression differs little in meaning from the word "residence" as used in the Acts; and I find it difficult to imagine a case in which a man while not resident here is yet ordinarily resident here.'

The practical importance of the distinction was that complete absence from the UK for an entire tax year would constitute non-residence for that year, but the circumstances will dictate whether the individual had also ceased to be not ordinarily resident for that year. The decision in *Reed v Clark* (see above) showed that the court had held that this was possible to achieve.

A Special Commissioners decision on ordinary residence was *Genovese v Revenue and Customs Comrs* [2009] STC (SCD) 373, SCD. The House of Lords had said that 'ordinarily resident' did not imply an intention to live in a place permanently or indefinitely but rather referred to an individual's abode in a particular country which had been voluntarily adopted as part of the regular order of life for the time being, whether of short or of long duration (*Shah v Barnet London Borough Council* [1983] 2 AC 309, [1983] 1 All ER 226). In this case the Special Commissioner found that Mr Genovese had in the September or October of the third year of his residence voluntarily adopted an abode in the UK as part of the regular order of his life for the time being. This, common law, test led to a conclusion which was at variance with IR20 (concerned as it was with matters of intention and what the individual decides). For the purposes of the charge to tax on employment income Mr Genovese was ordinarily resident in 2001/02 and it was not necessary to show that he was ordinarily resident throughout the year of assessment.

The effect of *Genovese* was that ordinary residence would commence at the beginning (and not after the end) of the tax year in which falls the third anniversary of arrival in the UK. Following the Upper Tribunal in *Tuczka* (see below), HMRC6 stated at para 3.2:

> ' When you come to the UK you do not have to intend to remain in the UK permanently or indefinitely in order to be ordinarily resident here. It is enough that your residence has all the following attributes:
>
> - Your presence here has a settled purpose. This might be for only a limited period, but has enough continuity to be properly described as settled. Business, employment and family can all provide a settled purpose, but this list is not exhaustive.
> - Your presence in the UK forms part of the regular and habitual mode of your life for the time being. This can include temporary absences from the UK. For example, if you come to live in the UK for three years or more then you will have established a regular and habitual mode of life here from the start.
> - You have come to the UK voluntarily. The fact that you chose to come to UK at the request of your employer rather than seek another job does not make your presence here involuntary.'

The Tribunal's decision in the case of *Tuczka v Revenue and Customs Comrs* [2010] UKFTT 53 (TC), [2010] SWTI 1594 was of interest in that the Tribunal Judge John Clark admitted that he had wrongly decided *Genovese* because he had failed to take account of the relevant authorities. That decision had established that a person not being clear about his purpose when he arrived in the UK would be held to have become ordinarily resident at the beginning of the tax year in which fell the third anniversary of his arrival. In this case Dr Tuczka had come to work in the UK expecting to be here for only a couple of years with no intention of staying in the UK. However, he did purchase a property as his residence as more financially sensible than to rent. Dr Tuczka's challenge to HMRC was not so much on the terms of IR20 but on the general law where the Tribunal said:

> 'Acquisition of a property would not necessarily prevent an individual from establishing that he or she was not ordinarily resident provided that the property was sold within the period specified in IR20; in other words, an individual could buy instead of renting, based on the same commercial approach as expressed by Dr Tuczka, and still not prejudice the ordinary resident status as long as the property was held for a limited period.'

Interestingly, the sale of the property and his departure from the UK within three years after arrival would not have made him ordinarily resident under IR20 where para 3.12 stated:

> 'If you are treated as ordinarily resident solely because you have accommodation here and you dispose of the accommodation and leave the UK within three years of your arrival, you may be treated as not ordinarily resident for the duration of your stay if this is to your advantage.'

The Upper Tribunal followed the First-tier Tribunal in deciding in favour of HMRC, finding that the First-tier Tribunal's conclusion was amply supported by the facts and that the Upper Tribunal would on those facts have reached the same view themselves. For an individual to be 'ordinarily resident' in a country did not require that he intended to stay there permanently or for an indefinite period. While there was a distinction between residence and ordinary residence, it was not as wide or as basic as was suggested for Dr Tuczka.

A final case on ordinary residence was decided on 8 March 2010, *Turberville v Revenue and Customs Comrs* [2010] UKFTT 69 (TC), [2010] SWTI 1619. After a long absence working overseas a Scots domiciliary was posted back to the UK in February 1997, leaving his employer in October 1998 and taking a three year contract to work in the United States with effect from 1 July 2010. He was made redundant in October 2002 and in December 2002 rented a flat in Monaco. During 2002/03 he spent 140 days in total in the UK of which 22 were caused by the death of his mother. The First-tier Tribunal agreed with HMRC that Mr Turberville had been ordinarily resident in the UK in 2001/02 but not in 2002/03. This was because in July 2001 there was a distinct break in his residence and his return to the UK in late 2002 before moving to Monaco had been 'a time of transition' during which he did not have 'a regular order of life anywhere'.

Appendix H

Trust Management Expenses Table

Trust management expenses table: what is allowable/not allowable

Item	Allowable	Not allowable
Accountancy	Identifiable or realistically estimated costs of: • accounting for the trust's income • returning the trust's income, including costs of tax return software incurred by the trustees • making Income Tax repayment claims • getting tax advice relating directly to the preparation of Income Tax returns or Income Tax repayment claims.	All other accounting costs. All other costs of making the tax return including return of capital gains. All other tax advice costs including costs that relate to Capital Gains Tax or Inheritance Tax.
Audit	Audit undertaken because of S22(4) Trustee Act 1925: where trustees exercise their discretion, expenses they decide to charge to income; where they do not, only the expenses associated with auditing income. Otherwise, identifiable costs of auditing the trust's income.	Audit undertaken because of S22(4) Trustee Act 1925: where trustees exercise their discretion, expenses they decide to charge to capital; where they do not, the expenses associated with auditing capital. Otherwise, all other audit costs.
Bank charges	Identifiable costs of operating a bank account that deals exclusively with income.	Charges to secure a facility that is for the better administration of the trust as a whole, for example, charges on a current account, whether or not it incidentally bears interest, or to keep open an overdraft facility.
Depreciation	None.	All.

Trust management expenses table: what is allowable/not allowable

Item	Allowable	Not allowable
Distributing trust funds – cost of	Identifiable or realistically estimated costs of deciding which income beneficiaries to pay and how much, and of paying income to beneficiaries.	All other distribution costs.
Insurance or assurance premiums	Only where: • the premiums relate to buildings insurance for a property, and • the lease contains an obligation to insure the property, and • the trustees are lessees of the property, and • the leasehold property is occupied by beneficiaries under the terms of the trust, and • neither the beneficiaries nor any tenants (as the case may be) are under a legal obligation to meet the insurance premium.	Premiums for insuring trust assets already allowed as a deduction against trading or rental income of the trustees. Insurance on trust assets other than buildings. Premiums payable for trust buildings used or occupied by a beneficiary where the terms of the beneficiary's use or occupation provide that they must meet the insurance premium. Annual premiums on assurance policies.
Interest	Interest on a loan taken out in order to purchase an income-bearing asset, such as shares, that is to be held in the trust for as long as the asset is held in the trust. Interest on a loan taken out or overdraft arranged by trustees for acquiring a non-income bearing property that is occupied by a beneficiary.	Interest on a loan taken out or overdraft arranged to pay for general administration or to buy a non-income bearing asset (other than property to be occupied) for the trust, or an asset that is to be sold. Interest on a loan used by the trustees to make a gift or non-commercial loan to a third party (not an income beneficiary of the trust). Interest incurred in the course of a trade or rental business and already allowed as a deduction against trading or rental income.

Trust Management Expenses Table

Item	Allowable	Not allowable
Interest on unpaid/overdue tax, etc.	Interest on overdue Income Tax.	Interest on overdue Capital Gains Tax. Interest on unpaid Inheritance Tax. Interest on loans taken out to pay Inheritance Tax. Tax penalties and interest on penalties.
	Surcharges and interest on surcharges relating to overdue Income Tax.	Surcharges and interest on surcharges relating to overdue Capital Gains Tax.
Investment advice	Exceptionally, identifiable costs incurred for the purpose of temporarily investing income while deciding whether or not to distribute income to beneficiaries, to the extent that the income was distributed and not accumulated.	Normally, all costs, including the costs incidental to the investment or change of investment of trust funds and the costs of getting investment advice.
Legal costs	Identifiable or realistically estimated costs that relate exclusively to the income beneficiaries.	All other costs including: • the costs of the appointment of new trustees • the costs of getting legal advice, and of taking the direction of the court • the costs of an administration action • the costs of paying money into court under the Trustee Act • the costs of bringing or defending actions against third parties for the protection of the estate (for example, against lessees for breach of their covenants to repair), and the like.
Personal expenses of beneficiaries	None.	All, including items that are the occupier's responsibility, as opposed to the owner's (trustee's) responsibility, for example, utility bills and Council Tax (including business rates, if appropriate).
Premiums on life policies	None.	All.

Trust management expenses table: what is allowable/not allowable

Item	Allowable	Not allowable
Property costs	Identifiable costs of: • maintenance of a freehold property • rent or maintenance of a leasehold property, paid by trustees pursuant to the terms of a lease of which they are the lessees where: • the property is properly held by the trust for the occupation of a beneficiary, and • is actually occupied by a beneficiary, or the only reason it is not is because the property is in a state of disrepair that makes it uninhabitable, and • the beneficiary is not occupying on terms that they meet those expenses personally.	Otherwise not allowable.
Property income business expenses	None.	All.
Reimbursement of expenses to trustees	Allowable or not according to what costs the reimbursement is for – see specific categories.	Allowable or not according to what costs the reimbursement is for – see specific categories.
Running costs	None.	All, including maintaining an office, salaries of personnel, expenses of accommodation, cleaning, and maintenance of equipment and premises.
Trading expenses	None.	All.
Travel and subsistence costs of trustees	Identifiable costs incurred exclusively to confer benefit on the income beneficiaries.	All other costs.
Trustees' fees – the public trustee	Costs specifically chargeable to income by statute – Public Trustee (Fees) Order SI 1999 No. 855.	All other costs.

Item	Allowable	Not allowable
Trustees' fees – other trustees	Identifiable or realistically estimated costs of conferring benefit exclusively on income beneficiaries, such as securing the income of the trust, and determining and making income distributions.	All other costs.

Table taken from HMRC Helpsheet 392 *Trust Management Expenses*. These notes are for guidance only and reflect the position at the time of writing. They do not affect the right of appeal.

Index

A

Accelerated payment notices
  anti-avoidance, and, 23.31–23.33
Accrued income scheme
  'accrued amount', 6.9
  capital gains tax, and, 7.123–7.125
  fixed interest trusts, 6.11
  generally, 6.7
  occasions of charge, 6.15–6.18
  personal representatives, 6.19
  rate of tax, 6.12–6.14
  'rebate amount', 6.8
  settlement day, 6.10
Accumulation and maintenance trusts
  age 18 to 25 trusts, and, 11.23–11.24
  charge to tax on failure, 11.29–11.31
  conditions, 11.6–11.15
  continuing arrangements, 11.22
  extra-statutory concession, Appendix B
  FA 2006 changes, and, 11.19–11.28
  generally, 2.49–2.50
  inheritance tax
    age 18-to-25 trusts, and, 11.23–11.24
    background, 11.1–11.3
    charge to tax on failure, 11.29–11.31
    choice of options, 11.26–11.28
    conditions, 11.6–11.15
    consequences, 11.16–11.18
    continuing arrangements, 11.22
    FA 2006 changes, and, 11.19–11.28
    meaning, 11.4–11.5
    relevant property trusts, 11.25
    transitional arrangements, 11.21
  meaning, 11.4–11.5
  relevant property, and, 8.29
  relevant property trusts, 11.25
  tax consequences, 11.16–11.18
  transitional arrangements, 11.21
Accumulation of income
  beneficiaries' interests, and, 3.6–3.12
  ten-year charge, and, 9.30–9.32
Accumulation trusts
  advance of capital, 6.80–6.85
  deceased estates, 6.59

Accumulation trusts – *cont.*
  deductibility of expenses, 6.26–6.27
  discretionary payments to beneficiaries
    advance of capital, 6.80–6.85
    generally, 6.65–6.67
    tax pools, 6.68–6.79
  dividend income rate, 6.57
  'good receipt', 6.86
  grossing up regime
    advance of capital, 6.80–6.85
    generally, 6.65–6.67
    tax pools, 6.68–6.79
  income charged as special rates
    exceptions, 6.63–6.64
    generally, 6.60–6.62
  income tax
    advance of capital, 6.80–6.85
    deceased estates, 6.59
    deductibility of expenses, 6.26–6.27
    discretionary payments to beneficiaries, 6.65–6.85
    dividend income rate, 6.57
    generally, 6.51
    'good receipt', 6.86
    grossing up regime, 6.65–6.85
    income charged as special rates, 6.60–6.64
    introduction, 6.50–6.51
    non-dividend income rate, 6.56
    payments to beneficiaries, 6.86–6.90
    special rates, 6.55–6.64
    standard rate band, 6.52–6.54
    tax pools, 6.68–6.79
    trust management expenses, 6.53
  introduction, 6.50–6.51
  management expenses, 6.53
  non-dividend income rate, 6.56
  payments to beneficiaries, 6.86–6.90
  special rates
    deceased estates, 6.59
    dividend income rate, 6.57
    generally, 6.55–6.58
    income charged, 6.60–6.64
    non-dividend income rate, 6.56

527

Index

Accumulation trusts – *cont.*
  standard rate band, 6.52–6.54
  tax pools, 6.68–6.79
Addition of property
  ten-year charge, and, 9.57–9.64
Administration of taxes
  charitable trusts, and, 14.68–14.73
  disabled persons' trusts , and, 15.18
Advance of capital
  accumulation trusts, and, 6.80–6.85
Advancement
  generally, 2.24–2.28
Age 18-to-25 trusts
  accumulation and maintenance trusts, and 11.23–11.24
  exit charge, and, 10.32–10.33
Age of donee
  running a trust, and, 18.4
Aggregation of funds
  running a trust, and, 18.2–18.3
Agricultural property relief
  agricultural property, 18.57
  claw-back, 18.66–18.70
  farmhouses, 18.58–18.63
  introduction, 18.56
  occupation and ownership tests, 18.64–18.65
  tax planning, 18.73–18.74
Annual exemption
  capital gains tax, and, 7.36–7.39
Anti-avoidance
  accelerated payment notices, 23.31–23.33
  'associated operations', 23.4
  avoidance/evasion distinction, 23.2–23.3
  bare trusts, 4.20–4.22
  capital gains tax
    deeds of variation, 4.37
    flip-flop scheme, 4.34–4.35
    generally, 4.33
    sub-funds, 4.36
  charitable trusts, and
    abnormal dividends, 14.60–14.61
    generally, 14.47–14.50
    non-qualifying expenditure, 14.53–14.55
    purpose of establishment condition, 14.51–14.52
    substantial donors, 14.57
    tainted donations, 14.58–14.59
  child settlements
    bare trusts, 4.20–4.22
    chargeability of trustees to tax, 4.23
    generally, 4.14–4.19
  conduct notices, 23.29

Anti-avoidance – *cont.*
  deeds of variation
    capital gains tax, 4.37
    income tax, 4.7
  disclosure of tax avoidance schemes (DOTAS)
    generally, 23.15–23.16
    inheritance tax, 23.17–23.23
    stamp duty land tax, 23.24–23.26
  disclosure regimes, 23.3
  evasion/avoidance distinction, 23.2–23.3
  flip-flop scheme, 4.34–4.35
  follower notices, 23.30
  general anti-abuse rule, 23.11–23.14
  gifts with reservation of benefit, 23.4–23.10
  heritage maintenance funds, 4.13
  high risk promoters
    accelerated payment notices, 23.31–23.33
    conduct notices, 23.29
    follower notices, 23.30
    generally, 23.27–23.28
    information powers, 23.29
  income tax
    bare trusts, 4.20–4.22
    capital sums, 4.26–4.31
    child settlements, 4.14–4.23
    exceptions, 4.10–4.12
    general anti-abuse rule, 23.11–23.14
    heritage maintenance funds, 4.13
    'income', 4.9
    'interest' under a settlement, 4.3–4.4
    non-UK resident trusts, 25.13–25.15
    overview, 4.2
    pre-owned assets regime, 4.32
    related property, 4.4
    'settlement', 4.6–4.7
    'settlor', 4.5
    waiver of dividends, 4.24–4.25
    wills, 4.7
  inheritance tax
    'associated operations', 23.4
    DOTAS, 23.17–23.23
    general anti-abuse rule, 23.11–23.14
    generally, 23.4–23.10
    gifts with reservation of benefit, 23.4–23.10
    pre-owned assets regime, 4.39–4.52
    reservation of benefit, 23.4–23.10
    settlors, and, 4.38–4.52
  interest in possession trusts, and, 12.28–12.29
  introduction, 1.17

Anti-avoidance – *cont.*
  non-UK resident trusts, and
    income tax, 25.13–25.15
  overview, 23.1–23.3
  pre-owned assets regime
    capital gains tax, and, 4.32
    chattels, 4.43
    de minimis exemption, 4.47
    exclusions, 4.45
    exemptions, 4.46–4.48
    intangible property comprised in a settlement with retained interest, 4.44
    land, 4.41–4.42
    post-death variations, 4.48
    scope, 4.51–4.52
    summary, 4.39–4.40
    transitional provisions, 4.49–4.50
  reservation of benefit, 23.4–23.10
  running a trust, and, 18.71
  settlors, and
    capital gains tax, 4.33–4.37
    income tax, 4.2–4.32
    inheritance tax, 4.38–4.52
    introduction, 4.1
  stamp duty land tax
    DOTAS, 23.24–23.26
  starting a trust, 17.59–17.60
  summary, 23.34
  tax evasion/avoidance distinction, 23.2–23.3
Appointment
  generally, 2.24–2.28
Appointments
  capital gains tax, and, 7.19–7.20
Appropriation
  generally, 2.27
Asbestos compensation settlements
  generally, 15.19
  relevant property, and, 8.29
Assessment
  discretionary trusts, and, 6.101–6.103
'Associated operations
  anti-avoidance, and', 23.4

Bare trusts – *cont.*
  income tax, and, 4.20–4.22
Base values at death
  capital gains tax, and, 7.40–7.42
Beneficiaries
  income tax returns, and, 20.31
Beneficiaries' interests
  accumulation of income, 3.6–3.12
  contingent interests, 3.4–3.5
  excessive accumulations, and, 3.9
  intermediate income, 3.13–3.15
  introduction, 3.1
  mere spes, 3.2
  possession interests 3.3
  pur autre vie, 3.4
  reversionary interests 3.3
  types, 3.1
  undistributed income, and, 3.6
  vested interests, 3.3
Bereaved minor trusts
  relevant property, and, 8.29
Building society interest
  discretionary trusts, and, 6.4–6.6
Business assets hold-over relief
  generally, 7.62–7.70
  overview, 7.60
  residence, and, 7.61
Business property relief
  AIM shares, 18.32–18.33
  claw-back, 18.66–18.70
  disqualified businesses, 18.34–18.47
  excepted assets, 18.48–18.50
  excluded property, 18.34–18.47
  groups, 18.51–18.53
  introduction, 18.28
  liquidations, 18.55
  period of ownership, 18.54
  qualifying businesses, 18.34–18.47
  relevant business property, 18.29–18.31
  sales, 18.55
  'see through' provisions, 18.31
  tax planning, 18.73–18.74

B

'Baker'-type trusts
  non-UK resident trusts, and, 25.5–25.6
Bank interest
  discretionary trusts, and, 6.4–6.6
Bare trusts
  generally, 2.44–2.48

C

Capital gains tax
  absolute entitlement
    gains, 7.6–7.14
    losses, 7.15–7.18
  accrued income scheme, and, 7.123–7.125
  administrative rules, 7.129–7.131

Index

Capital gains tax – *cont.*
  allowable expenditure
    base values at death, 7.40–7.42
    credit for IHT paid, 7.46–7.47
    expenses, 7.43–7.45
  annual exemption, 7.36–7.39
  anti-avoidance, and
    deeds of variation, 4.37
    flip-flop scheme, 4.34–4.35
    generally, 4.33
    sub-funds, 4.36
  appointments, 7.19–7.20
  base values at death, 7.40–7.42
  business assets hold-over relief
    generally, 7.62–7.70
    overview, 7.60
    residence, and, 7.61
  charitable trusts, and, 14.14
  connected persons, 7.3–7.5
  credit for IHT paid, 7.46–7.47
  deeds of variation
    generally, 7.112–7.117
    introduction, 4.37
  demergers, 7.21–7.24
  disabled persons' trusts, and
    administration, 15.18
    election for special treatment, 15.17
    generally, 15.12
    tax treatment, 15.14–15.16
  distributions, 7.19–7.20
  emigration, 5.25
  employee benefit trusts, 16.23–16.31
  employee ownership trusts, 16.38–16.40
  entitlement
    gains, 7.6–7.14
    losses, 7.15–7.18
  Enterprise Investment Scheme deferral relief, 7.97–7.100
  entrepreneur's relief
    conditions, 7.103
    extension to trustees, 7.104–7.106
    generally, 7.102
  exemption, 7.36–7.39
  expenses, 7.43–7.45
  flip-flop scheme
    generally, 4.34–4.35
    hold-over relief for inheritance tax purposes, 7.75
    non-UK resident trusts, 26.59–26.61
  gains, 7.6–7.14
  high value disposals of residential property, 7.126–7.128
  hold-over relief
    business assets, for, 7.62–7.70

Capital gains tax – *cont.*
  hold-over relief – *cont.*
    gain arising on transfer to settlor interested trust, and, 7.83
    inheritance tax purposes, for, 7.72–7.82
    introduction, 7.60–7.61
    non-business assets, for, 7.71
    residence, and, 7.61
    running a trust, 18.72
  hold-over relief for inheritance tax purposes
    accumulation and maintenance settlements, 7.84–7.90
    accumulation and maintenance trusts, and, 7.72
    age 18-to-25 trusts, and, 7.72
    agricultural property, and, 7.73
    anti-avoidance rules, 7.92–7.93
    bereaved minors' trusts, 7.72
    chargeable transfers, 7.72
    claims, 7.91
    double taxation, and, 7.95
    flip-flop schemes, 7.75
    generally, 7.72–7.74
    'half-gain' rule, 7.96
    heritage maintenance trusts, and, 7.83
    instalment relief, 7.94
    'Melville' arrangements, 7.78–7.82
    overview, 7.60
    relevant property settlements, 7.76–7.77
    relevant property trusts, and, 7.72
    residence, and, 7.61
  inheritance tax, and, 7.46–7.47
  interests under settlement, 7.134
  introduction, 1.7–1.9
  investor's relief, 7.107–7.111
  losses, 7.15–7.18
  main residence relief, 7.51–7.59
  non-business assets hold-over relief, 7.71
  non-UK resident trusts, and
    see also **Capital gains tax (non-UK resident trusts)**
    capital payments charge, 26.33–26.46
    exit charge, 26.5–26.16
    'flip-flop' schemes, 26.59–26.61
    heads of charge, 26.4–26.46
    information powers, 26.63–26.65
    introduction, 26.1–26.3
    overview, 7.1
    settlor charge, 26.17–26.32
    situs of assets, 26.62
    supplementary charge, 26.45–26.46
    temporary non-residence, 26.57–26.58
    2008/2009 changes, 26.47–26.52
    2017/2018 proposals, 26.53–26.56

Index

Capital gains tax – *cont.*
  non-UK resident trusts, and – *cont.*
    UK residential property held by non-residents, and, 26.66–26.68
  occasions of charge, 7.1–7.2
  overview, 1.7–1.9
  pooling land, 7.133
  post-death appointments
    generally, 7.112–7.117
    introduction, 4.37
  rate, 7.33–7.35
  recapture of held over gains, 5.21–5.24
  relief
    EIS deferral relief, 7.97–7.100
    entrepreneur's relief, 7.102–7.106
    hold-over relief, 7.60–7.96
    investor's relief, 7.107–7.111
    main residence relief, 7.51–7.59
    SEIS, 7.101
    taper relief, 7.48–7.50
  residence, and
    hold-over relief, 7.61
    introduction, 7.1
  residential property
    high value disposals, 7.126–7.128
  Seed Enterprise Investment Scheme, 7.101
  'settled property', 5.18
  settlor-interested trusts, and
    deeds of variation, 4.37
    flip-flop scheme, 4.34–4.35
    generally, 4.33
    sub-funds, 4.36
  starting a trust, and
    generally, 17.9–17.12
    hold-over relief, 17.13–17.17
    payment, 17.18–17.19
  sub-funds
    generally, 7.118–7.122
    settlor-interested trusts, 4.36
  taper relief, 7.48–7.50
  termination of qualifying life interest, 7.25–7.32
  transfer of assets by settlor, 7.2
  trust and estate tax return, and, 20.74
  trustees' liability, and
    emigration, 5.25
    generally, 5.18
    recapture of held over gains, 5.21–5.24
    'settled property', 5.18
  valuation of shares
    unquoted/unlisted companies, 7.132
  variation of trusts, 7.135
Capital gains tax (non-UK resident trusts)
  acquisition by dual resident trustees, 26.14

Capital gains tax (non-UK resident trusts) – *cont.*
  capital payments charge
    anti-avoidance provisions, 26.35–26.44
    generally, 26.33–26.34
    supplementary charge, 26.45–26.46
  death of trustee, 26.7
  disposal of interests in settlements, 26.11–26.13
  dual resident trustees, 26.9
  exit charge
    acquisition by dual resident trustees, 26.14
    death of trustee, 26.7
    disposal of interests in settlements, 26.11–26.13
    dual resident trustees, 26.9
    generally, 26.5–26.6
    hold-over restriction, 26.10
    immigration-emigration issue, 26.15
    introduction, 26.4
    past trustees' liability for tax, 26.8
    30 day rule for share identification, 26.16
    trustees becoming dual resident, 26.9
  'flip-flop' schemes, 26.59–26.61
  heads of charge, 26.4–26.46
  hold-over restriction, 26.10
  immigration-emigration issue, 26.15
  information powers, 26.63–26.65
  'interest in the settlement', 26.20–26.25
  introduction, 26.1–26.3
  overview, 7.1
  past trustees' liability for tax, 26.8
  settlor charge
    generally, 26.17–26.19
    'interest in the settlement', 26.20–26.25
    qualifying settlements, 26.26–26.27
    transitional provisions (1998/1999), 26.28–26.32
  situs of assets, 26.62
  supplementary charge, 26.45–26.46
  temporary non-residence, 26.57–26.58
  30 day rule for share identification, 26.16
  trustees becoming dual resident, 26.9
  2008/2009 changes, 26.47–26.52
  2017/2018 proposals, 26.53–26.56
  UK residential property held by non-residents, and, 26.66–26.68
Capital payments charge
  anti-avoidance provisions, 26.35–26.44
  generally, 26.33–26.34
  supplementary charge, 26.45–26.46
Capital sums
  discretionary trusts, and, 4.26–4.31

Charge to tax
  accumulation and maintenance trusts, and, 11.29–11.31
  interest in possession trusts, and
    death, on, 12.3–12.7
    lifetime termination, on, 12.8–12.12
  stamp duty land tax, and
    additional residential properties, 13.29–13.33
    introduction, 13.23–13.24
    mixed use land, 13.25–13.26
    non-residential land, 13.25–13.26
    other points, 13.35–13.36
    residential land, 13.27–13.28
Charitable companies
  see also **Charitable trusts**
  generally, 14.3
Charitable trusts
  abnormal dividends, 14.60–14.61
  administration, 14.68–14.73
  advancement of religion, 14.4
  anti-avoidance
    abnormal dividends, 14.60–14.61
    generally, 14.47–14.50
    non-qualifying expenditure, 14.53–14.55
    purpose of establishment condition, 14.51–14.52
    substantial donors, 14.57
    tainted donations, 14.58–14.59
  beneficial to the community, 14.4
  capital gains tax, 14.14
  cessation of charitable use, 14.78
  chargeable gains, 14.31
  'charity', 14.4–14.9
  claims for relief, 14.2
  community amateur sports clubs, 14.2
  covenanted payments, 14.31
  disaster funds, 14.74–14.75
  education, 14.4
  exemptions on setting up or gifts to charities
    capital gains tax, 14.14
    income tax, 14.15–14.27
    inheritance tax, 14.12–14.13
    stamp duty, 14.10
    stamp duty land tax, 14.10–14.11
  'fit and proper persons' test, 1.43–14.46
  fraudulent claims for relief, 14.2
  general rule, 14.1
  generally, 2.51
  Gift Aid
    'charity', 14.5
    income tax, 14.15–14.26
    introduction, 14.2

Charitable trusts – *cont.*
  Gift Aid – *cont.*
    'purpose of establishment' condition, 14.51–14.52
    Spotlights, 14.63–14.64
    tainted donations, 14.58
    tax exemptions, 14.33
  gift of qualifying investments, 14.65
  HMRC administration, 14.68–14.73
  income tax, 14.15–14.27
  inheritance tax, 14.12–14.13
  introduction, 14.1–14.3
  investment income, 14.31
  latest developments, 14.66
  non-qualifying expenditure, 14.53–14.55
  payroll giving, 14.2
  Press release, Appendix A
  'purpose of establishment' condition, 14.51–14.52
  purposes
    generally, 14.4
    tax exemptions, and, 14.32
  reforms of 2006 and 2011, 14.76–4.80
  relevant property, and, 8.29
  relief of poverty, 14.4
  rents, 14.31
  running a trust, and, 18.1
  savings income, 14.31
  schools, 14.79
  Spotlights
    Gift Aid, 14.63–14.64
    gift of qualifying investments, 14.65
    introduction, 14.62
  stamp duty, 14.10
  stamp duty land tax, 14.10–14.11
  substantial donors, 14.57
  tainted donations, 14.58–14.59
  tax exemptions, 14.31–14.42
  time charities, 14.67
  trading income, 14.33
  trading profits, 14.31
  transfer of family shareholdings, 14.28–14.30
  VAT, and, 14.41
Child settlements
  income tax, and, 4.14–4.23
  settlors, and
    bare trusts, 4.20–4.22
    chargeability of trustees to tax, 4.23
    generally, 4.14–4.19
Children's trusts
  non-UK resident trusts, and, 28.15–28.16
Civil partners
  running a trust, and, 18.5–18.10

Index

Clearance
  income tax returns, and, 20.22
Common Reporting Standard for Automatic Exchange of Tax Information
  generally, 28.33–28.35
Community amateur sports clubs
  charitable trusts, and, 14.2
Companies
  residence, and, 24.51–24.52
Compliance
  beneficiaries, 20.31
  capital gains tax, 20.74
  clearance, 20.22
  deceased estates, 20.32–20.36
  discovery assessment, 20.25–20.30
  enquiry window, 20.25
  estimates of value, 20.20
  finality for deceased estates, 20.21
  income tax
    payment, 20.17–20.19
    returns, 20.1–20.36
    trust and estate returns, 20.37–20.73
  income tax returns
    beneficiaries, and, 20.31
    capital gains, and, 20.74
    deceased estates, 20.32–20.36
    enquiry window, 20.25
    estimates of value, 20.20
    generally, 20.1–20.8
    'no income' trusts, 20.12–20.16
    notification of liability, 20.9–20.11
    provisional figures, 20.20
    trust and estate pages, 20.37–20.73
    trustee policy, 20.23–20.24
  inheritance tax
    account, 21.3–21.5
    chargeable gifts history, 21.12–21.13
    de minimis provisions, 21.8–21.11
    determination of chargeable amount, 21.3–21.18
    determinations, 21.17
    electronic delivery of returns, 21.31
    excepted settlements, 21.11
    excepted terminations, 21.10
    excepted transfers, 21.9
    instalment payments, 21.19–21.25
    introduction, 21.1–21.2
    late payment, 21.14
    liability, 21.26–21.29
    national heritage property, and, 21.30
    payment, 21.6–21.7, 21.19–21.25
    quick succession relief, 21.18
    reporting requirements, 21.15–21.16

Compliance – *cont.*
  inheritance tax – *cont.*
    tax account, 21.3–21.5
  interest
    due date for payment, and, 22.3
    generally, 22.3
    overpayments, 22.4–22.6
    overview, 22.1
    underpayments, 22.4–22.6
    unpaid tax, 22.4
  'no income' trusts, 20.12–20.16
  notification of liability, 20.9–20.11
  offshore tax liability
    criminal sanctions, 22.28–22.30
    penalties, 22.24–22.27
    policy developments, 22.31
  payment of tax
    due date, 22.3
    generally, 20.17–20.19
    interest, and, 22.3–22.6
    penalties, and, 22.7–22.30
  penalties
    failure to deliver returns, 22.19–22.20
    inaccurate returns, 22.9–22.20
    late-filed returns, 22.7–22.8
    overview, 22.2
    policy developments, 22.31
    reasonable care, 22.15
    reasonable excuse, 22.16–22.18
    unpaid tax, 22.21–22.27
  pre-filing date valuation service, 20.20
  provisional figures, 20.20
  tax returns
    income tax, 20.1–20.8
    penalties, and, 22.7–22.20
    trust and estate, 20.37–20.73
  trust and estate tax return
    capital gains, 20.74
    dividends from non-UK companies, 20.71–20.72
    main pages, 20.37–20.70
    statutory residence test, 20.73
    trustee policy, 20.23–20.24
  trusts with no income, 20.12–20.16
Conduct notices
  anti-avoidance, and, 23.29
Covenanted payments
  charitable trusts, and, 14.31
Credit for inheritance tax
  capital gains tax, and, 7.46–7.47
Criminal sanctions
  offshore tax evasion, and, 22.28–22.30

D

Deceased estates
  accumulation trusts, and, 6.59
  income tax returns, and
    finality, 20.21
    generally, 20.32–20.36
Decommissioning security settlements
  relevant property, and, 8.29
Deductibility of expenses
  accumulation trusts, and, 6.26–6.27
  capital gains tax, and
    base values at death, 7.40–7.42
    credit for IHT paid, 7.46–7.47
    expenses, 7.43–7.45
  discretionary trusts, and, 6.26–6.27
  fixed interest trusts, and, 6.24–6.25
  income tax, and
    accumulation trusts, 6.26–6.27
    discretionary trusts, 6.26–6.27
    fixed interest trusts, 6.24–6.25
    generally, 6.23
    interest paid by trustees, 6.41–6.43
    non-UK resident beneficiaries, 6.44
    order, 6.28–6.30
    trust management, 6.31–6.40
Deductibility of loans
  employee trusts, 16.32–16.34
Deduction of tax
  non-UK resident trusts, and, 25.51–25.52
Deeds of variation
  capital gains tax, and
    generally, 7.112–7.117
    introduction, 4.37
  income tax, and, 4.7
  running a trust, and, 18.3
  settlors, and
    capital gains tax, 4.37
    income tax, 4.7
Deemed domicile
  current rules to 2016/2017, 27.13–27.14
  introduction, 27.1
  proposed rules from
    2017/2018, 27.15–27.20
Defeasible absolute interests
  starting a trust, and, 17.41
Demergers
  capital gains tax, and, 7.21–7.24
Development of land
  discretionary trusts, and, 6.126
Disabled persons' trusts
  administration of tax, 15.18
  capital gains tax
    administration, 15.18
    election for special treatment, 15.17

Disabled persons' trusts – *cont.*
  capital gains tax – *cont.*
    generally, 15.12
    tax treatment, 15.14–15.16
  'disabled person', 15.3–15.6
  discretionary trusts, and, 2.37
  generally, 2.52
  HMRC administration, 15.18
  income tax
    administration, 15.18
    election for special treatment, 15.17
    generally, 15.12
    tax treatment, 15.14–15.16
  inheritance tax, 15.7–15.11
  overview, 15.1–15.2
  relevant property, and, 8.29
  running a trust, and, 18.1
  transfer of value, and, 15.13
Disaster funds
  charitable trusts, and, 14.74–14.75
Disclosure
  see also **Anti-avoidance**
  generally, 23.3
  non-UK resident trusts, and, 28.29–28.31
Disclosure of tax avoidance schemes
  (DOTAS)
  see also **Anti-avoidance**
  generally, 23.15–23.16
  inheritance tax, 23.17–23.23
  overview, 1.17
  stamp duty land tax, 23.24–23.26
  starting a trust, and, 17.24
Discounted gift trusts
  starting a trust, and, 17.51–17.54
Discovery assessment
  income tax returns, and, 20.25–20.30
Discretionary payments to beneficiaries
  accumulation trusts, and
    advance of capital, 6.80–6.85
    generally, 6.65–6.67
    tax pools, 6.68–6.79
Discretionary trusts
  advance of capital, 6.80–6.85
  deceased estates, 6.59
  deductibility of expenses, 6.26–6.27
  discretionary payments to beneficiaries
    advance of capital, 6.80–6.85
    generally, 6.65–6.67
    tax pools, 6.68–6.79
  dividend income rate, 6.57
  'good receipt', 6.86
  grossing up regime
    advance of capital, 6.80–6.85
    generally, 6.65–6.67

Index

Discretionary trusts – *cont.*
  grossing up regime – *cont.*
    tax pools, 6.68–6.79
  generally, 2.31–2.37
  income charged as special rates
    exceptions, 6.63–6.64
    generally, 6.60–6.62
  income tax
    advance of capital, 6.80–6.85
    deceased estates, 6.59
    deductibility of expenses, 6.26–6.27
    discretionary payments to beneficiaries, 6.65–6.85
    dividend income rate, 6.57
    generally, 6.51
    'good receipt', 6.86
    grossing up regime, 6.65–6.85
    income charged as special rates, 6.60–6.64
    introduction, 6.50–6.51
    non-dividend income rate, 6.56
    payments to beneficiaries, 6.86–6.90
    special rates, 6.55–6.64
    standard rate band, 6.52–6.54
    tax pools, 6.68–6.79
    trust management expenses, 6.53
  introduction, 6.50–6.51
  management expenses, 6.53
  non-dividend income rate, 6.56
  payments to beneficiaries, 6.86–6.90
  special rates
    deceased estates, 6.59
    dividend income rate, 6.57
    generally, 6.55–6.58
    income charged, 6.60–6.64
    non-dividend income rate, 6.56
    standard rate band, 6.52–6.54
    tax pools, 6.68–6.79
Disguised trusts
  interest in possession trusts, and, 12.23–12.27
Dispositive powers
  generally, 2.24–2.28
Distributions
  capital gains tax, and, 7.19–7.20
Dividend income rate
  accumulation trusts, and, 6.57
Dividend tax credit
  discretionary trusts, and, 6.1A
Dividends
  charitable trusts, and, 14.60–14.61
  discretionary trusts, and
    enhanced, 6.21
    generally, 6.20

Dividends – *cont.*
  non-UK companies, from, 20.71–20.72
Domicile
  see also **Residence**
  basic concept, 24.3
  deemed domicile
    current rules to 2016/2017, 27.13–27.14
    introduction, 27.1
    proposed rules from 2017/2018, 27.15–27.20
  generally, 24.26–24.38
  introduction, 24.1–24.2
  non-UK resident trusts, and
    deemed domicile, 27.13–27.20
    introduction, 27.1
    pre-owned assets regime, 27.63
    tax planning issues, 28.4–28.6
  policy developments, 24.39
DOTAS
  see also **Anti-avoidance**
  generally, 23.15–23.16
  inheritance tax, 23.17–23.23
  overview, 1.17
  stamp duty land tax, 23.24–23.26
  starting a trust, and, 17.24
Double charges
  running a trust, and, 18.92–18.93
'Double trust' arrangements
  running a trust, and, 18.90–18.91

E

Electronic delivery of returns
  inheritance tax, and, 21.31
Emigration
  capital gains tax, and, 5.25
Employee benefit trusts (EBTs)
  capital gains tax, 16.23–16.31
  corporation tax deduction, 16.4–16.5
  deductibility of loans, 16.32–16.34
  income tax, 16.11–16.22
  inheritance tax, 16.6–16.10
  introduction, 16.3
  settlement, and, 16.35
Employee ownership trusts (EOTs)
  capital gains tax, 16.38–16.40
  income tax, 16.41
  inheritance tax, 16.42–16.43
  introduction, 16.36
  qualification conditions, 16.37
Employee trusts
  discretionary trusts, and, 2.37

Employee trusts – *cont.*
  employee benefit trusts
    capital gains tax, 16.23–16.31
    corporation tax deduction, 16.4–16.5
    deductibility of loans, 16.32–16.34
    income tax, 16.11–16.22
    inheritance tax, 16.6–16.10
    introduction, 16.3
    settlement, and, 16.35
  employee ownership trusts
    capital gains tax, 16.38–16.40
    income tax, 16.41
    inheritance tax, 16.42–16.43
    introduction, 16.36
    qualification conditions, 16.37
  ending a trust, and, 19.8
  generally, 2.53
  overview, 16.1–16.2
  relevant property, and, 8.29
Ending a trust
  capital gains tax
    generally, 19.10–19.13
    overview, 19.2
    sale of trust assets, 19.10
  employee trusts, 19.8
  income tax, 19.14–19.19
  inheritance tax
    death of beneficiary, 19.6
    employee trusts, 19.8
    exit charge, 19.3–19.4
    generally, 19.3–19.8
    overview, 19.2
    qualifying IIP, 19.5
    relevant property trust, 19.3–19.4
    reliefs, 19.9
  methods, 19.1
  overview, 19.1–19.2
  planning points, 19.21
  stamp taxes, 19.20
Enquiry window
  income tax returns, and, 20.25
Enterprise Investment Scheme deferral relief
  capital gains tax, and, 7.97–7.100
Entrepreneur's relief
  conditions, 7.103
  extension to trustees, 7.104–7.106
  generally, 7.102
Equitable jurisdiction of the court
  mistake, and, 5.51–5.56
Estimates of value
  income tax returns, and, 20.20
Evasion of tax
  see also **Anti-avoidance**
  generally, 23.2–23.3

Excessive accumulations
  beneficiaries' interests, and, 3.9
Excluded property
  relevant property, and, 8.29
Excluded property trusts
  non-UK residents, and, 28.4
  running a trust, and, 18.1
Exit charge
  age 18-to-25 trust charge, 10.32–10.33
  before first ten-year anniversary, 10.20–10.27
  between ten-year anniversaries, 10.28–10.31
  chargeable amount, 10.17–10.19
  charities, 10.14
  employee trusts, 10.14
  excluded property, 10.8–10.9
  exemptions
    excluded property, 10.8–10.9
    gratuitous transfers, 10.10
    other, 10.14–10.16
    transfers within the first quarter, 10.11–10.13
  gratuitous transfers, 10.10
  introduction, 10.1–10.2
  maintenance funds for historic buildings, 10.14
  national heritage bodies, 10.14
  non-UK residents, and
    acquisition by dual resident trustees, 26.14
    death of trustee, 26.7
    disposal of interests in settlements, 26.11–26.13
    dual resident trustees, 26.9
    generally, 26.5–26.6
    hold-over restriction, 26.10
    immigration-emigration issue, 26.15
    introduction, 26.4
    past trustees' liability for tax, 26.8
    30 day rule for share identification, 26.16
    trustees becoming dual resident, 26.9
  occasions of charge, 10.3–10.7
  permanent charities, 10.14
  political parties, 10.14
  rate of charge, 10.20
  running a business, and
    business property relief, 18.28
    generally, 18.1
    income tax planning, 18.83
  transfers within the first quarter, 10.11–10.13
Expenses
  capital gains tax, and, 7.43–7.45

Index

Extra-statutory concessions
general, Appendix B

F

Failed PETs
ten-year charge, and, 9.78–9.80
Family companies
running a trust, and, 18.18–18.27
Family home
running a trust, and, 18.90–18.91
settlors, and, 4.20–4.22
stamp duty land tax, and, 13.5–13.9
starting a trust, and, 17.40
FATCA (US)
non-UK residents, and, 28.32
Favoured trusts
discretionary trusts, and, 2.37
relevant property, and, 8.29
Finality
income tax returns, and, 20.21
'Fit and proper persons' test
charitable trusts, and, 1.43–14.46
Fixed income trusts
accrued income scheme, 6.11
deductibility of expenses, 6.24–6.25
generally, 2.1
income tax, and
  accrued income scheme, 6.11
  deductibility of expenses, 6.24–6.25
  payments to beneficiaries, 6.86–6.90
payments to beneficiaries, 6.86–6.90
Flat management companies
discretionary trusts, and, 6.99–6.100
Flexible reversionary trust
starting a trust, and, 17.57–17.58
Flip-flop scheme
generally, 4.34–4.35
hold-over relief for inheritance tax purposes, 7.75
non-UK resident trusts, 26.59–26.61
Follower notices
anti-avoidance, and, 23.30
Football club trusts
relevant property, and, 8.29
Fraudulent claims for relief
charitable trusts, and, 14.2

G

Gains
capital gains tax, and, 7.6–7.14
'Garland'-type trusts
non-UK residents, and, 25.7
General anti-abuse rule (GAAR)
see also **Anti-avoidance**
generally, 23.11–23.14
overview, 1.17
running a trust, and, 18.73
starting a trust, and, 17.60
Gift and loan arrangement
starting a trust, and, 17.55–17.56
Gift Aid
see also **Charitable trusts**
'charity', 14.5
income tax, 14.15–14.26
introduction, 14.2
'purpose of establishment' condition, 14.51–14.52
Spotlights, 14.63–14.64
tainted donations, 14.58
tax exemptions, 14.33
Gifts with reservation of benefit
anti-avoidance, and, 23.4–23.10
ten-year charge, and, 9.81–9.82
Good receipt
accumulation trusts, and, 6.86
Gratuitous transfers
exit charge, and, 10.10
Grossing up
accumulation trusts, and
  advance of capital, 6.80–6.85
  generally, 6.65–6.67
  tax pools, 6.68–6.79

H

Hastings-Bass rule
generally, 5.31–5.47
Tax Bulletin, Appendix A
Held-over gains
trustees' tax liability, and, 5.21–5.24
Heritage maintenance funds
income tax, and, 4.13
relevant property, and, 8.29
High risk promoters
accelerated payment notices, 23.31–23.33

High risk promoters – *cont.*
  conduct notices, 23.29
  follower notices, 23.30
  generally, 23.27–23.28
  information powers, 23.29
High value residential property
  capital gains tax, and, 7.126–7.128
  stamp taxes, and, 1.13–1.15
HMRC administration
  charitable trusts, and, 14.68–14.73
  disabled persons' trusts, and, 15.18
Hold-over relief
  business assets, for
    generally, 7.62–7.70
    overview, 7.60
    residence, and, 7.61
  gain arising on transfer to settlor interested trust, and, 7.83
  inheritance tax purposes, for
    accumulation and maintenance settlements, 7.84–7.90
    accumulation and maintenance trusts, and, 7.72
    age 18-to-25 trusts, and, 7.72
    agricultural property, and, 7.73
    anti-avoidance rules, 7.92–7.93
    bereaved minors' trusts, 7.72
    chargeable transfers, 7.72, 17.14
    claims, 7.91
    double taxation, and, 7.95
    flip-flop schemes, 7.75
    generally, 7.72–7.74
    'half-gain' rule, 7.96
    heritage maintenance trusts, and, 7.83
    instalment relief, 7.94
    'Melville' arrangements, 7.78–7.82
    overview, 7.60
    relevant property settlements, 7.76–7.77
    relevant property trusts, and, 7.72
    residence, and, 7.61
  introduction, 7.60–7.61
  non-business assets, for, 7.71
  residence, and, 7.61
  running a trust, and, 18.72
  starting a trust, and
    categories, 17.14–17.15
    chargeable transfers for IHT purposes, 17.14
    claims, 17.16–17.17
    defined business assets, 17.14
    generally, 17.13

I

Identification of property
  ten-year charge, and, 9.77
Implied trusts
  generally, 2.29
Inaccurate returns
  penalties, and, 22.9–22.20
Income tax
  accrued income scheme
    'accrued amount', 6.9
    fixed interest trusts, 6.11
    generally, 6.7
    occasions of charge, 6.15–6.18
    personal representatives, 6.19
    rate of tax, 6.12–6.14
    'rebate amount', 6.8
    settlement day, 6.10
  accumulation trusts
    advance of capital, 6.80–6.85
    deceased estates, 6.59
    deductibility of expenses, 6.26–6.27
    discretionary payments to beneficiaries, 6.65–6.85
    dividend income rate, 6.57
    exceptions to charge at special rates, 6.63–6.64
    generally, 6.51
    'good receipt', 6.86
    grossing up regime, 6.65–6.85
    income charged as special rates, 6.60–6.62
    introduction, 6.50–6.51
    non-dividend income rate, 6.56
    payments to beneficiaries, 6.86–6.90
    special rates, 6.55–6.64
    standard rate band, 6.52–6.54
    tax pools, 6.68–6.79
    trust management expenses, 6.53
  anti-avoidance, and
    bare trusts, 4.20–4.22
    capital sums, 4.26–4.31
    child settlements, 4.14–4.23
    exceptions, 4.10–4.12
    general anti-abuse rule, 23.11–23.14
    heritage maintenance funds, 4.13
    'income', 4.9
    'interest' under a settlement, 4.3–4.4
    non-UK resident trusts, 25.13–25.15
    overview, 4.2
    pre-owned assets regime, 4.32
    related property, 4.4

Income tax – *cont.*
  anti-avoidance, and – *cont.*
    'settlement', 4.6–4.7
    'settlor', 4.5
    waiver of dividends, 4.24–4.25
    wills, 4.7
  assessment, 6.101–6.103
  bank interest, 6.4–6.6
  bare trusts, 4.20–4.22
  building society interest, 6.4–6.6
  capital sums, 4.26–4.31
  charitable trusts, and, 14.15–14.27
  child settlements, 4.14–4.23
  compliance, and
    payment, 20.17–20.19
    returns, 20.1–20.36
    trust and estate returns, 20.37–20.73
  deductibility of expenses
    accumulation trusts, 6.26–6.27
    discretionary trusts, 6.26–6.27
    fixed interest trusts, 6.24–6.25
    generally, 6.23
    interest paid by trustees, 6.41–6.43
    non-UK resident beneficiaries, 6.44
    order, 6.28–6.30
    trust management, 6.31–6.40
  development of land, 6.126
  disabled persons' trusts, and
    administration, 15.18
    election for special treatment, 15.17
    generally, 15.12
    tax treatment, 15.14–15.16
  discretionary trusts
    advance of capital, 6.80–6.85
    deceased estates, 6.59
    deductibility of expenses, 6.26–6.27
    discretionary payments to beneficiaries, 6.65–6.85
    dividend income rate, 6.57
    exceptions to charge at special rates, 6.63–6.64
    generally, 6.51
    'good receipt', 6.86
    grossing up regime, 6.65–6.85
    income charged as special rates, 6.60–6.62
    introduction, 6.50–6.51
    non-dividend income rate, 6.56
    payments to beneficiaries, 6.86–6.90
    special rates, 6.55–6.64
    standard rate band, 6.52–6.54
    tax pools, 6.68–6.79
    trust management expenses, 6.53
  dividend tax credit, and, 6.1A

Income tax – *cont.*
  dividends
    enhanced, 6.21
    generally, 6.20
  employee benefit trusts, 16.11–16.22
  employee ownership trusts, 16.41
  ending a trust, and, 19.14–19.19
  estimates of value, 20.20
  exceptions, 4.10–4.12
  fixed interest trusts
    accrued income scheme, 6.11
    deductibility of expenses, 6.24–6.25
    payments to beneficiaries, 6.86–6.90
  flat management companies, 6.99–6.100
  general anti-abuse rule, 23.11–23.14
  generally, 2.1
  heritage maintenance funds, 4.13
  'income', 4.9
  interest in possession (IIP) trusts, 6.45–6.49
  interest paid by trustees, 6.41–6.43
  interest received
    accrued income scheme, 6.7–6.19
    bank and building society, from, 6.4–6.6
  'interest' under a settlement, 4.3–4.4
  introduction, 6.1–6.3
  land transactions, and, 6.96–6.98
  non-UK resident beneficiaries
    deductibility of expenses, 6.44
    generally, 6.104–6.105
  non-UK resident trusts, and
    anti-avoidance, 25.13–25.15
    deduction of tax, 25.51–25.52
    FA 2008 reforms, 25.16–25.45
    identifying income of beneficiary, 25.4–25.12
    liability, 25.1–25.3
    temporary non-residence, 25.53–25.58
    transactions in land, 25.46–25.50
    transfer of assets abroad, 25.18–25.45
  notification of liability, 20.9–20.11
  overview, 1.19–1.11
  premiums on leases, 6.96
  pre-owned assets regime, 4.32
  provisional figures, 20.20
  related property, 4.4
  returns
    beneficiaries, and, 20.31
    capital gains, and, 20.74
    deceased estates, 20.32–20.36
    enquiry window, 20.25
    estimates of value, 20.20
    finality for deceased estates, and 20.21

539

Income tax – *cont.*
 returns – *cont.*
  generally, 20.1–20.8
  'no income' trusts, 20.12–20.16
  notification of liability, 20.9–20.11
  provisional figures, 20.20
  trust and estate pages, 20.37–20.73
  trustee policy, 20.23–20.24
 running a trust, and, 18.77–18.83
 sale of land, 6.126
 self-assessment, 6.101–6.103
 'settlement', 4.6–4.7
 'settlor', 4.5
 settlor-interested trusts, 5.11–5.17
 settlors, and
  bare trusts, 4.20–4.22
  capital sums, 4.26–4.31
  child settlements, 4.14–4.23
  exceptions, 4.10–4.12
  heritage maintenance funds, 4.13
  'income', 4.9
  'interest' under a settlement, 4.3–4.4
  overview, 4.2
  pre-owned assets regime, 4.32
  related property, 4.4
  'settlement', 4.6–4.7
  'settlor', 4.5
  waiver of dividends, 4.24–4.25
  wills, 4.7
 stock dividends
  enhanced, 6.21
  generally, 6.20
 tax pools, 6.68–6.79
 tax returns
  beneficiaries, and, 20.31
  capital gains, and, 20.74
  deceased estates, 20.32–20.36
  enquiry window, 20.25
  estimates of value, 20.20
  finality for deceased estates, and 20.21
  generally, 20.1–20.8
  'no income' trusts, 20.12–20.16
  notification of liability, 20.9–20.11
  provisional figures, 20.20
  trust and estate pages, 20.37–20.73
  trustee policy, 20.23–20.24
 temporary non-residence, 25.53–25.58
 transfer of assets abroad
  generally, 25.18–25.23
  'motive test', 25.24–25.27
  2005 replacement regime, 25.28–25.33
  2013 amendments, 25.34–25.40
  2017 proposed changes, 25.41–25.45
 transfers of income streams, 6.22

Income tax – *cont.*
 trust management expenses
  discretionary trusts, and, 6.53
  generally, 6.31–6.33
  HMRC Guidance, 6.36–6.40
  Peter Clay case, 6.34–6.35
 trustees' liability, and
  generally, 5.5–5.10
  settlor-interested trusts, 5.11–5.17
 vulnerable beneficiaries' trusts, 6.50
 waiver of dividends, 4.24–4.25
 wills, 4.7
Income tax returns
 beneficiaries, and, 20.31
 capital gains, and, 20.74
 deceased estates, 20.32–20.36
 enquiry window, 20.25
 estimates of value, 20.20
 finality for deceased estates, and 20.21
 generally, 20.1–20.8
 'no income' trusts, 20.12–20.16
 notification of liability, 20.9–20.11
 provisional figures, 20.20
 trust and estate pages, 20.37–20.73
 trustee policy, 20.23–20.24
Indemnity
 trustees' liability, and, 5.2
Information exchange
 Common Reporting Standard, 28.33–28.35
 disclosure facilities, 28.29–28.31
 FATCA (US), 28.32
 introduction, 28.27–28.28
 multinational disclosure arrangements, 28.32–28.36
Inheritance tax
 accumulation and maintenance trusts
  age 18-to-25 trusts, and, 11.23–11.24
  background, 11.1–11.3
  charge to tax on failure, 11.29–11.31
  choice of options, 11.26–11.28
  conditions, 11.6–11.15
  continuing arrangements, 11.22
  FA 2006 changes, and, 11.19–11.28
  meaning, 11.4–11.5
  relevant property trusts, 11.25
  tax consequences, 11.16–11.18
  transitional arrangements, 11.21
 'age 18-to-25 trusts'
  A&M trusts, and, 11.23–11.24
  generally, 8.13–8.15
 anti-avoidance, and
  'associated operations', 23.4
  DOTAS, 23.17–23.23

Inheritance tax – *cont.*
  anti-avoidance, and – *cont.*
    general anti-abuse rule, 23.11–23.14
    generally, 23.4–23.10
    gifts with reservation of benefit, 23.4–23.10
    pre-owned assets regime, 4.39–4.52
    reservation of benefit, 23.4–23.10
    settlors, and, 4.38–4.52
  'bereaved minors' trusts', 8.9–8.12
  capital gains tax, and, 7.46–7.47
  chargeable gifts history, 21.12–21.13
  charitable trusts, and, 14.12–14.13
  compliance, and
    account, 21.3–21.5
    chargeable gifts history, 21.12–21.13
    de minimis provisions, 21.8–21.11
    determination of chargeable amount, 21.3–21.18
    determinations, 21.17
    electronic delivery of returns, 21.31
    excepted settlements, 21.11
    excepted terminations, 21.10
    excepted transfers, 21.9
    instalment payments, 21.19–21.25
    introduction, 21.1–21.2
    late payment, 21.14
    liability, 21.26–21.29
    national heritage property, and, 21.30
    payment, 21.6–21.7, 21.19–21.25
    quick succession relief, 21.18
    reporting requirements, 21.15–21.16
    tax account, 21.3–21.5
  death of beneficiary, 19.6
  deemed domicile
    current rules to 2016/2017, 27.13–27.14
    introduction, 27.1
    proposed rules from 2017/2018, 27.15–27.20
  definitions, 8.1–8.42
  determination of chargeable amount
    chargeable gifts history, 21.12–21.13
    de minimis provisions, 21.8–21.11
    determinations, 21.17
    excepted settlements, 21.11
    excepted terminations, 21.10
    excepted transfers, 21.9
    late payment, 21.14
    payment, 21.6–21.7
    quick succession relief, 21.18
    reporting requirements, 21.15–21.16
    tax account, 21.3–21.5
  determinations, 21.17
  'disabled person's interest', 8.16

Inheritance tax – *cont.*
  disabled persons' trusts, and, 15.7–15.11
  double tax treaties, 27.53–27.54
  electronic delivery of returns, 21.31
  employee benefit trusts
    ending a trust, 19.8
    generally, 16.6–16.10
  employee ownership trusts
    ending a trust, 19.8
    generally, 16.42–16.43
  ending a trust, and
    death of beneficiary, 19.6
    employee trusts, 19.8
    exit charge, 19.3–19.4
    generally, 19.3–19.8
    overview, 19.2
    qualifying IIP, 19.5
    relevant property trust, 19.3–19.4
    reliefs, 19.9
  'excluded property'
    excluded settlements, 8.24–8.25
    FOTRA securities, 8.26–8.27
    introduction, 8.23
    reversionary interests, 8.28
  excluded property settlements, 8.24–8.25
  exit charge
    age 18-to-25 trust charge, 10.32–10.33
    before first ten-year anniversary, 10.20–10.27
    between ten-year anniversaries, 10.28–10.31
    chargeable amount, 10.17–10.19
    ending a trust, and, 19.3–19.4
    excluded property, 10.8–10.9
    exemptions, 10.8–10.16
    gratuitous transfers, 10.10
    introduction, 10.1–10.2
    occasions of charge, 10.3–10.7
    rate of charge, 10.20
    transfers within the first quarter, 10.11–10.13
  failed PETs, 5.28
  FOTRA securities, 8.26–8.27
  'gift with reservation'
    generally, 8.36–8.40
    protective trusts, 8.41–8.42
  'immediate post-death interest', 8.8
  instalment payments, 21.19–21.25
  interest, and
    due date for payment, and, 22.3
    generally, 22.3
    overpayments, 22.6
    overview, 22.1
    underpayments, 22.6

Inheritance tax – *cont.*
  interest, and – *cont.*
    unpaid tax, 22.4
  'interest in possession'
    ending a trust, and, 19.5
    generally, 8.6
    immediate post-death interest, 8.8
    qualifying interest, 8.7
  late payment, 21.14
  national heritage property, and, 21.30
  non-UK residents, and
    deemed domicile, 27.13–27.20
    domicile, and, 27.1
    double tax treaties, 27.53–27.54
    enforcement, 27.62
    excluded property, 27.2–27.12
    executors, 27..59–27.61
    exempt gifts, 27.28–27.38
    liabilities, 27.9–27.12
    pre-owned assets regime, 27.63
    reporting obligation, 27.55–27.58
    reversionary interests, 27.27
    settled property situated outside the UK, 27.4–27.6
    settlor, 27.7–27.8
    situs of property, 27.21–27.38
    trustees, 27..59–27.61
    UK residential properties held by offshore holding structure, 27.39–27.52
  overview, 1.4–1.6
  payment
    generally, 21.6–21.7
    instalments, by, 21.19–21.25
    introduction, 8.31
    late, 21.14
  penalties, and
    failure to deliver returns, 22.19–22.20
    inaccurate returns, 22.9, 22.17
    overview, 22.2
    policy developments, 22.31
    reasonable care, 22.15
    reasonable excuse, 22.16–22.18
    unpaid tax, 22.22–22.27
  'potentially exempt transfer', 8.32–8.35
  pre-owned assets regime
    capital gains tax, and, 4.32
    chattels, 4.43
    de minimis exemption, 4.47
    exclusions, 4.45
    exemptions, 4.46–4.48
    intangible property comprised in a settlement with retained interest, 4.44
    land, 4.41–4.42

Inheritance tax – *cont.*
  pre-owned assets regime – *cont.*
    post-death variations, 4.48
    scope, 4.51–4.52
    summary, 4.39–4.40
    transitional provisions, 4.49–4.50
  protective trusts, 8.41–8.42
  qualifying interest in possession trusts
    anti-avoidance, 12.28–12.29
    charge on death, 12.3–12.7
    charge on lifetime termination, 12.8–12.12
    disguised IIP, 12.23–12.27
    ending a trust, and, 19.5
    'interest in possession', 8.6–8.7
    introduction, 12.1–12.2
    'qualifying interest in possession', 8.7
    reservation of benefit, 12.19–12.22
    reversionary interests, 12.17–12.18
    revertor to settlor, 12.13–12.16
  'quarter', 8.31
  quick succession relief, 21.18
  'relevant property'
    exclusions, 8.29
    generally, 8.29–8.30
  relevant property settlements
    ending a trust, and, 19.3–19.4
    exit charge, 10.1–10.34
    ten-year charge, 9.1–9.84
  reversionary interests, 8.28
  running a trust, and
    agricultural property relief, 18.56–18.65
    anti-avoidance rules, 18.71
    business property relief, 18.28–18.55
    claw-back of relief, 18.66–18.70
    family companies, 18.18–18.27
    introduction, 18.1–18.10
    pre-March 1986 settlements, 18.17
    residence nil-rate band, 18.11–18.16
  settled property, 5.20
  'settlement', 8.2–8.5
  settlors, and
    introduction, 4.38
    pre-owned assets regime, 4.39–4.52
  situs of property, 27.21–27.38
  starting a trust, and
    agricultural property, 17.36–17.39
    business property, 17.36–17.39
    compliance, 17.22–17.23
    exceeding nil-rate band, 17.33–17.35
    exemptions, 17.21
    generally, 17.20
    life assurance trusts, 17.47–17.50
    nil-rate band, 17.33–17.35

Inheritance tax – *cont.*
  tax account, 21.3–21.5
  ten-year charge
    accumulations of income, 9.30–9.32
    addition of property, 9.57–9.64
    anti-avoidance measures, 9.69–9.76
    calculation of tax, 9.23
    change of character of property within settlement, 9.65
    chargeable amount, 9.12–9.23
    combination of relevant and non-relevant property, 9.49–9.54
    complicated example, 9.37–9.55
    failed PETs, 9.78–9.80
    FA 2006, and, 9.83–9.84
    gifts with reservation of benefit, 9.81–9.82
    identification of property, 9.77
    overview, 9.1–9.7
    pension death benefits, 9.68
    practical difficulties, 9.77–9.84
    rate of tax, 9.23
    related settlements, 9.37–9.43
    same-day additions, 9.44–9.48
    settled legacies, 9.66–9.67
    simple example, 9.24–9.36
    ten-year anniversary, 9.8–9.11
    undistributed income, 9.33–9.36
  'transitional serial interests', 8.17–8.22
  trustees' liability, and
    failed PETs, 5.28
    generally, 5.19–5.20
    settled property, 5.20
    'trustees', 5.19
    unusual events, 5.26–5.27
  'trusts for bereaved minors', 8.9–8.12
  UK residential properties held by offshore holding structure, 27.39–27.52
  usufructs, 8.5
Instalment payments
  inheritance tax, and, 21.19–21.25
Interest
  due date for payment, and, 22.3
  generally, 22.3
  overpayments, 22.4–22.6
  overview, 22.1
  self-assessment, and, 22.3
  underpayments, 22.4–22.6
  unpaid tax, 22.4
Interest in possession (IIP) trusts
  anti-avoidance, 12.28–12.29
  charge to tax
    death, on, 12.3–12.7
    lifetime termination, on, 12.8–12.12
  disguised IIP, 12.23–12.27

Interest in possession (IIP) trusts – *cont.*
  generally, 2.38–2.43
  income tax, and, 6.45–6.49
  introduction, 2.1
  qualifying interest in possession trusts
    anti-avoidance, 12.28–12.29
    charge on death, 12.3–12.7
    charge on lifetime termination, 12.8–12.12
    disguised IIP, 12.23–12.27
    generally, 2.1
    introduction, 12.1–12.2
    'qualifying interest in possession', 8.7
    reservation of benefit, 12.19–12.22
    reversionary interests, 12.17–12.18
    revertor to settlor, 12.13–12.16
  reservation of benefit, 12.19–12.22
  reversionary interests, 12.17–12.18
  revertor to settlor, 12.13–12.16
  running a trust, and, 18.1
Interest paid by trustees
  income tax, and, 6.41–6.43
Interest received
  income tax, and
    accrued income scheme, 6.7–6.19
    bank and building society, from, 6.4–6.6
'Interest' under a settlement
  generally, 4.3–4.4
Interests of beneficiaries
  accumulation of income, 3.6–3.12
  contingent interests, 3.4–3.5
  excessive accumulations, and, 3.9
  intermediate income, 3.13–3.15
  introduction, 3.1
  mere spes, 3.2
  possession interests 3.3
  pur autre vie, 3.4
  reversionary interests 3.3
  types, 3.1
  undistributed income, and, 3.6
  vested interests, 3.3
Intermediate income
  beneficiaries' interests, and, 3.13–3.15
Investment income
  charitable trusts, and, 14.31
Investor's relief
  capital gains tax, and, 7.107–7.111

L

Land transactions
  discretionary trusts, and, 6.96–6.98

Late-filed returns
  penalties, and, 22.7–22.8
Late payment of tax
  inheritance tax, and, 21.14
Lease premiums
  income tax, and, 6.96
Life assurance trusts
  starting a trust, and, 17.47–17.50
Lifetime settlements
  generally, 2.14–2.23
Location of trust
  non-UK residents, and, 28.17–28.19
Losses
  capital gains tax, and, 7.15–7.18

M

Main residence relief
  capital gains tax, and, 7.51–7.59
Maintenance funds for historic buildings
  income tax, and, 4.13
  relevant property, and, 8.29
Management expenses
  accumulation trusts, and, 6.53
Married couples
  running a trust, and, 18.5–18.10
Mere spes
  beneficiaries' interests, and, 3.2
Mistake
  trustees' liability, and, 5.51–5.56

N

National heritage property
  inheritance tax, and, 21.30
Newspaper trusts
  relevant property, and, 8.29
Nil-rate band
  running a trust, and
    generally, 18.2
    residences, for, 18.11–18.16
'No income' trusts
  income tax returns, and, 20.12–20.16
Non-business assets hold-over relief
  capital gains tax, and, 7.71
Non-dividend income rate
  accumulation trusts, and, 6.56
Non-domiciliaries
  overview, 1.16
Non-UK domiciled individuals
  tax planning issues, and, 28.20–28.26

Non-UK resident beneficiaries
  income tax, and
    deductibility of expenses, 6.44
    generally, 6.104–6.105
    identifying income, 25.4–25.12
Non-UK resident children's trusts
  generally, 28.15–28.16
Non-UK resident trusts
  anti-avoidance, 25.13–25.15
  'Baker'-type trusts, 25.5–25.6
  capital gains tax
    capital payments charge, 26.33–26.46
    exit charge, 26.5–26.16
    'flip-flop' schemes, 26.59–26.61
    heads of charge, 26.4–26.46
    information powers, 26.63–26.65
    introduction, 26.1–26.3
    introduction, 7.1
    settlor charge, 26.17–26.32
    situs of assets, 26.62
    supplementary charge, 26.45–26.46
    temporary non-residence, 26.57–26.58
    2008/2009 changes, 26.47–26.52
    2017/2018 proposals, 26.53–26.56
    UK residential property held by non-residents, and, 26.66–26.68
  capital payments charge
    anti-avoidance provisions, 26.35–26.44
    generally, 26.33–26.34
    supplementary charge, 26.45–26.46
  children's trusts, 28.15–28.16
  Common Reporting Standard for Automatic Exchange of Tax Information, 28.33–28.35
  companies, 24.51–24.52
  deduction of tax, 25.51–25.52
  deemed domicile
    current rules to 2016/2017, 27.13–27.14
    introduction, 27.1
    proposed rules from 2017/2018, 27.15–27.20
  disclosure facilities, 28.29–28.31
  domicile
    basic concept, 24.3
    generally, 24.26–24.38
    inheritance tax, 27.1
    introduction, 24.1–24.2
    tax planning issues, 28.5–28.6
  excluded property trusts, 28.4
  exit charge
    acquisition by dual resident trustees, 26.14
    death of trustee, 26.7

Non-UK resident trusts – *cont.*
  exit charge – *cont.*
    disposal of interests in settlements, 26.11–26.13
    dual resident trustees, 26.9
    generally, 26.5–26.6
    hold-over restriction, 26.10
    immigration-emigration issue, 26.15
    introduction, 26.4
    past trustees' liability for tax, 26.8
    30 day rule for share identification, 26.16
    trustees becoming dual resident, 26.9
  extra-statutory concession, Appendix B
  family context, 28.12–28.14
  FATCA (US), 28.32
  'Garland'-type trusts, 25.7
  income tax
    anti-avoidance, 25.13–25.15
    deduction of tax, 25.51–25.52
    FA 2008 reforms, 25.16–25.45
    identifying income of beneficiary, 25.4–25.12
    liability, 25.1–25.3
    temporary non-residence, 25.53–25.58
    transactions in land, 25.46–25.50
    transfer of assets abroad, 25.18–25.45
  information exchange
    Common Reporting Standard, 28.33–28.35
    disclosure facilities, 28.29–28.31
    FATCA (US), 28.32
    introduction, 28.27–28.28
    multinational disclosure arrangements, 28.32–28.36
  inheritance tax
    deemed domicile, 27.13–27.20
    domicile, and, 27.1
    double tax treaties, 27.53–27.54
    enforcement, 27.62
    excluded property, 27.2–27.12
    executors, 27..59–27.61
    exempt gifts, 27.28–27.38
    liabilities, 27.9–27.12
    pre-owned assets regime, 27.63
    reporting obligation, 27.55–27.58
    reversionary interests, 27.27
    settled property situated outside the UK, 27.4–27.6
    settlor, 27.7–27.8
    situs of property, 27.21–27.38
    trustees, 27..59–27.61
    UK residential properties held by offshore holding structure, 27.39–27.52

Non-UK resident trusts – *cont.*
  location of trust, 28.17–28.19
  multinational disclosure arrangements, 28.32–28.36
  ordinary residence
    generally, Appendix G
    introduction, 24.3
  overview, 1.16
  remittance basis charge, 28.3
  residence
    basic concept, 24.3
    companies, 24.51–24.52
    individuals before 2013/2014, 24.4–24.8
    individuals from 2013/2014, 24.9–24.21
    introduction, 24.1–24.2
    policy developments, 24.39–24.50
    statutory test, 24.9–24.20
    temporary non-residence, 24.21
    trustees, 24.22–24.25
  settlor charge
    generally, 26.17–26.19
    'interest in the settlement', 26.20–26.25
    qualifying settlements, 26.26–26.27
    transitional provisions (1998/1999), 26.28–26.32
  statutory residence test
    generally, 24.9
    rules, 24.10–24.20
  supplementary charge, 26.45–26.46
  tax planning issues
    children's trusts, 28.15–28.16
    Common Reporting Standard, 28.33–28.35
    disclosure facilities, 28.29–28.31
    domicile, 28.5–28.6
    excluded property trusts, 28.4
    family context, 28.12–28.14
    FATCA (US), 28.32
    information exchange, 28.27–28.36
    introduction, 28.1–28.4
    location of trust, 28.17–28.19
    multinational disclosure arrangements, 28.32–28.36
    opportunities for individuals, 28.20–28.26
    remittance basis charge, 28.3
    trust document, 28.7–28.11
  temporary non-residence
    capital gains tax, 26.57–26.58
    generally, 24.21
    income tax, 25.53–25.58
    transactions in land, 25.46–25.50
  transfer of assets abroad
    generally, 25.18–25.23

Index

Non-UK resident trusts – *cont.*
  transfer of assets abroad – *cont.*
    'motive test', 25.24–25.27
    2005 replacement regime, 25.28–25.33
    2013 amendments, 25.34–25.40
    2017 proposed changes, 25.41–25.45
  trust document, 28.7–28.11
Notification of liability
  compliance, and, 20.9–20.11

O

Offshore tax evasion
  criminal sanctions, and, 22.28–22.30
Offshore tax liability
  criminal sanctions, 22.28–22.30
  penalties, 22.24–22.27
  policy developments, 22.31
Offshore trusts
  see Non-UK resident trusts
Ordinary residence
  see also Residence
  generally, Appendix G
  introduction, 24.3
Overpayments
  interest, and, 22.4–22.6
Own share purchases
  running a trust, and, 17.84

P

Payment of tax
  due date, 22.3
  generally, 20.17–20.19
  inheritance tax, and
    generally, 21.6–21.7
    instalments, by, 21.19–21.25
    late, 21.14
  interest, and
    due date for payment, and, 22.3
    generally, 22.3
    overpayments, 22.4–22.6
    overview, 22.1
    underpayments, 22.4–22.6
    unpaid tax, 22.4
  penalties, and
    failure to deliver returns, 22.19–22.20
    inaccurate returns, 22.9–22.20
    late-filed returns, 22.7–22.8
    overview, 22.2
    policy developments, 22.31

Payment of tax – *cont.*
  penalties, and – *cont.*
    reasonable care, 22.15
    reasonable excuse, 22.16–22.18
    unpaid tax, 22.21–22.27
Payments to beneficiaries
  accumulation trusts, and, 6.86–6.90
Payroll giving
  charitable trusts, and, 14.2
Penalties
  failure to deliver returns, 22.19–22.20
  inaccurate returns, 22.9–22.20
  late-filed returns, 22.7–22.8
  overview, 22.2
  policy developments, 22.31
  reasonable care, 22.15
  reasonable excuse, 22.16–22.18
  unpaid tax, 22.21–22.27
Pension death benefits
  ten-year charge, and, 9.68
Pension funds
  relevant property, and, 8.29
Pooling land
  capital gains tax, and, 7.133
Possession interests
  beneficiaries' interests, and, 3.3
Post-death appointments
  capital gains tax, and, 7.112–7.117
Post-death variations
  running a trust, and, 18.3
Pre-filing date valuation service
  compliance, and, 20.20
Premiums on leases
  income tax, and, 6.96
Pre-owned assets regime
  chattels, 4.43
  de minimis exemption, 4.47
  exclusions, 4.45
  exemptions, 4.46–4.48
  income tax, and, 4.32
  intangible property comprised in a settlement with retained interest, 4.44
  land, 4.41–4.42
  post-death variations, 4.48
  scope, 4.51–4.52
  summary, 4.39–4.40
  transitional provisions, 4.49–4.50
Professional compensation funds
  relevant property, and, 8.29
Protective trusts
  relevant property, and, 8.29
Provisional figures
  income tax returns, and, 20.20

Pur autre vie
 beneficiaries' interests, and, 3.4

Q

Qualifying interest in possession trusts
 anti-avoidance, 12.28–12.29
 charge on death, 12.3–12.7
 charge on lifetime termination, 12.8–12.12
 disguised IIP, 12.23–12.27
 generally, 2.1
 introduction, 12.1–12.2
 'qualifying interest in possession', 8.7
 reservation of benefit, 12.19–12.22
 reversionary interests, 12.17–12.18
 revertor to settlor, 12.13–12.16
 running a trust, and, 18.1
Quick succession relief
 inheritance tax, and, 21.18

R

Reasonable care
 penalties, and, 22.15
Reasonable excuse
 penalties, and, 22.16–22.18
Recapture of held over gains
 capital gains tax, and, 5.21–5.24
Rectification
 trustees' liability, and, 5.48–5.50
Related property
 income tax, and, 4.4
Related settlements
 ten-year charge, and, 9.37–9.43
Relevant property regime
 exit charge
  age 18-to-25 trust charge, 10.32–10.33
  before first ten-year anniversary, 10.20–10.27
  between ten-year anniversaries, 10.28–10.31
  chargeable amount, 10.17–10.19
  excluded property, 10.8–10.9
  exemptions, 10.8–10.16
  gratuitous transfers, 10.10
  introduction, 10.1–10.2
  occasions of charge, 10.3–10.7
  rate of charge, 10.20
  transfers within the first quarter, 10.11–10.13
 generally, 2.1

Relevant property regime – *cont.*
 ten-year charge
  accumulations of income, 9.30–9.32
  addition of property, 9.57–9.64
  anti-avoidance measures, 9.69–9.76
  calculation of tax, 9.23
  change of character of property within settlement, 9.65
  chargeable amount, 9.12–9.23
  combination of relevant and non-relevant property, 9.49–9.54
  complicated example, 9.37–9.55
  failed PETs, 9.78–9.80
  FA 2006, and, 9.83–9.84
  gifts with reservation of benefit, 9.81–9.82
  identification of property, 9.77
  overview, 9.1–9.7
  pension death benefits, 9.68
  practical difficulties, 9.77–9.84
  rate of tax, 9.23
  related settlements, 9.37–9.43
  same-day additions, 9.44–9.48
  settled legacies, 9.66–9.67
  simple example, 9.24–9.36
  ten-year anniversary, 9.8–9.11
  undistributed income, 9.33–9.36
Relevant property trusts
 accumulation and maintenance trusts, and, 11.25
 generally, 2.1
 running a trust, and, 18.1
Relief
 capital gains tax, and
  EIS deferral relief, 7.97–7.100
  entrepreneur's relief, 7.102–7.106
  hold-over relief, 7.60–7.96
  investor's relief, 7.107–7.111
  main residence relief, 7.51–7.59
  SEIS, 7.101
  taper relief, 7.48–7.50
Remittance basis charge (RBC)
 background, 24.39–24.40
 generally, 24.41–24.43
 overview, 1.16
 quantum of charge, 24.44–24.45
 Summer Budget 2015 proposals, 24.46–24.50
 tax planning issues, 28.3
 transfer of assets abroad, and, 25.18
Rents
 charitable trusts, and, 14.31
Reservation of benefit
 anti-avoidance, and, 23.4–23.10

Reservation of benefit – *cont.*
  interest in possession trusts, and, 12.19–12.22
Residence
  basic concept, 24.3
  capital gains tax, and
    hold-over relief, 7.61
    introduction, 7.1
  companies, 24.51–24.52
  domicile, and
    basic concept, 24.3
    generally, 24.26–24.38
    introduction, 24.1–24.2
    policy developments, 24.39
  extra-statutory concession, Appendix B
  individuals before 2013/2014, 24.4–24.8
  individuals from 2013/2014, 24.9–24.21
  introduction, 24.1–24.2
  ordinary residence
    generally, Appendix G
    introduction, 24.3
  overview, 1.16
  policy developments
    FA 2008 revisions, 24.41–24.43
    generally, 24.39–24.40
    quantum of RBC charge, 24.44–24.45
    Summer Budget 2015 proposals, 24.46–24.50
  statutory residence test
    generally, 24.9
    rules, 24.10–24.20
  temporary non-residence, 24.21
  trustees, and
    generally, 24.22–24.25
    introduction, 5.29
    Non-UK Resident Landlord Scheme, 5.30
Residence nil-rate band (RNRB)
  civil partners, 18.15
  'closely inherited', 18.13
  conditions, 18.12–18.14
  disadvantages, 18.16
  generally, 18.11
  married couples, 18.15
  'residential property interest', 18.12
  transfer, 18.15
Residential property
  capital gains tax, and
    high value disposals, 7.126–7.128
Retention of title clauses
  meaning of trusts, and, 2.2
Reversionary interests
  beneficiaries' interests, and 3.3
  interest in possession trusts, and, 12.17–12.18

Revertor to settlor
  interest in possession trusts, and, 12.13–12.16
Romalpa clauses
  meaning of trusts, and, 2.2
Running a trust
  age of donee, 18.4
  aggregation of funds, 18.2–18.3
  agricultural property relief
    agricultural property, 18.57
    claw-back, 18.66–18.70
    farmhouses, 18.58–18.63
    introduction, 18.56
    occupation and ownership tests, 18.64–18.65
    tax planning, 18.73–18.74
  anti-avoidance rules, 18.71
  business property relief
    AIM shares, 18.32–18.33
    claw-back, 18.66–18.70
    disqualified businesses, 18.34–18.47
    excepted assets, 18.48–18.50
    excluded property, 18.34–18.47
    groups, 18.51–18.53
    introduction, 18.28
    liquidations, 18.55
    period of ownership, 18.54
    qualifying businesses, 18.34–18.47
    relevant business property, 18.29–18.31
    sales, 18.55
    'see through' provisions, 18.31
    tax planning, 18.73–18.74
  capital gains tax
    hold-over relief, 18.72
  charitable trusts, and, 18.1
  civil partners, 18.5–18.10
  deeds of variation, and, 18.3
  disabled persons trusts, and, 18.1
  donee's age, 18.4
  double charges, and, 18.92–18.93
  'double trust' arrangements, 18.90–18.91
  excluded property trusts, and, 18.1
  exit charge, and
    business property relief, 18.28
    generally, 18.1
    income tax planning, 18.83
  family companies, 18.18–18.27
  family home, 18.90–18.91
  future considerations, 18.75–18.76
  general anti-abuse rule, 18.73
  general principles, 18.1
  hold-over relief, 18.72
  income tax, 18.77–18.83

Index

Running a trust – *cont.*
  inheritance tax
    agricultural property relief, 18.56–18.65
    anti-avoidance rules, 18.71
    business property relief, 18.28–18.55
    claw-back of relief, 18.66–18.70
    family companies, 18.18–18.27
    introduction, 18.1–18.10
    pre-March 1986 settlements, 18.17
    residence nil-rate band, 18.11–18.16
  liabilities for financing relievable property, 18.71
  married couples, 18.5–18.10
  nil-rate band
    generally, 18.2
    residences, for, 18.11–18.16
  overview, 18.1
  own share purchases, 18.84
  post-death variations, and, 18.3
  pre-March 1986 settlements, 18.17
  qualifying IIP trusts, and, 18.1
  relevant property trusts, 18.1
  residence nil-rate band (RNRB)
    civil partners, 18.15
    'closely inherited', 18.13
    conditions, 18.12–18.14
    disadvantages, 18.16
    generally, 18.11
    married couples, 18.15
    'residential property interest', 18.12
    transfer, 18.15
  second homes, 18.85–18.89
  share buy-backs, 18.84
  tax planning
    agricultural property relief, 18.73–18.74
    business property relief, 18.73–18.74
    hold-over relief, 18.72
    income tax, 18.77–18.83
  ten-year charge, and
    age of donee, 18.4
    business property relief, 18.28
    generally, 18.1
    income tax planning, 18.83
  transferable nil-rate band, 18.5–18.6
  'washing the gain', 18.85–18.89

S

Sale of land
  income tax, and, 6.126
Sales at an undervalue
  starting a trust, and, 17.42–17.44

Same-day additions
  ten-year charge, and, 9.44–9.48
Savings income
  charitable trusts, and, 14.31
Schools
  charitable trusts, and, 14.79
Second homes
  running a trust, 18.85–18.89
Seed Enterprise Investment Scheme
  capital gains tax, and, 7.101
Self-assessment
  see also **Tax returns**
  due date for payment of tax, and, 22.3
  income tax, and, 6.101–6.103
Settled legacies
  ten-year charge, and, 9.66–9.67
Settlement
  employee benefit trusts, 16.35
  income tax, and 4.6–4.7
  meaning, 2.2
  stamp duty land tax, and., 13.10–13.11
Settlor charge
  generally, 26.17–26.19
  'interest in the settlement', 26.20–26.25
  qualifying settlements, 26.26–26.27
  transitional provisions (1998/1999), 26.28–26.32
Settlor-interested trusts
  anti avoidance, and
    capital gains tax, 4.33–4.37
    income tax, 4.2–4.32
    inheritance tax, 4.38–4.52
    introduction, 4.1
  bare trusts, 4.20–4.22
  capital gains tax
    deeds of variation, 4.37
    flip-flop scheme, 4.34–4.35
    generally, 4.33
    sub-funds, 4.36
  child settlements
    bare trusts, 4.20–4.22
    chargeability of trustees to tax, 4.23
    generally, 4.14–4.19
  deeds of variation
    capital gains tax, 4.37
    income tax, 4.7
  flip-flop scheme, 4.34–4.35
  heritage maintenance funds, 4.13
  income tax
    bare trusts, 4.20–4.22
    capital sums, 4.26–4.31
    child settlements, 4.14–4.23
    exceptions, 4.10–4.12
    heritage maintenance funds, 4.13

Settlor-interested trusts – *cont.*
  income tax – *cont.*
    'income', 4.9
    'interest' under a settlement, 4.3–4.4
    overview, 4.2
    pre-owned assets regime, 4.32
    related property, 4.4
    'settlement', 4.6–4.7
    'settlor', 4.5
    waiver of dividends, 4.24–4.25
    wills, 4.7
  inheritance tax
    introduction, 4.38
    pre-owned assets regime, 4.39–4.52
  pre-owned assets regime
    capital gains tax, and, 4.32
    chattels, 4.43
    de minimis exemption, 4.47
    exclusions, 4.45
    exemptions, 4.46–4.48
    intangible property comprised in a settlement with retained interest, 4.44
    land, 4.41–4.42
    post-death variations, 4.48
    scope, 4.51–4.52
    summary, 4.39–4.40
    transitional provisions, 4.49–4.50
  sub-funds, 4.36
  trustees' tax liability, and, 5.11–5.17
Share buy-backs
  running a trust, 18.84
Special rates
  accumulation trusts, and
    deceased estates, 6.59
    dividend income rate, 6.57
    generally, 6.55–6.58
    income charged, 6.60–6.64
    non-dividend income rate, 6.56
Sports trusts
  relevant property, and, 8.29
Stamp duties/taxes
  see also **Stamp duty land tax**
  annual tax on enveloped dwellings, 13.40–13.45
  charitable trusts, and, 14.10
  disclosure regime, 13.48
  ending a trust, and, 19.20
  high-value UK residential property, 1.13–1.15
  introduction, 1.12
  land and buildings transaction tax, 13.37–13.39
  overview, 1.12
  stamp duty, 13.46–13.47

Stamp duties/taxes – *cont.*
  stamp duty land tax
    bare trusts, 13.5–13.9
    chargeable consideration, 13.23–13.36
    disclosure regime, 13.48
    settlement, 13.10–13.11
    trustees' responsibilities, 13.12–13.22
  starting a trust, and, 17.25–17.26
  summary, 13.1–13.4
  transfer of stocks and securities, 13.46–13.47
Stamp duty land tax (SDLT)
  anti-avoidance, and, 23.24–23.26
  bare trusts, 13.5–13.9
  chargeable consideration
    additional residential properties, 13.29–13.33
    introduction, 13.23–13.24
    mixed use land, 13.25–13.26
    non-residential land, 13.25–13.26
    other points, 13.35–13.36
    residential land, 13.27–13.28
  charitable trusts, and, 14.10–14.11
  DOTAS, 23.24–23.26
  settlement, 13.10–13.11
  summary, 13.1–13.4
  trustees' responsibilities, 13.12–13.22
Starting a trust
  anti-avoidance, 17.59–17.60
  bare trusts, 17.40
  capital gains tax
    generally, 17.9–17.12
    hold-over relief, 17.13–17.17
    payment, 17.18–17.19
  charities, 17.27
  compliance
    Form 41G (Trust), 17.8
    introduction, 17.6–17.7
  defeasible absolute interests, 17.41
  disclosure of tax avoidance schemes, 17.24
  discounted gift trusts, 17.51–17.54
  DOTAS, and, 17.59
  flexible reversionary trust, 17.57–17.58
  General Anti-Abuse Rule, 17.60
  gift and loan arrangement, 17.55–17.56
  hold-over relief
    categories, 17.14–17.15
    chargeable transfers for IHT purposes, 17.14
    claims, 17.16–17.17
    defined business assets, 17.14
    generally, 17.13
  inheritance tax
    agricultural property, 17.36–17.39

Starting a trust – *cont.*
  inheritance tax – *cont.*
    business property, 17.36–17.39
    compliance, 17.22–17.23
    exceeding nil-rate band, 17.33–17.35
    exemptions, 17.21
    generally, 17.20
    life assurance trusts, 17.47–17.50
    nil-rate band, 17.33–17.35
  life assurance trusts, 17.47–17.50
  overview, 17.1–17.5
  sales at an undervalue, 17.42–17.44
  stamp taxes, 17.25–17.26
  tax planning, 17.28–17.32
Statutory residence test
  generally, 24.9
  rules, 24.10–24.20
  trust and estate returns, and, 20.73
STEP provisions
  trustees' powers, and, 5.3
Stock dividends
  income tax, and
    enhanced, 6.21
    generally, 6.20
Sub-funds
  capital gains tax, and
    generally, 7.118–7.122
    settlor-interested trusts, 4.36
Superannuation schemes
  relevant property, and, 8.29
Supplementary charge
  non-UK residents, and, 26.45–26.46

T

Taper relief
  capital gains tax, and, 7.48–7.50
Tax evasion
  see also **Anti-avoidance**
  generally, 23.2–23.3
Tax liability
  capital gains tax
    emigration, 5.25
    generally, 5.18
    recapture of held over gains, 5.21–5.24
    'settled property', 5.18
    equitable jurisdiction of the court, 5.51–5.56
  held over gains, 5.21–5.24
  income tax
    generally, 5.5–5.10
    settlor-interested trusts, 5.11–5.17

Tax liability – *cont.*
  inheritance tax
    failed PETs, 5.28
    generally, 5.19–5.20
    settled property, 5.20
    'trustees', 5.19
    unusual events, 5.26–5.27
  mistake, and, 5.51–5.56
  ordinary course, in
    capital gains tax, 5.18
    income tax, 5.5–5.17
    inheritance tax, 5.19–5.20
    introduction, 5.4
  'relevant trustees', 5.4
  'settled property', 5.18
  settlor-interested trusts, 5.11–5.17
  unusual events, for, 5.21–5.56
Tax pools
  accumulation trusts, and, 6.68–6.79, Appendix C
Tax returns
  income tax
    beneficiaries, and, 20.31
    capital gains, and, 20.74
    deceased estates, 20.32–20.36
    enquiry window, 20.25
    estimates of value, 20.20
    finality for deceased estates, and 20.21
    generally, 20.1–20.8
    'no income' trusts, 20.12–20.16
    notification of liability, 20.9–20.11
    provisional figures, 20.20
    trust and estate pages, 20.37–20.73
    trustee policy, 20.23–20.24
  inheritance tax, 21.3–21.5
  penalties, and
    failure to deliver returns, 22.19–22.20
    inaccurate returns, 22.9–22.20
    late-filed returns, 22.7–22.8
    overview, 22.2
    policy developments, 22.31
    reasonable care, 22.15
    reasonable excuse, 22.16–22.18
  trust and estate
    capital gains, 20.74
    dividends from non-UK companies, 20.71–20.72
    main pages, 20.37–20.70
    statutory residence test, 20.73
Temporary non-residence
  capital gains tax, 26.57–26.58
  generally, 24.21
  income tax, 25.53–25.58

Index

Ten-year charge
- accumulations of income, 9.30–9.32
- addition of property, 9.57–9.64
- anti-avoidance measures, 9.69–9.76
- calculation of tax, 9.23
- change of character of property within settlement, 9.65
- chargeable amount, 9.12–9.23
- combination of relevant and non-relevant property, 9.49–9.54
- complicated example, 9.37–9.55
- exit charge, and
  - before first ten-year anniversary, 10.20–10.27
  - between ten-year anniversaries, 10.28–10.31
  - failed PETs, 9.78–9.80
  - FA 2006, and, 9.83–9.84
  - gifts with reservation of benefit, 9.81–9.82
- identification of property, 9.77
- overview, 9.1–9.7
- pension death benefits, 9.68
- practical difficulties, 9.77–9.84
- rate of tax, 9.23
- related settlements, 9.37–9.43
- running a trust, and
  - age of donee, 18.4
  - business property relief, 18.28
  - generally, 18.1
  - income tax planning, 18.83
- same-day additions, 9.44–9.48
- settled legacies, 9.66–9.67
- simple example, 9.24–9.36
- ten-year anniversary, 9.8–9.11
- undistributed income, 9.33–9.36

Trading income
- charitable trusts, and, 14.33

Trade compensation funds
- relevant property, and, 8.29

Trading profits
- charitable trusts, and, 14.31

Transactions in land
- non-UK residents, and, 25.46–25.50

Transfer of assets abroad
- generally, 25.18–25.23
- 'motive test', 25.24–25.27
- 2005 replacement regime, 25.28–25.33
- 2013 amendments, 25.34–25.40
- 2017 proposed changes, 25.41–25.45

Transfer of assets by settlor
- capital gains tax, and, 7.2

Transfer of family shareholdings
- charitable trusts, and, 14.28–14.30

Transfer of income streams
- income tax, and, 6.22

Transfer of value
- disabled persons' trusts, and, 15.13

Transferable nil-rate band
- running a trust, 18.5–18.6

Trust and estate tax return
- capital gains, 20.74
- dividends from non-UK companies, 20.71–20.72
- form, Appendix F
- main pages, 20.37–20.70
- statutory residence test, 20.73

Trust management expenses (TMEs)
- discretionary trusts, and, 6.53
- generally, 6.31–6.33
- HMRC Guidance, 6.36–6.40
- Peter Clay case, 6.34–6.35
- table of allowable items, Appendix H

Trustees
- capital gains tax liability
  - emigration, 5.25
  - generally, 5.18
  - recapture of held over gains, 5.21–5.24
  - 'settled property', 5.18
- equitable jurisdiction of the court, 5.51–5.56
- held over gains, 5.21–5.24
- income tax liability
  - generally, 5.5–5.10
  - settlor-interested trusts, 5.11–5.17
- indemnity for liability, 5.2
- inheritance tax liability
  - failed PETs, 5.28
  - generally, 5.19–5.20
  - settled property, 5.20
  - 'trustees', 5.19
  - unusual events, 5.26–5.27
- mistake, 5.51–5.56
- personal liability, 5.1–5.3
- powers, 5.3
- rectification, 5.48–5.50
- 'relevant trustees', 5.4
- residence
  - introduction, 5.29
  - Non-UK Resident Landlord Scheme, 5.30
- rule in *Hastings-Bass*, 5.31–5.47
- settlor-interested trusts, 5.11–5.17
- stamp duty land tax, and., 13.12–13.22
- STEP standard provisions, 5.3
- tax liabilities
  - capital gains tax, 5.18
  - income tax, 5.5–5.17
  - inheritance tax, 5.19–5.20
  - ordinary course, in, 5.4–5.20

Trustees – *cont.*
tax liabilities – *cont.*
'relevant trustees', 5.4
'settled property', 5.18
settlor-interested trusts, 5.11–5.17
unusual events, 5.21–5.56

Trusts
definition, 2.2
dispositive powers, 2.24–2.28
general, 2.1–2.3
implied trusts, 2.29
lifetime settlements, 2.14–2.23
meaning, 2.2
no income, with, 20.12–20.16
practice, in
  accumulation and maintenance trusts, 2.49–2.50
  bare trusts, 2.44–2.48
  charitable trusts, 2.51
  disabled trusts, 2.52
  discretionary trusts, 2.31–2.37
  employee trusts, 2.53
  interest in possession trusts, 2.38–2.43
  introduction, 2.30
types, 2.1–2.50
will trusts, 2.4–2.13

Trusts with no income
compliance, and, 20.12–20.16

U

UK resident trusts
anti-avoidance, 1.17
capital gains tax
  see also **Capital gains tax**
  introduction, 1.7–1.9
income tax
  see also **Income tax**
  introduction, 1.19–1.11
inheritance tax
  see also **Inheritance tax**
  introduction, 1.4–1.6
non-domiciliaries, 1.16
overview, 1.1–1.3
stamp taxes
  see also **Stamp duties/taxes**
  high-value UK residential property, 1.13–1.15
  introduction, 1.12

Underpayments
interest, and, 22.4–22.6

Undistributed income
beneficiaries' interests, and, 3.6
ten-year charge, and, 9.33–9.36

Unpaid tax
interest, and, 22.4
penalties, and, 22.21–22.27

V

Valuation
estimates of value, 20.20
unquoted/unlisted companies, 7.132

Variation of trusts
capital gains tax, and, 7.135

VAT
charitable trusts, and, 14.41

Vested interests
beneficiaries' interests, and, 3.3

Vulnerable persons' trusts
administration of tax, 15.18
capital gains tax
  administration, 15.18
  election for special treatment, 15.17
  generally, 15.12
  tax treatment, 15.14–15.16
'disabled person', 15.3–15.6
discretionary trusts, and, 2.37
generally, 2.52
HMRC administration, 15.18
income tax
  administration, 15.18
  election for special treatment, 15.17
  generally, 15.12
  introduction, 6.50
  tax treatment, 15.14–15.16
inheritance tax, 15.7–15.11
overview, 15.1–15.2
relevant property, and, 8.29
transfer of value, and, 15.13

W

Waiver of dividends
income tax, and, 4.24–4.25

'Washing the gain'
running a trust, and, 18.85–18.89

Will trusts
generally, 2.4–2.13

Wills
income tax, and, 4.7